Lecture Notes in Computer Science 5900

Commenced Publication in 1973
Founding and Former Series Editors:
Gerhard Goos, Juris Hartmanis, and Jan van Leeuwen

Services Science

Subline of Lectures Notes in Computer Science

Luciano Baresi   Chi-Hung Chi
Jun Suzuki (Eds.)

Service-Oriented Computing

7th International Joint Conference, ICSOC-ServiceWave 2009
Stockholm, Sweden, November 24-27, 2009
Proceedings

Springer

Volume Editors

Luciano Baresi
Politecnico di Milano
Dipartimento di Elettronica e Informazione
via Golgi, 40, 20133, Milano, Italy
E-mail: baresi@elet.polimi.it; lbareis@gmail.com

Chi-Hung Chi
Tsinghua University
School of Software
Main Building Room 818, 100084, Beijing, China
E-mail: chichihung@mail.tsinghua.edu.cn

Jun Suzuki
University of Massachusetts
Dept. of Computer Science
100 Morrissey Blvd., Boston, MA 02125-3393, USA
E-mail: jxs@cs.umb.edu

Library of Congress Control Number: 2009939278

CR Subject Classification (1998): D.2, C.2, H.3.5, J.1, K.6, B.8, C.4

LNCS Sublibrary: SL 2 – Programming and Software Engineering

ISSN 0302-9743

ISBN 978-3-642-10382-7 Springer Berlin Heidelberg New York

springer.com

© Springer-Verlag Berlin Heidelberg 2009

Typesetting: Camera-ready by author, data conversion by Scientific Publishing Services, Chennai, India
Printed on acid-free paper   SPIN: 12797387   06/3180   5 4 3 2 1 0

Preface

Welcome to ICSOC-ServiceWave 2009. This volume contains the research and demo papers selected for presentation at the Seventh International Conference on Service-Oriented Computing, which was held in Stockholm, Sweden, November 24-27, 2009.

Continuing the tradition set in the previous six years, we are pleased to present a high-quality technical program. This year ICSOC ServiceWave worked together to convey a world-leading and unique opportunity for academic researchers and industry practitioners to report their state-of-the-art research findings in service-oriented computing. The joint conference aims to foster cross-community scientific excellence by gathering experts from various disciplines such as distributed systems, software engineering, computer networks, business intelligence, service science, grid and cloud computing, and security.

Consistent with the high quality of the conference, we received 228 paper submissions from a number of different disciplines. Thirty-seven papers were accepted as regular contributions, for a very competitive acceptance rate of 16%; eight further submissions were accepted as short papers. The program also comprised nine demonstrations of innovative tools and prototypes. All these elements contributed to a program that covered the many different areas of the discipline and provided an up-to-date synthesis of the research on service-oriented systems and applications.

Without the high-quality work of the authors of selected papers this volume would have not been possible. We thank these researchers and practitioners for the efforts and enthusiasm put in their contributions. We also appreciate the hard work of the members of our Program Committee. Some 100 people were involved in reviewing many good papers carefully and rigorously: it was our privilege to work with these respected colleagues. These efforts were the key elements for a program that represents a highly selective and high-quality set of research results. A big thank you also goes to Springer, and in particular to Ursula Barth, for helping us publish this volume.

It was our privilege and pleasure to compile these outstanding proceedings. We sincerely hope that you find the papers in this volume as interesting and stimulating as we did. Our last big thanks to all participants who, at the end of the day, are what this is all about.

September 2009

Luciano Baresi
Chi-Hung Chi
Jun Suzuki

Organization

General Chairs

Mohand-Said Hacid   Université de Lyon, UCBL, France (ICSOC)
Fernando Fournon   Telefónica R&D Labs, Spain (ServiceWave)
Gunnar Landgren   KTH, Sweden (Hosting partner)

Program Committee Chairs

Luciano Baresi   Politecnico di Milano, Italy
Chi-Hung Chi   Tsinghua University, China
Jun Suzuki   University of Massachusetts, Boston, USA

Industry Program Chairs

Stefano De Panfilis   Engineering Ingegneria Informatica, Italy
Santi Ristol   ATOS Origin, Spain

Workshops Chairs

Asit Dan   IBM Research, USA
Frédéric Gittler   HP Labs
Farouk Toumani   Université Blaise Pascal, France

PhD Symposium Chairs

Florian Daniel   University of Trento, Italy
Fethi Rabhi   UNSW, Australia

Demonstration Chairs

Hamid Motahari   HP, USA
Julien Vayssiere   CRC, Australia

Publicity Chairs

Fuyuki Ishikawa   NII, Japan
Hamamache Kheddouci   Université de Lyon, UCBL, France
Weider Yu   San Jose State University, USA
Andrea Zisman   City University London, UK

Organizing Committee

Véronique Pevtschin	Engineering Ingegneria Informatica, Italy (Coordination)
Gunnar Landgren	KTH, Sweden (Coordination)
Barbara Pirillo	Engineering Ingegneria Informatica, Italy
Rikard Lingström	KTH, Sweden
Mike Papazoglou	Tilburg University, The Netherlands
Bernd Krämer	ServTech, Germany
Samir Sebahi	Lyon University, France (Webmaster)

Sponsoring

Bruno François-Marsal	Thales, France

Scientific Program Committee

Marco Aiello	University of Groningen, The Netherlands
Alvaro Arenas	STFC Rutherford Appleton Laboratory, UK
Alistair Barros	SAP, Australia
Samik Basu	Iowa State University, USA
Boualem Benatallah	University of New South Wales, Australia
Salima Benbernou	University of Lyon, France
Djamal Benslimane	University of Lyon, France
Elisa Bertino	Purdue University, USA
Antonia Bertolino	CNR, Italy
Walter Binder	University of Lugano Switzerland
Athman Bouguettaya	CSIRO, Australia
Christoph Bussler	BEA, USA
Barbara Carminati	University of Insubria, Italy
Manuel Carro	Polytechnic University of Madrid, Spain
Fabio Casati	University of Trento, Italy
Shiping Chen	CSIRO, Australia
Lawrence Chung	University of Texas at Dallas, USA
Emmanuel Coquery	University of Claude Bernard, France
Paco Curbera	IBM Research, USA
Vincenzo D'Andrea	University of Trento, Italy
Flavio De Paoli	University di Milano Bicocca, Italy
Frederic Desprez	INRIA, France
Elisabetta Di Nitto	Politecnico di Milano, Italy
Khalil Drira	LAAS, Toulouse, France
Schahram Dustdar	University of Technology Vienna, Austria
Elena Ferrari	University of Insubria, Italy
Ioannis Fikouras	Ericsson, Germany
Howard Foster	Imperial College London, UK

Mathias Weske	Hasso Platner Institute, Germany
Andreas Wombacher	University of Twente, The Netherlands
Chou Wu	Avaya Laboratory, USA
Ramin Yahyapour	University of Dortmund, Germany
Jian Yang	Macquire University, Australia
Yelena Yesha	University of Maryland, USA
Weider D. Yu	San Jose State University, USA
Jia Zhang	Northern Illinois University, USA
Yan Zheng	Nokia Research, Finland
Andrea Zisman	City University London, UK
Joe Zou	IBM, Australia

Demonstration Program Committee

Claudio Bartolini	HP Labs, USA
Paco Curbera	IBM Research, USA
Vincenzo D'Andrea	University of Trento, Italy
Gero Decker	Hasso Plattner Institute, Germany
Keith Duddy	Queensland University of Technology, Australia
Marlon Dumas	University of Tartu, Estonia
Brian Elvesaeter	SINTEF, Norway
Howard Foster	Imperial College London, UK
Max Muhlhaeuser	Technische Universität Darmstadt, Germany
Anna Liu	University of New South Wales, Australia
Wasim Sadiq	SAP Research, Australia
Halvard Skogsrud	ThoughtWorks, Australia
Stefan Tai	University of Karlsruhe, Germany
Rainer Ruggaber	SAP Research, Germany
Liangzhao Zeng	IBM Research, USA

Table of Contents

Composition

Discovery

Design Principles

Customization and Adaptation

Negotiation, Agreements, and Compliance

Selection

Platforms and Infrastructures

Short Papers I

Security

Short Papers II

Modeling and Design

Validation and Verification

Reputation and Ranking

Service Management

Demonstrations

Facilitating Workflow Interoperation Using Artifact-Centric Hubs

Richard Hull[1,*], Nanjangud C. Narendra[2], and Anil Nigam[3]

[1] IBM T.J. Watson Research Center, USA
hull@us.ibm.com
[2] IBM India Research Lab, Bangalore, India
narendra@in.ibm.com
[3] IBM T.J. Watson Research Center, USA
anigam@us.ibm.com

Abstract. Enabling interoperation between workflows, and between web services, continues to be a fundamental challenge. This paper proposes a new approach to interoperation based on hubs that are designed using "business artifacts", a data-centric paradigm for workflow and business process specification. The artifact-centric interoperation hubs are focused primarily on *facilitating communication and business-level synchronization* between relatively autonomous stakeholders (and stakeholder organizations). Interoperation hubs provide a centralized, computerized rendezvous point, where stakeholders can read or write data of common interest and check the current status of an aggregate process, and from which they can receive notifications about events of interest. The paper describes the approach, including an extended example, access restrictions that can be placed on stakeholders, some preliminary theoretical results, and a discussion of work towards a prototype system that supports interoperation hubs.

Keywords: Business Artifact, Interoperation, Service, Workflow.

1 Introduction

Enabling interoperation between workflows, and between web services, continues to pose a fundamental challenge. Two traditional approaches to this challenge are orchestration and choreography [16]. Orchestration tackles interoperation by essentially creating an new application with a centralized set of goals to be achieved. The orchestrator is typically designed to fit with the various workflows or services that are to interoperate, thus limiting opportunities for re-use of the orchestration. Also, orchestrators become the primary controllers of the interoperation, and as a result reduce the autonomy of the different stakeholders (individuals and organizations) in acheiving their portions of the aggregate goal. On the other hand, choreography embraces the autonomy of the stakeholders, and attempts to enforce the achievement of aggregate goals by restricting how messages can be passed between the stakeholder workflows or services. A weakness of choreography, however, is that there is no single conceptual point or "rendezvous" where stakeholders can go to find current status and information about the aggregate process. This paper proposes a new approach to workflow and web service interoperation, that largely preserves the autonomy of participating stakeholders, and provides

---

* This author partially supported by NSF grants IIS-0415195, CNS-0613998, and IIS-0812578.

L. Baresi, C.-H. Chi, and J. Suzuki (Eds.): ICSOC-ServiceWave 2009, LNCS 5900, pp. 1–18, 2009.

a single conceptual point where stakeholders can obtain current status and information about a process, and can receive notifications about status changes of interest. We call our approach *interoperation hubs*.

The interoperation hubs proposed here focus primarily on *facilitating communication and business-level synchronization* between relatively autonomous stakeholders. The conceptual model used by the hubs is based on "business artifacts" [14,5,11], a data-centric paradigm for workflow and business process specification. An interoperation hub can be viewed as a stylized "whiteboard" for holding information relevant to the stakeholder community as they participate in a consensus-based aggregate process. The whiteboard is structured to ensure that certain constraints are satisfied about information access, information update, and task sequencing. The hub is primarily passive and re-active, allowing the stakeholder workflows to post new information of interest to the stakeholder community. The hub is pro-active in only one regard: stakeholders can subscribe for notification when certain steps of the aggregate process have occurred.

The interoperation hubs used here are fundamentally different from conventional orchestrators. The difference stems from the fact that *business artifacts*, or simply "artifacts", unlike BPEL, provide a holistic view of process and data. Artifacts are business-relevant objects that are created, evolve, and (typically) archived as they pass through the workflow. An artifact type includes both an *information model* (or "data schema"), that can hold data about the business objects during their lifetime in the workflow, and a *lifecycle model* (or "lifecycle schema"), that describes the possible ways and timings that tasks (a.k.a. services) can be invoked to manipulate these objects. A prototypical example of a business artifact type is "air courier package delivery," whose information model would include slots for data such as ID of the package, sender, recipient, arrival times at different points along the way, time delivered, and billing information, and whose lifecycle model would include the different ways that the package could be delivered and paid for.

In the context of individual workflows, experiences reported [6,5,7] by the business artifacts team at IBM Research show that an artifact-based perspective helps in improving stakeholder understanding of the workflows, and often leads to new insights. These experiences suggest that an artifact-based interoperation hub will be of significant business value to the many people in the stakeholder organizations. More specifically, it suggests that the business managers, business architects, and IT infrastructure specialists will be able to adapt their workflows, including both manual and automated portions, to take advantage of the interoperation hub, to draw upon the information that can be stored there, to write appropriate information there, and to help guide how the artifacts move through their lifecycles.

In addition to presenting an extended example to illustrate our approach, the paper includes formal definitions for three kinds of access restrictions. "Windows" provide a mechanism to restrict which artifacts a stakeholder can see; "views" provide a mechanism to restrict what parts of an artifact a stakeholder can see; and a variation of "Create-Read-Update-Delete (CRUD)" specifications is used to restrict the ways that stakeholders can read and modify artifacts. The paper also studies the question of *persistent visibility* of artifacts. An interoperation hub supports persistent visibility if, for each stakeholder p and artifact a, if a becomes visible (based on the window restrictions) to p at some point, then a remains visible to p for the remainder of its evolution through the workflow. In the general case testing this property is undecidable, but we show that it is decidable for a natural class of window specifications.

The approach of interoperation hubs can be used to facilitate interoperation between different enterprises or organizations. Indeed, companies such as PayPal or Salesforce.com can be viewed as providing massively scaled interoperation hubs, that facilitate interoperation between largely autonomous stakeholders. Conference submission management sites such as ConfTool or EasyChair also provide application-specific interoperation hubs. The framework and theoretical development of this paper provides a formal basis for analyzing application-specific interoperation hubs, such as those just mentioned.

Section 2 introduces an example of an interoperation hub along with its business artifacts. This example is used throughout the paper to illustrate different concepts related to interoperation hubs. Section 3 presents a more formal description of the framework for artifact-centric interoperation hubs. Section 4 incorporates various notions related to access control, and presents some preliminary theoretical results about the framework. Section 5 describes work towards a prototype implementation of interoperation hubs. Section 6 describes related work, and Section 7 offers brief conclusions.

2   Representative Example

This section presents an illustration of an artifact-based interoperation hub, which will be used through the rest of the paper. It is based on employee hiring an an enterprise.

2.1   Example Overview

Fig. 1 shows the six primary kinds of stakeholders and stakeholder organizations whose interoperation around hiring will be supported, viz., *Candidates, Human Resources Organization, Hiring Organizations, Evaluators, Travel Provider, Reimbursement*. There could be several hiring organizations, each with its own worklows for managing the recruitment process. We assume that the enterprise has a single HR organization responsible for recruitment purposes.

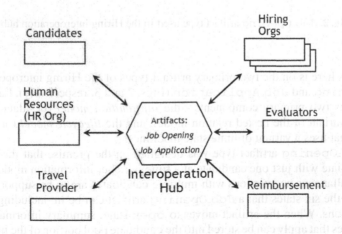

Fig. 1. Six types of stakeholder organizations using the Hiring Interoperation Hub

Participants can interact with the hub in several ways. For instance, a candidate may choose to interact directly with the designated *Travel Provider*, perhaps through their web-site, and create her itinerary. The hub can record the authorization for travel (perhaps from HR or perhaps from the Hiring Organization). The Travel Provider can the access the hub for the travel authorization, and place a link to the itinerary. This enables the Hiring Organization and the Evaluators to access the itinerary when preparing for interviews. Finally, the Reimbursement organization can access the airline and hotel invoices when processing the travel reimbursement request from the candidate. These interactions illustrate how an interoperation hub can facilitate information transfer between participant organizations, while giving them considerable autonomy and latitude with regards to how and when they provide the information or accomplish tasks.

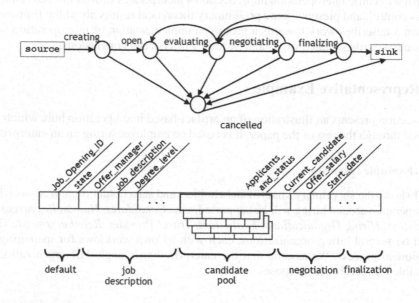

Fig. 2. Job_Opening artifact type used in the Hiring interoperation hub

Our focus here is on the two primary artifact types of the Hiring interoperation hub - Job_Opening and Job_Application (Figs. 2 and 3, respectively). Each artifact type contains two primary components - the *information model* (or "data schema"), that uses a variant of the nested relation model, and the *lifecycle model* (or "lifecycle schema"), that uses a variant of finite state machines.

The Job_Opening artifact type was designed on the premise that the enterprise would negotiate with just one candidate at a time; a richer information model could be used if simultaneous negotiations with multiple candidates are to be supported. Fig. 2 also depicts the six states that a Job_Opening artifact can be in, including the inter-state transitions. When the artifact moves to open state, summary information about the candidates that apply can be stored into the candidate pool portion of the information model. (However, the bulk of the candidate information will be stored in the corresponding Job_Application artifact instance.) In the evaluating state, one or more of

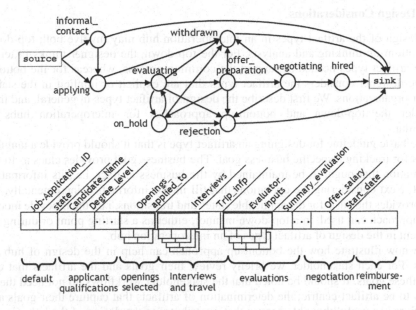

Fig. 3. Job_Application artifact type used in the Hiring interoperation hub

the applicants might start through the evaluation process. In the negotiating state, one candidate has been shortlisted for selection, and undergoes salary negotiations with the HR organization. At any point of time, HR or the Hiring Organization can cancel the job opening by moving the artifact instance to cancelled state.

The information model for Job_Opening consists of the following attribute clusters - an ID, job details (job description, offering manager, etc.), candidate pool (summary of each applicant being considered), negotiation details (current candidate, offered salary, start date), finalization (salary, start date, hiring manager, etc.). Similarly, the lifecycle specification of Job_Opening is specified as the states - creating, open, evaluating, negotiating, finalizing, cancelled - and transitions between them. Each stakeholder is responsible for adding appropriate information to the Job_Opening in some state and might also move it to the next state.

The Job_Application artifact type is intended to track job candidates from when the enterprise first thinks of someone as a potential recruit, through the formal application process, to the point of hiring, rejection, or the candidate withdrawing her application. As noted previously, the interoperation hub should be viewed as an electronic repository of selected information relevant to the stakeholders involved with a given applicant; it is not required that all information exchanged between the stakeholders be formally recorded into the hub. For example, the candidate and the travel provider might interact directly, and then have the travel provider record the planned itinerary into the interoperation hub. This illustrates another aspect of the flexibility in communication and business-level synchronization enabled with using interoperation hubs.

As per Fig. 3, a candidate can either apply formally (applying state) or come into informal contact with the Hiring Organization (informal_contact state). The rest of the state machine is self-explanatory.

2.2   Design Considerations

The design of the artifact types in an interoperation hub may involve both top-down and bottom-up thinking and analysis. For the top-down, the designer thinks in terms of the artifact types needed to support the common process, whereas for the bottom-up, the designer considers the artifact types that are explicit or implicit in the stakeholder organizations. We first describe the design of artifact types in general, and then consider the top-down and bottom-up approaches for interoperation hubs in particular.

The basic guideline for designing an artifact type is that it should provide a tangible means for tracking a specific business goal. The business goal provides clues as to the information that ought to be maintained by the business artifact, i.e., its information model. Next considering the operations that fill in this information incrementally, the goal provides the basis for the applicable states and transitions, i.e., the lifecycle model. This approach can used, in a top-down manner, either as a starting point or during refinement in the design of artifact types of an interoperation hub.

We now illustrate how the bottom-up approach can help in the design of hub artifacts. For each stakeholder, we briefly review their goals and the artifacts that can track these goals. It should be noted that the stakeholder workflows do not need themselves to be artifact-centric; the determination of artifacts that capture their goals and behaviors is a useful thought exercise that contributes to the design of the hub. *Candidates* strive to obtain suitable employment at the best terms; they will think primarily in terms of Job_Application artifact type of the Hiring hub. *HR* employees are focused on ensuring that the hiring policies are followed; towards this end their artifacts will also be based on Job_Opening and Job_Application. *Hiring Organizations* are primarily interested in recruiting highly qualified applicants who will be productive contributors in their organization; their artifacts would be Prospects (or "Leads"), which in some cases lead to the creation of Job_Application. *Evaluators* focus on providing effective input on the capabilities of Prospects/Candidates. The *Travel Provider* works to provide a friendly and effective service to help candidates finalize their travel arrangements, and as such is focused on managing the Itinerary. *Reimbursement* strives to reimburse applicants for travel expenses incurred, accurately and in a timely manner, and their primary artifact is an Expense Report.

Considering the goals that need to be tracked, the Job_Application artifact type addresses the needs of *Hiring Organization* and Candidates alike. It also incorporates information relevant to *Evaluators*, the *Travel Provider*, and *Reimbursement*. Additionally, the Job_Opening artifact can serve to track a union of the goals of *HR* and the *Hiring Organizations* with regards to Candidates and Prospects, respectively. A final observation is that both artifact types of the Hiring hub is of interest to more than one stakeholder; this makes the case for an interoperation hub that houses the aggregate process. As we will see later, each stakeholder will have differing abilities to view and modify the information in these artifacts.

3   A Framework for Artifact-Centric Interoperation Hubs

This section presents a succinct description of the framework for interoperation hubs, and illustrates the framework in terms of the Hiring example. Due to space limitations, only the most essential definitions are given in detail. For this formalism, we use the terms 'data schema' and 'lifecycle schema' rather than 'information model' and 'lifecycle model', to be more consistent with the database and workflow literature.

3.1 Nested Data and Artifact Types

The information model for the artifacts in interoperation hubs is based on nested data types, based on a nested relation model. These are built up using scalars and four types of identifier, namely artifact_ID, participant_ID, stakeholder_org_ID, and state_name (described below), and the record (formed with attribute names) and set constructs. We permit the use of an undefined value, denoted as $\perp$, for any type. We consider only nested data types that are in *Partitioned Normal Form* (PNF) [17,2], that is, so that for each set of (nested) tuples, the set of non-nested attributes forms a key for the overall set of tuples.

An *artifact data schema* is a nested record type of the form

$$D = \langle \mathbf{ID} : \text{artifact\_ID}, \mathbf{state} : \text{state\_name}, A_1 : T_1, \ldots, A_n : T_n \rangle$$

(where the T_j's range over nested data types). Intuitively, in an instance of an artifact data schema, the first field will hold a unique ID for the artifact being represented, and the second field will hold the state in the lifecycle that the artifact is currently in. We use the term *snapshot* to refer to instances of an artifact data schema; this is to reflect the intuition that artifacts persist as they evolve through a workflow, and pass through a sequence of "snapshots" over this time period. We informally use the term *"artifact instance"* to refer to the persisting object that underlies a sequence of artifact snapshots all having the same artifact ID.

An *artifact lifecyle schema* is a pair (S, E) where

1. S is a finite set of *states*, which includes the designated states **source** and **sink**.
2. E is a set of directed edges (ordered pairs over S), such that there are no in-edges into **source** and there are no out-edges from **sink**.

Intuitively, on a move from **source** to another state an artifact instance is created, and on a move from a state into **sink** an artifact instance is archived and effectively taken out of further evolution or participation in the workflow.

An *artifact type* is a triple $\mathcal{R} = (R, D, L)$ where R is the name of the type (a character string), D is an artifact data schema and L is an artifact lifecycle schema. Suppose that $L = (S, E)$. A *snapshot* of $\mathcal{R}$ is a snapshot of D such that the **ID** and **state** attributes are defined, and the **state** attribute is an element of $S - \{\mathbf{source}\}$.

3.2 Artifact Schemas and Hub Schemas

An *artifact schema* is a collection $\mathcal{S} = \{\mathcal{R}_1, \ldots, \mathcal{R}_n\}$ of artifact types that have pairwise distinct names $R_1, \ldots, R_n$. If *PID* is a set of participant IDs and *OID* a set of stakeholder organization IDs, then a *snapshot* of $\mathcal{S}$ over *PID, OID* is a function $I : \{R_1, \ldots, R_n\} \to$ sets of artifact snapshots that use participant (organization) IDs from *PID* (*OID*), where $I[R_j]$ is a set of artifact snapshots of type $\mathcal{R}_j, j \in [1..n]$; there are no pairs s_1, s_2 of distinct snapshots in $\cup_j I(R_j)$ with $s_1.\mathbf{ID} = s_2.\mathbf{ID}$; and for each artifact ID g occurring in any artifact snapshot of I, there is a snapshot s occurring in I with $s.\mathbf{ID} = g$.

Job_Opening_ID	State	Applicants_and_Date	...
J312	negotiating	A567	4/15/09	
		C123	3/10/09	
		B647	4/10/09	

Job_App_ID	State	Name	...
A567	evaluating	Alice	
C123	evaluating	Carl	
B647	offer_preparation	Bob	

(a) Partial snapshot of a Job_Opening artifact   (b) Partial snapshots of Job_Application artifacts

Fig. 4. Partial snapshot of the artifact schema from the Hiring example

Example 1. An example snapshot from the Hiring example is depicted in Fig. 4 (only some of the attributes are shown). Part (a) depicts a snapshot of a single Job_Opening artifact with ID of J312. This artifact instance is in the negotiating state, indicating that one candidate has been short-listed. Part (b) shows a portion of the snapshots of three artifact instances of type Job_Application, all of whom applied for opening J312. One of them, corresponding to Bob, is in the offer_preparation state. □

A *hub schema* is a pair $\mathcal{H} = (\mathcal{S}, \mathbf{Org})$ where $\mathcal{S}$ is an artifact schema and $\mathbf{Org}$ is a finite set of stakeholder organization types. In the Hiring example, $\mathbf{Org}$ has six types.

Let $\mathcal{H} = (\mathcal{S}, \mathbf{Org})$ be a hub schema. A *snapshot* of $\mathcal{H}$ is a 5-tuple

$$H = (I^{art}, OID, PID, I^{org}, I^{part})$$

where

1. I^{art} is a snapshot of $\mathcal{S}$ over OID, PID.
2. OID is a finite set of organization IDs.
3. PID is a finite set of participant IDs.
4. $I^{org} : OID \rightarrow \mathbf{Org}$ is the organization to organization type mapping.
5. $I^{part} : PID(\rightarrow 2^O - \{\emptyset\})$ is the participant to role mapping.

Here, each stakeholder organization in OID is associated with exactly one stakeholder organization type in $\mathbf{Org}$, and each participant in PID is a member of at least one, but possibly more than one, stakeholder organization in OID.

Example 2. Returning to our running example, two stakeholder organizations of the same type could be Software_Group and Research_Division, both acting as Hiring Organizations. As an example of a participant belonging to more than one stakeholder organization, an employee might be a member of Research_Division and involved with overseeing the recruiting for a staff researcher position, and also serve as an Evaluator for a candidate being considered by Software_Group. □

We now consider how the contents of an interoperation hub can evolve over time. Let $\mathcal{H} = (\mathcal{S}, \mathbf{Org})$ be a hub schema, and let H, H' be two snapshots of $\mathcal{H}$. Then H *transitions* to H', denoted $H \rightarrow_{\mathcal{H}} H'$, if one of the following holds

1. **(New artifact instance:)** H' is the result of adding a single, new artifact snapshot s to H, and the state of that snapshot is one state away from the **source** node of the state machine of the artifact schema of s.
2. **(Update to artifact instance:)** H' is the result of replacing a single snapshot s of H by a new snapshot s' having the same type, where $s.\mathbf{ID} = s'.\mathbf{ID}$ and $s.\mathbf{state} = s'.\mathbf{state}$, and for at least one top-level attribute A, $s.A \neq s'.A$.

3. **(Change state of artifact instance:)** H' is the result of replacing a single snapshot s of H by a new snapshot s' having the same artifact type $\mathcal{A} = (D, L)$, where $s.\mathbf{ID} = s'.\mathbf{ID}$, $(s.\mathbf{state}, s'.state)$ is a transition in L, and for each other attribute A, $s'.A = s.A$.

4. **(Modify participants or stakeholder organizations:)** H' is the result of adding or dropping an element to OID or PID, or making a change to the function I^{org} that impacts a single organization, or making a change to the function I^{part} that impacts a single participant.

3.3 Adding a Condition Language

We shall use a logic-based expression language for nested data types, that can be used to express conditions and queries on snapshots of artifact and schema snapshots. The language is modeled after the calculus defined in [1], and we provide here only the most salient details. Variables are typed using the nested complex types. Terms include $\tau.A$ for record type term τ and attribute name A. Constructors are provided to create record- and set-typed terms. Atomic formulas include $R(\tau)$ for artifact schema name R, $\tau = \tau'$ for scalar or ID types (but not set types), $\tau \in \tau'$ where the type of τ' is set of the type of τ. It also includes atomic formulas of the form $\tau \in \tau'$ where τ has type `participant_ID` and τ' has type `organization_ID`. Query expressions are created in the manner of relational calculus queries.

4 Views and Access Rights

An important component of the interoperation hub vision is that typically, stakeholders will not be able to see entire artifacts, nor will they be able to make arbitrary updates to them. This section introduces the notion of *views* of artifact schemas and snapshots which restrict what participants from a given organization type can see, *windows* into the set of artifacts that a given participant can see, and also access rights for making updates against them based on a generalization of "CRUD" restrictions. These notions embody an important aspect of the utility of interoperation hubs in facilitating communication and business-level synchronization between organizations, because they provide mechanisms for ensuring that information and events that should be kept private are indeed being kept private.

The section also develops a family of simple theoretical results, including a decidability result concerning whether an artifact, once visible to a participant, remains visible to the participant for the rest of its lifecycle.

4.1 Views

We begin with an example of the views presented to one kind of stakeholder.

Example 3. Figures 5 and 6 show the views of `Job_Opening` and `Job_Application`, respectively, that are made available to Candidates in the Hiring example. In these views, some of the attributes of the data schema are grayed out, because the view prevents a candidate from seeing those attributes. In terms of the lifecycle, some states are collapsed or "condensed" together. (These are shown as solid disks.) For example, in the view

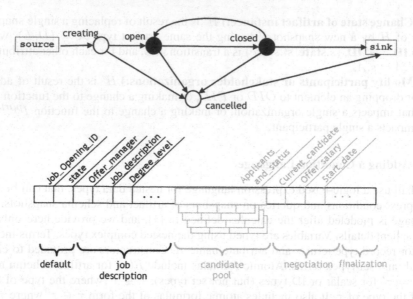

Fig. 5. The view of the `Job_Opening` artifact type that would be visible to Candidates

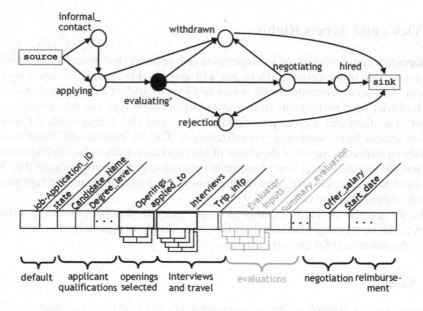

Fig. 6. The view of the `Job_Application` artifact type that would be visible to Candidates

of Job_Application, the enterprise will typically want to hide from the candidate whether it is in the evaluating, on_hold, or preparing_offer state. Similarly, as shown in the view of Job_Opening several states are collapsed into the two states open and closed. (The specific mapping of states to open and closed would depend on the business policy to be followed.) □

With regards to artifact types, the notion of view includes two components: a restriction on the attributes that can be seen, and a restriction on the set of states that can be seen. The first case will be achieved using projection, and the second by using node condensation.

Let $\mathcal{R} = (R, D, L)$ be an artifact type, where $D = \langle \mathbf{ID} : \text{artifact\_ID}, \mathbf{state} : \text{state\_name}, A_1 : T_1, \ldots, A_n : T_n \rangle$. A *projection mapping* over D is an expression of the form π_J where J is a subset of $A_1, \ldots, A_n$. Projection mappings operate at both the data schema level and the snapshot level in the natural manner. A *condensation mapping* over a lifecycle schema $L = (S, E)$ is an expression γ_f where f is a surjective function $f : S \to S'$, where S' is a set of state names, such that

1. **source** , **sink** $\in S'$.
2. $\gamma(\mathbf{source}) = \mathbf{source}$ and $\gamma(\mathbf{sink}) = \mathbf{sink}$.

(Note that multiple states of S might map into **source** or **sink**.) A condensation mapping works on the meta-data of a lifecycle schema; specifically, in the above case $\gamma_f(L) = (S', E')$ where $E' = \{(\gamma(\sigma_1), \gamma(\sigma_2)) \mid (\sigma_1, \sigma_2) \in E\}$.

A *view* on $\mathcal{R} = (R, D, L)$ is an ordered pair $\nu = (\pi_J, \gamma_f)$ where π_J is a projection mapping over D and γ_f is a condensation mapping over L. The result of applying ν to a snapshot s of $\mathcal{R}$ is defined in the natural manner. For an artifact schema $\mathcal{S} = \{\mathcal{R}_1, \ldots, \mathcal{R}_n\}$, with artifact type names $R_1, \ldots, R_n$, a *view mapping* of $\mathcal{S}$ is a function ν with domain $\{R_1, \ldots, R_n\}$ such that $\nu[R_j]$ is a view on $\mathcal{R}_j$ for $j \in [1..n]$. We use $\nu(\mathcal{S})$ to denote the schema $\{\nu[R_1](\mathcal{R}_1), \ldots, \nu[R_n](\mathcal{R}_n)\}$, and for a snapshot I of $\mathcal{S}$, $\nu[I]$ is a snapshot of $\nu(\mathcal{S})$ defined in the natural manner. Finally suppose now that $\mathcal{H} = (\mathcal{S}, \mathbf{Org})$ is a hub schema. A *view mapping* for $\mathcal{H}$ is a function ν with domain $\mathbf{Org}$, such that for each stakeholder organization type O in $\mathbf{Org}$, $\nu[O]$ is a view mapping of $\mathcal{S}$.

Example 4. The projection mapping of Job_Opening artifact for an Evaluator would include all of the attributes depicted in Fig. 5, except for Offer_salary. The condensation mapping, however, would include all states in the Job_Opening artifact. □

If ν is a view mapping, and there is a participant p who is a member of two or more organizations of different types, then $\nu[R](p)$ can be defined using a union on the projections and a variant of the cross-product construction for the condensations. The details are omitted due to space limitations.

Given a view mapping and an organization type O, we ask: when does it make sense for participants in an organization of type O to be able to request a transition in a lifecycle in their view? Let $\mathcal{H} = (\mathcal{S}, \mathbf{Org})$ by an interoperation hub, ν be a view mapping, and $\mathcal{R} = (R, D, (S, E))$ be an artifact type in $\mathcal{S}$. An edge $e = (\sigma_1, \sigma_2) \in E$ is *eligible* in $\mathcal{H}$ if for some $O \in \mathbf{Org}$ with $\nu[O](R) = (\pi_J, \gamma_f)$ we have: for each state $\sigma_1' \in f^{-1}(f(\sigma_1))$ there is exactly one state $\sigma_2' \in f^{-1}(f(\sigma_2))$ such that $(\sigma_1', \sigma_2') \in E$. Intuitively, this means that if a participant p in an organization of type O requests a transition in p's view from $f^{-1}(\sigma_1)$ to $f^{-1}(\sigma_2)$, then there is no ambiguity with regards to which transition in the base state machine (S, E) should be taken.

Although not done here due to space limitations, it is straightforward to characterize, given an interoperation hub $\mathcal{H}$ and view mapping ν, the full set of transitions $\rightarrow_{\mathcal{H},\nu}$ between snapshots of $\mathcal{H}$ that can be achieved by participants working through their views.

4.2 Windows

The notion of "window mapping" is used to restrict which artifact instances a participant can see. Recall the condition language from Section 3. Suppose that $\mathcal{S} = \{\mathcal{R}_1, \ldots, \mathcal{R}_n\}$ is an artifact schema with artifact type names $R_1, \ldots, R_n$. For $j \in [1..n]$, a query $Q_{\varphi(x,y)}$ is a *window mapping* for $\mathcal{R}_j$ using x for participant IDs and y for artifact IDs if

1. x has type participant_ID,
2. y has type artifact_ID, and
3. φ has the form $\exists z (R_j(z) \wedge z.\mathbf{ID} = y \wedge \psi(x, z))$ for some formula ψ.

When a window mapping $Q_{\varphi(x,y)}$ for $\mathcal{R}_j$ is applied to a snapshot I of $\mathcal{S}$, the result is $Q_{\varphi(x,y)}(I) = \{(p, g) \mid I \models \varphi[x/p, y/g]\}$. Note that in each element of the answer, the second coordinate will be the ID of an artifact snapshot in $I[R_j]$. Analogous to view mappings, a window mapping ω for an interoperation hub $\mathcal{H} = (\mathcal{S}, \mathbf{Org})$ is a function that maps a pair O, R (for $O \in \mathbf{Org}$ and R the name of some $\mathcal{R}$ in $\mathcal{S}$) to a window mapping $\omega[O, R]$ for $\mathcal{R}$.

Example 5. In the running example, the window query for Hiring Organizations might permit them to see only Job_Applications that are targeted at Job_Openings sponsored by that Hiring Organization. For the snapshot of Fig. 4, Software_Group would see all three candidates, but Research would see none of them. □

In many cases, a window mapping will focus on whether a certain pattern of values is found in the current snapshot. For example, an evaluator might be permitted to "see" all Job_Application artifact instances for which he is named in the *evaluators* attribute. Happily, the class of such window mappings, which have no negation and only existential quantifiers, correspond closely to the conjunctive queries with union in the relational model, about which many properties are known.

To illustrate, we briefly study the question of whether one window mapping ω is less restrictive than another one ω'. Let $\mathcal{H} = (\mathcal{S}, \mathbf{Org})$ be an interoperation hub. We say that ω *dominates* ω', denoted $\omega' \preceq \omega$, if for each instance I of $\mathcal{H}$ and each artifact type $\mathcal{R} = (R, D, L)$ of $\mathcal{H}$, $\omega'[O, R](I) \subseteq \omega[O, R](I)$. Using the fact that our nested types are in Partitioned Normal Form, the correspondance with conjunctive queries with union, and results from [18] we obtain the following.

Proposition 6. Let $\mathcal{H}$ be an interoperation hub, and assume that ω and ω' are window mappings based on queries that have no negation and only existential quantifiers. Then it is decidable whether $\omega' \preceq \omega$, and this decision problem is NP-complete.

4.3   Access Rights and CRUDAE

Windows and views give a first-tier, rather coarse-grained mechanism for specifying the access rights of participants to the contents of an interoperation hub. Following in the spirit of [19,8,10], we now introduce a finer-grained mechanism, that is based on providing "Create-Read-Update-Delete-Append (CRUDA)" and "Execute" permissions to a participant p, depending on what type of stakeholder organization(s) p is in, and what state an artifact instance is in. (More precisely, this is based on the state in p's view of the artifact instance.)

Suppose that $\mathcal{R} = (R, D, L)$ is an artifact schema, where $D = \langle$ **ID** : artifact_ID, **state** : state_name, $A_1 : T_1, \ldots, A_n : T_n \rangle$ and $L = (S, E)$. A *simple CRUDAE specification* for $\mathcal{R}$ is a mapping α with domain $\{A_1, \ldots, A_n\} \cup \{$'E'$\}$ and where

- $\alpha : \{A_1, \ldots, A_n\} \rightarrow 2^{\{\text{'C','R','U','D','A'}\}}$
- $\alpha($'E'$) \subseteq E$ (i.e., the set of edges in L)

Intuitively, if 'C' $\in \alpha(A_j)$, this indicates that under α, a participant can "create" a value for A_j (e.g., provide a value to a previously undefined attribute) and similarly for cases of 'R' $\in \alpha(A_j)$, 'U' $\in \alpha(A_j)$, 'D' $\in \alpha(A_j)$ and 'A' $\in \alpha(A_j)$; and α(E) indicates the set of edges that the participant can request a transition along.

In general, we associate a simple CRUDAE specification to each state of an artifact lifecycle, reflecting the intuition that access rights typically change based on state. A *CRUDAE specification* for $\mathcal{R} = (R, D, (S, E))$ is a mapping β with domain S, such that $\beta[\sigma]$ is a simple CRUDAE specification for $\mathcal{R}$ for each state $\sigma \in S$. Intuitively, for state $\sigma \in S$, $\beta[\sigma]$ is intended to indicate the access rights that a participant will have when the artifact instance is in state σ. Suppose that $\sigma \in S$, and consider $\beta[\sigma]$(E). It is natural to assume that each edge $e \in \beta[\sigma]$(E) has σ as source.

Suppose now that $\mathcal{H} = (\mathcal{S}, \mathbf{Org})$ is a hub schema, where $\mathcal{S} = (\mathcal{R}_1, \ldots, \mathcal{R}_n)$ with artifact type names $(R_1, \ldots, R_n)$. Suppose further that ν is a view mapping for $\mathcal{H}$. A *CRUDAE specification* for the pair $(\mathcal{H}, \nu)$ is a mapping δ with domain $\mathbf{Org} \times \{R_1, \ldots, R_n\}$, such that

1. $\delta[O, R_j]$ is a CRUDA specification for $\nu[O](\mathcal{R}_j)$, for each $O \in \mathbf{Org}$ and $j \in [1..n]$.
2. $\delta[O, R_j]$(E) $\subseteq \{e \mid e$ is an eligible edge in the lifecycle of $\nu[O](\mathcal{R}_j)$

To understand this intuitively, think of a stakeholder organization type $O \in \mathbf{Org}$. Recall that a participant p in an organization o of type O cannot "see" all of $\mathcal{S}$, but rather can "see" only $\nu[O]$. Furthermore, $\delta[O, R_j]$ will indicate, for each state in the lifecycle of $\nu[O](\mathcal{R}_j)$, which attributes of $\nu[O](\mathcal{R}_j)$ can be created, read, updated, or deleted by p, and also which transitions in the lifecycle of $\nu[O](\mathcal{R}_j)$ can be invoked by p.

Example 7. We recall that a candidate can view at most one Job_Application artifact instance, namely,, the one that the candidate created. For this instance, the candidate has Update permission only for attributes such as Degree_level, vita, experience, and only Read permission for the other attributes depicted in Fig. 6. The candidate will have execute permission to bring about a move his Job_Application artifact from evaluating' to withdrawn state, by withdrawing his/her application from consideration for the job opening.   □

Finally, an *extended hub schema* is a tuple $\mathcal{H} = (\mathcal{S}, \mathbf{Org}, \omega, \nu, \delta)$ where

1. $(\mathcal{S}, \mathbf{Org})$ is a hub schema.
2. ω is a window mapping for $(\mathcal{S}, \mathbf{Org})$
3. ν is a view mapping for $(\mathcal{S}, \mathbf{Org})$
4. δ is a CRUDAE specification for $(\mathcal{S}, \mathbf{Org})$

The notion of transitions between snapshots of a hub schema can be genealized to extended hub schemas in the natural manner, taking into account the restrictions on participants, based on the view they can "see", the artifacts accessible through the window mapping, and the CRUDAE mapping. For an extended hub schema $\mathcal{H}$, this relation is denoted by $\rightarrow_H$.

4.4 Persistence of Visibility

We conclude the section by studying the question: Given an extended interoperation hub $\mathcal{H} = (\mathcal{S}, \mathbf{Org}, \omega, \nu, \delta)$, and a participant p and artifact instance a, is it possible that p can "see" a at some point but not "see" a at a later point.

More precisely, let $I = I_0 \rightarrow_\mathcal{H} I_1 \rightarrow_\mathcal{H} \ldots \rightarrow_\mathcal{H} I_n$ be a sequence of snapshots of $\mathcal{H}$ satisyfing the $\rightarrow_\mathcal{H}$ relation as indicated, where I_0 is the empty snapshot, and in which there are no transitions involving changes to the particpants or the organizations. Suppose that for some participant ID p, artifact ID g, artifact type $\mathcal{R}$ with name R, and index j, we have $(p, g) \in \omega[O, R](I_j)$, and j is the first index with this property. Then g has *persistent visibility* for p in I if $(p, g) \in \omega[O, R](I_k)$ for each $k \in [j + 1, n]$. The sequence I has *persistent visibility* if each artifact ID occurring in I has persistent visibility for each participant occurring in I. $\mathcal{H}$ has *persistent visibility* if each such sequence I has persistent visibility.

In some cases it may be natural to not have persistent visibility. For example, a candidate p may see a Job_Opening while it is still in the Open state (in the view provided to candidates). If p did not apply for this particular opening, and if the Job_Opening moves to the Closed state, then it may be appropriate to hide this job opening from the candidate. An alternative, that might be more convenient to users so that things don't unexpectedly disappear, would be to still show the artifact instance to the candidate, but grayed out.

In other contexts, it may be desirable to ensure that a given artifact type has persistent visibility for a given stakeholder organization type. The following result states that this is decidable if the window queries correspond to conjunctive queries.

Proposition 8. Let $\mathcal{H} = (\mathcal{S}, \mathbf{Org}, \omega, \nu, \delta)$ be an extended interoperation hub, and suppose that ω has no negation, no disjunction, and only existential quantifiers. Then it is decidable whether $\mathcal{H}$ has persistent visibility. This problem is in PSPACE in terms of the size of $\mathcal{H}$.

Although space limitations prevent inclusion of the proof, we note that the result is demonstrated by showing that it suffices to look at a small set of sequences of snapshots, which are constructed from a bounded active domain and have bounded length.

This result leaves several questions open, including finding a tight bound for the complexity of testing persistent visibility under the assumptions of the proposition, and finding the limits of decidability.

In the case of no negation and only existential quantifiers, a straightforward sufficient condition can be developed, that guarantees persistent visiblity. The basic idea is that if some value in a field A of some artifact instance b is used as a witness for p to see an artifact a, then we need to ensure that for the state that b is in, and any state that it can reach from there, the field A can be read (and appended if it is of set type), but not created, deleted or updated.

5   Towards a Prototype Implementation

It is natural to ask how difficult it would be to build a system that supports the creation and deployment of artifact-centric interoperation hubs. It appears that such a system can be constructed in a straightforward manner from an artifact-centric workflow engine. To verify this conjecture, we have been working to create a generic interoperation hub capability on top of the Siena prototype system [8,10]. (As an alternative, one could use the BELA tool developed at IBM Research [19], which operates on top of IBM's WebSphere product line.)

The Siena system includes a user interface for designing artifact-based workflow schemas (that use a state-machine based lifecycle model), a capability to represent the workflow schemas as an XML file along with some XSDs for holding the arti-fact information models, and an engine that directly executes against the XML file in response to incoming events and tasks being performed. As described in [8], Siena schemas can be specified in Microsoft Powerpoint. To permit easier access to Siena schemas by multiple designers, the Siena team at IBM Research is currently developing

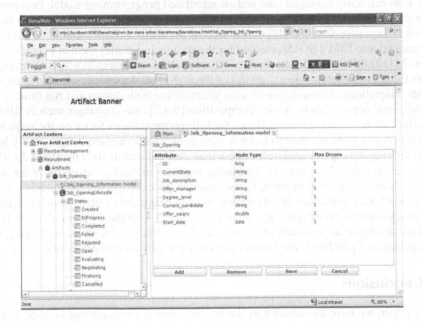

Fig. 7. Screen shot of Siena's web-based GUI, used here to specify the Hiring artifact schema

a web-browser-based tool for specifying artifact schemas. A screen shot of this interface, showing part of the artifact schema for the Hiring example, is shown in Fig. 7.

Siena provides REST and WSDL interfaces so that outside services can invoke the Siena capabilities, including changes to artifact values, and moving artifacts along their lifecycle. Siena provides the capabilities of sending notifications on a selective basis on entry into states, and of showing artifact instances to users, restricted according to a global, role-based specification of Read permissions, and it supports role-based access control based on CRUDE at the state level. (Restrictions on "append" capabilities are not currently supported.) Siena also provides numerous hooks for triggering of events and behaviors, along with guards on transitions and state entry. The main steps in creating a system for supporting inteoperation hubs on top of Siena include (i) enriching the current capability in Siena to recognize roles, so that participants, stakeholder organizations, and stakeholder organization types can all be specified and used during runtime; (ii) modifying the view of snapshots provided to participants to reflect the condensation of states in interoperation hub views; and (iii) incorporating the ability to specify access controls based on windows. Creating these extensions is a work in progress.

6   Related Work

Nigam and Caswell [15] present one of the earliest discussions of the artifact-centric model its application to business modelling. Here, we extend [15] to show how services and applications can interoperate using the artifact-centric approach. In [13], Nandi and Kumaran introduce the concept of Adaptive Business Objects (ABO) to integrate people, processes, information and applications. ABO presents an abstraction of a business entity with explicitly managed state and an associated programming model. In contrast, our interoperation hub model is at a higher abstraction level, understandable by those without IT expertise. Citation [19] describes how the artifact-centric technique has been incorporated into IBM's SOMA method for the design and deployment of business processes. In [12], Müller et al. present data-driven process structures in which Object Life Cycles (OLC) of different objects are linked through OLC dependencies. This approach enables adaptations of data-driven process structures at both design and run time.

Traditional approaches to service composition [9,4,3], use languages such as BPEL[1] to model low-level service interactions. Such implementations focus on the sequence of Web services to be invoked to reach a state goal, and do not explicitly specify how the underlying data is manipulated, or how that data constrains the operation. As a result, the approach is less intuitive than using business artifacts, especially in the case of large shared business processes. In the business process space, [20] models a business process as a collection of interacting process fragments called "proclets". Each proclet is autonomous enough to decide how to interact with the other proclets, and this provides flexibility in workflow execution. In that work, similar to choreography, the interoperation of proclets is not managed or facilitated by a centralized hub.

7   Conclusions

In this paper, we have illustrated how the artifact-centric approach can be used to create hubs that facilitate the interoperation of multiple automonous stakeholders who

---

[1] http://www-128.ibm.com/developerworks/library/specification/ws-bpel/

have a common goal. Because the basic building block of the artifact-centric approach, namely "business artifacts", combine data and process specification into a single unit, it is straightforward to incorporate three natural forms of access control into the framework, namely, windows (that restrict which artifact instances a participant can see), views (that restrict which attributes and states of an artifact a participant can see), and CRUDAE (a variant of the classical CRUD notion, that restricts the kinds of reads and updates a partipant can perform, based on the current state of an artifact).

The formal framework developed in the paper was used to develop results concerning some of the global implications of placing these access restrictions on a hub, and a prototyping effort indicates that these hubs can be created through a straightforward extension of an artifact-centric workflow engine. This paper provides the starting point for a rich exploration into this new style of interoperation hub. Some theoretical questions of particular interest involve the interplay of, on the one hand, the views and windows exposed to participants and, on the other hand, the sets of achievable sequencs of hub snapshots and integrity constraints on them.

Acknowledgements. The authors thank the extended ArtiFact^{TM} team at IBM Research for many informative discussions about the artifact-centric approach and its application in business contexts. The authors are also very grateful to Fenno (Terry) Heath III, Florian Pinel, and Sridhar Maradugu for facilitating the use of the Siena prototype system [8,10].

References

1. Abiteboul, S., Beeri, C.: The power of languages for the manipulation of complex values. The VLDB Journal 4(4), 727–794 (1995)
2. Abiteboul, S., Bidoit, N.: Nonfirst normal form relations: An algebra allowing data restructuring. Journal of Computer and System Sciences 33, 361–393 (1986)
3. Agarwal, V., Chafle, G., Mittal, S., Srivastava, B.: Understanding Approaches for Web Service Composition and Execution. In: Proc. of Compute 2008, Bangalore, India (2008)
4. Barros, A.P., Dumas, M., Oaks, P.: Standards for web service choreography and orchestration: Status and perspectives. In: Bussler, C.J., Haller, A. (eds.) BPM 2005. LNCS, vol. 3812, pp. 61–74. Springer, Heidelberg (2006)
5. Bhattacharya, K., Caswell, N.S., Kumaran, S., Nigam, A., Wu, F.Y.: Artifact-centered operational modeling: Lessons from customer engagements. IBM Systems Journal 46(4), 703–721 (2007)
6. Bhattacharya, K., et al.: A model-driven approach to industrializing discovery processes in pharmaceutical research. IBM Systems Journal 44(1), 145–162 (2005)
7. Chao, T., et al.: Artifact-based transformation of IBM Global Financing: A case study, 2009. To appear Intl. Conf. on Business Process Management (BPM) (September 2009)
8. Cohn, D., Dhoolia, P. (Terry) Heath III, F.F., Pinel, F., Vergo, J.: Siena: From powerpoint to web App in 5 minutes. In: Bouguettaya, A., Krueger, I., Margaria, T. (eds.) ICSOC 2008. LNCS, vol. 5364, pp. 722–723. Springer, Heidelberg (2008)
9. Decker, G., Zaha, J.M., Dumas, M.: Execution semantics for service choreographies. In: Bravetti, M., Núñez, M., Zavattaro, G. (eds.) WS-FM 2006. LNCS, vol. 4184, pp. 163–177. Springer, Heidelberg (2006)
10. (Terry) Heath III, F.F., Pinel, F.: Siena user's guide (2009) (in preparation)
11. Hull, R.: Artifact-centric business process models: Brief survey of research results and challenges. In: Meersman, R., Tari, Z. (eds.) OTM 2008, Part I. LNCS, vol. 5331, pp. 1152–1163. Springer, Heidelberg (2008)

12. Müller, D., Reichert, M., Herbst, J.: A New Paradigm for the Enactment and Dynamic Adaptation of Data-Driven Process Structures. In: Bellahsène, Z., Léonard, M. (eds.) CAiSE 2008. LNCS, vol. 5074, pp. 48–63. Springer, Heidelberg (2008)
13. Nandi, P., Kumaran, S.: Adaptive Business Objects - A New Component Model for Business Integration. In: Proceedings of ICEIS 2005, Miami, FL, USA (2005)
14. Nigam, A., Caswell, N.S.: Business artifacts: An approach to operational specification. IBM Systems Journal 42(3), 428–445 (2003)
15. Nigam, A., Caswell, N.S.: Business Artifacts: An Approach to Operational Specification. IBM Systems Journal 42(3) (2003)
16. Peltz, C.: Web services orchestration and choreography. IEEE Computer 36(10), 46–52 (2003)
17. Roth, M.A., Korth, H.F., Silberschatz, A.: Extended algebra and calculus for nested relational databases. ACM Trans. Database Syst. 13(4), 389–417 (1988)
18. Sabiv, Y., Yannakakis, M.: Equivalences among relational expressions with the union and difference operators. Journal of the ACM 27(4), 633–655 (1980)
19. Strosnider, J.K., Nandi, P., Kumarn, S., Ghosh, S., Arsanjani, A.: Model-driven synthesis of SOA solutions. IBM Systems Journal 47(3), 415–432 (2008)
20. van der Aalst, W.M.P., Barthelmess, P., Ellis, C.A., Wainer, J.: Proclets: A framework for lightweight interacting workflow processes. Int. J. Cooperative Inf. Syst. 10(4), 443–481 (2001)

Aspect Orientation for Composite Services in the Telecommunication Domain

Jörg Niemöller, Roman Levenshteyn, Eugen Freiter, Konstantinos Vandikas,
Raphaël Quinet, and Ioannis Fikouras

Ericsson GmbH
Ericsson Allee 1, 52134 Herzogenrath, Germany
{joerg.niemoeller,roman.levensteyn}@ericsson.com,
{eugen.freiter,konstantinos.vandikas}@ericsson.com,
{raphael.quinet,ioannis.fikouras}@ericsson.com

Abstract. Telecommunication network operators have specific requirements on services offered through their network, which are frequently independent of the core business logic of the service. As an example, these requirements ensure monitoring of user activities for charging purposes or allow controlling parameters that influence the quality of service. In order to satisfy these demands, services are typically tailor-made to support these supplementary features next to their core business logic. As a result, their implementation becomes tangled and specialized. This is identified as a major obstacle for efficient service composition, because more specialized services are less suitable for being reused in different contexts. This paper describes an approach to introduce concepts of aspect-oriented programming to service composition in order to keep the implementations of telecommunication-specific requirements separated from the core business function of a service.

Keywords: AOP, IMS, Service Composition, Telecommunication.

1 Introduction

Telecommunication network operators aim for a service infrastructure that allows a converged usage of heterogeneous services. They rely on cost-efficient and rapid design of new applications by re-use of already existing services. Another goal is differentiation form the competition by integrating telecommunication services with popular community services from the internet, because these services provide users with a new style of communication and social interaction. Service composition is a key technology for reaching the desired convergence within a heterogeneous service environment. This paper is based on an approach for service composition [1] that supports multiple service technologies to be used within a single composite service.

Typically, operators from the telecommunication domain require support for specific supplementary functions from all services provided through their network. These functions, for example, allow charging for service usage, collect statistics or help controlling the service quality.

L. Baresi, C.-H. Chi, and J. Suzuki (Eds.): ICSOC-ServiceWave 2009, LNCS 5900, pp. 19–33, 2009.

This paper analyzes the design of converged composite services that need to consider specific requirements of the telecommunication domain. Furthermore, this paper outlines that these requirements often imply cross-cutting implementations, therefore they are a severe obstacle for efficient composition of services. A solution is presented that combines data-driven composition of heterogeneous services with techniques from aspect oriented programming (AOP). This includes weaving based on the unique elements of the composition environment. The paper explores a solution in which aspects are modeled as services and selected through constraint-based service selection, thus concepts known from the underlying service composition approach are applied to AOP.

2 Related Work

The central problem of composing applications according to cross-cutting concerns is motivated in [2]. That paper defines common concepts and terminology of the AOP domain like cross-cutting concerns, aspects, point-cut, advice, and weaving. In our paper we follow this terminology.

AspectJ [3] was one of the first implementations of the AOP paradigms as proposed in [2]. AspectJ extends the Java language by new elements that allow the definition of point-cuts and advice code. Weaving is performed prior to execution, resulting in a regular Java application including injected advice code.

JBOSS-AOP [4] introduces weaving on byte-code level rather than on source code. This allows online weaving at runtime rather than offline weaving that is performed prior to runtime, like for example in AspectJ. In this paper we apply online weaving, since the dynamic run-time behavior of composite services means that information for effective identification of relevant join-points is not available at design time.

AO4BPEL [5] is an aspect-oriented extension for business process execution language (BPEL) [6], [7]. Online weaving is used in order to dynamically add or remove aspects from a BPEL process. Each activity within a BPEL workflow process can serve as join-point. Point-cuts can span over multiple BPEL processes and attributes of the BPEL processes can be used in order to identify relevant join-points.

A framework that uses aspect orientation for dynamic selection of web services is presented in [9]. The goal here is to dynamically select the web services to be used within client-applications. An intermediate layer for managing web services and decoupling them from applications is introduced based on AOP principles. Aspects are used in order to flexibly redirect web service invocations to alternative services, thus flexibly binding web services to clients.

This paper is based on the service composition technology described in [1]. According to this approach [1], an abstract description of constituent services function and capabilities is the base of composition. Service templates are used to describe which constituent services shall be used as components of the composition. This is achieved by using constraints for specifying the properties a service required to be selected for execution. The constituent services to be used as components of a composite application are therefore selected according to their abstract description, rather than pointing directly to a concrete service. A service skeleton represents a model of a composite service. It combines service templates with control elements that steer the composition process.

In order to execute the composite service, the skeleton is executed step-by-step by a composition engine. In this process, constituent services are selected by satisfying the constraints specified by a service template. These constraints perform a selection among the descriptions of all available services, stored in a service repository. The service descriptions contain abstract descriptions of the service function and capabilities, coupled with binding information. For example, a service that provides the geographical location of a subscriber might be described by its function "positioning" and by its capability to provide the position with certain accuracy. The composition is session based and all services within a composition session have access to a shared state, which can be used for data exchange between services.

3   Crosscutting in the Telecommunication Domain

The requirements of a telecommunication network operator are mainly driven by business models, legal requirements and standardization. Besides the functionality offered as end-user services to their subscribers, multiple supplementary functions are usually required. Examples include the collection of information for charging and billing purposes, or monitoring and control of service quality. Support for this kind of functionality is usually an integral part of a service that targets a telecommunication network, but it considerably increases the costs for service design and modification. Thus, methods reducing the investments into system integration, customization and new design are of particular importance for operators.

Furthermore, services from third-party providers often do not meet the very specific requirements of a network operator. Customization of these services is usually not feasible and not desired as this would create very specialized services that are not suitable for broad re-use in new contexts.

Service composition allows the creation of new applications by re-using existing constituent services. A composition technology like the one described in [1] provides simple tools that allow the creation and modification of composite applications in a very cost efficient way. Fig.1 shows a simplified skeleton of a composite service that provides a weather forecast for the user's geographical location. It combines services that retrieve the user position with a weather forecast service. Depending on the user preferences, further services might generate a map illustrating the forecast and finally send an SMS or MMS to the user.

When offering this service through a telecommunication network, the operator usually requires support for charging. In addition, logging of all used services for statistical purposes might be required as well as setting and monitoring of service quality parameters. These supplementary features do not provide a service directly to the end-user, but they help the operator controlling service and network operation. For this reason they are often referred to as non-functional requirements.

Using the design methods of service composition, the supplementary functions could be implemented by selecting only those constituent services that already contain support for such functions. Alternatively, additional services can be included into the composition, which contribute only the supplementary features to the overall composite service. The resulting composite service is depicted in Fig. 1 on the right side.

One observation is that additional services providing supplementary functions spread across the whole composition. They cannot be implemented within a single, well encapsulated entity due to their inherent need to interact with the constituent services throughout the whole composite application. These supplementary functions show a property that is referred to as cross-cutting in AOP terminology. Cross-cutting caused by supplementary functions is typical for telecommunication services. Although it is not further investigated within the scope of this paper, a similar observation can be made for the domain of enterprise applications.

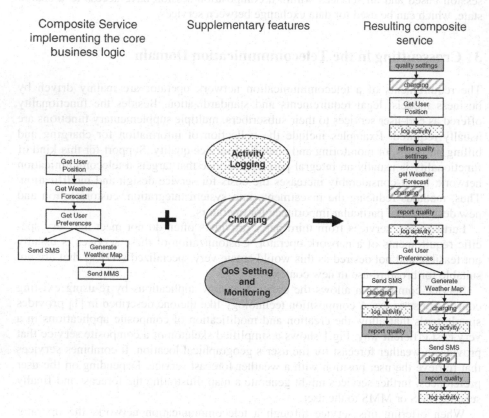

Fig. 1. Adding supplementary features to a composite service

The described method for service composition [1] is based on modules that are products of functional decomposition of an intended application. In this respect, it is not different than procedural or object oriented programming languages and equally affected from cross-cutting as described in [2]. Its advanced features like constraint-based service selection and service modeling based on abstract service descriptions are designed to handle services that are strongly encapsulated functional entities.

Therefore, they are weakly entangled with other services. As a result, the features of service composition do not help handling cross-cutting.

Another observation is that certain services have already included the support for supplementary features. In Fig. 1, for example, the support for charging was implemented into the service "get Weather Forecast". A service like this is multifunctional, which increases its specialization. It is tailor-made for certain scenarios and might not fit in other scenarios. Some of the multiple functions it provides might interfere with other services or it would need to operate differently. For example, the charging enhanced weather forecast service cannot be used if a different charging method needs to be applied although its basic function alone, the weather forecast, might fit.

Composite services can be created with comparably small investments into service design together with short lead-times. This cost efficiency of composite services depends to a great extent on the availability of constituent services that can be flexibly re-used in different contexts. Such a service is virtually lean and functionally pure, thus it focuses on its single main function. The more specialized a service is, the less suitable it becomes for broad use within composition.

Aspect orientation of the composition environment reduces the need for implementing supplementary functions into constituent services or into composition skeletons. They can be implemented separately and applied if needed. The following chapter outlines an AOP enhanced composition environment.

4 AOP for Composite Services

Aspect orientation is proposed to become an integral part of the composition engine that executes a composite service by interpreting the respective service skeletons. This integration is practical as most join-points lie within the execution steps of the composite service. In order to catch relevant join-points, a weaving function allocated within the composition engine monitors the skeleton execution and applies advice when necessary. This process is steered by point-cut definition expressed within a weaving language that is tailor-made for the underlying service composition technology.

Execution of composite services as described in [1] is based on service selection at runtime leading to late-binding of constituent services. Furthermore, the requirements and conditions for service selection, which are expressed in terms of constraints, are dynamic. They might, for example, depend on services that were executed previously within the same composition session. As this dynamic service selection is the central process of the described service composition technology, many useful join-points originate within this service selection process and are in turn volatile and dynamic. Thus, weaving prior to the execution of a composite service is in many cases not possible. For this reason an event driven online weaving approach was chosen.

4.1 Weaving Definition and Join-Points

Weaving refers to composing an application from a target application where an additional function and aspects are desired that implement this function. The base and target of the proposed aspect enabled environment is the step-by-step execution of composite service skeletons. At each step of the execution where a potential join-point resides, point-cut definitions are interpreted in order to identify and execute those point-cuts that apply here. If advice is defined for the currently reached point-cut, it is executed. The elements of the skeleton and therefore the steps in the execution of a composite service represent the source for join-points and the target for point-cuts and advices. Basic join-points in this environment are for example:

- The start and end of a skeleton execution. This join-point would allow to execute an advice prior to or after the execution of the actual composite service.
- The start of a service selection. This join-point would allow to analyze the starting of service selection and to influence it by e.g. the addition of constraints.
- A list of services that satisfy the constraints was returned from the service repository. This join-point occurs as one step within the constituent service selection. A list of all services that qualify for being selected according to constraints is available. This join-point is helpful if, for example, advice needs to further prioritize certain services.
- A service is invoked. This join-point marks the invocation of a selected service. Advice can be used here for example to influence the parameters that are used in the service call.
- A return value is received. This join-point marks the return of a result from an invoked service. Here an evaluation of the result is possible before it is processed by the target composite service.
- A message is received. This join-point marks the reception of a message from an external protocol in the composition engine, for example a SIP message.

Some of the aforementioned basic join-points correspond to the elements of the skeleton language like, for example, the start element or the service template, and some originate in the end-to-end communication session, like the SIP message reception. Furthermore, events from the composition environment and events in the composite service execution are reflected uniformly within the weaving language by considering that reaching a new execution step and sub-step is an event in itself.

It is important to note that weaving instructions are stored and managed separately from composite services. This way, they can be applied and modified separately, without opening the target service. Thus, aspects can be added or removed independently of composite service design.

The weaving language is kept simple and intuitive and it allows the definition of point-cuts by means of weaving instructions. These weaving instructions consist of condition, control instructions and advice.

```
IF(<condition>) DO <control instructions> <advice>
```

Reaching a potential join-point in the skeleton execution triggers an event. If such an event occurs, the applied weaving instructions are evaluated. At this point it is important to highlight that multiple, independently specified sets of weaving instructions might be applicable. All of them are considered.

The keyword "IF" marks the start of a weaving instruction and precedes the condition element. The purpose of the condition element is to verify if this particular weaving instruction matches the currently considered event representing a join-point.

Furthermore, it specifies if and which advice shall be executed. A central element here is the join-point or event type that triggers the weaving. Additionally, further conditions might exist, that evaluate variables stored in the shared state of the composition session. Depending on the event type, further data might be subject to conditions. For example, for join-points that reside within the context of service selection, the condition might be defined based on currently used selection constraints. If a condition cannot be evaluated because data is not available in the current context, this particular weaving instruction is ignored and weaving proceeds.

If the condition is found to be true, the respective advice is executed. The definition of advice and its mode of execution are specified after the keyword "DO" within a weaving instruction.

It is important to note that some combinations of join-points and additional conditions might fail. For example a condition based on constituent service selection combined with the event for skeleton start might never be evaluated because the required information is not available in this context. This weaving instruction will never apply.

By means of the optional control instruction, the execution of the advice code can be steered. By default the advice code is executed synchronously by halting the skeleton execution at the join-point. Skeleton execution resumes after the advice execution has been finished. By means of the control instruction, asynchronous advice execution can be selected (keyword "ASYNC"). Furthermore the advice execution can be delayed after the action in the skeleton execution that is marked by the join-point (Keyword "AFTER"). With this behavior, the start of the advice execution can for example wait for results of the action that is connected to the join-point. The default is to execute advice immediately at reaching the join-point.

4.2 Advice Selection and Execution

The presented approach allows different ways to implement advice:

- As separate composition skeleton
- As inline command within the weaving instruction
- As external service

If advice is implemented as separate skeleton, the weaving instruction explicitly refers to this skeleton. In the following example the join-point is the execution of a service template (event SERVICESELECT).

```
IF(event=SERVICESELECT, constraint="srv=user_profile")
DO AFTER SKELETON(alt_user_profile)
```

Here, the weaving only applies if this service template contains a selection constraint requiring a service that is described as "user_profile". This service, for example, loads a profile of the user from an external database into the shared state of the composition session. The weaving instruction specifies that once the service template is finished, thus after the selected service was executed, a skeleton called "alt_user_profile" is started as advice. This advice skeleton might, for example, contain functionality that processes and modifies user profile information. The composition engine continues execution within the advice skeleton. If the advice skeleton is finished, the execution resumes in the original skeleton. Being implemented as skeleton, advice can in turn be subject to further weaving when being executed.

Another possibility to implement advice would be an inline command given from within the weaving instruction. This way, simple operations like a change within a shared state variable can be initiated without the overhead of an external implementation of such a basic operation. The following example shows the usage of commands as advice:

```
IF(event=SKELETONSTART, $SIP.METHOD="INVITE") DO
COMMAND($PRIORITY=2)
```

At skeleton start and if a SIP INVITE message was received according to the value of a shared state variable $SIP.METHOD, the command sets the shared state variable $PRIORITY to the value 2.

The most flexible possibility to implement advice would be to implement it as an external service, for example as a web service. This separates the advice implementation from the implementation of the targeted composite services. Services are self contained entities with strongly encapsulated functions that interact through well defined APIs and protocols. Using an external service as advice implies the invocation of this advice service at join-points. Thus, a service invocation is directly weaved into the target application rather than the advice itself, which stays a separate process.

In the simplest cases, an external service could be used as advice by directly and statically addressing it from the weaving instruction.

Tooling of the underlying service composition environment provides an even more dynamic and flexible method.. The model-driven composition approach and in particular the data and constraint based selection of services may be applied to the selection of services that implement an aspect. For this purpose, the weaving instruction specifies selection constraints rather than pointing statically to an advice. Like any other service in the composition environment, services that implement advices are formally described within a service repository. Thus, aspects are implemented and exposed in the same way as the constituent services that are used in skeleton based composition.

The service description contains binding information and abstract description of the service function and capabilities. Being based on constraints, advice selection in the weaving process is based on abstract properties. The same constraint expressions that are used in skeleton controlled composition apply in weaving instructions.

The following example of a weaving instruction adds functionality to count the number of skeleton starts within the environment to composite services.

```
IF(event=SKELETONSTART) DO SELECT(srv="skeleton_count")
```

The keyword "SELECT" instructs to use the following parameters as constraints for service selection in order to find the advice to be executed. In this example, the constraint demands to use a service that is described by the property "srv" as "skeleton_count". This constraint is matched against the service repository in order to find applicable advice. The aspect is applied by executing the selected advice service.

In this example, the same function could be added to a skeleton by inserting an additional service template directly after the skeleton start element. Even the same constraint for service selection can be used, potentially finding and invoking the same service. This means that a service could be used either as a constituent service within a composition or the same service could serve as advice within aspect weaving.

The skeleton counting example above describes a typical supplementary function within a network. Its conventional implementation with additional service templates would cross-cut throughout all composite services. By means of the weaving instructions, an alternative mechanism is available that complements the composition without changing in the composition skeleton. In this respect, it is important to note that both the skeleton based composition and the weaving are based on the same enablers like constraint based service selection, abstract description of the services and the shared state of the composition session.

The underlying composition environment supports services from various service technology worlds. Currently, next to SIP and Web Services, AJAX services can be used and Enterprise Service Buses (ESBs) are supported. The composition core process of constraint based service selection is agnostic of the technology of constituent services due to using abstract description of a service's functional properties rather than the technological details of its implementation. For the application of aspects this means in principle, advice can be implemented based on any service technology that is supported by the composition environment. In practice, some service technologies like IMS/SIP, where services are persistent within end-to-end user communication sessions, is less suitable for advice implementation. Instead, aspects can be implemented using technologies like web services or AJAX, which are based on request-response usage schemes.

4.3 Data Exchange with Advice Services

An important issue is how access to data is granted to the advice. There are two philosophies for data handling: the full direct access to all data from the advice code or the encapsulation of the advice in a way that allows data exchange with the target application only through dedicated APIs. The presented approach uses both methods depending on the advice implementation.

If an aspect is implemented as separate skeleton, this skeleton would be executed as integral part of the target skeleton and within the same composition session. This implies full access to all run-time data of the composition.

If an aspect is implemented as separate external service, it is encapsulated and needs to exchange data through dedicated APIs. For this purpose, two possibilities are available:

- Data exchange through an API exposed by the composition environment.
- Data exchange defined in weaving instruction using the service API.

For the first alternative, access to shared state is provided through an external API of the composition engine. This API allows reading and writing shared state variables. This method requires the advice service to use this particular API.

The latter alternative takes into account that advice invocations are service calls, which can be parameterized and which might provide a return value. The service parameters to be applied to the advice service invocation are defined in the weaving instruction. The values used in parameters can for example originate in shared state variables within the composition session. Furthermore, the return-value of the advice service can be connected with a shared state variable. The following example shows the concept:

```
IF(event=SKELETONSTART) DO
SELECT(srv="userlog")($SIP.invite.userid,"24")
->$SERVICEUSEDCOUNT
```

Here, at every start of a skeleton, a service shall be called, that logs the skeleton usage per user. The user address, as received from SIP, was stored within a shared state variable and it is used here as first parameter. The second parameter is a constant that specifies the time interval for logging. Here 24 hours is used. As return value, the service provides the number of skeleton invocations by this user within the specified time interval. This return value is directed into the shared-state variable $SERVICEUSED-COUNT and available for further processing within the composition session. This processing might be implemented e.g. by further aspects applied to this composition. As shown above, shared state can be used by aspects for exchanging data between each other. Furthermore, shared state can be used to share data with the target application. The target application is not aware of the presence of aspects but it considers the variables that are used by the aspects as part of the run-time environment.

Data exchange through the weaving instruction and the API of the advice service allows implementing aspects without considering additional APIs that are specific to the composition environment. The resulting services are more generic, thus more suitable to be used in different contexts.

5   Example

This example demonstrates the addition of functionality that logs constituent service usage to a composite service. As a base, the service that was already outlined in Fig. 1 is used. It provides an automatically localized weather forecast service. Additionally, the service takes into account user preferences regarding the delivery of results.

Fig. 2 shows the composition skeleton that implements this service. The white boxes in the skeleton are service templates, which imply constraint based selection of services. They are complemented by structural elements that mark the start and end of the skeleton and provide conditional branching of the execution.

The function to be added is logging of constituent service usage. Implementing this within the skeleton would mean adding an additional service template after each already existing service template. This additional service is shown on the right side in Fig. 2. It shows the six locations in the skeleton where this service template would need to be added.

The same result can be achieved by means of weaving without changing the original skeleton. The following weaving instruction inserts the logging service at all six join-points:

```
IF(event=SERVICESLECT) DO AFTER
SELECT(srv="logging")($USERID, $LASTCONSTRAINT.SRV)
->$NUMBER
```

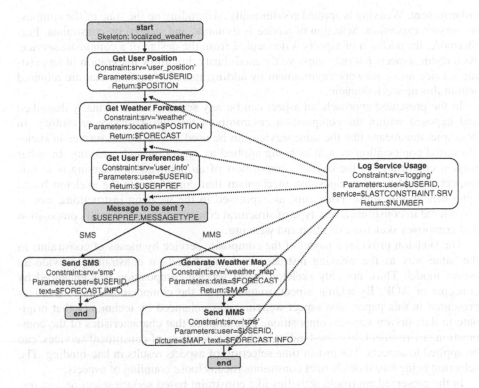

Fig. 2. Example skeleton implementing location based weather forecast service

The aspect shall be applied after each service selection. The respective join-points correspond to the event SERVICESELECT. The keyword 'AFTER' instructs to wait with the advice execution until the execution of the skeleton selected service was finished.

This example shows the similarities in the skeleton controlled composition and weaving of aspects. The selection of the additional logging service is based on the same constraint regardless if it is applied through additional service templates added to the skeleton or by means of weaving. The parameters for service invocation and the return value are connected to the same shared state variables. Nevertheless, the aspect oriented approach implies two important advantages. It does not modify the original service skeleton and it can easily be applied to multiple composite services at once. It therefore helps to keep the service lean and it allows a broad deployment and distribution of additional functionality within a service domain.

6 Summary and Discussion of the Approach

The presented approach uses dynamic weaving at run-time, based on intercepting events, which reflect the process of composition execution or originate in the run-time environment. Weaving is applied conditionally, depending on the state of the composite service execution. Selection of advice is dynamic and steered by constraints. Furthermore, the addition of aspects is decoupled from the design of a composite service. As a result, aspects not only improve the modularity, but allow integration of an existing service into a network environment by adding specific functions that are required within this network domain.

In the presented approach, an aspect can be any service that is formally described and exposed within the composition environment through a service repository. In principle, this means that the same service can be used as constituent service in skeleton based composition as well as being applied as aspect through weaving. In either way, it contributes to the overall composition of an application. Weaving is in this respect an additional composition mechanism that complements the skeleton based approach. In this sense, point-cuts, as expressed in the weaving instructions, can be considered to constitute a new type of structural constraint for the overall composition that comprises skeleton execution and weaving.

The skeleton provides a model of the composite service by means of constraints in the same way as the weaving instructions, being based on constraints, provide an aspect model. Thus, not only skeleton based service composition was enhanced by concepts of AOP. By adding aspect orientation to the composition environment as presented in this paper, also aspect weaving was enhanced by techniques that originate in data-driven service composition. This implies that characteristics of the composition environment, like late-binding and loose-coupling of constituent services, can be applied to aspects. The just-in-time selection of aspects results in late-binding. The selection being based on abstract constraints means loose coupling of aspects.

In the presented approach, activities like constraint based service selection and service invocation are treated as join-points regardless if they occur in the execution of skeletons or weaving instructions. This implies that weaving execution might in turn be subject to further weaving. Furthermore, a service being invoked as advice does not differ from a service being invoked from skeleton execution. Thus, the activities of an aspect service might be subject to further weaving.

Being implemented and exposed as services, aspects, as described in this paper, are strongly encapsulated entities in the sense of SOA (Service Oriented Architectures). They offer their function through clearly defined APIs, but they are in principle not dedicated to a certain application use-case scenario. The application of aspects is kept separate and it is entirely done within the weaving instruction. As a result, aspects are implemented in a generic way considering as less information about a specific application scenario as possible. Thus they are re-useable in many contexts. This is in contrast to aspects known from other AOP approaches like AspectJ and JBOSS-AOP, where an aspect itself often contains information about where and under which conditions it can be applied.

In many scenarios, AOP is used by a single developer who implements the target application along with the implementation and application of aspects. The presented approach additionally allows using AOP for target applications that might be provided by a different administrative domain, for example, a 3rd party service provider. In this context, the described aspect orientation concepts can be used as tools for system integration.

The composition engine is based on a separation of service selection and service execution. Thereby, it becomes service technology agnostic to a great extent. The described weaving approach inherits this characteristic by selecting and executing advice similar to constituent services. Thus, weaving becomes as technology agnostic regarding the used aspects as the skeleton based composition is agnostic regarding constituent services. Aspects can be implemented with a different programming language or even based on a different service technology than the target application or other aspects used within the same environment. In general, aspects can be implemented based on any of the various service technologies that are supported by the composition environment. It is possible to replace an aspect by another one that is implemented using a different service technology without the need to change the composition skeleton or the weaving instructions. Both the skeleton and the weaving instructions can accommodate changes in the available services. They can be deployed in a different environment with different services and work unchanged changes as long as services that satisfy the constraints are available. In this respect, the presented approach differs from other AOP enhanced environments like, for example, AO4BPEL [5]. In AO4BPEL the composition mechanism and the aspects are mostly based on BPEL workflow processes and web service technology. Aspects are not selected as dynamically as presented here though abstract modeling based on constraints.

Furthermore, the approach presented in this paper differs from the framework that was proposed in [9]. Rather than using aspects to modify the binding of web services and client applications as proposed in [9], services are considered to be the aspects themselves. In our approach, the binding flexibility lies within the expressiveness of the weaving instructions and the constraint based selection of advice implementing services.

Regular expressions in the weaving language, as they are known for example from JBOSS-AOP [4], would provide expressiveness to the join-point selection that is useful if complex language constructs are the base for point-cuts. Within the proposed skeleton based environment such a powerful mechanism is not needed due to the limited complexity of the join-point model based on skeleton elements and events.

The presented way of online weaving implies that the selection of aspects at different join points is decoupled from each other while alternative aspects for the same functionality are available. This might for example lead to the problem that whenever a logging aspect has to be applied, a different one is selected and the complete logging becomes inconsistent. In order to address this problem, we are working on coordination in-between the aspect selections.

The described online weaving evaluates the weaving instructions at every potential join point. If extensive collections of weaving instructions are applicable, this approach might considerably impact performance of the composite service execution. In order to improve in this respect and improve run-time performance of the composite application, static offline weaving might be applied if possible. Due to the dynamic nature of the weaving concept that is characterized by weaving instructions based on run-time conditions and dynamic constraint based advice selection, a full offline weaving is usually not possible, but partial weaving might be possible offline. It can be applied as pre-processing that optimizes the overall composition process.

In order to allow design, deployment and application of aspects in a user-friendly way, we are currently integrating the development of weaving instructions and the management of aspects into the existing development and management tools for composite services.

7 Conclusion

In this paper, we have identified how frequently required supplementary functions, which are essential in the telecommunication domain, affect service composition. We have outlined the cross-cutting nature of many of these supplementary functions. If these supplementary functions are implemented directly into the services, they lead to complex, multi-functional and therefore specialized services.

One major benefit promised by service composition is fast and cost-efficient design cycles enabled by re-using service components to a great extent. In order to reach this goal, service composition relies on the availability of lean constituent services. We have outlined how aspect oriented software design helps keeping services lean as it allows separating these cross-cutting supplementary functions from the core function of the service. This is achieved by the introduction of aspect weaving in the composition environment.

Furthermore, this paper has not only applied aspect oriented design principles to a new domain of composite services based on its specific composition paradigm and language. It has rather shown that aspect weaving can reside as an additional and complementary composition method besides a skeleton based approach. We have shown that aspects can be implemented as services and added to a composition following the same constraint based mechanism that is used for skeleton driven selection of constituent services. The implementation of the presented concepts is ongoing.

We have outlined that the described methodology does not only support the composite service designer, but it allows broad application and management of additional functions, e.g. applied to multiple services within a domain. Aspects can be applied to a number of applications at once and automatically. This way, services that are available from third-party providers could be adapted without changes. This feature is especially interesting for telecommunication network operators, considering their specific needs regarding supplementary functions. In this respect, the global management of weaving instructions deserves further investigation in order to control how new functions are distributed to multiple applications.

References

1. Dinsing, T., Eriksson, G., Fikouras, I., Gronowski, K., Levenshteyn, R., Pettersson, P., Wiss, P.: Service composition in IMS using Java EE SIP servlet containers. Ericsson Review 84(3), 92–96 (2007)
2. Kiczales, G., Lamping, J., Mendhekar, A., Maeda, C., Lopes, C., Loingtier, J.-M., Irwin, J.: Aspect-Oriented Programming. In: Aksit, M., Matsuoka, S. (eds.) ECOOP 1997. LNCS, vol. 1241, pp. 220–242. Springer, Heidelberg (1997)

3. Kiczales, G., Hilsdale, E., Hugunin, J., Kersten, M., Palm, J., Griswold, W.G.: An Overview of AspectJ. In: Knudsen, J.L. (ed.) ECOOP 2001. LNCS, vol. 2072, p. 327. Springer, Heidelberg (2001)
4. Burke, B., Flury, M.: JBOSS-AOP,
   http://www.jboss.org/developers/projects/jboss/aop.jsp
5. Charfi, A., Mezini, M.: Aspect-Oriented Web Service Composition with AO4BPEL. In: Zhang, L.-J., Jeckle, M. (eds.) ECOWS 2004. LNCS, vol. 3250, pp. 168–182. Springer, Heidelberg (2004)
6. Web Services Business Process Execution Language (WSBPEL), OASIS (2007),
   http://www.oasis-open.org/committees/
   tc_home.php?wg_abbrev=wsbpel
7. Khalaf, R., Mukhi, N., Weerawarana, S.: Service-Oriented Composition of Web Services (WS4BPEL). In: WWW 2003 Conference, Budapest, Hungary (2003)
8. Charfi, A., Mezini, M.: AO4BPEL: An Aspect-oriented Extension to BPEL. World Wide Web Journal 10(3), 309–344 (2003)
9. Cibran, M.A., Verheecke, B., Vanderperren, W., Suvee, D., Jonkers, V.: Aspect-Oriented Programming for Dynamic Web-Service Selection. World Wide Web Journal 10(3), 212–242 (2003)

Intelligent Overload Control for Composite Web Services

Pieter J. Meulenhoff[1], Dennis R. Ostendorf[2], Miroslav Živković[1],
Hendrik B. Meeuwissen[1], and Bart M.M. Gijsen[1]

[1] TNO ICT, P.O. Box 5050, 2600 GB Delft, The Netherlands
{pieter.meulenhoff,miroslav.zivkovic}@tno.nl,
{erik.meeuwissen,bart.gijsen}@tno.nl
[2] Quintiq, 's-Hertogenbosch, The Netherlands

Abstract. In this paper, we analyze overload control for composite web services in service oriented architectures by an orchestrating broker, and propose two practical access control rules which effectively mitigate the effects of severe overloads at some web services in the composite service. These two rules aim to keep overall web service performance (in terms of end-to-end response time) and availability at agreed quality of service levels. We present the theoretical background and design of these access control rules as well as performance evaluation results obtained by both simulation and experiments. We show that our access control rules significantly improve performance and availability of composite web services.

Keywords: Availability, Performance, Quality of Service, Service Oriented Architecture, Web Admission Control, Web Service Composition, Web Service Orchestration.

1 Introduction

Service oriented architectures (SOAs), based on Web Service technology, are becoming increasingly popular for the development of new applications due to the promises of easier development and shorter time-to-market. These so-called SOA-based composite services are offered by service providers, and typically consist of multiple web services, developed by third parties, which are executed in multiple administrative domains.

Currently, service developers and providers focus on the functional aspects of composite web services. However, too little attention is paid to the non-functional aspects of composite web services such as availability, performance, and reliability.

Since several composite web services can make use of the same web services, these popular web services used by multiple composite web services may experience high demand, resulting in more requests than they can handle, leading to degradation of all services that rely on these web services. These overload situations lead to reduced availability as well as higher response times, resulting in degraded quality as perceived by end users.

This paper concentrates on improving performance and availability of *composite* web services. In particular, a solution is proposed to improve the quality as perceived

L. Baresi, C.-H. Chi, and J. Suzuki (Eds.): ICSOC-ServiceWave 2009, LNCS 5900, pp. 34–49, 2009.
© Springer-Verlag Berlin Heidelberg 2009

by end users by increasing the average number of successfully served requests per second. This solution is based on intelligently preventing overload on any one of the services in the composition, by denying service to specific requests based on dynamic admission control rules.

To illustrate our problem setting, Fig. 1 shows a simplified SOA architecture with an orchestrating web service, also referred to as an orchestrating broker. Let us suppose that the composite web service consists of three web services identified by W1 thru W3.

The broker consists of a scheduler and a controller. The scheduler determines the order of the jobs submitted to web services W1 thru W3, since it may be different per client. Each web service, W1 thru W3, has implemented the Web Admission Control (WAC) mechanism. The broker's controller keeps track of the total request execution time, and decides if the latency is within the required limit.

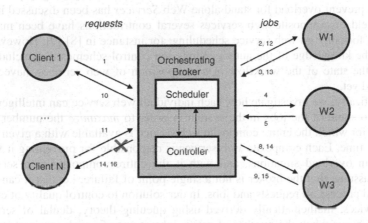

Fig. 1. Jobs for client requests are routed through a network of web services (W1, W2 and W3) by an orchestrating broker

To illustrate normal operation, let us suppose that a request from Client 1 (#1) arrives at the broker. The scheduler analyses the request, and determines that the web service W1, W2, and W3 should be invoked in that order. If the total execution time of the request is less than the required limit, the job is delegated to component W1 (#2). Before actually executing the job in W1, the WAC mechanism decides that W1 is not in overload and executes the job. On the response (#3) from W1, the scheduler checks with the controller that the total latency is less than the required limit and invokes the next job at W2 (#4). This is repeated until all web services are invoked, and the response (#10) to Client 1 is given within a maximum amount of time.

To illustrate an overload situation, let us suppose that a request from Client N (#11) arrives at the broker. The scheduler analyses the request, and determines that the web services W1 and W2 should be invoked in that order. When the job is delegated to web service W1 (#12), the WAC mechanism in W1 decides that W1 is not in overload and the job is executed. On the response (#13) from W1, the scheduler delegates the next job to W2 (#14). The WAC mechanism in W2 denies the job as W2 is in overload, and an unavailable message is returned to the broker (#15). As a result, the broker is able to respond to Client N with a service unavailable message (#16) within the maximum amount of time as well as to prevent escalation of the overload situation of W2. Obviously, in this described overload situation resources of web service W1 have been wasted.

Providers of web services W1 thru W3 may apply different state-of-the-art techniques, such as overdimensioning of computing resources, load balancing, and caching, to prevent overload in their own domain. *In this paper we focus on the use of admission control in the web services in combination with a simple response time limit check in the orchestrating broker to prevent the composite web service from becoming generally unavailable in an overload situation.* Admission control is already widely used in telecommunications. Research has also been performed on the use of admission control for Web *Servers*; see for instance [1]-[3], [7]. The use of WAC to prevent overload for stand alone Web *Services* has been discussed in [4]-[5]. In the field of composite web services several contributions have been made more recently, focusing on web service scheduling; for instance in [8]-[9]. However, to the best of the knowledge of the authors admission control schemes that include awareness of the state of the workflow in a composition of web services, have not been published yet.

Specifically, we investigate how each individual web service can intelligently deny service to some of the jobs in the system in order to *maximize* the number of client requests for which the entire composite web service is available with a given maximal response time. Each composite web service is responsible for preventing it from collapsing in overload situations, and with it the entire composite web service. We thereby assume that the broker is not a single point of failure, i.e. that it can instantly serve and process all requests and jobs. In our solution to control quality of composite web services, mathematically derived using queuing theory, denial of service will typically occur when the number of active jobs at specific web services reaches the allowed maximum. As a result, we serve as many client requests as possible with the requested end-user perceived quality, including a guarantee on the maximum response time.

The rest of the paper is organized as follows. In Section 2, we define the mathematical foundation of the admission control problem. In Sections 3 and 4, two algorithms for admission control by the web services are derived from the results in Section 2. In Section 5, the simulation setup to investigate our solutions is described as well as two simulation cases. In Section 6, the results of an experimental validation are described. In Section 7, we end with conclusions and suggestions for the future work.

2   Mathematical Foundation for Admission Control

In this section, we will derive a queueing model of an composition of web services, including an orchestrating web service (broker), see Fig. 1. This queueing model forms the mathematical foundation for our access control rules.

Let us suppose that the composite web service consists of web services from the set $W = \{W_1, W_2, ..., W_N\}$. In general, the $W_j \in W$ may be composite web services themselves. The incoming client requests at the broker are composed of jobs to be sequentially executed by a chain of web services from the set W. Thus, each job within the request is served by a single web service. Since the broker controls different composite web services, the order in which jobs are executed may differ per client request. The broker tracks job execution on a per request basis.

In practice, web services serve jobs using threading, which could be modeled using a round-robin (RR) service discipline in which jobs are served for a small period of time ($\delta \rightarrow 0$) and are then preempted and returned to the back of the queue. Since $\delta \rightarrow 0$, assuming there are n jobs with the same service rate μ_w, the per job service rate is μ_w/n. To simplify analysis, this process is modeled as an (egalitarian) processor sharing (PS) service discipline.

The service time distribution of web service W_j is assumed to be exponential with parameter μ_j. Jobs arrive at web service W_j with arrival rate λ_j and the web service load is defined as $\rho_j = \lambda_j/\mu_j$.

We define the latency L_i of an incoming client request i as the total time it takes for a request to be served. The sojourn time (i.e. time spent in the system) of job j at web service W_j from request i is denoted by S_{ij}. We ignore possible delay due to network traffic and broker activity, so it holds that

$$L_i = \sum_j S_{ij} \tag{1}$$

The clients are willing to wait only a limited amount of time for the request(s) to the composite web service to be completed. Within the SOA architecture, Service Level Agreements (SLAs) can be defined between the clients and the provider of the composite web service in order to quantify whether a request has been successful or not. For example, the SLA may contain the description that a client request i is considered successful when its latency L_i is smaller than maximum latency L_{max}. The maximum latency tolerated by clients may depend on the application itself. Some studies [6] show that users are on average willing to wait up to eight to ten seconds for the response from a website. However, atomic commercial transactions may require latencies that are much shorter [1]. The same SLA negotiation can be done between the broker and each composite service. An existing standard that serves as inspiration is WS Reliability [10]. Using the WS Reliability standard it is possible to give jobs so called 'expiry times', which define the maximum time it may take to receive a response.

We denote by c_j a maximum number of jobs allowed to be served simultaneously by web service W_j. When c_j requests are served and the next job arrives it is denied service by the admission control rules at the web service. This admission control rule for web service W_j can be modeled by the blocking probability p_{cj}. Since our objective is to serve as many requests as possible (within L_{max}) in an overload situation, our goal is to find the optimal values of the c_j.

To further simplify analysis, we assume that the web services W_j have the same values of c_j, λ_j, p_{cj}, and μ_j, denoted as c, λ, p_c and μ, respectively. We address this optimization problem by modeling the web services $W_j \in W$ as an $M/M/1/c$ Processor

Sharing Queue (PSQ). It is generally known that the blocking probability of the *M/M/1/c PSQ* equals

$$P_c = \frac{\rho^c}{\sum_{k=0}^{c} \rho^k} \tag{2}$$

And that the expected sojourn time at each of the web services equals

$$E(S) = \frac{1/\mu}{1 - \rho(1 - p_c)} \tag{3}$$

In the subsequent sections, two dynamic admission control algorithms S and D are derived from the model discussed in this section.

3 Dynamic Admission Control Algorithm S

The basic underlying principle of algorithm S is that the expected sojourn time $E(S)$ of a job in a web service should be less than or equal to the average available time for the jobs within the request. Thus, the problem of serving the client request within L_{max} is split up in consecutive steps. In each step, a limit on the expected sojourn time is calculated in the following way.

The broker, which is the only component that `knows' the structure of the request, divides the total allowed latency L_{max} over all jobs. The moment t^* when a request enters the broker the due date for the next job j^* is calculated. First, the total remaining time for this request, i.e. $L_{max} - \sum_{j=1}^{j^*-1} S_{ij}$, is determined. Then, it is divided over all remaining jobs in proportion to their service requirements. Let D_{ij*} be the due date of job j^* from request i, let J_i be the total number of jobs from request i, let t^* be the time at which the due date for job j^* is calculated, and let v_{ij} denote the expected service time of job j from request i. Now the following relation holds:

$$D_{ij*} = t^* + \left(L_{max} - \sum_{j=1}^{j^*-1} S_{ij} \right) \frac{v_{ij*}}{\sum_{j=j^*}^{J_i} v_{ij}}$$

As a result, the remaining time for job j from request i at time t is given by $R_{ij}(t) = D_{ij} - t$. When the total remaining time of a request is less than zero, the request is discarded by the broker and the client is notified. Let $\overline{R}$ denote the average remaining available service time of all jobs in the Web Service $R_{ij}(t)$. Now dynamic admission control algorithm S is derived based on the following constraint: *the expected sojourn time $E(S)$ of a job in a web service should be less than or equal to the average available time.* Now our optimization problem is defined as follows:

$$\max_{c} \left\{ c : E(S) \leq \overline{R} \right\} \tag{4}$$

In (4), both c and $\overline{R}$ are time-dependent, but we omit this to simplify our notation. Computation of $\overline{R}$ is straightforward since due times of all jobs within the composite service are known.

Substituting (3) in (4) yields:

$$\max_{c} \left\{ c : \frac{1/\mu}{1 - \rho(1 - p_c)} \leq \overline{R} \right\} \tag{5}$$

Substituting (2) in (5) yields:

$$\max_{c} \left\{ c : c \leq \log_{\rho}(1 + \mu\overline{R}(\rho - 1)) \right\} \quad for \quad \rho > 1 \tag{6}$$

Therefore, the admission control algorithm S is now defined as:

Allow arriving jobs service if $\rho < 1$ or $n \leq \log(1 + \mu\overline{R}(\rho - 1))$ still holds after the new job is allowed service.

In the remainder of this section, we discuss two issues of algorithm S. In order to compute c the value of ρ is needed and thus the values of λ and μ as well. It is assumed that the service requirement rate μ is known, but the value of λ is not. The arrival process (of a web service) will in reality not be known and thus must be estimated. Therefore, the question arises what is the time period to estimate λ and how to estimate this value.

Another issue is that the arrival rate is explicitly used to estimate the value of c. Intuitively the number of jobs, which can be simultaneously served, does not depend on the number of jobs which arrive at the system. The web service is capable of simultaneously serving c jobs. The blocking probability corrects for this fact, but further investigation of this issue is required.

In the next section, an alternative dynamic admission control rule is derived, in which the arrival rate λ (and hence ρ) is not used to determine the maximum value of the number of jobs allowed.

4 Dynamic Admission Control Algorithm D

The goal of algorithm D is to implement admission control without knowledge of the arrival rate λ. This algorithm is based on the relaxed constraint that only the average job has to be completed on time. Theoretically, the average job completes on time when the number of jobs in the system remains the same for the entire service time of each job. Although jobs may enter the jobs may enter the system or depart from the system, we investigate whether effective admission control is possible under the assumption that the number of jobs remains the same.

When the number of jobs n in the queue is assumed to be constant, the expected sojourn time for a job equals n/μ. When all jobs must be served before their due dates the problem is defined as follows:

$$\max_c \left\{ c : E(S) \le R_{ij}, \text{for all jobs in service} \right\} \tag{7}$$

In our case $E(S)$ equals c/μ, and R_{ij} is replaced by $\overline{R}$, where $\overline{R}$ determines the average remaining available service time for all jobs in service. These relaxations lead to the following optimization problem:

$$\max_c \left\{ c : \frac{c}{\mu} \le \overline{R} \right\}, \tag{8}$$

The solution of this trivial problem yields $c = \mu \overline{R}$. Hence we define the more practical admission control algorithm D as follows:

Allow arriving jobs service if $n \le \mu \overline{R}$ still holds after the arriving job is allowed service.

Note that for the calculation of the admission control parameter c, the arrival rate (and thus ρ) is not needed. This is a major advantage from a practical point of view compared to algorithm S.

5 Simulation Setup

A discrete-event simulation model is constructed to evaluate the proposed admission control algorithms. The model is implemented using the software package eM-Plant see [11]. The simulation model basically consists of four components, see Fig. 2. Component 'Client' generates new requests according to a Poisson process with rate λ. Requests are dispatched through the network by component 'Broker'. After a request has been generated a request type is randomly assigned, to indicate which web services need to be visited. Each web service is an instance of component 'WS'. The completed or denied requests arrive at component 'Output', where relevant data is collected.

When a job is sent to one of the web services in the composition, the web service checks whether it is allowed or denied service. In case admission control is not used, all incoming jobs are allowed. When admission control is used, the web service uses an access control rule to decide whether the incoming job may be served or not. Fig. 3 illustrates the flowchart of the broker component in case of admission control. When a new request comes in, the broker determines whether the latency of this request has already reached its limit, i.e. the remaining time for the request is less than zero. If the limit is reached, the request is denied service and sent to the output component. It may happen that the request has been allowed by the broker, but still the web service itself can not serve the request. Even when the remaining time is greater than zero, the broker determines whether the request has previously been denied service by the web

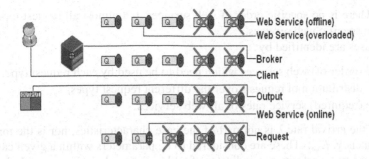

Fig. 2. Overview of the simulation model

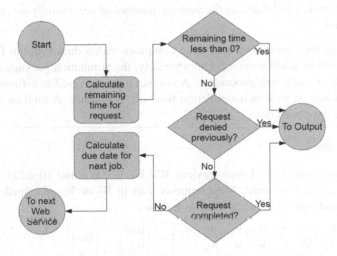

Fig. 3. Flowchart of the broker component in case of admission control

service component. If so, the request is also sent to the output component. If neither the latency limit has been reached nor the request has been denied service previously, the next web service needed to complete the request is determined. The web service calculates the due time for the next job, and then sends the job to the determined web service. For this calculation the total remaining time for the request is divided over all remaining jobs in proportion to their service requirements. When all jobs in the request are served, the request is sent to the output component as well.

Two simulation cases were designed to be used to compare the proposed admission control algorithms:

Case 1: The web services are placed in a specific order i.e. if web service X is before web service Y in one request type, it will be in every request type (in which both web services are present).

Case 2: There is no specific order of web services, but almost all request types make use of two specific web services.

Both cases are identified by

- the (order of) web services which need to be used by each request type.
- the distribution of requests over the different request types.
- the (required) service rates of all web services.

Note that the arrival rate λ is not part of the case characteristics, nor is the maximum allowed latency, L_{max}. These are considered to be parameters within a given case.

There are two performance indicators for the given admission control algorithms that we observed in greater detail

- Number of successfully served requests
- Goodput, which is defined as the average number of successfully served requests per second.

All simulations are executed on a desktop computer with a dual Pentium IV 3.2GHz processor and 1GB RAM memory. Unfortunately, the simulation package eM-Plant7 is not capable of using both processors. A bootstrap period (used to estimate λ) of 15 minutes is chosen as well as a simulation time of 15 minutes. A total of 15 simulations per case have been run.

Simulation Case 1

In the first case a total of 11 web services W_1, W_2, ..., W_{11} and 10 different request types r_1, r_2, ..., r_{10} were used. Most requests start in W_1 or W_5 and finish in W_{10} or W_{11}. The characteristics of this case are as follows:

$$Y = \begin{pmatrix} r_1 \\ r_2 \\ r_3 \\ r_4 \\ r_5 \\ r_6 \\ r_7 \\ r_8 \\ r_9 \\ r_{10} \end{pmatrix} = \begin{pmatrix} W_1 & W_2 & W_3 & W_7 & W_8 & W_9 & W_{11} \\ W_1 & W_2 & W_3 & W_8 & W_9 & W_{10} \\ W_1 & W_2 & W_7 & W_8 & W_9 & W_{10} \\ W_1 & W_2 & W_8 & W_9 & W_{10} \\ W_1 & W_4 & W_8 & W_9 & W_{10} \\ W_1 & W_4 & W_8 & W_9 & W_{11} \\ W_5 & W_{10} \\ W_1 & W_6 & W_8 & W_9 & W_{11} \\ W_2 \\ W_4 \end{pmatrix}, p = \begin{pmatrix} 0.05 \\ 0.20 \\ 0.05 \\ 0.05 \\ 0.05 \\ 0.10 \\ 0.40 \\ 0.05 \\ 0.03 \\ 0.02 \end{pmatrix}, \mu = \begin{pmatrix} 5 \\ 10/3 \\ 5 \\ 5 \\ 10/3 \\ 5 \\ 5 \\ 10 \\ 10 \\ 10/3 \\ 10 \end{pmatrix}$$

In this notation Y is a matrix which shows the (order of) web services which need to be used by each request. The vector p denotes the distribution of requests over the different types and vector μ denotes the (required) service rates of all web services. Using test runs, the system (with L_{max}=8s) is found to get in overload around λ=3s^{-1}. Therefore arrival rates around λ=3s^{-1} were investigated as well as other extreme values. Without WAC, the simulation runtime rapidly increases as λ increases. For λ=1s^{-1} the runtime (without WAC) is about half a minute. For λ=10s^{-1} the runtime has increased to about 45 minutes. To keep simulation run times acceptable, the extreme arrival rates are not investigated for the situation without admission control. It is expected that the fraction of successfully served request and the goodput both have value 0 in these situations. Total simulation time of this case was approximately 8 hours. Simulation results are summarized in Fig. 4, including 99.7% individual confidence intervals. Notice that the scale of the horizontal axis changes after $\lambda=10s^{-1}$.

It can be seen that both admission control rules have a positive effect on goodput. Both admission control schemes seem to perform equally well. Only at extreme arrival rates the difference with the theoretical maximum increases. Goodput drops when admission control is not used. However, when admission control is not used, there is a slight increase in goodput between $\lambda=5s^{-1}$ and $\lambda=9s^{-1}$. Especially at $\lambda=9s^{-1}$ the percentage of successful requests is much larger than expected. Given the (very small) confidence intervals it seems unlikely that this is due to the stochastic nature of the experiment results. This phenomenon will be called the *arrival paradox* and is explained by the following example:

Consider three web services, W_1, W_2 and W_3 (see Fig. 5) each with service rate 5. Requests go from W_1 or W_2 to W_3. If both W_1 and W_2 are not overloaded, the goodput

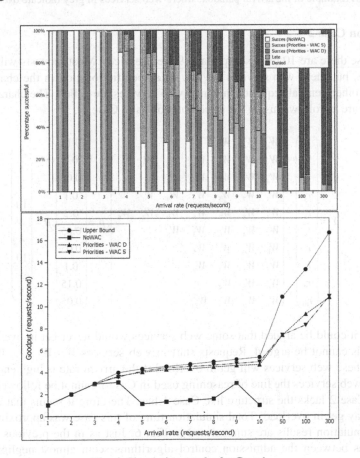

Fig. 4. Simulation results for Case 1

from these web services equals the arrival rate of these web services. Therefore the arrival rate at W_3 equals the sum of the arrival rates at W_1 and W_2 and hence W_3 is in overload and its goodput drops to zero. When the arrival rates are doubled, one of the web services W_1 and W_2 may get overloaded. Because admission control is not used, sojourn times will explode and requests will exceed their maximum allowed latencies. Recall that late requests are preempted at the broker. Therefore the arrival rate at web service W_3 decreases due to the higher overall arrival rate and W_3 no longer is in overload, hence its goodput increases.

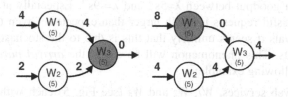

Fig. 5. Example of the arrival paradox, where web services in grey indicate overload

Simulation Case 2

In this case there are 10 request types and 9 web services. Most requests will visit W_5 and/or W_6, but these web services are not on a specific location in the chain, nor is there any other general sequence in which web services are called. The characteristics of Case 2 are as follows (using the same notation as in Case 1).

$$
Y = \begin{pmatrix} r_1 \\ r_2 \\ r_3 \\ r_4 \\ r_5 \\ r_6 \\ r_7 \\ r_8 \\ r_9 \\ r_{10} \end{pmatrix} = \begin{pmatrix} W_8 & W_6 & W_2 \\ W_5 & W_2 & W_3 & W_7 & W_6 & W_1 \\ W_4 & W_3 & W_7 & W_2 & W_6 \\ W_8 & W_7 & W_5 & W_5 & W_9 & W_1 \\ W_7 & W_8 & W_2 & W_5 & W_9 & W_1 & W_6 \\ W_7 & W_4 & W_6 & W_3 & W_5 \\ W_8 & W_9 & W_1 & W_5 \\ W_5 & W_8 & W_3 & W_9 \\ W_6 & W_5 & W_4 \\ W_1 & W_9 & W_8 & W_{21} \end{pmatrix}, p = \begin{pmatrix} 0.15 \\ 0.1 \\ 0.05 \\ 0.1 \\ 0.2 \\ 0.05 \\ 0.05 \\ 0.1 \\ 0.15 \\ 0.05 \end{pmatrix}, \mu = \begin{pmatrix} 5 \\ 5 \\ 4 \\ 10 \\ 4 \\ 4 \\ 10 \\ 5 \\ 5 \end{pmatrix}
$$

In Case 1 it could be argued that some web services would never get in overload. For Case 2 this cannot be argued. Requests start in web services W_1, W_4, W_5, W_6, W_7 or W_8, thus these web services will get in overload if the arrival rate is high enough. For the other web services the line of reasoning used in Case 1 cannot be followed. This is because Case 2 lacks the structure like Case 1 has. Therefore it seems that each web service may get in overload. Total simulation time of this case was approximately 11 hours. Simulation results are summarized in Fig. 6. Just as in the previous case, the differences between the admission control algorithms seem almost negligible. The only (relevant) difference occurs in terms of goodput for high arrival rates. For low arrival rates ($\lambda < 5s^{-1}$) the D rule results in a slightly worse situation than if admission control is not used. In all other cases the admission control rules both behave better than when admission control is not used.

The difference between the theoretical maximum for the goodput and the observed goodput is larger compared to case 1, even for small values of λ. In case 1 the goodput kept increasing, even at high arrival rates. In this case however, the goodput decreases after $\lambda = 12s^{-1}$.

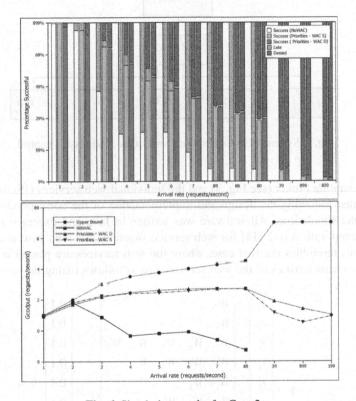

Fig. 6. Simulation results for Case 2

6 Experimental Validation

Besides theoretical analysis and simulation of admission control, an empirical experiment is set up to validate the simulations. Concrete web services were built and the results are compared to the simulation results. For this purpose of comparison it does not matter what function the web services perform. In addition, for setting up the tests it is convenient if the CPU demand of executing a web service can be controlled. Therefore, we implemented web services that calculate a specific Fibonacci number (each service has its own number to calculate) according to a CPU consuming algorithm. By choosing the Fibonacci number the CPU consumption of this web service can be influenced. During the experiments two scenarios were evaluated: One where admission control rule D is enabled (WAC D); the other where admission control is disabled (NOWAC). To obtain the results from the web service the software package JMeter [12] was used. A global overview of the experimental setup is given in Fig. 7.

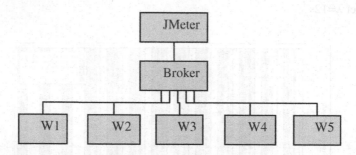

Fig. 7. System setup for empirical validation of admission control

The orchestrating broker (see Fig. 3) and the individual web services (W_1 thru W_5) are implemented following the design and implementation of the corresponding components in the simulations. All software was written in Java and executed on Tomcat [13] extended with Axis2 [14] for web service functionality. The case used in these experiments resembles the first case, where the web services are placed in a specific order. The characteristics of the web services are as follows (using the same notation as in Case 1):

$$Y = \begin{pmatrix} r_1 \\ r_2 \\ r_3 \\ r_4 \\ r_5 \\ r_6 \\ r_7 \\ r_8 \\ r_9 \\ r_{10} \end{pmatrix} = \begin{pmatrix} W_1 \\ W_4 \\ W_1 \quad W_2 \quad W_3 \quad W_4 \quad W_5 \\ W_1 \quad W_2 \quad W_4 \quad W_5 \\ W_1 \quad W_2 \\ W_1 \quad W_4 \quad W_5 \\ W_1 \quad W_3 \quad W_5 \\ W_1 \quad W_3 \quad W_4 \\ W_2 \quad W_5 \\ W_3 \quad W_4 \end{pmatrix}, p = \begin{pmatrix} 0.1 \\ 0.1 \\ 0.1 \\ 0.1 \\ 0.1 \\ 0.1 \\ 0.1 \\ 0.1 \\ 0.1 \\ 0.1 \end{pmatrix}$$

Note that no values for the service rate of each web service are given. All web services were configured to calculate the same Fibonacci number. Both the JMeter and the Broker run on the system equipped with 2GB RAM and single Pentium IV processors clocked at 3.2GHz. The web services $W_1,\ldots,W_5$ run on systems equipped with 0.5GB, 1GB, 1GB, 0.5GB, 0,5GB and with Pentium IV processors at 1GHz, 2.4GHz,

2.4Ghz, 1GHz, 1GHz respectively. JMeter was configured to generate the requests r_1, r_2, ..., r_{10} based on the probabilities p_1, p_2, ..., p_{10}. In each run of JMeter a fixed number of threads (between 1 and 200) were active. Each run used a warm-up time of 15 minutes, and a test time of 15 minutes; the latter has been used to gather the results shown here.

In any composite web service the orchestrating broker is a suspect to become a performance bottleneck and should therefore be kept light. In our case the admission control rules are executed by the web services, and the broker is only responsible for service orchestration and tracking total latency of a composite request. In our experimental validation the orchestration is implemented in such a way, that performing admission control does not add a bottleneck to the composite web service. If, the broker would become the bottleneck in the system due to its orchestration function, then it would be possible to distribute the work by using more brokers. This is possible since the admission control rules are implemented in the web services. An overview of the experimental results is given in Fig. 8.

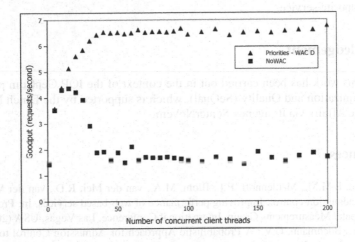

Fig. 8. Results of the empirical tests

The empirical and simulation results correlate well. Using WAC the overall goodput was noticeably higher than the NOWAC scenario. The NOWAC scenario reaches a maximum goodput when there are a little bit more than 4 requests per second at 15 concurrent threads. The WAC scenario seems to level between 6 to 7 requests per second at 50 concurrent threads.

7 Concluding Remarks

In this paper two different overload control algorithms for composite web services in service oriented architectures, were derived. These algorithms, S and D, were derived based on a $M/M/1/c$ Processor Sharing Queue. In addition, a simulation model was constructed and used to conduct simulations with these two rules and a benchmark (in which no admission control rule is used). Moreover, an experimental setup was constructed to conduct an empirical evaluation of rule D and the benchmark.

Based on simulation results, we conclude that in most situations both admission control rules S and D resulted in a higher objective value (measured in goodput) than the benchmark. While the difference is small, rule S does perform better than rule D. However, it can be observed that the results are dependent on the case, the structure and interaction patterns of the used web service components. The experimental evaluation of rule D gives similar results to the simulations performed for this rule.

To achieve further improvements, the empirical experiments should be scaled up to evaluate a broader range of different and larger service oriented infrastructures. Such experiments would be primarily focused on obtaining the most optimum goodput as well as incorporating business objectives in the admission control rules.

Another area of research is to extend the proposed admission control mechanisms in more complex environments, e.g. when the sequence of composite services is not known in advance, or when there is more variation in the resource requirements of each composite service.

Ackowledgement

Part of this work has been carried out in the context of the IOP GenCom project Service Optimization and Quality (SeQual), which is supported by the Dutch Ministry of Economic Affairs via its agency SenterNovem.

References

1. Gijsen, B.M.M., Meulenhoff, P.J., Blom, M.A., van der Mei, R.D., van der Waaij, B.D.: Web admission control: Improving performance of web-based services. In: Proceedings of Computer Measurements Group, International Conference, Las Vegas, USA (2004)
2. Xu, Z., Bochmann, G.V.: A Probabilistic Approach for Admission Control to Web Servers. In: Proceedings of Intern. Symp. on Performance Evaluation of Computer and Telecommunication Systems, SPECTS 2004, San Jose, California, USA, July 2004, pp. 787–794 (2004) ISBN 1-56555-284-9
3. Elnikety, S., Nahum, E., Tracey, J., Zwaenepoel, W.: A Method for Transparent Admission Control and Request Scheduling in E-Commerce Web Sites. In: Proceedings of the 13th international conference on World Wide Web, New York, USA, pp. 276–286 (2004) ISBN:1-58113-844-X
4. Urgaonkar, B., Shenoy, P.: Cataclysm: Scalable Overload Policing for Internet Applications. Journal of Network and Computer Applications (JNCA) 31, 891–920 (2008)
5. Xi, B.: Quality of service (QoS) for web-based applications. Technical report, TNO-ICT and Eindhoven University of Technology (2007)
6. Bouch, A., Kuchinsky, A., Bhatti, N.: Quality is in the eye of the beholder: Meeting user's requirements for internet quality of service. In: Proceedings of CHI 2000 Conference on Human Factors in Computing Systems (2000)

7. Abdelzaher, T., Bhatti, N.: Web server QoS management by adaptive content delivery. In: Proceedings of the International Workshop on Quality of Service, London, UK (June 1999)
8. Dyachuk, D., Deters, R.: Scheduling of Composite Web Services. In: Meersman, R., Tari, Z., Herrero, P. (eds.) OTM 2006 Workshops. LNCS, vol. 4277, pp. 19–20. Springer, Heidelberg (2006)
9. Dyachuk, D., Deters, R.: Improving Performance of Composite Web Services. In: Proceedings of IEEE International Conference on Service-Oriented Computing and Applications, June 2007, pp. 147–154 (2007) ISBN 0-7695-2861-9
10. Iwasa, K., Durand, J., Rutt, T., Peel, M., Kunisetty, S., Bunting, D.: Web Services Reliable Messaging TC, WS-Reliability 1.1. (2004), http://docs.oasis-open.org/wsrm/ws-reliability/v1.1/
11. Tecnomatix, eM-Plant 7.0 Manual. Tecnomatix GmbH (2004)
12. Apache JMeter, http://jakarta.apache.org/jmeter
13. Apache Tomcat, http://tomcat.apache.org
14. Apache Axis2, http://ws.apache.org/axis2/

Trust-Oriented Composite Service Selection and Discovery

Lei Li[1], Yan Wang[1], and Ee-Peng Lim[2]

[1] Department of Computing, Macquarie University, Sydney, Australia 2109
[2] School of Information Systems, Singapore Management University, Singapore 178902
{leili,yanwang}@science.mq.edu.au,
eplim@smu.edu.sg

Abstract. In Service-Oriented Computing (SOC) environments, service clients interact with service providers for consuming services. From the viewpoint of service clients, the trust level of a service or a service provider is a critical issue to consider in service selection and discovery, particularly when a client is looking for a service from a large set of services or service providers. However, a service may invoke other services offered by different providers forming composite services. The complex invocations in composite services greatly increase the complexity of trust-oriented service selection and discovery. In this paper, we propose novel approaches for composite service representation, trust evaluation and trust-oriented service selection and discovery. Our experiments illustrate that compared with the existing approaches our proposed trust-oriented service selection and discovery algorithm is realistic and more efficient.

1 Introduction

In recent years, Service-Oriented Computing (SOC) has emerged as an increasingly important research area attracting much attention from both the research and industry communities. In SOC applications, a variety of services across domains are provided to clients in a loosely-coupled environment. Clients can look for preferred and qualified services via a discovery service of registries, invoke and receive services from the rich service environments [18].

In SOC, a service can refer to a transaction, such as selling a product online (i.e. the traditional online service), or a functional component implemented by Web service technologies [18]. However, when a client looks for a service from a large set of services offered by different providers, in addition to functionality, the reputation-based trust is also a key factor for service selection. It is also a critical task for service registries to be responsible for maintaining the list of reputable and trustworthy services and service providers, and bringing them to clients [19].

Trust is the measure by one party on the willingness and ability of another party to act in the interest of the former party in a situation [11]. Trust is also the subjective probability by which, party A expects that another party B performs a given action if the trust value is in the range of [0,1] [8].

Different from P2P information-sharing networks or eBay reputation management system, where a binary rating system is used [25], in SOC environments, a trust rating is usually a value in the range of [0,1] [19,20,21] given by a service client, representing

L. Baresi, C.-H. Chi, and J. Suzuki (Eds.): ICSOC-ServiceWave 2009, LNCS 5900, pp. 50–67, 2009.

the subjective belief of the service client on the satisfaction of a service or a service provider. The trust value of a service or a service provider can be calculated by a trust management authority based on the collected trust ratings representing the reputation of the service or the service provider.

However, trust management is a very complex issue in SOC environments. To satisfy the specified functionality requirement, a service may have to invoke other services forming composite Web services with complex invocations and trust dependencies among services and service providers [16]. Meanwhile, given a set of various services, different compositions may lead to different service structures. Although these certainly enrich the service provision, they greatly increase the computation complexity and thus make trustworthy service selection and discovery a very challenging task.

In the literature, there are some existing studies for service composition and quality driven service selection [3,16,24,28,30]. However, for trust-oriented composite service selection and discovery, some research problems remain open.

1. The definition of a proper graph representation of composite services including both probabilistic invocations and parallel invocations is still lacking. The corresponding data structure is also essential. Both of them are fundamental and important for deploying the global trust evaluation of composite services.
2. From the definitions in [8,11], trust can be taken as the *subjective probability*, i.e. *the degree of belief an individual has in the truth of a proposition* [4,5], rather than the *objective probability* or *classical probability*, which is *the occurrence frequency of an event* [5]. A subjective probability is derived from an individual's personal judgment about a specific outcome (e.g. the evaluation of teaching quality or service quality). It differs from person to person. Hence, the classical probability theory does not fit for trust evaluation. Instead, *subjective probability theory* deals with *subjective probability* [4,5] and should be adopted for trust evaluation.
3. Although there are a variety of trust evaluation methods in different areas [19,21,25], no proper mechanism exists for evaluating the global trust of a composite service with a complex structure from the trust values of all service components.
4. Taking trust evaluation and the complex structure of composite services into account, effective algorithms are needed for composite service selection and discovery, and are expected to be more efficient than the existing approaches [16,28].

In this paper, we first present the service invocation graph and service invocation matrix for composite service representation. In addition, we propose a trust evaluation method for composite services based on Bayesian inference, which is an important component in subjective probability theory. Furthermore, we propose a service selection and discovery algorithm based on Monte Carlo method. Experiments have been conducted on composite services with various sizes to compare the proposed model with the existing exhaustive search method [16]. The results illustrate that our proposed algorithm is realistic and more efficient.

This paper is organized as follows. Section 2 reviews existing studies in service composition, service selection and trust. Section 3 presents our proposed composite services oriented service invocation graph and service invocation matrix. Section 4 presents a novel trust evaluation method for composite services. In Section 5, a Monte Carlo method based algorithm is proposed for trust-oriented composite service selection and discovery. Experiments are presented in Section 6 for further illustrating the properties of our models. Finally Section 7 concludes our work.

2 Related Work

In SOC environments, the composition of services offered by different providers enriches service provision and offers flexibility to service applications. In [14,15], Medjahed et al present some frameworks and algorithms for automatically generating composite services from specifications and rules.

In real applications, the criteria of searching services should take into account not only functionalities but also other properties, such as QoS (quality of service) and trust. In the literature, a number of QoS-aware Web service selection mechanisms have been developed, aiming at QoS improvement in composite services [3,24,30]. In [30], Zeng et al present a general and extensible model to evaluate the QoS of composite services. Based on their model, a service selection approach has been introduced using linear programming techniques to compute optimal execution plans for composite services. The work in [3] addresses the selection and composition of Web services based on functional requirements, transactional properties and QoS characteristics. In this model, services are selected in a way that satisfies user preferences, expressed as weights over QoS and transactional requirements. In [24], Xiao et al present an autonomic service provision framework for establishing QoS-assured end-to-end communication paths across domains. Their algorithms can provide QoS guarantees over domains. The above works have their merits in different aspects. However, none of them has taken parallel invocation into account, which is fundamental and one of the most common existing invocations in composite services [16,28].

Menascé [16] adopts an exhaustive search method to measure service execution time and cost involving probabilistic, parallel, sequential and fastest-predecessor-triggered invocations. However, the algorithm complexity is exponential. Yu et al [28] study the service selection problem with multiple QoS constraints in composite services, and propose two optimal heuristic algorithms: the combinatorial algorithm and the graph-based algorithm. The former one models the service selection as a multidimension multichoice 0-1 knapsack problem. The latter one can be taken as a multiconstraint optimal path problem. Nevertheless, none of these works addresses any aspect of trust.

The trust issue has been widely studied in many applications. In e-commence environments, the trust management system can provide valuable information to buyers and prevent some typical attacks [20,29]. In Peer-to-Peer information-sharing networks, binary ratings work pretty well as a file is either the definitively correct version or not [27]. In SOC environments, an effective trust management system is critical to identify potential risks, provide objective trust results to clients and prevent malicious service providers from easily deceiving clients and leading to their huge monetary loss [19].

In general, the trust from a service client on a service or a service provider can be taken as an extent with which the service client *believes* that the service provider can satisfy the client's requirement with desirable performance and quality. Thus, as we point out in Section 1, trust is a *subjective belief* and it is better to adopt *subjective probability theory* [5] to deal with trust. In contrast, *classical probability theory* is actually more suitable to deal with objective occurrence frequency of an event.

There are some works to deal with subjective ratings [7,22]. Jøsang [7] describes a framework for combining and assessing subjective ratings from different sources based on Dempster-Shafer belief theory. Wang and Singh [22] set up a bijection from subjective ratings to trust values with a mathematical understanding of trust in a variety of multiagent systems. However, their models use either a binary rating (positive or negative) system or a triple rating (positive, negative or uncertain) systems that are more suitable for security-oriented or P2P file-sharing trust management systems.

As pointed in [27], in richer service environments such as SOC or e-commerce, a rating in [0, 1] is more suitable. In [26], Xu et al propose a reputation-enhanced QoS-based Web service discovery algorithm for service matching, ranking and selection based on existing Web service technologies. Malik et al [13] propose a set of decentralized techniques aiming at evaluating reputation-based trust with the ratings from peers to facilitate trust-based selection and composition of Web services. However, in these works, no service invocation and composite service structure are taken into account. Taking the complex structure of composite services into account, effective algorithms are needed for trust-oriented composite service selection and discovery.

3 Service Invocation Model

In this section, we present the definitions of our proposed service invocation graph and service invocation matrix for representing the complex structures of composite services. They are essential for our trust-oriented composite service selection and discovery algorithm to be introduced in Section 5.

3.1 Composite Services and Invocation Relation

A *composite service* is a conglomeration of services with invocation relations between them. Six atomic invocations [16,28] are depicted as follows and in Fig. 1.

- *Sequential Invocation*: A service S invokes its unique succeeding service A. It is denoted as $Se(S : A)$ (see Fig. 1(a)).
- *Parallel Invocation*: A service S invokes its succeeding services in parallel. E.g., if S has successors A and B, it is denoted as $Pa(S : A, B)$ (see Fig. 1(b)).
- *Probabilistic Invocation*: A service S invokes its succeeding service with a probability. E.g., if S invokes successors A with the probability p and B with the probability $1 - p$, it is denoted as $Pr(S : A|p, B|1 - p)$ (see Fig. 1(c)).
- *Circular Invocation*: A service S invokes itself for n times. It is denoted as $Ci(S|n)$ (see Fig. 1(d)). A circular invocation can be unfolded by cloning itself n times [28]. Hence, it can be replaced by Se in advance.
- *Synchronous Activation*: A service S is activated only when all its preceding services have been completed. E.g., if S has synchronous predecessors A and B, it is denoted as $Sy(A, B : S)$ (see Fig. 1(e)).
- *Asynchronous Activation*: A service S is activated as the result of the completion of one of its preceding services. E.g., if S has asynchronous predecessors A and B, it is denoted as $As(A, B : S)$ (see Fig. 1(f)).

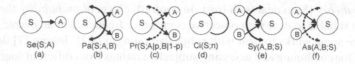

Se(S;A)   Pa(S;A,B)   Pr(S;A|p,B|1-p)   Ci(S;n)   Sy(A,B;S)   As(A,B;S)
(a)   (b)   (c)   (d)   (e)   (f)

Fig. 1. Atomic invocations

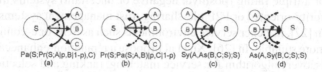

Pa(S;Pr(S;A|p,B|1-p),C)   Pr(S;Pa(S;A,B)|p,C|1-p)   Sy(A,As(B,C;S);S)   As(A,Sy(B,C;S);S)
(a)   (b)   (c)   (d)

Fig. 2. Complex invocations examples

With atomic invocations, some complex invocations can be depicted as Fig. 2, which are not clearly introduced in the existing works.

- *Probabilistic inlaid parallel invocation*, denoted as $Pa(S : Pr(S : A|p, B|1-p), C)$.
- *Parallel inlaid probabilistic invocation*, denoted as $Pr(S : Pa(S : A, B)|p, C|1-p)$.
- *Asynchronous inlaid synchronous activation*, denoted as $Sy(A, As(B, C : S) : S)$.
- *Synchronous inlaid asynchronous activation*, denoted as $As(A, Sy(B, C : S) : S)$.

3.2 An Example: Travel Plan

Here we introduce an example of composite services.

Smith in Sydney, Australia is making a travel plan to attend an international conference in Stockholm, Sweden. His plan includes conference registration, airline from Sydney to Stockholm, accommodation and local transportation.

Regarding conference registration *Reg*, Smith could pay *Online* or by *Fax* with a credit card *Ccard*. Regarding accommodation reservation *Acc*, Smith could make a reservation at Hotel *Ha*, *Hb* or *Hc* with credit card *Ccard*. According to the hotel choice, Smith could arrange the local transportation, e.g. take a *Taxi* to *Ha*, take a *Taxi* or a *Bus* to either *Hb* or *Hc*. Regarding airplane booking *Air*, Smith could choose from Airlines *Aa*, *Ab* and *Ac* with the credit card *Ccard* for the payment. Smith chooses the services according to their trust values. He will have a higher probability to choose the service with a better trust value.

In this example, with a starting service *START* and an ending service *END*, the composite services consisting of all possibilities of the travel plan can be depicted by a service invocation graph (*SIG*) (Fig. 3). One of all feasible travel plans is a service execution flow as depicted in Fig. 4.

3.3 Service Invocation Graph

The structure of a composite service can be represented by a service invocation graph (*SIG*), with the initial definition as follows.

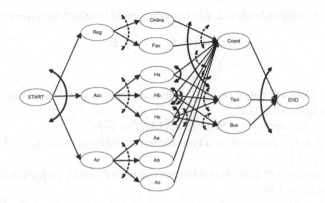

Fig. 3. The *SIG* for the travel plan of Smith

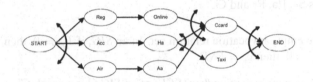

Fig. 4. A service execution flow

Definition 1. The *service invocation graph (SIG)* is a directed graph $G = (V, E, R)$, where V is a finite set of vertices, E is a finite set of directed edges and R is the set of atomic invocations Se, Pa, Pr, Ci, Sy and As. In G, each vertex $v \subset V$ represents a service. $\forall e = (v_1, v_2) \in E$ $(v_1, v_2 \in V)$ is a directed edge, where v_1 is the *invoking vertex* and v_2 is the *invoked vertex*. Here v_1 is the *direct predecessor* of v_2 and v_2 is the *direct successor* of v_1. It is denoted as $v_1 \succeq v_2$.

Definition 2. Given a service invocation graph $G = (V, E, R)$, vertex $v_2 \in V$ is *invocational* from vertex $v_1 \in V$ if $(v_1, v_2) \in E$ or there is a directed path P in G where v_1 is the staring vertex and v_2 is the ending vertex. If v_2 is invocational from v_1, it is denoted as $v_1 \succ v_2$.

In addition, if $v_1 \succ v_2$, v_1 is the predecessor of v_2 and v_2 is the successor of v_1. Obviously, the *invocational* relation is transitive, i.e. if $v_1 \succ v_2$, $v_2 \succ v_3$, then $v_1 \succ v_3$.

Definition 3. In a service invocation graph, the *service invocation root* is the entry vertex without any predecessors, and the *service invocation terminal* is the exit vertex without any successors.

Based on the above definitions, *SIG* is well-defined as follows.

Definition 4. A composite service can be represented by a *service invocation graph*

$$SIG = (V, I_p, R_p, I_s, R_s),$$ (1)

where

- In an *SIG*, there are only one service invocation root *START* and only one service invocation terminal *END*;
- $V = \{v_i | v_i$ is a vertex, $v_i = START$ or $START \succ v_i\}$;
- $I_p = \{I_{p_i}\}$ and I_{p_i} is a set of direct predecessors invoking v_i, i.e. $I_{p_i} = \{p_{ij} | p_{ij}, v_i \in V$ and $p_{ij} \succeq v_i\}$;
- R_p represents a set of activation relations between I_p and V, which includes atomic activations Sy and As;
- $I_s = \{I_{s_i}\}$ and I_{s_i} is a set of direct successors invoked by v_i, i.e. $I_{s_i} = \{s_{ij} | v_i, s_{ij} \in V$ and $v_i \succeq s_{ij}\}$;
- R_s represents a set of invocation relations between V and I_s, which includes atomic invocations Se, Pa, Pr and Ci.

Let $\emptyset$ denote the empty invocation relation set. In an *SIG*, if $I_{p_i} = \emptyset$, then $v_i = START$. Similarly, if $I_{s_i} = \emptyset$, then $v_i = END$.

Definition 5. A *service execution flow* (*SEF*) of an *SIG G* is a graph $G' = (V', E', R')$, where R' contains Se, Pa, Sy and Ci, $V' \subseteq V$ and $E' \subseteq E$. In addition, $\forall v' \in V'$, v' is invocational from service invocation root *START* of G, and service invocation terminal *END* of G is invocational from v'.

3.4   Service Invocation Matrix

In Section 3.3, *SIG* provides a clear picture of service invocation relations in composite services. However, an underneath data structure is essential to represent and store vertices and invocation relations. Here we propose *service invocation matrix* - an algebraic representation of composite services.

Definition 6. A composite service can be represented by a *service invocation matrix*

$$SIM = (M_{ij})_{1 \leq i \leq n, 1 \leq j \leq n},$$ (2)

where

- n is the number of vertices in the composite services;
- $M_{ij} = 0$ *iff* there is no invocation from vertex i to vertex j;
- $M_{ij} = <M_{ij}^{(1)}, M_{ij}^{(2)}, \ldots, M_{ij}^{(k)}> (i \neq j)$ represents the invocations from vertex i to vertex j, and k is the number of all invocations from i to j;
- $M_{ij}^{(h)}$ ($1 \leq h \leq k$) is an integer which represents an invocation type from vertex i to vertex j;
    - If it is a parallel invocation, $M_{ij}^{(h)} = 2m_1$ ($m_1 = 1, 2 \ldots$), where m_1 increases from 1 continuously and different m_1 values indicate different parallel invocations Pas;

– If it is a probabilistic invocation, $M_{ij}^{(h)} = 2m_2 - 1 \ (m_2 = 1, 2 \ldots)$, where m_2 increases from 1 continuously and different m_2 values indicate different probabilistic invocations Prs;

– M_{ii} is an integer to represent the number of circular times of Ci in vertex i.

According to Definition 6, we have the following property.

Property 1. $< M_{ij}^{(1)}, M_{ij}^{(2)} > = < M_{ij}^{(2)}, M_{ij}^{(1)} >$

Taking Travel Plan (Fig. 3) in Section 3.2 as an example, non-zero entities of the *SIM* are listed in Table 1. Our proposed *SIM* can cover all atomic invocation structures and the complex invocation structures derived from them.

Table 1. Non-zeros of *SIM* in Travel Plan

i	j	M_{ij}	i	j	M_{ij}	i	j	M_{ij}	i	j	M_{ij}
START	Reg	< 2 >	Air	Ab	< 1 >	Hc	Ccard	< 2 >	Fax	Ccard	< 1 >
START	Acc	< 2 >	Air	Ac	< 1 >	Hc	Taxi	< 2, 1 >	Ha	Ccard	< 1 >
START	Air	< 2 >	Reg	Online	< 1 >	Hc	Bus	< 2, 1 >	Ha	Taxi	< 1 >
Acc	Ha	< 1 >	Reg	Fax	< 1 >	Aa	Ccard	< 1 >	Ccard	END	< 1 >
Acc	Hb	< 1 >	Hb	Ccard	< 2 >	Ab	Ccard	< 1 >	Taxi	END	< 1 >
Acc	Hc	< 1 >	Hb	Taxi	< 2, 1 >	Ac	Ccard	< 1 >	Bus	END	< 1 >
Air	Aa	< 1 >	Hb	Bus	< 2, 1 >	Online	Ccard	< 1 >			

4 Trust Evaluation in Composite Services

In this section, we introduce our trust evaluation models for composite services. In Section 4.1, a trust estimation model is proposed to estimate the trust value of each service component from a series of ratings according to Bayesian inference[4,5], which is an important component in subjective probability theory. These ratings are provided by service clients and stored by the service trust management authority. In Section 4.2, a global trust computation model is proposed to compute the global trust value of a composite service based on the trust values of all service components.

4.1 Trust Estimation Model

Since subjective probability is a person's degree of belief concerning a certain event [4,5], the trust rating in $[0, 1]$ of a service given by a service client can be taken as the *subjective possibility* with which the service provider can perform the service satisfactorily. Hence, *subjective probability theory* is the right tool for dealing with trust ratings. In this paper, we adopt *Bayesian inference*, which is an important component in *subjective probability theory*, to estimate the trust value of a provided service from a set of ratings. Each rating is a value in $[0, 1]$ evaluated from the subjective judgements of a service client on multiple attributes of the provided service, such as availability, security, execution time and cost [8,23].

The primary goal of *Bayesian inference* [4,5] is to summarize the available information that defines the distribution of trust ratings through the specification of probability density functions, such as: prior distribution and posterior distribution. The *prior distribution* summarizes the subjective information about the trust prior to obtaining the ratings sample $x_1, x_2, \ldots, x_n$. Once the sample is obtained, the prior distribution can be updated. The updated probability distribution on trust ratings is called the *posterior distribution*, because it reflects probability beliefs posterior to analyzing ratings.

According to [6], if all service clients give ratings for the same service, the provided ratings conform to normal distribution. The complete set of ratings can be collected based on honest-feedback-incentive mechanisms [9,10]. Let μ and σ denote the mean and the variance of ratings in the normal distribution. Thus, a sample of ratings $x_1, x_2, \ldots, x_n$ ($x_i \in [0,1]$) has the normal density with mean μ and variance σ. In statistics, when a ratings sample with size n is drawn from a normal distribution with mean μ and variance σ, the mean of the ratings sample also conforms to a normal distribution which has mean μ and variance $\sigma/\sqrt{n}$ [4]. Let $\delta \in [0,1]$ denote the prior subjective belief about the trust of a service that a client is requesting for. We can assume that the prior normal distribution of μ has mean δ and variance $\sigma/\sqrt{n}$, i.e.

$$f(\mu) = \begin{cases} \frac{\sqrt{n}}{\sigma\sqrt{2\pi}} e^{\frac{n(\mu-\delta)^2}{-2\sigma^2}}, & 0 < \mu < 1; \\ 0, & \text{otherwise.} \end{cases} \tag{3}$$

Given μ, the joint conditional density of the ratings sample is

$$f(x_1, x_2, \ldots, x_n|\mu) = \frac{1}{\sigma^n(2\pi)^{\frac{n}{2}}} e^{\frac{\Sigma(x_i-\mu)^2}{-2\sigma^2}} = \frac{1}{\sigma^n(2\pi)^{\frac{n}{2}}} e^{\frac{\Sigma x_i^2 - 2\mu\Sigma x_i + n\mu^2}{-2\sigma^2}}. \tag{4}$$

Hence, the joint density of the ratings sample and μ is

$$f(x_1, \ldots, x_n; \mu) = \frac{\sqrt{n}}{\sigma^{n+1}(2\pi)^{\frac{n+1}{2}}} e^{\frac{\Sigma x_i^2 - 2\mu n\bar{x} + n\mu^2 + n(\mu-\delta)^2}{-2\sigma^2}}. \tag{5}$$

Based on Eq. (5), the marginal density of the ratings sample is

$$\begin{aligned} f(x_1, x_2, \ldots, x_n) &= \frac{\sqrt{n}}{\sigma^{n+1}(2\pi)^{\frac{n+1}{2}}} e^{\frac{\Sigma x_i^2 + n\delta^2}{-2\sigma^2}} \int_{-\infty}^{\infty} e^{\frac{n\mu^2 - (n\bar{x}+n\delta)\mu}{-\sigma^2}} \, \mathrm{d}\mu \\ &= \frac{\sqrt{n}}{\sigma^{n+1}(2\pi)^{\frac{n+1}{2}}} e^{\frac{\Sigma x_i^2 + n\delta^2 - \frac{n(\bar{x}+\delta)^2}{2}}{-2\sigma^2}} \int_{-\infty}^{\infty} e^{\frac{n(\mu-\frac{\bar{x}+\delta}{2})^2}{-\sigma^2}} \, \mathrm{d}\mu \\ &= \frac{1}{\sqrt{2}\sigma^n(2\pi)^{\frac{n}{2}}} e^{\frac{\Sigma x_i^2 + n\delta^2 - \frac{n(\bar{x}+\delta)^2}{2}}{-2\sigma^2}}, \end{aligned} \tag{6}$$

since a normal density has to integrate to 1.

Thus, the posterior density for μ is

$$f(\mu|x_1, x_2, \ldots, x_n) = \frac{f(x_1, x_2, \ldots, x_n; \mu)}{f(x_1, x_2, \ldots, x_n)} = \frac{\sqrt{n}}{\sigma\sqrt{\pi}} e^{\frac{n(\mu-\frac{\bar{x}+\delta}{2})^2}{-\sigma^2}}. \tag{7}$$

Therefore, the posterior distribution of μ is normal with mean $\frac{\bar{x}+\delta}{2}$ and variance $\sigma/\sqrt{2n}$. If the loss function is squared error [4,5], the mean of the posterior normal distribution can be used as the estimation of trust value from ratings. Hence,

Theorem 1. The Bayesian estimation of the trust value of a service with n ratings $x_1, x_2, \ldots, x_n$ ($x_i \in [0, 1]$) is

$$T(x_1, x_2, \ldots, x_n, \delta) = \frac{\bar{x} + \delta}{2} = \frac{\Sigma_{i=1}^n x_i + n\delta}{2n}, \tag{8}$$

where $\delta \in [0, 1]$ denotes the requesting client's prior subjective belief about the trust.

If the requesting client has no prior subjective information about the trust of the requested service, by default, let $\delta = \frac{1}{2}$ since $\frac{1}{2}$ is the middle point of $[0, 1]$ representing the neutral belief between distrust and trust. After the Bayesian inference, the Bayesian estimation of the trust can be taken as the requesting client's prior subjective belief about the trust for the Bayesian inference next time.

Now we can estimate the trust of a requested service by combining the requesting client's prior subjective belief about the trust and ratings. Since trust is subjective, it is more reasonable to include the requesting client's prior subjective belief about the trust.

4.2 Global Trust Computation in Composite Services

Our goal is to select the optimal one from multiple *SEF*s (service execution flows) in an *SIG* aiming at maximizing the global trust value of *SEF*, which is determined by the trust values of vertices and invocation relations between vertices in the *SEF*.

According to Definition 5, in *SEF* we only need consider Se (Fig. 1 (a)), Pa (Fig. 1 (b)) and Sy (Fig. 1 (e)) . From Se and Pa, Sy in *SEF* can be determined. Due to space constraint, the details are omitted. Hence, there are two kinds of atomic structures to determine the trust value of an *SEF*: Se and Pa. Se in the *SEF* can be selected from the service invocation relation Se (Fig. 1(a)) or Pr (Fig. 1(c)) in the *SIG*. Pa in the *SEF* can be selected from the service invocation relation Pa (Fig. 1 (b)) in the *SIG*.

Definition 7. The global trust value T_g of an Se structure where service S uniquely invokes service A (see Fig. 1 (a)) can be computed by

$$T_g = T_S \cdot T_A, \tag{9}$$

where T_S and T_A are the trust values of S and A respectively, which are evaluated from Theorem 1. Since S and A are independent, the probability that S and A both occur is equal to the product of the probability that S occurs and the probability that A occurs.

Definition 8. The global trust value T_g of a Pa structure where service S invokes services A and B in parallel (see Fig. 1 (b)) can be computed from T_S and the combined trust value T_{AB} by Definition 7, and

$$T_{AB} = \frac{\omega_1}{\omega_1 + \omega_2} \cdot T_A + \frac{\omega_2}{\omega_1 + \omega_2} \cdot T_B, \tag{10}$$

where T_S, T_A and T_B are the trust values of S, A and B respectively, which are evaluated from Theorem 1. ω_1 and ω_2 are weights for A and B respectively which are specified in a requesting client's preference or specified as the default value by the service trust management authority according to QoS.

According to Definitions 7 & 8, each atomic structure Se or Pa can be converted to a single vertex. Hence, in the process of trust computation, an *SEF* consisting of Se and Pa structures can be incrementally converted to a single vertex with its trust value computed as the global trust. Due to space constraint, we briefly introduce the following global trust computation algorithm. For details, please refer to [12].

Global Trust Computation Algorithm. In order to obtain the global trust value of an *SEF*, firstly the trust value of each atomic Se structure in the *SEF* should be computed by Definition 7. Each computed atomic Se structure is then taken as a vertex in the *SEF*. After that, the trust value of each atomic Pa structure is computed by Definition 8. Similarly, each computed atomic Pa structure is then taken as a vertex in the *SEF*. Thus, the computation can repeat until the final *SEF* is simplified as a vertex, and the global trust value is obtained.

5　Composite Service Selection and Discovery

Here we assume that a service trust management authority stores a large volume of services with their ratings. In response to a client's request, the service trust management authority first generates an *SIG* containing all relevant services and invocation relations. Then, the trust-oriented service selection and discovery algorithm is applied to find the optimal *SEF* with the maximized global trust value.

5.1　Longest *SEF* Algorithm

If there are only Pr (probabilistic invocation) structures in an *SIG* (i.e. there are only Se (sequential invocation) structures in the *SEF*), the *SEF* is a path in the *SIG*. In this case, the longest *SEF* algorithm is applied for searching the optimal *SEF*. By extending Dijkstra's shortest path algorithm [1], the longest *SEF* algorithm is to find an execution flow (path) from *START* to *END* so that the multiplication of trust values of all vertices in the path is the maximal according to Definition 7. Formally, given a weighted graph consisting of set V of vertices and set E of edges, find a flow (path) P from the service invocation root $START \in V$ to the service invocation terminal $END \in V$ so that

$$\prod_{v_j \in P, v_j \in V} (T(x_1(v_j), x_2(v_j), \ldots, x_n(v_j), \delta_j)) \tag{11}$$

is the maximal among all flows (paths) from *START* to *END*, where $x_i(v_j)$ denotes a rating for vertex v_j and δ_j denotes the requesting client's prior subjective belief about the trust of vertex v_j. Due to space constraint, we ignore the details of this algorithm.

5.2　Monte Carlo Method Based Algorithm (MCBA)

If there are only Pa structures in an *SIG*, the unique *SEF* is the same as the *SIG*.

If an *SIG* consists of both Prs and Pas, finding the optimal *SEF* is an NP-complete problem [28], and we propose a *Monte Carlo method based algorithm (MCBA)* to find the optimal *SEF*.

Algorithm 1. *MCBA* for Composite Service Selection and Discovery

---

Input: Simulation times l; *SIM*, and service ratings *Reputation*.
Output: The optimal *SEF* with maximum global trust value $Trust_{global}$.
```
 1: Let Trust be the trust value for each service evaluated from Reputation by Theorem 1;
 2: for all i such that 1 ≤ i ≤ l do
 3:     Initialize active = [root], SEF= [root];
 4:     while active ≠ ∅ do
 5:         Select a vertex vertex from active, and remove vertex from active;
 6:         Let vectors Pr and Pa be the Pr and Pa structures from vertex;
 7:         if vector Pa ≠ ∅ then
 8:             if vertex is in SEF then
 9:                 for all Pa(j) in Pa do
10:                     if Pa(j) is not in SEF then
11:                         Add Pa(j) into SEF
12:                     end if
13:                 end for
14:             end if
15:             for all Pa(j') in Pa(j) do
16:                 if Pa(j') is not terminal and Pa(j') is not in active then
17:                     Add Pa(j') into active
18:                 end if
19:             end for
20:         end if
21:         if vector Pr ≠ ∅ then
22:             if vertex is in SEF then
23:                 if none of Pr is in SEF then
24:                     for all Pr(k) in Pr do
25:                         Generate a uniform distributed random number rand in [0, 1];
26:                         Select the smallest k' such that rand <Trust(k')/sum(Trust(k))
27:                     end for
28:                     Add Pr(k') in SEF
29:                 end if
30:             end if
31:             if Pr(k') is not terminal and Pr(k') is not in active then
32:                 Add Pr(k') into active
33:             end if
34:         end if
35:     end while
36:     Let Trust_SEF be the trust value of SEF according to Global Trust Computation Algorithm
37:     Trust_global = max Trust_SEF;
38: end for
39: return Optimal SEF and Trust_global.
```

Monte Carlo method [2] is a computational algorithm which relies on repeated random sampling to compute results. It tends to be adopted when it is infeasible to compute an exact result with a deterministic algorithm. Monte Carlo method is useful for modeling phenomena with significant uncertainty in inputs, such as the calculation of risk in business [2]. The specific areas of application of the Monte Carlo method include computational physics, physical chemistry, global illumination computations, finance and business, and computational mathematics (e.g. numerical integration and numerical optimization) [2,17]. It is also one of the techniques for solving NP-complete problems [2,17]. Generally, Monte Carlo method consists of four steps: (1) defining a domain of inputs, (2) generating inputs randomly, (3) performing a computation on each input, and (4) aggregating the results into the final one.

The main strategy in *MCBA* is as follows. In an *SIG*, the direct successors of a service need to be selected according to their trust values. Usually, the direct successor with a larger trust value is preferred, which indicates higher probability to be invoked, and vice versa. Then, according to this, a uniform distributed random number is generated to decide which succeeding service is selected.

When determining the optimal *SEF* from an *SIG*, we only need *MCBA* for Pr structures. Let's take Pr in Fig. 1(c) as an example to explain the details of our *MCBA*. If successor A has a trust value T_A from Theorem 1 and successor B has a trust value T_B from Theorem 1, the probability for vertex S to choose successor A is

$$P_A = \frac{T_A}{T_A + T_B}. \tag{12}$$

Similarly, the probability to choose successor B is

$$P_B = \frac{T_B}{T_A + T_B}. \tag{13}$$

Obviously, $0 < P_A, P_B < 1$. Then a uniform distributed random number r_0 in $(0, 1)$ is generated to decide which successor is chosen. In detail, if $r_0 < P_A$, successor A is chosen; If $P_A < r_0 < P_A + P_B = 1$, successor B is chosen.

Therefore, given an *SIG*, an *SEF* could be obtained by repeating *MCBA* from the service invocation root *START* until the service invocation terminal *END* is reached. Once an *SEF* is generated, its global trust value can be calculated by global trust computation algorithm in Section 4.2. By repeating this process for l simulation times, a set of *SEF*s can be generated, from which the locally optimal *SEF* with the maximal global trust value can be obtained. A high value of l is necessary to obtain the optimal solution. *MCBA* for composite service selection and discovery is illustrated in Algorithm 1.

In Theorem 1, the trust estimation algorithm has a complexity of $O(n)$ with n ratings. Hence, in global trust computation algorithm in Section 4.2, the complexity of trust evaluation for a composite service with N services is $O(nN)$. Therefore, *MCBA* with l simulations incurs a complexity of $O(nlN)$.

6 Experiments

In this section, we will illustrate the results of conducted experiments for studying our proposed *MCBA*.

6.1 Comparison on Travel Plan Composite Services

In this experiment, we compare our proposed *MCBA* with the exhaustive search method by applying them to the travel plan composite services (with 16 vertices and 30 *SEF*s). The corresponding ratings and Smith's prior subjective belief of each service component are listed in Table 2. The weights of service components in all Pa structures of the composite services are listed in Table 3.

The exhaustive search method is inefficient as it aims to enumerate all solutions. In the work by Menascé [16], the exhaustive search method is adopted to calculate execution time and cost of all *SEF*s in a composite service.

According to global trust computation algorithm in Section 4.2, the global trust value T_i of *SEF* i ($i = 1, 2, \ldots, 30$) can be calculated. Let *trust-based SEF optimality* be

$$O_T(T_i) = \frac{T_i}{\max(T_i)}. \tag{14}$$

Table 2. Ratings and subjective belief of each service component in the travel plan

	Reg	Acc	Air	Online	Fax	Ha	Hb	Hc	Aa	Ab	Ac	Ccard	Taxi	Bus
x_1	0.88	0.83	0.78	0.92	0.51	0.17	0.35	0.89	0.30	0.95	0.25	0.95	0.94	0.32
x_2	0.84	0.82	0.87	0.92	0.38	0.18	0.32	0.86	0.36	0.98	0.30	0.95	0.86	0.37
x_3	0.97	0.85	0.77	0.94	0.25	0.22	0.46	0.82	0.34	0.91	0.24	0.96	0.86	0.34
x_4	0.87	0.82	0.83	0.96	0.40	0.12	0.34	0.87	0.29	0.91	0.31	0.96	0.89	0.18
x_5	0.91	0.74	0.79	0.95	0.41	0.16	0.28	0.88	0.41	0.97	0.29	0.96	0.90	0.35
δ	0.92	0.85	0.91	0.95	0.32	0.20	0.50	0.91	0.32	0.92	0.51	0.98	0.89	0.33

Table 3. Weights of service components in Pa

Reg	Acc	Air	Ccard	Taxi	Ccard	Bus
0.1	0.3	0.6	0.6	0.4	0.6	0.4

The corresponding histogram of $O_T(T_i)$ values of 30 *SEF*s is plotted in Fig. 5. From it, we can observe that 80% of $O_T(T_i)$ values are less than 0.8, implying that if we choose an *SEF* randomly, it is very likely to obtain an *SEF* with a low trust value .

In *MCBA*, there are multiple simulations, in each of which an *SEF* is generated and its global trust value is calculated. After l simulations, a locally optimal *SEF* can be obtained from l generated *SEF*s. In order to study the distribution of global trust of locally optimal *SEF*'s, we take l simulations as a repetition and repeat for m times.

Our experiments are using Matlab 7.6.0.324 (R2008a) running on a Dell Vostro V1310 laptop with an Intel Core 2 Duo T5870 2.00GHz CPU and a 3GB RAM. l, the number of simulation times, is set from 1 to 100. m, the number of repetition times, is set from 1 to 100. The experiment results are plotted in Fig. 7. We could observe that with a fixed number of repetitions, the more simulations, the closer to 1 O_T becomes. Namely more simulations lead to a higher probability to obtain the optimal *SEF*.

Furthermore, we compare the execution time of *MCBA* with that of the exhaustive search method. Each CPU time in this paper is the average of ten independent

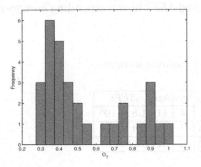

Fig. 5. Histogram of O_T for each *SEF*

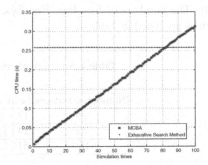

Fig. 6. CPU time of simulation times

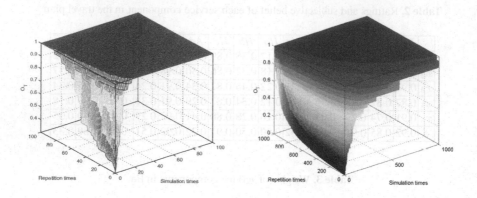

Fig. 7. O_T in the travel plan example   **Fig. 8.** O_T in composite service of 100 vertices

executions. In Fig. 6, we can observe that when the number of simulation times $l \leq 82$, our *MCBA* is faster than the exhaustive search method. From Figs 6 and 7, we can see that the probability to obtain the optimal *SEF* is 97% when there are 20 simulations. Meanwhile, the execution time of our *MCBA* is 27% of the one of the exhaustive search method. According to Table 2, theoretically the probability to obtain the optimal *SEF* for each simulation in *MCBA* is 17.8%, due to *SIG* and the strategy in *MCBA* in Section 5.2. Hence after 20 simulations theoretically *MCBA* has the probability of 98.04% to obtain the optimal *SEF*. Hence the experiment result about the probability to obtain the optimal *SEF* confirms to the theoretical conclusion.

With this simple travel plan example, *MCBA* outperforms the exhaustive search method. More significant performance differences can be observed with some complex composite services to be introduced in the next section.

6.2   Comparison on Complex Composite Services

In this experiment, we further compare our proposed Monte Carlo method based algorithm (*MCBA*) and the exhaustive search method on three more complex composite services. The number of vertices of these composite services is 35, 52 and 100 respectively. The numbers of Ses, Pas, Prs, Sys, Ass and *SEF*s in corresponding composite services are listed in Table 4.

Table 4. Structure of complex composite services

Number of vertices	Ses	Pas	Prs	Sys	Ass	SEFs
35	17	8	11	4	11	1.8×10^3
52	24	13	16	7	16	5.4×10^4
100	51	24	32	12	32	2.92×10^9

Table 5. CPU time in seconds of different examples

Number of vertices	16	35	52	100
Probability to obtain the optimal *SEF* for each simulation	17.84%	14.31%	5.71%	0.33%
Number of simulation times in *MCBA*	20	20	52	925
Probability to obtain the optimal *SEF* for *MCBA*	98.04%	95.45%	95.29%	95.12%
CPU time (seconds) of *MCBA*	0.0695	0.3219	0.8625	34.51
CPU time (seconds) of exhaustive search method	0.2578	17.09	–	–

In this experiment, we use the same platform as the experiment in Section 6.1. In the case of composite service with 35 vertices, the *MCBA* takes 0.3219 second to finish 20 simulations with the probability of 95.45% to obtain the optimal *SEF*, while the exhaustive search method uses 17.09 seconds. When the number of vertices becomes 52, our *MCBA* takes 0.8625 second to finish 52 simulations, with which the probability to obtain the optimal *SEF* is 95.29%. However, when taking the same time, the exhaustive search method can only search 0.42% of 5.4×10^4 *SEFs*. When taking 1000 times of the *MCBA* CPU time, it can only search approximately 1% of all *SEFs*. We further apply our *MCBA* to a composite service with 100 vertices. It takes 34.51 seconds to finish 925 simulations with a probability of 95.12% to obtain the optimal *SEF*. In contrast, when taking the same time, the exhaustive search method can only search $(9.56 \times 10^{-6})\%$ of 2.92×10^9 *SEFs*. When taking 100 times of the *MCBA* CPU time, it can only search $(1.01 \times 10^{-5})\%$ of all *SEFs*. The above results are listed in Table 5.

In the case of composite service with 100 vertices, the results of *MCBA* are plotted in Fig. 8. When there are $l = 925$ simulation times, *MCBA* can reach the optimal solution with the probability 95.2%. Also it has a great chance to obtain the near-optimal one, even when l is as small as 200. For example, in Fig. 8, when l is 200, the probability for the trust-based *SEF* optimality to be $O_T \geq 0.82$ is about 95.7%.

In summary, our proposed *MCBA* can obtain a near-optimal *SEF* after some simulations. As the CPU time for a single simulation in *MCBA* is extremely short, our experiments have illustrated that the overall performance of *MCBA* is good even with complex composite services. In addition, *MCBA* is suitable for parallel computing since each simulation in *MCBA* is independent. This can greatly speed up computations and shorten the overall CPU time. Thus, our proposed *MCBA* is realistic and efficient.

7   Conclusions

In this paper, we first propose our service invocation graph and service invocation matrix for composite service representation. In addition, a novel trust evaluation approach based on Bayesian inference has been proposed that can aggregate the ratings from other clients and the requesting client's prior subjective belief about the trust. Based on them, a Monte Carlo method based trust-oriented service selection and discovery algorithm has been proposed. Experiments have illustrated that our proposed approach can discover the near-optimal composite services efficiently.

In our future work, strategies for optimizing the Monte Carlo method based algorithm will be studied to further improve the efficiency. We will also study some heuristic approaches for trust-oriented optimal service selection and discovery.

References

1. Dijkstra, E.W.: A note on two problems in connexion with graphs. Numerische Mathematik 1, 269–271 (1959)
2. Gentle, J., Härdle, W., Mori, Y.: Handbook of Computational Statistics. Springer, Heidelberg (2004)
3. Haddad, J.E., Manouvrier, M., Ramirez, G., Rukoz, M.: QoS-driven selection of web services for transactional composition. In: ICWS 2008, pp. 653–660 (2008)
4. Hamada, M.S., Wilson, A.G., Reese, C.S., Martz, H.F.: Bayesian Reliability. Springer, Heidelberg (2008)
5. Hines, W.W., Montgomery, D.C., Goldsman, D.M., Borror, C.M.: Probability and Statistics in Engineering. John Wiley & Sons, Inc., Chichester (2003)
6. Hu, N., Pavlou, P.A., Zhang, J.: Can online reviews reveal a product's true quality?: empirical findings and analytical modeling of online word-of-mouth communication. In: ACM EC 2006, pp. 324–330 (2006)
7. Jøsang, A.: Subjective evidential reasoning. In: IPMU (2002)
8. Jøsang, A., Ismail, R., Boyd, C.: A survey of trust and reputation systems for online service provision. Decision Support Systems 43(2), 618–644 (2007)
9. Jurca, R., Faltings, B.: Collusion-resistant, incentive-compatible feedback payments. In: ACM EC 2007, pp. 200–209 (2007)
10. Jurca, R., Faltings, B.: Minimum payments that reward honest reputation feedback. In: ACM EC 2006, pp. 190–199 (2006)
11. Knight, D.H., Chervany, N.L.: The meaning of trust. Technical Report WP9604, University of Minnesota, Management Information Systems Research Center (1996)
12. Li, L., Wang, Y.: Trust evaluation in composite services selection and discovery. In: SCC 2009, Bangalore, India, September 21-25 (2009)
13. Malik, Z., Bouguettaya, A.: RATEWeb: Reputation assessment for trust establishment among web services. VLDB J. 18(4), 885–911 (2009)
14. Medjahed, B., Bouguettaya, A.: A multilevel composability model for semantic web services. IEEE Trans. Knowl. Data Eng. 17(7), 954–968 (2005)
15. Medjahed, B., Bouguettaya, A., Elmagarmid, A.K.: Composing web services on the semantic web. VLDB J. 12(4), 333–351 (2003)
16. Menascé, D.A.: Composing web services: A QoS view. IEEE Internet Computing 8(6), 88–90 (2004)
17. Morton, D.P., Popova, E.: Monte-Carlo simulations for stochastic optimization. In: Encyclopedia of Optimization, pp. 2337–2345. Springer, Heidelberg (2009)
18. Papazoglou, M.P., Traverso, P., Dustdar, S., Leymann, F.: Service-oriented computing: a research roadmap. Int. J. Cooperative Inf. Syst. 17(2), 223–255 (2008)
19. Vu, L.-H., Hauswirth, M., Aberer, K.: QoS-based service selection and ranking with trust and reputation management. In: Meersman, R., Tari, Z. (eds.) OTM 2005. LNCS, vol. 3760, pp. 466–483. Springer, Heidelberg (2005)
20. Wang, Y., Lim, E.-P.: The evaluation of situational transaction trust in e-service environments. In: ICEBE 2008, pp. 265–272 (2008)
21. Wang, Y., Lin, K.-J., Wong, D.S., Varadharajan, V.: Trust management towards service-oriented applications. Service Oriented Computing and Applications journal 3(1) (2009)

22. Wang, Y., Singh, M.P.: Formal trust model for multiagent systems. In: Proceedings 20th International Joint Conference on Artificial Intelligence (IJCAI 2007), pp. 1551–1556 (2007)
23. Wang, Y., Wong, D.S., Lin, K.-J., Varadharajan, V.: Evaluating transaction trust and risk levels in peer-to-peer e-commerce environments. Inf. Syst. E-Business Management 6(1), 25–48 (2008)
24. Xiao, J., Boutaba, R.: QoS-aware service composition and adaptation in autonomic communication. IEEE Journal on Selected Areas in Communications 23(12), 2344–2360 (2005)
25. Xiong, L., Liu, L.: PeerTrust: Supporting reputation-based trust for peer-to-peer electronic communities. IEEE Trans. Knowl. Data Eng. 16(7), 843–857 (2004)
26. Xu, Z., Martin, P., Powley, W., Zulkernine, F.: Reputation-enhanced QoS-based web services discovery. In: ICWS 2007, pp. 249–256 (2007)
27. Yu, B., Singh, M.P., Sycara, K.: Developing trust in large-scale peer-to-peer systems. In: 2004 IEEE First Symposium on Multi-Agent Security and Survivability, pp. 1–10 (2004)
28. Yu, T., Zhang, Y., Lin, K.-J.: Efficient algorithms for web services selection with end-to-end Qos constraints. TWEB 1(1) (2007)
29. Zacharia, G., Maes, P.: Trust management through reputation mechanisms. Applied Artificial Intelligence 14(9), 881–907 (2000)
30. Zeng, L., Benatallah, B., Dumas, M., Kalagnanam, J., Sheng, Q.Z.: Quality driven web services composition. In: WWW 2003, pp. 411–421 (2003)

A Two-Tiered Approach to Enabling Enhanced Service Discovery in Embedded Peer-to-Peer Systems*

Antonio Brogi, Sara Corfini, and Thaizel Fuentes

Department of Computer Science, University of Pisa, Italy
{brogi,corfini,fuentes}@di.unipi.it

Abstract. Recent technology advances are pushing towards a full integration of low-capacity networked devices in pervasive embedded P2P systems. One of the challenges of such integration is to allow low-capacity devices both to invoke and to provide services, while featuring enhanced service discovery mechanisms that are necessary to automate service invocation in pervasive environments. In this paper we present a two-tiered approach to enabling enhanced service discovery in embedded P2P systems. We first present a super-peer based overlay network featuring a matching capability aware routing of messages, and saving the resource consumption of low-capacity devices while keeping the overall network traffic low. We then present a service discovery protocol that exploits such underlying overlay network to suitably distribute service contracts on devices capable of analysing them, thus enabling enhanced service discovery even in nets mainly formed by low-capacity devices. Finally, we discuss some experimental results that confirm the viability of the proposed approach.

1 Introduction

Recent advances in hardware and wireless technologies have paved the way for a full integration of low-capacity networked devices in pervasive embedded P2P systems. In this perspective, Service-oriented Computing [1] has proven to provide suitable abstractions to master the complexity of large applications. The notion of *service* is used to represent sets of functionalities offered by a peer[1], service providers publish into service registries *contracts* describing the provided services, while service consumers query service registries to locate the services they need to interact with.

To achieve truly automated pervasive systems, service discovery and invocation should be entirely automated, which means that enhanced service discovery mechanisms should be featured to reduce the possibility of failures in automated discover-and-invoke steps. In particular, one of the desired enhancements in the

---

* Research partially supported by EU FP6-IST STREP 0333563 SMEPP.
[1] In this paper we will use the terms "*peer*" and "*device*" interchangeably.

L. Baresi, C.-H. Chi, and J. Suzuki (Eds.): ICSOC-ServiceWave 2009, LNCS 5900, pp. 68–82, 2009.

service discovery process concerns the quality of the results of the discovery process. Indeed while the need of including *signature information* in service contracts to enable interoperability is universally accepted (e.g., WSDL has prominently emerged as the de facto standard for defining the syntax of the functionalities featured by Web services), signature information is not enough to fully automate the discover-and-invoke step. For this reason, *ontological annotations* —to overcome non-relevant differences in the syntactic description of services— as well as *behavioural information* —to verify that service interactions will not lock— are starting to be included in service contracts of embedded P2P systems [2].

Achieving an effective implementation of enhanced service discovery is however one of the critical issues in pervasive embedded P2P environments for various reasons:

- Service registries cannot be centralised for obvious scalability and reliability reasons, thus service contracts have to be suitably distributed among the peers participating in the application.
- A distributed implementation of the service discovery process should aim at saving the resource consumption of low-capacity devices, which could otherwise consume all their resources by participating in the discovery protocol and then become unavailable when other peers will invoke the services they offered.
- Intuitively, contracts of services published by low-capacity devices should hence better be stored by higher-capacity devices. The implementation of such a policy is however complicated by the fact that devices storing contracts may (unexpectedly) disconnect from the network (e.g., because of mobility or battery exhaustion reasons). Also, not all devices are in general capable of analysing all types of information contained in service contracts.

Various service discovery architectures for (pervasive) P2P environments have been proposed over the last years. Those architectures are however typically tailored to efficiently deal with contracts and queries describing a specific type of information (e.g., [3,4,5] focus on syntactic information, while [6,7,8] focus on ontology-annotated queries), and they cannot be straightforwardly exploited to efficiently implement discoveries based on other types of information. Consider a query specifying both ontology-based and behaviour requirements. One could exploit for instance the approach of [6] to locate the service contracts matching the ontology-based requirements, and then check whether the partially matched services also satisfy the behaviour requirements of the query. The service contracts found by [6] may be however hosted by peers which do not feature behaviour-aware matching algorithms, and in those cases it would be necessary to discover other peers capable of performing a behaviour-aware analysis of contracts and to move the candidate contracts there to complete the matching. However, moving sets of contracts across a P2P network would seriously increase net traffic and severely affect the efficiency of the resulting discovery process.

In this paper we present a two-tiered approach to enabling enhanced service discovery (taking into account different types of information contained in service contracts) in embedded P2P systems for pervasive environments. We first present

a super-peer based overlay network featuring a matching-capability aware routing of messages, capable of *(o1) saving the resource consumption of low-capacity
devices* and *(o2) keeping the overall network traffic low.* We then present a service
discovery protocol that exploits such underlying overlay network to *(o3) suitably
distribute service contracts on devices capable of analysing them*, thus enabling
enhanced service discovery even in nets mainly formed by low-capacity devices.
Finally, we discuss some experimental results to assess the level of achievement
of objectives *(o1)*, *(o2)*, and *(o3)* and to confirm the viability of the proposed
approach.

The proposed overlay network is a slight extension of the classical super-peer
model [9], where a set of connected (*super*) peers acts as servers for the rest of
(*client*) peers. One of the novelties of our overlay network is the introduction
of the notion of *assistant* peers, which can provide functionalities (matching
functionalities, in our context) not provided by the super peers. While assistant
peers may not own enough resources to play the role of super peers, these can
exploit assistant peers to provide the functionalities they cannot provide by
themselves. A suitable *ranking function* is introduced to rank peers (and classify
them as client, assistant or super peers) with respect to the provided matching
functionalities and their physical resources.

The rest of the paper is organised as follows. Sections 2 and 3 present the overlay network and the service discovery protocol, respectively. Section 4 discusses
some optimisations which mainly concern the maintenance of the overlay network. Some experimental results are discussed in Section 5, while related work
is discussed in Section 6. Finally, Section 7 presents some concluding remarks.

2   Overlay Network

As anticipated in Section 1, the overlay network proposed in this paper slightly
extends the classical super peer model by introducing the notion of *assistant*
peers (Fig. 1). Intuitively, an assistant peer is a peer which provides some (matching) functionalities, yet not owning enough physical resources to be a super peer.
A super peer can exploit assistant peers in its vicinity to provide its client peers
with functionalities it cannot provide by itself. In order to classify a peer as
super, assistant or client peer we introduce a ranking function ρ which ranks
peers by taking into account the features (i.e., physical resources and provided
functionalities) described in peer advertisements.

Specifically, an advertisement A_P of a peer P is a tuple

$$A_P = \langle WL_P, CPU_P, RAM_P, MOB_P, POW_P, MF_P \rangle$$

where $WL_P \in [0..1]$ denotes the current workload of the peer in terms of both
the number of contracts stored by P and the requests managed in the last time
interval (i.e., 1 denotes an overloaded peer, 0 an idle peer), CPU_P and RAM_P
respectively denote the CPU speed and the RAM capacity of the peer, $MOB_P \in$
{stationary, moving} describes whether the peer is moving or not, $POW_P \in$
{power plugged, on battery} describes whether the peer is plugged to the power

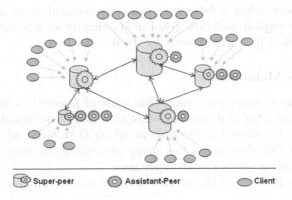

Super-peer   Assistant-Peer   Client

Fig. 1. Overlay network topology

or not, and $MF_P = MF_{self(P)} \cup MF_{assistants(P)}$ denotes the functionalities that the peer provides either by itself $(MF_{self(P)})$ or through its assistant peers $(MF_{assistants(P)})$.

The functionalities MF_P described in a peer advertisement are precisely the *matching functionalities* that the peer is able to provide. A matching functionality is a *type* of matching algorithm. The group of matching functionalities that we consider are $\langle syntactic \rangle$, $\langle syntactic, ontological \rangle$, $\langle syntactic, light\text{-}behavioural^2 \rangle$, $\langle syntactic, behavioural \rangle$, $\langle syntactic, ontological, light\text{-}behavioural \rangle$ and $\langle syntactic, ontological, behavioural \rangle$.

A ranking function $\rho : \mathcal{ADV} \times \mathbb{N} \longrightarrow \mathbb{R}$ is used to rank peers. A peer Q ranks a peer P by computing the value $\rho(A_P, D_{PQ})$, where A_P is the advertisement of P and D_{PQ} is the distance (i.e., number of physical hops) from P to Q. Intuitively, when ranking peers featuring similar physical resources, ρ ranks higher peers providing more matching functionalities. On the other hand, peer that advertise no matching functionalities (viz., $MF_P = \emptyset$) are always ranked 0, independently of their physical resources.The values computed by ρ are also inversely proportional w.r.t. the second parameter (i.e., $\rho(A_P, D_{PQ}) > \rho(A_P, D_{PQ} + \varepsilon))$ to take into account the physical vicinity among peers.

A peer Q can exploit ρ to classify a peer P (possibly itself) as client, assistant or super peer, as follows:

- P is a *client* peer if $\rho(A_P, D_{PQ}) = 0$,
- P may act as *assistant* peer if $\rho(A_P, D_{PQ}) > 0$, and
- P may act as *super* peer if $\rho(A_P, D_{PQ}) > t$

where t is a threshold to establish whether a peer can be a super peer or not, and $D_{PQ} = 0$ if $Q = P$. As illustrated in Fig. 1, client peers connect to a (single)

---

[2] We distinguish *light-behavioural* matching algorithms (checking the "may"-compatibility of service protocols, i.e., the existence of at least one successful interaction trace) from full *behavioural* matching algorithms (checking the full compatibility of service protocols, i.e., that all interaction traces are successful).

nearby super peer, while – differently from the classical super peer model – a super peer may exploit assistant peers in its vicinity to provide the matching functionalities that it cannot provide by itself.

2.1 Network Maintenance

A peer Q acting as super peer maintains a list of *fingers* to other super peers in its vicinity and a list of its current *assistants*. Both lists contain tuples of the form $\langle A_P, D_{PQ}, t \rangle$, where t is the time at which Q received advertisement A_P from P. A peer that does not act as super peer maintains only one super peer tuple, corresponding to the chosen super peer.

The core functionality of the overlay network can be summarised as follows:

- Each peer enters the net as a *client* peer, and it remains idle until it receives a routing request (from one of its upper layer protocols) or it receives a message from some other peer.
- When a client peer C needs to route a message, if it has not yet chosen its super peer then it broadcasts to its vicinity a SuperPeerDiscovery message carrying its advertisement A_C.
- When a peer P receives a SuperPeerDiscovery message from C:
  - If P is acting as super peer then P unicasts its advertisement A_P to C.
  - If P is not acting as super peer but $\rho(A_P, 0) > t$ or $\rho(A_P, D_{CP}) \geq \rho(A_C, D_{CP})$ then P unicasts A_P to C and self promotes itself to super peer.
- When a client peer C receives an advertisement A_P from P at time t:
  - If C does not have a super peer and $\rho(A_C, 0) < \rho(A_P, D_{PC})$ then C chooses P as its super peer and stores $\langle A_P, D_{PC}, t \rangle$ as its *super* tuple.
  - The same happens if C has a super peer $S \neq P$ but $\rho(A_P, D_{PC}) > \rho(A_S, D_{SC}) + \Delta$
  - If P was already the super peer chosen by C then C simply updates its *super* tuple into $\langle A_P, D_{PC}, t \rangle$.
  In any case, if C provides some matching functionality which is not provided by P, then C unicasts its advertisement A_C to P.
- A client C which has broadcasted a SuperPeerDiscovery message and which has not received any advertisement A_P such that $\rho(A_C, 0) < \rho(A_P, D_{PC})$ self promotes itself to super peer after a timed wait.

Super peers periodically broadcast their advertisements to their vicinity and unicast their *fingers* list to the super peers in such a list. When a super peer receives an advertisement or the list of another super peer, it updates its own *finger* and *assistant* lists by exploiting the ranking function ρ. Note that a super peer can be chosen as an assistant by another super peer.

2.2 Message Routing Protocol

The objective of the overlay network is to deliver messages to the peers which provide the required matching functionalities. The overlay network routes each message with respect to an associated key $k = \langle MF^S, MF^G \rangle$, which specifies the set MF^S of matching functionalities which *must* be strictly provided by the target peer, and the set MF^G of the matching functionalities which should be greedily provided by the target peer.

If the sender of the message is a client peer, the message is first routed to the super peer of the sender (if any, otherwise the sender peer broadcasts a SuperPeerDiscovery message to choose a super peer). If the target super peer provides the required matching functionalities, the message and – possibly – the link(s) to the assistant peer(s) necessary to satisfy $\langle MF^S, MF^G \rangle$, are dispatched to the upper service discovery layer. The super peer may also forward the message to those super peers in its fingers table which match the received key k. The radius of such forwarding is set by the service discovery layer.

3 Service Discovery Protocol

The service discovery layer features a service discovery protocol by storing service contracts in super peers and by exploiting matching functionalities provided by super and assistant peers to match contracts with queries.

The service discovery protocol exploits the overlay network to publish and to search for service contracts by passing a publication or query message and a key $k = \langle MF^S, MF^G \rangle$ to the overlay network. As described in the previous section, the key specifies the matching functionalities that the target peer(s) must provide (viz., MF^S) and should greedily provide (viz., MF^G). For instance, a message associated with the key $\langle \{ \langle syntactic,\ light\text{-}behavioural \rangle \}, \{ \langle syntactic,\ ontological, light\text{-}behavioural \rangle \} \rangle$ will be received by super peers capable of performing (possibly with the help of their assistants) both *syntactic* and *light-behavioural* matching and optionally, also ontological matching.

When a (service discovery) message and the associated key k are received by a target super peer, the overlay network dispatches the message, and the link(s) to the assistant peer(s) possibly necessary to satisfy the matching functionalities $\langle MF^S, MF^G \rangle$, to the service discovery layer. If the message is a publication message the (discovery layer of the) target super peer stores the contract of the published service. If the message is a query, the (discovery layer of the) target super peer first matches the contracts that it stores locally. If the super peer can provide all the required matching functionalities MF^S by itself, it returns the matched contracts to the peer that generated the request, otherwise, it forwards the query and the (partially matched) contracts to (some of) its assistant peers. Assistant peers match the received contracts by executing the matching functionalities requested by k, and return the matched contracts the peer that generated the request.

As anticipated in the previous section, the service discovery layer can specify the radius of the forwarding of messages among super peers. A peer can hence decide for instance to publish and search services only in its super peer.

Summing-up, the service discovery protocol (SDP) publishes and searches service contracts by invoking the overlay network (ON). To do this, the former invokes the later with calls of the form: route(m,k,forwardHops) where m is either publish(contract) or query(contractTemplate) and where k=$\langle MF^S, MF^G \rangle$. Suppose that the service discovery protocol of a peer Q invokes such a call. Then the behaviour of the overlay network of Q can be synthesised as follow:

If Q is not super peer **Then** {
  If $\nexists$ super peer **Then** Q starts discovering a super peer
  <m,k,forwardHops> is sent to the ON of the super peer of Q
}
Else { // this branch is also the code to be executed when a ON component receives a
      // message from another ON component
  If $MF_Q \supseteq MF^S$ **Then** {
    If $MF_{self(Q)} \not\supseteq MF^S$ AND m=query(ct) **Then**
    m is dispatched to the SDP (of Q), together with a subset H of the assistants of
    Q such that $(\cup_{h \in H} MF_h \cup MF_{self(Q)}) \supseteq MF^S \wedge$
                $\forall h \in H$ $(\cup_{k \in H \setminus \{h\}} MF_k \cup MF_{self(Q)}) \not\supseteq MF^S$
    Else m is dispatched to the SDP (of Q)
    dispatched = **true**
  }
  Else dispatched = **false**
  // to forward message m
  If (dispatched is **false**) OR (forwardHops > 0) **Then** {
    If (dispatched is **true**) **Then** forwardHops=(forwardHops−1)
    <m,k,forwardHops> is sent to all R in the fingers of Q such that $MF_R \supseteq MF^S$
  }
}

4   Optimisations

To simplify the reading, in Section 2 we have presented the core aspects of our overlay network. There are, however several important optimisations that have been implemented to reduce the number of messages exchanged for network maintenance and routing.

– *Limited broadcast.* We have seen that super peers periodically broadcast their advertisement. To control the number of potential clients, super peers dynamically update the radius of such broadcast according to their own current workload and available resources.
– *Passive mode.* If an (active) super peer does not receive routing message for a while, it switches to *passive mode* and stop periodically broadcasting its advertisement – until it will receive a routing message and switch back to active mode.
– *Checking the aliveness of super peers.* Whenever a peer routes a message to a super peer A, it firstly checks the time t_A when it received the advertisement from A. If t_A is up-to-date (i.e., the advertisement has been received recently), the message is sent *asynchronously* to the super peer. Otherwise, if t_A is out-of-date, the message is sent *synchronously* to the super peer, in

order to get an acknowledgement from it. If an acknowledgement is received, t_A is updated, otherwise A is not considered a valid super peer any more.

– *Avoiding network partitioning.* Network partitioning may especially occur in networks of mobile, limited-resource devices, where super peers advertise themselves in a short vicinity. To avoid that, whenever a peer chooses a new super peer, it notifies its old super peer (if any) of the availability of the new super peer, thus facilitating the inter-connection among super peers.

5 Evaluation

In order to assess the viability of the proposed overlay network and service discovery protocol, we analysed their behaviour with PlanetSim[10], an extensible discrete-event Java simulator for key-based routing protocols in P2P overlay networks.

We run a set of simulations for networks populated by heterogeneous peers, randomly distributed and moving in a $600 \times 600m^2$ area and capable of communicating within a $100m$ range. The matching functionalities provided by each peer were obtained according to the peer's randomly generated capabilities, and peers could unexpectedly leave the network due to battery exhaustion. In all the simulations, first all peers join the network, then 40% of peers (randomly chosen) started publishing service contracts, and then 60% of peers (randomly chosen) started issueing queries to discover services. The simulations were run by scaling the number n of peers from 10 to 150 (with a pace of 10), and for each n the result was obtained by taking the average of the results of 15 different tests run for 200 units of simulation time. In each test 20% of peers (randomly chosen) were high-capacity devices and 10% of peers (randomly chosen) were mobile devices, (randomly) moving in their vicinity during the entire simulation.

The first set of simulations was run to assess the degree with which the proposed service discovery protocol accomplished objective *(o3)* set in the Introduction, namely "*to suitable distribute service contracts on devices capable of analysing them*".

The metric we used to measure the accomplishment level of *(o3)* was the percentage of published contracts matching a query q that were successfully located by the service discovery protocol on devices capable of analysing them. Formally, let q be a query, let k be the key used to route q and let $MF^S(q)$ be the set of required matching functionalities specified with q. Then for each query q we computed the ratio:

$$\frac{\sharp\{c_h \mid \exists P : P \text{ stores } c_h \wedge h \bowtie k \wedge q \text{ hits } P \wedge MF_P \supseteq MF^S(q)\}}{\sharp\{c_h \mid \exists P : P \text{ stores } c_h \wedge h \bowtie k\}} \quad (1)$$

where c_h denotes a contract that was published with key h, $h \bowtie k$ denotes that the key h and k match, and MF_P denotes the set of matching functionalities provided by peer P (possibly with the help of its assistants).

Fig. 2 illustrates the results of the simulation, with only 1-hop routing forwarding among super peers. We can observe that even with a little percentage

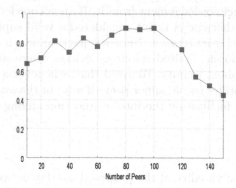

Fig. 2. Testing the ability of locating contracts on devices capable of analysing them

of high-capacity devices (20%), the accuracy of the discovery is very high up to 100 peers. After that it starts to decrease because of the incompleteness inherent to the super peer model (exacerbated here by considering only 1-hop routing forwarding among super peers).

The second set of simulations was run to assess the degree with which the proposed overlay network accomplishes objective *(o1)* set in the Introduction, namely *"saving the resource consumption of low-capacity devices"*.

The first metric we used to measure this was the percentage of (overlay) messages received by low-capacity devices w.r.t the overall number of messages exchanged due to routing activities (Fig. 3(a)). We compared our proposal with a basic implementation of the super-peer model (similar to [3][3]) and with the implementation of Chord DHT[11] provided by PlanetSim, customised to support mobility and to fit our statistics outputs.

We observed in Fig. 3(a) that, while Chord does not take into account device capabilities, when the number of peer grows, our proposal reduces the percentage of messages received by low-capacity devices w.r.t the basic super peer implementation.

The saving of resource consumption of low-capacity devices achieved by our proposal is even better highlighted in Fig. 3(b), where the used metric is directly the number of low-capacity devices still alive[4] at the end of the simulation.

A further set of simulations was done to assess the degree with which the proposed overlay network accomplishes objective *(o2)* set in the Introduction, namely *"keeping the overall network traffic low"*.

We first measured the number of (overlay network) messages generated by network maintenance activities. We can observe in Fig. 4(a) how the optimisations implemented in our proposal (Section 4) allow to reduce the network

---

[3] Super peer advertises right after joining the net, maintains a registry of their clients, and client requests are routed to super peers with compatible (numeric) keys.

[4] The simulation decrements the battery of a device every time it receives a message at the physical level (either for network maintenance or for routing).

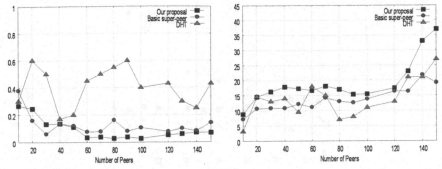

(a) Percent of messages received by low-capacity devices during routing

(b) Number of low-capacity devices alive at the end of the simulation

Fig. 3. Testing resource consumption of low-capacity devices

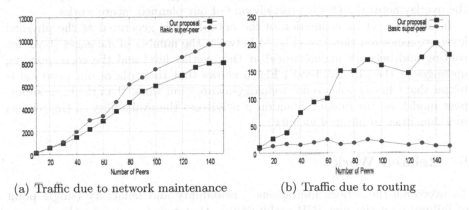

(a) Traffic due to network maintenance

(b) Traffic due to routing

Fig. 4. Testing network traffic

traffic generated for network maintenance by the basic super peer model. The numerical values for Chord –which generates only $O(\log_2^2(N))$ messages during network maintenances[11]– are not plotted in Fig. 4.

We then measured the number of (overlay network) messages generated by routing activity. Fig.4(b) shows that our proposal generates, as expected, quite more traffic for routing than the basic super peer implementation. The reason for this is that the implementation of our overlay network used in the experimentation routes messages with the objective of hitting devices providing the desired matching functionalities, but it does not take into account the other information included in contracts and queries (whose analysis is to be entirely performed by the upper service discovery level). A more fair comparison of the two approaches should consider an implementation of our overlay network capable of exploiting such information to reduce the number of fingers and assistants to which messages are routed. Such an implementation could be obtained by allowing the

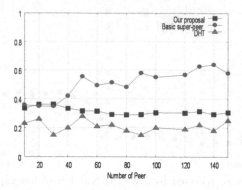

Fig. 5. Overlay/physical messages ratio

service discovery level to suitably configure the type of filters to be exploited by the overlay network. This is precisely one of our planned future works.

In order to get an estimation of the actual traffic generated at the physical level, we measured the ratio (Fig. 5) between the number of messages (both for routing and network maintenance) at the overlay level and the corresponding messages at the physical level[5]. Fig. 5 shows that the ratio of our proposal is better that Chord (which is not topology-aware), but worse than the basic super-peer model, as our ranking function ρ privileges the availability of (matching) functionalities to physical vicinity.

6 Related Work

To overcome the serious limitations —scalability and reliability (single point of failure)— of the first P2P architectures that relied on a centralised server (e.g., like in Napster's original design), a number of decentralised architectures have been proposed for P2P systems. These can be roughly partitioned into unstructured, structured and semi-structured architectures.

A main drawback of unstructured architectures (like Gnutella[12], JXTA[13,14]) is message explosion, caused by the use of message flooding to route messages. Moreover, each peer –target of a message routing– executes its own matching algorithm(s) without exploiting enhanced matching algorithms possibly provided by higher-capacity peers. This makes unstructured architectures unsuitable to implement enhanced service discovery mechanisms for embedded P2P systems.

Structured architectures, such as Distributed Hash Tables (DHTs [4,5]), sensibly reduce the number of (overlay) messages. However, the unawareness of the underlying physical topology and of peers'capacities make DHTs unsuitable to implement enhanced service discovery mechanisms for embedded P2P systems.

---

[5] The simulator determined the number of physical messages corresponding to an overlay message sent from A to B by counting one physical hop every $100m$ over the Euclidean distance between A and B.

Also, DHTs are not particularly well-suited for mobile environments, where frequent unexpected (dis)connections would cause frequent costly reorganisation of the overlay network. It is worth mentioning [15], an extension of Pastry DHT [16] which takes into account static physical capabilities of peers (viz., cpu speed, ram, etc.), but does not consider dynamic properties like vicinity, workload or battery consumption, and [17], which extends Chord's identifiers [11] to take into account any type of information regarding the service provider. Both [15] and [17] however present the other general drawbacks of DHTs.

Semi-structured architectures (like our proposal) set up a backbone of super peers which act as mini-servers for the other peers in the network. While they do not present the drawbacks of unstructured and structured approaches, network partitioning and cyclic message forwarding may occur in semi-structured approaches like [18], where peers autonomously choose their links to other peers. [7] and [19] build an overlay network among peers "sharing common interests" (e.g., semantic concepts or types of services). In [7] peers are organised in clusters, each mapping a semantic concept and storing "similar" files, while queries are forwarded to clusters that feature compatible concepts. In [19], each cluster has a coordinator, coordinators are linked one another, and coordinators do not take into account the physical capabilities of peers. Data-centered approaches like [7] and [19] are however tailored to handle specific types of data, and they cannot straightforwardly exploited to efficiently implement discoveries based on other types of information, as we already mentioned in the Introduction. In [20] super peers exchange a hierarchical XML representation of the data they store and use path expressions to process incoming queries. Such an approach cannot be however exploited in networks consisting of low-capacity devices only, because of the resources needed to process path expressions.

In [21] and [22], super peers constitute a DHT. In [21] low-capacity devices connect to a bootstrap node, which is chosen as super peer. If the chosen super peer is overloaded, the client is redirected to a non-overloaded super peer in the (Chord) ring, and service publication and discovery is based on keywords. In [22] peers discover and connect to super peers via JXTA protocols [13], and peers discover services by sending trivial semantic-based queries (a single taxonomy of types of services is considered) to super peers. Both [21] and [22] are not however well-suited for mobile networks of low-capacity devices, and they suffer from the previously discussed general drawbacks of structured architectures.

The approaches [23,24,25,3,6] are the most related with our proposal. In designing our architecture, we followed the guideline of [9] on how super peers can be selected, and we extended the concrete, yet partially defined, super peer network protocol of FastTrack [23] (inspired by Kazaa, http://www.kazaa.com). [24] ranks peers considering their static and dynamic capabilities. Super peers are dynamically elected in order to keep bounded the ratio between the number of clients peers and the number of super peers. Each super peer periodically compares its ranking against the ranking of its clients (and vice-versa). If the number of highest-ranked client peers exceeds a predefined threshold, then the super peer downgrades to client peer while the best ranked client peer promotes as super peer. In [25] super-peers are elected considering mainly the distance (measured as communication latency). Moreover, [25] deactivates super peers when they do not register clients, but (active) super peers advertise themselves even if they are not receiving queries from their clients. Instead, our proposal deactivates super peers when they do not receive service discovery messages for a while, thus saving network traffic. Differently from [24] and [25], we choose super peers by taking into account their matching functionalities mainly, but also our super peers do not register their clients to save memory consumption. Differently from [25], our proposal also dynamically sets the advertisement radius of super peers (i.e., the radius within which the super peers advertise themselves) with respect to their current capabilities, helping to keep bounded the ratio between client peers and super peers, similar to [24]. In the approaches [3] and [6], peers are organised into a semi-structured network similar to [25]. Super peers store service contracts and match them syntactically [3] and semantically [6]. The main novelty of our proposal with respect to [3] and [6] is that our architecture supports any matching approach, strengthened by the introduction of assistant peers, which are the key ingredient to implement an efficient and accurate service discovery mechanism capable of matching any type of query.

Last, but not least, we mention [26] that provides a high-level service discovery architecture enabling the coexistence of different contracts languages and (legacy) matching algorithms and allowing low-level communication among different (multi-radius) networks.

Different contract and query description languages and different matching algorithms are used in pervasive environments, ranging from syntactic [5], to semantics-based [8,27], to behaviour-based [28] service discovery. [26] provides a high-level service discovery architecture enabling the coexistence of such (legacy) matching algorithms. Our proposal can be integrated as a (vertical) middle-layer in multi-tiered architectures like[26]: We locate –and route messages to– devices capable to perform required matching functionalities, abstracting on the underlying multi-radius network –provided by [26]– and perimetrically w.r.t. both the contract (query) languages and the (legacy) matching algorithms, which will be locally provided by systems like [26].

7   Concluding Remarks

We have presented a two-tiered approach to enabling enhanced service discovery in embedded P2P systems. As we have seen, the proposed service discovery protocol exploits an overlay network featuring a matching capability aware routing of messages to suitably distribute service contracts on devices capable of analysing them, thus enabling enhanced service discovery even in nets mainly formed by low-capacity devices. We have also analysed the collected experimental data to assess the level of achievement of the three objectives that we set in the Introduction —(o1) saving the resource consumption of low-capacity devices, (o2) keeping the overall network traffic low, and (o3) suitably distributing service contracts on devices capable of analysing them— yielding a confirmation of the viability of the proposed approach.

Our plans for future work include to integrate first in our overlay network key-based data filters (such those employed in [6,8]) to drive message routing, as we already mentioned in Section 5. Then we plan to develop a full-fledged service discovery system where existing (both ontology-based and behaviour-aware) matchers can be plugged-in, so as to be able to start a thorough assessment of the versatility of the proposed overlay network and a comparative assessment at the service discovery level.

References

1. Papazoglou, M.P., Georgakopoulos, D.: Service-Oriented Computing. Communications of the ACM 46(10), 24–28 (2003)
2. Benigni, F., Brogi, A., Corfini, S., Fuentes, T.: Contracts in a Secure Middleware for Embedded Peer-to-Peer Systems. In: Proc. of the 2nd Workshop on Formal Languages and Analysis of Contract-Oriented Software (FLACOS) (2008)
3. Sailhan, F., Issarny, V.: Scalable Service Discovery for MANET. In: 3rd IEEE Int. Conf. on Pervasive Computing and Communications (PerCom), pp. 235–244. IEEE Computer Society, Los Alamitos (2005)
4. Lua, E.K., Crowcroft, J., Pias, M., Sharma, R., Lim, S.: A Survey and Comparison of Peer-to-Peer Overlay Network Schemes. IEEE Communications Surveys and Tutorials 7(2), 72–93 (2005)
5. Louati, W., Zeghlache, D.: SPSD: A Scalable P2P-based Service Discovery Architecture. In: IEEE Wireless Communications and Networking Conference (WCNC), pp. 2588–2593 (2007)
6. Mokhtar, S.B., Preuveneers, D., Georgantas, N., Issarny, V., Berbers, Y.: EASY: Efficient semAntic Service discoverY in pervasive computing environments with QoS and context support. Journal of Systems and Software 81(5), 785–808 (2008)
7. Garcia-Molina, H., Crespo, A.: Semantic Overlay Networks for P2P Systems. Stanford InfoLab, Technical Report 2003-75 (2003)
8. Skoutas, D., Sacharidis, D., Kantere, V., Sellis, T.K.: Efficient Semantic Web Service Discovery in Centralized and P2P Enviroments. In: Sheth, A.P., Staab, S., Dean, M., Paolucci, M., Maynard, D., Finin, T., Thirunarayan, K. (eds.) ISWC 2008. LNCS, vol. 5318, pp. 583–598. Springer, Heidelberg (2008)
9. Yang, B., Garcia-Molina, H.: Designing a Super-Peer Network. In: Proc. of the 19th Int. Conf. on Data Engineering (ICDE), pp. 49–60. IEEE Computer Society, Los Alamitos (2003)
10. Pujol Ahulló, J., García López, P., Sànchez Artigas, M., Arrufat Arias, M., París Aixalà, G., Bruchmann, M.: PlanetSim: An extensible framework for overlay network and services simulations. Universitat Rovira i Virgili, Tech. Rep. DEIM-RR-08-002 (2008)
11. Stoica, I., Morris, R., Karger, D.R., Kaashoek, M.F., Balakrishnan, H.: Chord: A scalable peer-to-peer lookup service for internet applications. In: ACM Conference on Applications, Technologies, Architectures, and Protocols for Computer Communication (SIGCOMM), pp. 149–160 (2001)
12. Gnutella team, Gnutella discovery protocol,
    http://www9.limewire.com/developer/gnutella_protocol_0.4.pdf
13. JXTA team, Jxta specification, https://jxta-spec.dev.java.net/
14. Srirama, S.N., Jarke, M., Zhu, H., Prinz, W.: Scalable Mobile Web Service Discovery in Peer-to-Peer Networks. In: 3rd Int. Conf. on Internet and Web Application and Services (ICIW), pp. 668–674. IEEE Computer Society, Los Alamitos (2008)

15. Liang, Q.A., Chung, J.-Y., Lei, H.: Service Discovery in P2P Service-oriented Environments. In: Proc. of the 8th Int. Conf. on E-Comemerce Technology and of the 3rd Int. Conf. on Enterprise Computing, E-Commerce, and E-Services (CEC/EEE). IEEE Computer Society, Los Alamitos (2006)
16. Rowstron, A., Druschel, P.: Pastry: Scalable, Decentralized Object Location, and Routing for Large-Scale Peer-to-Peer Systems. In: Guerraoui, R. (ed.) Middleware 2001. LNCS, vol. 2218, pp. 329–350. Springer, Heidelberg (2001)
17. He, Q., Yan, J., Yang, Y., Kowalczyk, R., Jin, H.: Chord4S: A P2P-based Decentralised Service Discovery Approach. In: IEEE Int. Conf. on Services Computing, pp. 221–228. IEEE Computer Society, Los Alamitos (2008)
18. Kobayashi, H., Takizawa, H., Inaba, T., Takizawa, Y.: A Self-Organizing Overlay Network to Exploit the Locality of Interests for Effective Resource Discovery in P2P Systems. In: Proc. of the 2005 Symposium on Applications and the Internet (SAINT), pp. 246–255. IEEE Computer Society, Los Alamitos (2005)
19. Doulkeridis, C., Nørvåg, K., Vazirgiannis, M.: DESENT: decentralized and distributed semantic overlay generation in P2P networks. IEEE Journal on Selected Areas in Communications 25(1), 25–34 (2007)
20. Thilliez, M., Delot, T.: A Localization Service for Mobile Users in Peer-to-Peer Environments. In: Crestani, F., Dunlop, M.D., Mizzaro, S. (eds.) Mobile HCI International Workshop 2003. LNCS, vol. 2954, pp. 271–282. Springer, Heidelberg (2004)
21. Hofstätter, Q., Zöls, S., Michel, M., Despotovic, Z., Kellerer, W.: Chordella – A Hierarchical Peer-to-Peer Overlay Implementation for Heteregeneous, Mobile Environments. In: 8th Int. Conf. on Peer-to-Peer Computing (P2P), pp. 75–76. IEEE Computer Society, Los Alamitos (2008)
22. Ayorak, E., Bener, A.B.: Super Peer Web Service Discovery Architecture. In: Proc. of the 23rd Int. Conf. on Data Engineering (ICDE), pp. 1360–1364. IEEE, Los Alamitos (2007)
23. FastTrack team, FastTrack protocol,
    http://cvs.berlios.de/cgi-bin/viewcvs.cgi/gift-fasttrack/
    giFT-FastTrack/PROTOCOL?revision=1.19
24. Xiao, L., Zhuang, Z., Liu, Y.: Dynamic Layer Management in Superpeer Architectures. IEEE Trans. on Parallel and Distributed Systems 16(11), 1078–1091 (2005)
25. Jesi, G.P., Montresor, A., Babaoglu, O.: Proximity-Aware Superpeer Overlay Topology. IEEE Tran. on Network and Service Management 4(2), 74–83 (2007)
26. Caporuscio, M., Raverdy, P.-G., Moungla, H., Issarny, V.: ubiSOAP: A Service Oriented Middleware for Seamless Networking. In: Bouguettaya, A., Krueger, I., Margaria, T. (eds.) ICSOC 2008. LNCS, vol. 5364, pp. 195–209. Springer, Heidelberg (2008)
27. Zhou, G., Yu, J., Chen, R., Zhang, H.: Scalable Web Service Discovery on P2P Overlay Network. In: IEEE Int. Conf. on Services Computing (SCC), pp. 122–129. IEEE Computer Society, Los Alamitos (2007)
28. Shen, Z., Su, J.: Web Service Discovery Based on Behavior Signatures. In: Proc. of the 2005 IEEE Int. Conf. on Services Computing (SCC), pp. 279–286. IEEE Computer Society, Los Alamitos (2005)

Web Service Selection with Incomplete or Inconsistent User Preferences

Hongbing Wang[1], Shizhi Shao[1], Xuan Zhou[2],
Cheng Wan[1], and Athman Bouguettaya[2]

[1] School of Computer Science and Engineering,
Southeast University, China
{hbw,szs,chw}@seu.edu.cn
[2] CSIRO ICT Centre, Australia
{xuan.zhou,athman.Bouguettaya}@csiro.au

Abstract. Web service selection enables a user to find the most desirable service based on his / her preferences. However, user preferences in real world can be either incomplete or inconsistent, such that service selection cannot be conducted properly. This paper presents a system to facilitate Web service selection in face of incomplete or inconsistent user preferences. The system utilizes the information of historical users to amend the active user's preference, so as to improve the results of service selection. We present a detailed design of the system and verify its efficiency through extensive experiments.

1 Introduction

As an increasing number of Web services have been deployed on the Web, service selection is becoming an important technique for helping users identify desirable Web services. To conduct effective service selection, we need (1) a model to adequately describe users' requirements or preferences over the nonfunctional properties of services, such as Quality of Web Service, and (2) an intelligent algorithm to select services according to a user's preferences. In recent years, a number of solutions have been proposed to address these two issues.

Most of existing solutions perform service selection based on quantitative criteria, such as a utility function [1,2]. These quantitative approaches are computationally efficient. However, they offer limited usability to end users, as it is difficult for users to express their preferences using quantitative metrics [2], such as *Utility(Qantas Airline)=0.9* and *Utility(Thai Airline)=0.7*. In many cases, users tend to express their preferences in a qualitative way, such as "I prefer *Qantas Airline* to *Thai Airline*". To obtain better usability, a number of qualitative methods [3,4] have recently been proposed to model users' preferences and to perform service selection.

Qualitative Web service selection is faced with a number of challenges as well. On the one hand, users may not provide complete descriptions of their preferences, such that service selection may produce too many results. On the other hand, as users are not completely rational, they may provide inconsistent

L. Baresi, C.-H. Chi, and J. Suzuki (Eds.): ICSOC-ServiceWave 2009, LNCS 5900, pp. 83–98, 2009.

descriptions of their preferences, such that no result will be obtained. According to [5,6], these cases are quite common in real life. To perform effective service selection, we need an intelligent system that is able to automatically complement users' incomplete preferences and remove inconsistencies.

This paper proposes a system for conducting qualitative Web service selection in face of incomplete or conflicting user preferences. To enable effective service selection, it finds a number of historical users with similar preferences, and uses their preferences to amend the preference of the active user. Then, it conducts service selection using the amended preferences to obtain improved results. This approach is in spirit similar to that of recommender systems [7,8]. We present a detailed design of this service selection scheme, which include the technique for finding similar users and the scheme for preference amendment. An experimental evaluation has been conducted to verify its efficiency and effectiveness.

The rest of the paper is organized as follows. Section 2 gives some background on qualitative service selection and recommender system. Section 3 presents our general service selection framework. Section 4 presents the heuristics and the algorithms for amending users' preferences. Section 5 gives the results of our experimental evaluation. Finally, Section 6 provides a conclusion.

2   Background

We first give a brief overview of Web service selection, and proceed to review the technologies of Conditional Preference Network (CP-Net) [10] and Recommender System.

2.1   Web Service Selection

In a typical scenario of service discovery, a user describes a desired service, and an agent identifies the relevant services or service compositions that satisfies the user's requirements. The entire process actually consists of two steps, as illustrated in Fig. 1. First, an abstract service or abstract service composition is identified, which offers the conceptual functionality required by the user. For example, if a user requests a service to store a data set, this step would returns an abstract service called Data Storage. If the user requires that her information be stored securely, this step would return an abstract composition consisting of a Data Encryption service and a Data Storage service. While the abstract service or composition is correct in functionality, it is not executable. In the second step, a set of concrete services are selected to turn the abstract service or composition into executable process. For example, either *Faidu File System* or *Doogle Database* can be selected to provide Data Storage service. Either *Universal Protection* or *PGP Cypher* can be selected to provide the Data Encryption service. *Service selection*, also known as service optimization [9], refers to the second step. Its objective is to select the concrete services which can best satisfy the user. The level of satisfaction of a user is mostly determined by a service's nonfunctional features, such as reliability, latency and etc. Therefore, service selection always

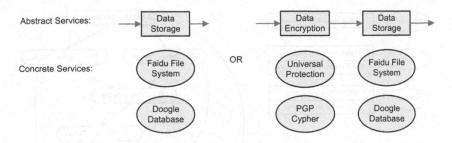

Fig. 1. Example of Service Selection

focuses on comparing the nonfunctional attributes of concrete services. However, as different users have different options on services' goodness, users' preferences are important information for conducting effective service selection.

2.2   CP-Net

Conditional Preference Network (CP-Net) [10,11] is a widely used model for qualitatively representing users' preferences. This model can be briefly defined as follows.

Definition 1 (CP-net). Let $V = \{X_1, ..., X_n\}$ be a set of attributes of Web services. A CP-net over V is a directed graph G (called *dependency graph*) over $X_1, ..., X_n$, in which each node is annotated with a Conditional Preference Table, denoted by $CPT(X_i)$. Each conditional preference table $CPT(X_i)$ associates a total order of X_i's values with each instantiation of X_i's parents.   ⊔

We illustrate the semantics of CP-net using the example in Fig. 2. A Data Storage service can be described by a number of attributes. They include *Platform*, which can be a file system or a database, *Location*, which can be USA or China, and *Provider*, which can be a private company or a public organization. As shown in Fig. 2 (a), the user has an unconditional preference on *Platform*. As indicated by the corresponding CPT, she always prefers databases to file systems. The user's preference on *Location*, however, depends on the platform she chose. As a file system offer less data processing capability than a database, the user may consume much more I/O traffics when using a file system. If the user is located in China, most likely she would like the file system to be located in China too. On the other hand, if the platform is a database, she prefers it to be located in USA, as she believes that database technologies in USA are more sophisticated. Moreover, the user's preference on *Provider* depends on the location of the service. For service providers in USA, she believes that private companies are more trustworthy than public organizations. For service providers in China, she believes that public sectors are more trustworthy than private companies. Based on the CP-net presentation of the user's reference, we can deduce the detailed preference graph of her, which gives the user's explicit preferences among all

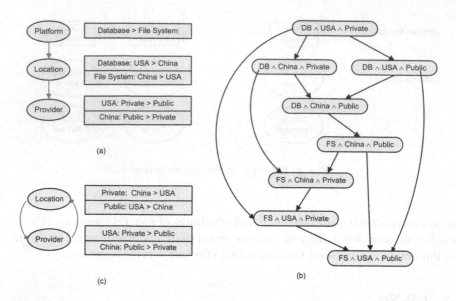

Fig. 2. Examples: (a) CP-net, (b) Induced Preference Graph, (c) Inconsistent CP-net

types of services. This induced preference graph is shown in Fig. 2 (b). Database services provided by private companies in USA are the user's first choice.

In real-world settings, a user may not want or be able to give a complete CP-net presentation of her preferences. For instance, the user's preference over platform in Fig. 2 (a) can be missing. In this situation, $FS \wedge China \wedge Public$ and $DB \wedge USA \wedge Private$ become incomparable. When preference specifications in a CP-net are sparse, service selection may not be useful anymore, as there can be too many candidate services that are possibly optimal. In a worse case, a user's specifications in the CP-net can be semantically inconsistent. As illustrated in Fig. 2 (c), a user may specify that the attributes Location and Provider are mutually dependent, and give four conditional preferences. However, based on the user's specification, we find conflicts in the induced preferences. (We can deduce both $China \wedge Public \succ USA \wedge Private$ and $USA \wedge Private \succ China \wedge Public$.) In this case, no optimal service can be found. According to [5,6], as users are not complete rational, such cases are very common.

Existing techniques for service selection are unable to deal with the above scenarios. In this paper, we provide solutions to service selection when information of user preferences is incomplete or conflicting.

2.3 Recommender System

Recommender system [7,8] is a technology attempting to select information items that are likely to be interesting for users. It analyzes a user's profile and predicts the user's interests through statistical methods. We found that similar approaches can be applied to complement a user's incomplete preferences or to

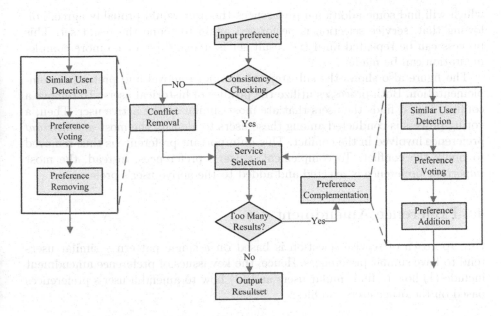

Fig. 3. Process of Service Selection

fix a user's inconsistent preferences. The most typical technique used in recommender system is collaborative filtering [12]. Collaborative filtering utilizes the regular pattern that like-minded users tend to have similar interest. It compares users' profiles to select users who share similar characteristic with the active user. Then it aggregates the interests of these like-minded users to predicate the possible interests of the active user. The method has been successfully applied to a number of leading commercial Web-sites, such as Amazon and Ebay. To solve the problems in service selection, we borrow the idea of collaborative filtering. We find historical users who share similar preferences with the active user, and use their preferences to amend the active user's preferences, such that service selection can be successfully conducted. In the following, we present a detailed design of this approach.

3   Service Selection Framework

The complete process of service selection in our system is shown in Figure 3. Upon receiving a user's preference description, the system first checks its consistency. If it contains conflicts, which are represented as cycles in the induced preference graph, a conflict removal process is conducted to remove all conflicts (cycles). The amended preference description is then passed to the service selector to retrieve the user's favorite Web services. If the result set is too big to be handled by the user, which means that the user's preferences is under-specified, the preference description is passed to the preference complementation process, which will find some additional preferences the user would probably agree. Following that, service selection is performed again to refine the result set. This process can be repeated until the result set is manageable or no more complementation can be made.

The figure also shows the sub-steps of conflict removal and preference complementation. Both processes utilize the profiles of historical users. To remove a conflict, it first finds the users that are most similar to the active user. Then, a voting process is conducted among these users to identify the most *unimportant* preference involved in the conflict. This unimportant preference is thus removed to break the conflict. To complement a user's preferences, instead, the most *important* preference is selected and added to the active user's preferences.

4   Preference Amendment

Our approach of service selection is based on a single pattern – similar users tend to have similar preferences. Hence, the key issues of preference amendment include (1) how to find similar users and (2) how to amend a user's preferences based on the other users' profiles.

4.1   Similar User Detection

To identify similar users, we compare the current user's preferences against the preferences of other users. The users with the most similar preferences are selected. As introduced in Section 2, we describe a user's preferences using CP-net. Thus the similarity between two users can be measured by the similarity between their CP-nets. An intuitive measure of this similarity is defined as follows.

Definition 2 (Distance between CP-nets). Let A and B be two CP-nets of an abstract service composition. Let $P(A)$ and $P(B)$ be the induced preference graphs of A and B respectively. Let e denote an edge in a preference graph. Thus, the distance from B to A is calculated as:

$$Dis(A:B) = \frac{|\{e : e \in P(A) \wedge e \in P(B)\}|}{|\{e : e \in P(A) \vee e \in P(B)\}| - |\{e : e \in P(A) \wedge e \in P(B)\}|}$$

□

According to Definition 2, the distance between CP-net B and CP-net A can be measured by the size of the overlap between A and B's induced preference graphs (as illustrated in Fig. 2 (b)) divided by the size of the non-overlapping parts. While this measure of distance is intuitive, its computation can be very expensive. According the definition of CP-net, the size of an induced preference graph grows exponentially with the number of attributes of services. Therefore, when a large number of attributes are considered in service selection, it will be infeasible to use Definition 2 to compute users' similarity. Fortunately, we can largely reduce the cost by utilizing the characteristics of CP-nets.

Given a particular abstract service or service composition, we assume that different users' CP-nets share the same dependency graph. This assumption is based on two facts. First, the dependencies among the attributes of a certain service type are usually determined by the inherent characteristics of these attributes themselves. For instance, as illustrated in Fig. 2, the dependency between Location and Provider is determined by the correlation between the quality of service and these two attributes. In contrast, it is difficult to argue that a dependency exists between Location and Platform. As another example, *Destination* and *Hotel* are two attributes of a Travel service. It is easy to understand that Hotel depends on Destination, as a tourist a choice of hotel usually depends on where he is visiting. However, it is difficult to justify that Destination depends on Hotel. Second, even when users specify different dependency graphs in their CP-nets, we can create a common dependency graph for them by combining their dependency graphs into one. The users' CP-nets can be adjusted accordingly to fit the more complex common dependency graph, without varying their semantics. When CP-nets share a common dependency graph, their distances can be directly calculated from their CPTs.

Lemma 1. Let $\{X_1, ..., X_n\}$ be the attributes of an abstract service S. Let $D(X_i)$ denote the set of attributes which X_i depends on. Let $R(X_i)$ be the set of values that can be assigned to X_i. Then, given a CP-net, each conditional preference in $CPT(X_i)$ forms $\prod_{X_j \notin D(X_i)} |R(X_j)|$ edges in the induced preference graphs. $\square$

For instances, in Fig. 2, the preference *Database* $\succ$ *File System* determines four edges in the induced preference graph, while the preference *China: Public* $\succ$ *Private* determines two edge in the induced preference graph. According Lemma 1, we can compute the distance between two CP-nets using the following formula.

Theorem 1. Let $\{X_1, ..., X_n\}$ be the attributes of an abstract service S. Let A and B be two CP-nets of S which share the same dependency graph. Let $D(X_i)$ denote the set of attributes which X_i depends on. Let $R(X_i)$ be the set of values that can be assigned to X_i. Then, the distance from B to A can be calculated by:

$$Dis(A:B) = \frac{\sum_{X_i} \left(|CPT_A(X_i) \cap CPT_B(X_i)| \times \prod_{X_j \notin D(X_i)} |R(X_j)|\right)}{\sum_{X_i} \left(|CPT_A(X_i) \cup CPT_B(X_i) - CPT_A(X_i) \cap CPT_B(X_i)| \times \prod_{X_j \notin D(X_i)} |R(X_j)|\right)}$$

$\square$

As discussed previously, it is expensive to compute the distance between CP-nets by counting the overlapped edges in the induced preference graphs. By applying Theorem 1, the computational cost can be reduced to the order of the size of CP-nets. Specifically, the cost is linear with the number of conditional preferences in the CPTS.

4.2   Preference Voting

Using distances between CP-nets, we can identify users with similar preferences. When a user's preference is incomplete or inconsistent, it can be amended using the preferences of his / her like-minded users. As we assume that different users' CP-nets share a common dependency graph, by incompleteness or inconsistency, we always refer to the conditional preferences in the CPTs. We apply the idea of collaborative filtering. If a user's preferences, i.e., the conditional preferences in her CPTs, is incomplete, we add to it some additional preferences which are most supported by the like-minded users. If a user's preferences contain a conflict, we find all the preferences involved in the conflict, and remove the one that is least supported by the like-minded users. To measure how much an individual preference is supported by a group of users, an voting scheme is utilized. If the preference can be deduced from a user's CP-net, we regard that the user votes for this preference. In the end, the preferences with the most votes are candidates for complementing an incomplete CP-net. The preferences with the least vote are candidates to be removed to break a conflict.

4.3   Conflict Removal

To remove conflicts from a CP-net, we need to first identify conflicts, which are actually cycles in the induced preference graph of the CP-net. As a number of algorithms for conflict detection or consistency check in CP-nets have been proposed [13,14], our system directly reuses them to detect conflicts (cycles). Once a cycle in the induced preference graph is detected, we go through its edges to find the corresponding conditional preferences in the CPTs. These preferences are candidates to be removed from the CP-net. Finally, our voting scheme is applied to determine the final preference to be removed.

According to Lemma 1, a conditional preference in a CPT can correspond to more than one edges in the induced preference graph. When choosing the most suitable conditional preference to remove, we consider two factors. First, the preference should be supported by as less like-minded users as possible. This indicates that the preference is likely to be a incorrect one, as most like-minded users do not have it. Second, the preference should correspond to as less edge in the induced preference graph as possible. This ensures that removal of the preference would not affect the user's preference graph too much. Let P be a conditional preference in the CPT of the attribute X. Let $R(X)$ be the attributes which X depends on. Let $Votes(P)$ be the number of votes P receives from the like-minded users. We use the following score to measure the suitability of removing P from the CP-net.

$$Score(P) = Votes(P) \times \prod_{X_j \notin D(X_i)} |R(X_j)| \tag{1}$$

The score is actually the production of the two factors mentioned above. Our system always chooses the preference with the lowest score to remove.

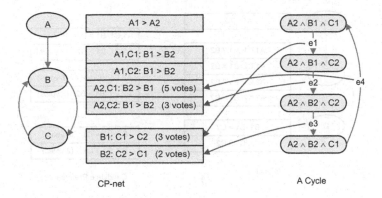

CP-net   A Cycle

Fig. 4. Example of Conflict Removal

An example of conflict removal is shown in Fig. 4. The CP-net in the figure is inconsistent, as its induced preference graph contains a cycle, as shown on left of Fig. 4. The edges of the cycle, i.e. $e1, e2, e3, e4$, are induced from the conditional preferences $B1 : C1 \succ C2$, $A2, C2 : B1 \succ B2$, $B2 : C2 \succ C1$ and $A2, C1 : B2 \succ B1$, respectively. Thus, these preferences are candidates to be removed from the CP-net. Based on Formula 1, the scores of the preferences are:

$Score(B1 : C1 \succ C2) = 3 \times 2 = 6,$
$Score(A2, C2 : B1 \succ B) = 3 \times 1 = 3,$
$Score(B2 : C2 \succ C1) = 2 \times 2 = 4,$
$Score(A2, C1 : B2 \succ B1) = 5 \times 1 = 5.$

Based on the scores, $A2, C2 : B1 \succ B2$ is finally removed from the CP-net. As we can see, even though $B2 : C2 \succ C1$ got the least votes, because it is a more significant preference, our conflict removal algorithm did not choose to remove it.

4.4 Preference Complementation

To complement a CP-net, we consider the unknown conditional preferences in the CPTs. Based on the voting of the like-minded users, the conditional preferences with the most votes is chosen to be added to the current CP-net. When adding a conditional preference in CPTs, it is important to ensure that the resulting CP-net should not contain conflicts. The conditional preferences that will form cycles in the induced preference graph are not considered in preference complementation. Preference complementation is an incremental process, in which one conditional preference is added to the CPT-net at a time. The process stops until the number of services returned by service selection is sufficiently small (e.g., less than 20 services) or no more preference can be added to the current CP-net.

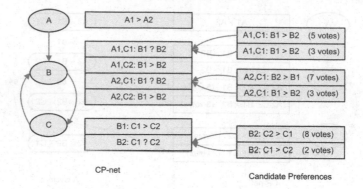

Fig. 5. Example of Preference Complementation

Fig. 5 shows an example of preference complementation. Three conditional preferences, i.e., $A1, C1 : B1?B2$, $A2, C1 : B1?B2$ and $B2 : C1?C2$, are unknown in the CPTs. Based on the voting results, which are shown on the left of Fig. 5, $B2 : C2 \succ C1$ is the most common preference among the like-minded users. Then, it is first chosen to be added to the current CP-net. If the results of service selection are still not satisfactory, the preference with the second highest votes is considered, and so on. As shown in Fig. 4, because $A2, C1 : B2 \succ B1$ will cause conflict, although it has many votes, we have to ignore it in preference complementation. Instead, $A1, C1 : B1 \succ B2$ is used to further complement the CP-net.

5   Experiment

As it is difficult to find sufficient real-world services and user records, we performed simulation to evaluate the efficiency and effectiveness of our approach. This section presents our results.

5.1   Simulation Setup

We simulated the scenario of service selection using randomly generated services and user preferences. To simulate different types of services, we varied the number of attributes and the number of possible values of each attribute. For each type of service we randomly generated 10,000 concrete services, which have different attribute values. To simulate user preferences, we generated random CP-nets. As mentioned previously, for each type of services, all users' CP-nets share a common dependency graph. In our simulation, we generated a random graph to represent each of the dependency graphs. Based on the dependency graph, we generate 5,000 sets of random CPTs to represent 5,000 historical users. Each CPT is filled with random conditional preferences, each of which is a random order of the attribute values. To simulate real-world situations, we

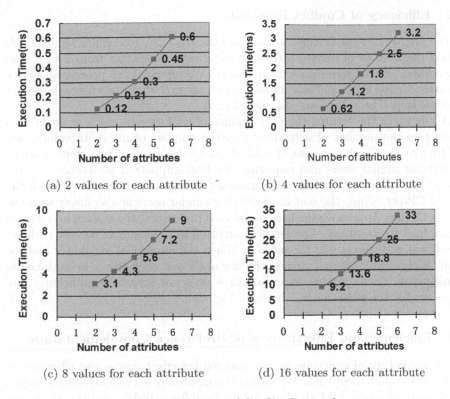

(a) 2 values for each attribute   (b) 4 values for each attribute

(c) 8 values for each attribute   (d) 16 values for each attribute

Fig. 6. Efficiency of Conflict Removal

divided the 5,000 users into 10 groups. Each group of users was based on a single CP-net with complete CPTs. We duplicated the CP-net for 500 times, and randomly varied and removed the conditional preferences in their CPTs, to obtain 500 incomplete CP-nets. Each CP-net then represented a user within that group. As a result, the users in a single group were similar to each other, and those from different groups were different. This enabled our system to easily find like-minded users.

To perform service selection, we randomly picked a service type and randomly selected a user from the 5,000 historical users, and executed the process in Fig. 3 to select the optimal service for that user. We repeated the whole process for multiple times, and recorded the average execution time of each step as well as the statistics of the result sets.

We implemented the service selection system using Java. The processes of conflict removal and preference complementation were based on Section 4. We reused the algorithm of [4] to perform CP-net based service selection. Our simulation was conducted in a personal computer with a CPU of 1.79GHz and a RAM of 768M. The operating system was Windows XP.

5.2 Efficiency of Conflict Removal

In the first set of experiments, we assessed the efficiency of conflict removal. We varied the number of service attributes involved in a conflict from 2 to 6, and the number of attribute values from 2 to 16. We repeated the process of service selection for 100 times and calculated the average execution time for each conflict removal step. The results are shown in Fig. 6.

As shown in the results, the performance of conflict removal is scalable with respect to the number of attributes and the number of attribute values. According to Fig. 3, the process of conflict removal consist of two steps, that is, identifying similar users and removing the least supported preference. As discussed in Section 4.1, the cost of computing CP-net distance is linear with the size of CP-net. Thus, the cost of identifying similar users is also linear with the size of CP-net. To remove the least supported preference, the system needs to go through all the conditional preferences involved in the conflict. Its cost is therefore linear with the size of CP-net too. When the number of attributes and the number of possible values increase, the size of CP-net normally does not increase significantly. Therefore, the execution time does not increase significantly too. This justifies the performance shown in Fig. 6.

5.3 Efficiency and Effectiveness of Preference Complementation

In the second set of experiments, we assessed the effectiveness and efficiency of preference complementation. We varied the number of service attributes from 6 to 15, and the number of attribute values from 2 to 16. We also varied the degree of completeness of user preferences. When the number of attributes is 6, we set users' CP-nets to be 50% complete. When the number of attributes is 10, we set users' CP-nets to be 20% complete. When the number of attributes is 15, we set users' CP-nets to be 10% complete. We repeated the process of service selection for 100 times. We recorded the average execution time for each complementation step and the number of selected services after each step.

Fig. 7 shows the numbers of services returned by service selection before and after each step of preference complementation. We assumed that preference complementation stops when less than 20 services are returned. We can see that when a user's preference description is incomplete, the number of services returned by service selection can be too many for the user to evaluate. When additional preferences are added to the description, the result set of service selection can be significantly reduced. As shown in Fig. 7 (a), by adding 3 preferences, the result set were reduced from 800 to only 20. The experiment results indicate that preference complementation is effective in pruning services.

Fig. 8 shows the efficiency of preference complementation. According to Fig. 3, the process of preference complementation consist of two steps, that is, identifying similar users and adding the most supported preference to the user's CP-net. As discussed previously, the cost of both steps is linear with the size of CP-net. When we increase the number of attributes and the number of possible attribute values, the size of CP-net normally does not increase significantly. Therefore, the

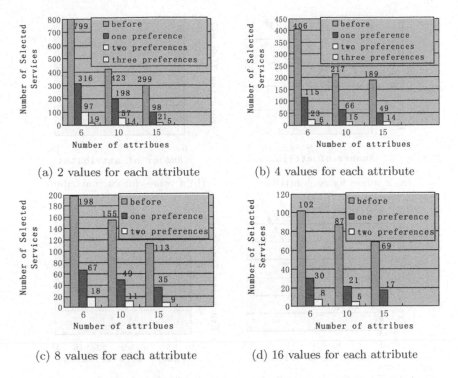

(a) 2 values for each attribute   (b) 4 values for each attribute

(c) 8 values for each attribute   (d) 16 values for each attribute

Fig. 7. Effectiveness of Preference Complementation

performance of preference complementation is scalable with the number of attributes and the number of attribute values.

6   Related Work

Service selection aims at helping user select the optimal service from the list of results returned by service discovery. It is an important process, when (1) users' queries are ambiguous or (2) there are too many services that meet the user's basic requirements. One approach to service selection is to provide interactive interfaces for users to refine their selection criteria. For instance, in [15] the authors proposed form based interfaces that allow user to refine the results of service discovery. In [16], the authors proposed to cluster services based on their various properties, so that users can prune services by choosing appropriate clusters. Another approach to service selection is to rank services according to users' preferences or utilities functions. The work of [1,2,4] as well as our approach fall in the second types of approach. To the best of our knowledge, little work has considered the case when users' qualitative preferences are faulty or incomplete. As this case can be common in real world, this paper proposes techniques to enable service selection in face of inconsistent or incomplete preferences.

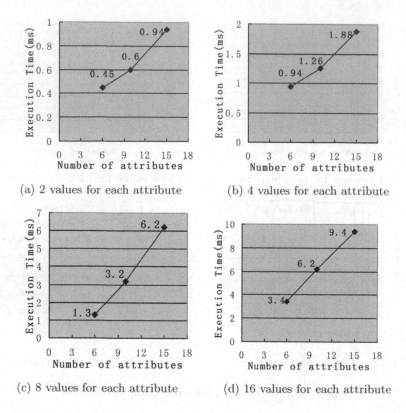

Fig. 8. Efficiency of Preference Complementation

Application of recommender system in service selection is not new. In [17], the authors proposed a scheme which applies collaborative filtering to facilitate service selection. Their approach directly works on services rather than user preferences. It utilizes users' ratings on various services to identify like-minded users and predicate user desired services. When the number of services is large and users' ratings are insufficient, this approach can be ineffective. In contrast, our approach utilizes users' preferences to identify like-minded users and select services. As user preferences, e.g. CP-nets, are described in the conceptual level, it requires much less information to be effective. Moreover, it can work on arbitrarily large repositories of services.

In [4], the authors proposed an algorithm for performing service selection with incomplete preferences. While the algorithm enable service selection to be correctly conducted using incomplete preferences, it may return too many results to be handled by the user, especially when preferences are under-specified. Our approach utilizes the preferences of historical users to complement an incomplete preference, so as to reduce the result set to a manageable size.

7   Conclusion

In this paper, we present an approach of service selection that can handle incomplete and inconsistent user preferences. Our approach uses CP-nets to model user preferences. It utilizes the preferences of historical users to predicate and amend the active user's preference, so that service selection can be performed properly. We conducted simulation to test our approach. The simulation results verified the effectiveness and efficiency of our techniques in conflict removal and preference complementation.

Acknowledgement. This work is partially supported by NSFC of China (No. 60473091 and No. 60673175).

References

1. Yu, T., Lin, K.J.: Service selection algorithms for composing complex services with multiple qos constraints. In: Benatallah, B., Casati, F., Traverso, P. (eds.) ICSOC 2005. LNCS, vol. 3826, pp. 130–143. Springer, Heidelberg (2005)
2. Lamparter, S., Ankolekar, A., Studer, R., Grimm, S.: Preference-based selection of highly configurable web services. In: WWW, pp. 1013–1022 (2007)
3. Balke, W.T., Wagner, M.: Towards personalized selection of web services. In: WWW (Alternate Paper Tracks) (2003)
4. Wang, H., Xu, J., Li, P.: Incomplete preference-driven web service selection. IEEE SCC (1), 75–82 (2008)
5. Tversky, A.: Contrasting rational and psychological principles of choice. In: Zeckhauser, R.J., Keeney, R.L., Sebenius, J.K. (eds.) Wise Choices. Decisions, Games, and Negotiations, pp. 5–21. Harvard Business School Press, Boston (1996)
6. Mellers, B.A., Schwartz, A., Cooke, A.D.J.: Judgment and decision making. Annual Review of Psychology 49, 447–477 (1998)
7. Adomavicius, G., Tuzhilin, A.: Toward the next generation of recommender systems: A survey of the state-of-the-art and possible extensions. IEEE Trans. Knowl. Data Eng. 17(6), 734–749 (2005)
8. Burke, R.D.: Hybrid recommender systems: Survey and experiments. User Model. User-Adapt. Interact. 12(4), 331–370 (2002)
9. Yu, Q., Bouguettaya, A.: Framework for web service query algebra and optimization. TWEB 2(1) (2008)
10. Boutilier, C., Brafman, R.I., Hoos, H.H., Poole, D.: Reasoning with conditional ceteris paribus preference statements. In: UAI, pp. 71–80 (1999)
11. Boutilier, C., Brafman, R.I., Domshlak, C., Hoos, H.H., Poole, D.: Cp-nets: A tool for representing and reasoning with conditional ceteris paribus preference statements. J. Artif. Intell. Res. (JAIR) 21, 135–191 (2004)
12. Sarwar, B.M., Karypis, G., Konstan, J.A., Riedl, J.: Item-based collaborative filtering recommendation algorithms. In: WWW, pp. 285–295 (2001)
13. Wilson, N.: Extending cp-nets with stronger conditional preference statements. In: AAAI, pp. 735–741 (2004)
14. Goldsmith, J., Lang, J., Truszczynski, M., Wilson, N.: The computational complexity of dominance and consistency in cp-nets. In: IJCAI, pp. 144–149 (2005)

15. Sirin, E., Parsia, B., Hendler, J.: Filtering and selecting semantic web services with interactive composition techniques. IEEE Intelligent Systems 19(4), 42–49 (2004)
16. Abramowicz, W., Haniewicz, K., Kaczmarek, M., Zyskowski, D.: Architecture for web services filtering and clustering. In: Second International Conference on Internet and Web Applications and Services, ICIW 2007, p. 18 (2007)
17. Manikrao, U.S., Prabhakar, T.V.: Dynamic selection of web services with recommendation system. In: NWESP 2005: Proceedings of the International Conference on Next Generation Web Services Practices, Washington, DC, USA, p. 117. IEEE Computer Society, Los Alamitos (2005)

Energy-Aware Design of Service-Based Applications

Alexandre Mello Ferreira, Kyriakos Kritikos, and Barbara Pernici

Dipartimento di Elettronica e Informazione
Politecnico di Milano, Italy
{ferreira,kritikos,pernici}@elet.polimi.it

Abstract. The continuous increase in electrical and computational power in data centers has been driving many research approaches under the Green IT main theme. However, most of this research focuses on reducing energy consumption considering hardware components and data center building features, like servers distribution and cooling flow. On the contrary, this paper points out that energy consumption is also a service quality problem, and presents an energy-aware design approach for building service-based applications. To this effect, techniques are provided to measure service costs combining Quality of Service (QoS) requirements and Green Performance Indicators (GPI) in order to obtain a better tradeoff between energy efficiency and performance for each user.

1 Introduction

Considering the arising amount of energy consumed in IT and the arising prices of electrical energy, strategies to achieve energy efficiency have been seen more attractive than ever as a way of cutting costs [1]. The US Department of Energy (DOE), for instance, reported that data centers consumed 1.5% of the total electricity in 2006 and it's projected to double up until 2011 [2]. Furthermore, it is expected that energy costs will exceed the hardware costs by 2015 according to the Efficient-Servers project (www.efficient-servers.eu).

In the last years, IT systems and Data Centers are moving towards the adoption of a Service-based Model, in which the available computing resources are shared by several different users or companies. In such systems, the software is accessed as-a-service and computational capacity is provided on demand to many customers who share a pool of IT resources. The Software-As-A-Service model can provide significant economies of scales, affecting to some extent the energy efficiency of data centers. Services and their composition, both at the providers' side (to provide new value-added services), and at the users' side (with mashups of services composed by the users themselves), are becoming more and more widespread in a variety of application domains. Hence, since the service-oriented approach is steadily increasing for many application domains, its impact on data and service centers will become more and more significant.

In order to develop and use computer resources efficiently, a new research field is growing under the denomination of Green Computing (GC). Essentially,

L. Baresi, C.-H. Chi, and J. Suzuki (Eds.): ICSOC-ServiceWave 2009, LNCS 5900, pp. 99–114, 2009.

GC focuses on sustainable computer resources development and usage through using less hazardous materials, maximizing energy efficiently, and promoting recyclability [3]. The Natural Edge Project (www.naturaledgeproject.net), for instance, presents an overall seven-step process to create and maintain data centers using minimal energy consumption with high quality, which includes airflow optimization and virtualization techniques.

Despite the substantial research work already performed in GC, most of this work relies on a very generic approach, trying to provide a holist view on the problem, or focuses only at the infrastructure layer, especially on hardware issues. This paper, on the other hand, tackles the data center energy efficiency problem at the service level as a nonlinear Service Concretization (SC) problem, taking into account infrastructure characteristics and service requirements. To this end, a new approach to design service-based processes in huge data centers is devised that takes into account both Key Performance Indicators (KPIs) and Green Performance Indicators (GPIs), expressed as user preferences, in order to obtain a better tradeoff between performance and energy efficiency. A new GPI metric is defined, namely service *energy efficiency* (ee), and its computation is based on classical service quality attributes like *execution time* (et) and physical energy measures like *energy consumption* (ec).

By being able to compute both quality and energy metrics for each service, a service-based process is designed by executing a novel constraint-based quality and energy-aware service composition algorithm that advances the state-of-the-art by: a) taking into account not only single (average or minimum) values of independent quality and energy metrics but a range of values, while also dependency functions are used in order to express tradeoffs between these metrics; b) using loop peeling [4] to transform an abstract execution plan into several execution paths and trying to satisfy all of the global constraints in every execution path and not in specific ones; c) producing a concrete execution plan even if the requirements set by the user are over-constrained through the use of appropriate normalization functions; d) allowing for the use of non-linear functions in the optimization (QoS-based Service Composition) problem to be solved.

The rest of this paper is organized as follows. Section 2 introduces the service energy efficiency metric, proposes a way to compute it, and correlates it with other known quality and energy attributes. Section 3 introduces our novel constraint-based quality and energy-aware service composition approach for the design of energy-aware Service-Based Applications (SBAs). Section 4 provides a motivating example that highlights the benefits of our approach. Finally, Section 5 concludes the paper and draws direction for further research.

2   Service Energy Efficiency Computation

Green IT techniques have to be taken in a holistic approach, in which the whole data center is considered, such as layout, airflow, cooling techniques, power management, eco-friendly IT equipments, virtualization, and service requirements. Although efforts have been performed to measure and control these items (mainly to measure energy efficiency on IT equipments), there is no widely accepted metric, which makes it difficult to compare the results of these efforts [5].

Even though metrics to measure data center electrical efficiency proposed by Green Grid, Uptime Institute, Lawrence Berkeley National Laboratory, and Greenpeace are quite similar, the comparison of their results should be made with caution. For instance, one of the most used metric to measure electrical efficiency is the Data Center infrastructure Efficiency (DCiE), in which a percentage expresses how much power consumed by the data center is being delivered to IT loads. In this way, higher percent number means higher energy efficiency, where 100% is the perfect efficiency.

Considering that energy efficiency is directly proportional to IT loads and most data center servers remain running at low utilization rates or in idle mode for a considerable amount of time, it seems consistent to balance their workload in such way to increase the utilization of low power servers, whenever is possible. Indeed, this impact will be reflected into all the other facility components, since less power will be needed to cooling, for example. Some crucial issues come up, the most important of which are the way service efficiency is measured and which standards are used to classify both services and servers.

Real data centers use many different IT equipments, where each equipment has different characteristics concerning electrical and computational power. For this reason, each server can be classified into a certain class, from the slowest to the fastest, at different energy consumption levels. For instance, Zenker [6] assumes that by using a multi-dimensional coefficient it is possible to compare results among different environments.

Based on the aforementioned fact, the first important assumption adopted during this paper is that energy consumption is directly proportional to computational power performance [7]. Although this is not true in all cases - e.g. very old equipments with low computational and high electrical power - we sustain that all the heterogeneous servers considered are new and are therefore homogeneous with respect to this aspect. According to this basic assumption, three classes of servers have been created that can be separated according to their performance and electrical power. This partition of servers into classes was inspired from Koomey's report [8], in which, servers were divided into: *volume*, *mid-range*, and *high-end* according to their overall system costs. Table 1 presents theses classes of servers (*slow, average, high*) and their weighs with respect to electrical power during three different utilization periods (*idle, normal,* and *burst*) that were measured in Watts. The latter numbers were derived from measurements performed by [9,10,11,8].

By inspecting the data shown in Table 1, the energy efficiency (ee) metric of a single service is computed based on which server class the service is executed, taking into account possible server modes during a fixed time period. Despite the fact that Table 1 presents the *burst* column with the maximum power, we will not consider these values for the following reasons: (a) the usage of a simple admission control scheme [12] is assumed, which is responsible to maintain the number of execution services under the *normal* utilization level by dropping the overload

Table 1. Classes of servers and their power for each utilization period

Server Class	Idle (0–0.12)	Normal (0.13–0.67)	Burst (0.68–1)
Slow	178	222	266
Average	486	607	728
High	6,485	8,106	9,727

requests; (b) beyond the *normal* utilization limit, although the energy efficiency will increase, the boundary of accepted performance, which involves execution time for example, will be exceeded. Energy efficiency can be computed by formula (1). According to this formula, the ee $ee_j^{\Delta t}$ of the service s_j executing in server class class(j) is computed by dividing the amount of energy consumption of the real execution of the service (i.e., when server is in *normal* mode) with the total energy consumed by the server in our specific unit of time reference.

$$ee_j^{\Delta t} = \frac{ec_{\text{class}(j)}^{\text{normal}} \cdot t_j^{\text{normal}}}{ec_{\text{class}(j)}^{\text{idle}} \cdot t_j^{\text{idle}} + ec_{\text{class}(j)}^{\text{normal}} \cdot t_j^{\text{normal}}} \tag{1}$$

For example, suppose we want to calculate the energy efficiency of service s_1 that is executed in a *slow* server in one specific time unit, where 45 percent of the time is executed in *normal* mode and 55 percent in *idle* mode. Then, from formula (1) and Table 1 we will have that : $ee_1^{\Delta t} = \frac{222 \cdot 0.45}{178 \cdot 0.55 + 222 \cdot 0.45} = 0.505$.

As can be easily seen from formula (1), there is a direct relationship between energy consumption, service execution time, and energy efficiency. The object of research is how to exactly compute this quantitative dependency based on formula (1). After a small analysis, formula (2) was derived from formula (1) by relying on the fact that the execution time of the service is measured according to our time unit reference and that the service is executed in a specific server class. The numerator of formula (2) calculates a service's total energy consumed in *normal* mode by multiplying the power in this mode ($ec_{\text{class}(j)}^{\text{normal}}$) with the total time spent by this service in this mode ($\frac{ec_j - ec_{\text{class}(j)}^{\text{idle}} \cdot et_j}{ec_{\text{class}(j)}^{\text{normal}} - ec_{\text{class}(j)}^{\text{idle}}}$) with respect to its total execution time et_j. The denominator of formula (2) is the total energy consumed ec_j by this service. In other words, formula (2) has the same physical meaning as formula (1), as it calculates the percentage of energy consumed by a service in *normal* mode with respect to the total energy consumed by this service. Moreover, this new formula expresses our inquired quantitative dependency as it dictates the way the energy efficiency of a single service can be computed by measuring its execution time and its total energy consumption. The latter two metrics can be computed for each service through a monitoring layer [13], which provides information on the fly about application workload, resource utilization and power consumption. As far as a composite service is concerned, its energy efficiency can be computed by taking the average from the energy efficiency of all its service components.

$$ee_j = \left\lceil \frac{ec_{\text{class}(j)}^{\text{normal}} \cdot \frac{ec_j - ec_{\text{class}(j)}^{\text{idle}} \cdot et_j}{ec_{\text{class}(j)}^{\text{normal}} - ec_{\text{class}(j)}^{\text{idle}}}}{ec_j} \cdot 100 \right\rceil \tag{2}$$

In addition to the aforementioned dependency, other types of dependencies and constraints can be derived from a service's past execution (in all classes of servers) and from its specification in a service profile. Without considering other quality attributes like availability and reliability, we can have constraints (3) and (4) on execution time and energy consumption defining the range of admissible values of these two dimensions. Equality constraint (5) defines how the price of the service is produced from a cost model that takes into account the service's execution time and energy consumption. We assume that the cost of a service depends linearly on the time it needs to execute and on the amount of energy consumed, where the first partial cost depends also on the server class (see constant $\alpha_{\text{class}(j)}$). Of course, apart from linear, other types of functions could be used instead [14].

$$et_{\text{class}(j)}^{min} \leq et_j \leq et_{\text{class}(j)}^{max} \tag{3}$$

$$ec_{\text{class}(j)}^{min} \leq ec_j \leq ec_{\text{class}(j)}^{max} \tag{4}$$

$$pr_j = \alpha_{\text{class}(j)} \cdot et_j + \beta \cdot ec_j \tag{5}$$

Based on the above analysis, a service can operate in different quality and energy levels and constraints can be used to capture the service's performance and energy efficiency in all these levels. Then, according to the application domain that this service is used, user preferences can be issued in the form of constraints and a service discovery process can be executed in order to select those services that satisfy the user needs.

3   Service-Based Application Design

While in the previous section the problem of energy and quality-aware selection of single services was analyzed, we consider now the case of composite services, for which a service is built from other services at runtime when the user's requirements are issued to a broker or service composition engine. The composite service construction is separated into two sequential phases: a) an abstract execution plan is built; b) one service is selected for each abstract task of the execution plan. Various techniques have been proposed for automatically or semi-automatically creating an abstract execution plan of a composite service based on the functional needs of the user and the functional capabilities of available services in the system's registry. This paper does not deal with this phase and regards that the execution plan is already in place as an outcome of the first phase or as a product of an expert that designs the process (e.g., in the form of Abstract BPEL).

In the second phase, based on the abstract execution plan, for each abstract service a set of functionally-equivalent services are selected as candidate services which implement the same functionality but differ in their non-functional characteristics, i.e, quality (and energy in our case). The functional selection of these candidate services is a very well known problem that has been efficiently solved with approaches like the one of Pernici and Plebani [15]. The final goal of this phase is achieved by solving the well-known Service Concretization (SC) or QoS-based Service Composition problem and is the focus of our paper. According to this problem, the best service available at runtime has to be selected among all candidate ones for each abstract service, taking into consideration the global and local quality (and energy in our case) constraints given by the user. It must be noted that by a user we mean specialized users like a service designer or provider or Data Center administrator and not simple users, as energy is usually not a concern of them. However, we do not rule out the fact that in the near future even simple users will be more concerned about energy issues and may provide energy constraints apart from those given for QoS and cost.

In order to guarantee the fulfilment of global constraints, SC approaches use optimization techniques like MIP [16,17] or Genetic Algorithms (GAs) [18]. However, most of these approaches usually consider the worst or most common case scenario for the composite service (that concerns the longest or hottest execution path, respectively) [16,18] or they satisfy the global constraints only statistically (by reducing loops to a single task) [19]. So they are either very conservative or not very accurate.

Moreover, most of these approaches present the following disadvantages, which will be solved by the approach proposed below: a) they do not allow non-linear constraints like the ones we have outlined in the previous section; b) they do not produce any solution when the requirements of the user are over-constrained, while we adopt soft constraints in order to allow constraint violations in less likely compositions; c) they are very conservative concerning the fact that all execution paths have to satisfy the global constraints – even the longest ones that are not so probable have to satisfy all of the global constraints so some good solutions are removed when these constraints are very tight – while we allow constraint violations for the improbable execution paths; d) they take into account only the worst or average value of a metric for each service and they also regard that all metrics are independent, while we allow ranges of possible values and metric dependencies; e) they do not take into account energy metrics, while we do.

Our proposed approach is analyzed in the following two subsections. Subsection 3.1 provides the main definitions and assumptions we make on the SC problem, while Subsection 3.2 defines our approach for solving this problem.

3.1   Main Definitions and Assumptions

The first main assumption is that a composite service is characterized by a single initial and end task and that the composition of tasks follows a block structure. In this way, only structured loops can be defined, i.e., loops with only one entry and exit point. We name each abstract service of the composite service with the term $task$ (t_i), while the set of services S_i to be executed for this task are called *candidate services* (s_j). We symbolize with I the total number of tasks of the composite service specification and with J the number of candidate services retrieved from the system's registry. The goal of the process that solves the SC problem is to find the optimum execution plan OEL^* of the composite service, i.e., the set of ordered couples $\{(t_i, s_j)\}$, indicating that task t_i is executed by invoking service s_j for all tasks of the composite service, such as that the overall trade-off between energy and quality is achieved by satisfying all the global constraints set by the user. The latter constraints are either explicitly specified by the user or can be implicit in the user profile. We assume that these constraints are expressed by the following upper or low bounds (depending on the monotonicity of the attribute) ET, PR, EE, and EC for the four quality dimensions under consideration, respectively.

Based on the past execution of the composite service stored in system logs or from the designer's experience, the following two types of information can be derived and evaluated [16,18,17]:

- *Probability of execution of conditional branches.* For every switch s, we symbolize with NB^s the number of disjoint branch conditions of s and with p_h^s the probability of execution of each disjoint conditional branch. For all these probabilities, the following constraint must hold: $\sum_{h=1}^{NB^s} p_h^s = 1$.
- *Loop constraints.* For every loop l, we define the expected maximum number of iteration IN^l as well as the probability p_h^l for every number of iteration h of the loop. For all these probabilities, the following constraint must hold: $\sum_{h=0}^{IN^l} p_h^l = 1$. A loop cannot have infinite number of iterations, otherwise the composite service could not be optimized since infinite resources might be needed and consequently global constraints cannot be guaranteed [16].

These two types of information can be used to transform the abstract execution plan of a composite process to a Directed Acyclic Graph (DAG) through the use of loop peeling [4]. The latter method is a form of loop unrolling in which loop iterations are represented as a sequence of branches whose branch condition evaluates if loop l has to continue with the next iteration (with probability $\{p_h^l\}$) or it has to exit.

After loop peeling, from the transformed DAG, we can derive a set of K *execution paths* ep_k that identify all possible execution scenarios of the composite service. An *execution path* is a set of tasks $\{t_1, t_2, \ldots, t_l\}$ where t_1 and t_I are the initial and final tasks, respectively, and no tasks t_{i_1} and t_{i_2} belong to alternative branches. Every execution path ep_k has an associated probability of execution $freq_k$ that can be evaluated as the product of the probability of execution of the branch conditions included in the execution path. Moreover, we associate to each execution path ep_k a set A_k of the indices of the tasks included in it. In addition, each execution path ep_k has a set of *subpaths* that are indexed by m and denoted by sp_m^k. A subpath of an execution path contains those tasks of the execution path, from the initial to the end task, so that it does not contain any parallel sequence. For every possible concrete execution plan CEP (including the optimum one), we evaluate the quality dimensions under consideration under the hypothesis that the composite service is executed along the corresponding execution path using the aggregation patterns that will be analyzed below.

Every service s_j is selected as a candidate service based on its advertised service profile sp_j that is stored in the system's registry. In this service profile, the functional, quality and energy capabilities of the service are defined based on information submitted by the service provider and the past execution of the service. Moreover, this service profile specifies the server class class(j) on which the service s_j executes. If the service runs also in a different server class class(j'), then it is considered as a different service $s_{j'}$ and its capabilities are stored in a different service profile $sp_{j'}$. It must be noted that each service profile will contain an attribute *run* indicating if the corresponding service is currently running on the designated service class. In this way, our proposed SC approach will fetch only those services from the service profiles stored in the system's registry that run on their corresponding server classes at that time. Thus, we accommodate for the case where the resources are dynamically allocated in a hosting site, as if a service stops running on a service class and starts running on a different class, then the corresponding service profiles of this (abstract) service will be updated according to their *run* attribute.

According to our approach described in Section 2, a service profile does not advertise only one quality and energy level of a service performance in a specific service class by storing only one (average or minimum) value for every possible quality and energy dimension but all the possible levels through the use of the constraint set we have introduced in the previous section. Thus, in our approach, the service profile sp_j of a service s_j contains a set of constraints that involve variables qd_j^n that are associated to the quality and energy dimensions qd^n (N is the total number of dimensions).

In this paper, we have considered two of the most representative quality dimensions, namely *execution time* and *price*, and two energy dimensions, namely *energy efficiency* and *energy consumption*. For these four dimensions, we consider the following information as relevant for them:

- Execution time is the expected duration in time that a service spends to fulfill a service request. For each service s_j it is represented as an integer variable et_j that takes values from the following domain of values: $[et^{min}, et^{max}]$. It is measured in a specific time unit like seconds.
- Price is the fee/cost that a service requester has to pay to the service provider for the service invocation. For each service s_j it is represented as an integer variable pr_j that takes values from the following domain of values: $[pr^{min}, pr^{max}]$. It is measured in euros. This dimension depends both on the execution time and energy consumption dimensions, as it was highlighted in Section 2.
- Energy efficiency is a measure of how efficiently a service uses energy (analyzed in the previous section). For each service s_j it is represented as an integer variable ee_j that takes values from the following domain of values: $[ee^{min}, ee^{max}]$. It depends on both execution time and energy consumption dimensions.

– Energy consumption is a measure of the total energy consumed by the service during its execution. For each service s_j it is represented as an integer variable ec_j that takes values from the following domain of values: $[ec^{min}, ec^{max}]$. It is usually measured in Watts-hours or Kilowatts-hours.

The aggregation pattern for each of these four dimensions for every execution path is given in Table 2. Execution time of a composite service is computed by the maximum execution time calculated in all possible subpaths of the execution path. For each subpath, the execution time is calculated as the sum of all the execution times of the services that are contained in it. The price of a composite service is computed by the sum of prices of all component services contained in the execution path. The energy efficiency of a composite service is computed by the average of the energy efficiency value of each component service contained in the execution path. Finally, the energy consumption of a composite service is computed by adding the energy consumption of all component services contained in the execution path.

Table 2. Aggregation patterns for each considered dimension

Dimension	Aggregation Function
Execution Time	$et_k\,(CEP) = \max_{sp_m^k \in ep_k} \sum_{\substack{t_i \in sp_m^k \\ (t_i, s_j) \in CEP}} et_j$
Price	$pr_k\,(CEP) = \sum_{\substack{t_i \in ep_k \\ (t_i, s_j) \in CEP}} pr_j$
Energy Efficiency	$ee_k\,(CEP) = \frac{1}{|A_k|} \sum_{\substack{t_i \in ep_k \\ (t_i, s_j) \in CEP}} ee_j$
Energy Consumption	$ec_k\,(CEP) = \sum_{\substack{t_i \in ep_k \\ (t_i, s_j) \in CEP}} ec_j$

3.2 Proposed Approach

In this subsection, we formulate the SC problem as a Constraint Satisfaction Optimization Problem (CSOP) [20]. The main decision variables of our problem are the following:

$z_{i,j} :=$ equals 1 if the task t_i is executed by service s_j, $j \in S_i$; 0 otherwise

The goal of the SC problem is to maximize the aggregated quality and energy value by considering all possible execution paths ep_k of the abstract execution plan and their corresponding probability of execution $freq_k$. To this end, we have used the following optimization function for defining our problem:

$$\max \sum_{k=1}^{K} freq_k \cdot sc_k$$

In this way, we try to find the solution that is the best at least for the most frequent execution paths.

According to the above optimization function, a score sc_k is produced from the aggregated quality and energy value for each execution path. This score is obtained by applying the Simple Additive Weighting (SAW) technique [21] to the list of considered dimensions. According to this technique, the raw aggregated values for each dimension are first normalized through the use of a corresponding evaluation function that is specific for each dimension and then multiplied by the weight (i.e., the impact) of this dimension. This weight is either given explicitly by the user or is obtained from his profile. So by denoting the aggregated value of each dimension along a specific execution path ep_k with q_n^k and the user-provided weights of this dimension as w_n, the score of ep_k is obtained from the following equation:

$$sc_k = \sum_{n=1}^{N} w_n \cdot f_n \left(q_n^k \right)$$

Based on the above equation, different evaluation functions can be used to normalize the values of different dimensions. We have carefully chosen a specific type that allows the use of soft instead of hard global constraints for restricting the aggregated values for each dimension and for each execution path. Depending on the monotonicity of the dimension, we have used the following two (denoted by (6) and (7)) evaluation functions for negative and positive dimensions, respectively:

$$f_n(x) = \begin{cases} a_n + \frac{q_n^{max} - x}{q_n^{max} - q_n^{min}} \cdot (1 - a_n), & q_n^{min} \leq x \leq q_n^{max} \\ \max \left(a_n - \frac{q_n^{min} - x}{q_n^{max} - q_n^{min}} \cdot (1 - a_n), 0 \right), & x < q_n^{min} \\ \max \left(a_n - \frac{x - q_n^{max}}{q_n^{max} - q_n^{min}} \cdot (1 - a_n), 0 \right), & x > q_n^{max} \end{cases} \quad (6)$$

$$f_n(x) = \begin{cases} a_n + \frac{x - q_n^{min}}{q_n^{max} - q_n^{min}} \cdot (1 - a_n), & q_n^{min} \leq x \leq q_n^{max} \\ \max \left(a_n - \frac{q_n^{min} - x}{q_n^{max} - q_n^{min}} \cdot (1 - a_n), 0 \right), & x < q_n^{min} \\ \max \left(a_n - \frac{x - q_n^{max}}{q_n^{max} - q_n^{min}} \cdot (1 - a_n), 0 \right), & x > q_n^{max} \end{cases} \quad (7)$$

where q_n^{min} is either the minimum domain value for this dimension or a user-provided bound, q_n^{max} is either the maximum domain value for this dimension or a user-provided bound, x is the value to be normalized, and a_n is a number between 0.0 and 1.0 given by the user or the composite service designer in order to allow values outside the ranges specified within the constraints. In order to give a more specific example, the evaluation function of the execution time quality dimension is given by the following formula:

$$f_{et}(x) = \begin{cases} a_{et} + \frac{ET - x}{ET - q_{et}^{min}} \cdot (1 - a_{et}), & q_{et}^{min} \leq x \leq ET \\ \max \left(a_{et} - \frac{q_{et}^{min} - x}{ET - q_{et}^{min}} \cdot (1 - a_{et}), 0 \right), & x < q_{et}^{min} \\ \max \left(a_{et} - \frac{x - ET}{ET - q_{et}^{min}} \cdot (1 - a_{et}), 0 \right), & x > ET \end{cases}$$

In this case, we can have that: $q_{et}^{min} = et^{min}$, or the user also provides another bound for the highest level (lowest value) of this dimension that is: $q_{et}^{min} = ET'$.

As it can be observed from the latter equation, the aggregated dimension's value is allowed to take values outside the user requested bound or range of values but the produced normalized value decreases and gets to zero when the aggregated value's distance from the bound increases. Actually, from which starting normalized value and how quickly this value decreases depends on both the design parameter a_n and the distance between the two bound values. For instance, if $a_{et} = 0.8$, $ET - q_{et}^{min} = 5$ and $ET = 7$, then if $x \in (12, 17]$, it will get a normalized value in $[0.0, 0.4)$; otherwise if $x \in (7, 12]$, it will get a normalized value in $[0.4, 0.8)$; and if $x \in [2, 7]$, it will get a normalized value in $(0.8, 1.0]$. So if we want to allow a very small amount of values outside the user requested bound, we have to use small values of the a_n parameter, depending also on the min and max bound values and their distance. It must be noted that the value of a_n can be predefined or produced from a predefined table that maps the distance between the min and max values of a dimension to the value of a_n. Similarly, the weights given to each dimension can be all equal. In this way, the user quantifies only the bounds of the dimensions and not any other parameter, so there is no cognitive overload for him.

The reason for using the above type of evaluation functions is because we do not want to rule out solutions that do not violate in a significant way the user's global constraints. In this way, if the SC problem is over-constrained, a solution can be found that violates in the smallest possible way the least number of global constraints. Of course, in the way the SC problem is formed, if this problem is not over-constrained, then violating solutions will always get a lower score than the correct solutions. Moreover, as the approach [17] we are extending is very conservative concerning the fact that all execution paths, even the longest non-probable ones, have to satisfy the global constraints, we relax this assumption by allowing solutions that violate some of the global constraints of the SC problem for the non-probable execution paths. In this way, solutions that satisfy the global constraints only for probable execution paths are not ruled out from the result set but they get a smaller score with respect to those solutions that satisfy the global constraints for all execution paths. We achieve this goal by using appropriate evaluation functions that return a zero normalized value for undesired aggregated dimension values and the following set of constraints: $[sc_k > 0, \forall k]$ that rule out those solutions that have a zero score for at least one execution path.

Based on the above analysis, the SCOP that has to be solved in order to determine the optimum execution plan OEP^* is the following:

$$\max \sum_{k=1}^{K} freq_k \cdot sc_k \tag{8}$$

$$sc_k = w_{et} \cdot f_{et}(et_k) + w_{pr} \cdot f_{pr}(pr_k) + w_{ee} \cdot f_{ee}(ee_k) + w_{ec} \cdot f_{ec}(ec_k), \forall k \tag{9}$$

$$sc_k > 0, \forall k \tag{10}$$

$$f_{et}(x) = \begin{cases} a_{et} + \frac{ET-x}{ET-q_{et}^{min}} \cdot (1-a_{et}), & q_{et}^{min} \leq x \leq ET \\ \max\left(a_{et} - \frac{q_{et}^{min}-x}{ET-q_{et}^{min}} \cdot (1-a_{et}), 0\right), & x < q_{et}^{min} \\ \max\left(a_{et} - \frac{x-ET}{ET-q_{et}^{min}} \cdot (1-a_{et}), 0\right), & x > ET \end{cases} \tag{11}$$

$$f_{pr}(x) = \begin{cases} a_{pr} + \frac{PR-x}{PR-q_{pr}^{min}} \cdot (1-a_{pr}), & q_{pr}^{min} \leq x \leq PR \\ \max\left(a_{pr} - \frac{q_{pr}^{min}-x}{PR-q_{pr}^{min}} \cdot (1-a_{pr}), 0\right), & x < q_{pr}^{min} \\ \max\left(a_{pr} - \frac{x-PR}{PR-q_{pr}^{min}} \cdot (1-a_{pr}), 0\right), & x > PR \end{cases} \tag{12}$$

$$f_{ee}(x) = \begin{cases} a_{ee} + \frac{x-EE}{q_{ee}^{max}-EE} \cdot (1-a_{ee}), & EE \leq x \leq q_{ee}^{max} \\ \max\left(a_{ee} - \frac{EE-x}{q_{ee}^{max}-EE} \cdot (1-a_{ee}), 0\right), & x < EE \\ \max\left(a_{ee} - \frac{x-q_{ee}^{max}}{q_{ee}^{max}-EE} \cdot (1-a_{ee}), 0\right), & x > q_{ee}^{max} \end{cases} \tag{13}$$

$$f_{ec}(x) = \begin{cases} a_{ec} + \frac{x-EC}{q_{ec}^{max}-EC} \cdot (1-a_{ec}), & EC \leq x \leq q_{ec}^{max} \\ \max\left(a_{ec} - \frac{EC-x}{q_{ec}^{max}-EC} \cdot (1-a_{ec}), 0\right), & x < EC \\ \max\left(a_{ec} - \frac{x-q_{ec}^{max}}{q_{ec}^{max}-EC} \cdot (1-a_{ec}), 0\right), & x > q_{ec}^{max} \end{cases} \tag{14}$$

$$\sum_{j \in S_i} z_{ij} = 1 \ , \qquad \forall i \tag{15}$$

$$et_i = \sum_{j \in S_i} z_{ij} \cdot et_j \ , \qquad \forall i \tag{16}$$

$$x_{i_2} - (et_{i_1} + x_{i_1}) \geq 0, \qquad \forall t_{i_1} \rightarrow t_{i_2} \tag{17}$$

$$\sum_{i \in sp_m^k} et_i \leq et_k \ , \qquad \forall k \tag{18}$$

$$pr_k = \sum_{i \in A_k} \sum_{j \in S_i} z_{ij} \cdot pr_j, \qquad \forall k \tag{19}$$

$$ee_k = \frac{1}{|A_k|} \cdot \sum_{i \in A_k} \sum_{j \in S_i} z_{ij} \cdot ee_j \ , \qquad \forall k \tag{20}$$

$$ec_k = \sum_{i \in A_k} \sum_{j \in S_i} z_{ij} \cdot ec_j \ , \qquad \forall k \tag{21}$$

$$et_{\text{class}(j)}^{min} \leq et_j \leq et_{\text{class}(j)}^{max} \ , \qquad \forall j \tag{22}$$

$$ec_{\text{class}(j)}^{min} \leq ec_j \leq ec_{\text{class}(j)}^{max} \ , \qquad \forall j \tag{23}$$

$$ee_j = \frac{ec_{\text{class}(j)}^{\text{normal}} \cdot \frac{ec_j - ec_{\text{class}(j)}^{\text{idle}} \cdot et_j}{ec_{\text{class}(j)}^{\text{normal}} - ec_{\text{class}(j)}^{\text{idle}}}}{ec_j} \ , \qquad \forall j \tag{24}$$

$$pr_j = \alpha_{\text{class}(j)} \cdot et_j + \beta \cdot ec_j \ , \qquad \forall j \tag{25}$$

$$et^{min} \leq et_j \leq et^{max} , \qquad \forall j \qquad\qquad (26)$$

$$et^{min} \leq et_k \leq et^{max} , \qquad \forall k \qquad\qquad (27)$$

$$et^{min} \leq et_i \leq et^{max} , \qquad \forall i \qquad\qquad (28)$$

$$pr^{min} \leq pr_j \leq pr^{max} , \qquad \forall j \qquad\qquad (29)$$

$$pr^{min} \leq pr_k \leq pr^{max} , \qquad \forall k \qquad\qquad (30)$$

$$ee^{min} \leq ee_j \leq ee^{max} , \qquad \forall j \qquad\qquad (31)$$

$$ee^{min} \leq ee_k \leq ee^{max} , \qquad \forall k \qquad\qquad (32)$$

$$ec^{min} \leq ec_j \leq ec^{max} , \qquad \forall j \qquad\qquad (33)$$

$$ec^{min} \leq ec_k \leq ec^{max} , \qquad \forall k \qquad\qquad (34)$$

The optimization function (8) and the constraints (9) and (10) have already been explained. The equation set from (11) to (14) defines the evaluation functions of the four quality and energy dimension under consideration. Constraint set (15) enforces the fact that only one candidate service should be selected for each task. Constraint set (16) expresses that the execution time for each task is the execution time of its selected service. Constraint set (17) represents precedence constraints for subsequent tasks in the abstract execution plan. To explain, if $t_{i_1} \rightarrow t_{i_2}$, $i_1, i_2 \in I$, then the task t_{i_2} is a direct successor of task t_{i_1} so the execution of the former should start after the termination of the latter. The variable x_i denotes the starting time point of task t_i. Constraint set (18) expresses that the execution time of every execution path is obtained by calculating the maximum execution time of all corresponding execution subpaths of this path. Constraint sets (19-21) express the price, energy efficiency, and energy consumption of every execution path, respectively, based on the aggregation rules highlighted in Table 2. Constraints sets (22-25) express the constraints obtained from the service profile of every candidate service for the four considered dimensions. Finally, constraints sets (26-34) define those variables of the problem that are related to the considered dimensions and are specific for each service, task and execution path.

Local constraints can be easily added in the above definition of the SC problem as they predicate on properties of a single task. For instance, if the ee for a task t_y has to be greater than or equal to a specific given value v, then the following constraint should be added to the above definition:

$$\sum_{j \in S_y} z_{yj} \cdot ee_j \geq v$$

Based on the above analysis, we have shown that the SC problem for a composite process with a block structure can be mapped to a SCOP. Unfortunately, solving SCOP is NP-hard. Thus, we have to experimentally evaluate our approach in order to discover if the solving time is very big in most of the cases. If this is true, then we may have to relax this problem, use heuristics or investigate if only linear constraints can be used in the problem so as to use MIP that is better than CSOP in problems with linear constraints. If this is not true, then our approach is appropriate for solving the energy-aware SC problem. Even if the solving time is big and we cannot find a way to reduce it, our approach can be used in the case of relatively stable compositions that are very resource demanding and for which any delta in optimization could have a benefit.

4   Motivating Example

In this section, we provide a proof-of-concept example that highlights the significance of our approach. In this example, our service-based process, under consideration, consists of six tasks, namely t_0, t_1, t_2, t_3, t_4 and t_5. According to this process, task t_0 runs first, then there is a split where tasks t_1 and t_2 run in parallel. After t_1 is executed, then we have a conditional branch, where t_3 is executed with probability 0.8 or t_4 is executed with probability 0.2. In the end, when either t_3 or t_4 and t_2 are executed, there is a join and the last task, t_5 is executed. Thus, this process has two execution paths, namely $ep_1 = \{t_0, t_1, t_2, t_3, t_5\}$ and $ep_2 = \{t_0, t_1, t_2, t_4, t_5\}$, that have the corresponding probabilities of execution $freq_1 = 0.8$ and $freq_2 = 0.2$, respectively. Execution path ep_1 has two subpaths, namely $sp_1^1 = \{t_0, t_1, t_3, t_5\}$ and $sp_2^1 = \{t_0, t_2, t_5\}$. Similarly, execution path ep_2 has two subpaths, namely $sp_1^2 = \{t_0, t_1, t_4, t_5\}$ and $sp_2^2 = \{t_0, t_2, t_5\}$. As can be easily seen, we have that $sp_2^1 = sp_2^2$.

Moreover, for the sake of simplicity, we assume that there are three services that can be used to execute any of the six tasks, where service s_1 runs in the slow server class (class(1) = slow), s_2 runs in the average server class (class(2) = average), and s_3 runs in the fast server class (class(3) = fast). For service s_1 we assume that we can derive the following information from its pro-

file: $7 \le et_1 \le 10, 1275.4 \le ec_1 \le 2088, ee_1 = \left\lceil \dfrac{222 \cdot \frac{ec_1 - 178 \cdot et_1}{222 - 178}}{ec_1} \cdot 100 \right\rceil$. Similarly,

for services s_2 and s_3 we have the following information: $4 \le et_2 \le 7, 1992.4 \le$

$ec_2 \le 3994.9, ee_2 = \left\lceil \dfrac{607 \cdot \frac{ec_2 - 486 \cdot et_2}{607 - 486}}{ec_2} \cdot 100 \right\rceil$ and $1 \le et_3 \le 4, 6647.1 \le ec_3 \le$

$30478.8, ee_3 = \left\lceil \dfrac{8106 \cdot \frac{ec_3 - 6485 \cdot et_3}{8106 - 6485}}{ec_3} \cdot 100 \right\rceil$, respectively. In addition, we assume the

following information: $\alpha_{class(1)} = 10, \alpha_{class(2)} = 50, \alpha_{class(3)} = 250, \beta = 0.5$, so the cost models of the services will be: $pr_1 = 10 * et_1 + 0.5 * ec_1$, $pr_2 = 50 * et_2 + 0.5 * ec_2$, and $pr_3 = 100 * et_1 + 0.5 * ec_3$, respectively.

The last assumptions made in this example concern the value domain of the quality and energy variables, the normalization functions and their weights, and the user constraints. Concerning the variables, we assume that all execution time variables et_x have the domain $[1, 10]$, all price variables pr_x have the domain $[500, 20000]$, all energy efficiency variables ee_x have the domain $[0,100]$, and all energy consumption variables ec_x have the domain $[1000, 31000]$. Moreover, we assume that all dimensions are equally important and should be evaluated in the same way, so we have that: $a_{et} = a_{pr} = a_{ee} = a_{ec} = 0.4, w_{et} = w_{pr} = w_{ee} = w_{ec} = 0.25$. Finally, we assume that the user provides the following constraints: $ET = 27, PR = 2400, EE = 0.55, EC = 6000$.

Based on the user-supplied information, it is easy to see that the problem is over-constrained, so all of the current approaches would fail and not return any solution. However, our approach does not fail and produces the following solution $z_{0,1} = z_{1,1} = z_{2,1} = z_{3,1} = z_{4,1} = z_{5,1} = 1$, which has the highest score (0.2825) and violates in the least possible way the user constraints. In other words, all tasks of the process have been assigned to the first service, which is the cheapest and less energy consuming. Based on this solution, both execution paths will have the following values for their aggregated dimensions: $et = 28, pr = 3770, ee = 0.45, ec = 6840$.

5 Concluding Remarks

Approaching the problem to find out the best tradeoff between performance and energy consumption, this paper presents a novel energy-aware and quality-based technique in order to solve the SC problem taking into account non-functional characteristics through a global approach. Hence, a new energy efficiency metric for a single service is introduced, which maps directly the relationship between energy consumption and execution time. The energy dimension requires to consider novel aspects for service quality evaluation. In particular, the proposed method considers soft constraints, nonlinear relationships among quality dimensions, and ranges for quality values.

As future work, we intend to develop a more detailed and easy-to-use framework tool for data centers, in which possible burst periods have to be taken into consideration, adding, thus, new elements into our energy efficiency metric. Furthermore, techniques to measure real electrical power consumed by a single server according to its workload will be used as well.

Acknowledgement. The research leading to these results has received funding from the European Community's Seventh Framework Programme FP7/2007-2013 under grant agreement 215483 (S-Cube) and the MIUR Tekne FIRB project.

References

1. GreenBiz.com. In Economic Downturn, Energy Efficiency and IT Take on Green Sheen (February 2009),
http://www.greenbiz.com/news/2009/02/26/
economic-energy-efficiency-green-it
2. Tschudi, W.: Save Energy Now – Data Center Briefing. Technical report, Lawrence Berkeley National Laboratory (October 2008)
3. Schmidt, N.H., Erek, K., Kolbe, L.M., Zarnekow, R.: Towards a Procedural Model for Sustainable Information Systems Management. In: HICSS 2009: Proceedings of the 42nd Hawaii International Conference on System Sciences, Hawaii, USA, pp. 1–10. IEEE Computer Society, Los Alamitos (2009)
4. Bacon, D.F., Graham, S.L., Sharp, O.J.: Compiler Transformations for High-Performance Computing. ACM Computing Surveys 26(4), 345–420 (1994)

5. Williams, J., Curtis, L.: Green: The New Computing Coat of Arms? IT Professional 10(1), 12–16 (2008)
6. Zenker, N., Rajub, J.: Resource Measurement for Services in a heterogeneous Environment. In: ICTTA 2008: Proceedings of the 3rd International Conference on Information and Communication Technologies: From Theory to Applications, Damascus, Syria, IEEE Communications Society, pp. 1–15 (2008)
7. Barroso, L.A., Hölzle, U.: The Case for Energy-Proportional Computing. Computer 40(12), 33–37 (2007)
8. Koomey, J.: Estimating total power consumption by servers in the U.S. and the world. Technical report, Analytics Press (February 2007),
   http://enterprise.amd.com/Downloads/svrpwrusecompletefinal.pdf
9. Orgerie, A.C., Lefèvre, L., Gelas, J.P.: Save Watts in Your Grid: Green Strategies for Energy-Aware Framework in Large Scale Distributed Systems. In: ICPADS 2008: Proceedings of the 2008 14th IEEE International Conference on Parallel and Distributed Systems, Melbourne, Victoria, Australia, pp. 171–178. IEEE Computer Society, Los Alamitos (2008)
10. U.S. Environmental Protection Agency (EPA): Report to Congress on Server and Data Center Energy Efficiency – Public Law 109-431. Technical report (August 2007)
11. Wang, D.: Meeting Green Computing Challenges. In: HDP 2007: Proceedings of the International Symposium on High Density packaging and Microsystem Integration, Shanghai, China, pp. 1–4. IEEE Computer Society, Los Alamitos (2007)
12. Xue, J.W.J., Chester, A.P., He, L.G., Jarvis, S.A.: Model-driven Server Allocation in Distributed Enterprise Systems. In: ABIS 2009: Proceedings of the 3rd International Conference on Adaptive Business Information Systems, Leipzig, Germany (March 2009)
13. Liu, L., Wang, H., Liu, X., Jin, X., He, W.B., Wang, Q.B., Chen, Y.: GreenCloud: a new architecture for green data center. In: ICAC-INDST 2009: Proceedings of the 6th international conference industry session on Autonomic computing and communications industry session, Barcelona, Spain, pp. 29–38. ACM, New York (2009)
14. Comuzzi, M., Pernici, B.: A Framework for QoS-Based Web Service Contracting. ACM Transactions on the Web (June 2009)
15. Plebani, P., Pernici, B.: URBE: Web Service Retrieval Based on Similarity Evaluation. IEEE Transactions on Knowledge and Data Engineering (2009)
16. Zeng, L., Benatallah, B., Ngu, A.H., Dumas, M., Kalagnanam, J., Chang, H.: QoS-Aware Middleware for Web Services Composition. IEEE Transactions on Software Engineering 30(5), 311–327 (2004)
17. Ardagna, D., Pernici, B.: Adaptive Service Composition in Flexible Processes. IEEE Transactions on Software Engineering 3(6), 369–384 (2007)
18. Canfora, G., Di Penta, M., Esposito, R., Villani, M.L.: QoS-Aware Replanning of Composite Web Services. In: ICWS 2005: Proceedings of the IEEE International Conference on Web Services, Orlando, FL, USA, pp. 121–129. IEEE Computer Society, Los Alamitos (2005)
19. Jaeger, M.C., Mühl, G., Golze, S.: QoS-Aware Composition of Web Services: A Look at Selection Algorithms. In: ICWS 2005: IEEE International Conference on Web Services, Orlando, FL, USA, pp. 807–808. IEEE Computer Society, Los Alamitos (2005)
20. Rossi, F., van Beek, P., Walsh, T.: Handbook of Constraint Programming. Elsevier Science Inc., New York (2006)
21. Hwang, C., Yoon, K.: Multiple Criteria Decision Making. LNEMS (1981)

Action Patterns in Business Process Models

Sergey Smirnov[1], Matthias Weidlich[1], Jan Mendling[2], and Mathias Weske[1]

[1] Hasso Plattner Institute, Potsdam, Germany
{sergey.smirnov,matthias.weidlich,mathias.weske}@hpi.uni-potsdam.de
[2] Humboldt-Universität zu Berlin, Germany
jan.mendling@wiwi.hu-berlin.de

Abstract. Business process management experiences a large uptake by the industry, and process models play an important role in the analysis and improvement of processes. While an increasing number of staff becomes involved in actual modeling practice, it is crucial to assure model quality and homogeneity along with providing suitable aids for creating models. In this paper we consider the problem of offering recommendations to the user during the act of modeling. Our key contribution is a concept for defining and identifying action patterns - chunks of actions often appearing together in business processes. In particular, we specify action patterns and demonstrate how they can be identified from existing process model repositories using association rule mining techniques. Action patterns can then be used to suggest additional actions for a process model. Our approach is challenged by applying it to the collection of process models from the SAP Reference Model.

1 Introduction

Business process management experiences a large uptake by the industry, as more and more companies analyze and improve their processes to stay competitive. Process models, being formal representations of business processes, facilitate many tasks in the domain of business process management. Thereby, instead of being an art of a few specialists, process modeling becomes a daily routine of office staff. This development implies several challenges in terms of an efficient and effective modeling support. In particular, many staff members have low modeling competence and model only on an irregular basis [20]. For this reason, process modeling tools have to incorporate techniques to help these casual modelers to conduct their work in a productive way.

Business process modeling research has revealed several approaches to make modeling more efficient. This research can be classified into two main categories. On the one hand, reference modeling aims to increase productivity based on the reuse principle: models are created for a specific domain and are meant to be customized in different application projects. On the other hand, different types of patterns describe recurring situations in a domain independent way. The potential of both approaches is hardly reflected by current tool features. Whilst most of the pattern sets for processes and workflows are mainly used for

L. Baresi, C.-H. Chi, and J. Suzuki (Eds.): ICSOC-ServiceWave 2009, LNCS 5900, pp. 115–129, 2009.

model verification and modeling language analysis, the existing reference models are tightly coupled with their partial domain and can hardly be used in other settings. Against this background, we define a concept of *action patterns*. In contrast to well known workflow patterns, action patterns are closely related to semantic content of a process model. Meanwhile, unlike reference models, action patterns are abstract enough to be applicable in various domains. In this context, the term *action* essentially refers to the verb that describes the work content of a textual activity label.

The contribution of this paper is a formal description of action patterns and an approach for identification of patterns in existing process model collections based on association rules mining. The mined action patterns can be used to suggest additional activities to the modeler during a modeling act. We specify two classes of patterns. Co-occurrence action patterns signify sets of actions that are likely to appear jointly in a model. Behavioral action patterns describe how co-occurring actions are related to each other in terms of behavioral constraints. This information allows us to identify the control flow position where an activity has to be added.

The rest of the paper is structured as follows. Section 2 provides a motivating example to illustrate our approach. Section 3 formalizes the action pattern concept and presents two classes of action patterns: co-occurrence action patterns and behavioral action patterns. Section 4 describes the evaluation of our approach by deriving action patterns from the SAP Reference Model. In Section 5 we present an outlook of the related work. Section 6 concludes the paper.

2   Motivating Example

An intrinsic complexity of business processes together with process models heterogeneity, originating from a variety of stakeholders and modeling purposes, calls for sophisticated support for process modeling. We distinguish two important drivers for such modeling support. On the one hand, the support aims at facilitating the design of a standalone process model. This kind of modeling support includes means to accelerate process model creation, assure correct model execution semantics, and increase model conciseness. However, the focus is purely on the *isolated* creation of a dedicated model: the application domain of this model is not taken into account. On the other hand, the rationale behind modeling support might be homogeneity of the modeling efforts. Process models created within a certain *domain*, might it be an organizational unit or a process model collection, should be modeled in a consistent and similar manner. In this case the emphasis is on avoiding redundancies and contradictions, as well as on enforcing modeling guidelines.

We illustrate the use case of *domain-aware* modeling support by means of the example in Fig. 1, which shows fragments of two EPCs from the SAP Reference Model [9]. Both business processes originate from the SAP material management and describe production planning. We see that the processes have a similar structure and semantics. For the long-term planning (Fig. 1(a)), as well as for the

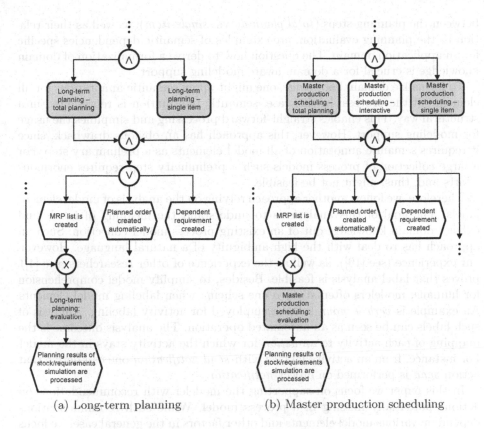

(a) Long-term planning   (b) Master production scheduling

Fig. 1. Fragments of two similar planning processes from the SAP Reference Model

master production scheduling (Fig. 1(b)), two similar planning steps are performed concurrently, and in both cases are succeeded by an evaluation. In Fig. 1 we highlight the activities which are interesting for us with grey color. Given these models, the creation of a model for a related process, e.g., a short-time production planning, might be supported as follows. After the modeler creates a function *Short-Term Planning - Total Planning*, we suggest to insert a concurrent function *Short-Term Planning - Single Item* on the fly. This recommendation can be derived from the analysis of the already existing models. We might also alert the modeler if he saves the model for short-term planning without having inserted a function for planning evaluation. The modeler might reconsider the modeling decisions and insert such a function, or rename an existing function, which has been intended to model the evaluation step, but was labeled differently (e.g., function *planning calculation* can be renamed to *planning evaluation*).

For obvious reasons, such *domain-aware* modeling support has to take into account semantics of existing process models. In this case semantics is not restricted to the model execution semantics. Instead, semantics has to be given in terms of concepts of the application domain. Applied to Fig. 1, a dependency between the planning steps (*total planning* vs. *single-item*), as well as their relation to the planning evaluation, are examples of semantic dependencies specific for an application domain. The question how to derive a formalization of domain knowledge is crucial for a domain-aware modeling support.

To formalize domain knowledge, one might apply semantic annotations for all elements of the process. In this case, semantic information is represented in a structural way. This enables straight-forward processing and simplifies the usage for modeling support. However, this approach has an obvious drawback, since it requires semantic annotation of all model elements as a preliminary step. For a large collection of process models such a preliminary step requires enormous efforts and, thus, might not be feasible.

Therefore, we follow another approach relying on the analysis of model element labels. The goal of this analysis is to understand the meaning of labels and extract domain knowledge out of an existing process model collection. Such an approach has to deal with the high ambiguity of a natural language. However, our experience (see [19]), as well as the experience of other researchers (see [4]), proves that label analysis is feasible. Besides, to simplify model comprehension for humans, modelers often stick to one schema when labeling model elements. An example is *verb + noun* schema employed for activity labeling. Analysis of such labels can be seen as an automated operation. The analysis outcome is the mapping of each activity to an *action* for which the activity stays in the model. For instance, from an activity labeled with *send notification* one can derive that action *send* is performed on object *notification*.

In this paper we focus on supporting the modeler with recommendations on actions potentially missing in a process model. While such recommendations depend on various model elements and other factors in the general case, we focus on the analysis of activities. There are two major drivers for our work. First, giving recommendations on the missing actions (i.e., activities on the model level) requires exhaustive investigation of the existing ones. Second, a lion's share of business process model semantics is given by the activities. Hence, we formulate the recommendations based on the analysis of activities. To formalize the knowledge extracted from a process model collection we propose to use the notion of *action patterns*—groups of actions which often appear together in business processes. In the next section we elaborate on the concept of action patterns. However, before we proceed with action patterns discussion, we would like to summarize the assumptions used in this work:

Assumption 1. A process model collection is large enough to extract domain knowledge.

Assumption 2. An activity label signifies an action.

Assumption 3. There is a mechanism interpreting an activity label as an action.

3   Action Patterns

In general, a pattern is a concept that organizes knowledge related to "a problem which occurs over and over again in our environment, and then describes the core solution to that problem, in such a way that you can use this solution a million times over, without ever doing it the same way twice" [3]. While originally defined for architecture, this concept was adapted to software engineering in the 1990s (see [6]). In business process management, patterns have been defined, among others, for control flow [25], data flow [21], resources [22], and collaboration [15]. Also the MIT Process Handbook [16] can be related to the idea of describing a core solution to a recurring problem.

This section discusses the notion of actions patterns in order to meet the requirements for modeling support outlined above. First, Section 3.1 presents our formal framework for action patterns. Then, Section 3.2 defines co-occurrence action patterns. Finally, Section 3.3 specifies behavioral action patterns based on behavioral profiles.

3.1   Formal Framework

In order to formalize the concept of an action pattern we need to introduce a number of auxiliary concepts. First, we postulate Γ to be the universal alphabet of labels. Based thereon, we define the notion of a process model enriched with labeling information.

Definition 1 (Process Model). A tuple $PM = (A, G, F, s, e, t, l)$ is a *process model* , where:
  - A is a finite nonempty set of activities;
  - G is a finite set of gateways;
  - $A \cap G = \emptyset$ and $N = A \cup G$ is a finite set of nodes;
  - $F \subseteq N \times N$ is the flow relation, such that (N, F) is a connected graph;
  - $s \in A$ is the only start activity, such that $\bullet s = \emptyset$, where $\bullet n = \{n' \in N | (n', n) \in F\}$ for node n;
  - $e \in A$ is the only end activity, such that $e\bullet = \emptyset$, where $n\bullet = \{n' \in N | (n, n') \in F\}$ for node n;
  - $t : G \mapsto \{and, xor, or\}$ is a mapping that assigns type to each gateway;
  - $l : A \mapsto \Gamma$ is a mapping assigning to each activity a label.

In the remainder, we do not formalize the execution semantics of a process model, but assume an interpretation of the model following on common execution semantics. Such semantics, in particular for the OR construct, has been presented in the existing work (see [17] as an example for EPCs).

To grasp the meaning of activities humans interpret their labels. In the context of this work interpretation of labels has great importance. Hence, we formalize it, introducing an alphabet of action terms T and a label interpretation function.

Definition 2 (Action Function).   For a given process model $PM = (A, G, F, s, e, t, l)$, the *action function* $v : \Gamma \mapsto T$ derives an action from a label. As a shorthand notation, we introduce $v_a : A \mapsto T$ for deriving an action from a label of an activity $a \in A$, i.e., $v_a(a) = v(l(a))$. We also use $V_{PM} = \bigcup_{a \in A}\{v_a(a)\}$ to denote the set of all actions of a process model.

Revisiting the example containing the label *send notification*, application of the action function v yields the action *send*. We also formalize the notion of a process model collection as follows.

Definition 3 (Process Model Collection). A tuple $C = (\mathcal{PM}, V)$ is a *process model collection* , where:

- $\mathcal{PM}$ is a nonempty finite set of process models with elements $PM_i = (A_i, G_i, F_i, s_i, e_i, t_i, l_i)$, where $i = 1, 2, \ldots, |\mathcal{PM}|$;
- $V = \bigcup_{i=1,2,\ldots,|\mathcal{PM}|} V_{PM_i}$ is the set of all actions in the model collection.

It is natural to expect that in a large collection of process models one can observe sustainable relations between actions (action patterns). Recognition of action patterns resembles uncovering patterns in large data collections. The latter problem is in the focus of data mining. In particular we are interested in association rule learning—a well established technique for discovering relations between variables in large databases. An example of an association rule in a commerce domain is a statement that if customers buy coffee and milk, they usually buy sugar as well. Association rule learning enables discovery of such statements from the analysis of basket data in supermarkets. The initial idea of association rule learning was presented by Agrawal, Imielinski, and Swami in [1]. More advanced algorithms were presented in [2].

Further, the generic formalism of association rule learning is adapted for both co-occurrence and behavioral action patterns. We introduce the set of items $\mathcal{I}$. Let us observe a collection of transactions C, where each transaction T is a set of items, i.e., $T \subseteq \mathcal{I}$. Given a set of items $X \subseteq \mathcal{I}$, we say that transaction T satisfies X, if $X \subseteq T$. An association rule in a collection C is an implication of the form $X \Rightarrow Y$, where $X \cap Y = \emptyset$ and $X, Y \subset \mathcal{I}$.

Based thereon, two elementary notions can be defined, i.e., *support* and *confidence*. A set $X \subseteq \mathcal{I}$ has support n in a collection C, if n transactions satisfy set X. We denote the support for set X with $supp(X)$. Support can be related to statistical significance. In the context of action pattern retrieval we are interested in sets that have high support. Let us require the minimum level of support for sets to be *minsup*. Then X is called a *large* set if $supp(X) \geq minsup$ (and a *small* set otherwise). An association rule $X \Rightarrow Y$ holds in transaction collection C with confidence $c = \frac{supp(X \cup Y)}{supp(X)}$, if at least c share of transactions satisfying X, satisfies Y as well. The confidence for a rule $X \Rightarrow Y$ is denoted as $conf(X \Rightarrow Y)$. A rule confidence reflects its strength. As in the case with support, we are interested in the rules with high confidence values. Hence, we introduce the minimal accepted level of confidence—*minconf*. Following [1], we claim that we are interested in the rules $X \Rightarrow Y$ for which $X \bigcup Y$ is large and the confidence is greater than user specified *minconf*.

3.2   Co-occurrence Action Patterns

The first class of action patterns is co-occurrence action patterns. *Nomen est omen*, these patterns capture sets of actions which often co-occur together in business processes, ignoring any ordering relations between these actions. In terms of association rules learning, we interpret actions as items and process models as transactions. Hence, a model collection is a collection of transactions. We say that a process model $PM = (A, G, F, s, e, t, l)$ satisfies an action set X, if $X \subseteq V_{PM}$. A co-occurrence action pattern is defined as an association rule on the domain of actions V associated with values for minimal support and confidence.

Definition 4 (Co-occurrence Action Pattern)
$CAP = (R, minsup, minconf)$ is a co-occurrence action pattern in process model collection $C = (\mathcal{PM}, V)$, where:
- R is an association rule $X \Rightarrow Y$, where $X, Y \subset V$;
- $minsup$ is the value of the required minimal support;
- $minconf$ is the value of the required minimal confidence.

From a user perspective such a pattern recommends the actions which are expected to appear in the process model given the current constellation of actions.

Mining of co-occurrence action patterns has two phases. In the first phase we seek for association rules $X \Rightarrow Y$, such that $X \bigcup Y$ is a large set. In the second phase the mined large sets are used for derivation of patterns—rules that have a high confidence level.

A search for large sets is a computationally intensive task. In this paper we set our choice on Apriori algorithm, since it is efficient and simple [2]. In terms of large action sets this algorithm works as follows. As the input the algorithm takes the process model collection $C = (\mathcal{PM}, V)$ and the minimal support value $minsup$. For every action $v \in V$, a one element action set is constructed, $\{v\}$. Then, for each action set, the algorithm checks its support. If the support is not less than $minsup$, the set is large. The derived 1-large sets are used as the input for the next step. In the k-th step the algorithm constructs sets of size k from $k - 1$ large sets and checks if they are large. The algorithm terminates, once all the large sets are found. Table 1 illustrates the first (see Table 1(b)) and the second steps (see Table 1(c)) of Apriori work for the model collection captured in Table 1(a) given $minsup = 5$.

After large sets have been retrieved, the second phase explores each large set for rules with high confidence level. A rule $A \Rightarrow B$ is defined by two sets: antecedent (A) and consequent (B). We consider all possible partitions of a large set into two sets, one of them to become an antecedent and the other—a consequent. For each partitioning we check, if it results in a rule with a confidence level greater than $minsup$.

3.3   Behavioral Action Patterns

Co-occurrence action patterns do not provide information about *how* the missing actions have to be introduced into the process model. As the next step, we consider action patterns that are enriched with information on relations between actions. First, we present preliminaries on behavioral relations and afterwards introduce the notion of a behavioral action pattern.

Table 1. Derivation of large action sets in a process model collection given $minsup = 5$

(a) Process model collection

Model	Actions
A	allocate analyze calculate collect evaluate settle summarize
B	allocate analyze asses calculate distribute entry evaluate reconcile repost settle split
C	allocate analyze calculate cost settle
D	allocate analyze calculate evaluate settle
E	allocate analyze collect calculate distribute evaluate settle summarize
F	allocate budget calculate copy define evaluate plan reconcile settle split transfer
G	allocate budget calculate copy cost define plan reconcile settle split transfer

(b) Large action sets of size 1

Set	Support
{allocate}	7
{analyze}	5
{calculate}	7
{evaluate}	5
{settle}	7

(c) Large action sets of size 2

Set	Support
{allocate, analyze}	5
{allocate, calculate}	7
{allocate, evaluate}	5
{allocate, settle}	7
{analyze, calculate}	5
{analyze, settle}	5
{calculate, evaluate}	5
{calculate, settle}	7
{evaluate, settle}	5

Behavioral Relations. In order to capture behavioral aspects of a process on the level of pairs of activities, we apply the notion of *behavioral profiles* [27]. Although Definition 1 does not specify execution semantics, we impose syntactical requirements for the definition of all complete traces of a process model to define its behavioral profile. That is, the (potentially unbounded) set of *complete process traces* T_{PM} for a process model $PM = (A, G, F, s, e, t, l)$ is a set of lists of the form $s \cdot A^* \cdot e$, such that a list entry contains the execution order of activities. Further on, we use $a \in \sigma$ with $\sigma \in T_{PM}$ to denote that an activity $a \in A$ is a part of a complete process trace. The behavioral profile is grounded on the notion of *weak order*. Two activities of a process model are in weak order, if there exists a trace in which one node occurs after the other.

Definition 5 (Weak Order Relation). Let $PM = (A, G, F, s, e, t, l)$ be a process model, and T_{PM}—its set of traces. The *weak order relation* $\succ_{PM} \subseteq (A \times A)$ contains all pairs (x, y), such that there is a trace $\sigma = n_1, \ldots, n_m$ in T_{PM} with $j \in \{1, \ldots, m-1\}$ and $j < k \le m$ for which holds $n_j = x$ and $n_k = y$.

Depending on how two activities of a process model are related by weak order, we define three relations forming the behavioral profile.

Definition 6 (Behavioral Profile). Let $PM = (A, G, F, s, e, t, l)$ be a process model. A pair $(x, y) \in (A \times A)$ is in one of the following relations:
- *strict order relation* $\leadsto_{PM}$, *if* $x \succ_{PM} y$ *and* $y \not\succ_{PM} x$;
- *exclusiveness relation* $+_{PM}$, *if* $x \not\succ_{PM} y$ *and* $y \not\succ_{PM} x$;
- *observation concurrency relation* $\|_{PM}$, *if* $x \succ_{PM} y$ *and* $y \succ_{PM} x$.

The set of all three relations is the *behavioral profile* of PM.

We illustrate the behavioral profile by means of the model in Fig. 2. For instance, *(Template allocation)* $\leadsto$ *(Overhead calculation)* holds as there exists no trace, such that the latter function occurs before the former. With $\leadsto_{PM}^{-1}$ as the inverse relation for $\leadsto_{PM}$, *(Revaluation completed)* $\leadsto_{PM}^{-1}$ *(Template allocation)* also holds. It is worth to mention that $\leadsto_{PM}, \leadsto_{PM}^{-1}, +_{PM}$, and $\|_{PM}$ partition the Cartesian product of activities $A \times A$ for a process model $PM = (A, G, F, s, e, t, l)$.

The Concept of Behavioral Action Patterns. We introduce behavioral action patterns as a mechanism enabling suggestions on how the missing actions should be introduced in an existing process model. Such patterns provide more information to the user than co-occurrence action patterns. However, we perceive behavioral patterns not as a mechanism replacing co-occurrence patterns, but rather as a complimentary mechanism: while co-occurrence action patterns suggest which actions are missing, behavioral action patterns hints on action relations. Assume a user designs a process model containing actions *allocate* and *calculate*; co-occurrence action pattern $\{allocate, calculate\} \Rightarrow \{settle\}$ is available (see Fig. 2). This pattern suggests to add action *settle* in the process model. Then, we can look up a suitable behavioral action pattern describing relations between these three actions. Behavioral action pattern $\{allocate \leadsto calculate\} \Rightarrow \{allocate \leadsto settle, calculate \leadsto settle\}$ provides a desired recommendation.

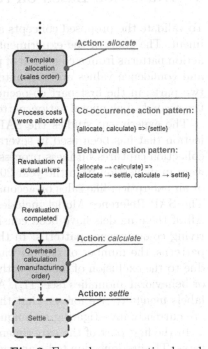

Fig. 2. Exemplary suggestion based on action patterns

To formalize the concept of relations between actions, we propose to adapt the behavioral relations between activities introduced earlier. We say that actions v_1 and v_2 are in relation R in a process model $PM = (A, G, F, s, e, t, l)$, if there are two activities $a, b \in A$, such that $(a, b) \in R \wedge v_a(a) = v_1 \wedge v_a(b) = v_2$. Within one process model a pair of actions (v_1, v_2) may be in more than one relation. This holds if there are several activities that signify action v_1, or action v_2, or both actions.

Definition 7 (Behavioral Action Pattern). $BAP = (R, minsup, minconf)$ is a *behavioral action pattern* in process model collection $C = (\mathcal{PM}, V)$, where:
- R is a rule $X \Rightarrow Y$, where $X, Y \subset V \times \{\rightsquigarrow, \rightsquigarrow^{-1}, +, \|\} \times V$, i.e., X and Y constitute of pairs of actions for which behavioral relations are specified;
- $minsup$ is the value of the required minimal support;
- $minconf$ is the value of the required minimal confidence.

Mining of behavioral action patterns resembles the approach introduced for co-occurrence action patterns. In the first phase we seek for large action sets. In the second phase we inspect the relations between the actions of each large set. In terms of association rules derivation, action relations are treated as items, while large action sets are interpreted as collections. Provided $minsup$ and $minconf$ values, we can derive behavioral action patterns.

4   Evaluation Based on the SAP Reference Model

To validate the proposed concepts and algorithms, we have conducted an experiment. The goals of the experiment were: 1) to check if it is possible to derive action patterns from a collection of process models and 2) to learn which support and confidence values are encountered in practice. The experiment consists of two parts: in the first part co-occurrence action patterns have been studied, in the second—behavioral action patterns.

The experiment studies the SAP Reference Model [9], a process model collection that has been used in several works on process model analysis [17]. The collection captures business processes that are supported by the SAP R/3 software in its version from the year 2000. It is organized in 29 functional branches of an enterprise, like sales or accounting, that are covered by the SAP software. The SAP Reference Model includes 604 Event-driven Process Chains (EPCs). All of these models have been considered in the first part of experiment for deriving co-occurrence patterns. In the second part, inspecting behavioral action patterns, the number of models was 421. The decrease in the model number is due to the exclusion of models with ambiguous instantiation semantics (see [5]) or behavioral anomalies (see [17]). At this stage we derived actions from activity labels manually. We foresee that this step can be automated in the future and are currently investigating techniques enabling the automation.

In the first part of the experiment, we have derived co-occurrence action patterns. The first question to be answered is which values of support and confidence indicate relevant patterns. While higher values indicate that the pattern is more reliable, we aim to understand which values can be expected. In the SAP Reference Model the support value for all action sets is under 10, which is quite low given the fact that some actions appear several hundred times [18]. As the minimally acceptable confidence level is hard to predict, we conducted a set of experiments varying the level of support from 2 to 9 and the level of confidence from 0.5 to 0.95. Table 2 summarizes the results of these experiments. It shows that there is almost half a million patterns with support 2, 17 patterns with support of 9, and not a single pattern has support 10. To illustrate how the derived

Table 2. Dependency of co-occurrence pattern number in the SAP Reference Model on *minsup* and *minconf* values

minconf \ minsup	2	3	4	5	6	7	8	9
0.50	522396	7395	2353	680	563	41	29	17
0.55	511373	6979	2247	665	550	34	23	13
0.60	510517	6123	2089	610	504	33	22	12
0.65	510498	6104	2070	591	497	26	16	9
0.70	484061	5569	1535	563	469	20	12	6
0.75	483415	4923	1477	505	421	19	11	6
0.80	483176	4684	1238	501	417	15	10	5
0.85	483135	4643	1197	460	417	15	10	5
0.90	483095	4603	1157	420	377	7	3	2
0.95	483093	4601	1155	418	375	5	1	0

Table 3. Derived behavioral profiles for action set {allocate, calculate, settle}

Model \ Action pair	(allocate, calculate)	(allocate, settle)	(calculate, settle)
A	⤳	⤳	⤳
B	⤳	⤳	⤳
C	⤳	⤳	⤳
D	⤳	⤳	⤳

patterns look like, we zoom into one cell of the table and list the patterns with $minsup = 7$ and $minconf = 0.95$:

- {pick} ⇒ {process}
- {level} ⇒ {evaluate}
- {permit} ⇒ {process}
- {archive, enter} ⇒ {process}
- {allocate, calculate} ⇒ {settle}

The results show that for the studied model collection the maximum support value is small. On the one hand, this is caused by unsystematic usage of labels: often the derived actions are semantically close, but are treated as different actions. On the other hand, this fact can be explained by the heterogeneity of process models. The presence of process variants in the collection leads to the fact that some action patterns, especially of size 5-7, identify these variants in the model set.

Behavioral action patterns originate from the inspection of behavioral constraints between actions in large action sets. Hence, derivation of behavioral patterns is possible only after *minsup* for action sets is given. In the experiment we considered those process models from the SAP Reference Model that can be mapped to free-choice Petri nets. Table 3 provides an example of relations for actions *allocate, calculate, settle*. Table 4(a) shows the number of patterns that

Table 4. Dependency of behavioral action patterns number for 2 action sets on *minsup* and *minconf* values

(a) Action set {allocate, calculate, settle}

minconf \ minsup	2	3	4	5
0.50	12	12	12	0
0.55	12	12	12	0
0.60	12	12	12	0
0.65	12	12	12	0
0.70	12	12	12	0
0.75	12	12	12	0
0.80	12	12	12	0
0.85	12	12	12	0
0.90	12	12	12	0
0.95	12	12	12	0

(b) Action set {analyze, allocate, settle}

minconf \ minsup	2	3	4	5	6
0.50	170	12	4	2	0
0.55	161	12	4	2	0
0.60	157	8	3	2	0
0.65	157	8	3	2	0
0.70	130	8	3	2	0
0.75	129	7	2	1	0
0.80	129	7	2	1	0
0.85	129	7	2	1	0
0.90	129	7	2	1	0
0.95	129	7	2	1	0

can be derived for this set depending on the *minsup* and *minconf* values for relations. A more vivid example is the action set {*analyze, allocate, settle*}, for which the number of behavioral patterns varies greatly (see Table 4(b)). A concrete example of a behavioral action pattern which can be derived from Table 3 is {*allocate* ⤳ *calculate*} ⇒ {*allocate* ⤳ *settle, calculate* ⤳ *settle*}. This pattern prescribes that the three actions are sequentially constrained. They should appear in the process model such that first it is *allocated*, then *calculated*, and finally *settled*, which is a standard sequence of activities for financial assets.

5   Related Work

Our work can be related to different contributions to business process modeling. We focus on the three areas, i.e., patterns for business processes, intelligent modeling support, and research on activity labels.

There is a wide variety of *patterns* proposed for business processes and business process modeling. On the technical level, the workflow pattern initiative has identified various patterns for the specification of control flow [25], data flow [21], and resources [22] in workflow management systems. On a more conceptual level, Lonchamp proposed a set of collaboration patterns defining abstract building blocks for recurrent situations [15]. Tran et al. formalize process patterns using UML concepts [24]. Most closely related to our work is the research by Thom et al. [23]. The authors identify so-called *activity* patterns that specify eight different types of micro workflows, like approval or decision. Further, in [14] the authors describe a method for patterns derivation. While [14,23] operates directly with activities, we use the concept of actions. As in real world models activities with different labels often signify the same action, usage of actions facilitates pattern derivation. Next, instead of direct analysis of a model graph structure, we rely on the concept of behavioral profiles. As relations captured by behavioral profiles are weaker than those defined by process models, [14] discovers only a subclass of behavioral action patterns.

The potential of improving business process modeling using *intelligent support and recommendations* has been recognized only recently. Hornung et al. define a concept to provide recommendations to the modeler based on search techniques [8]. The idea is to find similar models in the process repository and propose them as extensions to a process being currently modeled. This idea is in line with our approach, but requires a match not only in terms of actions, but also business objects and other textual content. We deem our approach to be more flexible and applicable across different modeling contexts. Further experiments are needed to check comparative strengths and weaknesses. A different stream of research investigates how far social software and Web 2.0 applications can provide recommendations to the modeler. Koschmider et al. propose a solution that enables collaborative modeling and user recommendations [11,12]. In contrast to our work, the approach builds on behavior and suggestions of other modelers. Control flow correctness issues are addressed in [13], where the authors offer continuous verification of process models during modeling. In [10] the authors study how cooperative modeling is supported by fragment-driven modeling approach. However, this paper primary focuses on describing the infrastructure for cooperative modeling, but not on the derivation of fragments (or action patterns). Gschwind et al. employ control flow patterns to accelerate business process modeling and minimize the number of modeling errors [7]. The authors develop a suggestion mechanism considering structural patterns and the model structure at hand.

Recent contributions identify a textual analysis of activity labels as an important step to improve the pragmatic quality of process models. For instance, different labeling schemata and their impact on model understanding have been analyzed in [19]. Textual labels are also used for matching and comparing process models [8,26]. Recent works by Becker et al. reuse parsing techniques from computer linguistics to efficiently identify the various parts of an activity label [4]. While we have derived the actions manually for our experiment reported in this paper, we are currently working on automating this step by using the approach taken by Becker et al.

6   Conclusion

In this paper we have addressed the challenge of assisting the designer in modeling a process. We defined the concept of action patterns, capturing co-occurrences of actions in existing process model collections. Our contribution is an approach based on association rules mining that identifies sets of actions that likely imply further actions. In this way, action patterns can be used to suggest additional activities to the modeler. Furthermore, we utilize behavioral profiles to capture behavioral relations between co-occurring actions. Therefore, we also provide information on how the additional action should be included in the process model. Our approach has been validated using the SAP Reference Model.

We assume that a mapping of an activity label to an action is given. However, derivation of actions from labels is a challenging research topic and is in the focus of our future work. Further, we analyze activity labels to derive actions only. We do not consider business objects referenced in the labels of model elements as well. While this might be regarded as a limitation, we made this design choice to identify recurring patterns holding for different business objects. Taking business objects into account offers several advantages, including object life cycle mining. A mined object life cycle is a helpful tool as it facilitates advanced modeling support. Another potential direction of the future work involves synonym recognition. Usage of thesauri, like WordNet, would allow to cluster actions that are closely related and gain stronger support for related patterns. In this context, one might also consider action hierarchies like the one developed for the MIT Process Handbook.

As process model collections are often incremented with new models, methods for action patterns derivation have to be efficient and adaptive. While in this paper derivation of action patterns relies on Apriori algorithm, there is a potential to improve the performance by substituting Apriori algorithm with a more efficient one. In addition, efficient strategies for adjusting the set of action patterns after creation of new process models have to be evaluated. Obviously, support and confidence values of existing patterns might easily be adapted. However, the detection of additional patterns, which have been ignored due to low support and confidence values before the model collection has been incremented, remains a serious issue. All these directions are rather unexplored for process models, and are on our future research agenda.

References

1. Agrawal, R., Imielinski, T., Swami, A.N.: Mining Association Rules between Sets of Items in Large Databases. In: COMAD, Washington, D.C, pp. 207–216 (1993)
2. Agrawal, R., Srikant, R.: Fast Algorithms for Mining Association Rules in Large Databases. In: VLDB, pp. 487–499. Morgan Kaufmann Publishers Inc., San Francisco (1994)
3. Alexander, C., Ishikawa, S., Silverstein, M.: A Pattern Language: Towns, Buildings, Construction. Oxford University Press, New York (1977)
4. Becker, J., Delfmann, P., Herwig, S., Lis, L., Stein, A.: Towards Increased Comparability of Conceptual Models - Enforcing Naming Conventions through Domain Thesauri and Linguistic Grammars. In: ECIS (June 2009)
5. Decker, G., Mendling, J.: Instantiation Semantics for Process Models. In: Dumas, M., Reichert, M., Shan, M.-C. (eds.) BPM 2008. LNCS, vol. 5240, pp. 164–179. Springer, Heidelberg (2008)
6. Gamma, E., Helm, R., Johnson, R., Vlissides, J.: Design Patterns. Addison-Wesley, Boston (1995)
7. Gschwind, T., Koehler, J., Wong, J.: Applying Patterns during Business Process Modeling. In: Dumas, M., Reichert, M., Shan, M.-C. (eds.) BPM 2008. LNCS, vol. 5240, pp. 4–19. Springer, Heidelberg (2008)
8. Hornung, T., Koschmider, A., Lausen, G.: Recommendation Based Process Modeling Support: Method and User Experience. In: Li, Q., Spaccapietra, S., Yu, E., Olivé, A. (eds.) ER 2008. LNCS, vol. 5231, pp. 265–278. Springer, Heidelberg (2008)

9. Keller, G., Teufel, T.: SAP(R) R/3 Process Oriented Implementation: Iterative Process Prototyping. Addison-Wesley, Reading (1998)
10. Kim, K.-H., Won, J.-K., Kim, C.-M.: A Fragment-Driven Process Modeling Methodology. In: Gervasi, O., Gavrilova, M.L., Kumar, V., Laganá, A., Lee, H.P., Mun, Y., Taniar, D., Tan, C.J.K. (eds.) ICCSA 2005. LNCS, vol. 3482, pp. 817–826. Springer, Heidelberg (2005)
11. Koschmider, A., Song, M., Reijers, H.A.: Social Software for Modeling Business Processes. In: Ardagna, D., et al. (eds.) BPM 2008 Workshops. LNBIP, vol. 17, pp. 642–653. Springer, Heidelberg (2009)
12. Koschmider, A., Song, M., Reijers, H.A.: Advanced Social Features in a Recommendation System for Process Modeling. In: Abramowicz, W. (ed.) BIS 2009. LNBIP, vol. 21, pp. 109–120. Springer, Heidelberg (2009)
13. Kühne, S., Kern, H., Gruhn, V., Laue, R.: Business Process Modelling with Continuous Validation. In: MDE4BPM, September 2008, pp. 37–48 (2008)
14. Lau, J.M., Iochpe, C., Thom, L., Reichert, M.: Discovery and Analysis of Activity Pattern Cooccurrences in Business Process Models. In: ICEIS, pp. 83–88. Springer, Heidelberg (2009)
15. Lonchamp, J.: Process Model Patterns for Collaborative Work. In: Telecoop (1998)
16. Malone, T.W., Crowston, K., Herman, G.A.: Organizing Business Knowledge: The MIT Process Handbook, 1st edn. The MIT Press, Cambridge (2003)
17. Mendling, J.: Metrics for Process Models: Empirical Foundations of Verification, Error Prediction, and Guidelines for Correctness. In: Mendling, J. (ed.) Metrics for Process Models. LNBIP, vol. 6, pp. 1–15. Springer, Heidelberg (2008)
18. Mendling, J., Recker, J.: Towards Systematic Usage of Labels and Icons in Business Process Models. In: EMMSAD, June 2008, vol. 337, pp. 1–13. CEUR Workshop Proceedings (2008)
19. Mendling, J., Reijers, H.A., Recker, J.: Activity Labeling in Process Modeling: Empirical Insights and Recommendations. Information Systems (to appear, 2009)
20. Rosemann, M.: Potential Pitfalls of Process Modeling: Part A. Business Process Management Journal 12(2), 249–254 (2006)
21. Russell, N., ter Hofstede, A.H.M., Edmond, D., van der Aalst, W.M.P.: Workflow Data Patterns. Technical Report FIT-TR-2004-01, QUT (2004)
22. Russell, N., van der Aalst, W.M.P., ter Hofstede, A.H.M., Edmond, D.: Workflow Resource Patterns. Technical Report WP 126, Eindhoven University of Technology (2004)
23. Thom, L.H., Reichert, M., Chiao, C.M., Iochpe, C., Hess, G.N.: Inventing Less, Reusing More, and Adding Intelligence to Business Process Modeling. In: Bhowmick, S.S., Küng, J., Wagner, R. (eds.) DEXA 2008. LNCS, vol. 5181, pp. 837–850. Springer, Heidelberg (2008)
24. Tran, H.N., Coulette, B., Dong, B.T.: Broadening the Use of Process Patterns for Modeling Processes. In: SEKE, July 2007, pp. 57–62. Knowledge Systems Institute Graduate School (2007)
25. van der Aalst, W.M.P., ter Hofstede, A.H.M., Kiepuszewski, B., Barros, A.P.: Workflow Patterns. Distrib. Parallel Databases 14(1), 5–51 (2003)
26. van Dongen, B., Dijkman, R., Mendling, J.: Measuring Similarity between Business Process Models. In: Bellahsène, Z., Léonard, M. (eds.) CAiSE 2008. LNCS, vol. 5074, pp. 450–464. Springer, Heidelberg (2008)
27. Weidlich, M., Mendling, J., Weske, M.: Computation of Behavioural Profiles of Process Models. Technical report, HPI (June 2009),
http://bpt.hpi.uni-potsdam.de/pub/Public/MatthiasWeidlich/
behavioural_profiles_report.pdf

Artifact-Centric Workflow Dominance

Diego Calvanese[1], Giuseppe De Giacomo[2], Richard Hull[3], and Jianwen Su[4]

[1] KRDB Research Centre
Free University of Bozen-Bolzano
I-39100 Bolzano, Italy
calvanese@inf.unibz.it

[2] Dipartimento di Informatica e Sistemistica
SAPIENZA Università di Roma
I-00185 Roma, Italy
degiacomo@dis.uniroma1.it

[3] IBM T.J. Watson Research Center
Yorktown Heights, NY, U.S.A.
hull@us.ibm.com

[4] Department of Computer Science
University of California at Santa Barbara
Santa Barbara, CA, U.S.A.
su@cs.ucsb.edu

Abstract. In this paper we initiate a study on comparing artifact-centric workflow schemas, in terms of the ability of one schema to emulate the possible behaviors of another schema. Artifact-centric workflows are centered around "business artifacts", which contain both a *data schema*, which can hold all of the data about a key business entity as it passes through a workflow, along with a *lifecycle schema*, which specifies the possible ways that the entity can evolve through the workflow. In this paper, the data schemas for artifact types are finite sets of attribute-value pairs, and the lifecycle schemas are specified as sets of condition-action rules, where the condition is evaluated against the current snapshot of the artifact, and where the actions are external *services* (or "tasks"), which read a subset of the attributes of an artifact, which write onto a subset of the attributes, and which are performed by an entity outside of the workflow system (often a human). The services are also characterized by pre- and post-conditions, in the spirit of semantic web services. To compare artifact-centric workflows, we introduce the notion of "dominance", which intuitively captures the fact that all executions of a workflow can be emulated by a second workflow. (In the current paper, the emulation is focused only on the starting and ending snapshots of the possible enactments of the two workflows.) In fact, dominance is a parametric notion that depends on the characterization of the policies that govern the execution of the services invoked by the workflows. In this paper, we study in detail the case of "absolute dominance", in which this policy places no constraints on the possible service executions. We provide decidability and complexity results for bounded and unbounded workflow executions in the cases where the values in an artifact range over an infinite structure, such as the integers, the rationals, or the reals, possibly with order, addition, or multiplication.

L. Baresi, C.-H. Chi, and J. Suzuki (Eds.): ICSOC-ServiceWave 2009, LNCS 5900, pp. 130–143, 2009.

1 Introduction

The importance of automation of workflow and business processes continues to increase, with a world economy moving towards increased globalization and the drive for more efficiency. A fundamental problem in workflow management is to understand when one workflow (schema) can emulate another one. At a practical level, this is important for workflow evolution and workflow integration, where one might need to verify that the new workflow can faithfully emulate the old workflow(s). Emulation has been studied in considerable depth in the form of simulation for process algebras, which can be viewed as an abstraction of process-centric workflow models. In the past several years a data-centric approach to modeling workflows has emerged, in which both data and process are tightly coupled in the basic building blocks of workflows. One class of data-centric workflow models is centered around "business artifacts" [12,16], which are augmented data records that correspond to key business-relevant entities, their lifecycles, and how/when services (a.k.a. tasks) are invoked on them. This "artifact-centric" approach provides a simple and robust structure for workflow, and has been demonstrated in practice to permit efficiencies in business transformation [2,3]. In the artifact-centric approach obviously the process is of interest, but differently from process-centric workflows the data play a key role.

This paper provides a first investigation into workflow emulation in the context of artifact-centric workflows. In particular, we develop a basic framework for characterizing when one artifact-centric workflow "dominates" another one, and then provide decidability and complexity results for bounded and unbounded workflow executions for a particular kind of dominance, called "absolute dominance."

In our formal model, which follows the spirit of [4,7], the artifact "data schema" is a set of attribute-value pairs, which is used to hold relevant information about the artifact as it passes through the workflow. The values range over an infinite structure, such as the integers, the rationals, or the reals, possibly with order, addition, or multiplication. The "lifecycle schema", which is used to specify the possible ways that the artifact can pass through the workflow, is specified as a set of condition-action rules, where the condition is evaluated against the current snapshot of the artifact, and where the actions are *services* (a.k.a. "tasks"), which read a subset of the attributes of an artifact, which write onto a subset of the attributes, and which are performed by an entity outside of the workflow system (often a human). Similar to the context of semantic web services [11], the behaviors of the services used here are characterized using pre- and post-conditions. The notion of dominance studied in the current paper focuses on the initial and final snapshots of the artifact as it passes through a workflow; in particular, workflow $\mathcal{W}_1$ dominates workflow $\mathcal{W}_2$ if for each execution of $\mathcal{W}_2$ on a given initial snapshot, there is an execution of $\mathcal{W}_1$ on that initial snapshot that yields the same final snapshot. This notion of dominance is in fact a parametric notion that depends on the characterization of the policies of the performers that execute the services invoked by the workflows. In this paper, we study in detail the case of "absolute dominance", in which this policy places no constraints on the possible executions. Alternative policies, which are the topic of future studies, might require that the service executions be deterministic, or that they be generic in the sense of database queries.

This paper develops results concerning absolute dominance for several variations of the underlying workflow model, based primarily on logical structure of the underlying domain of values. In the case of bounded-length executions, deciding absolute dominance can be reduced to first-order logic reasoning, which yields decidability if the underlying logical structure is, the integers with addition ($+$) and order ($<$), the rationals with addition and order, or the real closed field. For the unbounded case, we show that dominance is decidable if the logical structure has no function symbols and permits quantifier elimination, but it is undecidable for the cases of integers, rationals, or reals mentioned above.

Additional decidability results are obtained by focusing on FO logic/structures that have equality, order, and no function symbols. We borrow techniques from the powerful framework of Datalog with order constraints [9] to obtain decidability of absolute dominance in this case. In particular, we show decidability of absolute dominance for the cases of the integers with discrete order, and for rationals and reals with dense order. In all of these cases, we show that decidability is in exponential time.

Organizationally, Section 2 defines the formal model of artifact-centric workflow used in the paper, Section 3 defines the general notion of dominance, and absolute dominance in particular. Section 4 presents the theoretical results and Section 5 provides brief conclusions.

2   Artifact-Centric Workflows

In this paper we make use of a specific form of artifact-centric workflows, which we introduce in the following. We use a first-order logic $\mathcal{L}$ with equality, with predicates, constants, and possibly function symbols, over interpreted structures with a non-empty, possibly infinite domain. Examples of such interpreted structures are a dense or discrete order ($<$), Presburger arithmetic, or a real (closed) field. We will denote a structure $\mathbb{S}$ with domain $\Delta^{\mathbb{S}}$ over function symbols $f_1, f_2, \ldots$, and predicate symbols $p_1, p_2 \ldots$, as $\mathbb{S} = (\Delta^{\mathbb{S}}, f_1, f_2 \ldots, p_1, p_2 \ldots)$. We will assume to have one constant for each element of $\Delta^{\mathbb{S}}$, hence we usually omit constants (i.e., 0-ary functions) in the list of function symbols.

We assume an infinite alphabet $\mathcal{AN}$ of *attribute names*, which are also used as variables in logic formulas in $\mathcal{L}$ interpreted over $\mathbb{S}$. In the following, we use a, b for attribute names, c, d for values from the domain, and x, y, z for generic variables in formulas, all possibly with subscripts. Given a structure $\mathbb{S}$ with domain $\Delta^{\mathbb{S}}$, an *attribute-map* (w.r.t. $\mathbb{S}$), shortened as *amap*, is a total function from a finite set $X \subseteq \mathcal{AN}$ of attribute names into $\Delta^{\mathbb{S}} \cup \{\bot\}$, where the special symbol $\bot$ (which is not in $\Delta^{\mathbb{S}}$) has the intended meaning that the attribute is "undefined". Specifically, to represent that an attribute has an undefined value in an amap, i.e., has value equal to $\bot$, in formulas we shall use a syntactic shorthand: we introduce for each attribute name a an additional attribute $\bar{a}$, and use $\bar{a} = 0$ to indicate that a is undefined, where 0 (zero) is a distinguished constant of $\mathcal{L}$. Then, in formulas, we write $a = \bot$ as a shorthand for $\bar{a} = 0$ and, e.g., $R(a_1, \ldots, a_n)$ as a shorthand for $\bar{a}_1 \neq 0 \wedge \cdots \wedge \bar{a}_n \neq 0 \wedge R(a_1, \ldots, a_n)$, where R is any predicate symbol, including equality.

Definition 1. *An* artifact (data schema) *is a non-empty set $\mathcal{A}$ of attribute names. The names are partitioned into the following three sets:*
- *the set $I_{\mathcal{A}}$ of* input *attributes,*
- *the set $T_{\mathcal{A}}$ of* temporary *attributes, and*
- *the nonempty set $O_{\mathcal{A}}$ of* output *attributes.*

A snapshot *σ of $\mathcal{A}$ is an amap whose domain is $\mathcal{A}$. σ is* initial *if $\sigma(a) \neq \bot$ for each $a \in I_{\mathcal{A}}$ and $\sigma(a) = \bot$ for each $a \in \mathcal{A} \setminus I_{\mathcal{A}}$. σ is* complete *if $\sigma(a) \neq \bot$ for each $a \in O_{\mathcal{A}}$.*

If $\mathcal{A}$ is an artifact, σ a snapshot of $\mathcal{A}$, and $X \subseteq \mathcal{A}$, then the *projection* of σ onto X, denoted $\sigma|_X$, is the function from X to $\Delta^{\mathbb{S}}$ defined by $\sigma|_X(x) = \sigma(x)$, for each $x \in X$.

A fundamental concept in the workflow model is that an artifact gets modified by a service in a single step (see later). To model this, we also allow *primed* attribute names as variables in our logic, which are used to represent the artifact after the modification. Let φ be a formula in which each free variable is an unprimed or primed attribute name. Let X contain the set of attribute names that occur unprimed in φ and Y' contain the set of attribute names that occur primed in φ. Let σ_X be an amap with domain X and $\sigma_{Y'}$ be an amap with domain Y'. In this case, $(\sigma_X, \sigma_{Y'})$ *models* φ *in* $\mathbb{S}$, denoted $(\sigma_X, \sigma_{Y'}) \models_{\mathbb{S}} \varphi$ if φ is true in $\mathbb{S}$ under the assignment that maps each unprimed attribute name $x \in X$ to $\sigma_X(x)$, and each primed attribute name $y' \in Y'$ to $\sigma_{Y'}(y')$.

It is clear that the notion of a pair (σ, σ') of snapshots over an artifact $\mathcal{A}$ modeling a formula φ can be used whenever the set of attribute names occurring in φ is contained in $\mathcal{A}$. If one thinks of σ as a snapshot preceding σ', then we are following the tradition of using unprimed variables to indicate a "current" state and primed variables to indicate a "next" state.

We introduce now services, which are the atomic units that progress a system.

Definition 2. *Given an artifact $\mathcal{A}$, a* service *(specification) for $\mathcal{A}$ is a 4-tuple $S = (I_S, O_S, \delta_S, \xi_S)$ where*

- $I_S \subseteq I_{\mathcal{A}} \cup T_{\mathcal{A}}$ *is called the* input *of S.*
- $O_S \subseteq T_{\mathcal{A}} \cup O_{\mathcal{A}}$ *is called the* output *of S.*
- δ_S, *the* pre-condition *of S, is a formula in $\mathcal{L}$ where each free variable is an unprimed attribute name from I_S.*
- ξ_S, *the* post-condition *of S, is a formula in $\mathcal{L}$ where each free variable is an unprimed attribute name from I_S or a primed attribute name from O_S.*

The frame formula *of S is the formula $\Phi_S \equiv \bigwedge_{a \in \mathcal{A} \setminus O_S} (a = a')$.*

Intuitively, we require that a service takes its inputs either from the inputs to the workflow (i.e., the input attributes $I_{\mathcal{A}}$ of the artifact), or from the temporary attributes T_A of the artifact. The latter can be written by a service, together with the outputs of the workflow (i.e., the output attributes O_A of the artifact).

Definition 3. *Given an artifact A and a service $S = (I_S, O_S, \delta_S, \xi_S)$ for A, an execution of S is a pair (σ, σ') of snapshots of A such that $(\sigma, \sigma') \models_S \delta_S \wedge \xi_S \wedge \Phi_S$.*

Note that σ is in fact independent from σ' and that the frame formula Φ_S requires that in an execution (σ, σ') of S, each attribute not in O_S has in σ' the same value that it had in σ. Also, executions are in general *non-deterministic*, i.e., a service may have two executions (σ, σ') and (σ, σ''), with $\sigma' \neq \sigma''$.

We are interested in sequences of service executions that, from an initial snapshot of an artifact A may lead to a complete snapshot, i.e., one where all output attributes of A are defined. To formalize this notion, we first introduce the notion of *(artifact-centric) pre-workflow (schema)*, which is simply a pair $P = (A, S)$, where S a finite set of services for the artifact A. Each (initial, complete) snapshot of A is also an (initial, complete, resp.) snapshot of P. We can then provide the following definition of enactment.

Definition 4. *Given a pre-workflow $P = (A, S)$, an enactment E of P (of length n) is a sequence*

$$\sigma_0, S_1, \sigma_1, \ldots, S_n, \sigma_n$$

where

- *σ_0 is an initial snapshot of P,*
- *σ_i is a snapshot of P, for $i \in [1..n]$,*
- *$S_i \in S$, for $i \in [1..n]$,*
- *(σ_{i-1}, σ_i) is an execution of S_i, for $i \in [1..n]$.*

The enactment E is complete if σ_n is complete. The I/O-pair of a complete enactment E is the pair $IO(E) = (\sigma_0|_{I_A}, \sigma_n|_{O_A})$.

Observe that $\sigma_0|_{I_A} = \sigma_n|_{I_A}$ since the input attributes I_A of the artifact cannot be changed by services (see Definition 2)

We now introduce business rules, which specify the conditions under which a service may be executed. Given a pre-workflow $P = (A, S)$, a *(business) rule* ρ for P is an expression of the form "(**if** α **allow** S)" where α is a formula in which each free variable is an unprimed attribute name from A, and $S \in S$. With this notion in place, we are ready to provide the definition of artifact-centric workflows.

Definition 5. *Given a structure $\mathbb{S}$, a(n) (artifact-centric) workflow (schema) over $\mathbb{S}$ is a triple $W = (A, S, R)$ where (A, S) is a pre-workflow and R is a finite set of rules for (A, S). An enactment of W is an enactment of its pre-workflow (A, S)*

$$\sigma_0, S_1, \sigma_1, \ldots, S_n, \sigma_n$$

*such that for each $i \in [1..n]$, there is a rule "(**if** α **allow** S_i)" in R where $\sigma_{i-1} \models_S \alpha$.*

In the following, we will omit the specification of the structure $\mathbb{S}$ when it is clear from the context.

3   Dominance

Intuitively, services are executed by a *performer*. Performers are often humans, but they could also be software components. In this paper we do not address different "roles" that different performers might have. Performers choose how a service is executed. Indeed, as mentioned for a given service S and a snapshot σ there may be executions (σ, σ') and (σ, σ''), with $\sigma' \neq \sigma''$. This non-determinism corresponds to the possibility that the performer may execute the same service on the same inputs differently. Intuitively, this might be because the performer is exercising human judgement, or because there is information about the snapshot σ that is not modeled within the formal system, or both.

In order to capture formally the above intuitions on performers, we introduce the notion of a "performance policy", which specifies the possible behaviors of the performers of the services of a workflow. Given a set of attributes X, We denote with $\mathcal{M}[X]$ the set of amaps over X.

Definition 6. *A performance policy for a workflow $\mathcal{W} = (\mathcal{A}, \mathcal{S}, \mathcal{R})$ is a function π whose domain is $\mathcal{S}$. The value of π on $S = (I_S, O_S, \delta_S, \xi_S) \in \mathcal{S}$, denoted $\pi[S]$, is a subset of $\mathcal{M}[I_S] \times \mathcal{M}[O_S]$ such that, if $(\mu, \nu) \in \pi[S]$, then $\mu \models_S \delta_S$ and $(\mu, \nu) \models_S \xi_S$. An execution (σ, σ') of S is* compliant *with π if $(\sigma|_{I_S}, \sigma'|_{O_S}) \in \pi[S]$. An enactment of $\mathcal{W}$ is compliant with π if each execution in the enactment is compliant with π.*

With the notion of performance policy at hand, we can now compare two artifact-centric workflows. In particular, we are interested in comparing two workflows in terms of how values for the input attributes are mapped into values for the output attributes. Also, we ignore the order in which the output attributes are written in one enactment versus the other enactment. For this, we say that two workflows $\mathcal{W}_1 = (\mathcal{A}_1, \mathcal{S}_1, \mathcal{R}_1)$ and $\mathcal{W}_2 = (\mathcal{A}_2, \mathcal{S}_2, \mathcal{R}_2)$ are *compatible* if $I_{\mathcal{A}_1} = I_{\mathcal{A}_2}$ and $O_{\mathcal{A}_1} = O_{\mathcal{A}_2}$. Note that the temporary attributes ($T_{\mathcal{A}_1}$ and $T_{\mathcal{A}_2}$) may be different.

Definition 7. *Let $\mathcal{W}_1 = (\mathcal{A}_1, \mathcal{S}_1, \mathcal{R}_1)$ and $\mathcal{W}_2 = (\mathcal{A}_2, \mathcal{S}_2, \mathcal{R}_2)$ be two compatible workflows and Π a class of performance policies. Then $\mathcal{W}_1$ is Π-dominated by $\mathcal{W}_2$, denoted $\mathcal{W}_1 \preceq_\Pi \mathcal{W}_2$, if the following holds. For each perfomance policy $\pi_1 \in \Pi$ for $\mathcal{W}_1$ there exists a performance policy $\pi_2 \in \Pi$ for $\mathcal{W}_2$ such that: for every enactment E_1 of $\mathcal{W}_1$ compliant with π_1 there is an enactment E_2 of $\mathcal{W}_2$ compliant with π_2 such that $IO(E_1) = IO(E_2)$.*

We consider also the case where we compare two workflows only w.r.t. enactments of bounded length. To this purpose we introduce the notion of k-*dominance* between two compatible workflows, denoted $\mathcal{W}_1 \preceq_\Pi^k \mathcal{W}_2$, whose definition is analogous to the one above, except that we consider only enactments whose length is $\leqslant k$.

This framework permits us to study a variety of behaviours of performers, i.e., of performance policies, including, e.g., policies where $\pi[S]$ is required to satisfy certain properties, such as being computable or tractable. In this paper we concentrate on the most general performance policy, which states that the performers may use *any* execution of a service within the workflow (i.e., any execution that satisfies the pre- and post-conditions of the service), without further restrictions. We call this notion of dominance *absolute dominance*.

4   Absolute Dominance

We study now the problem of checking absolute dominance and absolute k-dominance. Let Abs denote the class of all performance policies. We say that $\mathcal{W}_1$ is *(k-)dominated absolutely* by $\mathcal{W}_2$ if $\mathcal{W}_1 \preceq_{Abs} \mathcal{W}_2$ (resp., $\mathcal{W}_1 \preceq^k_{Abs} \mathcal{W}_2$).

4.1   Enactments of Bounded Length

We deal first with the case of bounded absolute dominance, and show that we can characterize in a closed form the set of realizable I/O-pairs.

Lemma 1. *Let* $\mathcal{W} = (\mathcal{A}, \mathcal{S}, \mathcal{R})$ *be a workflow with service pre- and post-conditions and rule conditions expressed in FOL with equality. Let k be a positive integer. Then there is a FOL formula* $\Psi^k_{\mathcal{W}}$ *whose free variables are the input* ($I_{\mathcal{A}}$) *and output* ($O_{\mathcal{A}}$) *attributes of* $\mathcal{A}$, *that characterizes the set of all I/O-pairs of complete enactments of* $\mathcal{W}$ *compliant with Abs, for enactments whose length is bounded by k.*

Proof. We consider all possible sequences of services (possibly with repetitions) that may appear in enactments of length $n \leqslant k$, and characterize their I/O-pairs by means of a FOL formula.

Let $p = S_1, \ldots, S_n$ be such a sequence of services. Then, for $i \in [1..n]$, let

$$\alpha^p_i = \left(\bigvee_{(\text{if } \alpha \text{ allow } S_i) \in \mathcal{R}} \alpha\right) [a/a^{i-1} \mid a \in \mathcal{A}],$$
$$\delta^p_i = \delta_{S_i}[a/a^{i-1} \mid a \in \mathcal{A}],$$
$$\xi^p_i = \xi_{S_i}[a/a^{i-1} \mid a \in I_{S_i}][a'/a^i \mid a \in O_{S_i}],$$
$$\Phi^p_i = \Phi_{S_i}[a/a^{i-1} \mid a \in (\mathcal{A} \setminus O_{S_i})][a'/a^i \mid a \in (\mathcal{A} \setminus O_{S_i})],$$

where $\varphi[a/b \mid a \in X]$ denotes the formula obtained from φ by renaming each (occurrence of) attribute $a \in X$ to b. Using such formulas, we build inductively, for each $i \in [0..n]$, the "cumulative post-condition", denoted $\hat{\xi}^p_i$ as follows:

- $\hat{\xi}^p_i = true$,
- $\hat{\xi}^p_i = \exists\{a^{i-1} \mid a \in \mathcal{A}\}(\hat{\xi}^p_{i-1} \wedge \alpha^p_i \wedge \delta^p_i \wedge \xi^p_i \wedge \Phi^p_i)$,   for $i \in [1..n]$.

Note that $\hat{\xi}^p_i$, for $i \in [1..n]$, is a formula whose free variables are among $\{a^i \mid a \in \mathcal{A}\}$. It remains to project away the temporary attributes of the last step, and to impose that all output attributes are defined. Hence, we define

$$\Psi^p_{\mathcal{W}} = \left(\exists\{a^n \mid a \in T_{\mathcal{A}}\}(\hat{\xi}^p_n \wedge \bigwedge_{a \in O_{\mathcal{A}}} a^n \neq \bot)\right)[a^n/a \mid a \in I_{\mathcal{A}} \cup O_{\mathcal{A}}].$$

By quantifying over all possible sequences of services of length up to k, we obtain the desired formula

$$\Psi_W^k = \bigvee_{\substack{S_1, \ldots, S_n, \\ \text{for } S_i \in \mathcal{S}, i \in [1..n], n \leqslant k}} \Psi_W^{S_1, \ldots, S_n}.$$

It is not difficult to prove by induction on k that Ψ_W^k characterizes the set of all I/O-pairs of complete enactments of W compliant with Abs, for enactments whose length is bounded by k.   □

Using the above characterization of I/O-pairs, we can determine absolute k-dominance $W_1 \preceq_{Abs}^k W_2$ between two compatible workflows $W_1 = (\mathcal{A}_1, \mathcal{S}_1, \mathcal{R}_1)$ and $W_2 = (\mathcal{A}_2, \mathcal{S}_2, \mathcal{R}_2)$, where $I = I_{\mathcal{A}_1} = I_{\mathcal{A}_2}$ and $O = O_{\mathcal{A}_1} = O_{\mathcal{A}_2}$, by simply checking whether the following formula is true in $\mathbb{S}$:

$$\forall \{a \in I \cup O\}(\Psi_{W_1}^k \rightarrow \Psi_{W_2}^k). \tag{$\star$}$$

Hence, in all those cases where FOL over $\mathbb{S}$ is decidable, we obtain decidability of absolute k-dominance for workflows over $\mathbb{S}$.

Theorem 1. *For each positive integer k, absolute k-dominance between workflows over $\mathbb{S}$ is decidable for the following structures:*

1. $(\mathbb{Z}, +, <)$, *integers with additions.*
2. $(\mathbb{Q}, +, <)$, *rational numbers with additions.*
3. $(\mathbb{R}, +, \times, <)$, *real numbers with additions and multiplications (the real closed field).*

Proof (Sketch). By Lemma 1, absolute k-dominance between two workflows holds if and only if the formula shown in Equation $(\star)$ is true in the underlying structure. Thus the decidability results follow immediately from the decidability results for Presburger arithmetic [13] (Case 1) and the real closed field [17] (Cases 2 and 3).   □

We discuss briefly the complexity of the decisions problems. Given two workflows of length ℓ, the formula in Equation $(\star)$ has length at most $O(k^{k+1}\ell)$. For the domain of integers with additions, since the complexity of Presburger arithmetic is double exponential [6], it follows that the absolute k-dominance problem has complexity double expential in ℓ and triple exponential in k. On the other hand, since the complexity of the FO theory for the real closed field is exponential [1,14], the dominance problem is exponential in ℓ and double exponential in k. Note that the above analysis puts coarse upper bounds in the most general situations. If we focus on restricted classes, such as services only having quantifier free formulas as pre- and post-conditions, and put bounds on the number of temporary variables they can use, the complexity upper bounds can be refined.

$$ioPairs(I, O_1) \leftarrow initial(I, T, O), transStar(I, T, O, I_1, T_1, O_1),$$
$$complete(I_1, T_1, O_1).$$
$$initial(I, T, O) \leftarrow defined(I), undefined(T, O).$$
$$complete(I, T, O) \leftarrow defined(O).$$
$$transStar(I, T, O, I, T, O).$$
$$transStar(I, T, O, I_2, T_2, O_2) \leftarrow trans(I, T, O, I_1, T_1, O_1),$$
$$transStar(I_1, T_1, O_1, I_2, T_2, O_2).$$
$$trans(I, T, O, I_1, T_1, O_1) \leftarrow transByS_1(I, T, O, I_1, T_1, O_1).$$
$$\dots$$
$$trans(I, T, O, I_1, T_1, O_1) \leftarrow transByS_n(I, T, O, I_1, T_1, O_1).$$
$$transByS_i(I, T, O, I_1, T_1, O_1) \leftarrow \delta_{S_i}(I, T, O), rulesAllowS_i(I, T, O),$$
$$nextSnapshotByS_i(I, T, O, I_1, T_1, O_1).$$
$$nextSnapshotByS_i(I, T, O, I_1, T_1, O_1) \leftarrow \xi_{S_i}(I, T, O, I_1, T_1, O_1), \Phi_{S_i}(I, T, O, I_1, T_1, O_1).$$
$$rulesAllowS_i(I, T, O) \leftarrow \alpha_i^1(I, T, O).$$
$$\dots$$
$$rulesAllowS_i(I, T, O) \leftarrow \alpha_i^{m_i}(I, T, O).$$

Fig. 1. Constraint Datalog program $P_\mathcal{W}$ capturing the I/O-pairs of a workflow $\mathcal{W}$ for enactments of unbounded length

4.2   Enactments of Unbounded Length

We now turn to enactments of unbounded length. Oone might think that when the FO logic over the structure $\mathbb{S}$ admits quantifier elimination, the characterization in Lemma 1 could be extended to enactments of unbounded length. In general, it is not clear how this can be possibly done. In fact, the following can be established.

Theorem 2. *Absolute dominance between two workflows is undecidable for the following structures:*

1. $(\mathbb{Z}, +, <)$, *integers with additions.*
2. $(\mathbb{Q}, +, <)$, *rational numbers with additions.*
3. $(\mathbb{R}, +, \times, <)$, *real numbers with additions and multiplications (the real closed field).*

Proof (Sketch). The proofs are accomplished by reductions from Hilbert's 10th problem (computing integer roots of polynomials with integer coefficients), which is known to be undecidable (see [10]). Roughly, the idea of the reduction is to guess potential (integer) solutions (with a simple increment service) and then verify if they are indeed solutions. Over the given structures, one can easily compute multiplications with repeated additions. Thus, the verfication can also be expressed with a workflow. □

In the following, we explore more restricted FO logic/structures that consists of equality and order and without any functions. We borrow techniques from the powerful framework of Datalog with order constraints [9] to show that absolute dominance can still be decidable for these structures.

Specifically, we focus on workflows whose service pre- and post-conditions and rule conditions are quantifier free formulas over equality $(=)$ and order $(<)$ constraints. Given a workflow $\mathcal{W} = (\mathcal{A}, \mathcal{S}, \mathcal{R})$, we construct a constraint Datalog program $P_\mathcal{W}$ as shown in Figure 1, which views service pre- and post-conditions and rule conditions as constraint relations [9]. In the specification of the program, we have assumed that $\mathcal{S} = \{S_1, \ldots, S_n\}$, and that for $i \in [1..n]$, (if α_i^1 allow S_i), ..., (if $\alpha_i^{m_i}$ allow S_i) are all rules having S_i as consequent. Such a program provides a characterization of the set of all I/O-pairs of $\mathcal{W}$ under *Abs* for enactments of unbounded length. We briefly comment on the rules of $P_\mathcal{W}$.

- $ioPairs(I, O_1) \leftarrow initial(I, T, O), transStar(I, T, O, I_1, T_1, O_1),$
  $\qquad\qquad\qquad complete(I_1, T_1, O_1).$
  Generates all I/O-pairs of complete compliant enactments. Here, I, T, and O stand respectively for the input, temporary, and output attributes of the artifact in the initial snapshot. Similarly, I_1, T_1, and O_1 stand for the same attributes in the complete snapshot at the end of the enactment.

- $initial(I, T, O) \leftarrow defined(I), undefined(T, O).$
  States when a snapshot is initial, i.e., all input attributes are defined, and all temporary and output attributes are undefined.

- $complete(I, T, O) \leftarrow defined(O).$
  States when a snapshot is complete, i.e., all output attributes are defined.

- $transStar(I, T, O, I, T, O).$
  $transStar(I, T, O, I_2, T_2, O_2) \leftarrow trans(I, T, O, I_1, T_1, O_1),$
  $\qquad\qquad\qquad\qquad transStar(I_1, T_1, O_1, I_2, T_2, O_2).$
  Compute the reflexive transitive closure of *trans*, defined below.

- $trans(I, T, O, I_1, T_1, O_1) \leftarrow transByS_1(I, T, O, I_1, T_1, O_1).$
  $\qquad\qquad\qquad\qquad \cdots$
  $trans(I, T, O, I_1, T_1, O_1) \leftarrow transByS_n(I, T, O, I_1, T_1, O_1).$
  State that transition can be made by (and only by) services.

- $transByS_i(I, T, O, I_1, T_1, O_1) \leftarrow \delta_{S_i}(I, T, O), rulesAllowS_i(I, T, O),$
  $\qquad\qquad\qquad\qquad\qquad nextSnapshotByS_i(I, T, O, I_1, T_1, O_1).$
  States that a transition is made by service S_i when its preconditions hold and the rules allow S_i to execute. The service produces the next snapshot.

- $nextSnapshotByS_i(I, T, O, I_1, T_1, O_1) \leftarrow \xi_{S_i}(I, T, O, I_1, T_1, O_1),$
  $\qquad\qquad\qquad\qquad\qquad\qquad \Phi_{S_i}(I, T, O, I_1, T_1, O_1).$
  States that the execution of S_i produces the next snapshot on the basis of the service post-conditions and its frame formula. Note that ξ_{S_i} and Φ_{S_i} together constrain all variables I_1, T_1, O_1 w.r.t. I, T, and O, either with effect ξ_{S_i} or with the frame formula Φ_{S_i}.

- $rulesAllowS_i(I, T, O) \leftarrow \alpha_i^1(I, T, O).$
  $\qquad\qquad\qquad \cdots$
  $rulesAllowS_i(I, T, O) \leftarrow \alpha_i^{m_i}(I, T, O).$
  State that S_i is allowed to be executed.

We can show the following property regarding P_W.

Lemma 2. *Given a workflow* $W = (\mathcal{A}, \mathcal{S}, \mathcal{R})$ *over* $\mathbb{S}$, *let* P_W *be the constraint Datalog program constructed from* W *as specified above. Then an I/O-pair* (σ_I, σ_O) *is an I/O-pair of a complete enactment of* W *if and only if* (σ_I, σ_O) *is returned by the above constraint Datalog program when it is evaluated over* $\mathbb{S}$.

Proof (Sketch). The proof can be done via an induction argument on the length of the enactment producing the I/O-pair.   □

We note here that the above construction is rather general, and that the resulting Datalog program may not always terminate when the logic language includes at least one function symbol, regardless of whether the language/structure admits quantifier elimination.

   We now exploit results on constraint Datalog with order constraints that state, for some specific structures $\mathbb{S}$, that a constraint Datalog program P can be evaluated in closed form over $\mathbb{S}$ to produce a FOL formula φ_P over $\mathbb{S}$ (with the output variables of P as free variables). The resulting FOL formula is in fact equivalent to the Datalog program [9,15]. Specifically, from the results in [9,15] it follows that the program P_W is equivalent to a formula of $\mathcal{L}$ over the structure $\mathbb{S}$ having I and O_1 as free variables, in the cases where the logic $\mathcal{L}$ is FOL with equality, and $\mathbb{S}$ is a dense order over the rationals or reals (with all rationals as constants), or a linear order over the integers (with all integers as constants). Hence, extending Lemma 2, we obtain the following result.

Lemma 3. *Let* $W = (\mathcal{A}, \mathcal{S}, \mathcal{R})$ *be a workflow over a structure* $\mathbb{S}$ *with service pre- and post-conditions and rule conditions expressed as quantifier-free formulas in FOL. For each of the following structures, there is a quantifier-free FOL-formula* Ψ_W *whose free variables are the input* $(I_\mathcal{A})$ *and output* $(O_\mathcal{A})$ *attributes of* $\mathcal{A}$, *that characterizes the set of all I/O-pairs of complete enactments of* W *compliant with Abs:*

- $(\mathbb{Z}, <)$, *integers with the discrete order.*
- $(\mathbb{Q}, <)$, *rational numbers with the dense order.*
- $(\mathbb{R}, <)$, *real numbers with the dense order.*

Proof (Sketch). Clearly, for each service S, we can construct a constraint relation (quantifier-free formula in disjunctive normal form) [9] that represents its set of input and output pairs allowed by the pre- and post-conditions. Similarly, each rule condition can also be represented as a constraint relation. Let the constraint database consist of the constraint relations representing services and rule conditions. The Datalog program constructed above can then be evaluated as a query against the constraint database. Results from [9,15] state that the query answer can be computed effectively and represented as a constraint relation. The constraint relation is in fact a quantifier-free FOL formula.   □

For each structure listed in Lemma 3, we can proceed as for the case of bounded enactments, and exploit the formulas $\Psi_{\mathcal{W}_1}$ and $\Psi_{\mathcal{W}_2}$ to rephrase, also for unbounded enactments, absolute dominance between two workflows $\mathcal{W}_1$ and $\mathcal{W}_2$ over $\mathbb{S}$ in terms of evaluation over $\mathbb{S}$ of the FOL formula

$$\forall \{a \in I \cup O\}(\Psi_{\mathcal{W}_1} \to \Psi_{\mathcal{W}_2}).$$

From the decidability of FOL with equality over $\mathbb{S}$, we get the following result.

Theorem 3. *Absolute dominance between workflows over $\mathbb{S}$ is decidable in the following cases:*

- *$(\mathbb{Z}, <)$, integers with discrete order.*
- *$(\mathbb{Q}, <)$, rational numbers with dense order.*
- *$(\mathbb{R}, <)$, real numbers with dense order.*

The argument for the above theorem is similar to Theorem 1. We now briefly discuss the complexity of the above decision problems. Note that the query evaluation of the Datalog program can be done in exponential time and the size of the constraint relations that represent all possible enactments are of exponential size in the terms of the input workflow [9,15]. Applying known complexity of results in logic, checking the FOL formula that characterizes the dominance would add one additional level of exponentiation (in the cases of $(\mathbb{R}, <)$ and $(\mathbb{Q}, <)$) or two additional levels of exponentiation (in the case of $(\mathbb{Z}, <)$). However, this complexity for all three cases can be improved to overall single exponential time; we outline the algorithms in the following.

We call a conjunction of constraints *primitive* if it is satisfiable but not logically implied by but not equivalent to another conjunction. It is easy to see that for a given (finite) number of variables and a given finite set of constants, the number of pairwise non-equivalent primitive constraints is also finite (but exponential in terms of the total number of variables and constants).

For a given pair of workflows $\mathcal{W}_1, \mathcal{W}_2$, let V be the set of constants occurring in either $\mathcal{W}_1$ or $\mathcal{W}_2$. We convert the results of the Datalog program for $\mathcal{W}_1$ and $\mathcal{W}_2$ into two sets of primitive conjunctions of constraints, for $\mathcal{W}_1$ and $\mathcal{W}_2$, resp., of form "$x\theta v$" or "$x\theta y$" where v is in V and θ is either "$=$" or "$<$". We then remove each unsatisfiable primitive conjunction, which can be done in PTIME [8]. It can be shown that dominance holds for the workflows iff the containment of two sets of primitive conjunctions holds. Since the number of primitive conjunctions is exponential in the size of input, so is the complexity of the algorithms.

5   Conclusions

In this paper we have addressed the problem of comparing artifact-centric workflows by introducing a general notion of dominance between workflows. Such a notion is parametric with respect to a class of policies adopted by the performers of the services that are invoked by the workflow. Here we have focused on the most general type of performers, which may use any execution of a service within the workflow, resulting in the notion of "absolute dominance". We and have provided decidability and complexity results for this case.

The framework and results reported in this paper provide a basis and starting point for a rich study of dominance between artifact-centric workflows, and leave many questions yet to be explored. As noted above, our notion of dominance is focused only on the initial and final snapshots of a workflow execution; it would be useful to understand a richer notion of dominance that incorporates the order in which output values of the workflow execution are created. Also, the model used here assumes that all relevant data is held within the artifact. A useful extension would be to study the natural case in which there is also an external, basically fixed database that the conditions can refer to (for example, in the spirit of [5]). It is also of interest to study other types of performers, characterized by restrictions on the policy they may adopt. A notable case is the one where the performance policy is a deterministic function from the input attributes to the output attributes of the service. In other words, a performer deterministically takes its decision considering only the values of the input attributes of the service it is executing, and hence, if it re-executes a services with the same inputs, it takes the same decision, producing the same outputs, as in the previous execution.

References

1. Ben-Or, M., Kozen, D., Reif, J.: The complexity of elementary algebra and geometry. J. of Computer and System Sciences 32(2), 251–264 (1986)
2. Bhattacharya, K., Caswell, N.S., Kumaran, S., Nigam, A., Wu, F.Y.: Artifact-centered operational modeling: Lessons from customer engagements. IBM Systems Journal 46(4), 703–721 (2007)
3. Bhattacharya, K., et al.: A model-driven approach to industrializing discovery processes in pharmaceutical research. IBM Systems Journal 44(1), 145–162 (2005)
4. Bhattacharya, K., Gerede, C., Hull, R., Liu, R., Su, J.: Towards formal analysis of artifact-centric business process models. In: Alonso, G., Dadam, P., Rosemann, M. (eds.) BPM 2007. LNCS, vol. 4714, pp. 288–304. Springer, Heidelberg (2007)
5. Deutsch, A., Hull, R., Patrizi, F., Vianu, V.: Automatic verification of data-centric business processes. In: Proc. of the 12th Int. Conf. on Database Theory (ICDT 2009), pp. 252–267 (2009)
6. Fischer, M.J., Rabin, M.O.: Super-exponential complexity of Presburger arithmetic. In: SIAM-AMS Proceedings, vol. 7, pp. 27–41 (1974)
7. Fritz, C., Hull, R., Su, J.: Automatic construction of simple artifact-based workflows. In: Proc. of the 12th Int. Conf. on Database Theory (ICDT 2009), pp. 225–238 (2009)
8. Guo, S., Sun, W., Weiss, M.A.: Solving satisfiability and implication problems in database systems. ACM Trans. on Database Systems 21(2), 270–293 (1996)
9. Kanellakis, P.C., Kuper, G.M., Revesz, P.Z.: Contraint query languages. J. of Computer and System Sciences 51, 26–52 (1995)
10. Matiyasevich, Y.: Hilbert's 10th Problem. The MIT Press, Cambridge (1993)
11. Narayanan, S., McIlraith, S.: Simulation, verification and automated composition of web services. In: Proc. of the 11th Int. World Wide Web Conf. WWW 2002 (2002)

12. Nigam, A., Caswell, N.S.: Business artifacts: An approach to operational specification. IBM Systems Journal 42(3), 428–445 (2003)
13. Presburger, M.: Über die Vollständigkeit eines gewissen Systems der Arithmetik ganzer Zahlen, in welchem die Addition als einzige Operation hervortritt. In: Comptes rendus du premier Congrès des Mathématiciens des Pays Slaves, Warszawa, pp. 92–101 (1929)
14. Renegar, J.: On the computational complexity and geometry of the first-order theory of the reals. Journal of Symbolic Computation 13, 255–352 (1992)
15. Revesz, P.Z.: A closed-form evaluation for Datalog queries with integer (gap)-order constraints. Theoretical Computer Science 116, 117–149 (1993)
16. Strosnider, J., Nandi, P., Kumarn, S., Ghosh, S., Arsanjani, A.: Model-driven synthesis of SOA solutions. IBM Systems Journal 47(3), 415–432 (2008)
17. Tarski, A.: A Decision Method for Elementary Algebra and Geometry. University of California Press, Berkeley (1951)

Requirements-Driven Collaborative Choreography Customization

Ayman Mahfouz, Leonor Barroca, Robin Laney, and Bashar Nuseibeh

Computing Department, The Open University,
Walton Hall, Milton Keynes, MK7 6AA, UK
amahfouz@gmail.com,
{L.Barroca,R.C.Laney,B.A.Nuseibeh}@open.ac.uk

Abstract. Evolving business needs call for customizing choreographed interactions. However, conventional choreography description languages provide only a partial view of the interaction. Business goals of each participant and organizational dependencies motivating the interaction are not captured in the specification of messaging. Absence of this critical business knowledge makes it hard to reason if a particular customization satisfies the goals of participants. Furthermore, there is no systematic means to assess the impact of change in one participant's process (local view) on the choreography (global view) as well as on other participants' processes. To this end, we argue for the benefits of representing choreography at the level of requirements motivating the interaction. We propose a framework that allows participants to collaborate on customizing choreographed interactions, while reconciling their competing business needs. To bridge the worlds of messaging and requirements, we employ an automated technique for deriving a choreography description from the customized requirements.

Keywords: Choreography, Requirements, Evolution, Viewpoints.

1 Introduction

A choreography description specifies the behavioral contract of participants in an electronic interaction from a neutral point of view [1]. Mutual obligations of the participants are specified in terms of constraints on the sequences of messages they can exchange. Using a choreography description language (CDL), such as WS-CDL[2], is becoming a de facto way for describing the "global" view of service-oriented interaction protocols.

However, these languages focus almost entirely on operational aspects such as data formats and control flow. They fall short of capturing the business-domain knowledge behind the interaction. In particular, both the strategic motivations driving the participants to interact and the physical activities they are required to perform in order to fulfill their obligations are not directly represented in choreography.

This deficiency becomes critical when the choreography has to be customized to cater for emergent business needs. It is hard to ensure that a particular choice of customization to an existing choreography satisfies the business goals of participants.

L. Baresi, C.-H. Chi, and J. Suzuki (Eds.): ICSOC-ServiceWave 2009, LNCS 5900, pp. 144–158, 2009.

To this end, we propose an approach for customizing choreographed interactions at the level of organizational requirements that motivate the interaction. Organizational requirements models capture intentions of the participants, strategic dependencies driving them to interact, and all activities they undertake during the interaction. This knowledge is essential for rationalizing customizations made to the interaction.

Since business goals of one participant (local view) are often conflicting with those of other participants, a particular choice of customization of the choreography (global view) may not be agreeable to all participants. Hence, we propose a framework that allows participants to collaborate on finding an alternative for customizing the interaction agreeable to all of them.

Our framework adopts Tropos [3] for representing organizational requirements. Tropos provides suitable notations for capturing and reasoning about a choreographed interaction in stakeholder-friendly terms. Furthermore, whereas leading CDLs have been criticized for inadequate formal grounding [4], the Tropos framework employs the formal notations of Formal Tropos (FT) [5] for precisely describing constraints that govern the behavior of participants in the interaction.

The formality of FT allows us to maintain consistency between the two representations, organizational requirements and the choreographed-messaging specification. We have previously shown [6] how organizational dependencies motivate choreographed conversations. We have also detailed how choreographed messaging can be derived from requirements [7]. In this paper we build on this work by proposing a framework that bridges global and local views of the interaction. The framework guides the collaborative customization of the interaction protocol through an automatable process.

The rest of the paper is organized as follows: Section 2 introduces the notion of choreography customization and Abstract CDL (ACDL) using our running example. Section 3 motivates our work and gives an overview of our approach. Section 4 shows how we use Tropos to represent organizational requirements for an interaction. Section 5 outlines how we support impact analysis and traceability. Our customization process is detailed in section 6 and validated in section 7. Related work is discussed in section 8. Section 9 concludes and outlines future work.

2   Choreographed Interactions

A choreography description specifies a contract between a group of interacting roles in terms of sequences of messages they are allowed to exchange, i.e. it specifies a protocol. Messaging between actual participants that play the choreographed roles at runtime has to abide by this contract. For example, consider the three roles: a patient, a medical provider (MP), and an in insurance company (IC). One potential interaction between these roles can be choreographed as follows:

A patient who needs to visit an MP must get an authorization from her IC first. When the patient receives an authorization number from the IC, she requests an appointment from the MP. After getting the confirmation the patient visits the MP to get examined by a doctor who later sends a prescription. The MP then bills the IC and gets back an electronic payment (Figure 1).

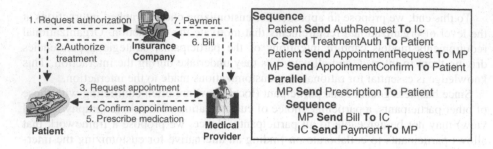

Fig. 1. Example choreographed medical interaction and its ACDL representation

In this paper we use a simple pseudo-language for representing choreography in order to focus on our approach without distracting the reader by the quirky details of a particular CDL. Nevertheless, ACDL constructs are directly drawn from the leading CDL, WS-CDL [2], which makes the mapping to WS-CDL constructs almost trivial.

The three ACDL constructs used in this paper are: "**Send**" message activity to represent a message sent by a participant, a "**Sequence**" of activities that have to execute in order, and a "**Parallel**" composition of activities that can proceed simultaneously. The grammar of the language is given in Figure 2 (terminal symbols in bold). The version of ACDL used here does not include constructs for representing repetition or conditional choice between alternative execution branches.

```
Choreography → Activity
Activity → Message I Sequence I Parallel I NoOp
Message → P1 Send Message Name To P2
Sequence → Sequence Activity *
Parallel → Parallel Activity *
```

Fig. 2. Abstract Choreography Description Language (ACDL) grammar

Message sending activities specify the participant who sends the message, P1, the participant who receives it, P2, and a literal "Message Name" that describes the message. All activities in a "**Sequence**" have to execute in order, where an activity cannot start unless the previous activity has completed. A "**Sequence**" activity is completed when the last activity in the sequence is completed. Individual branches of a "**Parallel**" can proceed concurrently. A "**Parallel**" activity is only completed when *all* branches are completed. The **NoOp** activity is a "do-nothing" activity. Figure 1 shows the ACDL for the medical example. Indentation represents nesting of activities.

3 Customizing Choreographed Interactions

We now motivate our work and present an overview of our approach.

3.1 The Problem

It is inevitable that the business requirements driving the interaction will change. As a result, the choreography description needs to be customized (adapted) to reflect the new contract.

For example, consider an emergent need for the IC to protect itself from abuse of coverage. To protect its assets, the IC needs to ensure that it only covers treatment expenses for eligible patients. One way to achieve this goal is to require the MP to verify the insurance coverage of each admitted patient. The MP is thus required to submit the patient's insurance information to the IC so that the IC checks the validity of the patient's insurance policy. The IC will not hold itself liable for covering treatment expenses unless the MP verifies the patient information before submitting a bill. This requirement imposes a constraint on the order in which the MP performs its activities. A naïve realization of this added requirement is to have the MP send a "Verify coverage" message before sending the billing message. With conventional choreography descriptions we face two challenges:

1. It is hard to rationalize this, or any other, choice for capturing the customization without considering how well it satisfies the emergent business need.
2. It is not clear how to assess the impact of any suggested change to the choreography (global view) on the process of each participant (local view). For a participant, e.g. the patient, to agree on the change they have to assess its impact on their business goals.

These issues are exacerbated by the lack of representation of physical activities in chorcography descriptions. Physical activities that are part of the interaction contract have to be taken into account when assessing a change.

3.2 Messaging Specification vs. Requirements

To rationalize a customization, it is crucial to consult problem-domain knowledge. However, choreographed messaging descriptions are operational in nature. They do not reveal much of the business rationale behind the interaction but rather focus on *how* the interaction is to be carried out, i.e. the control flow between activities. On the other hand, organizational requirements provide more abstract descriptions that focus on the *why* and *what* aspects of the interaction. We argue that Models of Organizational Requirements (MOR) are superior to messaging descriptions with respect to four representational areas, each of which is crucial to assessing alternative ways for capturing the required customization. These namely are:

1. Intention and Motivation: MOR for the interaction embody essential knowledge about motivations driving each participant including:

- Goals the participants wants to achieve
- Dependencies between participants enabling them to achieve their goals
- Risks and liabilities introduced by the dependencies

2. Refinement Mechanisms: MOR allow for refining high level goals into activities thereby providing rationalization of activities undertaken during the interaction. Refinement relates different levels of abstraction thereby providing traceability all the way down to the messaging specification.

3. Physical Activities: Electronic messaging is only part of the realization of the full interaction. Physical activities that the participants are obliged to perform as part of the interaction contract are not necessarily manifested in the messaging specification. For example, the patient's visit to the MP and its relation to other activities are not captured in the choreography description in Figure 1.

4. Behavioral Contract: MOR can be annotated with precise specification of participants' obligations. We employ these behavioral annotations to guide the refinement of models [7]. Furthermore, the use of formal logic enables automatic checking for the satisfaction of participants' goals.

3.3 Our Proposed Approach

We propose a framework for customizing choreographed interactions that combines the benefits of organizational requirements with the standards-based choreographed messaging descriptions.

While allowing the participants to collaborate on customizing the choreography (global view), our framework allows each participant to evaluate the impact of the customization on their individual business needs (local view). This dichotomy results in the four views (quadrants) of figure 3. We elaborate on Q1 and Q2 in section 4.

Our choreography customization framework entails: representing choreographed interactions at the level of organizational requirements models, performing required customizations to these models in a collaborative manner that benefits from the embodied domain knowledge, and deriving the resulting choreography description in an automated manner.

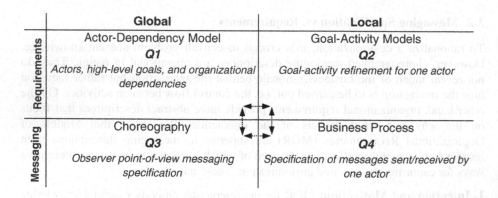

	Global	Local
Requirements	Actor-Dependency Model *Q1* Actors, high-level goals, and organizational dependencies	Goal-Activity Models *Q2* Goal-activity refinement for one actor
Messaging	Choreography *Q3* Observer point-of-view messaging specification	Business Process *Q4* Specification of messages sent/received by one actor

Fig. 3. The four views of our choreography customization framework

4 Modeling Interaction Requirements

Tropos [3] is an agent-oriented software development methodology with a focus on organizational requirements at various levels of abstraction. We use Tropos for modeling interaction requirements as it provides a suitable framework for representing and reasoning about the business context for a choreographed interaction. Its models capture goals of participants (actors) in the interaction, mutual dependencies that motivate them to interact, and activities they undertake to fulfill their goals. We introduce how we model the global view of a choreographed interaction using Actor-Dependency (AD) models, how we model the local view using Goal-Activity (GA) models, and how behavioral dynamics of the model are described using FT.

4.1 Global View: AD Modeling

Actor-Dependency (AD) models provide a notation for representing the global view of the interaction at a high-level of abstraction by capturing the actors (participants) in the interaction, their high-level goals, and the inter-dependencies driving them to interact. Figure 4 is an AD model representing the medical interaction at a high-level. An actor is an active entity that performs actions to achieve its goals. The patient, the MP, and the IC are all actors. Model elements can either be internal to an actor (inside the dotted ellipse) or define dependencies whose fulfillment is delegated to other actors. An actor may depend on another for fulfilling a goal, performing an activity, or making some resource available.

A goal is a state of the world desired by one of the actors. For example, the "Get Treated" goal represents the patient's desire to get cured from an ailment. An activity is an abstraction of a course of action with well-defined pre- and post-conditions. The patient is required to perform the "Appear for Exam" activity to visit the MP's office. A resource is an informational or physical entity. For example, the "Payment" resource represents the compensation that the MP gets from the IC in return for providing services to the patient.

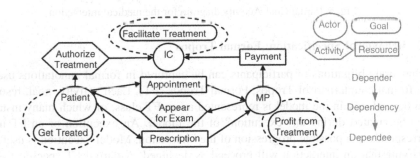

Fig. 4. Actor-Dependency model for the medical interaction

4.2 Local View: GA Modeling

To detail the specification of the interaction, we successively refine AD models into Goal-Activity (GA) models [3]. Each GA model represents an actor's local view of the interaction. In the process, goals are refined into sub-goals and eventually realized by activities. Each actor considers and evaluates refinement alternatives based on how well they satisfy their goals [8]. Activities can be further refined into sub-activities that are either implemented by a service or carried out by a human agent.

Figure 5 shows the GA model of both the MP and the patient. Goals and activities internal to an actor are refined inside the dotted ellipse for that actor. Each actor takes responsibility for carrying out their internal activities during the interaction. For example, the "Get Treated" goal was refined into activities to get an authorization from the IC followed by getting a prescription from the MP. The latter is further refined into activities for setting up an appointment followed by visiting the MP and then receiving a prescription from the MP.

The business goals of participants may dictate some ordering of activities. For example, in the analysis process the MP realized the need to manage office schedule. Hence, the MP requires every patient to setup an appointment before they visit. Also, physical activities may impose ordering. For example, the MP has to examine the patient before prescribing treatment.

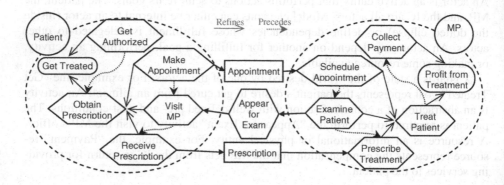

Fig. 5. Partial Goal-Activity diagram for the medical interaction

4.3 Behavioral Specification: Formal Tropos

Behavioral obligations of participants can be captured in formal annotations used by the formal counterpart of Tropos, Formal Tropos (FT). Each activity, goal, resource, and dependency in the model is represented as an FT class, of which many instances may be created during an "execution" of the model. An execution of an FT model corresponds to a possible progression of the interaction. Model execution is useful for verifying that an interaction will proceed as designed. A partial FT specification for the "MakeAppointment" activity and the "Appointment" dependency classes is shown in figure 6, parts of which can be deduced by applying some heuristics [5].

Each class has attributes that define associations with other instances in the model. For example, the "Appointment" class has "makeApp" attribute that references the associated instance of "MakeAppointment" class.

Valid progressions of the interaction are specified by constraining the lifecycle of model elements using temporal logic. **Creation** and **Fulfillment** conditions define when an instance of a class is created (instantiated) and when it becomes fulfilled.

4.3.1 Creation

Creation of a goal or a dependency is interpreted as the moment at which the actor begins to desire the goal or need the dependency to be fulfilled. For example, an "Appointment" dependency will be created if there is an instance of "MakeAppointment" activity that needs to be fulfilled. For an activity, creation is the moment at which the actor has to start performing it. Note how FT specifies that "MakeAppointment" is created when its "super" activity, "Obtain Prescription", needs to be fulfilled thereby bridging two levels of abstraction. We use Cr(X) to denote the creation event of X.

4.3.2 Fulfillment

Fulfillment condition marks the end of the lifecycle of an instance. Fulfillment condition should hold whenever a goal is achieved, an activity is completed, or a resource is made available. For example, the "MakeAppointment" activity is fulfilled when the associated "Appointment" dependency has been fulfilled (i.e. appointment confirmation was received by the patient) whereas an instance of "Appointment" is fulfilled when the MP has completed the activity of scheduling an appointment. We use Fi(X) to denote the fulfillment event of X.

Dependency Appointment	**Activity** MakeAppointment
Depender Patient	**Actor** Patient
Dependee MP	**Creation condition** ¬Fulfilled(super)
Attribute makeApp: MakeAppointment	**Fulfillment condition**
Creation condition ¬Fulfilled(makeApp)	∃ a:Appointment
Fulfillment condition	(a.depender = actor
∃ schedAp:SchedulApp	∧ a.makeApp = self ∧ **Fulfilled**(a))
(schedAp.actor = dependee ∧ **Fulfilled**(sa))	

Fig. 6. FT specification of "Appointment" and "MakeAppointment "

5 Traceability and Impact Analysis

Our goal here is twofold: first, facilitate collaboration between participants to find a customization on which they all agree and second: systematically determine the messaging specification resulting from customization of requirements models.

5.1 Impact Analysis: Bridging Local and Global Views

To allow participants to assess the suitability of a customization (from their point of view) we must be able to determine the effect of a change in the choreography on any participant's process. Conversely, we need to determine the impact of changes in any of the participant's local model on the choreography so that other participants get to assess suggested customizations to the choreography from their point of view.

We employ dependencies to link GA and AD models. GA models explicate which specific activities are at both ends of each dependency, thereby providing linkage between the local view of each participant with the global view of the interaction.

FT precisely relates the lifecycle of dependencies to that of activities at both ends of a dependency. For example, in figure 6, note how the state of "Appointment" dependency determines the state of "MakeAppointment" activity. The patient cannot make progress on their internal process flow unless "Appointment" dependency is fulfilled. On the other hand, the "Appointment" dependency is only fulfilled when the MP have complete the "ScheduleAppointment" activity.

5.2 Traceability: Bridging Requirements to Messaging

Using FT to relate the lifecycle of activities to their "super" activity enables us to bridge requirements models to messaging specification. We exploit this traceability mechanism to show how dependencies drive the interaction thereby outlining an abstract view of the choreography [6]. For example, "Appointment" dependency indicates that the patient depends on the MP for obtaining an appointment, which implies that both actors need to interact to fulfill the dependency.

We have exploited these semantics to automate the generation of choreographed messaging from requirements models [7]. First, we infer the set of choreographed events from creation/fulfillment events of activities and dependencies. Then, we use the semantics of refinement, dependencies, and precedence between activities to come up with a partial ordering relation over these events. Finally, from the ordering relation, we generate a choreography description that satisfies the requirements [7].

Even though GA modeling details the activities of the interaction, it provides an important flexibility. It defers the choice of the medium through which activities are carried out. For example, the choreography designer may choose to include the "Prescription" in choreographed messaging or have it be fulfilled otherwise, e.g. paper documents, fax, etc. We take advantage of this by including all activities, including physical activities, in the customization process.

6 Choreography Customization Process

Bridging requirements to choreography allows us to perform required customizations to requirements models then derive the customized messaging. On the other hand, bridging the local and global views helps ensure that customizations to a choreography description do not violate the goals of any participant. Thus, our proposed customization process covers the 4 quadrants of figure 3.

The driver behind choreography customization is to satisfy an emergent business need. Several customization alternatives that satisfy this need may exist. Our process enables participants to *collaborate* on finding an alternative acceptable to all of them. Each participant gets to evaluate the suitability of alternatives from their local point of view as well as suggest other alternatives.

An advantage of our process is that it has no fixed starting point. Customization may start in any of the four quadrants of figure 3 and *move* between them. Consider the following example manifestation of the process:

1. Participant P1 identifies an emergent business need.
2. P1 considers a change in their GA model (which is in Q2) to fulfill that need.

3. To determine the effect of the suggested change on the global view we use dependencies to relate P1 GA model to the AD model (moving from Q2 to Q1).
4. The change in the AD model may imply (again Q1 to Q2) changes to another participant's, P2, GA model.
5. P2 evaluates suggested change from their point of view (Q2 again – but for P2).
6. P2 deems the suggested change unacceptable and suggests an alternative way for fulfilling P1's need.
7. The effect of the alternative on the AD model is worked out (Q2 to Q1).
8. A change in the AD model implies a change in the GA model of P1 (Q1 to Q2).
9. P1 agrees to the suggested alternative.
10. The choreographed messaging is then derived from the customized AD and GA models [7] (moving from Q1 to Q3).

Each step of the process involves one of the following:

1. Switch Views. To assume one of the four views of figure 3 our customization framework allows moving between its four quadrants as follows:

- Q1-Q3: Choreographed messaging constraints obtained from AD models as per [7].
- Q1-Q2: Ends of every dependency appearing in the AD model are activities appearing in a GA model, as in section 5.
- Q2-Q4: Ordering of messages sent and received by one participant is constrained by refinement and precedence between the activities of that participant as per [7].
- Q3-Q4: Messages sent/received by every participant appear in the choreographed messaging specification. For example, as in [9], [10]

2. Evaluate Alternative. Each participant needs to ensure that a suggested customization is acceptable from their local point of view. When a change is suggested to their GA model (e.g. to reflect a change in the AD model), a participant can verify that the customized model still achieves their business goals. A systematic way to evaluate a GA model is by executing it using a simulator [5] and checking whether every possible execution state is acceptable. If the participant deems one of the states unacceptable, they can then suggest an alternative customization.

3. Suggest Alternative. To aid a participant suggest an alternative customization, we provide systematic ways for finding alternatives for certain classes of customizations. For example, by bridging requirements to messaging as in section 5, we can auto-enumerate all possible alternatives for a customization that requires *adding* an event to the choreography along with an ordering constraint [6].

4. Perform Customization. Customizations that we tackle here are those that result from incremental, rather than radical, changes to requirements. Section 7 shows examples of adding a dependency, an activity, and a precedence constraint.

5. Agree on an Alternative. The customization process concludes when none of the participants objects to the candidate customization alternative. However, there is no guarantee that a solution agreeable to all participants will be found. If a point is reached where at least one of the participants objects to the last remaining candidate solution, the requested customization may be deemed unreasonable. An alternative may then be sought at a higher level requirements model, e.g. as in [3] and [8].

7 Validation

We now demonstrate how our framework allows participants to collaborate on adapting the choreography to meet their emergent needs. Revisiting the medical example, we start the process from the customization to messaging as suggested by the IC in section 3.1. We arbitrarily break down the customization process into stages for readability:

Stage 1: The IC requests being asked to verify patient coverage

1. The IC suggests a customization where they get a message asking them to verify a patient's coverage prior to receiving a bill (Q4 in figure 3 for IC).
2. This translates (Q4-Q3) to adding a "verify coverage" message that precedes the billing message in the protocol.
3. Consequently (Q3-Q4 for the MP), the MP becomes obliged to send a "verify coverage" message before sending the billing message (Q3).
4. The added "verify coverage" request-response messages imply (through Q3-Q1) an added organizational dependency.

Stage 2: Adding the "Verification" dependency and required activities

5. We add a "Verification" dependency to the AD model (Q1).
6. To initiate the fulfillment of the dependency (Q1-Q2) the MP has to perform a "Verify Coverage" activity (Q2 for MP).
7. We add the new activity to the GA model of MP. From the original requirement imposed by the IC, the activity has to precede "Collect Payment" (see figure 5).
8. We have now found the first candidate solution which is to have the new activity immediately precede "Collect Payment".
9. The MP analyzes the suggested solution through simulation (Q2). The MP determines that the solution allows sending a prescription to a patient whose insurance information has not been verified. This state is deemed undesirable because if the coverage is not eventually verified, the MP will not get paid.
10. To find an alternative point for performing the "Verify Coverage" activity, the MP explores other alternatives [6]. Rather than directly preceding the billing activity, "Verify Coverage" can be made to precede any other activity that transitively-precedes the billing activity.
11. One such alternative is to have the "Verify Coverage" activity precede "Issue Prescription". But again, an execution of the model (Q2) deems this unacceptable as it allows a state where a doctor wastes his time examining the patient only to find later that she is not covered by the IC.
12. Continuing in the same manner, the MP finds the first viable solution which is to have "Verify Coverage" precede "Examine patient".

Stage 3: Adding the "Coverage" dependency and required activities

13. The MP adds a "Get Coverage Info" activity (Q2) which entails (Q1-Q2) adding a "Coverage Info" dependency (Q1). The MP requests that the patient provides coverage information prior to the examination,.
14. The patient adds "Provide Coverage" as a sub-activity of "Obtain Prescription". The new activity is assigned to fulfill "Coverage Info" dependency (Q1-Q2).

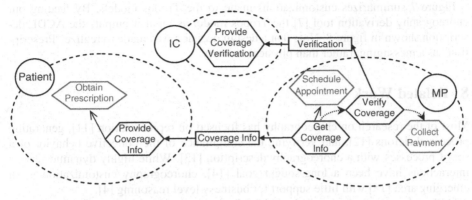

Fig. 7. Summary of the customizations made to the requirements model

15. The first point "Get Coverage Info" can be performed is right before Cr(Examine Patient) and right after Fi(Visit). This implies that the patient will physically carry the coverage information to the MP office.

16. The patient finds this option undesirable as an execution of the model (Q2 for patient) shows that she may go through the trouble of visiting the MP but not get examined, e.g. if verification fails due to some system outage.

17. Continuing as specified in [6], a viable solution is found where verification is made to precede the Fi(Appointment). Thus, the patient suggests providing coverage information prior to getting the appointment confirmation.

Stage 4: Agreeing on a customization and concluding the process

18. To add "Get Coverage Info" right before Fi(Appointment) the MP makes it a sub- activity of "Schedule Appointment".

19. The MP agrees the patient's suggestion.

20. All participants agree to the suggested solution.

21. Having agreed on a customization, the choreography messaging is then derived automatically from the Tropos models.

```
Sequence
    Patient Send AuthRequest To IC
    IC Send TreatmentAuth To Patient
    Patient Send AppointmentRequest To MP
    MP Send GetCoverageInfo To Patient
    Patient Send CoverageInfo To MP
    MP Send VerifyCoverage To IC
    IC Send CoverageVerification To MP
    MP Send AppointmentConfirm To Patient
    Parallel
        MP Send Prescription To Patient
        Sequence
            MP Send Bill To IC
            IC Send Payment To MP
```

Fig. 8. Choreography description derived from the customized requirements model

Figure 7 summarizes customizations made to the Tropos models. By feeding our choreography derivation tool [7] the Tropos model as input it outputs the ACDL description shown in figure 8. Note that a design decision was made to realize "Prescription" as a messaging, rather than physical, activity.

8 Related Work

Most of the research on choreography has focused on representation [11], generating process skeletons [12], and verifying the compliance of the collective behavior of a set of processes with a choreography description [13]. While highly-dynamic service interactions have been a long-sought goal [14], choreography customization is an emerging area [15] with little support for business-level reasoning [4].

Although, our work shares the spirit of attempts to integrate commitments with Tropos [16] [17], our structured customization process and automatic derivation set our approach apart, especially that it is not clear in [17] how activities can be related to messaging. The Amoeba methodology [18] for evolving cross-organizational interaction is promising, albeit it does not adequately distinguish between the local and global views of the interaction thereby obscuring the needs of each participant.

Attempts to adapt service interactions focused mostly on adapting orchestrations [19] [20] or dealing with changes in service interfaces, rather than adapting choreographed protocols. More importantly, with the exception of [21], the business needs driving the interaction are not addressed.

Representing organizational requirements for distributed actors is well-established [22], and also is evolution in agent-oriented systems [23]. However, both were yet to be applied to choreographed service interactions in a way that explicates the multiple views on the interaction. Our work is consistent with the dichotomy given in [24], albeit that work does not address customization. Otherwise, relating viewpoints in service interactions was established only at the messaging level [9]. Attempts to relate choreography to business rules have also only addressed operational aspects [25].

Finally, although UML activity diagrams [26] are widely used to represent choreographed interactions, the formality and the levels of abstractions of Tropos [3] make it superior for analyzing business goals and reasoning about their satisfaction.

9 Conclusions and Further Work

Ever-changing business needs call for adaptable choreographies. Conventional CDLs are not well-suited for adaptation as they embody little of the domain knowledge required to reason about participants' needs. In particular, the business goals of participants and strategic dependencies motivating the interaction are not explicitly represented. We proposed representing choreographed interactions at the level of organizational requirements. Tropos models embody knowledge about the goals of the participants, the dependencies driving the interaction, and all activities performed during the interaction including physical activities not represented in conventional CDLs.

We proposed a framework that enables participants to collaborate on customizing the choreography (global view) while at the same time ensuring their individual business needs (local view) are satisfied. We utilized the formality of FT to analyze the impact of choreography customization on each participant's processes. We provided systematic ways for finding customization alternatives and evaluating them.

Once participants have agreed on an alternative, we use our automated technique to derive the customized messaging specification from Tropos models. Using an example, we demonstrated how our framework exploits domain knowledge embodied in requirements models to decide how the required customization is to be performed.

The generated ACDL is a skeleton that needs to be refined in a design phase, e.g. by specifying message data types. In particular, ACDL employs request-response messaging whereas more complex patterns may realistically be needed. We will exploit the FT for inferring more detailed messaging, such as repetition and branching. Furthermore, we plan formalize data flow aspects of our analysis.

References

[1] Peltz, C.: Web Services Orchestration and Choreography. IEEE Computer 36, 46–52 (2003)

[2] Web Services Choreography Description Language Version 1.0. W3C (2005), http://www.w3.org/TR/ws-cdl-10/

[3] Bresciani, P., Perini, A., Giorgini, P., Giunchiglia, F., Mylopoulos, J.: Tropos: An Agent-Oriented Software Development Methodology. Journal of Autonomous Agents and Multi-Agent Systems 8, 203–236 (2004)

[4] Barros, A., Dumas, M., Oaks, P.: Standards for Web Service Choreography and Orchestration: Status and Perspectives. In: Bussler, C.J., Haller, A. (eds.) BPM 2005. LNCS, vol. 3812, pp. 61–74. Springer, Heidelberg (2006)

[5] Fuxman, A., Liu, L., Mylopoulos, J., Pistore, M., Roveri, M., Traverso, P.: Specifying and analyzing early requirements in Tropos. RE Journal 9, 132–150 (2004)

[6] Mahfouz, A., Barroca, L., Laney, R., Nuseibeh, B.: Customizing Choreography: Deriving Conversations from Organizational Dependencies. Presented at Enterprise Distributed Object Computing Conference (EDOC), Munich, Germany (2008)

[7] Mahfouz, A., Barroca, L., Laney, R., Nuseibeh, B.: From Organizational Requirements to Service Choreography. In: Congress on Services - I, pp. 546–553 (2009)

[8] Giorgini, P., Mylopoulos, J., Nicchiarelli, E., Sebastiani, R.: Formal Reasoning Techniques for Goal Models. In: Spaccapietra, S., March, S., Aberer, K. (eds.) Journal on Data Semantics I. LNCS, vol. 2800, pp. 1–20. Springer, Heidelberg (2003)

[9] Dijkman, R.M., Dumas, M.: Service-Oriented Design: A Multi-Viewpoint Approach. International Journal of Cooperative Information Systems 13, 337–368 (2004)

[10] Zaha, J. M., Dumas, M., ter Hofstede, A.H.M., Barros, A.P., Decker, G.: Service Interaction Modeling: Bridging Global and Local Views. Presented at EDOC, China (2006)

[11] Zaha, J.M., Barros, A.P., Dumas, M., ter Hofstede, A.H.M.: Let's Dance: A Language for Service Behavior Modeling. In: Meersman, R., Tari, Z. (eds.) OTM 2006. LNCS, vol. 4275, pp. 145–162. Springer, Heidelberg (2006)

[12] Mendling, J., Hafner, M.: From Inter-Organizational Workflows to Process Execution: Generating BPEL from WS-CDL. Presented at ACM / IEEE 8th International Conference on Model Driven Engineering Languages and Systems, Montego Bay, Jamaica (2005)

[13] Foster, H., Uchitel, S., Magee, J., Kramer, J.: Model-based Verification of Web Service Compositions. Presented at 18th International Conference on Automated Software Engineering, ASE 2003 (2003)

[14] Nitto, E.D., Ghezzi, C., Metzger, A., Papazoglou, M.P., Pohl, K.: A journey to highly dynamic, self-adaptive service-based applications. Automated Software Engineering 15, 313–341 (2008)

[15] Rinderle, S., Wombacher, A., Reichert, M.: On the Controlled Evolution of Process Choreographies. Presented at 22nd International Conference on Data Engineering (ICDE 2006), Atlanta, GA, USA (2006)

[16] Mallya, A.U., Singh, M.P.: Incorporating Commitment Protocols into Tropos. In: Müller, J.P., Zambonelli, F. (eds.) AOSE 2005. LNCS, vol. 3950, pp. 69–80. Springer, Heidelberg (2006)

[17] Telang, P.R., Singh, M.P.: Enhancing Tropos with Commitments: A Business Metamodel and Methodology. Presented at Conceptual Modeling: Foundations and Applications (2009)

[18] Desai, N., Chopra, A.K., Singh, M.P.: Amoeba: A Methodology for Modeling and Evolution of Cross-Organizational Business Processes. ACM Transactions on Software Engineering and Methodology (TOSEM) 19 (2009)

[19] Charfi, A., Mezini, M.: Aspect-Oriented Web Service Composition with AO4BPEL. In: Zhang, L.-J., Jeckle, M. (eds.) ECOWS 2004. LNCS, vol. 3250, pp. 168–182. Springer, Heidelberg (2004)

[20] Orriëns, B., Yang, J.: A Rule Driven Approach for Developing Adaptive Service Oriented Business Collaborations. Presented at IEEE International Conference on Services Computing (SCC), Chicago, Illinois, USA (2006)

[21] Kazhamiakin, R., Pistore, M., Roveri, M.: A Framework for Integrating Business Processes and Business Requirements. Presented at Enterprise Distributed Object Computing Conference (EDOC 2004), Monterey, California, USA (2004)

[22] Yu, E.: Towards Modeling and Reasoning Support for Early-Phase Requirements Engineering. Presented at 3rd IEEE Int. Symp. on Requirements Engineering, Washington D.C., USA (1997)

[23] Khallouf, J., Winikoff, M.: Goal-Oriented Design of Agent Systems: A Refinement of Prometheus and its Evaluation. International Journal Agent-Oriented Software Engineering 3, 88–112 (2009)

[24] Traverso, P., Pistore, M., Roveri, M., Marconi, A., Kazhamiakin, R., Lucchese, P., Busetta, P., Bertoli, P.: Supporting the Negotiation between Global and Local Business Requirements in Service Oriented Development. ITC-irst, Trento, Italy (2004)

[25] Berry, A., Milosevic, Z.: Extending Choreography With Business Contract Constraints. International Journal of Cooperative Information Systems (IJCIS) 14, 131–179 (2005)

[26] Vitolins, V., Kalnins, A.: Semantics of UML 2.0 Activity Diagram for Business Modeling by Means of Virtual Machine. Presented at EDOC 2005, Enschede, The Netherlands (2005)

An Automatic Approach to Enable Replacement of Conversational Services*

Luca Cavallaro[1], Elisabetta Di Nitto[1], and Matteo Pradella[2]

[1] Politecnico di Milano, DEI, Piazza L. Da Vinci, 32, 20133 Milano, Italy
{cavallaro,dinitto}@elet.polimi.it
[2] CNR IEIIT-MI, Via Golgi, 40, 20133 Milano, Italy
pradella@elet.polimi.it

Abstract. In Service Oriented Architectures (SOAs) services invoked in a composition can be replaced by other services, which are possibly discovered and bound at runtime. Most of the research efforts supporting this replacement assume that the interface of the interchangeable services are the same and known at design time. Such assumption is not realistic since it implies that providers of the same kinds of services agree on the interfaces the services offer. By *interface mapping* we mean the class of approaches aiming at relaxing this assumption. Most of those approaches available in the literature focus on stateless services and simply address mapping operation names and data structures. Instead, this paper focuses on *conversational services* for which the sequence of required operation calls, i.e., the *interaction protocol*, matters. We use model checking to automatically identify the interaction protocols mapping. We validate our technique both by applying it to the invocation of two real services (Flickr and Picasa), and by quantitatively comparing it to a related approach.

1 Introduction

Service oriented architectures (SOAs) offer the mechanisms to build software systems integrating loosely coupled services, possibly made available by third party vendors. As services may be controlled by third parties, they may be out of service consumers control. This means that the traditional closed world assumption, which mandates that developers know a priori all the components involved in the system and can model and plan their interactions, is no more verified [1] because services involved in the composition may change during the system life cycle to react to failures and service unavailabilities. When this happens, a new service semantically equivalent to the one not responding properly could be discovered and bound to the composition. When this replacement occurs at runtime, the composition (or the framework where the composition is running) should be able to perform the replacement requiring as little human intervention as possible.

In recent years, research about service oriented architectures produced many frameworks that can provide run time reconfigurations of service compositions (see for instance [2], [3]), but most of them make the hypothesis that all semantically equivalent

---

* This research has been funded by the European Community's FP7/2007-2013 Programme, grant agreement 215483 (S-Cube), and IDEAS-ERC Programme, Project 227977 (SMSCom).

L. Baresi, C.-H. Chi, and J. Suzuki (Eds.): ICSOC-ServiceWave 2009, LNCS 5900, pp. 159–174, 2009.

services have the same interface. This hypothesis, however, is not realistic as services can be released by independent vendors. Therefore in common practice interfaces lack standardization. Consequently there is no guarantee that services discovered and bound at runtime can perfectly fit in a preexistent composition.

To address this problem, in a previous work [4], we have developed an approach to allow invocation of services whose interfaces and behaviors differ from each other. The approach was based on the definition of proper *mapping scripts* that, when interpreted at runtime, could solve complex mismatches and perform the needed adaptations.

In this paper we extend the previous work by providing an approach and a tool to support the automation of the mapping scripts definition. The approach is able to handle *conversational services*, that is, services whose operations are expected to be called in some specific sequences, which define the services *interaction protocols*. We assume that, when developing a service composition, a service integrator uses the component services that are available at the time he/she is developing the system. We call these *abstract services* to highlight the fact that they are not necessarily the ones that will be actually used at runtime, which we call *concrete services*. We also assume that services are described not only in terms of their syntactic interface (i.e., their WSDL or any equivalent description), but also in terms of a model that defines the order in which service operations need to be invoked.

Given these assumptions and given a certain sequence of operations to be invoked on an abstract service, our approach is able to propose a possible mapping of this sequence to a sequence of operations on a concrete service. The result of this analysis is a mapping script fragment that, combined with other fragments that deal with data and operation names mappings, allows us to actually adapt abstract service invocations to their concrete implementations. Data and operation names mappings are disregarded in this paper as they appear to be much simpler than the mapping of interaction protocols and are covered in [5] and in other approaches in the literature (see Section 2).

The rest of the paper is organized as follows: Section 2 presents the current state of the art and highlights some open issues. Section 3 presents a real world example that motivates our work, Section 4 summarizes the background work that has been developed in [4], Section 5 discusses our approach to support semi-automatic generation of mapping scripts for what concerns protocol-level mismatches and refines the execution model associated to this specific case of mismatches. Section 6 evaluates our approach quantitatively and qualitatively, and, finally, Section 7 draws some conclusions.

2 Related Work

The approaches that support interface mapping can be categorized in those that require human intervention in the definition of mapping scripts or equivalent mechanisms (see for instance [6], [7], [8] and [9]) and those that offer some automatic tool.

Among the approaches in the first category, we mention here the one in [7] as it offers a model checking approach to verify the correctness of *adaptation contracts* that are manually defined by humans, and the one in [9] as it assists humans in the interface adapters development by offering a tool that provides hints about possible mismatches between an abstract and a concrete service interface. Both approaches, however, assume that, before execution, a developer can identify all potential pairs of abstract and concrete services and specify all needed adapters. This may not work properly in the cases of systems supporting run-time substitutions of services as the substitutions could have not be foreseen in advance.

Automated approaches try to solve this issue by generating adapters that are inferred from specifications associated to services. Many of these approaches are based on the use of ontologies. Among the others, our previous work [5] and [10] exploit a domain ontology (specified in SAWSDL[1]) to annotate service interfaces. At run-time, when a service bound to a composition needs to be substituted, a software agent generates a mapping by parsing the ontological annotations in the interfaces. *SCIROCO* [11] offers similar features focusing on stateful services. It requires all services to be annotated with both a SAWSDL description and a WS-ResourceProperties[2] document, which represents the state of the service. When an invoked service becomes unavailable, *SCIROCO* exploits the SAWSDL annotations to find a set of candidates that expose a semantically matching interface. Then, the WS-ResourceProperties document associated to each candidate service is analyzed to find out if it is possible to bring the candidate in a state that is compatible with the state of the unavailable service. If this is possible, then this service is selected for replacement of the one that is unavailable. All of these three approaches offer full run-time automation for service substitution, but can address only those mismatches that concern data and operation names while they disregard those concerning the interaction protocol.

An approach that generates adapters covering the case of interaction protocols mismatches is presented in [12]. It assumes to start from a service composition and a service behavioral description both written in the BPEL language [13]. These are then translated in the *YAWL* formal language [14] and matched in order to identify an invocation trace in the service behavioral description that matches the one expected by the service composition. The matching algorithm is based on graph exploration and considers both control flow and data flow requirements.

The approach presented in [15] offers similar features and has been implemented in an open source tool.[3] While both these approaches appear to fulfill our need for supporting interaction protocol mapping, they may present some shortcoming in terms of performances due to the high cost of exhaustive graph exploration algorithms that could prevent their usage in on-the-fly mapping derivation. While no data about performances are available for the approach in [12], we could exploit the tool offered by [15] to verify our guess. As discussed in Section 6, the processing time required by the tool is remarkably high in complex cases. Our goal is, therefore, to exploit some alternative technique to significantly improve these performances.

3 Motivating Example

To motivate our work we refer to an example based on some significant conversational services available on the Internet. Our example application is a photo management tool

---

[1] http://www.w3.org/2002/ws/sawsdl/

[2] http://docs.oasis-open.org/wsrf/wsrf-ws_resource_properties-1.2-spec-os.pdf

[3] http://sourceforge.net/projects/dinapter

designed for working on a mobile phone. A user can take some photos with his mobile, upload them to the web, and share them with his friends using an external service.

The tool expects to interact with the *Flickr* service[4]. *Flickr* makes available to its users a space where to upload photos and a REST[16] service to access it. Photos can have assigned one of the following levels of visibility: public, private, and family, where the latter lets only some members see the photos uploaded by a user. Once the user has uploaded some photos the service lets him group (part of) them in sets. Of course it is always possible to change the visibility of a photo or of a set.

Flickr is not the only service offering a photo repository. Another analogous service is called *Picasa*[5]. *Flickr* and *Picasa* are equivalent in a broad sense, but analyzing their interfaces in more detail some differences emerge. In particular, *Picasa* does not support the upload of photos if they are not grouped in a set. For this reason a user should first create a set and then upload pictures directly into the created set. In addition, while *Flickr* identifies three levels of visibility for photos and sets, *Picasa* only supports two (private and public) and, given the central role of sets, associates these levels only to sets and not directly to photos. Of course, other differences concern the names and the parameters of the equivalent operations made available by the two services. For instance the operation *addToSet* of *Flickr* and the operation *createPhoto* of *Picasa* both add a photo to a set, but they show different names and accept different input parameters (Tables 1 and 2 summarize the Flickr and Picasa operations we focus on.

Even if our photo management tool is built to be used with *Flickr*, many users may be subscribed to *Picasa* or to any other popular photo sharing service. In order to allow them to use any of these alternative services, either we hardcode in our tool the instructions to interact with any possible service, or we build a mapping mechanism that handles the mismatches on our behalf. Such mapping mechanism could state, for example, that the sequence of *Flickr* operations *uploadPriv*, *addToSet*, *makeSetPub* maps on the following sequence of *Picasa* operations: *createPublicSet* and *createPhoto*, which can therefore be invoked to obtain the required behaviour. The approach we discuss in this paper is focusing specifically on how to automatically and efficiently infer such kinds of mapping without or with limited human intervention.

4   Adaptation Approach: Overview

In order to describe possible differences that can arise between an abstract and a concrete service we need to define our model of a service. A service can be described as a *Labeled Transition System* (LTS) characterized by tuple $P = (S, O, \tau)$, where:

- S is the set of states the service can go through.
- O is the set of operations that can be invoked on the service together with the corresponding parameters. In formal terms, this is the input alphabet of the LTS.
- τ is the transition function $\tau : S \times O \rightarrow 2^S$ that describes how the service can evolve from state to state when operations are invoked. 2^S indicates that the transition function can non-deterministically lead the service to different states depending on the context (e.g., a state representing a correct functioning of the service

---

[4] http://www.flickr.com/services/api/
[5] http://code.google.com/apis/picasaweb/overview.html

Table 1. A subset of *Flickr* operations and required data

Operation name	Parameters	Return value	Description
uploadPub	photo photoName	success	Uploads a photo with *public* visibility
uploadPriv	photo photoName	success	Uploads a photo with *private* visibility
uploadFam	photo photoName	success	Uploads a photo with *family* visibility
makePhotoPub	photoName		Makes a photo visibility *public*
makePhotoPriv	photoName		Makes a photo visibility *private*
makePhotoFam	photoName		Makes a photo visibility *family*
addToSet	albumName photoName	success	Adds a previously uploaded photo to a (new or existent) set
makeSetPub	albumName		Makes a set visibility *public*
makeSetPriv	albumName		Makes a set visibility *private*
makeSetFam	albumName		Makes a set visibility *family*

Table 2. A subset of *Picasa* operations and required data

Operation name	Parameters	Return value	Description
createPublicSet	albumName	success	Creates a photo set with *public* visibility
createPrivateSet	albumName	success	Creates a photo set with *private* visibility
createPhoto	albumName photoName photo	success	Uploads a new photo and adds it to an existent set
makePub	albumName		Makes a set visibility *public*
makePriv	albumName		Makes a set visibility *private*

can be reached only after the user has been identified, otherwise an error state has to be reached), or on possible service failures (e.g., when an a timeout expires the corresponding transition leads to an error state).

Each operation $o \in O$ is a triple $\langle name, in, out \rangle$, where $name$ is the operation name, in and out are possibly empty multisets of data the operation requires as input and returns as output, respectively. A datum is a triple $\langle name, type, value \rangle$. $name$ is the name of the datum, $type$ is the type of the datum and $value$ is the value that the datum assumes.

Given an abstract and a concrete service, we say that a *mismatch* occurs when an operation request expressed in terms of the abstract interface cannot be understood by the concrete service that should handle it. We distinguish between two mapping classes:

- *Interface-level mismatches* concern differences between names of operations exposed by an abstract and a concrete service and parameters of these operations.
- *Protocol-level mismatches* concern differences in the order the operations offered by an abstract service and by its concrete representation are expected to be invoked.

As discussed in Section 2, interface-level mismatches have been threated in the literature and addressed either through methodological approaches involving human designers [9] or through automatic approaches able to reason in the presence of some reference ontology [10,11]. Thus, we do not go into further details on this aspect and handle it by exploiting the approach we reported in [5].

Protocol-level mismatches are those we want to focus on in this paper. As mentioned before, they apply to stateful conversational services for which the sequence in which operations are invoked matters. In this case, we can distinguish between the following classes of mismatches:

- *One to one binding*: an operation in the abstract service has a direct counterpart in the concrete service that can replace it. This case is addressed directly as an interface-level mismatch and therefore is not further considered in this paper.
- *One to many binding*: an operation in the abstract service does not have a direct counterpart in the concrete service but it can be mapped into two or more of its operations.
- *Many to one binding*: two or more operations in the abstract service do not have a direct counterpart in the concrete services, but, all together, can be mapped into one operation of the concrete service.
- *Many to many binding*: a sequence of operations on the abstract service can be mapped into a different sequence of operations on the concrete service.

Our aim is to focus on the general case of many to many binding and, based on it, deal also with the simpler cases. In particular, we aim at defining *mapping scripts* that contain histories which associate sequences of operations on the abstract services into sequences of operations on the corresponding concrete services.

At runtime, the mapping scripts are interpreted by adapters that are then able to invoke concrete services thus overcoming their mismatches with respect to the abstract services. Figure 1 shows the main components of our runtime infrastructure. Also, it shows how these components interact when a service composition tries to call a sequence of operations of an abstract service S1 and this sequence is then translated into a sequence of operations on a concrete service S2 that shows a different interaction protocol. The sequence of calls from the composition is intercepted by a proxy that passes it to an adapter. This last one, by interpreting the mapping script, translates it into a sequence of calls on S2 and returns the results back to the proxy. The runtime infrastructure shown in the figure is part of the *SCENE* framework [17] that, thanks to the intermediation of proxies, supports dynamic binding of services to a certain service composition. *SCENE* has been originally designed under the hypothesis that all services would exhibit identical interfaces or protocols. In our extension this limiting hypothesis is overcome by the introduction of the adapter, a piece of software integrated in *SCENE* proxy that supports mismatches solution by interpreting some mapping scripts. These scripts can be manually provided by a system integrator, as described in [4], or can be automatically generated by the proxy when the service to be bound to the composition is selected. Next section provides details about automatic generation of mapping scripts.

5   Generation of Adaptation Scripts for Protocol-Level Mismatches

In previous section we outlined how adaptation takes place once a mapping script is provided. Building the script may be a hard task for humans and in [5] we proposed an automated solution limited to interface level mismatches. In this section we focus on protocol-level mismatches and on how to build, possibly in an automatic way, a suitable adaptation script.

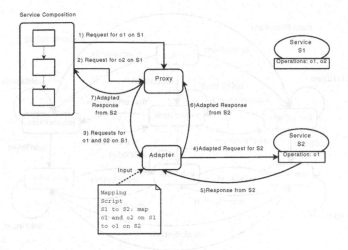

Fig. 1. The adaptation process

5.1   Problem Statement

We assume to know for each service the following information:

- A table which associates to each service operation its input and output parameters. For the example of Section 3 this information is represented by Tables 1 and 2.
- A description of the LTS model associated to the service. This is used to derive the order in which service operations may be invoked. A human-readable version of the LTS models of *Flickr* and *Picasa* is shown in Figures 2 and 3.

We make the hypothesis that both these pieces of information come as a service description that can be accessed and interpreted by both a human or a machine service requestor as *facets* (see [18] for details). The protocol mapping between an abstract and a concrete service assumes that two compatibility relationships have been previously defined. The first relationship states the *compatibility between states* of two LTS models. The second relationship concerns the *compatibility between name and data* associated to some operation $o_{abs} \in O_{abs}$ in the abstract service and those associated to some operation $o'_{conc} \in O_{conc}$ in the concrete service. For the sake of simplicity, we assume in this paper that compatible states, operation names, and data have been already identified someway (for instance, as described in [5]). For this reason, the triple $\langle name, type, value \rangle$ fully characterizing each datum is synthesized here only by the *name* element.

Given these definitions and considering the LTS models P_{abs} and P_{conc}, referring, respectively, to an abstract and concrete service, we say that, given a sequence of operations in P_{abs} (let us call it seq_{abs}), leading from a state s^i_{abs} to some state s^f_{abs}, this can be *substitutable* by another sequence of operations in P_{conc}, seq_{conc}, provided that:

1. seq_{conc} starts from a state s^i_{conc} compatible with s^i_{abs} and ends into a state s^f_{conc} compatible with s^f_{abs}. Note that LTSs may be non-deterministic: in this case the

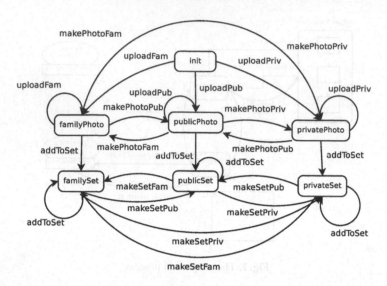

Fig. 2. A representation of the *Flickr* protocol

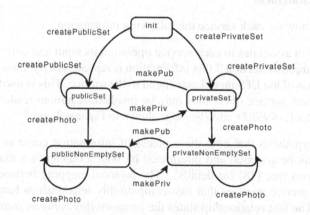

Fig. 3. A representation of the *Picasa* protocol

constraint is that at least one of the ending states $s_{conc}^{f_1} \ldots s_{conc}^{f_a}$ of the concrete service is compatible to one of the ending states $s_{abs}^{f_1} \ldots s_{abs}^{f_b}$ of the abstract service. From now on we will assume, without loss of generality, that both the LTSs are deterministic.

2. For all operations of seq_{conc}, all data parameters are compatible with those appearing in seq_{abs}.

On this basis we can build a reasoning mechanism that, given some $seq_{abs} = o_{abs}^1 \ldots o_{abs}^n$ returns a sequence of operations $seq_{conc} = o_{conc}^1 \ldots o_{conc}^m$ that can replace the first one according to the substitution relationship defined above. We use two different reasoning strategies for identifying seq_{conc}, depending on whether the composition execution environment supports a synchronous or an asynchronous request-reply semantics for operation calls.

The synchronous semantics requires that in a sequence of operation calls not only the operations are called in the required sequence, but also each operation call cannot be performed before the previous one has returned its foreseen result. An example of this semantics is offered by a BPEL *sequence* block. This mandates that the activities it contains should be executed sequentially.

The asynchronous semantics does not prevent the execution of an operation call even if the previous one has not returned the corresponding value yet, unless there is an explicit dependency between the two in terms of input parameters required by the operation to be started and output parameters produced by the previous operation. Using again an example from BPEL, the asynchronous semantics can be mapped on a *flow* block containing various invoke activities together with the corresponding receives. In this case the BPEL executor interprets the flow block by spanning an independent thread for each activity, still ensuring that each receive statement will be performed after the corresponding invoke, and, if dependent invokes are present, that their execution is properly ordered as well.

The strategies adopted by the reasoning mechanism are then the following:

- *Strategy 1 - Synchronous request-reply semantics.* Given the initial state s_{abs}^i of the abstract sequence seq_{abs} and the corresponding compatible state in the concrete LTS model s_{conc}^i, each transition departing from s_{conc}^i is considered as a candidate to be the o_{conc}^1 operation in seq_{conc} provided that all the data it requires as input can be available at the time it will be executed, and the data o_{conc}^1 produces as output include those expected by the consumer of o_{abs}^1, if any. The same line of reasoning is applied starting from any s_{conc}^x until the state s_{conc}^f is reached.
  From the runtime perspective, this results in the fact that an operation $o_{abs} \in seq_{abs}$ can be invoked only if the previous one in the sequence has been completed, that is, the corresponding counterpart in the concrete service has returned the proper value.
- *Strategy 2 - Asynchronous request-reply semantics.* Given the initial state s_{abs}^i of the abstract sequence seq_{abs}, the corresponding compatible state in the concrete LTS model s_{conc}^i, and the final state s_{abs}^f, the transitions $o_{conc}^1...o_{conc}^m$ are considered as possible candidate operations for seq_{conc} provided that:
  1. all the data each operation in seq_{conc} requires as input are available at the time the operation is executed;
  2. all the data expected as output by operations in seq_{abs} will be produced by the operations in seq_{conc} by the time s_{conc}^f is reached.
  At runtime, this implies that, given an invoked operation $o_{abs} \in seq_{abs}$ which returns some data, the next operation in sequence can be invoked without necessarily waiting that the result of o_{abs} has been provided. Consequently, any kind of binding can be established from some operations $o_{abs}^1...o_{abs}^n \in seq_{abs}$ into one or more operations in seq_{conc}, since, for every $x \in [1, n]$ the service consumer may invoke an operation o_{abs}^{x+1} even if o_{abs}^x has not returned yet. Of course this statement is valid if o_{abs}^{x+1} does not require any of the return parameter of o_{abs}^x as input.

Intuitively, the synchronous semantics limits the kind of mismatches for which a solution can be found. In this situation, many to one and many to many bindings can be treated in the general case only if operations involved in the mismatch require no return values. Consider for instance the example in Section 3. Given the trace: *uploadPriv*, *addToSet*, *makeSetPub* departing from the *init* state on *Flickr*, there is no possibility to build a mapping script allowing for the usage of *Picasa* in the synchronous case. In fact, applying the synchronous request-reply semantics reasoning schema, the first operation to be invoked on *Picasa* should accept as input a set of parameters included in those provided to *uploadPriv* on *Flickr*, and should return at least all the parameters expected in return by the same *Flickr* operation. Since all the operations outgoing from *init* on *Picasa* require as input a *albumName* and this datum is not provided by *uploadPriv*, no operation on *Picasa* is a valid candidate and, consequently, it is impossible to build a mapping script.

In the case the asynchronous request-reply semantics schema is applied, a mapping can be identified. In fact, *addToSet* in seq_{abs} can be invoked even if the operation call *uploadPriv* has not produced its return value yet as it does not have a direct counterpart in seq_{conc}. After *addToSet* is invoked, *createPublicSet* or *createPrivateSet* in *Picasa* can be invoked as their input parameter (*albumName*) is available. Indeed, both produce a *success* output, which is expected by the service requestor as output of one of the invoked abstract operations. Assuming that *createPublicSet* is chosen for invocation, there are two possible operations candidate for being part of the concrete sequence: *makePriv* and *createPhoto*. Between those *createPhoto* is chosen because it is the only operation that returns the second *success* output, which is expected by the service requestor. This last operation leads *Picasa* into the *publicNonEmpty* state that is compatible with final state of the abstract sequence, that is, *publicSet*.

From the above examples the reader should notice that both strategies are based on the assumption that the substitution is totally transparent to the service consumer, who invokes the abstract service operations, provides input data for those operations and expects some return data from them. The invocations performed to the abstract service operations are translated into invocations to concrete service operations: input data provided by the consumer are used as input for the invoked concrete service operations and return data provided by the invoked concrete operations are returned to the consumer as needed. Any input parameter provided by the consumer is stored and can be used as input for a concrete operation requiring it. When this happens the parameter is removed from the storage. The same line of reasoning is valid for output parameters, if we consider that they are provided by the concrete service and are returned to the service consumer.

5.2   Implementation and Practical Issues

The reasoning mechanism has been formulated using the linear temporal logic language TRIO [19]. Our model features some application-independent TRIO formulas that represent the reasoning strategies as expressed in the previous section, and some application-dependent formulas, which represent the interfaces and protocols of the abstract and concrete services.

Given this model and an operations sequence seq_{abs}, the approach formulates the problem of finding a substitutable operation sequence seq_{conc}. If this sequence exists, a mapping script is generated. The script is executed by the adapter that, as shown in Figure 1, receives the sequence of invocations that the service consumer expects to perform and transforms them into invocations suitable for the concrete service.

We have chosen to implement the model of the reasoning mechanism using Zot^6, an agile and easily extensible bounded model- and satisfiability-checker. In general, Zot returns a history (i.e., an execution trace of the specified system) which satisfies the given model. The history contains a finite number of steps, each one consisting of a possible configuration of the system.

In our approach the history returned by Zot is a mapping script that is then passed as input to the adapter (see Section 4 for details). Each history step contains the state in which each one of the analyzed LTS (the ones of the abstract and concrete services) is, the operations in seq_{abs} and in seq_{conc} that should be invoked in that step, and the exchanged data, if any. In the current implementation, we make the hypothesis that at most one operation in seq_{abs} and at most one in seq_{conc} can be executed at each history step.

Consider again the operations *uploadPriv, addToSet, makeSetPub* as seq_{abs} departing from the *init* state on *Flickr*. Let us assume an asynchronous semantics and specify as compatible the *init* states of the two services and the states *publicSet* of *Flickr* and *publicNonEmptySet* of *Picasa*. In this case, a possible history returned by *Zot* is reported in Table 3. In the first two steps the history only reports invocations on *Flickr*. This means that the adapter only expects to receive invocations from the service consumer and to keep trace of provided inputs and required outputs. On step 3 there are enough data to invoke the operation *createPublicSet* on *Picasa*. The adapter performs the invocation on the concrete service, uses as input for that invocation the *albumName* stored in memory, and removes the parameter from storage. The *success* value returned by this operation is forwarded to the service consumer. On step 4 the history reports again an invocation on *Flickr*. In this case the adapter behaves exactly as in steps 1 and 2. Finally on step 5 the history mandates the invocation on *Picasa* of the operation *createPhoto* and on step 6 *Flickr* is in a state *publicSet*, considered final for the considered sequence and *Picasa* is in a state compatible to *publicSet*.

6 Evaluation

The experiments were conducted to prove the effectiveness in solving protocol level mismatches and the performance of the approach both as an interactive and on-line solution to determine feasible mappings[7]. In particular, we conducted two classes of experiments.

- We ran experiments with *Flickr* and *Picasa* trying to map various abstract sequences into some concrete ones in order to see if the approach was behaving as expected in terms of the identification of correct mappings.

---

[6] *Zot* can be downloaded from http://home.dei.polimi.it/pradella

[7] The input set of experiments is available at http://home.dei.polimi.it/cavallaro/evaluation-experimentsInputs.zip

Table 3. An history generated for the seq_{abs} = *uploadPriv, addToSet, makeSetPub*

Step	History Content
1	FlickrState = init; FlickrInvoke = uploadPriv FlickrInput = photo, photoName; FlickrOutput = success PicasaState = init
2	FlickrState = privatePhoto; FlickrInvoke = addToSet FlickrInput = albumName, photoName; FlickrOutput = success PicasaState = init
3	FlickrState = privateSet PicasaState = init; PicasaInvoke = createPublicSet PicasaInput = albumName; PicasaOutput = success
4	FlickrState = privateSet; FlickrInvoke = makeSetPub FlickrInput = albumName PicasaState = publicSet
5	FlickrState = publicSet PicasaState = publicSet; PicasaInvoke = createPhoto PicasaInput = photo, photoName, albumName; PicasaOutput = success
6	FlickrState = publicSet PicasaState = publicNonEmptySet

- We compared the performance of our approach with the one shown by a similar approach found in the literature [15].

All the experiments had the goal of exploring the possibility for our tool to derive (whenever possible) correct mappings between an abstract and a concrete service. The experiments were conducted on a 2.5 Ghz Intel Core2 duo machine, equipped with 4 GBytes of memory, running Linux. The Common Lisp compiler used for running *Zot* was SBCL, version 1.0.18.

The main inputs used in each experiment have been: a) the LTSs of the abstract service and the candidate concrete service b) the associations between service operations and their inputs and outputs; c) the compatibility relationship between the operation names and parameters of the abstract and concrete services; and d) a possible seq_{abs}. The results obtained by the experiments have been a possible seq_{conc} in the cases this could have been identified by the tool as well as information about the time needed by the tool to produce a result or to signal the impossibility of producing it.

As additional input, since *Zot* is based on a SAT-solver, it is necessary to set the size k of the periodic temporal structure on which the verification is performed. In this case, all the periodic behaviors of the system, with period up to k are considered by the tool. The identification of a proper value for k is always a critical issue when exploiting a SAT-solver. High values for k usually imply long execution times for the tool while small values may result in the fact that the tool is not able to find a solution that would have been identified if the considered temporal structure was longer. Our approach is essentially based on constructing the product of the abstract and concrete LTSs, hence the upper bound for non-cyclic behaviors is $ns_{abs} \cdot ns_{conc} - 1$, where ns_{abs} and n_{conc} are the number of states of the LTS models of the abstract and concrete

Table 4. Results for the experiments on examples in Section 3

			Time (s)			
Uploaded photos	Sequence length	ns	ns	$2ns$	$3ns$	$4ns$
1	3	12	0.59	1.87	3.72	5.80
2	6	12	0.59	1.94	4.06	7.32
3	9	12	0.55	1.81	4.14	7.35
4	13	12	0.55	1.86	4.82	7.72

services, respectively. In practice, we empirically found that in most of the cases a good estimate for k is $ns = ns_{abs} + ns_{conc}$. With $k = 2ns$ we were able to find solutions for every considered case. Therefore the algorithm first tries with $k = ns$, then considers $k = 2ns$, and so on, keeping $ns_{abs} \cdot ns_{conc}$ as an upper bound. In the experiments we considered four possible values for k: $2ns$, $3ns$, and $4ns$, to see how the tool speed is affected by increasing bounds.

Experiments with Flickr and Picasa. We ran the tool starting from the *Flickr* abstract sequence we have used through this paper. Moreover, we have complicated it considering the case in which up to 4 pictures are uploaded (this results in the fact that the operations *uploadPriv* and *addToSet* are called more than one time. The results are reported in Table 4. We started with a bound $k = ns = 12$. In the first two cases reported in the table (upload of one and two pictures) we succeeded in determining a sequence with ns, while in the last two cases we needed to use $k = 2ns$. The overheads introduced to produce a working mapping script are between 0.59 and 1.86 seconds. This makes the approach suitable for both on-line and off-line use at least in this specific case. The histories produced by *Zot* were analyzed by a human to prove their correctness and were executed by the adapter as mapping scripts. The performed tests succeeded in using *Picasa* in place of *Flickr*.

Comparison with [15]. We compared our technique with the one presented in [15] and summarized in Section 2. The tool is called Dinapter, and its package contains several examples of abstract and concrete services. We took some of the most significant ones and used them both with Dinapter and *Zot*.

In the original example, the tested services were all described using abstract BPEL. They contain branches, loops and non-determinism. In order to use them with our tool we translated the abstract BPEL description into LTS using the following criteria:

- For what concern the BPEL descriptions representing sequences of calls, we considered invoke activities as operation invocations, and receive activities associated with invocations and featuring parameters as responses to the invoked operations.
- For BPEL description representing service interfaces, we considered receive activities as invocation expected by the service, and invoke operations featuring parameters and associated with the receives as issued responses.
- We considered those activities included in a BPEL *sequence* block as having a synchronous semantics.

Table 5. Results of the comparison with [15]

		[15]	Our approach (Time (s))			
Example name	ns	Time (s)	ns	$2ns$	$3ns$	$4ns$
e001-ftp-tiny	6	1.4	0.06	0.34	0.54	0.9
e002-ftp-small	8	30.65	0.11	0.53	0.95	1.54
e002c-ftp-small	7	37.15	0.12	0.39	0.81	1.30
e003-ftp-full	8	Out of memory	0.17	0.26	0.48	0.75
e004-wich-Pick	10	45.10	0.75	2.37	4.81	8.60
e005-start-Switch	8	51.05	0.53	1.62	2.87	4.45
e010-Pick-Pick	12	6.01	0.64	2.09	3.51	7.03
e013-deceptive-Pick	12	54.90	0.68	2.01	3.47	6.95
e017-2Switch-2Pick-carry	10	Out of memory	0.34	0.91	1.92	3.49
vod-1	8	14.41	0.09	0.23	0.71	1.10

The results of the comparison are reported in Table 5. In each row, the name of the example taken from the test set bundled with Dinapter is reported. The time needed to run Dinapter (third column) is the one we calculated by executing the tool on our reference machine. The other times in the last four columns are those referred to our tool with the temporal structure bound k set to the first four multiples of ns, i.e., the sum of the abstract and concrete LTSs states.

Our approach was able to find a solution in every case with the bound estimated as ns and with an execution time shorter than 1 second (clearly the time increases for higher values of the bound). This, again, is promising for on-line use of the tool. Moreover, our approach outperformed Dinapter that in some cases has not been able to terminate with success because of out of memory problems. The output sequences produced by *Zot* were inspected by a human to verify correctness and, in those cases in which Dinapter was able to produce a result, were compared with those produced by Dinapter and found out to be equivalent.

7   Conclusion

In this work we presented an approach to identify an interaction protocol mapping between compatible conversational services. The mapping is deduced by using *Zot*, a recent, efficient model checker based on a SAT-solver.

We validated our technique by considering two real-life services, *Flickr* and *Picasa*, obtaining both correct protocol mappings between the two and good performance. Moreover, we compared our approach with Dinapter [15] on some significant cases that have been made available together with this last tool. *Zot* outperformed Dinapter in all cases, with times suitable for on-line application of the technique. The research work is currently ongoing and disregards some important aspects that need to be considered for successful service replacement. Currently we analyzed only services featuring conversations that can be represented by LTSs, while some real world cases need more powerful formalisms (e.g. services featuring branches executed in parallel, services featuring not only a conversational state but also an internal state). Finally services are usually invoked in complex processes that may feature a state or transactional support. Consequently service substitution may require house keeping work of the running processes. Thus, as future work we plan to extend our approach to allow consistent substitution of stateful and transactional services.

References

1. Baresi, L., Nitto, E.D., Ghezzi, C.: Toward open-world software: Issue and challenges. IEEE Computer 39(10), 36–43 (2006)
2. Verma, K., Gomadam, K., Sheth, A.P., Miller, J.A., Wu, Z.: The METEOR-S approach for configuring and executing dynamic web processes. University of Georgia, Athens, Tech. Rep. (June 2005)
3. Antonellis, V.D., Melchiori, M., Santis, L.D., Mecella, M., Mussi, E., Pernici, B., Plebani, P.: A layered architecture for flexible web service invocation. Software Practice and Experience 36(2), 191–223 (2006)
4. Cavallaro, L., Di Nitto, E.: An approach to adapt service requests to actual service interfaces. In: Proceedings of SEAMS (2008)
5. Cavallaro, L., Ripa, G., Zuccalà, M.: Adapting service requests to actual service interfaces through semantic annotations. In: Proceedings of PESOS (2009)
6. Moser, O., Rosenberg, F., Dustdar, S.: Non-intrusive monitoring and service adaptation for WS-BPEL. In: Proceedings of WWW (2008)
7. Mateescu, R., Poizat, P., Salaün, G.: Adaptation of service protocols using process algebra and on-the-fly reduction techniques. In: Bouguettaya, A., Krueger, I., Margaria, T. (eds.) ICSOC 2008. LNCS, vol. 5364, pp. 84–99. Springer, Heidelberg (2008)
8. Dumas, M., Spork, M., Wang, K.: Adapt or perish: Algebra and visual notation for service interface adaptation. In: Dustdar, S., Fiadeiro, J.L., Sheth, A.P. (eds.) BPM 2006. LNCS, vol. 4102, pp. 65–80. Springer, Heidelberg (2006)
9. Nezhad, H.R.M., Benatallah, B., Martens, A., Curbera, F., Casati, F.: Semi-automated adaptation of service interactions. In: Proceedings of WWW 2007 (2007)
10. Drumm, C.: Improving schema mapping by exploiting domain knowledge. Ph.D. dissertation, Universitat Karlsruhe, Fakultat fur Informatik (2008)
11. Fredj, M., Georgantas, N., Issarny, V., Zarras, A.: Dynamic service substitution in service-oriented architectures. In: Proceedings of SERVICES (2008)
12. Brogi, A., Popescu, R.: Automated generation of BPEL adapters. In: Dan, A., Lamersdorf, W. (eds.) ICSOC 2006. LNCS, vol. 4294, pp. 27–39. Springer, Heidelberg (2006)
13. WS-BPEL specification,
   http://www.oasis-open.org/committees/tc_home.php?wg_abbrev=wsbpel
14. van der Aalst, W.M.P., ter Hofstede, A.H.M.: Yawl: yet another workflow language. Information Systems 30(4), 245–275 (2005)
15. Martìn, J.A., Pimentel, E.: Automatic generation of adaptation contracts. In: Proceedings of FOCLASA (2008)
16. Fielding, R.T.: Architectural styles and the design of network-based software architectures. Ph.D. dissertation, chair-Taylor, Richard N (2000)

17. Colombo, M., Di Nitto, E., Mauri, M.: Scene: A service composition execution environment supporting dynamic changes disciplined through rules. In: Dan, A., Lamersdorf, W. (eds.) ICSOC 2006. LNCS, vol. 4294, pp. 191–202. Springer, Heidelberg (2006)
18. Colombo, M., Di Nitto, E., Penta, M.D., Distante, D., Zuccalà, M.: Speaking a common language: A conceptual model for describing service-oriented systems. In: Benatallah, B., Casati, F., Traverso, P. (eds.) ICSOC 2005. LNCS, vol. 3826, pp. 48–60. Springer, Heidelberg (2005)
19. Ghezzi, C., Mandrioli, D., Morzenti, A.: Trio: A logic language for executable specifications of real-time systems. Journal of Systems and Software 12(2) (1990)

Towards Adaptable SOA:
Model Driven Development, Context and Aspect

Valérie Monfort[1,2] and Slimane Hammoudi[3]

[1] Université Paris IX Dauphine LAMSADE
Place du Maréchal de Lattre Tassigny, Paris Cedex 16 France
[2] Université Paris 1 - Panthéon –Sorbonne
Centre de Recherche en Informatique, France
[3] ESEO 4, Rue Merlet de la Boulaye B.P. 926
49 009 ANGERS Cedex 01 France
valerie.monfort@univ-paris1.fr, slimane.hammoudi@eseo.fr

Abstract. Service-Oriented Architectures (SOA) are broadly used by companies to gain in flexibility. Web service is the fitted technical solution used to
support SOA by providing interoperability and loose coupling. However, there
is still much to be done in order to obtain a genuine flawless Web service, and
current market implementations still do not provide adaptable Web service behavior depending on the service contract. In this paper, we propose two different approaches to increase adaptability of Web services and SOA. The first one
is based on a technical solution which considers Aspect Oriented Programming
(AOP) as a new design solution for Web services. We implemented an infrastructure to enrich services with aspects and to dynamically reroute messages
according to changes, without redeployment. The second one combines Model
Driven Development (MDD) and Context-Awareness to promote reusability
and adaptability of Web services behavior depending on the service context.

Keywords: Aspect Based services, Meta Modeling, Model Composition.

1 Introduction

Economical context impacts companies and their Information System (IS). With SOA
(Service Oriented Architecture), each application owns interfaces, offering services
and masking implementation details. Applications are seen as black boxes independently connected to a middleware as Enterprise Application Integration bus (EAI) with
its connectors (connecting the bus to the applications). However, this integration solution does not allow connecting heterogeneous applications or infrastructures, as distant IS. Web services [4][10] are the cheapest and simplest technical solution to
resolve this problem. They offer interoperability because they are based on standards
as XML (eXtensible Markup Language) and allow loose coupling. Web services
(WS), like any other middleware technologies, aim to provide mechanisms to bridge
heterogeneous platforms, allowing data to flow across various programs. The WS
technology looks very similar to what most middleware technologies looks like. Consequently, each WS possesses an Interface Definition Language, namely WSDL

L. Baresi, C.-H. Chi, and J. Suzuki (Eds.): ICSOC-ServiceWave 2009, LNCS 5900, pp. 175–189, 2009.

(Web Service Description Language), which is responsible for the message payload, itself described with the equally famous protocol SOAP (Simple Object Access Protocol), while data structures are explained by XML. Very often, WS are stored in UDDI (Universal Description Discovery and Integration) registry. In fact, the winning card of this technology is not its mechanism but rather the standards upon which it is built. Indeed, each of these standards is not only open to everyone but, since all of them are based on XML, it is pretty easy to implement these standards for most platforms and languages. For this reason, WS are highly interoperable and do not rely on the underlying platform they are built on, unlike many ORPC (object remote procedure call). According to a vast majority of industrial leaders, WS is the best fitted technology for implementing Service Oriented Architectures. With WSs, the message contract (WSDL) is the central meeting point which connects applications. The WSDL contract constitutes the design view upon which developers can generate both client and server sides (proxy and stub).

We noticed code is very monolithic it encapsulates different concerns as business, security... Moreover, we used to change Web service code according to new needs, to redeploy Web service. Each change is time costly and Web service is not available. So, flexibility to changes is not optimal. We proposed aspects based solutions to gain in code simplicity without re deploying code with a non intrusive manner [3][22]. We based our more recent approach on extended BPEL (Business Process Execution Language) [2][18] and temporized automatons [1][15], that we prototyped by providing client, and server adaptability.

Nevertheless, we are convinced this pragmatic and efficient solution is too complex for non expert users and developers and difficult to maintain, because it requires strong technical knowledge.

Recently, we have investigated a model driven approach and context awareness to provide developers mechanisms that allow them representing an application in abstract way (in a model) and, then, automatically generating the corresponding code. We broadly discussed about adaptability according to context in [23].

We aimed to explore adaptability and flexibility on a service platform using context with the benefits of an MDD (Model Driven Development) [26] development strategy. These benefits are related to productivity, quality, adaptability and maintenance. Model Driven Architecture (MDA) is based on standards from the Object Management Group (OMG); it proposes an architecture with four layers [24]: meta meta model, meta model, model and information (i.e. an implementation of its model). Object-oriented and component technology seem insufficient to provide satisfactory solutions to support the development and maintenance of these systems. To adapt to this new context, software engineering has applied an old paradigm, i.e. models, but with a new approach, i.e. Model Driven Development (MDD). In this new global trend, MDA is a particular variant. Adaptable Service platforms have been proposed for the development of mobile context-aware applications.

The development of such platforms involves a number of challenges from which we consider two main issues in the context of our approach of model driven development : i) the definition of a meta model to describe the contextual domain in which a given application or service is defined, ii) A mechanism to integrate the context into the business application using a model driven approach.

We propose to discuss about the pertinence to merge these two solutions. The section 2 explains our technical approach based on services and aspects to implement adaptability in Web services. The section 3 shows how our first step researches about MDD approach assure service adaptability while using context mechanisms. The section 4 comments the needs of merging and extending these two research works: aspect based services and context modeling with parameterized transformation. It launches our future research in this topic. Finally, we will discuss our solution and conclude this work. Let us see now Aspect based services.

2 Aspects for Web Services Adaptability

2.1 Applying AOP to Web Services with ASW

Aspect Oriented Programming (AOP) is viewed as an answer to improve Web services flexibility. AOP [5][20] is a paradigm that enables the modularization of crosscutting concerns into single units called aspects, which are modular units of crosscutting implementation. Aspect-oriented languages are implemented over a set of definitions:

1. Joinpoints: They denote the locations in the program that are affected by a particular crosscutting concern.
2. Pointcuts: They specify a collection of conditional joinpoints.
3. Advices: They are codes that are executed before, after or around a joinpoint.

In ΛOP, a tool named weaver takes the code specified in a traditional (base) programming language, and the additional code specified in an aspect language, and merges the two together in order to generate the final behavior. The weaving can occur at compile time (modifying the compiler), load time (modifying the class loader) or runtime (modifying the interpreter).

We developed an AOP based tool named Aspect Service Weaver (ASW) [3][18][22]. The ASW intercepts the SOAP messages between a client and an elementary Web service, then verifies during the interaction if there is a new behavior introduced (advice services). We use the AOP weaving time to add the new behavior (before, around or after an activity execution). The advice services are elementary Web services whose references are registered in a file called "aspect services file descriptor". The pointcut language is based on XPath [6]. XPath queries are applied on the service description (WSDL) to select the set of methods on which the advice services are inserted. We extended this approach to BPEL processes. The ASW controls the BPEL process execution instead of intercepting SOAP messages. It is integrated in the BPEL engine in order to interpret the BPEL process and apply the aspect services. It verifies before the execution of each BPEL activity if some Aspect service has to be inserted. Then, it executes the corresponding advice service. We also add a new functionality to the ASW. The tool dynamically generates messages called execute messages, encapsulating the identifier and the interaction protocol of the advice service. These messages are sent to the client to advertise it about a new behavior inserted at runtime. This message is necessary since the new behavior can require new information exchange involving messages not expected by the client, leading to execution failures. We defined a new process algebra semantics that associates a timed automaton [1] with an abstract process as shown in [13] . Let us see now related works.

2.2 Adaptability with Aspects Based Services : Related Works

In [3], the authors define specific AOP languages to add dynamically new behaviors to BPEL processes. But, neither of these approaches addresses the client interaction issue. The client has no mean to handle the interactions that can be added or modified during the process execution. The Web Service Management Layer (WSML) [22] is an AOP-based platform for Web services that allows a more loosely coupling between the client and the server sides. WSML handles the dynamic integration of new Web services in client applications to solve client execution problems. WSML dynamically discover Web services based on matching criteria such as: method signature, interaction protocol or quality of service (QOS) matching. In a complementary way, our work proposes to adapt a client to a modified Web services. Some proposals have emerged recently to abstractly describe Web services, most of them [7][13] are grounded on transition system models (Labeled Transition Systems, Petri nets, etc.). [9] Introduces WComp middleware model, which federates three main paradigms: event-based Web services, a lightweight component-based approach to design dynamic composite services, and an adaptation approach using the original concept called Aspect of Assembly.

These paradigms lead to two ways to dynamically design ubiquitous computing applications. The first implements a classical component-based compositional approach to design higher-level composite Web Services and then allow incrementing a graph of cooperating services for the applications. This approach is well suited to design the applications in a known, common, and usual context. The second way uses a compositional approach for adaptation using Aspect of Assembly, particularly well-suited to tune a set of composite services in reaction to a particular variation of the context or changing preferences of the users. In these approaches adaptability is resolved with AOP and /or with specific middleware.

We noticed some research works propose to formally specify composite Web services and handle the verification and the automatic composition issues. But, neither of these works proposes to formalize the dynamics of SOA architectures and to handle runtime interaction changes. Even if this solution addresses our (contextual) adaptability and interoperability aims, nevertheless, it may be felt as complex by non expert users or developers.

We are convinced adding an abstraction layer with metamodeling will facilitate usage of this technology and guaranty interoperability. We are also convinced parameterized Meta modeling is the fitted solution to our contextual adaptability need.

3   Context for Service Adaptability with Model Driven Approach

3.1 MDD and Context for Service Adaptability

3.1.1 A Context Meta Model with Example
Previous research works allowed us to define adaptability and context [23]. In the MDD approach, the use of a metamodel not only guarantees a strong and focused

semantics tied to a particular application domain, but also offers a precise abstract syntax and a common representation to any developed model. We are interested in our research in user centered mobile application [7][8]. Thus, we consider that the defining context here is a set of information structured in three dimensions [26] :

- Actor: A person which is a central entity in our system.
- Environment: in which the person evolves and
- Computational entities which are used by a person to invoke services and capture the different states of the environment.

All the information related to the three dimensions can also be shared by other mobile applications. Figure 1 shows our context metamodel. Our metamodel identifies and adds the most relevant and generic contextual entities that will be held in account in modeling any mobile and context aware application. This context metamodel consists of six generic contextual entities and four deduced entities specific to a category of mobile applications. The class "ContextView" groups all contextual entities involved in a given application. It is identified by name attribute and has two types of relation: the aggregation "involves" and the association "belongsTo". The first relation expresses that a given "ContextView" is composed of many "ContextEntity" that are involved in a context-aware application. The second relation "belongsTo" expresses the use of historical context information. A given context entity may have participated in different context views. This information can be helpful in the design of future context views. The second generic entity of the metamodel is the "ContextEntity". As we see on the figure bellow, it is specialized in three generic entities: Actor, ComputationalEntity and Environnement. Actor may be a person or another object that has a state and profile. It evolves in an environment and uses computational devices to invoke services. With the ComputationalEntity, the computational device is used by the actor to access the services and to capture contextual information from the environment. Usually, a mobile device is used in context aware mobile applications, and can obtain information concerning the type of device it is (PDA, laptop, cellular phone...), the application, the network, etc. The environment is constituted of all the information surrounding the actor and its computational device that can be relevant for the application. It includes different categories of information as :(i) Spatial context information can be location, city, building, (ii) Temporal context information comprises time, date, season, (iii) Climate can be temperature, type of weather.... The last entity is a profile. We are convinced this entity is important in any user centred context aware application. In fact, profile is strongly attached to the actor and contains the information that describes it. An actor can have a dynamic and/or a static profile. The static profile gathers information relevant for any mobile context-aware application. It can be the "date of birth", "name" or "sex". On the opposite, dynamic profile includes customized information depending on the specific type of application and/or the actor. It can be goals, preferences, intentions, desires, constraints, etc. For example the goal of a tourist searching for a restaurant is to have dinner. A profile in this case can give information concerning culinary habitude or constraints of a tourist. Let us see now the benefits of parameterized transformation for context binding.

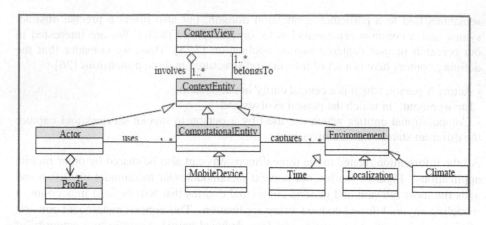

Fig. 1. A context Meta Model

3.1.2 Parameterized Transformation for Context Binding

MOF (Meta Object Facility) is a standard from OMG for meta models specification. The development is based on the separation of concerns (e.g. business and technical concerns), which are afterwards transformed between them. So, business concerns are represented using Platform-Independent Model (PIM), and technical concerns are represented using Platform- Specific Model (PSM). PIM models are more stable over time while PSM models are subject to frequent modification. So, this approach preserves the business's logic (i.e. PIM models) against the changes or evolutions of technologies (i.e. PSM models). The separation of concerns (business and context) is emphasized at a model level of our approach where PIM and context models are defined independently, and then merged by suitable transformation technique. Parameterized transformation allows merging context information with business logic at model level. We have investigated [12] this type of transformation which is not explored and there is not a standard transformation language implementing it. We will discuss shortly this type of transformation. A CPIM model (Contextual Platform Independent Model) is then obtained and fits together business requirements with contextual data. According to [25], "A parameter specifies how arguments are passed into or out of an invocation of a behavioral feature like an operation. The type and multiplicity of a parameter restrict what values can be passed, how many, and whether the values are ordered". In [12] David Frankel mentions the importance of parameterization in model operations using the association of tagged values with PIM and PSM models. Tagging model elements allows the model language to easily filter out some specific elements.

In our proposition these parameters are context or context-aware and after the transformation the application will join the context information specified into the parameters as illustrated in Figure 2. A PIM model can be developed without contextual details. User name, profiles, device type, location can be added as parameters in transformations. The same PIM can be re-transformed and refined many times adding, deleting or updating context information. The designer has to specify into the application model the elements that will receive the context information. A mark, identified by the symbol #, is given for these elements to be recognized by the transformation

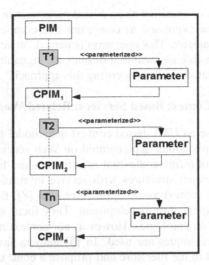

Fig. 2. Parameterized Transformation

engine. The marked elements represent context-aware elements, in others words, the model elements that can be contextualized.

The transformation language must support parameterization techniques. In our case the parameters can be a Context Property and/or a Context Data Type. We use templates to specify which elements in application model are potentially context-aware as depicted in Figure. 3.

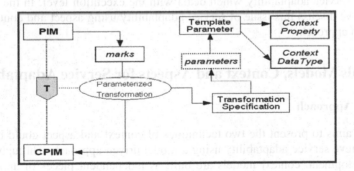

Fig. 3. Parameterized Transformation for context binding

The transformation engine has to navigate into the PIM model verifying the parameters and the elements marked and then make the transformation which consists in an update of contextual properties in a PIM. Template parameter [12] is an element used to specify how classifiers, packages and operations can be parameterized. UML 2.0 presents that any model element can be templateable. For independent context-aware models we need to identify context elements that could be parameterable. A parameterable element is an element that can be exposed as a formal template parameter for a template, or specified as an actual parameter in a binding of template. Context parameter can be expressed as constraint and compared with the elements signature in template parameter. This operation is named "matching operation". UML presents a Template Signature element that defines the signature for binding the template. Lets us see now related works concerning this approach.

3.2 Adaptability with Context Based Services: Related Works

In [7], the authors propose an UML based context metamodel for the development of context-aware mobile applications implemented on Web services platform. The proposed metamodel does not refine contextual information and focuses on the association between basic contextual structures with service invocation interfaces for both contextual providers and context-aware applications. In [8], they have been applied MDA in context-aware application development. They focus on.the development of context-awareness based on ontologies. However, nor context metamodel is proposed neither transformation techniques are used. In [5] authors investigate a number of context models described in the literature and propose a context metamodel based on the main concepts and strengths found on these models. The metamodel is formally described using MOF and has been used as a basis for the development of context-aware applications and an associated service platform. All these works aim to explore adaptability and flexibility on a service platform using context and models. But, neither of these works proposes an explicit approach to integrate context into business logic. By the use of a parameterized transformation technique the contextual parameter identified into the business logic model will be completed and contextualized with the "parameterable elements" which represents context information.

While our approach allows binding contextual data at model level, it doesn't take into account service adaptability which deals with the execution level. In the following section, we discuss this issue of service adaptability using aspect and context in a model driven approach.

4 Towards Models, Context and Aspects for Service Adaptability

4.1 Global Approach

This section aims to present the two techniques of context and aspect could be combined to achieve service adaptability using a model driven approach. Through Model Driven Development, context models are built as independent pieces of application and at different abstraction levels then attached by suitable transformation techniques called parameterized transformation. Context model specify contextual entities that are involved in a given context aware application. From a context model, an aspect model is derived. This aspect model specifies the behaviors linked to the context model. Figure 4 illustrates the main models and transformations techniques involved in our MDD approach. Five main objectives are illustrated:

- A separation between Context Model information (CM) and business logic (PIM) in individual models,

- The derivation of an Aspect Model (AM) from a context model. A Context Model specify the contextual entities with their properties (static view), while the aspect model specify behaviors (dynamic view).
- The integration of the Context Model into the business logic using parameterized transformation techniques. At this stage, the CPIM model is enriched by contextual data but the behavior part for adaptability at execution level is missing.
- The Weaving process add adaptability mechanism producing a CPSM model (Context Platform Specific Model) .
- Finally, a CPSM model is mapped into a service platform for future execution of context-aware services.

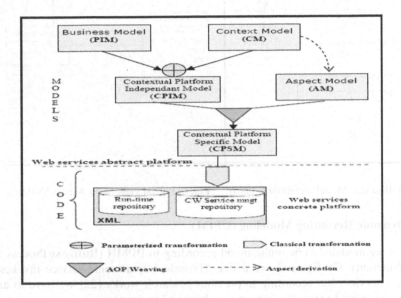

Fig. 4. Models, context and aspect for service adaptability

4.2 Concrete Examples

Figure 5 shows a simplified Business Model (BM) that is underlined. It is comes from a genuine industrial feedback. The company uses to let apartments for holidays (sea side, country side, mountain). If the client chooses an apartment a contract is established according to client profile and apartment characteristics. According to client profile, apartment availability, date in the location schedule, a specific offer may be proposed to the client. So, price will dynamically change according to these parameters. Moreover, Location Manager component will expose an interface with public methods as "ToSelectAppartment" and "ToContract". These methods are services and may be invoked through the Web as Web services in future implementations. Figure 6 expresses a part of an Aspect Model (AM). An aspect includes advices and pointcuts that include pointcut expressions. JoinPoints denote the locations in the program that are affected by a particular crosscutting concern. Advices implements Crosscutting concerns.

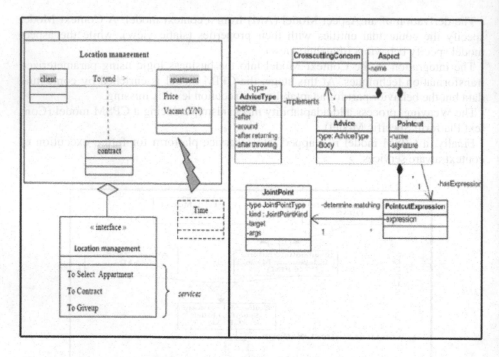

Fig. 5. Business Model including Context   **Fig. 6.** Partial view of an Aspect Model

4.3 Dynamic Rerouting Modeling (CPIM)

Services are modeled to be orchestrated according to BPMN (Business Process Modeling Notation). On figure 7, we notice "To select apartment" service invokes "To contract" service, but according to previous research works [22] we have to extend BPMN semantics to introduce aspect paradigm and to express:

- Contextual parameters and variability as with vacancy and season parameters
- Message rerouting according to parameters evaluation and context. Here, invocation is dynamically rerouted via "To give up" service.

CPSM includes paradigms of the chosen platform. We chose to extend and ESB (Enterprise Service Bus), an open source called MULE. This ESB will be extended with ASW techniques. We have to develop this modeling and mapping rules still remain to do.

4.4 Model Transformation

Previous research works [26] proposed a static solution by extending OCL (Object Constraint Language) language to adapt some model transformation operations used to attach context into application models. Differently from traditional model transformations, the parameterized one has as source model a set of contextual parameters and as target model the PIM marked model. The designer determines which model

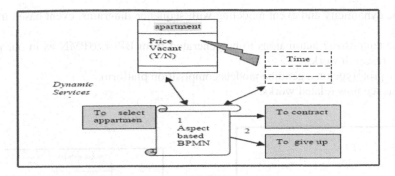

Fig. 7. Dynamic services orchestration models approach

element will be transformed by tagging parameters. The *match* operation is realized before the transformation one. The match binds and checks the concerned (marked) elements that will be transformed. It is also responsible for determining if a parameterable element is compatible with another one. Semantical interpretation among these elements can be supplied by the ontologies use. Our context meta model is ontology supported by the RDF interpretation. According to W3C RDF Semantic a RDF logical semantic is identified by a *triple(x,y,z)* where x and z are semantical elements, data types or resources in our case (represented by a string), and y is the relation between them. The context can be represented by N-triples in URI references. Nevertheless, previous research work propose a semantic solution for context representation; Aspect based services are not taken into account. Dynamicity and adaptability have to be added. The Match class, as illustrated in Figure 8, is responsible for navigating over models. The OCL Rules class specifies the navigation rules using OCL. OCL permits filter expressions to add platform requirements and context information. The *match* operation generates the correspondences between the elements of the Parameterable Element and its correspondents into the Template Parameter. This can be realized by the use of the new SQL queries supported by OCL 2.0. OCL owns a set of types and operations defined in its OCL Library. Some of the types are integer, string, real and boolean. Although, OCL is easily adapted for new types insertion and provides mechanisms for language extension. For example, the *let* expression permits definitions of variables and expressions. OCL also allows attachment of the new variables defined to a method or property. In [26] we defined extensions with the presence of the *match* operation. As aforementioned, the match operation checks the correspondence of the elements evolved in the parameterized transformation. The return value can be a type, property or N-triple. The match navigates over the model searching the marked elements and their correspondences. We are convinced Aspect Based Services Weaving refers to related works in dynamic models composition. We know many questions are till now unresolved as :

- The complete formal description of our meta models.
- The complete specification of our model transformations including context parameters.
- The study of the dynamic models composition including CPIM and AM.

- The dynamicity and event modeling with sequence diagrams, event based modeling.
- The temporized automatons to be generated from BPEL/BPMN as in our previous research works.
- The prototype on a genuine models composition platform.

Let us see now related works.

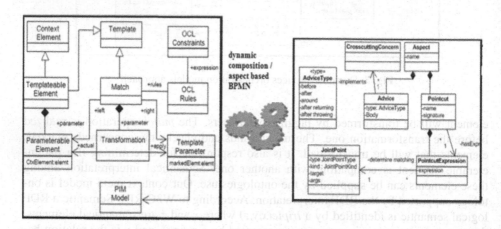

Fig. 8. Parameterized Transformation Metamodel

4.4 Related Works and Discussion

We noticed several related research works and also very interesting approaches to consolidate our work.

For instance [19], have a simpler approach as us. They notice behavioral meta modeling languages were fitted and powerful to perform aspects weaving. They define a semantic-based aspect weaving algorithm for Hierarchical Message Sequence Charts (HMSCs). The algorithm proposed uses a set of transformations that take into account the compositional semantics of HMSCs to weave an initial HMSC and a behavioural aspect expressed with scenarios and with UML sequence diagrams. Other research works about reactive objects, as Hennicker and al [16][17], allow to model synchronous and asynchronous messages by making a clear distinction between inactive (stable) states and activations occurring in different activation phases that follow as a reaction to synchronous operation call. His approach is activity-driven in the sense that during the transformation process different activations occurring in different scenarios but following the same incoming message (in the same state) are integrated into one single activity which models the behavior of an operation across many scenarios. For the integration of the asynchronous scenarios different strategies have been proposed and future work aim to merge these approaches. Context can be stored and recovered as stored variables. This approach seems to be interesting to express services orchestration and context recovering.

[14] notices in software engineering everything evolves very fast: user requirements, technologies, methodologies and applications. Software Product Lines (SPL) modeling technology together with source-code generative tools seem fitting to manage diverse environments with complex, constantly changing relationships. In the context of SPL, they propose an approach based on SmartModels, They propose a meta model to describe business models and a mechanism to compose them. One of the originalities of the meta model is that the designer of the business model can use descriptions of generic entities with a genericity degree which is defined during the model design. Meta-Object Protocol (MOP) which lays the foundation of SmartModels is a mechanism to fill the gap between the semantics and the reification of a model entity. SmartModels may also use AOP paradigm. AOM (Aspect Oriented Modeling) [21] is used to compose models introducing cross cutting concerns in business models to generate with mapping rules aspects based Java code. The aim is to simplify change management with models composition. These research works may be possibly taken into account in the future evolutions of our approach.

5 Conclusion and Future Works

Service-oriented architecture brings new perspectives not only to software architecture but also to enterprise business processes. SOA promotes the use of loosely coupled services to automate business processes. The automation of business processes raises several challenges for enterprises. One of those challenges relates to the how to adapt existing business processes, possibly even at run time. Thus, changing a collaborative business process can have an impact on the contract specified between the parties involved. Thus, a business process may need to adapt to meet a new contract. We have proposed two different approaches aiming to support service and business process adaptability; however, they both suffer from two important weaknesses:

- Aspect oriented approach, even pragmatic and efficient solution is too complex for non expert users and developers, because it requires strong technical knowledge.
- Context_aware model driven development, using parameterized transformation techniques, is suitable for a contextualization of a service model defined as a PIM. However, it doesn't take into account service orchestration which deals more with a dynamic part and interactions between services.

To overcome the above mentioned limitations, we propose in our future work to mix the two approaches. We propose a Model Driven Development Context_Aware Service Aspect approach with the following features:

- Context modeling allows providing information and situation which intervene in the process of service adaptability.
- Services are unaware of their context and the aspects adapt them to the current environment according to the current context. Context-dependant behaviors are extracted into aspects and weaved with the base service during execution.
- Using model driven development, context models are built as independent pieces of application models and at different abstraction levels then attached by suitable transformation techniques.

- Parameterized transformation technique allows binding context information to a service at a model level, and therefore, which aspect should be weaved at execution level.

We are developing CPSM part and we are working now on the mapping rules definition.

References

[1]   Alur, R., Dill, D.L.: A theory of timed automata. Theoretical Computer Science 126(2), 183–235 (1994)

[2]   Andrews, T., et al.: Business Process Execution Language for Web Services. 2nd public draft release, Version1.1 (2003), http://www.ibm.com/developerworks/

[3]   Baligand, F., Monfort, V.: A concrete solution for Web Services adaptability using policies and aspects. In: ACM-International Conference on Service Oriented Computing (ICSOC), New York, USA (2004)

[4]   Tidwell, D.: Web services: The web's next revolution (2000)

[5]   Charfi, A., Mezini, M.: Aspect-oriented Web service composition with AO4BPEL. In: Zhang, L.-J., Jeckle, M. (eds.) ECOWS 2004. LNCS, vol. 3250, pp. 168–182. Springer, Heidelberg (2004)

[6]   Clark, J., DeRose, S.: XML path language (xpath) ver. 1.0 (1999), http://www.w3.org/tr/xpath

[7]   Strang, T., Linnhoff-Popien, C.: A Context Modeling Survey. In: First International Workshop on Advanced Context Modelling, Reasoning and Management, UbiComp (2004)

[8]   De Farias, C.R.G., Pires, L.F., van Sinderen, M.: A MOF Metamodel for the Development of Context-Aware Mobile Applications. In: Proceeding of the 22nd ACM Symposium on Applied Computing SAC 2007 (2007)

[9]   Tigli, J.Y., Lavirotte, S., Rey, G., Hourdin, V., Cheung-Foo-Wo, D., Callegari, E., Riveill, M.: WComp Middleware for Ubiquitous Computing: Aspects and Composite Event-based Web Services. Annals of Telecommunications 64(3-4), 197 (2009)

[10] Staab, S., van der Aalst, W., Benjamins, V.R.: Web services: been there, done that? IEEE Intelligent Systems [see also IEEE Intelligent Systems and Their Applications] 18(1), 72–85 (2003)

[11] Ferrara, A.: Web services: a process algebra approach. In: ICSOC 2004: Proceedings of the 2nd international conference on Service oriented computing, pp. 242–251. ACM Press, New York (2004)

[12] David, F.S.: Model Driven Architecture: Applying MDA to Enterprise Computing. Wiley Publishing, Inc., Chichester (2003)

[13] Gottschalk, F., van der Aalst, W.M.P., Jansen-Vullers, M.H., La Rosa, M.: Configurable Workflow Models. International Journal of Cooperative Information Systems, IJCIS (2008)

[14] Tundrea, E., Lahire, P., Pescaru, D., Chirila, C.B.: SmartModels — an MDE platform for the management of software product lines Automation, Quality and Testing, Robotics. In: IEEE International Conference on AQTR 2008, May 22-25, vol. 3, pp. 193–199 (2008)

[15] Haddad, S., Moreaux, P., Rampacek, S.: Client synthesis for web services by way of a timed semantics. In: Proceedings of the 8th Int. Conf. on Enterprise Information Systems (ICEIS 2006), pp. 19–26 (2006)

[16] Henricksen, K., Indulska, J., Rakotonirainy, A.: Modeling context information in pervasive computing systems. In: Mattern, F., Naghshineh, M. (eds.) PERVASIVE 2002. LNCS, vol. 2414, p. 167. Springer, Heidelberg (2002)

[17] Hennicker, R., Knapp, A.: Activity-Driven Synthesis of State Machines. In: Dwyer, M.B., Lopes, A. (eds.) FASE 2007. LNCS, vol. 4422, pp. 87–101. Springer, Heidelberg (2007)

[18] Hmida, M.B., Tomaz, R.F., Monfort, V.: Applying AOP concepts to increase web services flexibility. Journal of Digital Information Management (JDIM) 4(1), 37–43 (2006)

[19] Klein, J., Hélouet, L., Jézéquel, J.M.: Semantic-based weaving of scenarios. In: Proceedings of the 5th International Conference on Aspect-Oriented Software Development (AOSD 2006), Bonn, Germany. ACM, New York (2006)

[20] Kiczales, G., Lamping, J., Maeda, C., Lopes, C.: Aspect-oriented programming. In: Aksit, M., Matsuoka, S. (eds.) ECOOP 1997. LNCS, vol. 1241, pp. 220–242. Springer, Heidelberg (1997)

[21] Lundesgaard, S., Solberg, A., Oldevik, J., France, R., Oyvind Aagedal, J., Eliassen, F.: Construction and Execution of Adaptable Applications Using an Aspect- Oriented and Model Driven Approach. In: Indulska, J., Raymond, K. (eds.) DAIS 2007. LNCS, vol. 4531, pp. 76–89. Springer, Heidelberg (2007)

[22] Tomaz, R.F., Hmida, M.B., Monfort, V.: Concrete solutions for web services adaptability using policies and aspects. The International Journal of Cooperative Information Systems (IJCIS) 15(3), 415–438 (2006)

[23] Monfort, V., Hammoudi, S.: On the Challenge of Adaptable SOA: Model Driven Development, context and Aspect Oriented Programming. In: Proceedings of the second International conference on Web and Information Technologies, ICWIT 2009, ACM SIGAPP, June 12-14, Kerkennah Island Sfax Tunisia (2009)

[24] OMG. Model driven architecture. Document ormsc/2001-07-01 (2001)

[25] OMG. QVT-Merge Group. Query, View and Transformations for MOF 2.0. OMG (2005)

[26] Vale, S., Hammoudi, S.: Model Driven Development of Context-aware Service Oriented Architecture. In: PerGrid 2008, São Paulo – Brazil, July 16-18 (2008)

Modeling Service Level Agreements with Binary Decision Diagrams

Constantinos Kotsokalis, Ramin Yahyapour, and Miguel Angel Rojas Gonzalez

Dortmund University of Technology, Germany
constantinos.kotsokalis@udo.edu, ramin.yahyapour@udo.edu,
miguel.rojas@udo.edu

Abstract. The vision of automated service composition for enabling service economies is challenged by many theoretical and technical limitations of current technologies. There is a need for complete, dependable service hierarchies created on-the-fly for critical business environments. Such automatically-constructed, complex and dynamic service hierarchies imply a similarly automated process for establishing the contracts that specify the rules governing the consumption of services; and for binding them into respective contract hierarchies. Deducing these required contracts is a computationally challenging task. This also applies to the optimization of such contract sets to maximize utility. We propose the application of (Shared) Reduced Ordered Binary Decision Diagrams, a suitable graph-based data structure well-known in the area of Electronic Design Automation. These diagrams can be used as a canonical representation of SLAs, thus allowing their efficient and unambiguous management independent of their structure's specifics. As such, this representation can facilitate the process of negotiating SLAs, subcontracting parts of them, optimizing their utility, and managing them during runtime for monitoring and enforcement.[1]

1 Introduction

Recent trends in service computing are lead by the vision of an *Internet of Services*, a marketplace without boundaries where service economies can flourish through composition and re-use. Suitable mechanisms, and the automation achieved through smart agents, will be the key enabler for this goal. It is anticipated that, eventually, full potential can be achieved through the automation of contracting for such services. More specifically, it is desired that service consumption can be enabled with determinism, under well-specified contracts that define all parameters and govern the use of a service by its customer.

Such a contract is encoded in a *Service Level Agreement* (SLA). A SLA is essentially a set of *facts*, and a set of *rules*. Facts are globally (with respect to the contract) applicable truths, such as parties involved, monetary unit, etc. Rules include:

---

[1] The research leading to these results is supported by the European Community's Seventh Framework Programme (FP7/2007-2013) and the SLA@SOI project under grant agreement no.216556.

L. Baresi, C.-H. Chi, and J. Suzuki (Eds.): ICSOC-ServiceWave 2009, LNCS 5900, pp. 190–204, 2009.

1. the *conditions* that must hold for a certain *clause* to be in effect;
2. the clause itself, typically describing the expected result that the customer wishes to receive – and which is usually referred to as *Service Level Objective* (SLO); and
3. a fall-back clause in the case that the aforementioned clause is not honored.

As an example, for the condition "time of day is after 08:00", the clause could be "response time is less than 5 seconds", and the fall-back clause could be an applicable penalty. This kind of format actually reflects real-life contracts and their *if-then-else* structure, which might apply either as the default or as the exception to such default respectively.

In this paper we propose that a *graph-based* data structure, well-known in the domain of *Computer Aided Design* (CAD) for *Very Large Scale Integrated* (VLSI) circuits, is suitable for modeling SLAs in a way which is both expressive enough, and very efficient. *Reduced Ordered Binary Decision Diagrams* (ROBBDs) were introduced by R. Bryant in 1986 [1] as an evolution of C.Y. Lee's [2] and S. Akers' [3] work on BDDs. The hardware industry race has further contributed to the optimization of the structure itself with a significant amount of relevant research, and a large number of methods already exist for taking advantage of ROBDDs' inherent properties.

The essential reason that ROBDDs are useful for modeling SLAs, is that they are canonical representations generated on the grounds of *if-then-else* rules. As such, they can express SLAs unambiguously: equivalent SLAs which are *structurally* different, are eventually represented by the same ROBDD. On the contrary, using formats developed for *on-the-wire* representation such as WS-Agreement [4] or WSLA [5] does not guarantee this property. We propose that ROBDDs are used internally in systems which have to manage SLAs, as a representation that facilitates their management. Suitable interpreters should then be developed to convert from standardized, interchangeable formats such as WS-Agreement and WSLA, to this more convenient data structure and vice-versa.

This paper continues with Section 2, which is discussing related work on SLA representation, management of hierarchies, and previous efforts to relate them to Logic. Following, Section 3 elaborates on (Shared) ROBDDs. Section 4 details their relationship with SLAs and the specific proposal on how to use them for our purposes. Section 5 illustrates initial experimental results. Finally, Section 6 concludes the paper with a summary of core results, and an outlook to future work.

2 Related Work

BDDs are classified as a tool in the area of symbolic model checking. This is the scientific discipline looking into the problem of verifying that a given system satisfies specific requirements, given any kind of input. To our best knowledge, this is the first work that uses BDDs to model and verify SLAs and SLA dependencies. That said, BDDs have been used in service computing before, albeit in very few occasions. In [6] the authors are using a special form of BDDs, called *Zero-Suppressed* BDDs, to create compact digests of service advertisements. Then, the digests are distributed to interested parties which use them for their service composition needs. In [7], the authors are using BDDs for matching service advertisements in publish-subscribe systems (making use of equivalence checking).

As regards SLA modeling in general, the most well-known efforts are WS-Agreement and WSLA. As also mentioned in the previous section, the focus of these specifications is on-the-wire representations for enabling interoperability between independent agents. This is an area we are not targeting with the work presented in this paper; rather, our focus is a system-internal representation, that will enable efficient mechanisms for decision making.

With regards to applying logic-based approaches to the topic of SLA management, the work which comes closest to ours is the one described in [8]. There, the authors look at the problem in more detail, defining constructs also for things such service description, pricing, QoS, etc. On the other hand, we face everything in an abstract way here, and assume external syntactical definitions and appropriate architectural patterns for applying these definitions. Additional differences include our explicit focus on managing hierarchies of SLAs and associations between them as such. The necessary constructs for this kind of functionality also exist in [8], however there is no mention of essential facilities such as equivalence checks and translation between different vocabularies for different layers of a complete IT stack.

3   Binary Decision Diagrams

This section serves as a general, high-level introduction to BDDs and their basic properties. Motivated readers are encouraged to consult with the bibliography for in-depth material. Most of the definitions provided in this section, are summaries of the definitions that can be found in [9].

A BDD is a graph-based representation of one or more boolean functions. This kind of diagram is based on *Shannon's decomposition theorem* [10], which states that, assuming a boolean function $f : X_n \to X_m$, where $X_n = \{x_1, ..., x_n\}$ and $X_m = \{x_1, ..., x_m\}$, then for any boolean variable x_i, $i \leq 1 \leq n$:

$$f = x_i \cdot f_{x_i=1} + \overline{x_i} \cdot f_{x_i=0} \qquad (1)$$

What Equation 1 provides, is the *if-then-else* representation we are looking for: If x_i is *true*, then $f_{x_i=1}$ must be evaluated, or *else* $f_{x_i=0}$ must be evaluated. A BDD then, is a *directed acyclic graph* $G = (V, E)$, where V denotes the vertices (nodes) and E the edges. Vertices can be either *terminal* (i.e. their out-degree is equal to zero), or *non-terminal*. The former can carry a value of either **1** (*true*) or **0** (*false*). The latter are labelled with a variable $x_i \in X_n$; if u is the node, the variable x_i is referred to as $var(u)$. Of the two children nodes, the one followed if x_i evaluates to *true* is referred to as $then(u)$, and the other as $else(u)$.

An illustrative example can be found in [9]. This example is shown in Figure 1(a), where we see a BDD representation of the boolean function $f =$

$x_1 \cdot x_2 + \overline{x_1} \cdot x_3$. We typically use solid lines for the edge between u and $then(u)$, and dashed lines for the edge between u and $else(u)$. Additionally, non-terminal nodes are denoted as circles, while terminal nodes as squares.

Let π be an ordering of the boolean variables involved in the function to represent. Then, the pair (π, G) is the *Ordered BDD* (OBDD) representation of the function, as long as (additionally to simple BDD definitions) it is true that on each path from the root to a terminal node the variables are encountered at most once and in the same order. Looking into the previous example, Figure 1(b) is illustrating exactly this ordering of variables, and how it affects the diagram. A diagram with more than one roots (i.e., representing more than one boolean functions which depend on the same boolean variables) is a *Shared BDD* (SBDD). It must be noted that a root node here does not necessarily imply that the in-degree of this node is equal to zero. For a specific function within a BDD or a SBDD, a *path* is a subset of G which connects the root with a terminal node, without any duplicate occurrences of a node or an edge. We denote the set of all paths for function f as Γ_f.

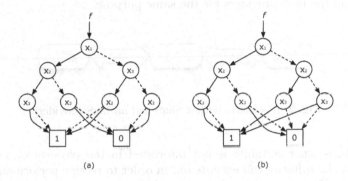

(a)   (b)

Fig. 1. Simple/Ordered BDD representations of $f = x_1 \cdot x_2 + \overline{x_1} \cdot x_3$

Last before looking at how this kind of diagrams facilitates our work for SLAs, is a short introduction to their operations for reduction. BDDs can be reduced in two ways:

1. *Deletion*: If for a non-terminal node u of G it is true that $then(u) = else(u) = u'$, the node can be removed from the graph. All edges pointing to it, if any, must now point to u', and if u was a root node, then u' must be upgraded to a root node.
2. *Merging*: If for two non-terminal nodes u and u' it is true that $var(u) = var(u')$, $then(u) = then(u')$ and $else(u) = else(u')$, then it is possible to remove u and have all edges pointing to it redirected to point to u'. Additionally, if u is a root node, then u' must be made into a root node.

Remark. In the text that follows, we will use the term *BDD* universally, to refer to Reduced Ordered BDDs. Also, we will not distinguish between single-rooted and shared diagrams. Whenever single-rooted BDDs are *explicitly excluded*, we will denote that by pre-pending "shared" or just the letter "S".

4   SLAs as BDDs

4.1   A Motivating Scenario

Let us now consider a somewhat typical (albeit reduced, for this example) scenario, where SLA management is necessary. We are assuming an *Infrastructure as a Service* (IaaS) provider; a *Software as a Service* (SaaS) provider which is also a customer to the IaaS provider; and an end-customer of the SaaS provider. We are therefore working on the assumption that the SaaS provider has no infrastructure of its own, therefore all operations are outsourced to the IaaS provider who owns the infrastructure for the software to be executed. This kind of business scenario involves two SLAs, as shown in Figure 2. The first (SLA-1) is established between the end-customer and the SaaS provider, to govern their interactions and apply guarantees. The second (SLA-2) is established between the SaaS and the IaaS providers for the same purpose.

Fig. 2. A scenario with a SaaS and an IaaS provider

The end-customer certainly is not interested in the physical or virtual resources that the software will execute on, in order to receive performance which is acceptable. Therefore, the customer would try to engage in a SLA with the SaaS provider, which would involve –for instance– metrics for service availability, and service invocations completion time (CT). The SaaS provider would typically have some understanding about the software based on modeling principles or historical monitoring evidence, starting from which it can derive expected resource requirements, possibly varying throughout a day's, month's or other period. The infrastructure resource requirements, on the other hand, would be the guarantees that the SaaS provider's SLA with the IaaS provider would need to include. Our example SLAs are described as follows:

SLA-1: For service "Service-1", and given that business hours are between 09:00 and 17:00: During business hours, operation "Operation-1" must complete within 5 seconds, and the service's availability must be more than 99%. Outside business hours, completion time for the same operation can be up to 10 seconds, and the service's availability must be more than 95%.

SLA-2: For service "VMpool", and given that business hours are between 09:00 and 17:00: During business hours, 10 virtual machines must be allocated to this contract. Outside business hours, 5 virtual machines must be allocated.

Table 1. Example clauses

SLA	Variable	Proposition	Proposition type
SLA-1	x_1	ServiceName = 'Service1'	Fact
SLA-1	x_2	BusinessHours = 09:00 - 17:00	Fact
SLA-1	x_3	TimeOfDay in BusinessHours	Condition
SLA-1	x_4	'Operation1' CT < 5 sec	Clause
SLA-1	x_5	Service1 availability > 99%	Clause
SLA-1	$\overline{x_3}$	TimeOfDay not in BusinessHours	Condition
SLA-1	x_6	'Operation1' CT < 10 sec	Clause
SLA-1	x_7	Service1 availability > 95%	Clause
SLA-2	y_1	ServiceName = 'VMpool'	Fact
SLA-2	y_2	BusinessHours = 09:00 - 17:00	Fact
SLA-2	y_3	TimeOfDay in BusinessHours	Condition
SLA-2	y_4	Number of VMs = 10	Clause
SLA-2	$\overline{y_3}$	TimeOfDay not in BusinessHours	Condition
SLA-2	y_5	Number of VMs = 5	Clause

Table 1 illustrates the set of facts and clauses that we will use for this example scenario. It is straightforward to see that, given these facts and clauses in the form of boolean variables which evaluate to *true* or *false*, the SLAs can also evaluate correctly if they are modeled according to Equations 2 and 3 respectively. In the upcoming Section 4.2 we will formalize the problem of expressing SLAs as boolean functions. Then in Section 4.3 we will show how these specific example SLAs map to BDDs.

$$f = x_1 \cdot x_2 \cdot (x_3 \cdot x_4 \cdot x_5 + \overline{x_3} \cdot x_6 \cdot x_7) \tag{2}$$

$$g = y_1 \cdot y_2 \cdot (y_3 \cdot y_4 + \overline{y_3} \cdot y_5) \tag{3}$$

4.2   SLAs and SLA Hierarchies

In Section 1 we referred briefly to service hierarchies and the corresponding SLA hierarchies. Each SLA governs the consumption of one or more services, by one or more consumers. Involved parties have specific obligations to comply with and/or specific gains to expect. In order to carry out its obligations, a service provider involved in a SLA may have to *subcontract*, that is to establish one or more additional SLAs with parties not directly involved in the initial one. This kind of dependency between the original contract and the subcontracts may take many different forms. It may be related to capacity, functionality limitations, failover capabilities, or may represent some other aspect of the provider's *modus operandi* and business model. As such, it is very generic and makes it difficult to identify exactly how the state of one contract affects the state of another.

We formulate a proposed SLA representation as follows: Let Φ^n be the universe of *facts* applicable to contracts as indisputable truth, $\Phi^n = \{\phi_1, ..., \phi_n\}$. Also let

Y^m be the universe of *clauses* which can be evaluated to either *true* or *false*, $Y^m = \{y_1, ..., y_m\}$. A Service Level Agreement is the boolean function f:

$$f : F^k \cup Z^l \rightarrow \{0, 1\} \tag{4}$$

where $F^k \subseteq \Phi^n$, $F^k = \{\phi_1, ..., \phi_k\}$ and $Z^l \subseteq Y^m$, $Z^l = \{z_1, ..., z_l\}$.

We therefore have a representation of a SLA as a boolean function, taking advantage of a SLA's binary nature upon evaluation as *possible / impossible* to satisfy (at negotiation time) or *honored / violated* (at runtime, i.e. while the service is being consumed). The variable terms of a SLA are taking values from Z^l, while pre-agreed understanding and in general facts about the world is encoded in facts accepting values from F^k. This definition is broad enough to encompass various previous definitions, both conceptual (e.g. [11]) and syntactical (e.g. WS-Agreement).

We are now ready to codify SLA dependencies in a generic way, that allows enough flexibility to describe any such kind. Let:

- $f : F^k \cup Z^l \rightarrow \{0, 1\}$, the dependent SLA
- $f_i : F^{ki} \cup Z^{li} \rightarrow \{0, 1\}$, $i \in \mathbb{N}$, the depending SLAs
- $F^{ki} \subseteq \Phi^n$, $F^{ki} = \{\phi_{1i}, ..., \phi_{ki}\}$
- $Z^{li} \subseteq Y^m$, $Z^{li} = \{z_{1i}, ..., z_{li}\}$

We define the dependency of f upon $\{f_i\}$ (and therefore the resulting hierarchy) as a function g:

$$g : Z^l \rightarrow \cup_i (Z^{li}) | F^k \cup_i (F^{ki}) \tag{5}$$

Simply said, a function of any number of *variable* terms from SLA f equals a function of any number of *variable* terms from one or more SLAs f_i, under the circumstances defined by the relevant fact sets. Operating under this highly abstract definition allows us the required flexibility to describe contracts with dependencies of any kind, as long as each of them does eventually evaluate to either *true*, or *false*.

4.3   BDD Mapping

We now have a formal representation of SLAs (Equation 4) and SLA dependencies (Equation 5). The gain in using BDDs lies in *reduction*. Through this process, a BDD becomes a *canonical* representation of the boolean function it describes, as proven in [1]. Therefore, a SLA described as a boolean function in the form of a BDD takes a unique, well-specified and minimal form, eliminating redundancy and allowing to make the mapping which describes SLA dependencies far more efficient than what it would be if we operated on complete graphs. Additionally, the canonical form of the SLAs allows objective evaluation and comparison for maximizing utility.

The exact method to construct a BDD from a SLA depends on the format in which this SLA is originally expressed, and therefore it cannot be algorithmically defined in a universal way. In the case of WS-Agreement we would use the

Context and Service Description Terms as facts; Qualifying Conditions as conditions; Guarantee Terms as clauses; and Term Compositor Terms could be classified as either conditions or clauses. In fact, WS-Agreement's Term Compositor Terms are essentially boolean operators: All (AND), OneOrMore (OR), ExactlyOne (XOR). Using this pre-defined knowledge for such a specific SLA language, it is straightforward to implement a parser that can read the documents and construct a (Reduced Ordered) BDD on-the-fly as described in [12] with the revised "APPLY" operation.

To illustrate the reduced form of BDDs representing SLAs, we will use the example scenario from Section 4.1. As mentioned, Equations 2 and 3 represent the two example SLAs as boolean functions of the variables from Table 1. Then, assuming an ordering corresponding to the numbering of the variables, the two resulting BDDs would be as in Figure 3.

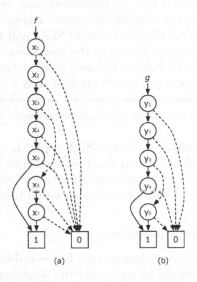

(a)   (b)

Fig. 3. The BDDs corresponding to functions from Equations 2 and 3

The main deficiency of BDDs is their reliance on the ordering of the variables. The size of a BDD for the same function may vary from linear to exponential, depending on how variables are ordered [1]. Generic algorithms for near-optimal orderings of variables during or after BDD construction have been researched extensively in the past (e.g. [13,14]). Our application to the domain of SLA management and the involvement of *facts* as variables, whose *else* edge always points directly to terminal node **0**, provides already a possibility for optimizing the BDD by pushing all facts to the top of the diagram. Although this kind of ordering does not reduce the total number of nodes, it allows us to ensure that indisputable facts are honored by all parts of the SLA, otherwise it will evaluate to false at runtime (i.e. it is violated). Also, at negotiation time, this ordering may speed up the negotiation process significantly, since the first thing to be confirmed as acceptable (or not) is the agreement of the involved parties on the essentials of the contract (for instance, monetary unit). It should be underlined, at this point, that facts are propositions which apply to the complete contract, and govern all terms included. Therefore, in certain cases, additional attention is required for choosing what is a fact and what is not. Let us consider, for instance, the case of a two-party contract with two sections describing the obligations of each party, starting each section with an indication as to which party it applies. The statement "section (a) describes the obligations of party (A)" is certainly true for the complete contract. Nevertheless, if reference to the section includes some contract-locality constraint, e.g. "*this* section describes the obligations of party (A)", then this causes ambiguity and cannot apply to the whole contract any more – therefore should be modeled as a *condition*.

Having ordered *facts* at the beginning of the diagram, we assume some BDD method to optimize the ordering of *conditions* and *clauses*. Additionally to generic methods described in relevant literature, a kind of structural optimization that takes advantage of the semantics of SLAs and may be applied here is one that considers what is more crucial to the user. Certain SLA representations contain sections on *Business Values*, that may reference specific terms as regards their importance. Given proper formalization of such sections, a constructor of BDDs from SLAs can take them into account and order clause variables from maximum to minimum importance, thus allowing faster evaluation of business-critical terms.

We can now discuss principles for the SLA application domain, and for outsourcing parts or all of the contract. Starting from the very semantics of SLAs represented as BDDs, we have to distinguish between the meaning of a boolean variable (and the whole diagram) during negotiation time, and during runtime.

4.4   Negotiation Time Operations

During negotiation time, the evaluation of a fact variable to *true* or *false* shows whether the fact is recognized as such from the receiving party. For conditions and clauses, it indicates whether there is any reachable state based on assignments of respective variables, so that the condition / clause under examination can eventually evaluate to *true*. Extending this to the complete diagram, at negotiation time we are interested to see if there exist, in general, truth assignments for the whole set $F^k \cup Z^l$ which satisfy the diagram and lead to **1**. At this point lies an implicit decision. The party that receives the offer needs to have some certainty that it can honor it after signing. It is a policy issue if this certainty needs to be 100%, or near that, or even much lower (perhaps indicating a high-risk strategy). Whatever the policy, the decision will have to be taken based on some objective criteria. A certainty of 100% would mean that paths of the BDD must be checked for *tautology*, that is, any truth assignment for a path will lead to terminal node **1**. If tautology applies for a single path, that should be enough to accept the offer. If not, it is necessary to make an educated guess whether the offer is acceptable, and whether some part needs to be subcontracted.

A simple calculation that can be performed, is the following: Let Γ_f^1 be the set of all paths for f that connect the root to terminal node **1**, and Γ_f^0 the respective set of paths leading to terminal node **0**. We assume that by means of historical monitoring information, forecasting, or simply common sense (e.g. time of day) there is assigned to each node u_i in $h \in \Gamma_f^1$ a probability $P'(u_i)$ to evaluate to a result so that node u_{i+1} is (also) on the same path, and $1 - p$ to evaluate otherwise. If the variables of the nodes in the path are *dependent*, then we need to take this into account and calculate the *conditional probability* of each variable, given the evaluation of all previous variables on this path:

$$P(u_{i+1}) = P'(u_{i+1}|u_1 \cap u_2 \cap ... \cap u_i) \tag{6}$$

In somewhat less formal notation, we have represented the variables (and the events of them taking a value of *true* or *false*) by the names of their nodes. If the variables are *independent*, then $P(u_i) = P'(u_i)$, $\forall i$. The probability p_h that the complete path evaluates to *true*, is

$$p_h = \prod_u P(u)|u \in h \tag{7}$$

Then, the total probability that the SLA can be honored if established, is

$$C = \sum_h (p_h)|h \in \Gamma_f^1 \tag{8}$$

Assuming that the acquisition of this probability per node can be performed in constant time, then the complexity of estimating this probability per path is $O(n)$. The consequent requirement to minimize the total number of paths at construction time or variable ordering time, should also be taken into account.

A negotiating party will want C to exceed some threshold, in order to agree to an offer that was received. If this is not the case, then the party (typically, a service provider) will have to either reject the offer, or try to increase C by sub-contracting one or more paths and thus increasing their contribution to the total success probability. Representing SLAs as BDDs is most useful at this point: The canonical and reduced form of a BDD produces a tractable list of options with regard to what we can assign to subcontractors. For items in such a list, due to the specific ordering of variables, we can devise unique and unambiguous signatures. The latter may then be associated to different boolean functions, which represent candidate subcontracts. Domain-specific intelligence can be applied by area experts before operation starts, and define the dependencies of certain variables on others for subcontracts. Then, a system based on these principles can make use of this knowledge, and construct proper offers towards third parties. As long as these offers are accepted, and the respective second-level SLAs are established, it should be the case that the corresponding path has increased certainty to complete successfully as regards honoring the first-level SLA. The negotiating party has a choice, according to policies and strategies, to modify the offer and return it with specific values for the variables of that path (practically suggesting the SLA equivalent of the path), or to accept the complete SLA as long as the increase in C is sufficient.

Coming back to the example scenario from Section 4.1, we can see two possible ways where this kind of subcontracting is / may be needed. The first, is the explicitly mentioned subcontracting from the SaaS to the IaaS provider. Conceptually, since the SaaS provider has no infrastructure, they cannot offer the service at all unless they subcontract for infrastructure. Terms x_4, x_5, x_6 and x_7 would always evaluate to *false* unless infrastructure resources are available for the software to execute on. As such, the SaaS provider has to go through this translation process in any case, to calculate infrastructure requirements and make a respective offer to the IaaS provider. If an agreement with the IaaS provider already exists, the contracting system in use should find this automatically after the translation occurs, try to reuse it if possible, otherwise resolve to making a new offer. It must be noted here that, since the outsourcing concerns *paths*, the SaaS provider may just as well make two different offers to two different infrastructure providers (one for each of the two paths in Γ_f^1), or can make a single offer to one infrastructure provider for both paths (this is our assumption in the example scenario).

The second case, is if it so happens that the IaaS provider cannot satisfy the incoming offer – for instance, does not have the resources to offer the requested performance during business hours. This means that, according to its estimation, y_4 would evaluate to *false* most of the times, and therefore path $y_1 - y_2 - y_3 - y_4 - 1$ would contribute minimally or not at all to the whole agreement's C-value. In this case, the IaaS provider can reject the offer, or —depending on projected utility— try to outsource this path to another IaaS provider. Further translation of the terms may occur or not in this case, depending on the structural and qualitative agreement properties that are accepted by the second IaaS provider.

It should be mentioned that an offer may be for a single SLA, or for multiple SLAs (typically for different services or groups of services) in the form of a Shared BDD. Our working assumption of an offer for a single SLA does not affect generality.

Another relevant point is that we are referring to SLA terms in a most abstract way, and that is on purpose in order to define a generic model. However, from an implementation point of view, we need to define proper *term signatures* (term templates), and to select "good" values to replace in them. For example, the expression *"completion time < 5 seconds"* evaluates to true or false and therefore can be modeled as a single boolean variable. Yet, if we assume that the expression *"completion time < 4 seconds"* is a term with a different signature, then naturally the complexity of mapping between different signatures increases enough to make the problem unfeasible. Therefore, from an implementation point of view, we need a single signature like *"completion time < duration"*, allowing to set duration to a preferred ("good") value as mentioned before. Here, "good" has to do with the notion that there is some utility coming out of each SLA, and this utility we wish to maximize. Structural optimization of the SLA's BDD supports better decisions from a SLA computability point of view, and possibly reduces time to reach an agreement. However, the utility itself is domain-specific again, and falls into the same realm with choosing a "SLA probability to succeed" threshold over which an offer is acceptable.

Solutions to the open issues elaborated in the previous paragraph are outside the scope of the work presented in this paper. *Technology mapping* [15,16] is a concept which matches the problem of templating terms and their combinations, and provides a starting point for further research. The topic of selecting values that increase total utility falls under *multi-objective optimization* [17]. As a matter of fact, the optimization logic may affect the negotiation process itself. An entity negotiating over a set of variables may find that small modifications to the negotiating party's requirements may increase significantly the resulting utility. In this case, it may just as well modify the proposed term slightly, and return a counter-offer which does not match the other entity's requirements, but may provide much better results if accepted. Such negotiation-time risk-taking attitudes can be modeled with *game theory* methods [18,19]. Technologies from all three areas will be tested in the future as part of this work and a complete implementation.

4.5   Runtime Operations

For this part of our work, we are assuming a monitoring subsystem that can capture service execution-related events from various sources and detect if some SLA term is being violated. The process actually starts much earlier, during negotiation. At that time already, we must verify that terms of an agreement *can* actually be monitored [20]. Following this verification step, as part of the negotiation process, a SLA may be formally established, perhaps relying on other SLAs for its existence.

While the service is being consumed, incoming events are processed and terms (in the form of boolean variables of the BDD) are examined to see if a violation has occurred. The ordering of the variables allows the linear-time confirmation, starting from the root and traversing the diagram towards terminal nodes. As each variable evaluates to *true* or *false*, the respective child (*then/else*) is followed until a terminal node is reached. If that node is **0**, then there exists a violation, and the reason of failing at that specific part of the SLA must be assessed. Depending on whether this failure happened on a path which was outsourced, or not, there may be a re-negotiation initiated, penalties claimed, or simply adjust the method to estimate success probabilities for different paths. Additionally to corrective actions, such an event must be logged to be reused in next negotiation cycles.

The exact methodology to use in order to avoid unnecessary evaluations of the complete diagram, depends on the monitoring system, the way to evaluate each variable, and the acceptable time thresholds for reaction to violations. A complete definition of such methodologies is out of scope for this work.

5   Experimental Verification

As a proof of concept, we built a very simple prototype that accepts a SLA already expressed as a boolean function in *Reverse Polish Notation* (RPN) form, produces a BDD from it and assigns probabilities to the nodes in a semi-random way. Then, it calculates the paths leading to 1, their probabilities to be followed and the total probability that the SLA can be honored without any subcontracting. We experimented with a single SLA offer, which was crafted not to contain dependent variables, according to the following description:

> *The SLA concerns service "Service-1" (fact). Business hours are set to 09:00-17:00 (fact). The whole system must run in isolation from other customers of the service provider (fact). If the operation invoked is "Operation-1" (condition), and time is within business hours (condition), then: completion time should be less than 5 seconds (clause); availability should be more than 99% (clause); and throughput should be more than 100 operations per minute (clause). For times outside business hours: completion time should be less than 10 seconds, availability should be more than 95%, and throughput should be more than 50 operations per second. For operations other than "Operation-1", invocations should be authenticated (clause) and availability should be more than 98%.*

With regard to the assignment of probabilities to the nodes and the paths to follow, we assigned a probability equal to 1.0 to facts and to the proposition of authenticated invocations (this being a functional requirement that the provider should be aware of). We then assumed that invocations of "Operation-1" are one out of three, i.e. a probability of roughly 0.33, and the same for the time of day being within business hours – so we imply that invocations of the service are equally distributed throughout the day. Finally, for the propositions of completion time, availability and throughput, we randomly assigned on each node a probability between 0.8 and 1.0 that the provider can satisfy it or will fail (a second random number indicates which of the two applies). In a real scenario, the provider would calculate these probabilities based on monitoring, forecasting or other information. Eventually, we run this simple scenario 10000 times, to see under these semi-random conditions how the SLA success estimations behave. Constructing the BDD for this specific SLA took place in a mere 2.2 seconds. Running the 10000 probability tests took approximately 4 seconds on a 2.4 GHz processor. The diagram contained 16 levels, excluding terminal nodes. Of the 21 paths leading to terminal node 1, the shortest was 6-nodes long (excluding 1), and the longest was 13-nodes long. Figure 4 illustrates the overall calculated probability that the SLA will be successful if established.

From this preliminary evaluation, the feasibility and validity of the approach is exhibited for all SLAs that consist of propositions evaluating to *true* or *false*. As long as all invariable statements of a SLA (e.g. references to other SLAs) can be expressed as facts, and all variable statements can be expressed as conditions and clauses, this assumption is valid for any SLA. In this experiment, a simple but not trivial expression was built fairly quickly, producing a vector of 21 paths to evaluate and monitor. Allowing some certainty for individual terms (80%-100% probability of success or failure) results in a clear gap between SLAs projected to fail, and those projected to succeed. This is an indication that, using BDDs

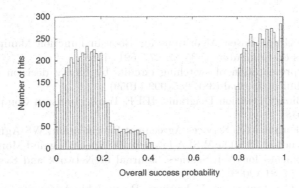

Fig. 4. Experimental result

in this context and under such circumstances, we can calculate in only a few milliseconds and with a reasonable amount of certainty, whether the complete SLA can be satisfied or not. Future application of this methodology on real-world use cases will allow for further evaluation.

6   Conclusions and Future Work

In this paper we presented a novel application of (Shared) Reduced Ordered Binary Decision Diagrams, for representing and managing SLAs, as well as facilitating the construction of SLA hierarchies. BDDs are graph-based structures which have been used for decades in the field of VLSI design and verification, with particular success. They are one of the main tools of the VLSI industry for testing prototypes, and therefore BDDs are a topic under heavy research for decades. The depth and breadth of existing ideas and research can be applied to SLA management for further advancement of this complex service management area. In this particular work we elaborated on the representation through a formal definition of SLAs as boolean functions and from there as BDDs; explained the advantages of this approach; and showed how such kind of use is possible for negotiating SLAs, subcontracting (leading to implicit SLA hierarchies) and detecting SLA violations. Finally, we briefly discussed the encouraging experimental results of applying BDDs to SLA representation.

In the near future we will fully implement these ideas as part of a more general SLA management design. It is our purpose to explore the topic of BDD structural optimization, in addition to that of multi-objective optimization, the latter being necessary for increasing a SLA's utility. Technology mapping appears to fit well the requirement to translate between abstract logic representations, and game theory is suitable for negotiation mechanisms. These technologies will also be evaluated and possibly applied to our implementation.

References

1. Bryant, R.: Graph-Based Algorithms for Boolean Function Manipulation. IEEE Transactions on Computers C-35(8), 677–691 (1986)
2. Lee, C.: Representation of switching circuits by binary decision diagrams. Bell System Technical Journal (38), 985–999 (1959)
3. Akers, S.: Binary Decision Diagrams. IEEE Transactions on Computers C-27(6), 509–516 (1978)
4. Open Grid Forum: Web Services Agreement Specification, WS-Agreement (2007)
5. Keller, A., Ludwig, H.: The WSLA Framework: Specifying and Monitoring Service Level Agreements for Web Services. Journal of Network and Systems Management 11(1), 57–81 (2003)
6. Binder, W., Constantinescu, I., Faltings, B.: Scalable Automated Service Composition Using a Compact Directory Digest. Database and Expert Systems Applications, 317–326 (2006)
7. Campailla, A., Chaki, S., Clarke, E., Jha, S., Veith, H.: Efficient filtering in publish-subscribe systems using binary decision diagrams. In: ICSE 2001: Proc. 23rd International Conference on Software Engineering, pp. 443–452 (2001)
8. Paschke, A., Bichler, M.: Knowledge representation concepts for automated SLA management. Decision Support Systems 46(1), 187–205 (2008)
9. Ebendt, R., Drechsler, R., Fey, G.: Advanced BDD optimization. Springer, Heidelberg (2005)
10. Shannon, C.E.: A symbolic analysis of relay and switching circuits. AIEE (57), 713–723 (1938)
11. Bhoj, P., Singhal, S., Chutani, S.: SLA management in federated environments. Computer Networks 35(1), 5–24 (2001)
12. Bryant, R.E.: Symbolic Boolean manipulation with ordered binary-decision diagrams. ACM Comput. Surv. 24(3), 293–318 (1992)
13. Friedman, S., Supowit, K.: Finding the optimal variable ordering for binary decision diagrams. IEEE Transactions on Computers 39(5), 710–713 (1990)
14. Rudell, R.: Dynamic variable ordering for ordered binary decision diagrams. In: ICCAD 1993: Proc. 1993 IEEE/ACM international conference on Computer-aided design, pp. 42–47. IEEE Computer Society Press, Los Alamitos (1993)
15. Keutzer, K.: DAGON: Technology Binding and Local Optimization by DAG Matching. In: 24th Conference on Design Automation, June 1987, pp. 341–347 (1987)
16. Detjens, E., Rudell, R., Gannot, G., Wang, A., Sangiovanni-Vincentelli, A.: Technology mapping in MIS. In: Proc. International Conference on Computer Aided Design, November 1987, pp. 116–119 (1987)
17. Ehrgott, M.: Multicriteria Optimization. Springer, Heidelberg (2005)
18. Fatima, S., Wooldridge, M., Jennings, N.: A Comparative Study of Game Theoretic and Evolutionary Models of Bargaining for Software Agents. Artificial Intelligence Review 23(2), 187–205 (2005)
19. Figueroa, C., Figueroa, N., Jofre, A., Sahai, A., Chen, Y., Iyer, S.: A Game Theoretic Framework for SLA Negotiation. Technical report, HP Laboratories (2008)
20. Comuzzi, M., Kotsokalis, C., Spanoudakis, G., Yahyapour, R.: Establishing and Monitoring SLAs in Complex Service Based Systems. In: ICWS 2009: Proceedings of the 2009 IEEE International Conference on Web Services, pp. 783–790 (2009)

Provider-Composer Negotiations for Semantic Robustness in Service Compositions*

Nikolay Mehandjiev, Freddy Lécué, and Usman Wajid

The University of Manchester
Booth Street East, Manchester, UK
(firstname.lastname)@manchester.ac.uk

Abstract. Research in automating service composition is rarely concerned with service providers, apart from work in quality guarantees and contracts. This perspective is arguably valid for comparatively static and cheap web services, which do not warrant continuous involvement of their providers in the process of service procurement and use by service consumers. However, opportunities for optimisation and fine-tuning of compositions are thus missed. We have created an approach which uses automated agent-based negotiation between service composer and service providers to address the issue of semantic robustness in large-scale service compositions by preventing cases where the wrong type of data is passed on from one service to the next. Starting from a service composition template which is not semantically robust, we allow the selection of semantically robust combinations of actual services. The approach is characterised with a linear complexity and also allows service providers to tune their services to the requirements of service compositions which may be lucrative business opportunities.

Keywords: service composition, semantic services, semantic robustness, autonomic agents, negotiation, template-based composition.

1 Introduction

Services are perceived as ubiquitous software-based units which can be procured by their consumers at the point of need to deliver certain functionality [1]. When a consumer desires functionality which cannot be provided by a single existing service, we can either develop a new service "from scratch", or attempt to compose one using existing services. Service composition is thus a valuable activity, and automating it has become a popular topic for service researchers, which have created a bewildering variety of approaches and methods.

One such approach [2,3] uses formalised knowledge about generic problem-solving approaches to break-up the desired functionality into a set of simpler units, called tasks. These tasks are interlinked into a service composition template, and suitable services are then sought for each task. If a number of services are found, one is selected aiming to optimise the composition according to certain criteria. For example, [4] shows how we can select a set of services which fit in terms of input and output data types.

---

* Foundation Project: Supported by European Commission VII Framework IP Project Soa4All.

L. Baresi, C.-H. Chi, and J. Suzuki (Eds.): ICSOC-ServiceWave 2009, LNCS 5900, pp. 205–220, 2009.

We say that such composition is *semantically robust* if we cannot have the wrong type of data passed on from one service to the next. Reasoning about services in general and semantic robustness in particular is greatly facilitated by tagging services with formal semantic descriptions of their functionality, inputs, outputs, pre-conditions, etc. These services are then known as *Semantic web services* [5].

Their formal semantic descriptions are based on Description Logics (DL) [6], such as OWL-S [7], WSMO [8] or SA-WSDL [9] (through annotations). These are in general specialisations of semantic tagging languages such as the Web Ontology Language (OWL) [10]. The latter are used to provide semantic annotations for general web resources, including documents and media streams, thus creating the Semantic Web [11].

The problem we address in this paper is how to achieve semantic robustness of the service composition if the composition template we use is not semantically robust itself. This may occur for a number of reasons, for example when we modify a semantically robust template to include specialised functionality, or if the service composition template is created manually by people. For brevity we will use "robust" instead of "semantically robust" in the remainder of this paper. A non-robust template will specify the desired services in a way which permits the selection of incompatible services, i.e., one service generates output which does not conform to the specifications for the input of the follow-up service. For example, a voice transcription service may handle English and German, whilst the follow-up grammar checking service may be specialised in English only. The latter will thus fail if it is given a German text as an input. The failure could be at the level of functionality, in that it will detect all phrases as grammatically incorrect, but it may also raise exception regarding bad input since the input string will now have extra characters from the German language (e.g., ä, ü or ö) which are not expected by an English grammar checker software.

There are several approaches to resolving this issue. For example, we can convert the composition template to one which is robust by narrowing down the specifications of the respective service outputs, and only then we start searching for candidate services. This may exclude many valid compositions and produce sub-optimal results, especially if some inputs are "over specified" unnecessarily. For example, there may be many multi-lingual grammar checker services available to complement our example bilingual voice transcription service and result in a robust composition.

Such combinations will be detected and used by an alternative approach which analyses every combination from the two sets of candidate services in the hope of finding robust matches. This will work for small numbers of candidate services, but its complexity is exponential and thus not applicable for large-scale compositions. In addition, the resulting combinations may deviate from the template prescriptions significantly, impeding the straightforward substitution of a failing service in the future.

In this paper we address the issue of robustness by approaching it from a multi-agent systems perspective which is rarely used in web service research. We involve the service composer and the corresponding providers of the candidate services in a negotiation process aiming to result in a robust composition optimised according to their perspectives. The composer and providers can be represented by autonomous software entities, called agents, which are pre-programmed to negotiate according to the business interests of the organisations they represent, and to reason over the semantic specifications of requirements and candidate services.

To drive the negotiation dialogue, we use a formal model of semantic robustness [12] described in Section 2. The model allows us to analyse each data link between tasks in our template, and for those links which are not robust, calculate precise semantic specifications of the *extra description* necessary for these links to become robust.

The negotiation process is guided by negotiation protocols, involving the service composer agent and the agents providing candidate services for every two tasks linked by a non-robust link. An informal outline of the protocols, together with overall approach proposed here, is described in Section 3, whilst the formal details of sub-protocols and negotiation strategies are specified in Section 4.

The combination of agent-based negotiation with semantic reasoning results in an innovative solution to the problem of robust service composition. Section 5 demonstrates how the approach can be used in a specific case study, delivering results with greater flexibility than the approaches based on centralised reasoning. Section 6 compares the approach with related work in the area, and Section 7 concludes this paper.

2   Preliminaries

This section describes in further detail the overall ideas of template-based service composition, and proceeds to define the formal model of their semantic robustness.

2.1   Template-Based Service Composition

An intuitive view to service composition would see it as an activity which aims to satisfy the need for a (non-existing) service by bringing together existing ones. For example, if we need a letter dictation service we can bring together a voice transcription service, a grammar checker service, a letter layout service and a printing service.

This integration activity can be done manually, yet automating it makes it more in tune with the vision of composing services at the point of need [1]. Automating can be done using program synthesis and AI planning techniques [13], employing reasoning over the pre- and post-conditions of available services, trying to create a plan of putting them together to jointly achieve the aim of the target composite service. This approach starts "from scratch" every time, yet significant performance improvements may be offered by reusing composition results as a template for new compositions, or creating such a template through the use of domain-specific knowledge about how the problem addressed by the sought service would decompose into sub-problems [14].

We follow this template-based composition, and focus on the stage of *template instantiation* [2,3], where we need to allocate a specific service for each the generic "service slots" in the template. From the perspective of template instantiation, we use the specification of each task $T_{i,1\leq i\leq n}$ to procure a set of candidate services $s_{j,1\leq j\leq m}$ for this task, and to select one of these services to instantiate the task. The precise manner in which we propose to implement both the procurement and selection activities so that we achieve semantically robust composition even in the cases where the template itself is not semantically robust, will be described in Section 3.

2.2 Formal Semantic Model

Using tasks specifications of inputs, outputs, pre- and post-conditions of templates, we should be able to infer additional dependencies between tasks, for example we can infer data flow dependencies between tasks using their input and output specifications.

In the following we present such dependencies as *semantic links* [15] between services. Then we define the concept of their *robustness* and finally we describe *semantic-link-based web service composition*.

Semantic Links. Since input and output parameters of semantic web services are specified using concepts from a common ontology[1] or Terminology $\mathcal{T}$ (an example of such is given in Figure 2), retrieving links between output parameters $Out\_s_i \in \mathcal{T}$ of services s_i and input parameters $In\_s_j \in \mathcal{T}$ of other services s_j could be achieved by using some DL reasoner such as Fact++[2] [16]. Such a link, also known as semantic link [15] $sl_{i,j}$ (Figure 1) between two functional parameters of s_i and s_j is formalized as

$$\langle s_i, Sim_{\mathcal{T}}(Out\_s_i, In\_s_j), s_j \rangle \tag{1}$$

Thereby s_i and s_j are partially linked according to a matching function $Sim_{\mathcal{T}}$. This function expresses which matching type is employed to chain services. The range of $Sim_{\mathcal{T}}$ is reduced to the four well known matching type introduced by [17] and the extra type Intersection [18]:

- **Exact.** If the output parameter Out_s_i of s_i and the input parameter In_s_j of s_j are equivalent; formally, $\mathcal{T} \models Out\_s_i \equiv In\_s_j$.
- **PlugIn.** If Out_s_i is sub-concept of In_s_j; formally, $\mathcal{T} \models Out\_s_i \sqsubseteq In\_s_j$.
- **Subsume.** If Out_s_i is super-concept of In_s_j; formally, $\mathcal{T} \models In\_s_j \sqsubseteq Out\_s_i$.
- **Intersection.** If the intersection of Out_s_i and In_s_j is satisfiable; formally, $\mathcal{T} \not\models Out\_s_i \sqcap In\_s_j \sqsubseteq \bot$.
- **Disjoint.** If Out_s_i and In_s_j are incompatible i.e., $\mathcal{T} \models Out\_s_i \sqcap In\_s_j \sqsubseteq \bot$.

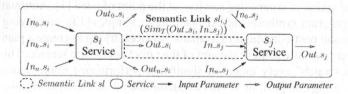

Semantic Link sl   ◯ *Service*   ⟶ *Input Parameter*   ⟶ *Output Parameter*

Fig. 1. A Semantic Link $sl_{i,j}$

In the same way as semantic links $sl_{i,j}$ between web services s_i and s_j, we define abstract semantic links $sl_{i,j}^A$ between tasks T_i and T_j. In the following we extend the definition of semantic link by introducing its concrete form (Definition 1).

---

[1] Distributed ontologies are not considered here but are largely independent of the problem addressed in this work.

[2] http://owl.man.ac.uk/factplusplus/

Definition 1 *(Concrete Semantic Link)*
A concrete semantic link $sl_{i,j}^{\alpha,\beta}$ is a concretization of its abstract form $sl_{i,j}^{A}$ if and only if s_α and s_β can respectively concretize tasks T_i and T_j.

Robust Semantic Link. The matching function Sim_T of semantic links enables, at design time, determining the degree of semantic compatibility among independently defined web service descriptions, from the strongly compatible *Exact* through *PlugIn*, *Subsume* and *Intersection* to the strongly incompatible *Disjoint*. However, as emphasized by [19], the matching types Intersection and Subsume need some refinements to be usable for semantic-links-based web service composition.

Example 1 *(Semantic Link & Subsume Matching Type)*
Suppose T_1 and T_2 are two tasks such that the output parameter NetworkConnection *of T_1 is semantically linked to the input parameter* SlowNetworkConnection *of T_2. According to the example ontology in Figure 2, this abstract semantic link $sl_{1,2}^{A}$ is valued by a Subsume matching type since* $NetworkConnection \sqsupseteq SlowNetworkCon\text{-}nection$. *It is obvious that such an abstract semantic link should not be directly applied in a service composition since the* NetworkConnection *is not specific enough to be used by the input parameter* SlowNetworkConnection, *which may cause data-based exception during execution. Indeed the output parameter* NetworkConnection *requires further restrictions to ensure a data-robust composition of T_1 and T_2.*

A semantic link valued by the Intersection matching type requires a comparable refinement. In this direction, [19] defined a robust semantic link and their composition.

Definition 2 *(Robust Semantic link)*
A semantic link $\langle s_i, Sim_T(Out\_s_i, In\_s_j), s_j \rangle$ is robust iff the matching type between Out_s_i and In_s_j is either Exact or PlugIn.

$NetworkConnection \equiv \forall netPro.Provider \sqcap \forall netSpeed.Speed$

$VeryRestrictedNetworkConnection \equiv NetworkConnection \sqcap \forall netSpeed.AdslVeryRestricted$

$LimitedNetworkConnection \equiv NetworkConnection \sqcap \forall netSpeed.AdslLimited$

$SlowNetworkConnection \equiv NetworkConnection \sqcap \forall netSpeed.Adsl1M$

$FastNetworkConnection \equiv NetworkConnection \sqcap \forall netSpeed.AdslMax$

$AdslVeryRestricted \equiv Speed \sqcap < 1mBytes$

$AdslLimited \equiv Speed \sqcap \geq 0.5\,mBytes \sqcap \leq 1.5mBytes$

$Adsl1M \equiv Speed \sqcap \geq 1mBytes$

$AdslMax \equiv Speed \sqcap \geq 8mBytes$

$AdslSuperMax \equiv Speed \sqcap \geq 16mBytes$

$Address \sqsubseteq \top, IPAddress \equiv Address \sqcap \forall protocol.IP$

$VoIPId \equiv Address \sqcap \forall network.Telecom$

Fig. 2. Sample of an $\mathcal{ALN}$ Terminology T

A possible way to replace an Intersection-, or Subsume-type link $\langle s_i, Sim_T(Out\_s_i, In\_s_j), s_j \rangle$ with its robust form consists of computing the information (as DL-based description) contained in the input parameter In_s_j and not in the output parameter Out_s_i. This information is then used as an additional restriction on the Out_s_i data type when a suitable web service is procured. We say that adding this latter restriction "transforms" the non-robust semantic link in its robust form. To do this, we apply initial ideas of [12], which adapt a non standard inference matching type i.e., the *Abduction* operation [20] (Definition 3) for comparing $\mathcal{ALN}$ DL-based descriptions.

Definition 3 *(Concept Abduction)*
Let $\mathcal{L}$ be a DL, C, D be two concepts in $\mathcal{L}$, and T be a set of axioms in $\mathcal{L}$. A Concept Abduction Problem (CAP), denoted as $\langle \mathcal{L}, C, D, T \rangle$ aims at finding Extra Description, as a the most general concept $H_{C,D} \in \mathcal{L}$ such that $T \models C \sqcap H_{C,D} \sqsubseteq D$.

According to Definition 3, a compact representation of *"difference"* $H_{Out\_s_i, In\_s_j}$ (henceforth H_{s_i, s_j}) between DL-based descriptions Out_s_i and In_s_j of a semantic link $sl_{i,j}$ can be computed. Such a description H_{s_i, s_j} can be formally defined by $T \models Out\_s_j \sqcap H_{s_i, s_j} \sqsubseteq In\_s_i$ as a solution of the *Concept Abduction* problem $\langle \mathcal{L}, Out\_s_i, In\_s_j, T \rangle$. In other words the *Extra Description* H_{s_i, s_j} refers to information required by In_s_j but not provided by Out_s_i to ensure a correct data flow between web services s_i and s_j.

In the same way robustness can be computed in template-based composition e.g., in case of non robust abstract semantic links $sl_{i,j}^A$ between tasks T_i and T_j. In the following H_{T_i, T_j} will refer to *Extra Description* between T_i and T_j in template-based composition (with non robust abstract semantic links).

Example 2 *(Robustness and Extra Description)*
Suppose the abstract semantic link $sl_{1,2}^A$ in Example 1. The additional restriction which has to be provided to the NetworkConnection *if this output is to be used by the input parameter* SlowNetworkConnection *is referred by the* Extra Description H_{T_1, T_2} *of the Concept Abduction Problem $\langle \mathcal{L}, NetworkConnection, SlowNetwork-Connection, T \rangle$ i.e., $\forall netSpeed.Adsl1M$ (see Figure 2).*

In other words, we can turn non-robust semantic links into robust ones by retrieving their *Extra Description*.

Semantic Link Composition Model. Here, we aggregate the concept of web service composition and semantic link in a same model. Therefore the process model of web service composition and its semantic links is specified by a directed graph which has the web service specifications s_i as its nodes, and the semantic links $sl_{i,j}$ (data dependencies) as its edges. In the same way a template-based composition, pre-computed for instance by *template-based* and *parametric-design-based* approaches [2,3], has the tasks specifications T_i as its nodes, and abstract semantic links $sl_{i,j}^A$ as its edges.

Given a template-based composition and an approach to compute robust semantic links (Definition 3), we address the issue of automating robustness in web service composition by using agent-based negotiation.

3   Negotiating Robust Interfaces with Candidate Service Providers

In an ideal template-based service composition, all semantic links between tasks (service placeholders) would be semantically robust. In practice this may not be the case, for example because the template has been created manually, or a generic template such as "object loan" has been modified with a domain-specific task such as checking credit record (for high-value objects such as expensive cars).

In such cases, we propose an agent-based approach to achieve robust instantiation of the non-robust template, which uses the formal model of semantic composition defined in the previous section. The approach is based on the following:

1. Every service provider and the service composer are represented by software agents.
2. The service composer agent "advertises" the service composition template on a shared notice board. It also calculates which semantic links in the template are not robust.
3. Service provider agents monitor the notice board. When they see requirements (task specifications) which one of their services can satisfy, they would "bid" for their service to instantiate the task.
4. Once the bids have been placed, the service composer agent initiates a three-phase negotiation protocol for each non-robust abstract link $sl_{i,j}^A$ in the template. The protocol involves the providers of services s_i and s_j which are candidates to instantiate the tasks T_i and T_j, respectively. The protocol should select services which provide robust instantiation of the semantic link.
5. The service composer agent can now instantiate the remaining tasks in the template by choosing the most appropriate service (in term of its semantic links with other services) for each such task.

In the remainder of this section, we will detail the suitability criteria used by service provider agents, followed by details of the three-phase negotiation protocol detailed in Step 4 above.

3.1   Service Suitability

Here we consider that a task T of a template can be instantiated by a service s if and only if the following conditions are true:

1. The service s achieves the same goal as T, assuming an ontology of goals [8].
2. The pre-conditions of s are implied by the pre–conditions of T.
3. The post-conditions of s imply the post-conditions of T.
4. The matching type between the input specification In_T of T and the input specification In_s of s i.e., $Sim_T(In\_T, In\_s)$ is PlugIn.
5. The matching type between the output specification Out_s of s and the output specification Out_T of T i.e., $Sim_T(Out\_s, Out\_T)$ is PlugIn.

Conditions (1) to (3) above ensure the candidate service s has the desired effect of the target task T, whilst conditions (4) and (5) ensure the semantic (functional) fit between

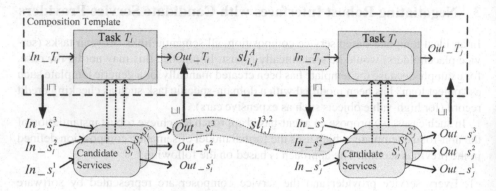

Fig. 3. Links between Tasks and Their Candidate Services

the candidate service and the target task. Condition (4) ensures that all the data which can be passed onto T can be processed by s. Condition (5) ensures that the output of s fits within the output specifications of T. Fig. 3 demonstrates the nature of the semantic fit between tasks and their candidate services.

Example 3 *(Tasks and Suitable Services)*
We illustrate our approach by considering two different tasks T_1 and T_2 such that:

- *AdslEligibility task T_1, starting from a PhoneNum, a ZipCode and an Email address, returns the NetworkConnection of a desired geographical zone;*
- *VoiceOverIP task T_2, starting from a PhoneNum and a SlowNetworkConnection, returns the VoIPId of the ADSL line a Telecom operator needs to install the line;*

On the one hand T_1 can be concretized by three services:

- *s_1^1, s_1^2 and s_1^3, that, starting from a PhoneNum, a ZipCode and an Email address, returns respectively a SlowNetworkConnection, VeryRestricted-NetworkConnection and LimitedNetworkConnection of the desired geographical zone;*

On the other hand T_2 can be concretized by two services:

- *s_2^1 and s_2^2, that, respectively starting from a NetworkConnection and Slow-NetworkConnection, returns the VoIPId of the ADSL line a Telecom operator needs to install the line;*

Note that s_1^1, s_1^2 and s_1^3 are suitable services for achieving task T_1 since they fulfil conditions (1), (2), (3) and (4). In the same way s_2^1 and s_2^2 are suitable services for T_2. In the rest of the paper we will focus on concretizing tasks by adequate services to achieve semantically robust links.

3.2 Negotiation Protocol

The service composer agent has identified all non-robust abstract semantic links $sl_{i,j}^A$ between tasks T_i and T_j in the composition template. The composer agent has also calculated H_{T_i,T_j} for each non-robust link. Once all the bids to instantiate the tasks involved in these links with services have come through (say an announced deadline for bidding has passed), the service composer will initiate a 3-phase negotiation protocol with the service providers for each *non-robust link* as follows.

Phase 1: In this phase all agents operate on the basis that they may achieve robust composition "for free" (i.e. without the use of extra services or modifying the behaviour of the ones proposed), using differences in specifications between a task and its candidate services (c.f. Section 3.1). We start by contacting all providers of services s_i for task T_i (on the left of Figure 3) sending them H_{T_i,T_j}. They compare it with their output specification as detailed in Section 4.1 to check if their (more specific) outputs turn $sl_{i,j}$ into a robust link. This is feasible since for each such output we have $Out\_s_i \sqsubseteq Out\_T_i$. If one or more service providers confirm this is indeed the case, the composer agent can terminate the protocol and, using the same selection criteria as the ones applied for a robust link, select one of them, and also any service provider for T_j. The actual selection criteria for choosing an instantiation could be based on a number of configurable parameters such as price, quality guarantees, etc. and will be application-specific. Alternatively, some service provider agents can provide their precise output specifications, if they have satisfiable intersection with the request (see Section 4).

In the second step of this phase, the service composer circulates the counter-offers (Out_s_i) to all providers of services s_j for task T_j (on the right of Figure 3), to check if their In_s_j (which subsume the input specification of their task In_T_j), covers at least one of the counter-offers in a PlugIn type of link and thus make the link robust. If $Sim_T(Out\_s_i, In\_s_j)$ is of PlugIn type for at least one pair of candidate services, the respective service provider for s_j will respond to the service composer, and the protocol will terminate with success. Otherwise each service provider will return a counter-offer which is the extra description required for this concrete semantic link $sl_{i,j}$ i.e., $T \models Out\_s_i \sqcap H_{s_i,s_j} \sqsubseteq In\_s_j$.

Phase 2: In this phase all agents operate on the basis that additional services will be required to make the link robust, and that the service consumer will have to pay additional usage fees for these extra services. They attempt to find just a single additional service per non-robust link, and to avoid having to modify or create services. This phase starts with the service composer contacting the service providers s_i ("on the left"), with either the specific "paired" counter-offers H_{s_i,s_j} generated from Phase 1, or, where the agent has not secured such a "paired" offer, with the general H_{T_i,T_j}.

The service providers then try to find the extra service (possibly in coalition with another service provider), which provides the missing semantic information and thus can narrow Out_s_i and thus convert $Sim_T(Out\_s_i, In\_s_j)$ into the robust PlugIn type. If they succeed, they will respond with the cost of using this extra service. In this case the service composer agent will terminate the protocol, and select one of the services with such offers, using its usual criteria. Therefore, in that specific case, the agent does not actively modify the service behaviour, but rather finds new services that support this extra description to ensure compliance to the restriction at run-time.

If no such offer is received, the service composer agent will contact all service providers "on the right", asking them to consider finding extra services which can act in parallel with their offerings and extend their specification of In_s_j to a degree where there is a PlugIn relationship with any of the Out_s_i. If no such offers are found, the negotiation proceeds to Phase 3.

Phase 3: At this phase all agents operate on the basis that some degree of service adaptation and/or development is necessary to achieve robustness of the specific semantic link, and the expectations of monetary values are thus also increased. Again we use the pairs of offers and counter-offers derived in the previous phases, and we contact in turn agents "on the left" and then the ones "on the right" to negotiate the best conditions (price, quality, etc.) needed to turn the specific link into a robust form.

Formal details of the agent protocol driving this approach are described in Section 4, whilst an example of its operation is found in Section 5.

4   Details of Protocol and Agent Decisions

In the previous section we have introduced a multi-phase negotiation mechanism to enable service composer agent to manage several negotiation processes (with providers of services s_i and s_j). The details described here relate to a single non-robust link only. Interdependencies between non-robust links are not considered in this work.

4.1   Phase 1

We start with the service composer agent calculating H_{T_i,T_j}.

Step 1: The first negotiation step comprises one-shot interaction between the service composer and all providers of services s_i, triggered by a Call-for-Proposals message from the service composer, which has H_{T_i,T_j} as its content. The negotiation protocol is shown in Figure 4 a). The type of response generated by service providers in the protocol is based on the following conditions.

a) `Proposal`: Each service provider will check if $T \models Out\_s_i \sqsubseteq H_{T_i,T_j} \sqcap Out\_T_i$. If so, that provider will respond positively and the process will terminate.
b) `Refuse`: Alternatively, services for which $T \models Out\_s_i \sqcap H_{T_i,T_j} \sqsubseteq \bot$ will be deemed unsuitable for further negotiation and their providers will refuse participating in the negotiation.
c) `Counter-Proposal`: If there is satisfiable intersection, i.e., $T \not\models Out\_s_i \sqcap H_{T_i,T_j} \sqsubseteq \bot$, these providers will respond to the service composer with their output specifications Out_s_i.

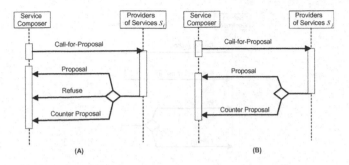

Fig. 4. Protocols to Support First Phase of Negotiation

Step 2: In case Step 1 ends up with counter proposals from providers of s_i, the service composer will use the negotiation protocol shown in Figure 4 b) to initiate negotiation with the providers of services s_j, sending them a Call-for-Proposals message with the set of all counter-proposals Out_s_i from Step 1 as its content. Step 2 can result in a robust composition if any of the services s_j has an input In_s_j which subsumes any of the counter-offers. The following response options are available to service provider agents.

a) `Proposal`: if $Sim_T(Out\_s_i, In\_s_j)$ is of a PlugIn type, the agent responds positively;

b) `Counter-Proposal`: If $Sim_T(Out\_s_i, In\_s_j)$ is an Intersection type, the agent responds with a counter-proposal which is the extra description required for this concrete semantic link $sl_{i,j}$ i.e., $T \models Out\_s_i \sqcap H_{s_i,s_j} \sqsubseteq In\_s_j$. Below we refer to this as a "paired offer" between two provider agents.

If the second step ends up with counter-proposals rather than proposals, the composer will initiate the second phase of negotiation.

4.2 Phases 2 and 3

Step 1: In the second and third phase of negotiation the service composer uses the protocol shown in Figure 5, to solicit offers of using additional services (in Phase 2), or adapting or even developing services (in Phase 3), which can turn the particular link in its robust form. These phases build on the data about semantic fit gathered during Phase 1, in a way of a matrix linking service providers for s_j as rows and service providers for s_i as columns. The matrix, an example of which is shown in Table 1, contains the specific "paired offer" Extra Descriptions H_{s_i,s_j} in the respective cells, and the abstract Extra Description H_{T_i,T_j} elsewhere. The initial `Call-for-Proposals` message will refer to this matrix in its contents.

In response to the CFP the negotiation protocol presents the following response options.

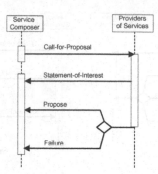

Fig. 5. Protocol to Support Second Phase of Negotiation

a) `Statement-of-Interest`: This is an optional response option. The service provider can send a `Statement-of-Interest` to buy time for finding other service providers (or coalition formation) that can help in delivering the required information.

b) `Proposal`: A service provider agent may use one of their services, or employ coalition formation techniques [21,22] and enlist a service from other agents for providing the needed additional specification. If these attempts succeed, the provider will responds positively with a proposal. For Phase 3, the service provider may propose adaptation of their service to provide the required specification, or the development of the extra filters required.

c) `Failure`: It is possible that the service provider agent is not able to form a coalition, in this case the service provider will responds with `Failure`.

Table 1. Matrix for Advertising Paired Services

	s_1^1	s_1^2	s_1^3
s_2^1	H_{T_1,T_2}	H_{T_1,T_2}	H_{T_1,T_2}
s_2^2	H_{T_1,T_2}	H_{s_3,s_2}	H_{T_1,T_2}

If any proposals are received, the service provider agent can terminate the protocol and select the best proposal. Otherwise they initiate Step 2.

Step 2: The service composer will initiate the negotiation with providers of services s_j using the same protocol (shown in Figure 5). The service providers are presented with the relevant specifications Out_s_i, gathered during Phase 1, and with the same response options. In Phase 2, the providers of services s_j should find extra services which can act in parallel with their offering to achieve a PlugIn relationship in relation to Out_s_i. In Phase 3, the providers should consider the costs and feasibility of adapting their services to handle the inputs specified by Out_s_i.

In case the protocol ends with a Failure then the negotiation proceeds to the third phase, where the service composer agent uses the same protocol template to check whether service providers are willing/able to develop new service that can complement their services for robust composition.

5 An Example Negotiation

Here we demonstrate how our approach can be applied to the example service composition covered in the Examples 1 to 3. We are focusing on the semantic link $sl_{1,2}^A$ in Example 1, which is non-Robust. The Service Composer Agent will calculate $H_{T_1,T_2} \equiv \forall netSpeed.Adsl1M$ (Example 2).

5.1 Phase 1

The Service Composer Agent will issue a CFP with an objective of H_{T_1,T_2} to all providers of candidate services for T_1, namely s_1^1, s_1^2, and s_1^3.

According to Example 3, we have $T \models Out\_s_1^1 \sqsubseteq H_{T_1,T_2} \sqcap Out\_T_2$. Therefore the agent providing s_1^1 will respond with Proposal message, where they specify the conditions (price, QoS,etc.) for using their service. The agent providing s_1^2 will respond with Refuse message since, according to Example 3: $T \models Out\_s_1^2 \sqcap H_{T_1,T_2} \sqsubseteq \bot$. And the agent providing s_1^3 will respond with Counter-Proposal($Out\_s_1^3$) since $T \not\models Out\_s_1^3 \sqcap H_{T_1,T_2} \sqsubseteq \bot$ (Example 3).

Having received all three responses, the Service Composer Agent will choose s_1^1 and terminate the negotiation over this semantic link. If the system did not contain s_1^1 or its service provider agent did not send a response, the Service Composer Agent will take the payload of the Counter-Proposal message $Out\_s_1^3$ and send it as the objective of a CFP message to the agents providing services s_2^1 and s_2^2. Since $Sim_T(Out\_s_1^3, In\_s_2^1)$ is of PlugIn matching type (Example 3), the provider of s_2^1 will respond with Proposal message, where they specify the conditions (price, QoS,etc.) for using their service.

This is not the case for the provider of s_2^2, where $Sim_T(Out\_s_1^3, In\_s_2^2)$ is of Intersection matching type. This provider will calculate $H_{s_1^3,s_2^2}$ using the following: $T \models Out\_s_1^3 \sqcap H_{s_1^3,s_2^2} \sqsubseteq In\_s_2^2$ which results in the $NetworkConnection$ to be $\forall netSpeed.Adsl1M \sqcap \forall netSpeed.AdslLimited$ (speed limited between $1mBytes$ and $1.5mBytes$).

The provider will then respond with this value as contents (payload) in a Counter-Proposal message.

Upon receiving all responses, the Service Composer agent will accept the best of all Proposal messages (the first and only one here). If such messages are not returned, the Service Composer agent will initiate the second phase of the negotiation, using the results $H_{s_1^1,s_2^1}$ from the first phase.

5.2 Phases 2 and 3

In the second phase, the Service Composer will ask the candidate service providers if they can provide an additional service (that provides the missing description H) to ensure the semantic link is robust. The phase starts by the Service Composer issuing a CFP message to the providers of s_1, where the content of the message refers to the matrix shown on Table 1. The matrix will contain H_{T_1,T_2} for all pairs of candidate services apart from the cell (s_1^3, s_2^2), where the content will be H_{s_3,s_2} based on the "paired" counter-proposal reached at the end of Phase 1. Service providers will attempt to find additional services by potentially building coalitions and send either an agreement or a rejection. If the service composer does not receive any agreements, they will contact the two providers of s_2 with a CFP message, containing the output specifications received in the first phase of the negotiation. The two service providers will attempt to find an additional service to handle these output specifications, and respond accordingly. The third phase will repeat the interaction pattern of the second phase.

6 Related Work

We review some works related to our main contributions i.e., i) *Robustness* in semantic web service composition and ii) *Agent-based Negotiation* for service composition.

6.1 Robustness in Composition

An intuitive method [12] to immediately retrieve the *Extra Description* consists in discovering services that return this description as output parameters. Such a solution can be employed and implemented in any composition approach. In case of a non-robust semantic link, the *Extra Description* is exposed to a Web service discovery process which is in charge of retrieving relevant Web services. The latter services are able to provide the *Extra Description* as output parameters. The *Extra Description* can be reached by one or a conjunction of Web services, depending on the *Extra Description* and the discovery process. In contrast we use agent based negotiation for obtaining robust compositions of web services. This reduced the complexity of the whole approach by assuming agents interfacing sets of services that can resolve robustness of some semantic links. In more particular the proposed approach is of linear complexity i.e., each (distributed) agent only needs to look through several options/counter-offers.

Alternatively the set of Extra Descriptions is suggested to the end user in order to be relaxed in [23]. This user is then responsible of providing the Extra Description that the system needed to elaborate the final composition. The new information that end users will provide to the system is necessary to compute and elaborate a robust composition of web services, hence satisfying the initial user request. The suggested method has the advantage of relaxing constraints on the end user. In contrast we suggest an automated approach which does not require any end user support.

6.2 Agent-Based Negotiation

Agent-based approaches have recently been used to provide effective automated solutions to web service composition. This is partly because agent negotiations provide an effective way of addressing the complete issues associated with automated service composition [23]. Negotiation between software agents is one of the fundamental research issues in multi-agent systems. In this respect, this paper introduces several negotiation processes that an be employed by agents to manage different issues within a service composition problem. The negotiation processes range from simple one-shot interactions to handling counter proposals across different processes and facilitating agent-based coalition-formation. The subject of coalition-formation is explored in [22] and agent-based coalition formation for service composition is discussed in [21]. In future we intend to focus on the coalition formation strategies and the trade-offs that can be offered to service provider agents within the service composition problem.

7 Conclusion

Ensuring robust semantic links between elements of composite services is very important in real scenarios of composition, and a mechanism to achieve this in an automated, effective and efficient fashion is needed for scalable and practical applications of web service composition. In this paper we propose such an automated approach which uses a formal model of semantic robustness, and agent-based negotiation protocol to ensure automation, effectiveness and efficiency. As shown by the example application and the specification of the approach, it can find automated solutions without involving humans, and also satisfy the criteria for effectiveness since innovative solutions can be found using coalition formation, and agents can customize services for lucrative opportunities of use. The dynamic nature of the negotiation protocol results in a number of requirements (in real-world scenarios) on the service providers side i.e., their willingness to create a new service on demand or to customize an existing service according to the composer's requirements. Finally, the approach is designed to ensure efficiency by exploring the free solutions first, then the low-cost use-based solutions, and only at last resort it considers service adaptation and development.

Our approach goes beyond the prevalent one-shot procedure (sending request and collecting results) by allowing agents to play a more active role in the composition process. The main direction for future work is to consider robustness in more expressive composition of web services (e.g., in case of conditional branching: multiple successors for on task with different input parameters). In addition, since running the negotiation protocol process during composition instantiation will affect the composition performance, some heuristics-based experiments on that specific point need to be driven. Finally optimization of robustness along web service composition needs to be investigated.

Acknowledgments

This work is conducted within the European Commission VII Framework IP Project Soa4All (Service Oriented Architectures for All) (*http://www.soa4all.eu/*), Contract No. IST-215219.

References

1. Bennett, K., Munro, M., Xu, J., Gold, N., Layzell, P., Mehandjiev, N., Budgen, D., Brereton, P.: Prototype implementations of an architectural model for service-based flexible software. In: Hawaii International Conference on System Sciences, vol. 3, p. 76b (2002)
2. Wielinga, B., Schreiber, G.: Configuration-design problem solving. IEEE Expert: Intelligent Systems and Their Applications 12(2), 49–56 (1997)

3. Motta, E.: Parametric Design Problem Solving - Reusable Components for Knowledge Modelling Case Studies. IOS Press, Amsterdam (1999)
4. Lécué, F., Mehandjiev, N.: Towards scalability of quality driven semantic web service composition. In: ICWS (2009)
5. Sycara, K.P., Paolucci, M., Ankolekar, A., Srinivasan, N.: Automated discovery, interaction and composition of semantic web services. J. Web Sem. 1(1), 27–46 (2003)
6. Baader, F., Nutt, W.: The Description Logic Handbook: Theory, Implementation, and Applications (2003)
7. Ankolenkar, A., Paolucci, M., Srinivasan, N., Sycara, K.: The owl-s coalition, owl-s 1.1. Technical report (2004)
8. Fensel, D., Kifer, M., de Bruijn, J., Domingue, J.: Web service modeling ontology submission, w3c submission (2005)
9. Sivashanmugam, K., Verma, K., Sheth, A., Miller, J.: Adding semantics to web services standards. In: ICWS, pp. 395–401 (2003)
10. Smith, M.K., Welty, C., McGuinness, D.L.: Owl web ontology language guide. W3c recommendation, W3C (2004)
11. Berners-Lee, T., Hendler, J., Lassila, O.: The semantic web. Scientific American 284(5), 34–43 (2001)
12. Lécué, F., Delteil, A., Léger, A.: Applying abduction in semantic web service composition. In: ICWS, pp. 94–101 (2007)
13. McIlraith, S.A., Son, T.C.: Adapting golog for composition of semantic web services. In: KR, pp. 482–496 (2002)
14. ten Teije, A., van Harmelen, F., Wielinga, B.: Configuration of web services as parametric design. In: Motta, E., Shadbolt, N.R., Stutt, A., Gibbins, N. (eds.) EKAW 2004. LNCS (LNAI), vol. 3257, pp. 321–336. Springer, Heidelberg (2004)
15. Lécué, F., Léger, A.: A formal model for semantic web service composition. In: Cruz, I., Decker, S., Allemang, D., Preist, C., Schwabe, D., Mika, P., Uschold, M., Aroyo, L.M. (eds.) ISWC 2006. LNCS, vol. 4273, pp. 385–398. Springer, Heidelberg (2006)
16. Horrocks, I.: Using an expressive description logic: Fact or fiction? In: KR, pp. 636–649 (1998)
17. Paolucci, M., Kawamura, T., Payne, T., Sycara, K.: Semantic matching of web services capabilities. In: Horrocks, I., Hendler, J. (eds.) ISWC 2002. LNCS, vol. 2342, pp. 333–347. Springer, Heidelberg (2002)
18. Li, L., Horrocks, I.: A software framework for matchmaking based on semantic web technology. In: WWW, pp. 331–339 (2003)
19. Lécué, F., Delteil, A.: Making the difference in semantic web service composition. In: AAAI, pp. 1383–1388 (2007)
20. Colucci, S., Noia, T.D., Sciascio, E.D., Donini, F., Mongiello, M.: Concept abduction and contraction for semantic-based discovery of matches and negotiation spaces in an e-marketplace. In: ECRA, vol. 4, pp. 41–50 (2005)
21. Muller, I., Kowalczyk, R., Braun, P.: Towards agent-based coalition formation for service composition. In: IAT 2006: Proceedings of the IEEE/WIC/ACM international conference on Intelligent Agent Technology, Washington, DC, USA, pp. 73–80. IEEE Computer Society, Los Alamitos (2006)
22. Shehory, O., Kraus, S.: Methods for task allocation via agent coalition formation. Artif. Intell. 101(1-2), 165–200 (1998)
23. Hassine, A.B., Matsubara, S., Ishida, T.: A constraint-based approach to horizontal web service composition. In: Cruz, I., Decker, S., Allemang, D., Preist, C., Schwabe, D., Mika, P., Uschold, M., Aroyo, L.M. (eds.) ISWC 2006. LNCS, vol. 4273, pp. 130–143. Springer, Heidelberg (2006)

Evaluating Contract Compatibility for Service Composition in the SeCO$_2$ Framework*

Marco Comerio[1], Hong-Linh Truong[2], Flavio De Paoli[1],
and Schahram Dustdar[2]

[1] University of Milano - Bicocca, Milano, Italy
{comerio,depaoli}@disco.unimib.it
[2] Distributed Systems Group, Vienna University of Technology
{truong,dustdar}@infosys.tuwien.ac.at

Abstract. Recently, the Software-as-a-Service (SaaS) model has been increasingly supported, becoming a major part of the new emerging cloud computing paradigms. Although SaaS exists in different forms, supporting and providing SaaS developed based Web services has attracted a large effort from industries and academics because this form of SaaS allows software to be easily composed and integrated to offer new services for customers. Even though various service composition techniques, based on functional and non-functional parameters, have been proposed, the issue of service contract compatibility has been neglected. This issue is of paramount importance in the Web services-based SaaS model because services are provided by different providers, associated with different contracts which are defined by different specifications. This paper proposes techniques for supporting service composers to deal with the heterogeneity of service contracts in service composition. We describe a novel approach for modeling and mapping different service contract specifications, and a set of techniques for evaluating service contract compatibility. Our techniques consider contract terms associated with data and control flows, as well as composition patterns. Illustrating scenarios are proposed to demonstrate the efficiency of our techniques.

1 Introduction

We have recently observed the rise of cloud computing and SaaS as a part of the cloud computing paradigm [1]. In particular, many providers have provided SaaS using the Web services model. This form of SaaS has been widely supported because it enables service composition and integration.

Techniques supporting service composition and integration have been developed for a long time. It is important that when services are selected and composed from different SaaS providers, their contracts, which govern how the services should be used, have to be compatible. We need to support both, users and tools, to deal with issues related to service contracts. This support is of

---

* This work is partially supported by the European Union through the FP7-216256 project COIN.

L. Baresi, C.-H. Chi, and J. Suzuki (Eds.): ICSOC-ServiceWave 2009, LNCS 5900, pp. 221–236, 2009.

paramount importance because how services are used is bound to the service contract. However, there is a lack of supporting tools to deal with the evaluation of service contract compatibility, which is actually just one of many open questions about the relationship between service contracts and service composition discussed in [2]. Current techniques, such as service license compatibility [3], are not suitable because they assume that service contracts follow the same specification and they do not support service contracts for service compositions. To our best knowledge, until now, there is no work supporting service contract compatibility that takes into account the heterogeneity of service contract specifications and different aspects associated with data and control flows of the composition.

In this paper, we present an overview of $SeCO_2$, a novel framework for supporting service composers to deal with the heterogeneity of service contracts in service compositions. The framework is a part of tools and systems for supporting the life-cycle management of the ecosystem of service contracts. Within this paper we present the following contributions: (i) a novel approach for modeling and mapping different service contract specifications, and (ii) a set of techniques for service contract compatibility evaluation. Our techniques consider contract terms associated with *data* and *control flows*, as well as *composition patterns*.

The rest of this paper is structured as follows: Section 2 elaborates the context, motivation, and related work of this paper. We discuss our approach and give an overview of $SeCO_2$ in Section 3. We present techniques to achieve the modeling and mapping of service contract specifications in Section 4. We present the compatibility evaluation in Section 5. Experiments are presented in Section 6. We conclude the paper and give an outlook to the future work in Section 7.

2   Motivation and Related Work

2.1   Motivation

The main motivation of our work is, in general, how to ensure the compatibility of service contracts for service compositions. In the current service composition landscape there is the need to compose different services to provide converged services. In the SaaS model it is assumed that the service customer uses the software deployed as a service. This model allows service providers to combine different services, potentially characterizing by different service contracts specified by different languages. With the techniques developed so far, it is not so difficult for consumers to compose different services based on published service interfaces. For example, existing platforms like The Process Factory[1] and Boomi[2] provide different connectors for consumers to compose their services from various SaaS providers. However, the consumers need to ensure that the service compositions do not include conflicting service contracts. This assurance cannot be given by a single SaaS provider and currently is not available in existing composition tools.

In the SaaS and cloud computing model, no single specification would be agreed by all, making the service contract compatibility evaluation hard. Past

---

[1] http://www.theprocessfactory.com
[2] http://www.boomi.com

research has neglected contracts of composite services when performing service composition by considering only functional parameters (service interfaces) or assume that contracts associated with services being composed are described by a single language. Furthermore, past research has not focused on tools and algorithms dealing with contract compatibility evaluation when combining different services from different providers. Typically, they deal with only contract negotiation between consumer and service in a point-to-point manner.

Service contract compatibility is also strongly dependent on the structure of composition. This is related to not only control flows but also data flows and composition patterns. While certain works address QoS-based compatibility for control flows, currently there is a lack of a good understanding of how to check contract compatibility for data, the input/output of services, whose contract terms are not always the same to that of the service operations. We stress that contract terms associated with the use of service and the use of data are different and our objective is to address the compatibility for both data and service.

2.2   Related Work on Service Contract Compatibility

As stated in [2], the understanding between a service consumer and a service provider can be established using different approaches (e.g., policies, licenses, service level agreements). Even if some philosophical differences exist among these approaches, in this paper we identify them under the common term *service contract* which specifies conditions that a service consumer and a service provider agree. Besides functional terms, a service contract is composed of the specification of *Quality of Service (QoS)*, *Business*, *Service Context* and *License* terms of a service. *QoS* terms (e.g., response time) represent technical aspects of the service. *Business* terms (e.g., service price) describe financial terms and conditions. *Service Context* terms (e.g., service delivery location) define the characteristics of the context associated with the service. Finally, *License* terms (e.g., limitation of liabilities and usage permissions) state responsibilities among involved parties and conditions on service usage.

Currently, service contracts can be described using several specifications, such as ODRL-S [4], WSLA [5], and WSOL [6]. Even though these specifications have some common parts, there exists no reference ontology/thesaurus for describing contract properties. This means that service consumers and providers specify their service contracts as they wish, causing many issues when multiple services governed by different contracts are utilized (e.g., in a composition). Until now we are not aware of any work dealing with the definition of techniques to evaluate the compatibility among contract terms specified in different languages.

The most cited works [7,8,9] are related to contract-based service composition and reduce the problem to the evaluation of QoS constraints among composite services and user requirements. The AgFlow framework [7] evaluates the QoS of composite services with an extensible multidimensional quality model and considering the control flow of the service composition. Other examples of QoS-based composition are in [8] that aims at defining composition rules to evaluate global values of QoS dimensions according to specific workflow patterns. The constraint-driven Web service composition tool presented in [9] reduces the service composition problem to a constraint satisfaction problem focusing on business and process constraints. These works consider only a small set of service contract terms (i.e., QoS). The evaluation of qualitative properties (e.g., license terms) are not tackled. Moreover, they assume that property descriptions are always available and specified using a common language.

3   Overview of the SeCO2 Framework

The objective of the SeCO2 framework is to support service composers to deal with the heterogeneity of service contracts in service composition. In this paper we focus on techniques used by SeCO2 to support the modeling and mapping of service contracts defined using different specification languages and the evaluation of the compatibility among these service contracts. Figure 1 provides an overview of actors and data involved in these activities.

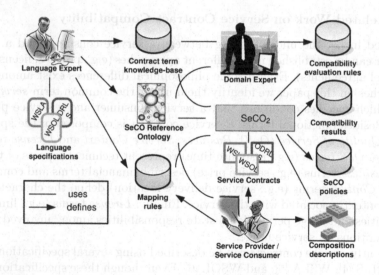

Fig. 1. The SeCO2 Framework

The SeCO2 framework overcomes the heterogeneity in service contract specifications using the *SeCO Reference Ontology* containing semantic descriptions of service contract properties and the *Contract term knowledge-base* specifying additional information about these properties. The *SeCO Reference Ontology* is built based on the Policy-Centered Metamodel (PCM) [10]. The PCM offers (i) the concept of *Policy* that aggregates property descriptions into a single entity with an applicability condition, and (ii) a set of constraint operators that allows for the description of both qualitative and quantitative properties.

The SeCO2 framework deals with service contracts specified in different languages (e.g., ODRL-S, WSLA and WSOL). In this paper we assume that SeCO2 receives these contracts from service providers and we show how it makes them comparable by wrapping them into *SeCO Policies*. In order to do this, *Language Experts* analyze *language specifications* and create, modify, update and delete the knowledge stored in the *SeCO Reference Ontology* and in the *Contract term knowledge-base*. The mapping between ontological concepts and contract-specific terminologies is defined by *Language Experts, Service Providers and Consumers* with *mapping rules*. In order to define techniques for service contract compatibility evaluation, the $SeCO_2$ framework supports *Domain Experts* in the definition of *compatibility evaluation rules* by means of the $SeCO_2$ *Reference Ontology* and the *Contract term knowledge-base*. *Mapping rules* and *compatibility evaluation rules*, as well as the *SeCO Reference Ontology* and the *Contract term knowledge-base*, are shared information for the users. This aspect reduces the effort for their definition and improves reusability. These rules allow $SeCO_2$ to receive *Service contracts* and *Composition descriptions* as inputs, perform the wrapping to *SeCO policies* and verify the compatibility among them.

One of the most innovative characteristics of our framework is how the compatibility evaluation is performed. Currently, there is no distinction between the description of properties related to service usage (e.g., `Request Limit`) and properties related to the data produced by the service (e.g., `Data Ownership`). This produces ambiguities in service contract specifications. As an example, the property `Price` can refer to the amount of money needed for invoking a service or it can refer to the amount of money needed for receiving an amount of data from a service. This distinction is critical for the service contract compatibility evaluation. The $SeCO_2$ framework performs the compatibility evaluation considering both the *control flow* and the *data flow* of the service composition. Dependencies between each service contract property and *control* and *data flow* are identified and considered during the definition of *compatibility evaluation rules*. Furthermore, another characteristics of the service contract compatibility evaluation performed by $SeCO_2$ is that it is not limited to *QoS* but it is also extended to other types of property that can be included in a service contract like *Business, Service Context* and *License* terms. Table 1 shows the influences between each identified service contract property type and *control* and *data flow*.

Table 1. Data and control flows in contract compatibility evaluation

	control flow	data flow	independent
Quality of Service (QoS)	X		
Service Context			X
Business	X	X	
License	X	X	

4   Modeling and Mapping Service Contract Specifications

The first step in order to achieve the service contract compatibility is that we have to develop techniques to map different service contracts described in different specifications and terminologies. In our view, the mapping of service contract specifications are not a static, but a dynamic process because specifications and terminologies as well as knowledge about them change over the time.

4.1   Typology of Contract Specifications

Starting from the analysis of ODRL-S, WSLA and WSOL we have identified three types of languages for the specification of service contract properties:

- **Type A**: includes *languages allowing the specification of predefined properties.* In this type, e.g., ODRL-S, the properties that can be specified are known by the Language Expert.
- **Type B**: includes *languages allowing the specification of user-defined properties.* In this type, e.g., WSLA, the Language Expert knows only the structure of the specification but the properties are defined by the Service Provider.
- **Type C**: includes *languages allowing the specification of properties defined in user ontologies.* In this type, e.g., WSOL, the Language Expert knows only the structure of the specification while the properties are specified by the Service Provider using external ontologies.

We use the SeCO Reference Ontology for mapping different specifications and for allowing compatibility evaluation. This ontology is composed of: (i) a core part containing the specification of common properties (e.g., QoS) and (ii) a plug-in part that can be enriched by Language Experts with new properties.

Languages in **Type A** (e.g., ODRL-S) are characterized by profile models describing all the properties that can be included in a service contract. In this case, the Language Expert enriches the plug-in part to model all the properties not included in the ontology. Moreover, the Language Expert can define fixed mapping rules between properties and ontological concepts.

Languages in **Type B** (e.g., WSLA) allow new properties to be defined. This characteristic limits the possibility to perform the modeling and mapping of properties in these languages into $SeCO_2$ in advance. Thus, interactions to the Service Providers are still needed when wrapping a concrete service contract into SeCO policies. However, users of the same domain (e.g., the logistic operator domain) typically utilize common terminologies, e.g., logistic operator service providers utilize the term **Shipping Location** in their specifications which has the same meaning of the property **Service Delivery Location** available in the core part of the SeCO Reference Ontology. Common terminologies and domain-specific knowledge are used by Language Experts and Domain Experts to define customized mapping rules which will reduce the interactions needed for the wrapping of service contracts.

Languages in **Type C** (e.g., WSOL) are similar to the ones in **Type B** but here the properties are semantically described in external ontologies. Thus, the possibility to perform the modeling and mapping activities is limited and we need to define customized mapping rules between concepts in the most common user ontologies and concepts specified in the SeCO Reference Ontology.

Since contract specifications use different representations, ontology alignment tools [11,12,13], which supports mappings between concepts defined in different ontologies, cannot be used to fully automate the mapping between different specifications. Furthermore, as the interpretation of contract terms may vary from different service providers, fully automatically generation of mapping rules cannot be achieved. However, these tools can support the definition of mapping rules when we deal with ontology-based specifications. In this paper, we consider the use of these tools as external activities triggered by the user of SeCO$_2$.

4.2 Modeling and Mapping Service Contract Terminologies into the Reference Ontology

When an XML-based profile model defining properties is available (i.e., Languages in Type A), a set of general rules is used to extract properties from XML-based specifications and semantically describe them into the SeCO Reference Ontology. General rules link an XML-structure to a proper PCM-based description. The same structure can be associated with several rules because also the nature of the property must be considered. Examples are: (i) the XML-structure in which an element $C1$ has a set of sub-elements can be linked to the InstanceOf-rule that consider each sub-element as possible values assumed by $C1$; (ii) the XML-structure in which different elements (e.g., $C2$ and $C3$) have the same sub-element $C1$ is linked to the IsA-rule that considers $C2$ and $C3$ as specializations (i.e., sub-concepts) of $C1$.

To illustrate the above-mentioned techniques, we focus on modeling and mapping ODRL-S terminology. Figure 2 shows how general rules can be used to model ODRL-S properties into the SeCO Reference Ontology. The following ODRL-S terms [4] are considered: (i) Permission Rights: defines types of uses of the service, such as Adaptation, Composition and Derivation; (ii) Payment: describes the financial terms assuming values, such as PrePay and PostPay.

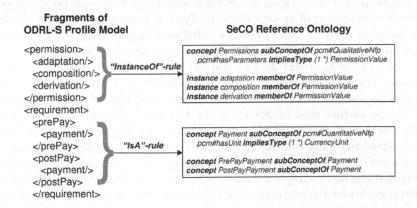

Fig. 2. Modeling ODRL-S properties in the SeCO Reference Ontology

In ODRL-S, `Adaptation`, `Composition` and `Derivation` are sub-elements of `Permission`. For this property the ODRL-S Language Expert uses the `InstanceOf`-rule to define a new concept `Permissions` in the ontology which can assume a fixed set of values (i.e., `pcm#hasParameters impliesType PermissionValue`) that are `Adaptation`, `Composition` and `Derivation`. `PrePay` and `PostPay` are super-elements for `Payment`. In this case the `IsA`-rule is applied considering them as specializations of the term `Payment`. A new concept `Payment` and two sub-concepts (`PrePayPayment` and `PostPayPayment`) are added to the ontology.

After the modeling of a property in the SeCO Reference Ontology, the Language Expert defines a mapping rule between the property and the related ontological concept; the rule is used in the wrapping of service contract specifications to SeCO Policies. Moreover, the Language Expert stores information into the Contract term knowledge-base about the influences of the property on the data and control flows of the composition. This information is used by Domain Experts for the definition of the related compatibility evaluation rule.

4.3   Wrapping Service Contract Specifications to SeCO Policy

A proper technique for each type of language must be defined to perform the wrapping from service contracts to SeCO Policy specifications. The wrapping of specifications in `Type A` language is directly performed by applying the mapping rules defined by Language Experts. For what concern specifications in `Type B` and `Type C` languages the wrapping activity may require interactions with the Service Providers to handle the absence of knowledge (i.e., mapping rules) on specified properties. The Service Providers must define the mapping between their properties (i.e., text labels for `Type B` and ontological concepts for `Type C`) and concepts available in the SeCO Reference Ontology.

For what concern specifications in `Type B` languages, lexical databases like WordNet support Service Providers to define mapping rules identifying synonyms between text labels and ontological concepts defined in the SeCO Reference Ontology. Different types of ontology alignment tools can be also used to support the wrapping of specifications in `Type C` languages: (i) tools for defining a mapping between concepts in two different ontologies by finding pairs of related concepts (e.g., `ANCHORPROMPT` [11]) or by evaluating semantic affinity between concepts (e.g., `H-MATCH` [12]) and (ii) tools for defining mapping rules to relate only relevant parts of the source ontologies (e.g., `ONION` [13]).

In this section, we describe a solution for the wrapping of a WSLA specification. The procedure used by $SeCO_2$ is the following: (i) parse the specification in order to detect properties (i.e., `SLAParameters`); (ii) search the availability of customized mapping rules related to the detected properties; (iii) if mapping rules are not identified, use WordNet to identify a possible mapping between the `SLAParameters` and concepts available in the SeCO Reference Ontology and ask confirmation about the correctness of the mapping to the Service Provider; and (iv) if the mapping is not correct or not available, ask to the Service Provider to perform the mapping manually.

Figure 3 illustrates the above-mentioned steps when wrapping a WSLA-based service contract consisting `PrePayment = 9.99` Euros and `ServiceUsage = ''adaptation''`. In this example, a customized mapping rule for `PrePayment` is identified. On the contrary, the term `ServiceUsage` is not known and no rules are available. Moreover, no synonym relations are specified in WordNet between `ServiceUsage` and terms defined in the SeCO Reference Ontology. In order to handle this absence of knowledge, the Service Provider is asked to navigate the ontology and map the SLAParameter `ServiceUsage` to any ontological concept. The result is the mapping of `ServiceUsage` with `Permissions`.

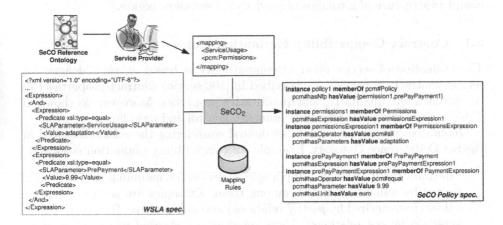

Fig. 3. Mapping between WSLA and ScCO Policy

After this preliminary step, the mapping proceeds considering the `Expressions` defined in each `Service Level Objective` of the WSLA specification. Each `Expression` follows the first order logic, including predicates and logic operators. According to the logic operators, different mapping rules can be applied. The simplest form of a logic expression is a plain predicate. The mapping to a SeCO policy includes the following steps: (i) the mapping rule is used to identify in the SeCO Reference Ontology the concept related to the `SLAParameter` specified by the Service Provider; (ii) a new instance of this concept is created. It must be characterized by an expression having constraint operator and parameter equals to `Type` and `Value` of the `Service Level Objective`; (iii) a new SeCO Policy containing the concept instance is created.

In Figure 3, the logic operator "*And*" is used to specify the aggregation of two plain predicates stating conditions on `PrePayment` and `ServiceUsage`. The mapping to a SeCO Policy consists in defining the concept instances related to all the plain predicates. The final result for the considered example is a SeCO Policy containing: (i) an instance of `Permissions` characterized by an expression stating that the value `adaptation` is assumed (i.e., `pcm#hasOperator hasValue pcm#all`; `pcm#hasParameters hasValue adaptation`) and (ii) an instance of

PrePayPayment stating that the amount is equal to 9.99 Euros (i.e., pcm#hasOper ator hasValue pcm#equal; pcm#hasParameter hasValue 9.99; pcm#hasUnit hasValue euro).

5   Contract Compatibility Evaluation for Service Composition

The service contract compatibility evaluation supported by the SeCO$_2$ framework accepts a full or part of a full description of service compositions, e.g., the complete structure of a composite service or a workflow region.

5.1   Contract Compatibility Evaluation Rules

The evaluation of service contract compatibility is based on rules defined for service contract properties. As described in [10], service contract properties can be classified into qualitative and quantitative properties. Moreover, as shown in Table 1, properties can differently influence control and data flows.

Qualitative properties must be evaluated considering the relations stored in the SeCO Reference Ontology. Examples of compatibility evaluation rules are:

- *"Relation-based"* rule: it is applicable to properties assuming values characterized by semantic relations among them. Examples are *partnership* (i.e., values characterized by *partOf* relations) and *subsumption* (i.e., values characterized by *isA* relations). These relations are checked to verify the compatibility among values associated to a property.
- *"Compatible value list"* rule: it is applicable to properties assuming a small set of possible values. The compatibility list among these values is stored into the reference ontology by the definition of *isCompatibleWith* relations.

Quantitative properties must be evaluated considering the constraint operators used to specified the offered values. As described in [10], constraint operators can be *binary* (e.g., $=, \leq, \geq$) or *ternary* (e.g., range of values). *"Binary operator"* and *"Ternary operator"* rules (see [14] for details) evaluate a numeric values in the range [0..1] stating the degree of compatibility between two offered values and the overlap between ranges of values respectively.

Table 2 presents some common rules for the evaluation. We explain some of them in the following. The **Service Delivery Location** property is independent from data and control flows since its value must be checked in all the contracts of the services involved in the composition. The compatibility is evaluated applying a *"Relation-based"* rule focusing on partnership relations ($\sqsupseteq$). In particular, services s_1 and s_2 are compatible if $s_1.value \sqsupseteq s_2.value$ or $s_2.value \sqsupseteq s_1.value$. For example, let us assume that s_1 delivers in the **Worldwide**, s_2 in **Europe** and s_3 in the **US**. The following partnership relations are hold: **Worldwide**$\sqsupseteq$**Europe** and **Worldwide**$\sqsupseteq$**US**. Thus, services s_2 and s_3 cannot be included in the same composition since their provision is limited to different geographical area.

Table 2. Examples of common rules

Property	Type	Data Flow	Control Flow	Rule
Service Delivery Location	Service Context			partnership
Pricing	Business	X		compatible value list
Payment (for data usage)	Business	X		binary, ternary
Payment (for service usage)	Business		X	binary, ternary
Scalability	QoS		X	binary, ternary
Request Limit	QoS		X	binary, ternary
Availability Time Range	QoS		X	ternary
Data Ownership	License	X		compatible value list
Permissions	License		X	subsumption

The compatibility on `Pricing` terms in service contracts is checked considering the data flow. The evaluation is performed using a *"Compatible value list"* rule stating the compatibility among possible pricing models. For example, `flat rate` is compatible with `pay per use with subscription` but it is incompatible with `free per use`.

The property `Scalability` is checked considering the *composition patterns* included in the control flow specification and applying a *"Binary operator"* rule. For example, assume that service s_1 and s_2 follow a *sequential execution* and that s_1 and s_2 have `Scalability` = sc_1 and `Scalability` = sc_2, respectively. Services s_1 and s_2 are compatible if $sc_1 \leq sc_2$.

5.2 An Algorithm for Contract Compatibility Evaluation

Let $S = \{s_1, s_2, \cdots, s_m\}$ denote the set of services involved in the composition. Each service is characterized by a service operation associated with one or more SeCO Policies. Let $P(s_i) = \{p_1, p_2, \cdots, p_n\}$ indicate the set of policies associated to service s_i. Each policy is composed of one or more offered properties. Let $PR(p_i) = \{pr_1, pr_2, \cdots, pr_w\}$ be the set of properties offered by policy p_i. Each property is specified by: (i) a **name** stating the related ontological concept; (ii) a **type** defining if the property is *CF-inf* (i.e., influence the *control flow*), *DF-inf* (i.e., influence the *data flow*) or *F-ind* (i.e., flow independent); (iii) an **operator**; (iv) a **value** and (v) a **unit** of measure.

Let $CF(s_i) = \{cf_1, cf_2, \cdots, cf_m\}$ denote the *control flow* where each cf_j in $CF(s_i)$ specifies the *composition pattern* between s_i and s_j. Possible values are *sequential, parallel* and *conditional execution*. Let $DF(s_i) = \{df_1, df_2, \cdots, df_m\}$ denote the *data flow* where each df_j in $DF(s_i)$ specifies if there is a dependency in data provisioning between s_i and s_j.

Our service contract compatibility algorithm is listed in Algorithm 1. The algorithm evaluates the compatibility among all the policies of all the couples of services available in the composition. Line 3 defines $\Omega(s_i, s_j)$ as a set of triples. Each triple will contain a policy p_w associated to s_i, a policy p_z associated to s_j, and the result of the compatibility evaluation $\lambda(p_w, p_z)$ among them. The evaluation of $\lambda(p_w, p_z)$ starts in Line 7 defining $\Upsilon(p_w, p_z)$ as a set of comparable properties $[pr_1, pr_2]$ specified in p_w and p_z. $\Upsilon(p_w, p_z)$ is populated by the `Matching` procedure (Line 8) that applies matching rules similar to the ones

---

Algorithm 1. Compatibility Evaluation

1: **for all** $s_i \in S$ **do**
2:    **for all** $s_j \in S(j \neq i)$ **do**
3:       $\Omega(s_i, s_j) = \phi$ where $\Omega(s_i, s_j)$ is a set of triples $[p_w, p_z, \lambda(p_w, p_z)]$
4:       **for all** $p_w \in P(s_i)$ **do**
5:          **for all** $p_z \in P(s_j)$ **do**
6:             $\lambda(p_w, p_z) = \phi$, where $\lambda(p_w, p_z)$ is a set of triples $[pr_i, pr_j, result]$
7:             $\Upsilon(p_w, p_z) = \phi$, where $\Upsilon(p_w, p_z)$ is a set of comparable properties $[pr_1, pr_2]$

8:             $\Upsilon(p_w, p_z) = Matching(p_w, p_z)$
9:             **for all** $[pr_1, pr_2] \in \Upsilon(p_w, p_z)$ **do**
10:                $rule = Extract(pr_1.name)$
11:                **if** $pr_1.type =' CF - inf'$ **then**
12:                   $\lambda(p_w, p_z) = \lambda(p_w, p_z) \cup EvalRuleF(rule, pr_1, pr_2, cf_j \in CF(s_i))$
13:                **else**
14:                   **if** $pr_1.type =' DF - inf'$ **then**
15:                      $\lambda(p_w, p_z) = \lambda(p_w, p_z) \cup EvalRuleF(rule, pr_1, pr_2, df_j \in DF(s_i))$
16:                   **else**
17:                      $\lambda(p_w, p_z) = \lambda(p_w, p_z) \cup EvalRule(rule, pr_1, pr_2)$
18:                   **end if**
19:                **end if**
20:             **end for**
21:             $\Omega(s_i, s_j) = \Omega(s_i, s_j) \cup [p_w, p_z, \lambda(p_w, p_z)]$
22:          **end for**
23:       **end for**
24:    **end for**
25: **end for**

---

shown in [10]. For each identified couple $[pr_1, pr_2]$ of comparable properties, the algorithm retrieves the related evaluation rule using the procedure Extract and specifying the property *name* (Line 10). As stated above, at this point the evaluation proceeds considering the property type. If the property is *CF-inf* then procedure EvalRuleF is invoked specifying the retrieved rule, the two comparable properties $[pr_1, pr_2]$ and the *control flow* information about the services s_i, s_j that offer the properties (Line 12). If the property is *DF-inf* then the same procedure EvalRuleF is invoked but specifying the *data flow* information about the services s_i, s_j (Line 15). Finally, if the property is *F-ind* then the procedure EvalRule that does not consider composition flows is invoked (Line 17). The result of the evaluation is saved in $\lambda(p_w, p_z)$ that contains the evaluation of all the comparable properties in p_w and p_z. Finally, the triple $[p_w, p_z, \lambda(p_w, p_z)]$ is saved in $\Omega(s_i, s_j)$ (Line 21) that contains the evaluation for all the policies offered by s_i and s_j.

6 Illustrating Scenarios

In order to demonstrate the contract compatibility evaluation techniques proposed in Section 5, we consider a process of purchase data analysis inside a supply chain management scenario. This process involves multiple services collaborating with each others: (i) a Request Service (RS) issuing a purchase request; (ii) a Purchase Processing Service (PPS) managing the standard e-commerce process; (iii) a Merchant Validation Service (MVS) verifying and providing data about a shopping merchant; (iv) a Payment Verification Service (PS) validating data related to the payment (e.g., the credit card number); (v) Shipping Evaluation Service (SES) calculating shipping charges and (vi) a Purchase Validation Service (PVS) analyzing data and validating the purchase. These services can be composed using different control and data flows. Figure 4 shows two different possible composition structures.

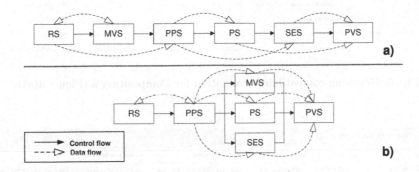

Fig. 4. Different composition structures for the *Purchase Data Analysis* service

Let us assume that a service consumer wants to create a Purchase Data Analysis (PDA) service by composing his/her RS with the following Web services: (i) *Yahoo! Shopping Web Service*[3] as MVS; (ii) *XWebCheckOut Web Service*[4] as PPS; (iii) *Aivea Shipping Web Service*[5] as SES; (iv) *ValidateCreditCard Web Service*[6] as PS and (v) *DOTS Lead Validation Web Service*[7] as PVS. For our experiments, we focus only on service contracts. Thus, let us assume that these Web services match the functionalities required for the PDA service.

The selected Web services are characterized by service contracts available only as HTML texts in their Websites (i.e., ODRL-S, WSLA and WSOL specifications are not available). Moreover, these contracts are unclear, ambiguous and limited to few information. This forces the service consumer to manually compare them and, often, further information from the service providers are needed. Modeling and mapping techniques presented in Section 4 are not applicable due to the absence of structured specifications. In order to overcome this strong limitation, we produce SeCO Policies using information described in the HTML texts and

---

[3] http://developer.yahoo.com/shopping/V1/merchantSearch.html
[4] http://www.xwebservices.com/Web_Services/XWebCheckOut/
[5] http://www.aivea.com/shipping-web-service.htm
[6] http://www.webservicex.net/WCF/ServiceDetails.aspx?SID=14
[7] http://www.serviceobjects.com/products/composite/lead-validation

Table 3. Contracts offered by services involved in the composition

	Del.Loc.	Data Own.	Request Limit	Pricing	Scalability
Request Service (RS)	US	personal-use	unlimited	free	100tr/min
Yahoo! Shopping (MVS)	Worldwide	copyrighted	5000q/day	free	100tr/min
XWebCheckOut (PPS)	Worldwide	free-distrib.	unlimited	100$/year	100tr/min
Aivea Shipping (SES)	Europe	free-distrib.	unlimited	49$/month	100tr/min
ValidateCreditCard (PS)	Worldwide	free-distrib.	unlimited	free	500tr/min
DOTS Lead Valid. (PVS)	Worldwide	free-distrib.	unlimited	free	500tr/min

Service Contract Compatibility

Property	Caller Service	Callee Service	Incompatibity
Scalability	Payment Verification Service	Shipping Evaluation Service	500tr/min not compatible with 100tr/min
Pricing	Request Service	Purchase Processing Service	free not compatible with 100$/year
Service Delivery Location	Request Service	Shipping Evaluation Service	US not compatible with Europe
Request Limit	Request Service	Merchant Validation Service	unlimited not compatible with 5000q/day

Fig. 5. Resulting compatibility evaluation for Composition a (Figure 4(a))

Service Contract Compatibility

Property ▲	Caller Service	Callee Service	Incompatibity
Data Ownership	Merchant Validation Service	Purchase Validation Service	copyrighted not compatible with free-distribution
Pricing	Request Service	Purchase Processing Service	free not compatible with 100$/year
Request Limit	Purchase Processing Service	Merchant Validation Service	unlimited not compatible with 5000q/day
Service Delivery Location	Request Service	Shipping Evaluation Service	US not compatible with Europe

Fig. 6. Resulting compatibility evaluation for Composition b (Figure 4(b))

inserting realistic properties in case of limited descriptions. These policies are summarized in Table 3. For each selected Web service, we consider the properties `Service Delivery Location`, `Pricing` and `Scalability` described in Section 5. Moreover, we consider `Data Ownership` (a license term stating how the data produced by the service are protected) and `Request Limit` (a license term defining the maximum number of requests that a user can submit to the service in a day).

Applying evaluation rules like the ones described in Section 5, the compatibility evaluation results produced by our SeCO$_2$ framework are given in Figures 5 and 6. The following results must be underlined: (i) incompatibility on `Service Delivery Location` is found in both the compositions since the property is independent from data and control flows; (ii) incompatibility on `Pricing` is found in both the compositions because both are characterized by a data flow from RS and PPS; (iii) incompatibility on `Request Limit` is found in both the compositions but between different services. This is determined by the different data flows involving MVS; (iv) incompatibility on `Scalability` is found only in `composition a`. This result depends on the different control flows (i.e., in `composition a` SES is invoked after PS instead in **composition b** it is invoked after PPS); (v) incompatibility on **Data Ownership** is found only in **composition b**. This result depends on the different data flows (i.e., in **composition a** MVS data are managed by RS instead in **composition b** they are managed by PVS).

7 Concluding Remarks

In this paper, we have presented our approach to checking service contract compatibility for service compositions. Our SeCO$_2$ framework provides support to define, update, and share knowledge about service contracts specified by different specifications. Our work can map different service contracts and determined the compatibility based on control and data flows, as well as composition patterns.

Our approach is currently tested with ODRL-S, WSLA, and WSOL. There is no way to automatically determine the typology of a language, thus mapping rules still involve domain experts. We think that it is inevitable, unless terminologies are well-defined and agreed by all service providers. Currently, we do not consider the dynamic changes of contracts during the composition. For example, when performing the composition, the customer and service providers might negotiate the contracts, as the contract changes certain steps have to be rerun. However, currently we consider this change can be solved only by re-running the compatibility checking. Our future work includes enhancing this dynamic interaction among actors when dealing with service contracts. Furthermore, data specific contract compatibility will be improved.

References

1. Armbrust, M., Fox, A., Grifth, R., Joseph, A.D., Katz, R., Konwinski, A., Lee, G., Patterson, D., Rabkin, A., Stoica, I., Zaharia, M.: Above the clouds: A berkeley view of cloud computing. Technical report, University of California at Berkeley (2009)
2. Truong, H.-L., Gangadharan, G.R., Treiber, M., Dustdar, S., D'Andrea, V.: On reconciliation of contractual concerns of web services. In: NFPSLASOC 2008 (2nd Non Functional Properties and Service Level Agreements in SOC Workshop), Dublin, Ireland (2008)
3. Gangadharan, G.R., Weiss, M., D'Andrea, V., Iannella, R.: Service License Composition and Compatibility Analysis. In: Krämer, B.J., Lin, K.-J., Narasimhan, P. (eds.) ICSOC 2007. LNCS, vol. 4749, pp. 257–269. Springer, Heidelberg (2007)
4. Gangadharan, G.R., D'Andrea, V., Iannella, R., Weiss, M.: ODRL Service Licensing Profile (ODRL-S). In: Proceedings of the 5th International Workshop for Technical, Economic, and Legal Aspects of Business Models for Virtual Goods (2007)
5. Ludwig, H., Keller, A., Dan, A., King, R., Franck, R.: Web Service Level Agreement (WSLA) Language Specification. IBM Coporation (2003)
6. Tosic, V., Pagurek, B., Patel, K., Esfandiari, B., Ma, W.: Management Applications of the Web Service Offerings Language (WSOL). Information Systems 30(7), 564–586 (2005)

7. Zeng, L., Benatallah, B., Ngu, A., Dumas, M., Kalagnanam, J., Chang, H.: Qos-aware middleware for web services composition. IEEE Trans. Softw. Eng. 30(5), 311–327 (2004)
8. Jaeger, M., Rojec-Goldmann, G., Muhl, G.: Qos aggregation for web service composition using workflow patterns. In: EDOC 2004: Proceedings of the Enterprise Distributed Object Computing Conference, Eighth IEEE International, Washington, DC, USA, pp. 149–159. IEEE Computer Society, Los Alamitos (2004)
9. Aggarwal, R., Verma, K., Miller, J., Milnor, W.: Constraint driven web service composition in meteor-s. In: Proceedings of the 2004 IEEE International Conference on Services Computing (SCC 2004), pp. 23–30 (2004)
10. De Paoli, F., Palmonari, M., Comerio, M., Maurino, A.: A Meta-Model for Non-Functional Property Descriptions of Web Services. In: Proceedings of the IEEE International Conference on Web Services (ICWS), Beijing, China (2008)
11. Noy, N.F., Musen, M.A.: The prompt suite: Interactive tools for ontology merging and mapping. International Journal of Human-Computer Studies 59 (2003)
12. Castano, S., Ferrara, A., Montanelli, S.: H-match: an algorithm for dynamically matching ontologies in peer-based systems. In: Proc. of the 1st VLDB Int. Workshop on Semantic Web and Databases (SWDB 2003), Berlin, Germany (2003)
13. Mitra, P., Wiederhold, G., Decker, S.: A scalable framework for the interoperation of information sources, Stanford University, pp. 317–329 (2001)
14. Comerio, M., De Paoli, F., Maurino, A., Palmonari, M.: NFP-aware Semantic Web Services Selection. In: Proceedings of the 11th IEEE International Enterprise Distributed Object Computing Conference, EDOC (2007)

Explaining the Non-compliance between Templates and Agreement Offers in WS-Agreement**

Carlos Müller, Manuel Resinas, and Antonio Ruiz-Cortés

Dpto. Lenguajes y Sistemas Informáticos
ETS. Ingeniería Informática - Universidad de Sevilla (Spain - España)
41012 Sevilla (Spain - España)
{cmuller,resinas,aruiz}@us.es

Abstract. A common approach to the process of reaching agreements is the publication of templates that guide parties to create agreement offers that are then sent for approval to the template publisher. In such scenario, a common issue the template publisher must address is to check whether the agreement offer received is compliant or not with the template. Furthermore, in the latter case, an automated explanation of the reasons of such non-compliance is very appealing. Unfortunately, although there are proposals that deal with checking the compliance, the problem of providing an automated explanation to the non-compliance has not yet been studied in this context. In this paper, we take a subset of the WS-Agreement recommendation as a starting point and we provide a rigorous definition of the explanation for the non-compliance between templates and agreement offers. Furthermore, we propose the use of constraint satisfaction problem (CSP) solvers to implement it and provide a proof-of-concept implementation. The advantage of using CSPs is that it allows expressive service level objectives inside SLAs.

Keywords: Service Level Agreement, SLA, WS-Agreement, Compliance Checking, Debugging, Quality of Service, Explanations.

1 Introduction

A common approach to the creation of agreements is by means of templates. For instance WS-Agreement specification [5] defines an XML-based language and a protocol for advertising the capabilities and preferences of services providers in templates, and creating agreements based on them. Specifically, WS-Agreement allows to specify templates that are published by a responder party, for instance an Internet service provider could have two public templates for a "basic" and

---

* This work has been partially supported by the European Commission (FEDER), Spanish Government under the CICYT projects Web-Factories (TIN2006-00472), and SETI (TIN2009-07366); and project P07-TIC-2533 funded by the Andalusian local Government.

L. Baresi, C.-H. Chi, and J. Suzuki (Eds.): ICSOC-ServiceWave 2009, LNCS 5900, pp. 237–252, 2009.

a "premium" Internet service. A typical interaction process using templates and offers could be as follows: (1) an initiator party take a public template from a responder party, describing the agreement terms and some variability that must be taken into account by initiator in order to achieve an agreement; (2) an agreement offer may be sent to the responder party, including several changes, or not, into the initial template; (3) finally, the responder party may accept or not the agreement offer received. To use such approach of templates and offers, once established that the agreement offer is consistent [15], the problem is to ensure the compliance between agreement templates and offers. Some proposals such as [13,19] focus on checking whether an SLA is compliant with another one, and, hence, they could be adapted to check the compliance between agreement templates and offers. However, if they are not compliant, an explanation would make it easier to solve problems between parties. This explanation may be provided as the subset of terms of both template and agreement offer, that causes the non-compliance. For example, the Internet service provider could establish inside a template the bandwidth limit, allowing the user to customise of download and upload speeds as follows:

- Template: $\{t1 : downloadSpeed > 5Mb, t2 : uploadSpeed < 0.768Mb,$
  $t3 : downloadSpeed + uploadSpeed < 5.768Mb\}$
- Agreement Offer: $\{o1 : downloadSpeed = 10Mb, o2 : uploadSpeed = 0.7Mb\}$

The explanation for the non-compliance of the previous example would be the following set of terms: $\{t3, o1, o2\}$.

Generally speaking, finding an explanation for the non-compliance is not as easy as in previous example. It is especially complex when a high expressiveness of the language used to specify the service terms is needed.

Solution overview and contribution: This paper is focused on providing explanations of the non-compliance between templates and agreement offers. To this end, we take our previous work in [15], in which we detail an approach to explain the inconsistencies in one SLA, as a starting point and we extend it to enable the checking of the compliance between templates and agreement offers and to provide explanations of the non-compliance.

Specifically, we extend the definition of the WS-Agreement subset of [15] to provide rigorous definitions of templates, the compliance between templates and offers and the explanation for the non-compliance. Then, we use such definitions to map agreement offers and templates into constraint satisfaction problems (CSPs) [21]. The CSP is sent to a constraint solver with an explanation engine [8,20] to get the terms that are causing the non-compliance. The advantage of using CSPs is that it allows the use of expressive assertions inside SLA terms, including arithmetic, comparison and logic operations such as $+, -, *, \div, >, \geq, <$ $, \leq, \rightarrow, \ldots$. Furthermore, we have developed a proof-of-concept which is available for testing at http://www.isa.us.es/wsag.

The remainder of the paper is organized as follows: Section 2 describes the used subset of WS-Agreement in Section 2.1, rigorous definitions for agreement offers and templates in Section 2.2, the compliance between WS-Agreement* templates and offers in Section 2.3, and the explanation for the non-compliance between templates and offers in Section 2.4; Section 3 describes the process of explaining the non-compliance of WS-Agreement* templates and offers using CSP; Section 4 informs about the related work; and finally Section 5 conclude this paper anticipating some future work.

2   WS-Agreement*-Non-compliant Offers and Templates

2.1   WS-Agreement* Offers and Templates

Due to the flexibility and extensibility of WS-Agreement, we focus on WS-Agreement*, which is a subset of WS-Agreement (cf. http://www.isa.us.es/wsag, for details about these differences). WS-Agreement* just imposes several restrictions on some elements of WS-Agreement but it keeps the same syntax and semantics, therefore any WS-Agreement document that follows these restrictions is a WS-Agreement* document. Furthermore, note that, although WS-Agreement* is not as expressive as WS-Agreement, it does allow to express complex agreement documents as those in Figure 1, in which the elements of several WS-Agreement* documents in a computing services providing scenario are depicted. The complete XML documents are available at http://www.isa.us.es/wsag.

- **Name & Context** identifies the agreement and other information such as a template name and identifier, if any, referring to the specific name and version of the template from which the current agreement is created. For instance, context of Figure 1(c) refers to Template of Figure 1(a).
  Terms can be composed using the three term compositors described in [5]: All (∧), ExactlyOne (⊕), and OneOrMore (∨). All terms in the document must be included into a main All term compositor. Figure 1(a) includes All and ExactlyOne term compositors. Terms can be divided into:
  Service Terms including:
    - **Service properties** must define all variables that are used in the guarantee terms and other agreement elements, explained later. In Figure 1(a), the variables defined are the *availability of the computing service* (Availability), the *mean time between two consecutive requests of the service* (MTBR), and the *initial cost for the service* (InitCost). The type and general range of values for each variable is provided in an external document such as the ad-hoc XML document depicted in Figure 1(b).
    - **Service description terms** provide a functional description of a service, i.e. the information necessary to provide the service to the consumer. They may set values to variables defined in the service properties (e.g. InitCost=20 in Figure 1(a)) or they may set values to new variables. Type and domains are defined in external files such as XML Schemas (e.g. CPUsType=Cluster in Figure 1(a)).
  Guarantee terms describe the service level objectives (SLO) that a specific obligated party must fulfill, and a qualifying condition that specifies the

validity condition under which the SLO is applied. For instance the Lower-Availability guarantee term included in Figure 1(a).

In [5], a WS-Agreement template is an agreement document with the structure of a WS-Agreement document described above, but including agreement creation constraints that should be taken into account during the agreement creation process. These **Creation Constraints** describe the variability allowed by the party who makes the template public. They include (1) general **Constraints** involving the values of one or more terms, for instance the FinalCost definition of "Constraint 1" of Figure 1(a); or (2) **Items** specifying that a particular variable of the agreement must be present in the agreement offer, typically as a service description term, and its range of values. For instance, the item elements of Figure 1(a) define three variables: the *number of Dedicated Central Processing Units* (CPUs), the *increase of the cost due to the selected MTBR* (ExtraMTBRCost), and the *final cost for the service* (FinalCost).

2.2   What's in WS-Agreement*?

To automate the explaining of the non-compliance, it is necessary to define the compliance between template and agreement offers and provide a rigorous definition of the explaining for the non-compliance. A first step toward this goal is to extend the definition of WS-Agreement* in [15] to provide rigorous definitions of templates, the compliance between templates and offers and the explanation for the non-compliance.

Definition 1 (A WS-Agreement* agreement offer). *A WS-Agreement* agreement offer* α *is a three-tuple composed of the variables defined in service properties and service description terms, their domains and a set of terms:*

$$\alpha = (v^\alpha, \delta^\alpha, T^\alpha), \ where$$

- $v^\alpha = v_p^\alpha \cup v_d^\alpha \neq \emptyset$ *is the finite set of variables defined in service properties* (v_p^α), *and in service description terms* (v_d^α), *respectively.*
- $\delta^\alpha = \delta_p^\alpha \cup \delta_d^\alpha \neq \emptyset$ *is the finite set of domains for those variables.*
- $T^\alpha = \{t_i^\alpha\}_{i=1}^n \neq \emptyset$ *is a finite set of terms, including service description terms, guarantee terms and terms compositors as follows:*

$$where \ t_i^\alpha = \begin{cases} \lambda^\alpha = (v_i, value(v_i)) & if \ t_i^\alpha \ is \ a \ service \ description \ term & (1) \\ \gamma^\alpha = (\kappa^\alpha(v), \sigma^\alpha(v)) & if \ t_i^\alpha \ is \ a \ guarantee \ term & (2) \\ (t_{i1}^\alpha \wedge \ldots \wedge t_{im}^\alpha) & if \ t_i^\alpha \ is \ an \ \texttt{All} \ term \ compositor \\ (t_{i1}^\alpha \oplus \ldots \oplus t_{im}^\alpha) & if \ t_i^\alpha \ is \ an \ \texttt{ExactlyOne} \ term \ compositor \\ (t_{i1}^\alpha \vee \ldots \vee t_{im}^\alpha) & if \ t_i^\alpha \ is \ an \ \texttt{OneOrMore} \ term \ compositor \end{cases}$$

Where Clause (1) defines the value of variable $(value(v_i))$, $v_i \in v^\alpha$, $value(v_i) \in \delta_i$; *and Clause (2) defines a guarantee term which includes:*

$$\kappa^\alpha(v) = \begin{cases} true \ if \ there \ is \ no \ qualifying \ condition \ or \ (\forall v_i \in v^\alpha) \ satisfies \ it \\ false \ otherwise \end{cases}$$

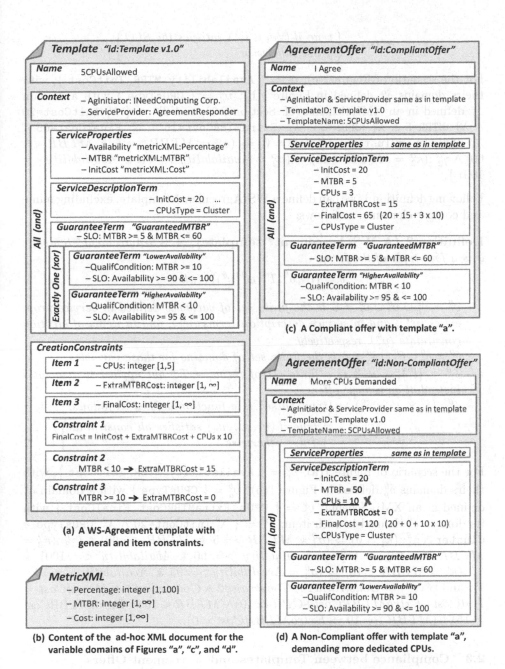

Template *"id:Template v1.0"*

Name   5CPUsAllowed

Context
  – AgInitiator: INeedComputing Corp.
  – ServiceProvider: AgreementResponder

All (and)

ServiceProperties
  – Availability "metricXML:Percentage"
  – MTBR "metricXML:MTBR"
  – InitCost "metricXML:Cost"

ServiceDescriptionTerm
  – InitCost = 20   ...
  – CPUsType = Cluster

GuaranteeTerm *"GuaranteedMTBR"*
  – SLO: MTBR >= 5 & MTBR <= 60

Exactly One (xor)

GuaranteeTerm *"LowerAvailability"*
  –QualifCondition: MTBR >= 10
  – SLO: Availability >= 90 & <= 100

GuaranteeTerm *"HigherAvailability"*
  –QualifCondition: MTBR < 10
  – SLO: Availability >= 95 & <= 100

CreationConstraints

Item 1   – CPUs: integer [1,5]

Item 2   – ExtraMTBRCost: integer [1, ∞]

Item 3   – FinalCost: integer [1, ∞]

Constraint 1
FinalCost = InitCost + ExtraMTBRCost + CPUs x 10

Constraint 2
   MTBR < 10 ➜ ExtraMTBRCost = 15

Constraint 3
   MTBR >= 10 ➜ ExtraMTBRCost = 0

(a) A WS-Agreement template with
general and item constraints.

MetricXML
  – Percentage: integer [1,100]
  – MTBR: integer [1,∞]
  – Cost: integer [1,∞]

(b) Content of the ad-hoc XML document for the
variable domains of Figures "a", "c", and "d".

AgreementOffer *"id:CompliantOffer"*

Name   I Agree

Context
  – AgInitiator & ServiceProvider same as in template
  – TemplateID: Template v1.0
  – TemplateName: 5CPUsAllowed

All (and)

ServiceProperties   *same as in template*

ServiceDescriptionTerm
  – InitCost = 20
  – MTBR = 5
  – CPUs = 3
  – ExtraMTBRCost = 15
  – FinalCost = 65   (20 + 15 + 3 x 10)
  – CPUsType = Cluster

GuaranteeTerm *"GuaranteedMTBR"*
  – SLO: MTBR >= 5 & MTBR <= 60

GuaranteeTerm *"HigherAvailability"*
  –QualifCondition: MTBR < 10
  – SLO: Availability >= 95 & <= 100

(c) A Compliant offer with template "a".

AgreementOffer *"id:Non-CompliantOffer"*

Name   More CPUs Demanded

Context
  – AgInitiator & ServiceProvider same as in template
  – TemplateID: Template v1.0
  – TemplateName: 5CPUsAllowed

All (and)

ServiceProperties   *same as in template*

ServiceDescriptionTerm
  – InitCost = 20
  – MTBR = 50
  – CPUs = 10 ✗
  – ExtraMTBRCost = 0
  – FinalCost = 120   (20 + 0 + 10 x 10)
  – CPUsType = Cluster

GuaranteeTerm *"GuaranteedMTBR"*
  – SLO: MTBR >= 5 & MTBR <= 60

GuaranteeTerm *"LowerAvailability"*
  –QualifCondition: MTBR >= 10
  – SLO: Availability >= 90 & <= 100

(d) A Non-Compliant offer with template "a",
demanding more dedicated CPUs.

Fig. 1. Template and Offers WS-Agreement* documents

$$\sigma^\alpha(v) = \left\{ \begin{array}{l} true \ if \ (\forall v_i \in v^\alpha) \ satisfies \ the \ SLO \\ false \ otherwise \end{array} \right\}$$

For the scenario of Figure 1(c), $v_p^\alpha = \{$ Availability, MTBR, InitCost $\}$, with theirs domains δ_p^α defined in Figure 1(b); $v_d^\alpha = \{$ CPUsType $\}$ with a domain δ_d^α defined in an XML-Schema (cf. Section 2.1); and $T^\alpha = \{$ λ_1^α:InitCost=20 $\wedge$ λ_2^α :MTBR=5 $\wedge$ λ_3^α :CPUs=3 $\wedge$ λ_4^α :ExtraMTBRCost=15 $\wedge$ λ_5^α :FinalCost=65 $\wedge$ λ_6^α :CPUsType=Cluster $\wedge$ γ_1^α :$(\kappa_1^\alpha = \emptyset) \Rightarrow (\sigma_1^\alpha = MTBR >= 5 \ \& \ MTBR <= 60) \wedge \gamma_2^\alpha$:$(\kappa_2^\alpha = MTBR < 10) \Rightarrow (\sigma_2^\alpha = Availability >= 95 \ \& \ Availability <= 100)$ $\}$.

Following definition 1, we can define a WS-Agreement* template, excluding name and context elements, as follows:

Definition 2 (A WS-Agreement* template). *A WS-Agreement* template θ is a four-tuple of the form:*

$$\theta = \left(v^\theta, \delta^\theta, T^\theta, \phi^\theta(v^\theta) \right), \ where$$

- $v^\theta = v_p^\theta \cup v_d^\theta \cup v_c^\theta \neq \emptyset$ *is the finite set of variables defined in service properties (v_p^α), and in service description terms (v_d^α), and in items of creation constraints (v_c^θ), respectively.*
- $\delta^\theta = \delta_p^\theta \cup \delta_d^\theta \cup \delta_c^\theta \neq \emptyset$ *is the finite set of domains for those variables.*
- $T^\theta = \{t_i^\theta\}_{i=1}^n \neq \emptyset$ *is a finite set of terms $\equiv T^\alpha$ but applied to templates instead of agreement offers.*
- $\phi^\theta : (\delta_1^\theta \times \ldots \times \delta_n^\theta) \rightarrow \{true, false\}$ *is a function defined as follows:*

$$\phi^\theta(v_1, \ldots, v_n) = \left\{ \begin{array}{l} true \ if \ (v_1, \ldots, v_n) \ satisfies \ all \ constraints \\ false \ otherwise \end{array} \right\}$$

For the scenario of Figure 1(a), $v_p^\theta = \{$ Availability, MTBR, InitCost $\}$, with theirs domains δ_p^θ defined in Figure 1(b); $v_d^\theta = \{$ CPUsType $\}$ with a domain δ_d^θ defined in an XML-Schema; $v_c^\theta = \{$ CPUs, ExtraMTBRCost, FinalCost $\}$ with its domain δ_c^θ defined in each item; $T^\theta = \{$ λ_1^θ:InitCost=20 $\wedge$ λ_2^θ :CPUsType = Cluster $\wedge$ γ_1^θ :$(\kappa_1^\theta = \emptyset) \Rightarrow (\sigma_1^\theta = MTBR >= 5 \ \& \ MTBR <= 60) \wedge (\gamma_2^\theta$:$(\kappa_2^\theta = MTBR >= 10) \Rightarrow (\sigma_2^\theta = Availability >= 90 \ \& \ Availability <= 100) \oplus \gamma_3^\theta$:$(\kappa_3^\theta = MTBR < 10) \Rightarrow (\sigma_3^\theta = Availability >= 95 \ \& \ Availability <= 100)$ $)\}$; and $\phi^\theta(v^\theta) = Constraint1 \wedge Constraint2 \wedge Constraint3 = (FinalCost = InitCost + ExtraMTBRCost + CPUs \times 10) \wedge (MTBR < 10 \Rightarrow ExtraMTBRCost = 15) \wedge (MTBR >= 10 \Rightarrow ExtraMTBRCost = 0)$.

2.3 Compliance between Templates and Agreement Offers

In WS-Agreement [5] the compliance of offers with templates is defined as follows:

*"**Agreement template compliance**: An agreement offer is compliant with a template advertised by an agreement responder if and only if each term of service described in the* **Terms** *section of the agreement offer complies with the term*

constraints expressed in the `CreationConstraints` section of the agreement template. In addition, in the `Context` of the offer, the `Agreement Responder` value must match the value specified in the template; and the `Template Id` must exactly match the name provided in the template document against which compliance is being checked."

This compliance is summarised with discontinuous arrows in Figure 2. Note that this definition of compliance does not state anything about the terms of the template. In other words, the party that creates the agreement offer may ignore the terms specified in the template. The problem with this definition is that the template creator can specify terms in the template, but the party that creates the agreement offer cannot do anything with them because the definition of compliance does not provide any semantics with regard to them. Thus, it is unknown for the party that creates the agreement offer whether the terms of the template specify default values, or preferred values, or mandatory values that could not be expressed by means of creation constraints, or any other meaning.

To solve this issue, we provide an extended definition of compliance, the so-called t-compliance, that extends the previous definition of compliance with the requirement that the terms of the agreement offer must be compliant with the terms of the template. This is depicted in Figure 2 by means of continuous arrows.

This new notion of compliance raises another issue: *does the compliance between the terms of the agreement offer and the terms of the template implies that agreement offer terms must syntactically match with template terms or they must match semantically?*

A syntactic match means that terms that appear in the template must appear as is in the agreement offer, perhaps after selecting some of the alternatives provided by the term compositors. For instance, the guarantee terms of the agreement offer of Figure 1(c) syntactically matches the guarantee terms of the template of Figure 1(a).

A semantic match means that all possible assignment of values to the variables that satisfies the terms of the template must satisfy the terms of the agreement offer. as well. For instance, the guarantee term $MTBR >= 3$ & $MTBR <= 60$ semantically matches the guarantee term `GuaranteedMTBR` of the template. In this paper we choose the semantic match because syntactic match is just a particular case of semantic match.

Then, assuming the context compliance between documents, we can define the compliance and t-compliance between WS-Agreement* offers and templates. But previously we define an auxiliary operation to represent if a vector of value assignments to all variables `satisfies` a concrete term.

Definition 3 (Satisfies Operation: $satisfies(t_i, v)$)
We define operation $satisfies(t_i, v)$, as a function such that, given a term t_i and a vector $(v_1, \ldots, v_n)$ of value assignments to all variables, it returns true if $(v_1, \ldots, v_n)$ satisfies the term and false, otherwise:

$$satisfies : T \times (\delta_1 \times \ldots \times \delta_n) \rightarrow \{true, false\}, \text{ where}$$

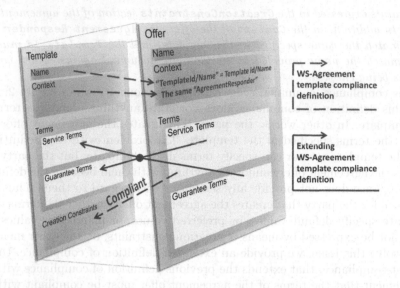

Fig. 2. Summary of Compliance between WS-Agreement templates and offers

$$satisfies(t_i, v) \Leftrightarrow \begin{cases} v_i = value(v_i) & (1) \\ \sigma(v) & (2) \\ \kappa(v) \Rightarrow \sigma(v) & (3) \\ \bigwedge_{i=1}^{n} satisfies(t_i, v) & (4) \\ \bigwedge_{i=1}^{n} satisfies(t_i, v) \Leftrightarrow (\bigwedge_{j=1 \setminus j \neq i}^{k} \neg satisfies(t_i, v)) & (5) \\ \bigvee_{i=1}^{n} satisfies(t_i, v) & (6) \end{cases}$$

Clause (1) is applied when t_i is a service description term $\lambda = (v_i, value(v_i))$. Clause (2) is applied if t_i is a guarantee term without qualifying condition $\gamma = (\emptyset, \sigma)$. Clause (3) is applied if t_i is a guarantee term with qualifying condition $\gamma = (\kappa, \sigma)$. And Clauses (4, 5, and 6) are applied if t_i is an All($\wedge$), ExactlyOne($\oplus$), and OneOrMore($\vee$) term compositor, respectively.

Definition 4 (WS-Agreement* template compliance)

A WS-Agreement* offer $\alpha = (v^\alpha, \delta^\alpha, T^\alpha)$ is compliant with a WS-Agreement* template $\theta = (v^\theta, \delta^\theta, T^\theta, \phi^\theta(v^\theta))$, iff the following operation is true:

$$compliance(\alpha, \theta) \Leftrightarrow \begin{cases} v_p^\theta = v_p^\alpha \wedge \delta_p^\theta = \delta_p^\alpha \wedge & (1) \\ \wedge\ v_d^\alpha = v_c^\theta \cup v_d^\theta \wedge \delta_d^\alpha = \delta_c^\theta \cup \delta_d^\theta \wedge & (2) \\ \wedge\ matches(T^\alpha, \phi^\theta) & (3) \end{cases}$$

where $matches(T^\alpha, \phi^\theta) \Leftrightarrow \forall v \in (\delta_1 \times \ldots \times \delta_n),\ \phi^\theta(v) = true \Rightarrow (\ \forall t_i \in T^\alpha, matches(t_i, v)\ )$.

Clause (1) means that variables and domains defined inside service properties of a compliant agreement offer must be the same as defined inside template. Clause (2) ensures that all variables and domains defined inside service description term of a compliant agreement offer are defined inside service description term of template or inside item element of template creation constraints. This does not allow to add any more variables and domains inside service description terms of a compliant agreement offer to such defined in template. Finally, Clause (3) means that each terms of a compliant agreement offer must match general constraints of template creation constraints.

Definition 5 (WS-Agreement* template t-compliance)
A WS-Agreement* offer $\alpha = (v^\alpha, \delta^\alpha, T^\alpha)$ is t-compliant with a WS-Agreement* template $\theta = (v^\theta, \delta^\theta, T^\theta, \phi^\theta(v^\theta))$, iff the following operation is true:

$$t\text{-}compliance(\alpha, \theta) \Leftrightarrow compliance(\alpha, \theta) \ AND \ matches(T^\alpha, T^\theta)$$

where $matches(T^\alpha, T^\theta) \Leftrightarrow \forall \ v \in (\delta_1 \times \ldots \times \delta_n), \ (\forall t_j \in T^\theta, \ matches(t_j, v)) \Rightarrow (\forall t_i \in T^\alpha, \ matches(t_i, v))$. In other words, each term of a compliant agreement offer must match template terms.

Figure 1(c) and 1(d) depict two possible responses for the agreement template of Figure 1(a). Figure 1(c) is a compliant agreement offer because all template general constraints are taken into account for the agreement offer service description term specification (clause (3) of compliance definition); and it is a t-compliant offer because it does not include neither different value definitions for variables, nor any term which were not semantically matched with template terms (t-compliance definition). However, Figure 1(d) depicts a non-compliant agreement offer, and the explanation for such non-compliance must be provided. Note that we do not detail yet the explanation for the non-compliance to highlight the advantages of having a system capable of providing them.

2.4 Explaining the Non-compliance

We consider an explanation for a non-compliance between agreement offers and templates as a minimum set of terms of both agreement offer and template that makes them not compliant. However, before defining rigorously the explanation, we must define two auxiliary operations.

Definition 6 (Closure of a set of terms: T^*)
The closure of a terms set (T^*) is the set of all possible agreements that can be obtained after selecting all the alternatives provided by the term compositors (All, ExactlyOne, and OneOrMore). T^* can be obtained by appliying the closure to non-composite terms (t_i^*), All term compositor (AND^*), ExactlyOne term compositor (XOR^*), and OneOrMore term compositor (OR^*) as follows:

$$T^* \Leftrightarrow \begin{cases} t_i^* = \{\{t_i\}\} \\ AND^*(t_1, \ldots, t_n) = \{\{i_1 \cup \ldots \cup i_n\} | i_1 \in t_1^* \wedge \ldots \wedge i_n \in t_n^*\} \\ XOR^*(t_1, \ldots, t_n) = \bigcup_{i=1}^n t_i^* \\ OR^*(t_1, \ldots, t_n) = \bigcup_{p \in P(\{t_1, \ldots, t_n\}) - \emptyset} \{\{i_1 \cup \ldots \cup i_n\} | \\ \qquad | i_1 \in p_1^* \wedge i_n \in p_n^* \wedge p = \{p_1, \ldots p_n\}\} \end{cases}$$

Where P(S) is the power set of S.

For example, the closure of template of Figure 1(a) is: $T^{\theta*} = \{\{$ Init-Cost=20, CPUsType=Cluster, GuaranteedMTBR, LowerAvailability $\}\{$ Init-Cost=20, CPUsType=Cluster, GuaranteedMTBR, HigherAvailability $\}\}$.

Definition 7 (Terms Extraction Operation: $terms(T)$)
We define operation $terms(T)$, where T is a set of terms including service description terms, guarantee terms, and term compositors; as an operation which obtain the set of service descriptions and guarantee terms of T.

This operation applied to template of Figure 1(a) is: $terms(T^{\theta}) = \{$ InitCost=20, CPUsType=Cluster, GuaranteedMTBR, LowerAvailability, HigherAvailability$\}$.

   Finally, the explanation could be rigorously defined, using the `closure` definition and `terms(T)` operation, as follows:

Definition 8 (Explanation for WS-Agreement* template non-compliance)
Given a WS-Agreement* offer $\alpha = (v^{\alpha}, \delta^{\alpha}, T^{\alpha})$ which is non-compliant with a WS-Agreement* template $\theta = \left(v^{\theta}, \delta^{\theta}, T^{\theta}, \phi^{\theta}(v^{\theta})\right)$ (i.e. $\neg compliance(\alpha, \theta)$), the explanation (E) is a minimal subset of terms defined as follows:
$E = \epsilon^{\alpha} \cup \epsilon^{\theta} \cup \epsilon^{\phi}$, *where* $\epsilon^{\alpha} \in P(terms(T^{\alpha}) - \emptyset)$, $\epsilon^{\alpha} \subseteq n \in T^{\alpha*}$, *and* $\epsilon^{\theta} \in P(terms(T^{\theta}) - \emptyset)$, $\epsilon^{\theta} \subseteq n \in T^{\theta*}$, *and* $\epsilon^{\phi} \in P(\phi^{\theta})$. *Where P(S) is the power set of S.*
   In other words, E is a minimal subset of conflictive terms extracted from the agreement offer terms, template terms and template creation constraints.

In the non-compliance between Figures 1(a) and 1(d), the resulting explanation would be: $\epsilon^{\phi} = \{$Item 1$\}$, and $\epsilon^{\alpha} = \{$CPUs=10$\}$. In such term the consumer is demanding more dedicated CPUs than the allowed by the provider template. Such underlined terms and the domain defined inside "Item 1" are the origin for the non-compliance situation and they are considered as the `explanation` for the non-compliance between such offer and template.

   Other examples of non-compliance in the example of Figure 1(a) and 1(d), would be the following: (a) if we change the value of `CPUsType` inside the agreement offer there will be two different values for the same variable; (b) if we change the value of `ExtraMTBRCost` inside service description term of the agreement offer, it there will be in conflict with the `Constraint 3` of template; if we change the guarantee term `MTBRDomain` in the agreement offer, there will be in conflict with such guarantee term definition inside template.

   The complexity of automating the search for explanations depends on the expressiveness of the language used to specify the agreement terms. An approach to automate this search is by means of constraint satisfaction problems (CSPs) and it is detailed in the following section.

3 Explaining the Non-compliance Using CSPs

3.1 Preliminaries

Constraint Satisfaction Problems. Constraint Satisfaction Problems (CSP) [21] have been an object of research in Artificial Intelligence over the last few decades. A CSP is a three–tuple of the form (V, D, C) where $V \neq \emptyset$ is a finite set of variables, $D \neq \emptyset$ is a finite set of domains (one for each variable) and C is a constraint defined on V. Consider, for instance, the CSP: $(\{a, b\}, \{[0, 2], [0, 2]\}, \{a + b < 4\})$. The solution of such CSP is whatever valid assignment of all elements in V that satisfies C. $(2, 0)$ is a possible solution of previous example since it verifies that $2 + 0 < 4$.

3.2 Mapping WS-Agreement* Templates onto CSP

In [15] we define the mapping (μ) of a WS-Agreement* offer document (α) onto an equivalent CSP, (ψ^α). The variables (v) defined inside the service properties are the CSP variables; the variable domains (δ) included in the document specified by the metric attribute are the CSP variable domains; and the constraints from the service description terms (λ_v), guarantee terms (γ) and term compositors ($\wedge$ as a logic "AND", $\oplus$ as logic "XOR", and $\vee$ as logic "OR") are the CSP constraints.

Then, we have to study now how the creation constraints mapping should be included in order to get a complete WS-Agreement* template to CSP mapping. Figure 3 summarizes how the creation constraints, expressed as items are mapped as CSP variables (v_c) and domains (δ_c); and expressed as general constraints (ϕ) are mapped as CSP constraints.

Thus, in general, our WS-Agreement* template to CSP mapping can be defined as follows:

Definition 9 (Mapping an WS-Agreement* template to CSP). *The mapping $(\mu : \theta \rightarrow \psi)$ of a WS-Agreement* template (θ) to a CSP (ψ) can be defined as follows:*

$$\mu(\theta) = \mu\left(v_i, \delta_i, T_i, \phi_i\right) = \left(\{v_i\}, \{\delta_i\}, \{\mu_T(T_i)\}, \{\mu_\phi(\phi_i)\}\right) = \psi^\theta$$

where $\mu_\phi : \phi \rightarrow C$ is a direct mapping function of WS-Agreement general constraints into constraints, defined as follows: $\mu_\phi \equiv \{\phi\}$, and where $\mu_T : T \rightarrow C$ is a mapping function of terms into constraints defined in [15].*

Using the previous mapping, the ψ^θ for the template of Figure 1(a) is mapped as follows: (1) a set of variables where the three last are mapped from the creation constraints *{ Availability, MTBR, InitCost, CPUsType, CPUs, ExtraMTBR-Cost, FinalCost }*; (2) a set of domains for such variables *{ [1 ... 100], [1 ... ∞), [1 ... ∞), [Cluster, Multicore, Distributed], [1 ... 5], [1 ... ∞), [1 ... ∞) }*; and (3) a set of constraint where the three last are mapped from the creation constraints *{ InitCost = 20, CPUsType = Cluster, MTBR ≥ 5 ∧*

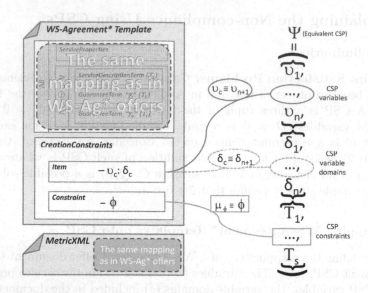

Fig. 3. Summary of WS-Agreement* template to CSP mapping

$MTBR \leq 60$, $((MTBR \geq 10) \Rightarrow (Availability \geq 90 \land Availability \leq 100)) \Leftrightarrow \neg ((MTBR < 10) \Rightarrow (Availability \geq 95 \land Availability \leq 100)) \land ((MTBR < 10) \Rightarrow (Availability \geq 95 \land Availability \leq 100)) \Leftrightarrow \neg ((MTBR \geq 10) \Rightarrow (Availability \geq 90 \land Availability \leq 100))$, $FinalCost = InitCost + ExtraMTBRCost + CPUs \times 10$, $(MTBR < 10) \Rightarrow (ExtraMTBRCost = 15)$, $(MTBR \geq 10) \Rightarrow (ExtraMTBRCost = 0)$ $\}$.

3.3 Explaining the Non-compliance between WS-Agreements* Documents

To perform the explaining of the Non-Compliance between templates and agreement offers, we have developed aa proof-of-concept implementation which is available at http://www.isa.us.es/wsag. The input to the system is threefold: the WS-Agreement* offer, the WS-Agreement* template, and the XML document with the metrics of service properties. The whole process implemented by the proof-of-concept involves four parts:

1. A simple checking of the document contexts is carried out to ensure that the offer refers to the template that has been provided. If an error is returned, it must be reported to user.
2. Each WS-Agreement* documents are mapped into a CSP: (1) the CSP mapped from the WS-Agreement* offer $(V^\alpha, D^\alpha, C^\alpha)$, as defined in [15]; and (2) the CSP mapped from the WS-Agreement* template $(V^\theta, D^\theta, C^\theta)$, as defined in Section 3.2. To explain the non-compliance between both CSPs we have to join them in an unique CSP as it is described in [19]:

$(V^\alpha \cup V^\theta, D^\alpha \cup D^\theta, C^\theta \rightarrow C^\alpha)$. Once the joined CSP is generated, we can check if it can be solved or not using CSP solvers. In the former case both documents are compliant.

3. An explanation engine obtains the explanations for the unsolved CSP and they are sent to the last part of our process.

4. Finally, a tracing component converts the explanations into the equivalent original agreement terms in order to classify the error to be reported to the user. The possible types of errors returned are:
   - If the explanations involve terms from both documents, then there is a non-compliance between them.
   - If the explanations involve terms from only one document, then this document is inconsistent.

For instance, if we check the disagreement between the non-compliant agreement offer of Figure 1(d) and the template of Figure 1(a), the first part would be passed due to the correct offer context. However, the explainer part will return, a minimal subset of the conflicting elements. Such elements are the underlined service description term of the offer against the item element of template creation constraint which detail the possible values for the dedicated CPUs. Then, the minimal subset of the example would be "CPUs = 10" and "CPUs >= 1 and CPUs <= 5". Each previous constraint would be traced back to its respective agreement element. In this case the constraints are traced back to the CPUs service description term inside offer and the CPUs item element inside template. Since the two conflictive elements come from the two agreement documents, the type of error occurred is a non-compliance between them.

4   Related Work

As far as we know, there are no proposals that deal with providing explanations for the non-compliance between agreement documents. This paper extends with template elements the definition of the WS-Agreement subset of [15] in which a first approach to explaining SLA inconsistencies was proposed. Previously, in [19], we studied mapping SLAs to CSPs, aimed at checking their consistency and conformance, which is a synonym of compliance. However, in that paper no explanation about the inconsistency or non-conformance of the documents was provided. In addition, [19] dealt with its own SLA specification instead of using a proposed standard format such as WS-Agreement.

Some proposals with similarities with our paper in their problem domain are the following ones: (1) The closest problem tackled in a research work is [16], in which Oldham et al. create a description logic-based ontology of WS-Agreement that could be used to check consistency and conformance of SLAs using a description logic reasoner. However, the authors do not detail what the consistency or conformance checking process is. Furthermore, they do not support the explanations for the inconsistent or non-conform terms. (2) A second group of proposals with some similarities in their problem domain deal with web service monitoring. For instance [22] checks the SLA compliance of web services compositions at a design time, but only for concrete types of SLOs and without providing any explanation for the non-compliance; [7] proposes a framework to audit if the execution of a web service is compliant with an unique SLA; [4] proposes the use of aspect oriented programming to monitor a concrete type of variables of an SLA; and [12] proposes a solution for managing SLAs in composite services. However, neither of them provide any explanation for the non-compliance. (3) Finally, [18] deals with the problem of compliance between SLOs and penalty clauses of an SLA, classifying the possible situations and using WS-Agreement as case study, but again without providing any explanations for the non-compliance.

Other proposals with similarities with our paper but in their solution domains are the following: (1) The closest solution used in a research work is [1], in which Aiello et al. uses rigorous definitions about WS-Agreement element such as terms, agreement, and several states because they study the different agreement states of an agreement process. (2) There are many authors that deal with constraint-based paradigms to tackle different SLA aspects as for instance: in [9,10] constraint-based problem are used to solve web services requests in a web services interaction process; in [3] a constraint-based language is proposed to specify SLAs; in [2] constraints are used to optimize web services composition taking into account quality of service. However the scope of these works is completely different in comparison with this paper because they do not provide any explanation for the non-compliance between agreement documents. (3) A third group of proposals deal with explanation-based solution for the following problems: [17] proposes an explanation-based tool to be integrated into solvers and make the detection of conflicts more user-friendly, and [6,11] improves the use of explanations to perform the solution of CSPs more efficient.

5   Conclusions and Future Work

In this paper we have motivated the need for explaining the non-compliance between WS-Agreement documents and we have presented a first approach to reach this goal in an automated manner. More specifically, we present the problem of explaining the non-compliance in an implementation-independent manner using rigorous definitions for agreement offers, templates, their compliance, and the explanation for their non-compliance. Then we propose to map templates and agreement offers into a constraint satisfaction problem (CSP), in order to use a CSP solver together with an explanation engine to perform the compliance checking and return the non-compliant terms in an automated manner.

In summary, this paper provides the following contributions:

1. A rigorous definition of compliance between WS-Agreement* templates and offers. Additionally, the rigorous definition of compliance has allowed us to extend template compliance definition of WS-Agreement.
2. A rigorous definition of explanations for the non-compliance between WS-Agreement* templates and offers.

3. A description of a process that materialises the previous definitions by means of a constraint satisfaction problem (CSP) solver combined with an explanation engine.

Finally, we have developed a proof-of-concept implementation that is available at http://www.isa.us.es/wsag.

However, there are still some open issues that require further research: first, extending the rigorous definitions and the mapping to CSPs to full WS-Agreement specification; second, checking the consistency and compliance of WS-Agreement documents with the temporal extension we detailed in [14].

References

1. Aiello, M., Frankova, G., Malfatti, D.: What's in an Agreement? An Analysis and an Extension of WS-Agreement. In: Benatallah, B., Casati, F., Traverso, P. (eds.) ICSOC 2005. LNCS, vol. 3826, pp. 424–436. Springer, Heidelberg (2005)
2. Alrifai, M., Risse, T.: Combining global optimization with local selection for efficient qos-aware service composition. In: 18th WWW Conf., p. 881 (2009)
3. Buscemi, M.G., Montanari, U.: Cc-pi: A constraint-based language for specifying service level agreements. In: De Nicola, R. (ed.) ESOP 2007. LNCS, vol. 4421, pp. 18–32. Springer, Heidelberg (2007)
4. Chen, C., Li, L., Wei, J.: Aop based trustable sla compliance monitoring for web services, October 2007, pp. 225–230 (2007)
5. Andrieux, et al.: OGF Grid Resource Allocation Agreement Protocol WG. Web Services Agreement Specification (WS-Agreement), v. gfd.107 (2007)
6. Grimes, D.: Automated within-problem learning for constraint satisfaction problems (2008)
7. Hasan, Stiller, B.: Auric: A scalable and highly reusable sla compliance auditing framework, pp. 203–215 (2007)
8. Jussien, N., Barichard, V.: The PaLM system: explanation-based constraint programming. In: Proceedings of TRICS, pp. 118–133 (2000)
9. Lazovik, A., Aiello, M., Gennari, R.: Encoding requests to web service compositions as constraints. In: van Beek, P. (ed.) CP 2005. LNCS, vol. 3709, pp. 782–786. Springer, Heidelberg (2005)
10. Lazovik, A., Aiello, M., Gennari, R.: Choreographies: using constraints to satisfy service requests, February 2006, p. 150 (2006)
11. Lecoutre, C., Sais, L., Tabary, S., Vidal, V.: Recording and minimizing nogoods from restarts. JSAT 1(3-4), 147–167 (2007)
12. Ludwig, A., Francyk, B.: COSMA - An Approach for Managing SLAs in Composite Services. In: Bouguettaya, A., Krueger, I., Margaria, T. (eds.) ICSOC 2008. LNCS, vol. 5364, pp. 626–632. Springer, Heidelberg (2008)
13. Martín-Díaz, O., Ruiz-Cortés, A., Durán, A., Müller, C.: An approach to temporal-aware procurement of web services. In: Benatallah, B., Casati, F., Traverso, P. (eds.) ICSOC 2005. LNCS, vol. 3826, pp. 170–184. Springer, Heidelberg (2005)
14. Müller, C., Martín-Díaz, O., Ruiz-Cortés, A., Resinas, M., Fernández, P.: Improving Temporal-Awareness of WS-Agreement. In: Krämer, B.J., Lin, K.-J., Narasimhan, P. (eds.) ICSOC 2007. LNCS, vol. 4749, pp. 193–206. Springer, Heidelberg (2007)

15. Müller, C., Ruiz-Cortés, A., Resinas, M.: An Initial Approach to Explaining SLA Inconsistencies. In: Bouguettaya, A., Krueger, I., Margaria, T. (eds.) ICSOC 2008. LNCS, vol. 5364, pp. 394–406. Springer, Heidelberg (2008)
16. Oldham, N., Verma, K., Sheth, A., Hakimpour, F.: Semantic WS-Agreement Partner Selection. In: 15th International WWW Conf., pp. 697–706. ACM Press, New York (2006)
17. Ouis, S., Tounsi, M.: An explanation-based tools for debugging constraint satisfaction problems. Applied Soft Computing 8(4), 1400–1406 (2008)
18. Rana, O.F., Warnier, M., Quillinan, T.B., Brazier, F., Cojocarasu, D.: Managing violations in service level agreements, pp. 349–358 (2008)
19. Ruiz-Cortés, A., Martín-Díaz, O., Durán, A., Toro, M.: Improving the Automatic Procurement of Web Services using Constraint Programming. Int. Journal on Cooperative Information Systems 14(4) (2005)
20. Schiex, T., Verfaillie, G.: Nogood recording for static and dynamic constraint satisfaction problems. In: Proceedings of the Fifth International Conference on Tools with Artificial Intelligence, TAI 1993, November 8-11, pp. 48–55 (1993)
21. Tsang, E.: Foundations of Constraint Satisfaction. Academic Press, London (1995)
22. Xiao, H., Chan, B., Zou, Y., Benayon, J.W., O'Farrell, B., Litani, E., Hawkins, J.: A framework for verifying sla compliance in composed services, September 2008, pp. 457–464 (2008)

A Probabilistic Approach to Service Selection with Conditional Contracts and Usage Patterns

Adrian Klein[1,2,3], Fuyuki Ishikawa[4], and Bernhard Bauer[1]

[1] University of Augsburg, Germany
bauer@informatik.uni-augsburg.de
[2] Technical University Munich, Germany
[3] Ludwig-Maximilians-University Munich, Germany
adrian.klein@campus.lmu.de
[4] National Institute of Informatics, Tokyo, Japan
f-ishikawa@nii.ac.jp

Abstract. Service selection is a central challenge in the context of a Service Oriented Architecture. Once functionally sufficient services have been selected, a further selection based on non-functional properties (NFPs) becomes essential in meeting the user's requirements and preferences. However, current descriptions of NFPs and approaches to NFP-aware selection lack the ability to handle the variability of NFPs, that stems from the complex nature of real-world business scenarios. Therefore, we propose a probabilistic approach to service selection as follows: First, to address the inherent variability in the actual values of NFPs at runtime, we treat them as probability distributions. Then, on top of that, we tackle the variability needed in describing NFPs, by providing conditional contracts. Finally, from usage patterns, we compute user-specific expectations for such NFPs. Further, we depict a typical scenario, which serves both as a motivation for our approach, and as a basis for its evaluation.

1 Introduction

A Service Oriented Architecture (SOA) lays the ground for loose coupling of interoperable services [1]. In a SOA, there are service providers, that offer services under certain conditions, and service users, that need services that fulfill certain criteria. Service contracts provide the basis necessary for the interaction between both of them, by describing the functional and non-functional properties (NFPs) [2] of a service. Service selection deals with finding the service that best matches the user's criteria and, as such, is a central challenge in the context of any SOA. The selection process is usually twofold: First, consider only the services matching the functional criteria. Then, to find the best one, rank those services according to which extent they fulfill the non-functional criteria.

While functional matching is a necessary part of any service selection, it has already been studied intensively [3]. On the other hand, matching based on NFPs such as price, response time, availability, or reliability has been drawing more

L. Baresi, C.-H. Chi, and J. Suzuki (Eds.): ICSOC-ServiceWave 2009, LNCS 5900, pp. 253–268, 2009.

and more attention, but it is far from being as well-understood. Sure, there is a consensus on the need for Service Level Agreements (SLAs), and several standards, like WSML [4] or WSLA [5], exist to define SLAs. Still, we think that probabilistic aspects are not covered in the necessary detail at the moment. Therefore, we want to focus on the aspect of variability found both in NFPs' values and their contractual descriptions.

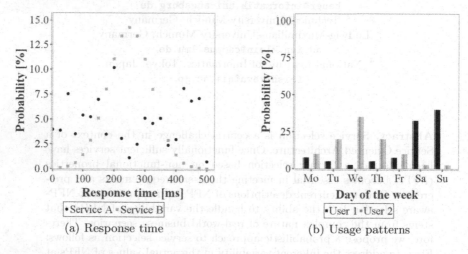

(a) Response time   (b) Usage patterns

Fig. 1. Examples

The values of a lot of NFPs exhibit an inherent variability. For instance, response time is not a constant value at all. Yet, in typical contracts, NFPs are represented by their maximum value only, whereas probability distributions would be much more accurate. As you can see in Fig. 1(a), the distributions of two services regarding response time can be quite different, though they share the same maximum value. This means that different users might prefer one over the other, which we think should be reflected in the selection. We therefore propose using probability distributions throughout the whole selection process.

The description itself also often exhibits variability. Commonly, in a contract, there is only one description for each NFP, specifying its value(s). A provider can, of course, offer multiple contracts, but, since customization is not possible, cannot really tailor a single contract for a specific kind of user. For example, if we take a look at mobile phone providers: They succeeded in catering to specific kinds of users, because what is charged per minute depends on several conditions, enabling each user to find a contract that best matches his needs. We think that, in a SOA, this possibility for providers to differentiate themselves is becoming increasingly important, as more and more functionally equivalent services are made available. We therefore propose the concept of conditional contracts. Providers can specify several descriptions of each NFP in a contract, and conditions according to which one of them will be chosen. Additionally, to help users finding the service that best matches their needs, the selection process should be adapted accordingly by taking usage patterns into account: A usage pattern tells us how and when a service is expected to be used by a user, and, as such, can be represented by a probability distribution. For instance, consider a contract for a service s that, compared to the average, is very expensive during the week, yet very cheap during the weekend: Given two users u_1 and u_2 and their corresponding usage patterns from Fig. 1(b), that tell us exactly which days of the week they usually use s, it is clear that u_1 should use s, whereas an average service would be a better choice for u_2.

In a nutshell, we propose a probabilistic approach to leverage the variability of NFPs: we use conditional contracts and usage patterns, while treating NFPs as probability distributions throughout the whole selection process. This gives providers an opportunity to differentiate themselves and users a very easy way to find the best match. Our evaluation shows that not only does our approach make novel kinds of scenarios possible, it also allows for better selection in existing scenarios.

The structure of this paper is as follows: Section 2 gives an overview over related work. Section 3 introduces a realistic scenario. Section 4 describes our approach. Section 5 evaluates our approach against our scenario, and finally Section 6 concludes the paper.

2 Related Work

In this section we survey work that is related to ours. We show both the impact and the differences in relation to our work.

Regarding NFPs, while, in general, there is a lot of research out there, probabilistic approaches are less common. Probability distributions for NFPs have mainly been used in computing the NFPs of service compositions with different kinds of techniques: Dynamic programming and the greedy method [6], as well as Monte-Carlo simulations [7] have been applied for this purpose. This gives us confidence that using probability distributions for NFPs is feasible, because even calculating those for composed services works reasonably well. Besides, to the best of our knowledge, there is no work that uses probabilistic NFPs directly for service selection, as we do in our approach.

While we have not seen conditional contracts, as such, there exists an approach [8] that formalizes the obligations of a service provider as logical rules, which are specified with the Web Service Modeling Language (WSML) [4]. This allows to use reasoning on top of those rules to compute the actual NFPs for a specific service request. In a way, this is quite similar to what you can do with conditional contracts, yet we found two important differences: First, there exists no designated way to use such logical rules in conjunction with probabilistic computations. Second, given the possible complexity of such rules in WSML, it might not be feasible to derive direct conditions that imply certain values for NFPs. As we will see, both are strictly necessary for our approach. Hence, we deem conditional contracts a better choice for our purposes.

Concerning usage patterns, there seems to be little research besides the introduction of the notion to refer to patterns in how users usually compose services [9]. On the contrary, we only refer to usage patterns in how a single service is used, e.g. at which day of the week, or at which time, a user usually calls a service

In conclusion, our contribution does not only lie in defining conditional contracts and usage patterns, but in combining them together with probability distributions into a probabilistic approach, which leverages the variability of NFPs both in their values and descriptions.

3   Scenario

Now, we start by depicting a realistic scenario to illustrate the real-world problems that we are trying to solve. First, we describe the setting, the service in question and the assumed infrastructure in a general overview. Then, we give detailed descriptions of the involved providers and users. Finally, we pinpoint the challenges that arise from this scenario.

3.1   Overview

Our overall setting is the stock market. The service we envision provides mobile news about companies listed in the stock market. A stock market, in general, is only open on certain days of the week during specific time slots. For our means, we assume a stock market that is open from Monday to Friday during 9 and 17 o'clock. Consequently, the demand for the service is generally highest when the stock market is open, and lowest on the weekend.

Through their mobile clients, users can request news when and how often they want. Payment is specified per service request. The service discovery happens through brokers, that are commonly found in a SOA. These brokers have access to all service contracts available from different providers. Furthermore, brokers not only provide service discovery, but can also compute the contract that best matches a user's requirements and preferences. However, as consulting the broker incurs a notable fee, the users' clients usually only update their contracts once in a while, e.g. once a month.

3.2   Providers

Providers all offer functionally equivalent services. Therefore, they differentiate themselves only through the NFPs defined in their contract(s). Though, to make things comparable, all providers have agreed on a common pricing schema. First, to distinguish them based on their quality, providers are classified into different service classes $A, B, \ldots$ according to their maximum response times. For those classes, base prices are fixed. Starting from the best service class, A, for each class the maximum response times increases, while the base price decreases.

Then, to cater to specific kinds of users or to differentiate themselves, providers can introduce as many different service options as needed. These options modify the base price, given by the service class, depending on the time of usage, which can be classified into: Stock market open (Mo-Fr 9-17), during the week (Mo-Fr else), and during the weekend (Sa-Su). While this discretization of the time of usage is standardized, the providers are free to choose the according prices.

Therefore, the final price for the user is calculated by multiplying the base price, determined by the service class, with a constant factor, determined by the service option.

3.3 Users

As for the users, of course, each of them has different needs and uses the service differently. Nevertheless, most can either be categorized as business users, that deal with the stock market for a living, or as casual users, that engage in the stock market as a hobby.

The most essential difference is the time when they use the service. Business users mostly use the service when the stock market is open, sometimes during the rest of the week, and only rarely on the weekend. Casual users, on the other hand, use the service rarely when the stock market is open, also sometimes during the rest of the week, but mostly on the weekend.

Additionally, they have different needs, resulting in different requirements and preferences that mainly relate to the following two NFPs: Response time and price. Regarding response time, both value the response time in terms of the throughput, which means the number of news updates they can receive in a certain time interval. Also, both have an optimal throughput that allows them to make the best use of the service, and a minimum throughput that is the limit of what is actually usable or tolerable for them in terms of productivity or patience. Naturally, business users have much higher requirements for the throughput than casual users. Regarding the price, both, similarly, have optimal and maximum values, and, as expected, casual users are more price sensitive than business users. Throughput and price each contribute a part to the overall utility of the service for the users: Business users value throughput the most, while casual users are more concerned about price.

3.4 Challenges

So far, we have described the scenario, but not yet analyzed what actually is challenging about it. On a top level, we identify two areas that pose new challenges: The definition and the selection of contracts.

Definition. The definition of contracts that meet the needs of the providers is the first challenge, because, with normal contracts, it is not possible to realize the service options mentioned: Representing an option as a separate contract would only allow to realize a base option that offers a constant price. On the other hand, any meaningful option would have to specify multiple alternatives at least for the price, depending on the time of the usage of the service. Otherwise, there would be no way for the service providers to cater to business or casual users by tailoring their contracts.

Selection. Selecting the best contract that accurately matches the users' needs poses the second challenge. While choosing the right service class according to its maximum response time is not that hard, choosing the best contract of providers from the same class is. The same maximum response time tells us nothing about the actual distribution of the response time's values: What is the average value, or how probable is an interval of values that is of special interest to the user? So selecting the best contract by choosing the right service class and service option is not trivial, because not only the needs, but also the usage patterns of users might differ, which might have a high impact on selection. Hence, accurately taking the long term prospect of a contract for a user into account is not easy, but especially important, as the contract can only be changed so often, because of the incurred fee when invoking the broker.

4   Approach

In this section we introduce our approach. While we want to illustrate how it can solve the challenges posed by the scenario, we first present it in its generality here, and then adapt it specifically to our scenario later on in the evaluation. First, we introduce our notions of conditional contracts, usage patterns and probability distributions, before going into the details of our probabilistic approach.

4.1   Conditional Contracts

First, we need contracts that allow us to express the services of our scenario. As already mentioned, we could model each service option with a separate contract, but we also would have to model the conditional pricing for each option. Therefore, we propose conditional contracts.

Definition 1. *A conditional contract (cc ∈ CC) consists of a conditional statement. A conditional statement (cs ∈ CS) can either be a statement (s ∈ S) or a tuple of a condition (c ∈ C) and two conditional statements, of which the first corresponds to the condition being true and the second to it being false.*

$$< cc > ::= < cs >$$
$$< cs > ::= < s > \mid (< c >, < cs >, < cs >) \tag{1}$$

As syntax we propose something similar to typical programming languages, so a sample conditional contract could look like this:

```
contract {
        if time.weekDay = Monday
            if 8 <= time.hour <= 9
                    price = 4
            else
                    price = 2
        else
            price = 1
}
```

The semantics are also similar to what one would expect in a typical programming language, so by evaluating the conditions, one can easily deduce which statement actually holds when a service is called.

4.2 Usage Patterns

Then, to select the best service option for a user, we need to know how he uses the service. Thus, we introduce usage patterns.

Definition 2. *A usage pattern function up takes a condition $c \in \mathcal{C}$ as a parameter and returns a probability between 0 and 1 for the likeliness that c is true.*

$$up : \mathcal{C} \to [0, 1] \tag{2}$$

For a given user, we compute[1] his usage pattern function, so we can evaluate the contracts for him.

4.3 Probability Distributions

Finally, to find the best provider not only on a service class level, but also within a service class, we treat all our NFPs as probability distributions. This way, we can later differentiate even between providers within the same service class.

Given an utility function, instead of applying it only to maximum values, we can apply it first to the values of the probability distributions themselves, before aggregating everything into a single utility value. To aggregate these utility values properly, we need the probability for each combination of values for the NFPs involved. Therefore, we introduce a NFP function.

Definition 3. *A NFP function nfp defined for several NFPs $P_1, \dots, P_n \in \mathcal{NFP}$ takes possible values for those NFPs as parameters and returns a probability between 0 and 1 for the likeliness of this combination of values.*

$$nfp : P_1 \times \cdots \times P_n \to [0, 1] \tag{3}$$

---

[1] There are many ways how to compute or approximate such a usage pattern function, e.g. one could compute it from the history of the user's previous requests.

4.4   Probabilistic Selection

Now, that we have introduced our notions of conditional contracts, usage patterns and probability distributions, we can introduce our probabilistic approach in its entirety. In the following we layout the steps of our approach one by one.

Setup. Our approach finds the best contract cc_u for a given user u from a given list of contracts $\mathcal{CC}_a \subseteq \mathcal{CC}$. For that, we only consider a limited number of NFPs, $P_a := \{P_1, \ldots, P_n\} \subseteq \mathcal{NFP}$, for which we also define the following notation:

$$\overrightarrow{P_a} := P_1 \times \cdots \times P_n \tag{4}$$

To compute the utility of a contract cc, we need the user's utility function $util_u$ that implies certain values for our NFPs P_a:

$$util_u : \overrightarrow{P_a} \to \mathbb{R} \tag{5}$$

Compute Conditions. As a first computation step, we compute all "full" conditions that directly determine if statements in the given contracts hold or not. For this, we need the following auxiliary function ac:

$$ac(cc, c_{ctx}) := \begin{cases} \{c_{ctx}\} & \text{for } cc = s \\ ac(cs_1, c_{ctx} \wedge c) \\ \cup\, ac(cs_2, c_{ctx} \wedge \neg c) & \text{for } cc = (c, cs_1, cs_2) \end{cases} \tag{6}$$

Then, we compute the relevant conditions $\mathcal{RC}_a$ for all given contracts, as follows:

$$\mathcal{RC}_a := \bigcup_{cc \in \mathcal{CC}_a} ac(cc, true) \tag{7}$$

Compute Usage Patterns. The next step is to compute[2] the user's usage pattern. While the usage pattern function may only be partial, it is important that it is defined for all relevant conditions:

$$\forall c \in \mathcal{RC}_a \,.\, up_u(c) \text{ is defined} \tag{8}$$

Compute NFPs. In the next step, we compute the user-specific probability distributions of all NFPs for each contract cc. In order to do this, we determine the relevant statement that corresponds to a given condition c with an auxiliary function rs:

$$rs(cc, c_x, c_{ctx}) := \begin{cases} \{s\} & \text{for } cc = s \wedge c_x = c_{ctx} \\ \{\} & \text{for } cc = s \wedge c_x \neq c_{ctx} \\ rs(cs_1, c_x, c_{ctx} \wedge c) \\ \cup\, rs(cs_2, c_x, c_{ctx} \wedge \neg c) & \text{for } cc = (c, cs_1, cs_2) \end{cases} \tag{9}$$

---

[2] There are several ways to compute this, but we do not focus on this in our approach.

Furthermore, for all statements s of cc, we compute[3] the NFP function $nfp_{cc,s}$ that returns the likeliness of a combination of values under the assumption that statement s holds:

$$nfp_{cc,s} : \overrightarrow{P_a} \rightarrow [0,1] \tag{10}$$

Given all this, we can now compute the probability distribution for NFPs specified in cc, as follows:

$$nfp_{cc,u}(\vec{p}) = \sum_{\substack{c \in ac(cc,true) \\ s \in rs(cc,c,true)}} up_u(c) \cdot nfp_{cc,s}(\vec{p}) \tag{11}$$

Compute Utility. As a last step, we compute the utility of the contract cc for the user u, using the utility function $util_u$. As already explained, we first apply the function to the values of the probability distributions itself, before aggregating everything into one utility value uv to make full use of the probability distributions:

$$uv_u(cc) := \sum_{\vec{p} \in \overrightarrow{P_a}} nfp_{cc,u}(\vec{p}) \cdot util_u(\vec{p}) \tag{12}$$

Thus, we can compute the utility value for any given contract, and then select the contract cc_u with the highest utility value for our user u.

5   Evaluation

In this section, we evaluate our approach against the scenario introduced before. The goal is to show two points:

1. Applying our approach to existing scenarios improves selection.
2. Using our approach allows for selection in novel scenarios.

Response time is a suitable NFP to show (1), because its variability is already inherent, independent of any scenario. So we take our scenario without its pricing aspects and show that applying our approach improves selection. Because our results do not depend on introducing novel pricing schemes, they can be generally applied to existing scenarios.

Price, on the other hand, is a NFP for which we can clearly show (2), directly following our scenario. Nevertheless, because of the prominence of pricing schemes, we think our results can be easily transfered to other scenarios as well, given some domain specific adaptation.

Hence, we conduct our evaluation in two parts, focusing on response time in the first part and on price in the latter to show (1) and (2), respectively.

---

[3] The complexity of the computation mainly depends on what kind of statements are allowed. For example, computation of $nfp_{cc,s}$ should be easy when directly assigning constant values or probability distributions to specific NFPs.

5.1   Response Time

In order to evaluate our approach for the NFP response time, we first define concrete providers and users. Then, we compute the utility of the providers for each user.

Users. We have four users: u_1, u_2, u_3 and u_4. Out of them, u_1 and u_2 are business users, and u_3 and u_4 are casual users. Therefore, u_1 and u_2 have sharper requirements regarding response time, meaning a higher optimal and minimum throughput.

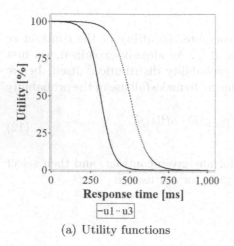
(a) Utility functions

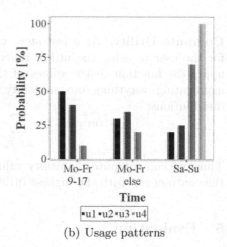
(b) Usage patterns

Fig. 2. Users

In Fig. 2(a) we see the corresponding utility functions for them[4], that are of the following form[5], similar to those described in [10]:

$$f(x) := \frac{1}{1+e^{a(x+c)}} \tag{13}$$

Additionally, our users have usage patterns, as seen in Fig. 2(b), that are typical for business and casual users, respectively. Two aspects are of special interest: First, while the usage pattern of u_1 directly corresponds to the load of p_1, u_2's usage pattern is still similar, but slightly different. Second, while both u_3 and u_4 represent casual users, only u_4 uses the service solely on the weekend.

Providers. We have two providers, p_1 and p_2, with the same maximum response time. This implies, they are in the same service class and therefore share the same base price. Thus, it makes sense to compare them just in terms of their response time. The probability distributions of their (aggregated) response times are shown in Fig. 3.

---

[4]   The utility functions of $u1$ and $u2$ are identical. The same is valid for $u3$ and $u4$.
[5]   Both a and c can be computed from the optimal and minimum throughput.

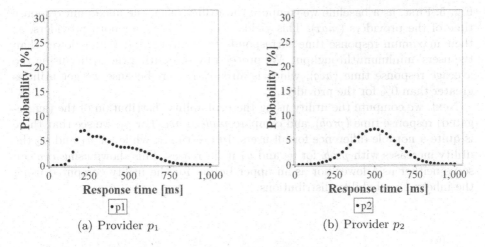

Fig. 3. Aggregated response time

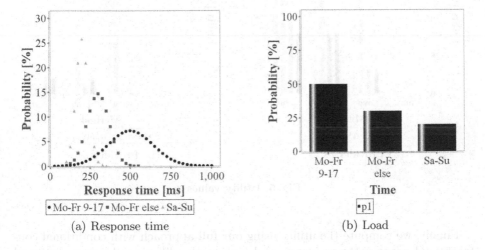

Fig. 4. Provider p_1

As you can see, for p_2 the probability distribution follows a simple normal distribution, while for p_1 it seems to follow no obvious pattern. That is, because, contrary to p_2, the response time of p_1 is dependent on the load, which varies throughout the week, as shown in Fig. 4(b). So actually, the distribution of p_1 is made up of all the normal distributions from Fig. 4(a), that, when aggregated, result in the distribution from Fig. 3(a).

Selection. Now, we compute the utility of each provider for each user, using four different methods: *max*, *avg*, *prob*, and *cond*. This yields the results seen in

Fig. 5. First, as a baseline we compute the utility using the maximum response time of the providers (*max*). This yields a utility of 0% for both providers, as their maximum response time corresponds to a throughput that is lower than the users' minimum throughput. We proceed by computing the utility using the average response time (*avg*), which is already better, because we get utilities greater than 0% for the providers.

Next, we compute the utility using the probability distribution of the (aggregated) response time (*prob*), and compare *prob* to *avg*. For p_1, we see that there is quite a notable difference for all users. Interestingly, while for u_1 and u_2 the utility increases with *prob*, for u_3 and u_4 it decreases. This shows using *avg* can serve neither as a lower nor as an upper bound for the utility computed using the inherent probability distributions.

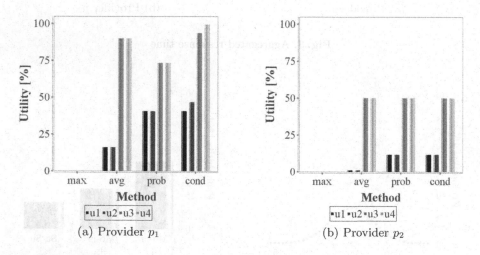

(a) Provider p_1 (b) Provider p_2

Fig. 5. Utility values

Finally, we compute the utility using our full approach with conditional contracts and usage patterns (*cond*), and look at the difference between *prob* and *cond*. This means that instead of just having one probability distribution for the aggregated response time in each provider's contract, we give three conditional definitions with different distributions, one for each time of usage. In the case of p_1, those conditional definitions correspond to the probability distributions given in Fig. 4(a). For p_2, on the other hand, there is just a single distribution from Fig. 3(b), so introducing conditions in p_2's contract does not change anything. This explains why the utility of p_2 does not change for a single user, as, without conditions, the usage patterns have no impact on the utility computation. So for p_1, we can see differences for all users, except for u_1, which is because of the correspondence of the load of p_1 and the usage pattern of u_1: The different normal distributions of p_1's response time are aggregated according to p_1's load, and each distribution corresponds to conditions in the contract; the same conditions the usage patterns correspond to. Hence, the bigger the difference between usage pattern and load, the bigger the difference in utility. For u_1 this means no difference, for u_2 a slight difference, and for u_3 and u_4 big differences, as their usage patterns are quite different from p_1's load. Overall, the comparison between *max* and *cond* shows quite remarkable differences in utility, especially regarding p_1: For u_3 and u_4 the utility goes up from 0% to over 40%, and for u_3 and u_4 it even goes up from 0% to over 90%.

5.2   Price

In order to evaluate our approach for the NFP price, we first refine the concrete providers and users, we already introduced. Then, we again compute the utility of the providers for each user, now considering price and response time.

Users and Providers. In order to compute the utility of a provider for our users, we first define the additional utility functions you can see in Fig. 6.[6]

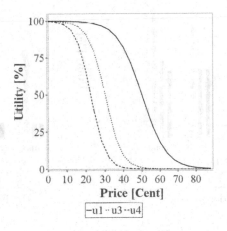

Fig. 6. Utility functions

Then, we use a typical weighted sum, as for instance used in [8] and [11], to combine the utilities for response time and price. Figure 7(a) shows the corresponding weights for each user, which reflect that u_1 and u_2 are business, and u_3 and u_4 are casual users. As you can see in Fig. 7(b), similar to response time, the price for p_1 also depends on the load, while p_2's price is constant.[7]

---

[6]   Both u_1 and u_2 have the same utility function.

[7]   The aggregated average price (according to the load) for p_1 is equal to p_2's price.

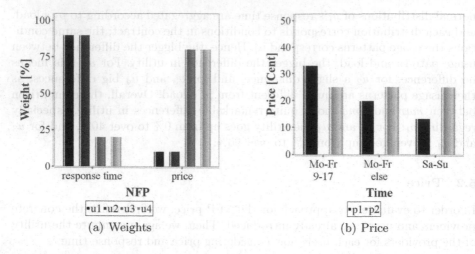

(a) Weights

(b) Price

Fig. 7. Distributions

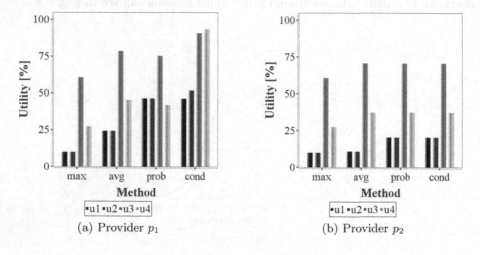

(a) Provider p_1

(b) Provider p_2

Fig. 8. Utility values

Selection. Again, we compute the utility of each provider for each user. The results from Fig. 8 are interesting in many respects, but we will pick just some observations: Comparing p_1's utility for u_4 to the previous evaluation, we see that, while the *max* utility is not 0% anymore, it is still less than 30%.

Also there is a sharp drop-off in *avg* and *prob* utility, that is not visible in the *cond* utility, which still is over 90%. The utilities for p_2, on the other hand, are not that much different, except that you can clearly see the different price expectations of u_3 and u_4 reflected in the increase of utility for u_3 and decrease for u_4, who is more price sensitive.

6   Conclusion

In this paper, we have proposed a probabilistic approach that leverages the variability of NFPs by using conditional contracts and usage patterns, together with probability distributions. We also have described a realistic scenario to illustrate the settings in which such variabilities occur. Furthermore, we have evaluated our approach against this scenario, with concrete examples, focusing on the two NFPs response time and price. The results of our evaluation show that our approach improves selection for existing scenarios and makes selection for novel scenarios possible.

Applying our approach in practice could yield some insights into how different ways of computing usage patterns or utility functions would fare, or what the impact of introducing conditional contracts in existing systems would be.

Last but not least, our work could also be extended in several ways. First, if anyone is going to use conditional contracts, the question is how to best formalize them, which could e.g. be done using WSLA [5]. Second, while we introduced conditional contracts, our approach could also, more generally, be applied to conditional descriptions of NFPs that are not necessarily contained in a contract. This also leaves the questions how to get such descriptions, and from where and from whom to get them. Finally, we have only looked into selection so far, but applying our approach to adaptation could be very interesting, because conditional descriptions of NFPs, and usage patterns could probably change at runtime.

References

1. Papazoglou, M.P., Traverso, P., Dustdar, S., Leymann, F.: Service-oriented computing. Communications of the ACM 46, 25–28 (2003)
2. O'Sullivan, J., Edmond, D., Ter Hofstede, A.: What's in a Service? Distributed and Parallel Databases 12(2-3), 117–133 (2002)
3. Paolucci, M., Kawamura, T., Payne, T.R., Sycara, K.P.: Semantic Matching of Web Services Capabilities. In: Horrocks, I., Hendler, J. (eds.) ISWC 2002. LNCS, vol. 2342, pp. 333–347. Springer, Heidelberg (2002)
4. de Bruijn, J., Lausen, H., Krummenacher, R., Polleres, A., Predoiu, L., Kifer, M., Fensel, D., Toma, I., Steinmetz, N., Kerrigan, M.: The Web Service Modeling Language WSML. Technical report, WSML, WSML Final Draft D16.1v0.3 (2007), http://www.wsmo.org/TR/d16/d16.1/v0.3/
5. Ludwig, H., Keller, A., Dan, A., King, R., Franck, R.: Web Service Level Agreement (WSLA) Language Specification, Version 1.0, IBM Corporation (2003), http://www.research.ibm.com/wsla/WSLASpecV1-20030128.pdf
6. Hwang, S., Want, H., Tang, J., Srivastava, J.: A probabilistic approach to modeling and estimating the QoS of web-services-based workflows. Information Sciences: an International Journal 177(23), 5484–5503 (2007)
7. Rosario, S., Benveniste, A., Haar, S., Jard, C.: Probabilistic QoS and Soft Contracts for Transaction-Based Web Services Orchestrations. IEEE Transactions on Services Computing 1(4), 187–200 (2008)

8. Toma, I., Roman, D., Fensel, D., Sapkota, B., Gomez, J.M.: A Multi-criteria Service Ranking Approach Based on Non-Functional Properties Rules Evaluation. In: Krämer, B.J., Lin, K.-J., Narasimhan, P. (eds.) ICSOC 2007. LNCS, vol. 4749, pp. 435–441. Springer, Heidelberg (2007)
9. Balke, W., Wagner, M.: Towards Personalized Selection of Web Services. In: WWW 2003 (May 2003)
10. Menasce, D.A., Dubey, V.: Utility-based QoS Brokering in Service Oriented Architectures. In: ICWS 2007, July 2007, pp. 422–430 (2007)
11. Haddad, J.E., Manouvrier, M., Ramirez, G., Rukoz, M.: QoS-Driven Selection of Web Services for Transactional Composition. In: ICWS 2008, September 2008, pp. 653–660 (2008)

ServiceTrust: Supporting Reputation-Oriented Service Selection

Qiang He[1,2], Jun Yan[3], Hai Jin[1], and Yun Yang[2]

[1] School of Computer Science and Technology
Huazhong University of Science and Technology, Wuhan, 430074, China
hjin@hust.edu.cn
[2] Faculty of Information and Communication Technologies
Swinburne University of Technology, Melbourne, Australia 3122
qhe@ict.swin.edu.au, yyang@swin.edu.au
[3] School of Information Systems and Technology
University of Wollongong, Wollongong, Australia 2522
jyan@uow.edu.au

Abstract. Service transactions, although attached with service level agreements, may still fail due to various reasons, intentionally or accidentally, in the open and volatile service-oriented environment. In service selection, consumers often need to estimate the trustworthiness of the provider with limited prior experience and knowledge about them. Moreover, the service-oriented environment exposes consumers to unique threats including malicious reputation manipulation and quality-of-service (QoS) abuse. This paper presents Service-Trust – a novel trust management approach to support reputation oriented service selection by quantifying and comparing the trustworthiness of providers based on their historic performance over service transactions. ServiceTrust combines a consumer's and other consumers' personal trust to estimate the provider's trust value. Our experimental results demonstrate that ServiceTrust can significantly increase the success rate of service transactions and is effective in resisting malicious reputation manipulation and QoS abuse.

Keywords: Service-oriented computing, Web services, service selection, trust, service reputation.

1 Introduction

Service-oriented computing (SOC) has been attracting tremendous attention from both the academic and industrial communities. Using SOC, various services across a spectrum of domains can be provided to service consumers over the Internet. Service consumers can look for preferred and qualified services through service registries, invoke services in a loosely coupled manner, and receive desired outcomes from invoked services. Moreover, services from distributed locations can be composed to create new value-added composite services. In the service-oriented environment, services are essentially considered merchandises so that *service level agreements*

L. Baresi, C.-H. Chi, and J. Suzuki (Eds.): ICSOC-ServiceWave 2009, LNCS 5900, pp. 269–284, 2009.

(SLAs) can be established between service consumers and providers to specify mutually-agreed understandings and expectations of the *quality-of-service* (QoS) [10].

However, service providers would not always successfully enforce the SLAs due to various reasons. SLA violations occur from time to time, intentionally or accidentally. For example, malicious service providers may strategically fail service transactions despite of the penalty specified in the previously established SLA. Service providers' failures to enforce SLAs may result in unpredictable consequences and noncompensable loss which cannot be specified in SLAs beforehand. In service selection, the QoS can be negotiated over, but the success rate of the service transaction cannot be provided by the service providers. This problem is especially severe in the service composition scenarios where the composite services are composed of several component services. The failure of an individual component service in this scenario may result in exceptions in the composite service. When searching for service providers, service consumers usually prefer those who are most likely to successfully enforce the SLAs.

In addition, the open and volatile service-oriented environment exposes service consumers to various threats. A widely recognised one is that malicious service providers manipulate service consumers to report incorrect feedbacks in order to boost their reputations or to ruin their competitors' reputations [13]. Another major threat is QoS abuse, where service providers strategically alter their QoS offering behaviour and then provide fraudulent services in order to earn profits [24].

Due to the above issues, in service selection, solutions should be provided to help the service consumers estimate the trustworthiness of the service providers, as suggested but not specified by [1, 12, 28]. However, it is difficult for a service consumer to determine how much it can trust a service provider due to the lack of sufficient experience and knowledge about the service provider. A direct approach to address this issue is to use a reputation system which collects and processes feedback about service providers' past behaviour [11, 18, 20, 25]. To the best of our knowledge, no reputation system has been tailored for service selection in the service-oriented environment and the threats described earlier have not been properly addressed.

Furthermore, the service providers in the service-oriented environment usually have unique identifications in order to allow the service consumers to identify their services. In contrast, the peers in the P2P environment are usually anonymous. This feature makes it difficult to stimulate the peers to develop and maintain long-term reputations. Therefore, existing trust and reputation systems in the P2P environment, which usually put a lot of effort in maintaining peers' anonymity property, are somehow unsuitable to be directly applied in the service-oriented environment where long-term reputation is desirable.

This paper proposes ServiceTrust, a novel reputation-based trust approach which supports reputation-oriented service selection by estimating service consumers' trust over service providers based on their historic performance for SLA enforcement. ServiceTrust can improve the success rate of service transactions by helping service consumers identify trustworthy service providers in the open and volatile service-oriented environment. Through analysing service providers' long-term performance, ServiceTrust can effectively resist malicious reputation manipulation. In addition, ServiceTrust can effectively resist QoS abuse by calculating transactional trust in consideration of the QoS of the past successful service transactions that a service provider has performed. ServiceTrust is independent of the underlying communication model so that it can be applied to different distributed computing architecture such as client-server and P2P.

The rest of the paper is organised as follows. Section 2 analyses the requirements of a reputation-oriented trust management approach for the service-oriented environment. Section 3 introduces the ServiceTrust mechanisms. After that, section 4 demonstrates the performance of the proposed ServiceTrust mechanisms with experimental evaluation. Section 5 introduces the major related work, and finally, section 6 summarises the key contribution of this paper and outlines the future work.

2 Requirements Analysis

To design a trust approach that supports reputation-oriented service selection, the following two threats that exist in the service-oriented environment must be addressed.

Malicious reputation manipulation. Malicious service providers may manipulate service consumers through techniques such as bribery to provide incorrect ratings in order to boost their reputations or to ruin their competitors' reputations. Malicious service providers can also inject incorrect ratings by faking service consumers.

QoS abuse. Malicious service consumers and providers may strategically alter their behaviour in QoS offering in order to obtain profits. For example, malicious service providers may use successful service transactions with small amounts to obtain service consumers' trust and then defraud the service consumers of their money with fraudulent service transactions with large amounts. Genuine service providers may also strategically alter their behaviour under certain circumstances, e.g. given an order of a service transaction with an unusually large amount; a genuine service provider might make the transition into being a malicious service provider and then provide a fraudulent service transaction.

To resist the threat of malicious reputation manipulation, service consumers' trust over service providers should be built on service providers' long-term reputations which are evaluated based on service providers' long-term performance. Long-term reputations can smooth out short-term fluctuations and highlight long-term trends of service providers' reputations. Another benefit of basing service consumers' trust on service providers' long-term reputation is that it encourages service providers' trustworthy and consistent behaviour at present.

To resist the threat of QoS abuse, when evaluating service consumers' trust for individual service transactions, namely *transactional trust*, the QoS of the past successful service transactions that the service providers have performed must be taken into account. By doing so, potential fraudulent service transactions can be identified and avoided.

3 ServiceTrust Mechanisms

The reasons why long-term reputation can help the service consumer with evaluating the trustworthiness of the service providers are twofold. First, service consumers can obtain information to estimate service providers' abilities to successfully perform the forthcoming service transactions. Second, service providers' expectation of long-term reputations creates an incentive for their good performance at present. In this section, we will introduce a hierarchical trust structure which consists of *local transactional rating*, *local trust*, *global trust* and *transactional trust*, and the supporting mechanisms.

3.1 Generating Local Transactional Ratings

A local transactional rating describes a service consumer's experience of an individual service transaction with a service provider. Some early works [11, 25, 27], which use binary rating systems for calculating peers' reputations, prove that binary-value ratings work well for file-sharing systems, in which a file is either a complete or an incomplete version. An SLA in the service-oriented environment can be seen as an equivalent of a file in a file-sharing system because an SLA also only has two finalised status: fulfilled or unfulfilled, representing a successful service transaction or a failed one. Using binary values to rate service transactions is simple and does not require service consumers' physical participation. Another advantage of adopting binary-value ratings is that the ratings are explicit – a service transaction is either successful or unsuccessful in fulfilling the attached SLA. However, some recent works [23, 26] adopt numeric rating systems, in which the ratings are in a certain interval, e.g. [0, 1]. Compared to binary-value ratings, numeric-value ratings can model more accurately a service consumer's experience of a service transaction. But it requires service consumers' direct participation in the rating process which might become an obstacle to the extensive use of the application. Moreover, service consumers' lack of incentive and knowledge to report authentic and accurate ratings over service transactions may result in undesired, inaccurate or even incorrect ratings.

To give application developers flexible choices, ServiceTrust supports both binary-value and numeric ratings. For binary-value ratings, *0* represents a failed service transaction and *1* represents a successful one. The definition of service consumer *i*'s local transactional rating over the nth service transaction with service provider *j*, denoted as $r_{i,j}^{(n)}$, is defined as follows:

$$r_{i,j}^{(n)} = \begin{cases} 0 & service\ transaction\ failed \\ 1 & service\ transaction\ succeeded \end{cases} \tag{1}$$

Service consumer can also rate service transactions using a value in the interval of [0, 1], with 0 and 1 representing complete dissatisfaction and complete satisfaction respectively. Considering that service consumers might lack the knowledge of QoS satisfaction, it is advisable for application developers to provide the service consumers with necessary assistance in the rating process.

3.2 Aggregating Local Transactional Ratings

To obtain a service consumer's local trust over a service provider, local transactional ratings generated from the service consumer's past service transactions with the service provider need to be aggregated. In the aggregation, we consider the temporal dimension when evaluating the credibility of the local transactional ratings. It is not only their values that matter, but also at what time they are recorded – we assume that the local transactional ratings are recorded upon the completion of the service transactions. The credibility of a local transactional rating diminishes as time elapses. The ratings over a service consumer's recent service transactions with a service provider are more credible than the old ones. Also, when combining a service consumer's and other service consumers' personal local trust (as detailed in Section 3.3), the recent ratings provided by one service consumer are more credible than the old ones provided by another service consumer.

We use exponential moving average (EMA) scheme [3] to aggregate a service consumer's local transactional ratings over a service provider. Weights are computed to represent the credibility of the ratings according to how old the ratings are. The weight of each older rating decreases exponentially, giving more credibility to recent ratings whilst not entirely discarding older ratings. By doing so, short-term fluctuation of ratings can be smoothed out and long-term trend can be highlighted. Since the threshold between short-term and long-term is application specific, ServiceTrust uses parameter θ, as a time window, to specify valid ratings when aggregating the local transactional ratings. Ratings lying outside of θ are considered obsolete and thus discarded in the aggregation. θ can be set accordingly by the application developers to meet the requirements of applications.

The elapsed time since a service transaction has been performed is used to express how old the corresponding rating is. In order to compute the elapsed time of the ratings, ServiceTrust requires the rating time, i.e. the time when the transaction is rated, to be recorded along with the rating in the form of 2-tuple: $(r_{i,j}^{(n)}, t_{i,j}^{(n)})$.

The process of calculating service consumer i's local trust over service provider j by aggregating the series of local transactional ratings over the past service transactions between them, i.e. $[(r_{i,j}^{(1)}, t_{i,j}^{(1)}), (r_{i,j}^{(2)}, t_{i,j}^{(2)}),...,(r_{i,j}^{(n)}, t_{i,j}^{(n)})]$, consists of the following five steps.

1. Compute the elapsed time, denoted as $et_{i,j}^{(n)}$, since each transaction was rated. The series of local transactional ratings becomes:
   $[(r_{i,j}^{(1)}, et_{i,j}^{(1)}),(r_{i,j}^{(2)}, et_{i,j}^{(2)}),...,(r_{i,j}^{(n)}, et_{i,j}^{(n)})]$;
2. Determine the value of the time window, θ ;
3. Divide the time frame confined by θ into s time slots;
4. Compute the arithmetic average value of the local transactional ratings in each time slot, denoted as $ar_{i,j}^{(1)}, ar_{i,j}^{(2)},..., ar_{i,j}^{(s)}$;
5. Aggregate $ar_{i,j}^{(1)}, ar_{i,j}^{(2)},..., ar_{i,j}^{(s)}$ to obtain service consumer i's local aggregated rating over service provider j, denoted as $R_{i,j}$, using exponential averaging scheme as follows:

$$R R_{i,j} = \sum_{k=1}^{s} \alpha(1-\alpha)^k ar_{i,j}^{(k)} \qquad (2)$$

where $0 < \alpha < 1$ controls how fast the credibility of the ratings decreases over time.

Besides θ, two other parameters, s and α, are manoeuvrable. They can be set by application developers to control the weight decrease in order to meet application specific requirements. The bigger s and α are, the faster the weight decreases, meaning the faster the old ratings in θ become incredible.

3.3 Combining Personal Trust

The local trust introduced in Section 3.2 reflects a service consumer's personal opinion of a service provider. To comprehensively evaluate a service consumer's global trust over a service provider, the service consumer's local trust should be combined with other service consumer's local trust. By doing so, the service consumer can obtain a global and comprehensive view of the service provider. A simple approach to the combination is to simply average all the local trust. An advanced approach is to compute a weighted average of all the local trust, where the weights represent the credibility of the local trust.

The credibility of a service consumer's local trust over a service provider depends not only on how old the local transactional ratings are (see Section 3.1), but also on how long the service consumer has had interactions with the service provider. Experience with the service provider in the longer-term gives the service consumer more information and knowledge about the service provider, thus enabling the service consumer to predict the service provider's ability and behaviour better [6, 21]. It also provides a firmer basis for calculating the credibility of the service consumer's local trust over the service provider. Therefore, when incorporating other service consumers' local trust into evaluating a service consumer's global trust over a service provider, we consider the relationship duration between the service consumers and the service provider, measured by the number of past service transactions between them. The longer relationship duration a service consumer has with the service provider, the more credible its local trust over the service provider is.

We adopt Rayleigh cumulative distribution functions [19] to calculate the weights according to the number of a service consumer's past service transactions with the service provider. The credibility of service consumer i's local trust over service provider j, denoted as $\beta_{i,j}$, is calculated as follows:

$$\beta_{i,j} = 1 - exp(\frac{-x^2}{2\sigma^2}) \quad (\sigma > 0) \tag{3}$$

where σ is a parameter that inversely controls how fast $\beta_{i,j}$ increases as the number of interactions, denoted as x, increases. σ can be set by the application developers, from 0 to theoretically ∞, to capture the characteristics of different application scenarios.

Compared to other service consumers' local trust, a service consumer can choose to trust its own local trust more or less when evaluating its global trust over the service provider. To reflect this nature, the weight assigned to the service consumer's own local trust over the service provider, denoted as $\beta'_{i,j}$, is computed as follows:

$$\beta'_{i,j} = 1 - exp(\frac{-x^2}{2(\sigma+\varepsilon)^2}) \quad (\sigma+\varepsilon) > 0 \tag{4}$$

where x is the number of service transactions that service consumer i has had with service provider j and ε specifies *how much more* (using a negative number) or *how much less* (using a positive number) the service consumer trusts its own local trust over service provider j than other service consumers'.

Then service consumer i's global trust over service provider j, denoted as $\tilde{R}_{i,j}$, can be calculated as follows:

$$\tilde{R}_{i,j} = \beta'_{i,j} \cdot R'_{i,j} + \sum_k \beta_{k,j} \cdot R_{k,j} \qquad (5)$$

where $R'_{i,j}$ is service consumer i's own local trust over service provider j and $R_{k,j}$ is the kth other service consumer's local trust over service provider j.

3.4 Evaluating Transactional Trust

The scheme presented in this section can be applied to prevent various types of QoS abuse, e.g. execution time, availability and throughput, etc. Since transaction amount is usually one of a service consumer's most important concerns about the service in the service-oriented environment, we present the solution to transaction amount abuse for demonstration.

To prevent service consumers from transaction amount abuse, we incorporate the transaction amount into estimating service consumers' transactional trust for individual service transactions. We define transactional trust as the probability at which a service consumer believes the service provider will perform an individual service transaction and deliver expected outcomes specified in the attached SLA.

Transaction amount abuse usually consists of two steps. First, the malicious service provider fulfils service transactions with relatively small amounts in order to obtain a service consumer's trust. Second, the malicious service provider entices the service consumer to give it an order for a service transaction with a large amount, and then defrauds the customer with fraudulent service transactions or inferior goods afterwards. Under other circumstances, a fraudulent service transaction might also be performed, e.g. a genuine service provider may make the transition into being malicious when it gets an order for a service transaction with an unusually large amount which reaches or crosses its threshold for being genuine.

We address this issue by evaluating the transactional trust in consideration of the similarity between the quote on the forthcoming service transaction and the average transaction amount of the successful service transactions the service provider has performed. The base for this approach is the spirit of situational trust [15]: experience from situations of a similar nature will give a means of determining risk accurately. When evaluating the transactional trust, we consider two factors:

1.   The average amount of successful service transactions that the service provider has performed. In general, the larger the quote on a service transaction is than the average amount of its past successful service transactions, the more likely that the service provider will provide a fraudulent service transaction.
2.   The extent of amounts of successful service transactions that the service provider has performed. If a service provider has a large extent of amounts of successful service transactions, the chance that it will provide a fraudulent service transaction is slim.

Combining the considerations on the above two factors, we evaluate service consumer i's transactional trust for a forthcoming service transaction provided by service provider j, denoted as $\overline{R}_{i,j}$, using formula (6).

$$\overline{R}_{i,j} = \gamma \cdot \tilde{R}_{i,j} \tag{6}$$

$$\gamma = (\frac{1}{\Delta^2})^k \tag{7}$$

$$\Delta = \frac{q_{new}}{a_j^{ave}} \cdot \frac{1}{cv_j} \tag{8}$$

$$cv_j = \frac{\sqrt{\sum_{m=1}^{M}(a_j^m - a_j^{ave})^2}}{a_j^{ave}} \tag{9}$$

where γ is the *transactional amount impact factor*, k is the parameter that controls how fast the transactional trust decreases as Δ increases, q_{new} is the quote on the forthcoming service transaction, a_j^{ave} is the average amount of the successful service transactions provider j has performed, a_j^m is the amount of the mth successful service transaction provider j has performed, and cv_j is the coefficient of variation of $a_j^1, a_j^2, ..., a_j^m, ..., a_j^M$. Parameter k can be set by application developers according to the requirements of the applications. For example, in the scenario where the fluctuation of prices is relatively violent, such as the global crude oil market, a small k is advisable.

Usually the smaller the transaction amount is, the better it is for the service consumers. However in relation to some QoS such as availability and throughput, the higher the better it is for the service consumers. In those cases, formula (10) can be used to replace formula (8):

$$\Delta = \frac{a_j^{ave}}{q_{new}} \cdot \frac{1}{cv_j} \tag{10}$$

3.5 Initial Trust for New Services

In the discussion so far, we assume that a service provider provides one type of service. However, in the service-oriented environment, a service providers might be able to provide multiple types of services with respective service identifications. Accordingly, in ServiceTrust, a service consumer's trust over a service provider is service specific, and is estimated based on the service provider's historic performance over an individual type of services. It is possible that when a service provider starts offering a new service, there is no historic performance information about the new service for service consumers to refer to. In this case, a service consumer's trust for this new service cannot be evaluated as described above.

The development of a service consumer's initial trust for a new service usually goes through two stages: an exploratory stage and a commitment stage, which reflect the general belief in the trust literature [2]. At the exploratory stage, the service provider's reputation will influence the service consumer's intention to trust the service provider. At the commitment stage, experience-based knowledge will readily replace the tentative trust built at the exploratory stage [16]. Another factor that influences a service provider's tentative trust over a service provider is its familiarity with the service provider [7, 14]. Familiarity is referred to as the understanding of the context which the service transaction is involved, and hence is considered the precondition for tentative trust [14].

From the perspectives of both reputation and context, we assume that a service provider with good reputation obtained from its existing services tends to provide the new service at a high success rate. This assumption is acceptable at least at the early stage of the new service's appearance because the service provider has to cater for the service consumers in order to quickly develop its reputation for the new service and to attract more potential service consumers [17]. Therefore, a service consumer's initial trust for a new service can be estimated through looking into the service provider's *global reputation* which is obtained by aggregating its reputations for its other services. And the estimation of a service consumer's initial trust for the new service is based on the service provider's global reputation. After interacting with the service provider, the service consumer can gradually incorporate its own experience and knowledge into developing its trust for the service following the procedure presented above (Sections 3.1-3.4). In ServiceTrust, service consumer i's global trust over service provider j, denoted as $\hat{R}_{i,j}$, based on its trust for service provider j's N individual existing services is calculated as:

$$\hat{R}_{i,j} = \frac{1}{N} \sum_{n=1}^{N} \tilde{R}_{i,j}^{(n)} \tag{11}$$

where $\tilde{R}_{i,j}^{(n)}$ is service consumer i's trust for the nth individual existing service provided by service provider j.

4 Experiments

In this section, we will assess the effectiveness of ServiceTrust as compared to a random service selection with no trust and reputation systems enabled. And then we will demonstrate our approach's resistibility against the threats of malicious reputation manipulation and QoS abuse. The issue of initial trust for new services is not directly related to either effectiveness on service selection or resistibility against threats and hence is not included in the experiments.

4.1 Experiments Configuration

Network model. We set up a service-oriented environment based on our previous work [8] in which peers look up each other in an efficient decentralised way. The simulation environment consists of 2000 service consumers and 200 service providers. Service consumers can request for services and service providers respond to these requests. Service consumers can access all the information about service providers' historic performance.

Node model. 20 types of services are provided by the 200 service providers, 10 for each. Each service provider has an inherent success rate randomly picked from a certain interval for its past and forthcoming service transactions. Different intervals for inherent success rates, including [0.9, 1], [0.8, 1] [0.7, 1], [0.6, 1], [0.5, 1] and [0.4, 1], are used to describe different volatile environments, [0.9, 1] being the best and [0.4, 1] being the worst. Throughout all experiments, service providers perform service transactions at their inherent success rates except under threat model #5. In the experiments with ServiceTrust enabled, genuine service consumers select the available service provider they have the highest trust over (global trust in experiments #1 to #5 and transactional trust in experiment #6), and rate service transactions honestly. Malicious service consumers select service providers and rate service transactions under corresponding threat models. The threat models are detailed in Table 1. In experiments where ServiceTrust is disabled, service consumers randomly select service providers.

Table 1. Threat models

Threat Models	Malicious Service Providers	Malicious Service Consumers	
		Service Selection	Rating
Threat Model #1	NA	randomly select service providers	rate 1 over all service transactions with malicious service providers
Threat Model #2	NA	select only malicious service providers	rate 1 over all service transactions with malicious service providers
Threat Model #3	NA	randomly select service providers	rate 0 over all service transactions with genuine service providers
Threat Model #4	NA	select only genuine service providers	rate over to all service transactions with genuine service providers
Threat Model #5	provide fraudulent services at the probability of $1 - \lambda$	NA	NA

ServiceTrust parameters. Table 2 summarises the parameters carefully chosen for the simulation in order to calculate service consumers' trust over service providers based on their historic performance in the long term.

Simulation execution. The simulation proceeds in simulation cycles. Each simulation cycle is subdivided into an evaluation cycle, a transaction cycle and a rating cycle. In an evaluation cycle, service consumers look up service providers and then evaluate

Table 2. ServiceTrust parameters used in simulation

α	θ	s	σ	ε	k
0.1	10 simulation cycles	10	15	-5	1/7

their global trust or transactional trust over the service providers. In a transaction cycle, each service consumer requests one service based on the results from trust evaluation in the evaluation cycle. Service providers correspond and complete service transactions. In each simulation cycle, each service provider can accommodate up to a maximum of 40 service consumers. If a service provider is fully loaded, the service consumer will turn to the service provider it has the next highest trust over. In a rating cycle, service consumers rate the service transactions honestly or under corresponding threat models. Binary rating values, described in Section 3.1, are used[1]. Upon the completion of each simulation cycle, statistics are collected at each service consumer. Each experiment is run 20 times and the results of all runs are averaged. We analyse the statistics to assess ServiceTrust by measuring the average success rates of overall service transactions.

4.2 Experimental Results

In experiment #1, we compare the average success rates of overall service transactions with ServiceTrust enabled against disabled in volatile environments without malicious service consumers and providers.

Figure 1 depicts results from experiment #1, showing that ServiceTrust can significantly increase the average success rates of overall service transactions in different volatile experiments. As the environment gets more volatile, the average success rate decreases drastically in the absence of ServiceTrust. However, with ServiceTrust enabled, even when different service providers' success rates vary in the large interval, i.e. [0.4, 1], the average success rate of overall service transactions still remains at 93%.

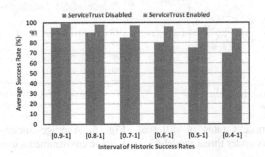

Fig. 1. Increase of average success rates of overall service transactions with ServiceTrust enabled

Then we conduct experiments #2-# 5 to evaluate ServiceTrust's resistibility against the threats of malicious reputation manipulation. Malicious reputation manipulation includes patterns described by four threat models: individual and collective malicious reputation boost, individual and collective malicious reputation ruin (threat models #1-#4). As shown in Figures 2-5, the experimental results demonstrate that

---

[1] We choose not to use numeric ratings to avoid unnecessary issue of modeling service consumer's satisfaction from QoS.

ServiceTrust can well protect the trust management from being undermined by these four threats in the long term.

Finally we test ServiceTrust's resistibility against the threats of QoS abuse (threat model #5) via experiment #6. This threat model describes the providers' strategic change of behaviour in QoS offering. We simulated the scenarios in which malicious service providers provide fraudulent services at the probability of $1-\gamma$. The results, as depicted in Figure 6, show that ServiceTrust can almost perfectly protect the consumers from being deceived by QoS abuse. In the most volatile environment with 70%

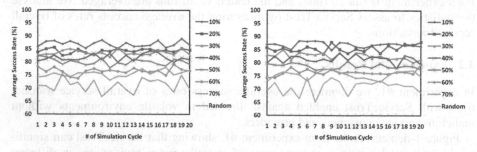

Fig. 2. Average success rates in different volatile environments under threat model #1

Fig. 3. Average success rates in different volatile environments under threat model #2

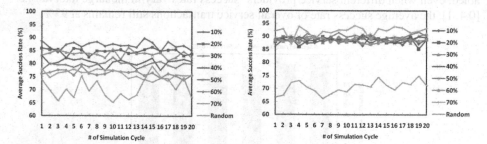

Fig. 4. Average success rates in different volatile environments under threat model #3

Fig. 5. Average success rates in different volatile environments under threat model #4

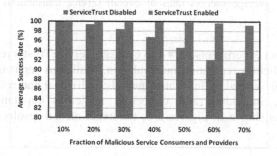

Fig. 6. Average success rate in different volatile environments under threat model #5

malicious service consumers and providers, the average success rate is still above 99%. The reason is that when the QoS is unusually better than the normal QoS that a service provider used to provide, the service consumer's transactional trust over that service provider drops immediately and drastically. The chance is very slim that a malicious service provider will be selected by a service consumer.

5 Related Work

Reputation-based trust research is being carried out in several distinct areas, most notably computer science and economics. An overview of many trust systems for online service provision can be found in [9]. And many key issues in reputation-based trust evaluation mechanisms in e-commerce environments are discussed in [22].

In the domain of distributed computing, several reputation systems have been proposed. Cornelli et al. [4] proposes P2PRep, a P2P protocol which complements Gnutella - an existing P2P file-sharing protocol. In P2PRep, peers can keep track of and share information about other peers' reputation. However, there are no formalised approaches to evaluate the reputation and credibility of the peers and no experimental evaluation is provided. Damiani et al. [5] enhance their previous work in [4] by introducing XRep, a distributed polling protocol that inquires the P2P network for peers' opinions (votes) on targeted resources. Votes are clustered based on IP address to prevent Sybil and collaboration attack. XRep focuses on supporting anonymous and secure services while preserving anonymity to a degree. Kamvar et al. [11] proposes EigenTrust, a distributed method for P2P file-sharing networks. Unique global trust values are computed and assigned to each peer in the network. EigenTrust requires pretrusted peers in the network to address the collusion problem. The limitation of their approach is that pretrusted peers may not always be available in all cases. Xiong et al. [25] proposes PeerTrust, a feedback based trust management system. PeerTrust incorporates three basic trust parameters (the feedback, the total number of transactions a peer performs and the credibility of the feedback sources) and two adaptive factors (transaction context factor and the community context factor) into computing the trustworthiness of peers. However, the solution adopted to measure feedback credibility, namely Trust-Value based credibility Measure (TVM), assumes that trustworthy nodes be more likely to be honest on the feedback they provide. This assumption is not generally true because peers may send incorrect feedbacks to ruin the reputations of its competitors. Srivatsa et al. [20] proposes TrustGuard, a safeguard framework in decentralised overlay networks, aiming at countering various vulnerabilities in reputation management. In TrustGuard, a peer rates credibility of feedback from other peers using a personalised similarity measure (PSM). Feedbacks that are similar to the peer's own are considered more credible. This method is limited in the cases where peers with long-term reputation are preferable and credible. For example, if a provider peer delivers a bad service transaction to a consumer peer by accident, malicious peers can flood bad feedbacks to rapidly ruin the consumer peer's trust over the provider peer.

Wang et al. [24] presents a model which incorporates transaction amount into trust evaluation. A simple method is proposed to measure the difference between old and new transaction amounts. However, no amount-related malicious behaviour is modelled and no experimental results are presented to validate their approach.

Our work focuses on the crossroad of SOC, electronic ecommerce and distributed computing, and differs from the above works in a number of ways. First, ServiceTrust evaluates service consumers' trust over service providers based on their performance over past service transactions in the long term. Second, the temporal factor and relationship duration between a service consumer and a service provider are taken into account when evaluating the credibility of the service consumer's local trust of the service provider. Third, we address two unique and critical threats faced by reputation-based trust systems in the service-oriented environment, namely, malicious reputation manipulation and QoS abuse. Finally, we implement ServiceTrust and demonstrate the effectiveness of ServiceTrust on service selection, and the resistibility against the two threats.

6 Conclusions and Future Work

We have presented ServiceTrust – a novel trust management approach to support reputation-oriented service selection. The proposed approach aims at addressing unique threats in the service-oriented environment including malicious reputation manipulation and QoS abuse. In ServiceTrust, we evaluate a consumer's trust over a provider based on the provider's historic performance over service transactions in the long term. A consumer's local trust over a provider is combined with other consumers' to evaluate the consumer's global trust over the provider. The credibility of a consumer's local trust over a provider is calculated by considering the temporal factor and the relationship duration between the consumer and the provider. In order to resist QoS abuse, the comparison between the QoS of the forthcoming service transaction and the QoS of the successful service transactions that a provider has performed is taken into account when calculating a consumer's transactional trust. We have demonstrated experimental results which show that ServiceTrust can significantly improve the average success rate of service transactions by facilitating reputation-oriented service selection. In addition, experimental results show that ServiceTrust can well resist the following malicious threats: 1) individual malicious reputation boost; 2) collective malicious reputation boost; 3) individual malicious reputation ruin; 4) collective malicious reputation ruin; and 5) QoS abuse.

In the future, we will develop a complementary scheme to offer incentive to consumers to participate in ServiceTrust and provide correct ratings over service transactions. The resistibility against more threats will be further investigated in ServiceTrust.

Acknowledgement

This work is partly funded by the Australian Research Council Discovery Project Scheme under grant No.DP0663841, National Science Foundation of China under grant No.90412010 and ChinaGrid project from Ministry of Education of China. We are grateful for S. Hunter's help with conducting the experiments.

References

1. Ardagna, D., Pernici, B.: Adaptive Service Composition in Flexible Processes. IEEE Transactions on Software Engineering 33(6), 369–384 (2007)
2. Blau, P.: Exchange and Power in Social Life. John Wiley & Sons, New York (1964)
3. Chou, Y.-l.: Statistical Analysis: With Business and Economic Applications. Holt, Rinehart and Winston (1969)
4. Cornelli, F., Damiani, E., di Vimercati, S.D.C., Paraboschi, S., Samarati, P.: Choosing Reputable Servents in a P2P Network. In: Proceedings of 11th International Conference on World Wide Web, pp. 376–386. ACM Press, Honolulu (2002)
5. Damiani, E., Vimercati, D.C.D., Paraboschi, S., Samarati, P., Violante, F.: A Reputation-Based Approach for Choosing Reliable Resources in Peer-to-Peer Networks. In: Proceedings of 9th ACM Conference on Computer and Communications Security, pp. 207–216. ACM Press, Washington (2002)
6. Doyle, S.X., Roth, G.T.: Selling and Sales Management in Action: The Use of Insight Coaching to Improve Relationship Selling. Journal of Personal Selling & Sales Management 12(1), 59–64 (1992)
7. Gefen, D.: E-Commerce: the Role of Familiarity and Trust. Omega 28(6), 725–737 (2000)
8. He, Q., Yan, J., Yang, Y., Kowalczyk, R., Jin, H.: Chord4S: A P2P-based Decentralised Service Discovery Approach. In: Proceedings of IEEE International Conference on Services Computing, pp. 221–228. IEEE Computer Society, Honolulu (2008)
9. Jøsang, A., Ismail, R., Boyd, C.: A Survey of Trust and Reputation Systems for Online Service Provision. Decision Support Systems 43(2), 618–644 (2007)
10. Jin, L.-j., Machiraju, V., Sahai, A.: Analysis on Service Level Agreement of Web Services. Technical Report, HP Laboratories (2002), http://www.hpl.hp.co.uk/techreports/2002/HPL-2002-180.pdf
11. Kamvar, S.D., Schlosser, M.T., Garcia-Molina, H.: The EigenTrust Algorithm for Reputation Management in P2P Networks. In: Proceedings of 12th International World Wide Web Conference, pp. 640–651. ACM Press, Budapest (2003)
12. Ko, J.M., Kim, C.O., Kwon, I.-H.: Quality-of-Service Oriented Web Service Composition Algorithm and Planning Architecture. Journal of Systems and Software 81(11), 2079–2090 (2008)
13. Lam, S.K., Riedl, J.: Shilling Recommender Systems for Fun and Profit. In: Proceedings of 13th International Conference on World Wide Web, pp. 393–402. ACM Press, New York (2004)
14. Luhmann, N.: Trust and Power. Wiley, Chichester (1979)
15. Marsh, S.P.: Formalising Trust as a Computational Concept, in Department of Mathematics and Computer Science Stirling, Scotland, UK, University of Stirling (1994)
16. McKnight, D.H., Choudhury, V., Kacmar, C.: Trust in E-Commerce Vendors: A Two-Stage Model. In: Proceedings of 21st International Conference on Information Systems, pp. 532–536. ACM Press, Brisbane (2000)
17. Mitchell, W.: Dual Clocks: Entry Order Influences on Incumbent and Newcomer Market Share and Survival When Specialized Assets Retain Their Value. Strategic Management Journal 12(2), 85–100 (1991)
18. Resnick, P., Kuwabara, K., Zeckhauser, R., Friedman, E.: Reputation Systems. Communications of the ACM 43(12), 45–48 (2000)
19. Ross, S.M.: Introduction to Probability and Statistics for Engineers and Scientists. Academic Press, Cleveland (2000)

20. Srivatsa, M., Xiong, L., Liu, L.: TrustGuard: Countering Vulnerabilities in Reputation Management for Decentralized Overlay Networks. In: Proceedings of 14th International Conference on World Wide Web, pp. 422–431. ACM Press, Chiba (2005)

21. Swan, J.E., Nolan, J.J.: Gaining Customer Trust: A Conceptual Guide for the Salesperson. Journal of Personal Selling & Sales Management 5(2), 39–48 (1985)

22. Wang, Y., Lin, K.-J.: Reputation-Oriented Trustworthy Computing in E-Commerce Environments. IEEE Internet Computing 12(4), 55–59 (2008)

23. Wang, Y., Varadharajan, V.: A Time-Based Peer Trust Evaluation in P2P E-commerce Environments. In: Zhou, X., Su, S., Papazoglou, M.P., Orlowska, M.E., Jeffery, K. (eds.) WISE 2004. LNCS, vol. 3306, pp. 730–735. Springer, Heidelberg (2004)

24. Wang, Y., Wong, D.S., Lin, K.-J., Varadharajan, V.: Evaluating Transaction Trust and Risk Levels in Peer-to-Peer E-Commerce Environments Information Systems and E-Business Management 6(1), 25–48 (2008)

25. Xiong, L., Liu, L.: PeerTrust: Supporting Reputation-Based Trust for Peer-to-Peer Electronic Communities. IEEE Transactions on Knowledge and Data Engineering 16(7), 843–857 (2004)

26. Yu, B., Singh, M.P., Sycara, K.: Developing Trust in Large-Scale Peer-to-Peer Systems. In: Proceedings of 1st IEEE Symposium on Multi-Agent Security and Survivability, pp. 1–10. IEEE CS Press, Philadelphia (2004)

27. Yu, B., Singh, M.P., Sycara, K.: A Reputation-Based Approach for Choosing Reliable Resources in Peer to Peer Networks. In: Proceedings of 9th ACM Conference on Computer and Communications Security, pp. 207–216. ACM Press, Washington DC (2002)

28. Zeng, L., Benatallah, B., Dumas, M., Kalagnanam, J., Sheng, Q.Z.: Quality Driven Web Services Composition. In: Proceedings of 12th International Conference on World Wide Web, Budapest, Hungary, pp. 411–421 (2003)

QoS Browsing for Web Service Selection

Chen Ding[1], Preethy Sambamoorthy[1], and Yue Tan[2]

[1] Department of Computer Science, Ryerson University, Canada
[2] School of Software, Tsinghua University, China
cding@scs.ryerson.ca, preethy.sambamoorthy@ryerson.ca

Abstract. In most of current research works on Quality of Service (QoS) based web service selection, searching is usually the dominant way to find the desired services. However, sometimes, requestors may not have the knowledge of the available QoS attributes and their value ranges in the registry, or they may only have vague QoS requirements. Under this situation, we believe that browsing is a more appropriate way to help the QoS-based service selection process. In this paper, we propose an interactive QoS browsing mechanism to first show an overview of the QoS value distribution to requestors and then gradually present more and more detailed views on some requestor interested value ranges. We find that interval data (or more generally symbolic data) is a more proper type to represent the QoS value, compared with the single valued numerical data. So we use interval clustering algorithms to implement our browsing system. The experiment compares the performance of using different distance measures and shows the effectiveness of the interval clustering algorithm we use. We also use a sample data set to illustrate the interactive QoS browsing process.

1 Introduction

Web service discovery and selection have been extensively studied in recent years. There are two major categories of approaches. The first one is based on the functional descriptions of web services and usually the syntactic or semantic matching is done [9] [18]. The second category is based on the non-functional properties of services, such as various QoS attributes and trust and reputation measurements [1] [3] [12] [14] [15] [19] [21]. QoS values can be obtained from publishers' descriptions, signed contracts between publishers and requestors such as Service Level Agreement (SLA), and monitoring engines set up by the service registry or a third party. Trust and reputation [20] value is calculated based on previous requestors' experiences of using those services or dealing with those providers. It could also be considered as a special type of QoS attributes, and therefore, in this paper, we simply refer to this category of approaches as the QoS-based selection method. In QoS-based service selection, requestors submit their QoS requirements, then services are chosen based on the obtained QoS data, which is usually a multi-factor decision making process.

There is one fundamental problem in this QoS-based selection process. Most of current approaches assume that requestors can formulate a QoS query correctly, which might not be true sometimes. Requestors may not have the knowledge about which QoS attributes are measured by the registry, or more commonly, what are the

L. Baresi, C.-H. Chi, and J. Suzuki (Eds.): ICSOC-ServiceWave 2009, LNCS 5900, pp. 285–300, 2009.
© Springer-Verlag Berlin Heidelberg 2009

exact value ranges of those QoS attributes, which usually leads to an unsuccessful search. For instance, a service requestor wants to find a service with a high reliability level, and thus he puts the request as "reliability>99%", however, none of the services in the registry achieves this level, and the maximum reliability is 97%. In this case, no matching result could be returned, but when no other choices are available, the requestor can accept a service with reliability 97%. This example shows the problem with searching when improper query is submitted. Also many of the QoS requirements are considered as soft constraints, which means requestors only have a fuzzy requirement on QoS values and it is often negotiable. For this kind of QoS requirements, searching on a fixed value is not a good option.

Information seeking on the web [5] is usually considered as an integrated activity of browsing and searching. When users have a particular information need, searching is a better way of finding information; when users don't have a clear idea about what they are looking for until the available options are presented, or users don't know how to formulate a query properly due to the lack of knowledge on the vocabulary or the corpus, browsing is a better way. Browsing is also better on keeping the relevant context information, which is crucial in some information seeking tasks.

We believe that QoS-based service selection should also be an integration of browsing and searching. Based on requestors' QoS requirements and their knowledge level, sometimes searching is a better choice, and sometimes browsing is a better choice. When a requestor first enters a service registry, browsing is the most appropriate way to navigate through a set of services which implement the similar functionalities. After the requestor gains some knowledge on the QoS value distribution in the registry, a QoS query could be formulated in a more accurate way and thus the subsequent searching could be more accurate. The requestor can also continue the interactive browsing until the desired service is identified. One advantage of the interactive browsing over searching is that requestors can be more actively involved in the whole selection process, which is especially helpful for vague and negotiable QoS requirements. In this paper, we focus more on the browsing part.

Since interval data is a more proper type to represent QoS values, compared with the single valued numerical data, we propose to use interval clustering to group services together based on their QoS values, and present the QoS clusters to requestors so that they could have a better knowledge on the QoS value distribution pattern in the registry. Based on the initial clustering, requestors could choose a few clusters they are interested in, then the system would re-cluster this subset and present the re-clustered results, and it could repeat until requestors find their desired services. During this process, searching is always an alternative route of selecting services.

There are three major contributions of the paper. Firstly, to the best of our knowledge, it is a novel idea of considering QoS-based service selection as an integrated activity of searching and browsing and proposing an interactive QoS browsing mechanism. Secondly, we use an efficient clustering algorithm iteratively to help requestors get more refined and focused view of their interested QoS values in the interactive browsing process. Thirdly, we represent the QoS data for each service as a vector of interval data, which is more accurate, and use interval clustering instead of the traditional clustering algorithms so as to avoid the loss of information.

The rest of the paper is organized as follows. Section 2 reviews the related works. Section 3 describes the properties of the QoS data, explains the interval clustering algorithm which we believe is the most appropriate clustering algorithm for QoS data, and defines our interactive QoS browsing algorithm. Then in section 4, we explain our experiment steps, analyze the results, and then use one example to illustrate the interactive browsing procedure. Finally in section 5, we conclude the paper.

2 Related Works

There are three areas of research works we will review: QoS-based service selection, information seeking and interactive browsing on the web, and interval clustering.

Web service selection is a two-step process: searching for services which could match requestors' functional requirements, and making a selection of services which could also satisfy requestors' non-functional (i.e. QoS) requirements. In the second step, similar services are filtered on the hard-constraint QoS requirements, and then ranked based on the soft-constraint QoS requirements. There are many issues in QoS-based service selection. We mainly review the QoS models and selection algorithms.

Different QoS models have been proposed to include various QoS attributes. In [15], the author defines four categories of QoS attributes: runtime related, transaction support related, configuration management and cost related, and security related. In [20], QoS attributes are categorized into four types: performance, dependability, security, and finally the application-specific metrics. In many other papers [3] [12] [14], the necessity to include domain specific QoS is also recognized, as well as the individual requestor's unique need on the QoS criteria.

There are many different QoS-based selection mechanisms. In [14], a fair and open QoS computation model is proposed and implemented in a service registry. QoS values are normalized and similar qualities are grouped. Then a linear combination with user preference based weights is used to calculate the final QoS value. They also enforce a policing mechanism to prevent the manipulation of QoS values from requestors. In [12], optimal service selection is achieved through the multi-attribute decision theory methods, the declarative logic-based matching rules are specified instead of the hard-coded matching algorithms, and therefore the whole algorithm is more flexible. In [19], for each service, based on the previously collected quality data with its trustworthiness and credibility, a time series forecasting technique is used to predict its future quality conformance level, and a simple additive weighting method is used to calculate the final QoS value. In [3], the service domains and QoS specifications are treated as subspaces in a multidimensional space. The QoS parameters published by providers are modeled as point data, whereas the requestor's parameter specifications are represented as constraints on these points. So the subspace clustering can be used to identify the matching services.

Browsing and searching are considered as two complementary ways of accessing information on the web [5]. When users have specific information needs, they would submit a query to a search engine such as Google, and then try to find the result from the returned ranked list of web pages. When users are not looking for anything in particular, or don't know how to formulate a query properly, they could go to a directory site such as Yahoo, or use some navigation tools such as Scatter/Gather [6].

The basic idea of the Scatter/Gather browsing method [6] is that: given a document collection, the system scatters it into a small number of clusters, and generates a summary for each cluster and presents to the user; the user can then select one or more clusters for further study based on summaries; the selected clusters are gathered together and the system then applies clustering again to scatter this sub-collection into a small number of clusters and presents to the user; this process could continue until the individual desired document is identified. Since the efficiency is really important in this interactive browsing process, there are a few follow-up works such as [11] trying to improve the efficiency of the on-the-fly clustering algorithm to make the system more feasible for the real use.

Clustering is an unsupervised learning technique to identify the natural groupings of data objects based on distance or similarity measures between them. There are two types of clustering algorithms, namely, partitioning and hierarchical. The first type generates flat clusters where each object is distinctly grouped into separate clusters by iteratively relocating the cluster centers. The second type produces a tree like structure that progressively join the most similar data at each level of the hierarchy.

Most of the clustering algorithms deal with the vector data, and in the vector, each item is a numerical value. There is a branch of clustering algorithms which specially deal with the interval data or more generally symbolic data. Symbolic data analysis [8] is a novel way of analyzing multi-valued data variables. It can handle variables of type numerical, interval, categorical, enumeration and modal, in which interval data is the most common type of study. For the interval data, interval clustering algorithms could produce more accurate clustering results than applying traditional clustering algorithms on representative single point values (e.g. midpoints of intervals), and furthermore, the structure information of the interval data will not be lost.

In [7], a dynamic clustering algorithm is used for the interval data with a two-step relocation process, which involves identification of prototypes representing each cluster by the local optimization of an adequacy function, followed by the allocation of data individuals to the correct clusters using their proximity from the prototypes. The algorithm repeatedly re-identifies new cluster prototypes followed by the re-allocation step until the adequacy function converges. The proximity is measured by two adaptive versions of the city-block distance. In another paper [4], the dynamic clustering algorithm is used with Hausdorff distance measure and the two-component dissimilarity measure. Other than the partitioning algorithms discussed in above papers, the hierarchical clustering also can be used for interval data. In [10], an agglomerative algorithm for symbolic data based on the combined usage of similarity and dissimilarity measures are presented, and these proximity measures are defined on the basis of the position, span and content of symbolic objects. There are also various other methods available for interval clustering, which are not reviewed here.

The work described in [13] is quite similar to ours because it also uses interval clustering to group QoS data. But there are two key differences: firstly, it is more for service providers, to present the clustered QoS values to them so that they could have a better idea about what range of QoS values they should provide in order to attract more requestors and compete with other providers, whereas our approach is more for requestors to select desired services; secondly, it only considers a single QoS attribute for clustering whereas our method considers QoS vectors which include the whole range of QoS attributes.

3   Interactive QoS Browsing for Service Selection

3.1   QoS Attributes of Web Services

There are many QoS attributes [15] [20] proposed for the web service selection. A few common ones include response time, throughput, reliability, availability, scalability, reputation, cost, and a few security properties such as authentication, confidentiality, etc. In this paper, we consider three important quality attributes – reliability, response time, and cost. Reliability is defined as the ability of a service to perform its required function following the stated conditions for a specified time period. Response time is defined as the difference between the time when a service is invoked and when the service invocation is completed. And cost or price is given by the amount of money paid by requestors to service providers on invoking and using the service successfully or with failure depending on the terms signed in agreement documents. Although cost is not part of QoS as specified in [20], it is considered as a QoS attribute in many other papers. In this paper, for the simplicity reason, we still consider it as a QoS attribute. Our proposed algorithm is flexible to include any number of quality attributes. However, in the experiment, it is only tested on these three attributes.

In many QoS selection papers [12] [15] [19] [21], QoS value is assumed to be numerical. Below is a segment of a sample tModel with the QoS information [21]:

>   *<keyedReference tModelKey= "uddi:uddi.org:QoS:Price"*
>   *keyName= "Price Per Transaction" keyValue= "0.01">*
>   *<keyedReference tModelKey= "uddi:uddi.org:QoS:ResponseTime"*
>   *keyName= "Average Response Time" keyValue= "0.05">*
>   *<keyedReference tModelKey= "uddi:uddi.org:QoS:Availability"*
>   *keyName= "Availability" keyValue= "99.99">*
>   *<keyedReference tModelKey= "uddi:uddi.org:QoS:Throughput"*
>   *keyName= "Throughput" keyValue= "500">*

From this example, we could see that each QoS attribute is measured by a single numerical value. However, it is only a simplified representation of the real values. For instance, response time is usually different in different service invocations, and so an average value like in this example can only approximate the actual delivered values. It would be more useful if the requestor could know the provider-promised upper and lower bound of this value. It is also more reasonable for providers to publish a value range of the response time instead of an average value. Even as in this example, an interval such as (0, 0.05) would be more clear. If we look at the availability, 99.99 refers to the minimum required availability, and in a more accurate way, availability should be (99.99, 100). Similarly throughput is also represented using the minimum value, it might be higher than this published value and the maximum possible value is restricted by the system capacity. The observation on these QoS attributes is also true for many other attributes, and therefore, we believe that the interval data should be a more accurate type to represent the QoS attribute. Sometimes, if the range is only fixed on one end (e.g. availability>99), it could be converted to two ends (e.g. 99<availability<100); or if the quality (e.g. price) is a single numerical value, it could still be converted to the interval data with both ends equal to this value. As pointed out in [3] [14], QoS values could also be Boolean or enumeration or other types. So the symbolic data is the most appropriate type to represent the QoS attribute. In this paper, since the three QoS attributes we choose are all interval data, we use interval data analysis instead of the more generic symbolic data analysis.

3.2 Iterative Clustering for QoS Browsing

In QoS-based web service selection, the main task for requestors is to find a service among a set of functionally similar services which also satisfies their quality requirements. It is very likely that requestors may not have any knowledge about the QoS value distribution in this set, and QoS offered by different providers might also change over time. Due to requestors' lack of knowledge and the dynamism of QoS values, we propose an interactive QoS browsing mechanism which could guide requestors in this selection process. Pure browsing is not feasible for a big collection such as the web, but for a smaller collection, it is an effective information seeking approach, which in fact is the case for our study. Another reason we choose the interactive browsing approach is that QoS-based selection usually involves the decision-making on the tradeoff among different QoS attributes, and it is more reasonable to include requestors in this process than doing it automatically for them. Automatic decision making algorithms need requestors to specify their preferences and constraints very clearly, which could be very hard for them due to their lack of knowledge or the vagueness of the QoS requirements. We believe that the user involvement in this QoS selection process is very important to make the best decision.

Clustering could organize a big collection into a small number of clusters so that it is more comprehensible. In this paper, we propose an interval cluster based interactive browsing algorithm which implements the similar functionality as Scatter/Gather [6] and is catered for the QoS data set instead of the document collection as in Scatter/Gather. Since the QoS values are symbolic data, we are going to use symbolic clustering algorithms or more specifically the interval clustering algorithms.

3.2.1 Interval Clustering

The input to our clustering algorithm is a set of QoS vectors, and each QoS vector includes intervals of p QoS attributes. Let $QS = \{Q_1, Q_2, ..., Q_n\}$ be a set of n QoS vectors described by p interval variables. Each QoS vector Q_i ($i = 1, 2, ..., n$) is represented as $([q_{1s,i}, q_{1e,i}], [q_{2s,i}, q_{2e,i}], ..., [q_{ps,i}, q_{pe,i}])$ where $q_{js,i}$ and $q_{je,i}$ ($j = 1, 2, ..., p$) represent the start and end points of interval values for the j-th QoS attribute of this vector. In this paper, we choose three QoS attributes and so the value of p is 3.

Both partitioning and hierarchical algorithms can be used for the interval data clustering. Through our preliminary experiment, we found that the partitioning algorithm is more efficient and also more effective than the hierarchical algorithm for the interval data. Therefore, we decide to use the partitioning interval clustering algorithm. Among different partitioning algorithms, we choose to use the dynamic clustering algorithm which is widely used in different interval clustering systems and known for its ability to globally optimize the data using simulated annealing [4] [7].

According to the dynamic clustering algorithm, our method searches for a partition $P = (C_1, C_2, ..., C_K)$ of QS in K clusters and a set of cluster prototypes $G = (G_1, G_2, ..., G_K)$ which locally optimizes an adequacy criterion $W(P, G)$ defined as,

$$W(P, G) = \sum_{k=1}^{K} \sum_{CQ_i \in C_k} D(CQ_i, G_k) \tag{1}$$

Where $D(CQ_i, G_k)$ is a dissimilarity measure between a QoS vector $CQ_i \in C_k$ and the cluster prototype G_k of C_k.

We use two different distance measures namely, city block [7] or Hausdorff [4] to calculate the dissimilarity between two QoS vectors. The city block distance and the Hausdorff distance are defined respectively as,

$$D_{CB}(Q_i, Q_j) = \sum_{h=1}^{p} (|q_{hs,i} - q_{hs,j}| + |q_{he,i} - q_{he,j}|) \tag{2}$$

$$D_H(Q_i, Q_j) = \sum_{h=1}^{p} \max(|q_{hs,i} - q_{hs,j}|, |q_{he,i} - q_{he,j}|) \tag{3}$$

We now discuss the steps of the dynamic interval clustering algorithm. It requires user input in the form of K, the desired number of clusters in the result. The steps are described below.

1. The algorithm is initialized by choosing a partition randomly, or choosing K distinct QoS vectors as prototypes $G_1, G_2, ..., G_K$ and then assigning the remaining vectors to the closest prototype to construct the initial partition.
2. The next step is to represent the cluster prototypes for the generated clusters as the median of the intervals. G_k $(k = 1, 2, ..., K)$ is represented as $([gq_{1s,k}, gq_{1e,k}], [gq_{2s,k}, gq_{2e,k}], ..., [gq_{ps,k}, gq_{pe,k}])$ where $gq_{js,k}$ is the median of $\{cq_{js,i}, CQ_i \in C_k\}$ and $gq_{je,k}$ is the median of $\{cq_{je,i}, CQ_i \in C_k\}$ $(j = 1, 2, ..., p)$.
3. This step allocates all the QoS vectors to the closest prototypes to form the new partitions.
4. The above two steps will be repeated until achieving the convergence of the algorithm, when the adequacy criterion (formula 1) reaches a stable value.

At the end, all the web services are clustered according to their QoS attributes and the result K clusters are presented to requestors.

3.2.2 Interactive Browsing

In order to implement the interactive browsing system, we use the dynamic interval clustering algorithm repeatedly. The whole browsing procedure is explained below.

1. Assume that we have used some algorithms to find out all the web services satisfying requestors' functional requirements. Given the QoS vectors of this set of services as the input to the dynamic clustering algorithm, we could get an initial clustering of all QoS vectors and these K clusters will be presented to requestors along with the prototype for each cluster, the size of the cluster, and the range of all QoS attribute values in the cluster. With these clusters and their attached information, requestors could have a rough idea about how the QoS values are distributed within the set.

2. Based on requestors' QoS requirements, they could choose one or more clusters among these K groups. Then the selected QoS vectors are input to the dynamic clustering algorithm again, and requestors could see the newly formed K_1 clusters, with a finer view on their interested QoS vectors.

3. Step 2 could be repeated iteratively until a desired service is identified, or requestors have had enough knowledge to formulate a good QoS query so that they could continue the selection process with searching. Each time, K_i ($i = 2$, 3, ...) clusters are constructed and presented to requestors and requestors can make their choices accordingly.

One of the problems we are facing is how we choose the K or K_i value. There are many possibilities. We could let requestors choose this value each time, or fix it as a pre-defined small number, or use some measurements to find an optimal value. In this paper, we use *nbclust* method [8] which tries to find a value that optimizes three different statistical indices as listed below.

- *C-H index:* $(B/(c-1))/(W/(n-c))$, where n is the total number of QoS vectors, and c is the number of clusters in the partition of the data set. B and W denote the total between-cluster sum of squared distances (distance between cluster prototypes) and the total within-cluster sum of squared distances, respectively.

- *C-index:* $(V - V_{min})/(V_{max} - V_{min})$, where V is the sum of within-cluster pair-wise distance. Optimal K value is fixed for the best minimal value 0 for *C-index*. This absolute minimum is attained when in a partition the biggest within-cluster dissimilarity is less than the smallest between-cluster dissimilarity.

- *Γ-index:* $(\Gamma_+ - \Gamma_-)/(\Gamma_+ + \Gamma_-)$. This measure compares the within-cluster and between-cluster pair-wise distances. The comparison is consistent (Γ_+) if within-in-cluster distance is strictly smaller than between-cluster distance and is inconsistent (Γ_-) otherwise. The maximum value for the index indicates an optimal K value.

The combination of a greater value for C-H index, a value closer or equal to 0 for C-index and a value closer or equal to 1 for Γ-index corresponds to the optimal K value. We will explain more details in the experiment part.

Our work is inspired by the Scatter/Gather system. However, there are some key differences between our approach and the Scatter/Gather method. Firstly, in Scatter/Gather system, the item to be clustered is a document, and it is usually represented as a vector of term weights which are numerical values. Whereas in our system, the clustering unit is a vector of service QoS values, and oftentimes, the QoS attribute is represented as symbolic data, or more commonly interval data. Secondly, the Scatter/Gather method uses partitioning clustering algorithm to form clusters, and in order to find seeds, they use two agglomerative hierarchical clustering algorithms: one is Buckshot which is faster and used in the real-time clustering, and the other is Fractionation which is more accurate and used in initial offline clustering. Whereas in our system, we use the dynamic interval clustering algorithm in both initial offline and the later iterative on-the-fly clustering and the seed points are chosen randomly. It is more efficient than using the hierarchical clustering algorithm to choose the seed points as in Scatter/Gather, whereas the effectiveness is not sacrificed according to our experiment results. Thirdly, the number of seeds in Scatter/Gather is a randomly chosen small number, whereas in our system, an optimal K could be identified by optimizing some statistical indices.

4 Experiments

There are two main purposes of the experiment: one is to show the effectiveness of the dynamic clustering algorithm; the other is to illustrate the interactive QoS browsing process with a sample data set, especially how iterative clustering can help zoom-in to requestor selected QoS vectors.

4.1 Experiments on Interval Clustering Algorithm

Since there are no standard data sets of web service QoS values available, we conducted our experiment on simulated data sets. In order to make sure the simulated data is close to the real data, we referred to the value ranges and distribution patterns of different QoS attributes in a real data set [1], and for service cost, we referred to a few publicly available services [2] [16]. The data sets comprise a collection of interval type vectors depicting various distribution patterns of QoS values, mainly for scenarios when there are natural data groupings. When the data is otherwise distributed, our approach may not work well. The data points are generated following a multivariate normal distribution with the independent components using mean vectors (μ) and covariance matrices (σ). Altogether we generated 15 data sets, representing different distribution patterns, e.g. distinct clusters, overlapping clusters, clusters close to each other, clusters far apart from each other, densely distributed clusters, sparsely distributed clusters, etc. Some data sets also have noise data added to make them closer to real data. Two representative data sets are shown in Table 1. The first group consists of 300 data points that are spread across three distinct clusters while the second group consists of 350 data points across three overlapping clusters.

Table 1. Distribution parameters for generating two data sets

	Input parameters
Data set 1: distinct clusters Total # of points = 300 Total # of clusters = 3	Group 1: (# of points = 100) $\mu_1 = 155$, $\mu_2 = 700$, $\mu_3 = 180$, $\sigma_1^2 = 64$, $\sigma_2^2 = 225$, $\sigma_3^2 = 144$ Group 2: (# of points = 100) $\mu_1 = 170$, $\mu_2 = 770$, $\mu_3 = 210$, $\sigma_1^2 = 25$, $\sigma_2^2 = 169$, $\sigma_3^2 = 196$ Group 3: (# of points = 100) $\mu_1 = 180$, $\mu_2 = 840$, $\mu_3 = 240$, $\sigma_1^2 = 9$, $\sigma_2^2 = 256$, $\sigma_3^2 = 169$
Data set 2: overlapping clusters (group 1 & 2 are overlapping) Total # of points = 350 Total # of clusters = 3	Group 1: (# of points = 150) $\mu_1 = 150$, $\mu_2 = 210$, $\mu_3 = 280$, $\sigma_1^2 = 25$, $\sigma_2^2 = 16$, $\sigma_3^2 = 9$ Group 2: (# of points = 100) $\mu_1 = 140$, $\mu_2 = 212$, $\mu_3 = 275$, $\sigma_1^2 = 25$, $\sigma_2^2 = 16$, $\sigma_3^2 = 9$ Group 3: (# of points = 100) $\mu_1 = 133$, $\mu_2 = 1745$, $\mu_3 = 90$, $\sigma_1^2 = 0.5$, $\sigma_2^2 = 9$, $\sigma_3^2 = 4$

The data points generated are used as seed points to compute normally distributed interval vectors using the equation: $([a-\gamma_1/2, a+ \gamma_1/2], [b-\gamma_2/2, b+ \gamma_2/2], [c-\gamma_3/2, c+ \gamma_3/2])$ [7]. The variables γ_1, γ_2 and γ_3 are values randomly drawn from predefined intervals and a, b and c refer to the three attributes of the seed point vectors. We used SODAS software [17] to run the clustering algorithm. A total of 50 replications per data set are generated to run and evaluate the performance.

In order to measure the performance, we use the corrected Rand (CR) index [7]. It compares the clusters produced in an a priori classification with the results of the clustering algorithm. The a priori classification in our case refers to the partition in the seed points generated, which equals to 3 for our data sets. CR index is a good choice of assessment because it is insensitive to the number of clusters in a given partition and to the distribution of data vectors within a cluster. The index value ranges from either [0,1] or [-1,1], with values closer to 1 indicating the correctness of the clustering results and values closer to 0 or -1 indicating a lower level of agreement between the clustering results and the prior classification.

First we compare the performance of dynamic clustering algorithm when using city block and Hausdorff distance measures respectively. Table 2 shows CR index values on two data sets when the value of K is set to 3. We could see that Hausdorff distance yields a slightly better result for data set 1 (distinct clusters), and we get mixed results for data set 2 (overlapping clusters). We conducted the same experiment on all 15 data sets, Hausdorff always performs better for distinct clusters, and when data overlaps more, city block sometimes performs better. Usually there is no big difference between their CR index values. It is also obvious that when the degree of overlapping becomes higher, CR index is getting lower. When data is well separated, we can achieve a very high CR index value.

Table 2. CR index for different distance measures on two data sets

Predefined intervals	Data set 1		Data set 2	
	City block	Hausdorff	City block	Hausdorff
$\gamma_1 = [1,4]$ $\gamma_2 = [1,8]$ $\gamma_3 = [1,8]$	0.9899	0.9899	0.7456	0.7593
$\gamma_1 = [1,8]$ $\gamma_2 = [1,16]$ $\gamma_3 = [1,16]$	0.9701	0.9701	0.7390	0.7390
$\gamma_1 = [1,12]$ $\gamma_2 = [1,24]$ $\gamma_3 = [1,24]$	0.9800	0.9899	0.7737	0.5287
$\gamma_1 = [1,16]$ $\gamma_2 = [1,32]$ $\gamma_3 = [1,32]$	0.9799	0.9799	0.4346	0.4806

We also tested whether we can find the optimal K value using the *nbclust* method. The optimal K value found is always 3, which matches with the actual value for our a priori partition. So it verifies the feasibility of using this method to find optimal K. Efficiency-wise, in average, the time to run the dynamic clustering algorithm (by using SODAS) is 5 seconds, and when *nbclust* method is used, the time is increased to 33 seconds, and we believe that both are acceptable for real-time usage.

4.2 Illustrating the Interactive QoS Browsing Process

The data set we used here is different from the previous ones. We generate 3 clusters, within each cluster, there are 3 sub-clusters which follow the multivariate normal distribution, and then we add some random points in each cluster and randomly in the whole space. With random points, we believe that it is closer to the real scenario. Table 3 shows the input parameters and the min-max value ranges for generating random points in the order of reliability, response time and price. The 3D representation of the data set is shown in Figure 1.

Table 3. Distribution parameters for generating data set 3

	Input parameters
Cluster 1 (150 points)	1: $\mu_1 = 154$, $\mu_2 = 212$, $\mu_3 = 188$, $\sigma_1^2 = 0.45$, $\sigma_2^2 = 6.5$, $\sigma_3^2 = 3$ 2: $\mu_1 = 157$, $\mu_2 = 213$, $\mu_3 = 189$, $\sigma_1^2 = 0.45$, $\sigma_2^2 = 7.25$, $\sigma_3^2 = 5$ 3: $\mu_1 = 155$, $\mu_2 = 220$, $\mu_3 = 190$, $\sigma_1^2 = 0.65$, $\sigma_2^2 = 10$, $\sigma_3^2 = 4$ $\gamma_1 = [0.5, 1]$, $\gamma_2 = [1, 2]$ and $\gamma_3 = [1, 5]$
Cluster 2 (140 points)	1: $\mu_1 = 165$, $\mu_2 = 420$, $\mu_3 = 160$, $\sigma_1^2 = 2.5$, $\sigma_2^2 = 6$, $\sigma_3^2 = 1.75$ 2: $\mu_1 = 178$, $\mu_2 = 435$, $\mu_3 = 162$, $\sigma_1^2 = 2.98$, $\sigma_2^2 = 3$, $\sigma_3^2 = 1.5$ 3: $\mu_1 = 186$, $\mu_2 = 420$, $\mu_3 = 161$, $\sigma_1^2 = 1.95$, $\sigma_2^2 = 6$, $\sigma_3^2 = 1.5$ $\gamma_1 = [0, 1]$, $\gamma_2 = [1, 2]$ and $\gamma_3 = [2, 3]$
Cluster 3 (150 points)	1: $\mu_1 = 191$, $\mu_2 = 250$, $\mu_3 = 240$, $\sigma_1^2 = 0.65$, $\sigma_2^2 = 6$, $\sigma_3^2 = 3$ 2: $\mu_1 = 195$, $\mu_2 = 251$, $\mu_3 = 241$, $\sigma_1^2 = 0.95$, $\sigma_2^2 = 8$, $\sigma_3^2 = 3$ 3: $\mu_1 = 192$, $\mu_2 = 248$, $\mu_3 = 261$, $\sigma_1^2 = 0.5$, $\sigma_2^2 = 6$, $\sigma_3^2 = 5$ $\gamma_1 = [0, 1]$, $\gamma_2 = [3, 7]$ and $\gamma_3 = [5, 10]$
Random set 1 (50)	[(74-80), (75-81)], [(100-113), (102-114)], [(89-95), (93-99)]
Random set 2 (50)	[(80-91), (89-100)], [(197-224), (205-225)], [(69-83), (78-91)]
Random set 3 (40)	[(88-96), (97-105)], [(111-132), (118-136)], [(114-127), (124-138)]
Random set 4 (100)	[(69-104), (82-116)], [(94-185), (120-210)], [(47-114), (59-127)]

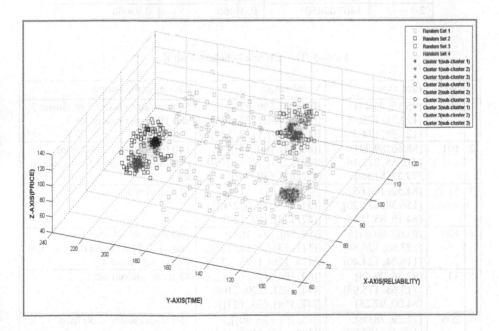

Fig. 1. 3D representation of data set 3

Now we illustrate the interactive QoS browsing using this data set. First the whole data set is fed into the dynamic clustering algorithm. In order to find the optimal K, we measure the three indices when $0 < K < 9$, and the result is shown in Table 4. In *nbclust* method, the ideal case is that we could find a K value which is consistently the best for all three indices. If there is a conflict on the best K value for different indices, we should try to find a K which performs the best for two indices, or the next optimal option is a K which has a more obvious advantage on one index than the other two. Following this principle, we choose optimal K as 6 because it is the best for C-index and Γ-index, although it is not the best for C-H index.

After we set K as 6, we do the first iteration of clustering. Since we haven't implemented the full prototype yet, we just show the result in a table format. Table 5 shows the clustering result in the first level. For each cluster, we present its size

Table 4. C-H index, C-index and Γ-index for different K values in the first round

K	C-H index	C-index	Γ-index
9	804.96862	0.01479	0.95104
8	910.78817	0.01091	0.94830
7	743.93457	0.02902	0.93490
6	*1182.20291*	*0.00525*	*0.96293*
5	1144.69582	0.01144	0.95409
4	1274.30594	0.02241	0.94014
3	1068.44013	0.08229	0.81188
2	1407.47450	0.04466	0.93666

Table 5. The first level clusters with K=6

	Size	Prototype	Value range	Cluster composition
1	69	[95.75, 96.44], [122.21, 125.8], [125.98, 134.35]	[[95, 97], [96, 97]], [[119, 125], [122, 128]], [[124, 129], [132, 137]]	50 from sub-cluster 3 of cluster 3, and 19 from random set 3
2	191	[88.66, 89.34], [210.55, 212.16], [79.27, 81.88]	[[80, 94], [80, 95]], [[207, 213], [208, 215]], [[77, 81], [80, 84]]	140 from cluster 2, 50 from random set 2, and 1 from random set 4
3	51	[84.52, 100.65], [156.39, 174.20], [84.19, 85.18]	[[69, 104], [82, 116]], [[94, 185], [120, 210]], [[47, 114], [59, 127]]	51 from random set 4
4	130	[96.02, 96.64], [123.60, 126.84], [116.04, 124.40]	[[88, 96], [97, 104]], [[111, 131], [118, 135]], [[114, 126], [125, 137]]	100 from sub-cluster 1 and 2 of cluster 3, 21 from random set 3, 9 from random set 4
5	33	[82.36, 99.48], [113.65, 175.93], [84.00, 97.28]	[[69, 104], [82, 116]], [[94, 185], [120, 210]], [[47, 114], [59, 127]]	33 from random set 4
6	206	[77.29, 78.06], [106.35, 107.98], [92.82, 95.89]	[[75, 79], [76, 80]], [[102, 113], [103, 114]], [[89, 96], [92, 99]]	150 from cluster 1, 50 from random set 1, 6 from random set 4

(the number of points in the cluster), the prototype - $[gq_{1s,k}, gq_{1e,k}], ([gq_{2s,k}, gq_{2e,k}], [gq_{3s,k}, gq_{3e,k}])$ (1 for reliability, 2 for response time and 3 for price, and k is from 1 to 6), the value range for each QoS attribute ([min-reliability, max-reliability] [min-time, max-time] [min-price, max-price]), and the composition of the cluster. From this table, we could see that all 3 clusters in the original data set have been correctly identified, and the random data is clustered into different groups based on their values.

By checking these clusters, suppose a requestor selects cluster 2 and 4 based on price and reliability. Again we need to find optimal K for this level. Table 6 shows the results for the 3 indices. We only show K values up to 5 due to the space constraint.

Table 6. C-H index, C-index and Γ-index for different K values in the second round

K	C-H index	C-index	Γ-index
5	2090.66573	0.01459	0.78485
4	2615.39297	0.01775	0.78276
3	3763.48829	0.01364	0.85353
2	6961.86844	0.00002	1.00000

From the table, we could see that the optimal choice is $K=2$. But since we have 2 clusters already and we want to zoom in to see more details about these two clusters, we would choose the second optimal choice instead, which is $K=3$. Now we set K as 3 and do the second iteration of clustering. Table 7 shows the clustering result in the second level. We could see that sub-clusters have been successfully identified. If we choose cluster 2 and continue the process, we could get results as shown in Table 8.

Table 7. The second level clusters with K=3

	Size	Prototype	Value range	Cluster composition
1	44	[82.65, 83.13], [209.00, 210.58], [78.61, 81.13]	[[80, 85], [80, 86]], [[207, 212], [209, 214]], [[77, 81], [80, 83]]	40 from sub-cluster 1 of cluster 2, 3 from random set 2, and 1 from random set 4
2	130	[96.02, 96.64], [123.60, 126.84], [116.04, 124.40]	[[88, 96], [97, 104]], [[111, 131], [118, 135]], [[114, 126], [125, 137]]	100 from sub-cluster 1 and 2 of cluster 3, 21 from random set 3, and 9 from random set 4
3	147	[89.50, 90.22], [211.26, 212.87], [79.51, 82.16]	[[80, 94], [80, 95]], [[207, 213], [208, 215]], [[77, 81], [80, 84]]	100 from sub-cluster 2 and 3 of cluster 2, and 47 from random set 2

From these three rounds of running clustering algorithm, natural clusters existing in the original data set could be identified, and we could also achieve the zoom-in effect in the re-clustering step, which is very helpful to give requestors more and more detailed views on their interested QoS values. In the above illustration, each time we try to find the optimal K first, and then do the clustering. Alternatively, requestors could specify a fixed K value, skip the step of finding optimal K and make the process

Table 8. The third level clusters with K=4

	Size	Prototype	Value range	Cluster composition
1	52	[82.65, 83.13], [209.00, 210.58], [78.61, 81.13]	[[94, 96], [95, 97]], [[121, 127], [124, 130]], [[113, 117], [121, 126]]	50 from sub-cluster 1 of cluster 3, 1 from sub-cluster 2 of cluster 3, and 1 from random set 4
2	20	[96.02, 96.64], [123.60, 126.84], [116.04, 124.40]	[[88, 96], [97, 105]], [[111, 132], [118, 136]], [[114, 127], [124, 138]]	20 from random set 3
3	6	[89.50, 90.22], [211.26, 212.87], [79.51, 82.16]	[[69, 104], [82, 116]], [[94, 185], [120, 210]], [[47, 114], [59, 127]]	6 from random set 4
4	52	[89.50, 90.22], [211.26, 212.87], [79.51, 82.16]	[[96, 98], [97, 99]], [[121, 128], [123, 130]], [[114, 119], [122, 128]]	49 from sub-cluster 2 of cluster 3, 1 from random set 3, and 2 from random set 4

faster. The problem is that user-defined K value might not work well for a tightly formed cluster in which all data points are very close to each other, and in this case, the cluster will be randomly partitioned into a few highly overlapping groups.

5 Conclusions

In this paper, we explain our idea of using interactive QoS browsing mechanism to help the web service selection process. Because of requestors' lack of knowledge on QoS distributions in the registry, vagueness of the QoS requirements, and dynamism of the QoS values offered by providers, we believe that browsing is necessary for QoS-based service selection. Since most of the QoS data is interval data, or more generally symbolic data, we propose using interval clustering algorithm for the QoS browsing. Starting from the initial set of services with the similar functionality, we apply the dynamic interval clustering algorithm on their QoS vectors to get the initial clusters. Then with requestors' selection on a subset of clusters and re-clustering on this subset, they could have more and more detailed views on their preferred QoS vectors. The experiment results show the effectiveness of the interval clustering algorithm, and we also illustrate the process of the interactive QoS browsing.

There are a few directions we can work on in the future. We could implement a prototype of the QoS browsing system. With a visual interface showing the distribution of data points in the clusters and related information such as prototypes, sizes, value ranges, and deviation levels of the clusters, requestors could make a more informed decision to choose the best service satisfying their QoS requirements. We are aware that the proposed approach may not work well for all QoS data distribution patterns, and therefore we would like to find out under what situations it works better. In order to evaluate the performance, we could define some objective measurements (e.g. the time or the path length of locating the desired service), or conduct a user study to get users' subject opinions on the performance. We would also like to apply the more generic symbolic clustering algorithms and test the performance.

Acknowledgments. This work is partially sponsored by Natural Science and Engineering Research Council of Canada (grant 299021-07) and the 863 Program of China under award 2008AA01Z12.

References

1. Al-Masri, E., Mahmoud, Q.H.: QoS-based Discovery and Ranking of Web Services. In: 6th International Conference on Computer Communications and Networks, pp. 529–534 (2007)
2. Amazon, http://aws.amazon.com
3. Bianchini, D., De Antonellis, V., Melchiori, M.: QoS in Ontology-based Service Classification and Discovery. In: 15th International Workshop on Database and Expert Systems Applications, pp. 145–150 (2004)
4. Chavent, M., De Carvalho, F.A.T., Lechevallier, Y., Verde, R.: New Clustering Methods for Interval Data. Computational Statistics 21(2), 211–229 (2006)
5. Choo, C.W., Detlor, B., Turnbull, D.: Information Seeking on the Web – an Integrated Model of Browsing and Searching. In: 62nd Annual Meeting of the American Society for Information Science, pp. 3–16 (1999)
6. Cutting, D., Karger, D.R., Pederson, J., Turkey, J.: Scatter/Gather: A Cluster-based Approach to Browsing Large Documents. In: 15th Annual International ACM SIGIR Conference on Research and Development in Information Retrieval, pp. 318–329 (1992)
7. De Souza, R.M.C.R., De Carvalho, F.A.T.: Clustering of Interval Data Based on City-Block Distances. Pattern Recognition Letters 25(3), 353–365 (2004)
8. Diday, E., Noirhomme-Fraiture, M.: Symbolic Data Analysis and the SODAS Software. Wiley-Interscience, Hoboken (2008)
9. Dong, X., Halevy, A., Madhavan, J., Nemes, E., Zhang, J.: Similarity Search for Web Services. In: 30th International Conference on Very Large Data Bases, pp. 372–383 (2004)
10. Gowda, K.C., Ravi, T.R.: Agglomerative Clustering of Symbolic Objects Using the Concepts of Both Similarity and Dissimilarity. Pattern Recognition Letters 16(6), 647–652 (1995)
11. Ke, W., Sugimoto, C.R., Mostafa, J.: Dynamicity vs. Effectiveness: A User Study of a Clustering Algorithm for Scatter/Gather. In: 32nd Annual International ACM SIGIR Conference on Research and Development in Information Retrieval, pp. 19–26 (2009)
12. Lamparter, S., Ankolekar, A., Studer, R., Grimm, S.: Preference-based Selection of Highly Configurable Web Services. In: 16th International Conference on World Wide Web, pp. 1013–1022 (2007)
13. Li, S.M., Ding, C., Chi, C.H., Deng, J.: Adaptive Quality Recommendation Mechanism for Software Service Provisioning. In: IEEE International Conference on Web Services, pp. 169–176 (2008)
14. Liu, Y.T., Ngu, A.H., Zeng, L.Z.: QoS Computation and Policing in Dynamic Web Service. In: 13th International Conference on World Wide Web, pp. 66–73 (2004)
15. Ran, S.: A Model for Web Services Discovery with QoS. ACM SIGecom Exchanges 4(1), 1–10 (2003)
16. Salesforce, http://www.salesforce.com
17. SODAS software, http://www.info.fundp.ac.be/asso/
18. Stroulia, E., Wang, Y.: Structural and Semantic Matching for Assessing Web-Service Similarity. International Journal of Cooperative Information Systems, Special Issue: Service-Oriented Computing 14(4), 407–437 (2005)

19. Vu, L.H., Hauswirth, M., Aberer, K.: QoS-based Service Selection and Ranking with Trust and Reputation Management. In: International Conference on Cooperative Information Systems, pp. 446–483 (2005)
20. Wang, Y., Vassileva, J.: Toward Trust and Reputation Based Web Service Selection: A Survey. International Transactions on Systems Science and Applications 3(2), 118–132 (2007)
21. Xu, Z., Martin, P., Powley, W., Zulkernine, F.: Reputation-Enhanced QoS-based Web Services Discovery. In: IEEE International Conference on Web Services, pp. 249–256 (2007)

An Orchestration as a Service Infrastructure Using Grid Technologies and WS-BPEL

A. Höing[1], G. Scherp[2], S. Gudenkauf[2], D. Meister[3], and A. Brinkmann[3]

[1] Technische Universität Berlin, Complex and Distributed IT Systems,
Einsteinufer 17, 10587 Berlin, Germany
andre.hoeing@tu-berlin.de
[2] OFFIS Institute for Information Technology, Technology Cluster EAI,
Escherweg 2, 26121 Oldenburg, Germany
{stefan.gudenkauf,guido.scherp}@offis.de
[3] University of Paderborn, Paderborn Center for Parallel Computing,
Fürstenallee 11, 33100 Paderborn, Germany
{dmeister,brinkmann}@uni-paderborn.de

Abstract. The BIS-Grid project, as part of the German D-Grid initiative, investigates service orchestration using Grid service technologies to show how such technologies can be employed for information systems integration, especially when crossing enterprise boundaries. Small and medium enterprises will be enabled to integrate heterogeneous business information systems and to use external resources and services with affordable effort.

In this paper, we discuss our Orchestration as a Service (OaaS) paradigm and present the BIS-Grid OaaS infrastructure. This infrastructure is based upon service extensions to the Grid middleware UNICORE 6 to use an arbitrary WS-BPEL workflow engine and standard WS-BPEL to orchestrate both plain Web services and stateful, WSRF-based Grid services. We report on the evaluation scenarios at our industrial application partners and on the applied service modeling methodology.

1 Introduction

The integration of heterogeneous information systems, referred to as Enterprise Application Integration (EAI), is crucial in order to map business processes to the technical system level. To do so, integration is often achieved by service orchestration in service-oriented architectures (SOA). Web services are commonly used to create SOA since they enable service orchestration and hide the underlying technical infrastructure. SOA and Web service technologies are also the basic technologies for the newly emerging Cloud computing paradigm. Cloud computing provides easy access to IT infrastructures, computing platforms, or complete applications. This characteristics of cloud computing are also referred to as *Infrastructure as a Service* (IaaS), *Platform as a Service* (PaaS), and *Software as a Service* (SaaS). As example, Amazon offers its IaaS product Elastic

L. Baresi, C.-H. Chi, and J. Suzuki (Eds.): ICSOC-ServiceWave 2009, LNCS 5900, pp. 301–315, 2009.

Compute Cloud (EC2)[1], but also others in the context of its Amazon Web Services platform. An IaaS open source implementation using the same Web services interfaces as EC2 is available from the EUCALYPTUS project [9].

Cloud services are designed as on-demand services as they only charge what users actually consume. Therefore, they are especially interesting for small, medium, and start-up enterprises that need highly scalable IT infrastructures and/or do not want to run the respective IT infrastructures on their own. However, such companies also have the need to map their business processes to the technical system level, integrating outsourced cloud services as well as in-house-hosted services. Nowadays, many companies offer consultant services supporting small enterprises to identify their key business processes and to create integrated IT environments by the introduction of in-house orchestration engines. This brings up the idea of *Orchestration as a Service* (OaaS), meaning that the orchestration engine is hosted in a cloud environment, directly to be maintained by the OaaS provider. Considering the security and privacy of the deployed workflows and their data, such an orchestration engine should be designed as a multi-tenant service, decreasing costs since hardware can be shared over several customers.

In the BIS-Grid project, we focus on realizing EAI using Grid service technologies. Our major objective is to proof that Grid technologies are feasible for information systems integration, especially when traversing enterprise boundaries. Small and medium enterprises shall be enabled to integrate heterogeneous business information systems and to use external resources and services with affordable effort, even across company boundaries. To do so, we propose and regard *Orchestration as a Service* (OaaS) as the primary infrastructure paradigm. This paper is organized as follows. OaaS is discussed in Sec. 2, and the BIS-Grid OaaS infrastructure is presented in Sec. 3, including our OaaS-capable workflow engine and the general security infrastructure. Section 4 presents our application scenarios and describes the applied service modeling methodology. After the presentation of related work in Sec. 5 a conclusion is given in Sec. 6.

2   Orchestration as a Service

Integration is a topic for both industry and research for many years in order to enable the seamless interaction of (heterogeneous) applications. Modern integration solutions adopted the service-oriented architecture (SOA) design paradigm which is tightly coupled with the representation of business logic. This means that all applications are encapsulated by enclosed, loosely coupled, often low-level services which are composed to business processes. Such a business process, often referred to as service orchestration, is often modeled graphically in order to develop executable workflow representations. The Web Services Business Process Execution Language (WS-BPEL) [10], an OASIS standard to orchestrate Web services, is an example of such a representation. Commonly, it is regarded as a key technology to build SOA, and to offer service orchestrations itself as Web

---

[1] http://aws.amazon.com/ec2

services. This enables the use of low-level processes to build complex services on a higher level.

The use of loosely coupled services in SOA allows to dynamically switch the location of invoked services in order to utilize services offered by an external provider instead of local services. Thus, SOA can be considered as an enabling technology to outsource IT infrastructure and corresponding services to reduce IT costs. Grid and the upcoming Cloud technologies are examples for realizing such outsourcing scenarios. Based on SOA and the rapid development of Internet technologies several service providers emerged that offer services known as *Cloud*. The general idea behind Cloud is that services can be accessed on demand after a short setup time based on a pay-per-use utility model. As the range of Cloud services is highly diverse a classification in the manner of "* as a Service" is widely adopted at present. Such services can be divided into three categories: Infrastructure as a Service (IaaS), Platform as a Service (PaaS) and Software as a Service (SaaS) [12]. In brief, IaaS represents the service-based access to (virtualized) computing resources as storage and processing power, PaaS represents the service-based access to a software platform that enables the custom development of (scalable) applications that are normally executed on a virtualized infrastructure. SaaS represents the service-based access to a specific software product (e. g., ERP software) or a certain functionality (e. g., creditworthiness check). Furthermore, in the following order, IaaS, PaaS, and SaaS are considered as subsequent abstraction layers to the executing infrastructure. In our opinion such services can also be provided by utilizing Grid technologies which are in general highly related to Cloud technologies [12].

Microsoft BizTalk Server[2] or SAP XI[3] are actual commercial integration platforms that can execute business processes and suitable for SOA integration. In order to run such a platform costs such as licenses, hardware and system administrators have to be considered. Many companies such as small and medium enterprises (SMEs) are not able to finance or operate such an infrastructure although they certainly have needs for integration. Even freely available products like Sun's OpenESB[4] are hard to set-up and maintain in a productive manner. Thus, our approach is to offer such an integration platform as an external service which we call *Orchestration as a Service*(OaaS). Thereby, we regard OaaS as a specialization of PaaS, as process developers are able to develop, deploy and manage custom business processes, and SaaS, as end users can use the functionality of deployed business processes as services. Our OaaS solution is build upon the WS-BPEL-based BIS-Grid engine which is developed in the BIS-Grid project and described in Sec. 3 in detail.

In summary, the described OaaS scenario must meet the requirements *Grid compatibility*, *SOA compatibility* and *WS-BPEL compatibility*. Beside OaaS we considered further deployment scenarios depending on the degree of Grid utilization of the involved components, namely the BIS-Grid engine and orchestrated

---

[2] http://www.microsoft.com/biztalk/en/us/default.aspx

[3] http://www.sap.com/platform/netweaver/pdf/BWP_SB_ExchangeInfrastructure.pdf

[4] https://open-esb.dev.java.net

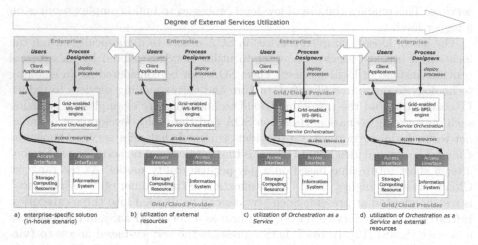

Fig. 1. Degree of Grid utilization

services as information systems. This ranges from (a) a pure in-house scenario, in which all components are deployed within a company, up to (d) a complete Grid scenario, in which each component is located in a Grid or Cloud infrastructure, see Fig. 1. The scenarios (b) and (c) are alternatives in which involved components are partially outsourced. In our case the in-house scenario (a) and the OaaS scenario (c) are currently regarded as most realistic since outsourcing information systems to Grid or Cloud providers often raises serious security concerns. So the philosophy is to keep all data services in-house and relevant data for orchestration and integration may leave the company on demand under ensuring certain security standards[5], see Sec. 3.2.

3   BIS-Grid OaaS Infrastructure

This section describes the BIS-Grid engine that is used to realize the technical side of the OaaS infrastructure. First, in Sec. 3.1 we describe the architecture of the orchestration engine, including the components of the engine and how they interact with each other. Second, we describe the security infrastructure for authentication and authorization in Sec. 3.2, also addressing privacy issues for realizing a multi-tenant environment.

3.1   BIS-Grid Engine Architecture

The BIS-Grid engine was designed with regard to its applicability in our OaaS scenario, see Sec. 2. This means the engine meets the following requirements:

---

[5] Beside the technical and organizational issues discussed in this paper, this also involves legal issues to be covered which are not part of the BIS-Grid project.

- *Grid compatibility*: The BIS-Grid engine is based on the Grid middleware UNICORE 6.
- *SOA compatibility*: As UNICORE 6 is based on Web services which is a key technology to build SOA.
- *WS-BPEL compatibility*: The BIS-Grid engine utilizes an arbitrary standard WS-BPEL engine to execute workflows.
- *Security*: The BIS-Grid engine supports authorization and authentication supporting a fine-grained role-based access control.

A more detailed view on the BIS-Grid engine's architecture is depicted in Fig. 2. The key concept is to use an arbitrary WS-BPEL engine, in our case ActiveBPEL, for workflow execution that is encapsulated by a *Grid proxy* based on service extensions to UNICORE 6. These service extensions enable interoperability between WS-BPEL and Grid environments by the support of the Web Service Resource Framework (WSRF) and Grid security. WSRF is an OASIS standard developed by the Grid community in order to enable stateless Web services to become stateful. This is essential, for instance, for job submission and data transfer services since they have a state by nature. WSRF-based Web services are also called Grid services, their states are represented by service instances and are stored in so called *resource properties*. Such properties can be accessed or manipulated by corresponding WSRF Web service methods. We discuss Grid security separately in Sec. 3.2.

The BIS-Grid service extensions mentioned above are the *Workflow Management Service* and the *Workflow Service* which are both realized as Grid services.

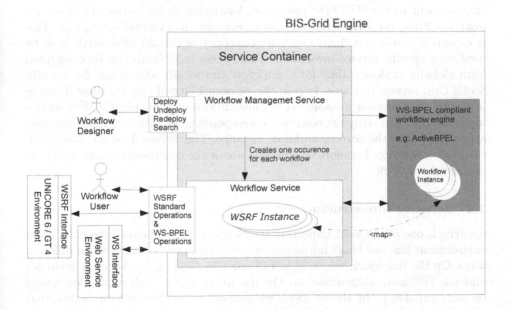

Fig. 2. The BIS-Grid engine architecture

The Workflow Management Service is initially deployed in the UNICORE 6 service container and provides methods for workflow management (i. e., deployment, redeployment, and undeployment of workflows). When a WS-BPEL workflow is deployed, a specialized version of the generic Workflow Service is created on-demand and hot-deployed to the UNICORE 6 service container. Thus, each deployed workflow in the WS-BPEL engine has a corresponding Workflow Service in UNICORE 6. A Workflow Service provides the same interface as its WS-BPEL workflow counterpart. The state of a workflow execution and additional configurations such as security credentials (see Sec. 3.2) are exposed by the corresponding Grid service instance as resource properties according to the WSRF standard. Since a workflow execution in the WS-BPEL engine is also regarded as an instance, each workflow execution is represented by two instances, one Grid service instance in the UNICORE 6 service container of the BIS-Grid engine, and one workflow instance in the WS-BPEL engine.

The communication between the BIS-Grid service extensions and the WS-BPEL engine depends on the used functionality. For management functions like workflow deployment and undeployment or workflow monitoring an engine-specific adapter is used. This adapter is pluggable and can be exchanged to support other WS-BPEL engines. The communication during workflow execution is based on standard Web service calls (SOAP) whereas outgoing messages (i. e., the invocation of external services within the workflow) must be sent to a HTTP proxy running in the UNICORE 6 container. Most Web service containers should provide a HTTP proxy configuration. If supported, the secure HTTPS protocol can be used, too. As each workflow execution has two instances, it is ensured that outgoing messages that originate from a workflow instance and that are sent to the HTTP(S) proxy, are forwarded to the correct Grid service instance. Then, the Grid service instance performs the external service call. This is especially important due to security concerns as certain credentials may be used for a specific service invocation. Thus, these credentials can be configured both globally at design time for a workflow and locally at runtime for a workflow's Grid service instance. It is in the responsibility of the workflow designer to ensure that ingoing messages (i. e., invocations of a workflow's Web service method), that primarily are send to a corresponding Workflow Service instance, are forwarded to the correct workflow instance. This is based on the WS-BPEL correlation concept. For more information about the described instance mapping please refer to [5,6].

3.2   Security Infrastructure

Security is one of the most important issues when setting up a Cloud computing environment like our OaaS infrastructure. Security can be achieved on different ways. On the one hand, we could install one BIS-Grid engine for each customer and use IP-based authentication. On the other hand, such a solution would be very expensive. In this section, we propose a security infrastructure that guarantees authentication, role based access control, and information privacy. To lower start-up and maintenance costs, we require a solution with minimal costs and maintenance overhead. Furthermore, credential delegation is an urgently needed feature. This enables the user to delegate rights to the OaaS environment to invoke external services in his name meanwhile the OaaS provider himself has naturally no access to that service.

Nowadays, Grid security is based on personalized X.509 certificates issued by a Certificate Authority (CA). Everyone participating in the Grid must trust this CA and authenticate himself with this CA or an associated Registration Authority (RA). Rights are not granted on business roles but on membership to a virtual organization. This scenario is not applicable for the business domain. A company, possibly having several hundred employees and high employee fluctuation can not send each new employee to a RA. To reduce maintenance overhead, rights must be bound to business roles and not to organizational membership. Hence, a distributed identity management system with the possibility to grant or revoke role-based permissions in a short time is necessary for OaaS.

We decided to build the security infrastructure up on well-known standards. SAML Assertions [11] are capable to fulfill most of our requirements. Arbitrary attributes, as roles and affiliation, can be included into an assertion. Such assertions are issued by an identity management system. SAML also provides the capability to express fine-grained credential delegation rights, expressing what entity is allowed to process what activity until what timestamp. For describing rights, we use XACML Policies [8] that are also well-known and very flexible and fine-grained if required. Access decisions can be described as rules, that define the applicability of a rule by means of the user, targeted resource, and the desired action. Furthermore, conditions that express dependencies between these can be formulated. Users are identified by the sum of all attributes included in the SAML assertion or/an via additional attributes requested during authorization process. Therefore, the policy designer must be aware of the organizational structures of the enterprises to describe the access rights correctly.

As technical infrastructure for an appropriate distributed identity management system with low maintenance costs and the capability to integrate different identity management systems we suggest the Shibboleth-based system[6]. This solution prevents the users from all complex security configurations. In combination with Grid-Shib[7], the system is able to automatically issue short-lived certificates (SLC) together with a SAML assertion including the user's business roles. Welch et al. described such an architecture in more detail [13]. The SLC is used to establish a SSL connection between the user and the BIS-Grid engine so that transport layer security is guaranteed. The major advantage is the seamless integration of existing identity management systems such as Active Directory or OpenLDAP with the Shibboleth system. These internally hosted and maintained systems can obtain and check credentials as well as supply attributes, so-called campus attributes. SLCs only have short lifetimes, usually one million seconds (circa 11 days), so that all roles and the connected rights are invalid after this period.

---

[6] http://shibboleth.internet2.edu/

[7] http://gridshib.globus.org/

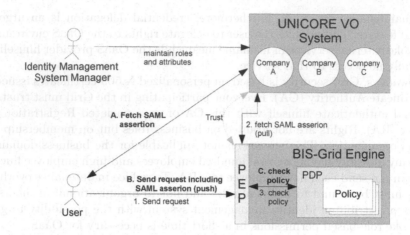

Fig. 3. Interaction between the BIS-Grid engine and UVOS

Because of simplicity of the exemplary evaluation, we decided not to set up a complete Shibboleth environment for our OaaS prototype but we use a similar solution that also provides the urgently needed SAML Attribute Assertions. The UNICORE Virtual Organisations System (UVOS)[8] allows the administration of user identities combined with arbitrary attributes for each identity. Additionally, hierarchical organizations can be mapped to hierarchical organized groups as well as attaching attributes to all members of a group. Groups or sub-groups members and attributes can be managed by different administrators. All UVOS-managed information can be queried by SAML2-compatible applications [3] and UVOS answers with a signed SAML assertion including all attributes (groups affiliations, group attributes, and global attributes). The combination of UVOS and UNICORE 6 are fully integrated and well-tested in the Chemomentum project, wherein UVOS was developed[9].

UNICORE 6 (and for this reason the BIS-Grid engine, too) supports two mechanism for assertion retrieval: push and pull. Push (cp. Fig. 3 A-C) means that the user authenticates himself at the UVOS server and retrieves his signed assertion that he attaches to the request to the BIS-Grid engine. Pull (cp. Fig. 3 1-3) uses the distinguished name of the user's certificate to fetch the assertion itself from the UVOS server. Nevertheless, there are two major disadvantages of UVOS compared to the Shibboleth solution. First, the user does not obtain a SLC for establishing TLS or for signing credential delegation assertions to delegate trust to the BIS-Grid workflow engine. Hence, each user must still own a standard X.509 certificate. Second, there is no integration of local identity management systems. This means that all identity information must be maintained a second time, beside the already existing company-local identity management system, either by the OaaS provider or by the companies themselves.

---

[8] http://uvos.chemomentum.org/
[9] http://chemomentum.org/

Hot deployment of Workflow Service also demands the hot deployment of security policies. We established such a hot deployment of XACML policies by adding new rules to the Policy Decision Point (PDP) that is part of the BIS-Grid deployment package. However, the possibility to add new policies also brings up the danger of misuse, for example, adding policies that affects other services. We limit the degree of freedom of newly inserted XACML rules in such a way that the rules must be limited to the newly created Workflow Service. Otherwise the deployment of the policy will fail.

After discussing authentication and authorization, we have to consider privacy. If several companies work with the same OaaS infrastructure, it must be ensured that only authorized users can see *what workflows are deployed* or *what workflows are currently running*. Authorized, in this case, does not only mean that the user must have the right to deploy a workflow but the system must also distinguish between affiliations or even departments during information retrieval operations. The same applies to running workflow instances.

We established means to filter information when discovery operations are used that must be accessible from different companies due to architectural issues, for example, creating new Workflow Management Service instances or searching for already created instances. Therefore, we store enriched information about the creator of an instance in the instances itself. As an example, instances of the Workflow Management Service store the creator's distinguished name, his affiliation, and his business role. When someone else searches for all deployed workflows, the BIS-Grid engine will only show deployed workflows matching the same affiliation and business role. Both must be included in the signed SAML assertion the requester presents. A similar filter also guarantees privacy for searching for instances of a Workflow Service. All other information depends on WSRF instances and are protected via the XACML policies.

4   Application Scenarios

We evaluate our OaaS approach in two business scenarios motivated by our industrial project partners, CeWe Color[10] and KIESELSTEIN Group[11]. CeWe Color is the number one services partner for first-class trade brands on the European photographic market supplying stores and internet retailers with photographic products, and KIESELSTEIN Group is one of the global market leaders in the field of wire drawing and draw-peeling for the automotive industry. Both partners have strong needs for enterprise application integration: CeWe Color to integrate enterprise data for unified access for call center agents, and KIESELSTEIN Group to improve access to, and retrieval and maintenance of product and project data. The overall goal of these application scenarios is to investigate the feasibility of EAI based on Grid technologies and the OaaS paradigm by prototypical realization.

---

[10] http://www.cewecolor.de
[11] http://www.kieselstein-group.com

For CeWe Color, the impact of digital photography affected requirements to business information systems (BIS) and processes, opened up new distribution channels, and facilitated new product lines. Product mass customization and the need to flexibly respond to market development demand BIS that can adapt dynamically. Regarding the call center scenario, information of different sources must be accessed by call center agents to provide feedback to customers, for example about order status, production failures, or accounting data. This access has to be provided unified and with hard constraints to the quality of the demanded services. For KIESELSTEIN Group, the main challenge is to integrate enterprise resource planning (ERP) data and product (CAD/PDM) data that are distributed across different sites. At these sites, BIS store information redundantly, since KIESELSTEIN Group grew together from three different producing factories, each providing their own information systems.

4.1 Workflow Modeling Methodology

Within the business application scenarios, we employed a top-down workflow modeling methodology. Figure 4 presents an overview of this methodology. Within a concrete workflow development process, the individual modeling activities may be applied in different orders. The upper half of the picture shows the creative part of the modeling methodology, and the lower half shows the components during the operational service. Additionally, the business roles are annotated to each component. The arrows depict main dependencies between the components.

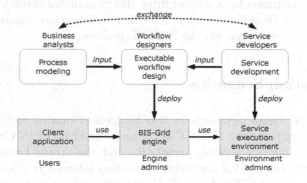

Fig. 4. Overview of the workflow modeling methodology

The design of a workflow mainly depends on the process model of a business analyst that uses BPMN as an high-level abstraction model to describe the desired business process, and on a service developer to identify existing services that can be reused or to design new services that have to be implemented and deployed. Furthermore, there is also an information exchange between a business analyst and a service developer, for example, to gain a common view of a global data model. To provide executable workflows, the workflow must be deployed on the BIS-Grid engine and, of course, all used services must be available on their service execution environments (cp. use-dependency in Fig. 4). Finally, users can initiate workflows using an appropriate client application.

For the evaluation of our application scenarios, we used a top-down development approach to identify, model, and deploy business workflows. The individual process steps were as follows.

(1) *Domain analysis.* The respective business domain(s) had to be analyzed to gain a thorough domain understanding. This included, for example, the analysis of the current enterprise architecture, expert interviews, on-site investigations, and requirements analysis.

(2) *Control-flow modeling.* This activity included the following sub-activities:
   (a) The current business processes (as-is state) were described as diagrams using the Business Process Modeling Notation (BPMN).
   (b) From the as-is state a first version of the to-be processes were developed and described using the BPMN, too, representing the basis for the realization of the prototype scenarios.
   (c) Data sources and simple data-flows were annotated in the to-be BPMN diagrams as far as possible using the BPMN (cp. Figure 5 lane 4).
   (d) The to-be BPMN diagrams were iteratively expanded to regard different layers of abstraction directly within the diagrams. Thereby, we focused on the operational layer, the services layer, the business process layer, and the consumer layer. We especially found this activity to be very helpful in order to separate concerns at an early stage of development (cp. SOA reference architecture in [4]). Figure 5 illustrates a such-layered call center process for read-only data retrieval (layers are ordered from the bottom to the top).

(3) *Data structure modeling.* Upon the relevant BIS and databases, the logical structure of the required information was modeled. To do so, we used entity-relationship (ER) diagrams that represent the relevant data structures whereas the BIS/database origin of the structures was annotated.

(4) *Data-flow modeling.* In addition to control-flow modeling, we modeled the data-flows of business processes using data flow diagrams (DFDs).

(5) *Service signature description.* Based upon the results of the previous activities, we textually described the signatures of the services of the respective business processes as a basis for service interface definition.

(6) *Service utilization description.* In addition to signature description, we described the usage protocol of the services regarded as black-boxes using protocol state machines. Although representing an overhead for services with small signatures, we think that this activity is of great importance for services that provide several operations and where the operations have strong service lifecycle dependencies.

(7) *Service implementation.* Starting with WSDL interface design, the services were implemented by our partners.

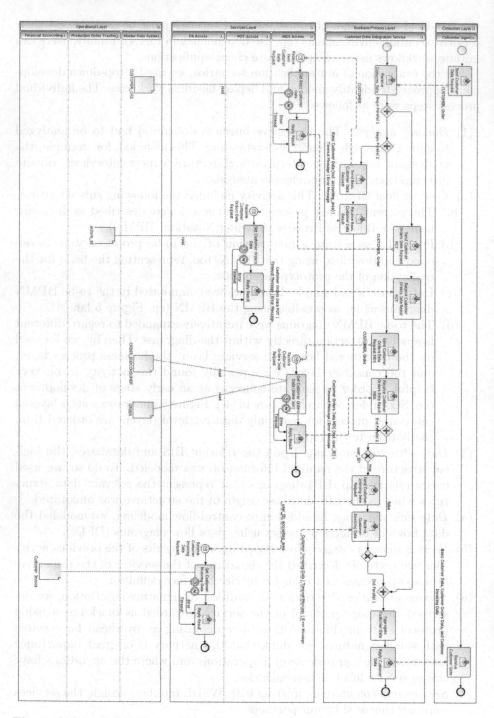

Fig. 5. A layered BPMN describing a call center process for read-only data retrieval as a basis for customer orders feedback

(8) *Service deployment.* The services were deployed by our partners under consideration of the enterprise architecture and the scenario requirements, for example, security requirements.

(9) *Workflow design.* Finally, we implemented WS-BPEL workflows for the modeled business processes.

(10) *Workflow use.* Users can now execute workflows via appropriate client applications. Within the application scenarios, we developed a prototypical user client on basis of the GridSphere Portal Framework[12], and use Net-Beans IDE[13] as a workflow modeling tool.

5 Related Work

There are several upcoming and new projects regarding service orchestration in cloud environments, proving the relevance of the Orchestration as a Service paradigm. Unfortunately, these are all new projects and aim at commercial issues and hence the infrastructures are not described neither scientifically nor in detail. Here, we present some of these projects but also regard related work concerning service orchestration in Grid environments.

For example, Microsoft is recently providing the .NET Workflow Service as part of the .Net Services of the Azure Services Platform[14] in order to execute user-defined declarative workflows as lightweight service orchestrations. These services facilitate the idea of an *Internet Service Bus* that addresses the need for cross-enterprise service orchestration, supporting both the Software as a Service paradigm as well as Microsoft's Software-plus-Services strategy.

CSC[15], as another example, recently announced Cloud Orchestration Services and Trusted Cloud Services promising various features such as service level management, remote monitoring, reporting, data transparency, and security while ensuring industry-specific compliance and auditing services. Thereby, Business Process as a Service (BPaaS) is named as one category of Trusted Cloud Services. Unfortunately, there is very little information on the concrete services, their realization, and the respective Service Level Agreements.

As a third example, Cordys also promotes cloud-based service orchestration, called Enterprise Cloud Orchestration[16]. Thereby, they emphasize the still-traditional nature of the SaaS distribution model in contrast to the Cloud idea as a federation of different Clouds, that may range from general-purpose Clouds to specialized Clouds in the future. Fundamentally this requires an orchestration layer in the Cloud to enable enterprises developing new business models and facilitate Application Service Provisioning.

The Chemomentum project already provides workflow extensions for UNI-CORE 6, consisting of two UNICORE 6 service containers. The first represents

---

[12] http://www.gridsphere.org/
[13] http://www.netbeans.org/
[14] http://www.microsoft.com/azure/workflow.mspx
[15] http://www.csc.com/cloud/
[16] http://www.cordys.com/cordyscms_com/enterprise_cloud_orchestration.php

a workflow engine that processes workflows on a logical level, the second represents a service orchestrator that transforms so-called Work Assignments into jobs, given in the Job Submission Description Language (JSDL) [1]. Both, this UNICORE 6 workflow system and the BIS-Grid engine, are implemented as service extensions to the UNICORE 6 service container. However, the UNICORE 6 workflow system does not support the integration of a WS-BPEL workflow engine well-adopted in industry.

In [2], Amnuaykanjanasin and Nupairoj present a solution to orchestrate Globus Toolkit services secured with the Grid Security Infrastructure. For each Grid service, a proxy implementation is generated automatically when the user requests one. To overcome the GSI, Proxy Certificates are requested dynamically from a MyProxy implementation. This architecture aims on scientific workflows without considering role-based access control or providing the workflow itself securely.

Many other paper present the possibility to model and execute workflows in Grid environments but without using the industrial de-facto standard WS-BPEL nor addressing the new cloud computing paradigm (e. g., see [7,14]).

6   Conclusion

In this paper, we discussed our Orchestration as a Service (OaaS) paradigm as a specialized form of PaaS. Since Oaas decreases the start-up costs for introducing EAI and SOA by outsorcing the operation and maintenance of a service orchestration infrastructure, we regard it as a viable option for small and medium enterprises. We also presented the BIS-Grid OaaS infrastructure, enabling enterprises to deploy workflows based on service-oriented architectures and opening up new possibilities for outsourcing IT to Grid or Cloud providers. Thereby, we regard different degrees of service outsourcing relying on the same technology underlying. The definition of service-level agreements (SLA) that are adequate to OaaS is future work.

Acknowledgement

The underlying work for this paper would not have been possible without the support of and close cooperation with our project partners. We especially thank our colleagues Herbert Nase, Manfred Neugebauer, and Christoph Rüger for their engagement.

References

1. Job Submission Description Language (JSDL) Specification, Version 1.0 (November 2005), http://www.gridforum.org/documents/GFD.56.pdf
2. Amnuaykanjanasin, P., Nupairoj, N.: The BPEL Orchestrating Framework for Secured Grid Services. In: International Conference on Information Technology: Coding and Computing, vol. 1, pp. 348–353 (2005)

3. Benedyczak, K.: UNICORE Virtual Organisations Service Overview. Technical report, Interdisciplinary Centre for Mathematical and Computational Modelling Warsaw University, Poland (2007)
4. Bieberstein, N., Laird, R.G., Jones, K., Mitra, T., Weisser, J.: A Methodology for Service Modeling and Design. In: Executing SOA: A Practical Guide for the Service-Oriented Architect, May 2008. DeveloperWorks Series, pp. 57–81. IBM Press (2008); Dimensions 7x9-1/4 240 Edition: 1st. 0-13-235374-1 ISBN-13: 978-0-13-235374-8
5. Brinkmann, A., Gudenkauf, S., Hasselbring, W., Höing, A., Kao, O., Karl, H., Nitsche, H., Scherp, G.: Employing WS-BPEL Design Patterns for Grid Service Orchestration using a Standard WS-BPEL Engine and a Grid Middleware. In: Bubak, M., Turala, M., Kazimierz, W. (eds.) CGW 2008 Proceedings, Cracow, Poland, pp. 103–110 (2009); ACC CYFRONET AGH
6. Gudenkauf, S., Höing, A., Scherp, G.: Catalogue of WS-BPEL Design Patterns. Technical report (May 2008)
7. Hoheisel, A.: User Tools and Languages for Graph-based Grid Workflows: Research Articles. Concurr. Comput.: Pract. Exper. 18(10), 1101–1113 (2006)
8. Moses, T.: eXtensible Access Control Markup Language (XACML) Version 2.0 (February 2005),
   http://docs.oasis-open.org/xacml/2.0/access_control-xacml-2.0-core-spec-os.pdf
9. Nurmi, D., Wolski, R., Grzegorczyk, C., Obertelli, G., Soman, S., Youse, L., Zagorodnov, D.: The Eucalyptus Open-source Cloud-computing System. In: Proceedings of 9th IEEE International Symposium on Cluster Computing and the Grid (2009)
10. OASIS WSBPEL Technical Committee. Web Services Business Process Execution Language (WSBPEL) Primer (May 2007),
    http://www.oasis-open.org/committees/download.php/23974/wsbpel-v2.0-primer.pdf
11. Ragouzis, N., Hughes, J., Philpott, R., Maler, E., Madsen, P., Scavo, T.: Security Assertion Markup Language (SAML) V2.0 Technical Overview, Working Draft (February 2007),
    http://www.oasis-open.org/committees/download.php/22553/sstc-saml-tech-overview-2%200-draft-13.pdf
12. Vaquero, L.M., Rodero-Merino, L., Caceres, J., Lindner, M.: A Break in the Clouds: Towards a Cloud Definition. SIGCOMM Comput. Commun. Rev. 39(1), 50–55 (2009)
13. Welch, V., Barton, T., Keahey, K., Siebenlist, F.: Attributes, Anonymity, and Access: Shibboleth and Globus Integration to Facilitate Grid Colloboration. In: Proceedings of the 4th Annual PKI R&D Workshop (2005)
14. Yu, J., Buyya, R.: A Novel Architecture for Realizing Grid Workflow using Tuple Spaces. In: GRID 2004: Proceedings of the 5th IEEE/ACM International Workshop on Grid Computing, Washington, DC, USA, pp. 119–128. IEEE Computer Society, Los Alamitos (2004)

The FAST Platform: An Open and Semantically-Enriched Platform for Designing Multi-channel and Enterprise-Class Gadgets

Volker Hoyer[1,6], Till Janner[1,6], Ivan Delchev[2], Andrea Fuchsloch[1], Javier López[4], Sebastian Ortega[4], Rafael Fernández[4], Knud Hinnerk Möller[5], Ismael Rivera[5], Marcos Reyes[3], and Manuel Fradinho[7]

[1] SAP Research St. Gallen, 9000 St. Gallen, Switzerland
[2] SAP Research Zurich, 8000 Zurich, Switzerland
[3] Telefonica I+D, 28043 Madrid, Spain
[4] Universidad Politecnica de Madrid, 28660 Madrid, Spain
[5] DERI, National University of Ireland, Galway
[6] University of St. Gallen, =mcm*institute*, 9000 St. Gallen, Switzerland
[7] Cyntelix Corporation, Galway, Ireland
{volker.hoyer,till.janner}@sap.com,
{ivan.delchev,andrea.fuchsloch}@sap.com,
{jlopez,sortega,rfernandez}@fi.upm.es,
{knud.moeller,ismael.rivera}@deri.org,
mru@tid.es, mfradinho@cyntelix.com

Abstract. The transfer of the mashup paradigm in corporate environments needs additional capabilities beyond those typically associated with consumer mashups. In this paper, we present the architecture of the FAST platform which allows creating enterprise-class and multi-channel visual building blocks (so called gadgets) in an ad-hoc manner. The design of complex enterprise-class gadgets is supported by an integrated semantic concept which hides the complexity from the actual users. The architectural components of the platform, a technical life cycle model for enterprise mashups, and the FAST gadget ontology are presented. By means of a cross-organizational real-world scenario from the marketing/ promotion event area, we demonstrate the value and potential of the FAST platform.

Keywords: Enterprise Mashups, Gadgets, Situational Applications, Semantics, Multi-Channel Visual Building Blocks, FAST Project.

1 Introduction and Motivation

After introducing transaction systems such as enterprise resource planning (ERP), customer relationship management (CRM), or supply chain management (SCM) since the beginning of 1990, a next wave in corporate technology adoption, the Web 2.0/ peer production philosophy, addresses ad-hoc and situational applications [1]. It integrates actual end users in order to generate new information or edit the work of

L. Baresi, C.-H. Chi, and J. Suzuki (Eds.): ICSOC-ServiceWave 2009, LNCS 5900, pp. 316–330, 2009.

others. Renowned management scholars such as Andrew McAfee and Don Tapscott envision an Enterprise 2.0 [2, 3]. It leverages new consumer-driven technologies in order to put people in the center of the information-centric work.

In this context, a new software development paradigm, known as enterprise mashups, has gained momentum. At the core of the mashup paradigm are two aspects: First, empowerment of the end user to cover ad-hoc and long tail needs by reusing and combining existing software artefacts. Second, broad involvement of users based on the peer production concept. In contrast to traditional software development concepts aligned with Service-Oriented Architectures (SOAs), enterprise mashups usually aren't constructed by a team of traditional software developers. Instead, they are created by users from the business units characterized by no or limited programming skills. They desire specific functionality that mainstream SOA-based enterprise applications don't provide [4]. In this kind of grassroots computing [5, 6], the focus on delivering a set of user friendly building blocks rather than finished applications enables users to automate also tactical and opportunistic applications.

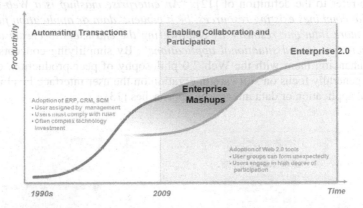

Fig. 1. From Automating Transactions to an Enterprise 2.0, adapted from [1]

Market research companies like Gartner [7], Forrester [8], or Economic Intelligence Units [9], and leading management consulting firms like McKinsey [10], forecast a growing practical relevance for the mashup paradigm over the next few years. Gartner sees mashup applications at the mainstream adoption in less than two years in its hype cycle for Web and user interaction technologies 2008 [7]. In addition, several mashup tools came up in the recent years [11], i.e., IBM Mashup Center, Intel Mash Maker, SAP Research RoofTop, Microsoft Popfly, Yahoo Pipes, etc. However, the transfer of the consumer-driven mashup paradigm to corporate environments needs additional capabilities beyond those typically associated with consumer mashup offerings.

The goal of this paper is to fill this gap by designing an open and semantically-enriched platform which allows creating enterprise-class and multi-channel visual building blocks (so called gadgets). In the course of the EU funded project FAST[1], we are currently implementing the platform. By means of a first cross-organizational

---

[1] http://fast.morfeo-project.eu, last checked 2009-08-13

real-world scenario from the marketing/ promotion event area, the platform and indirectly the underlying concepts are evaluated.

The remainder of the article is structured as follows: After introducing the terminology of enterprise mashups and elaborating on the requirements for corporate purposes in section two, we present the FAST platform in section three. In particular a life cycle for enterprise mashups, the architectural components, and the designed FAST gadget onotology are presented. Section four includes a demonstration by means of a first B2B mashup scenario. Finally, section five concludes with a brief summary and provides an outlook on future work.

2   Related Work and Background

2.1   Enterprise Mashups – Definition and Terminology

In the literature, the exact definition of enterprise mashups is open to debate. In this work, we refer to the definition of [12]: *"An enterprise mashup is a Web-based resource that combines existing resources, be it content, data or application functionality, from more than one resource by empowering the end users to create individual information centric and situational applications"*. By simplifying concepts of SOA and by enhancing them with the Web 2.0 philosophy of peer production, enterprise mashups generally focus on software integration on the user interface level instead of traditional application or data integration approaches [13].

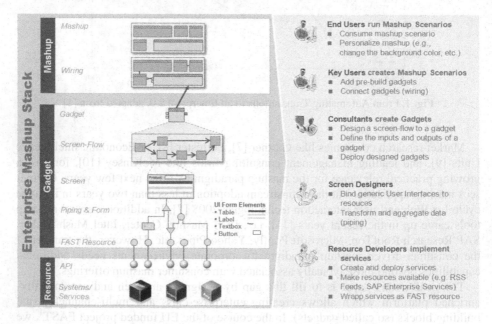

Fig. 2. Enterprise Mashup Development Layers, Terminology and User Roles

The relevant architectural components of the enterprise mashup paradigm can be structured in an enterprise mashup stack comprising three main layers (mashup, widget, resource) [5, 12]. On the gadget layer (visual building blocks), we introduce the concepts of screens and screen-flows in order to create powerful gadgets for enterprise purposes. Fig. 1 depicts the resulting terminology which is applied in the FAST project and in this paper. In addition, the relevant user roles including their tasks are mapped to the different architectural terms.

Resources (services) contain content, data or application functionality and represent the core building blocks of enterprise mashups. They are encapsulated via well-defined public interfaces (*Application Programming Interfaces*; i.e., WSDL, RSS, Atom Feeds, etc.) allowing for a loose coupling of existing resources – an important feature from the SOA paradigm. These resources are provided by enterprise systems or by external Web providers (i.e., Amazon, Google, etc.) and are created by traditional developers who are familiar with development concepts.

The layer above contains *gadgets* or *widgets* which provide a simple user interaction mechanism abstracting from the complexity of the underlying resources. Thereby, the *piping* composition integrates heterogeneous resources by defining composed data processing chains concatenating successive resources. Aggregate, transform, filter or sort operations adapt, mix, and manipulate the content of the underlying resources. A graphical user interface *form* is put on the composed resource. The combination of a form and the piping composition is called a *screen* which is created by the screen designer. This user role is characterized by basic programming skills in order to bind the resources to user interfaces. Screens are fully functional by themselves, and their pre- and post-conditions drive the transitions between them to tie them together, forming a *screen-flow*. A FAST gadget consists of various screens and allows the handling of lots of information in several steps. In a similar way to the resource, input and output ports of a gadget (so-called events and slots) can be defined by a consultant (gadget developer). In addition, the user playing the consultant role is able to deploy a gadget to different mashup platforms. A consultant plays a primary role in IT departments and works quite closely together with key users from the business units.

Now, a key user who understands the business challenge is able to combine such visual gadgets in a mashup platform according to their individual business needs, thus creating a *mashup*. This visual composition by linking the in-/ outports of a gadget is called *wiring* and requires no programming skills. Finally, the end users consume and run the created mashup scenario. If necessary, they are able to configure the mashup to some extent, e.g. (de)activation of functionalities, moving gadgets, etc.

In summery, the composition principle of the resource layer of traditional SOA environments is transferred to the user interface level where the end users are empowered to create an ad-hoc enterprise-class application. The power of the composition and also the required IT skills are different. A first discussion regarding the composition pattern in enterprise mashup environments can be found at [14].

2.2 Requirements

The existing discussion of the mashup principle in the scientific community is driven by technical aspects. In particular, several research activities deal with the lightweight provision of IT-enabled components [15, 16] as well as their composition on the resource layer [17, 18]. Coming instead from a business perspective, researchers also started to analyse the underlying structure of the resulting open mashup ecosystem [19] and derived first managerial implications for API providers.

However, the discussion about the layers on top of the resources is still missing. By means of a literature analysis of market research institute reports [1, 4, 8, 20] and by taking experiences from first mashup implementations into account [21, 22], we identify the following open challenges concerning the enterprise adoption of the mashup paradigm. They are clustered in three dimensions: technical, organizational, and business perspective.

Table 1. Challenges of Enterprise Mashups

Challenges	Description
Technical Perspective	
Interoperability	▪ Discovery and composition of gadgets ▪ Underlying information model for in-/ output parameters for wiring gadgets
Gadget Portability	▪ Moving gadgets between different mashup environments ▪ First standardization activities (e.g., OpenAjax, OpenSAM, OpenSocial, DataPortability, etc.)
Information Security	▪ Gadget-to-resource security ▪ Single Sign On (SSO) to multiple company internal and external component sources ▪ AJAX Web browser-based mashup execution engine
Organizational Perspective	
Availability of Components	▪ Integration in the existing IT infrastructure (legacy enterprise systems) ▪ Creation of enterprise-class gadgets representing the actual content of enterprise mashup platforms
Governance	▪ Managing grassroots and community-driven mashup environments ▪ Balancing between organization concerns such as manageability and fostering user involvement
Culture	▪ Exploitation of enterprise mashups to the right user groups ▪ Users have a new kind of freedom
Business Perspective	
Building the Business Case	▪ Business value for enterprises and the users to introduce the mashup paradigm ▪ Providing key performance indicators for the IT management
Use Cases	▪ Real-world scenarios demonstrating the potential

In course of this paper, we focus on the technical interoperability, gadget portability, and the availablity of gadgets.

3 FAST Platform

3.1 Enterprise Mashup Life Cycle

Before elaborating on the actual architecture of the FAST platform, we introduce a life cycle for enterprise mashups in order to understand how enterprise-class gadgets are designed and executed. The model is organized by means of two dimensions. First, according to the terminology as presented in Sect. 2, the relationship between the mashable components and the related user roles are structuring the vertical axis. Second, the horizontal axis focuses on the actual life cycle of mashable components. Thereby, each component of the enterprise mashup stack (*mashup*, *gadget*, and *resource*) goes through the four phases *design*, *store*, *deploy*, and *execution*. The resulting enterprise mashup life cycle is depicted in the figure below.

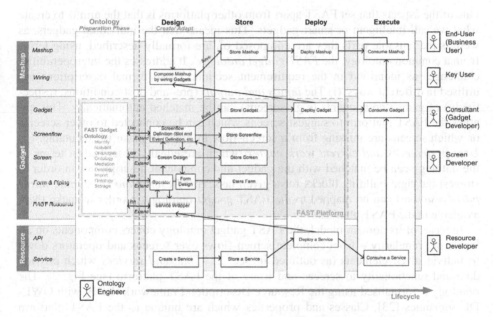

Fig. 3. Enterprise Mashup Life Cycle

As already mentioned, the FAST platform leverages semantics in order to hide the composition complexity from the users. Therefore, in a *preparation phase*, an ontology engineer identifies relevant domain specific ontologies. After importing of and mediating between existing ontologies, the FAST gadget ontology is used in the actual *design phase* by the users. On the other hand, users are able to extend the FAST gadget ontology with new instances by using the FAST platform. Mashable components can be annotated with additional semantics – in the FAST scope this is done by the consultants (gadget developers) and the screen developers. After finishing the design of a mashable components (screen-flow, screen design, form design, piping operation, and service wrapper), the persistence is handled in the *store phase*. A catalogue provides a URI to access the components and also allows the reuse of it during the design phase. In order to consume one of the three executeable components (resource, gadget, mashup), the *deployment phase* takes care of the publication to external platforms. In context of a gadget, the FAST platform provides a set of potential target mashup environments (enterprise, social, mobile, and desktop environments). Now, the key user is able to compose deployed gadgets with each other (design phase of the mashup layer). Finally, in the *execution phase*, the gadget in a mashup scenario is consumed.

As depicted in Fig. 3, the enterprise mashup life cycle is characterized by permanent loops between the different phases of the life cycle. The result of the FAST platform is self-contained gadget, i.e., a piece of code that is executeable without using the infrastructure of the FAST platform in the execution phase.

3.2 FAST Gadget Ontology

One of the aspects that set FAST apart from other platforms is that the aim is to create what we call intelligent or smart gadgets. This means that the individual gadgets, as well as the reusable parts they are composed of, are formally described, using terms from a common ontology, the *FAST gadget ontology*[2]. It addresses the interoperability challenges as identified in the requirement section. These formal descriptions are utilised in different ways. (i) The *inputs and outputs* (pre- and post-conditions, respectively) of gadget components (e.g., screens) can be matched automatically. This enables the FAST platform to suggest screens which can be connected to other screens, or which screens are missing from a screen-flow in order to make it executable. (ii) *User preferences and current work context* which are equally described in terms of the ontology can be matched with the gadget and component descriptions, in order to suggest the right building blocks for a given task. (iii) *Descriptions of existing third-party resources* can be mapped to the FAST gadget ontology in order to make them available to the FAST platform.

In terms of its domain model, the FAST gadget ontology covers components on all levels of granularity – from complete screen-flows over screens and operators down to individual UI elements (as outlined in Sec. 2) –, *backend services* which provide data and functionality to screens and *users* of the FAST platform (see Fig. 2). The ontology is formalised using the Resource Description Framework (RDF) with OWL-DL semantics [23]. Classes and properties which are unique to the FAST platform (e.g., screens and screen-flows) have been modelled in the dedicated FAST namespace, whereas more generic terms (e.g., users, properties for annotation) have been adopted from external vocabularies and ontologies, such as FOAF and Dublin Core. For an in-depth discussion of the FAST gadget ontology we refer the reader to [24], which includes details on the methodology adopted for its development, the scope and domain model and a complete list of classes and properties with documentation.

However, at this point we would like to highlight a central feature of the ontology, namely the modelling of pre- and post-conditions, which is crucial both for the composition of screen-flows, as well as their execcution. Each such condition is expressed as a graph pattern, i.e., a set of one or more RDF triple patterns. The patterns of post-conditions will be instantiated into a common RDF graph, while the patterns of

---

[2] http://purl.oclc.org/fast/ontology/gadget, last checked 2009-08-13.

pre-conditions will be executed as SPARQL queries against this graph to determine if they are fulfilled. For example, if the pre-condition of a product selection screen P is that a user has successfully logged into the system, then this could be expressed as simple graph pattern saying *"There is a resource of type* `sioc:User"` as follows[3]:

```
?user a sioc:User.
```

Now, if the post-condition of any screen currently present in the screen-flow contains this pattern (e.g., from a login screen L), then P is executable. Obviously, graph patterns can be more complex. We could imagine that the post-condition of the login screen L is *"There is a user resource which has an account name. There is also a person resource which has a name, and which has the user resource as its online account"*. Formally in FAST, this could be expressed as follows:

```
?user a sioc:User;
   foaf:accountName ?account_name.
?person a foaf:Person;
   foaf:holdsAccount ?user;
   foaf:name ?person_name.
```

In defining pre- and post-conditions of screens in this way, the FAST platform is capable of suggesting to a user which screens out of the set of available screens could be added to a given screen-flow during its development, or which of the screens already present in the screen-flow are executable or not.

3.3 Architecture

In order to support the presented enterprise mashup life cycle and FAST gadget ontology, we have designed a high level architecture of the FAST platform. By using the Fundamental Modeling Notation (FMC), we model the architectural components, their relationships and how the different user roles interact with the platform. In contrast to the technical-oriented UML notations, FMC focuses on human comprehension of complex systems[4].

Taking into account that the main objective of FAST is to allow users to compose gadgets from reusable building blocks and deploy them on various mashup platforms, the most natural mean is providing a rich internet application. Therefore, we have devised a robust architecture comprising the FAST client running on a Web-based FAST client, which deals with user interactions, and the FAST server, which takes care of the semantics, the storage capabilities and the deployment to external parties. Fig. 4 depicts the resulting FAST architecture.

The FAST client, which is called *Gadget Visual Storyboard (GVS)*, consists of three main architectural components.

Workspace Manager (GUI). This component is responsible for building and rendering the user interface and then populating it with the pieces required for designing an enterprise-class gadget. The AJAX-based user interface is composed by several areas: the building block palette, which shows a domain-specific subset of the existing building blocks stored in the server-side catalogue; the design area, in which the user

---

[3] Using SPARQL notation and terms from the SIOC and FOAF vocabularies.
[4] http://www.fmc-modeling.org, last checked 2009-08-13.

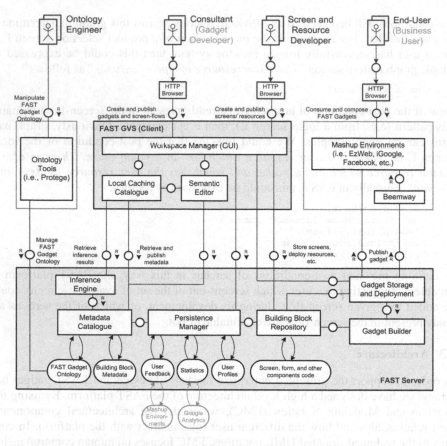

Fig. 4. FAST High Level Architecture (FMC Notation)

composes the gadget by mixing the pieces coming from the palette in a visual manner; and finally, a number of property editors and inspectors which show to the user the most relevant information about the screen-flow (or the screen). Fig. 6 in case study section depicts a screenshot of the FAST GVS user interface.

Local Caching Catalogue. The local catalogue retrieves and caches building block metadata coming from the FAST server metadata catalogue and being used for the designing of a gadget (or another lower-level piece, such as a screen). Moreover, this component provides the workspace manager with recommendations about what building blocks to use among other assistive features. These recommendations are provided by the server-side inference engine which is described below.

Semantic Editor. Building block reuse is empowered by the exploitation of semantics. Therefore, during their design and creation, it is necessary to use the existing semantic information and important to further enrich the elements being composed with semantic annotations. The semantic editor component allows the user to perform this duty in an integrated and user-friendly fashion.

The FAST server in the backend implements a REST API that offers the required functionality to deal with building block management, workspace persistence, gadget storage and its deployment. Additionally, the open APIs allow the integration of required third party tools (i.e., Protégé for managing domain-specific ontologies). In order to request information about the mashable components, we provide JSON and RDF/XML payloads. In particular, JSON reduces the programming effort in the FAST client. The FAST server-side itself is modularized into several cohesive components allowing independent development, even using different technologies. The main components are explained below.

Metadata Catalogue. The FAST metadata catalogue is in charge of the storage and indexing of information about every piece of a gadget, ranging from components such as screens or screen-flows all the way down to ontology terms describing the scope of a gadget. The structure of these components is formally defined in the FAST gadget ontolgy. Hence, every element in the catalogue is an instance of a concept from the FAST gadget ontology (or any other ontology), or indeed the ontology terms themselves. Consequently, its three main purposes are: (i) finding the most relevant building blocks for a given context (domain, user preferences and current workspace). (ii) The support for social interactions allowing community enrichment of the mashable component base (see semantic editor of the FAST client). (iii) The ability to deal with different domain-specific building blocks allowing users to create enterprise-class gadgets. In order to appropriately infer within those different domains, different ontologies must be used by the metadata catalogue. The main problem is that the most valuable gadgets usually are created by mashing up several application domains, so the catalogue component is also designed to manage the relationship between different ontologies (i.e., using ontology mapping techniques). The metadata catalogue is based on the RDF repository Sesame 2 which also provides a RESTful HTTP interface for SPARQL Protocol for RDF. As an abstraction to access the triple store, the RDF2Go library is integrated.

Inference Engine. Due to the importance of semantics, we distinguish the inference engine as the sub-component responsible for reasoning. It allows extracting and deriving new information given a certain knowledge base. It interacts directly with the triple store of the metadata catalogue and follows a forward-chaining policy, hence whenever new data is added to the catalogue, it also triggers a set of rules, and newly inferred data is added to the catalogue. Following a forward-chaining policy in the metadata catalogue makes sense, because it allows for faster query answering which is crucial for the performance of the overall FAST platform. Insertion of new data which would be favoured by backward-chaining is much less crucial in FAST. The set of rules being used by the inference engine is composed by a subset of the RDFS entailment rules[5] and the inverse of some of these rules.

Persistence Manager. The persistence manager is responsible for storing the relevant information between different browsing sessions. It stores user information (e.g., user profile) and settings, some usage statistics and user feedback, which can be used by the metadata catalogue to retrieve building blocks more accurately. As indicated in Fig. 4, data from external systems such as Google Analytics for monitoring designed

---

[5] http://www.w3.org/TR/rdf-mt/#RDFSRules, last checked 2009-08-13.

and deployed gadgets as well as user feedback from the runtime environments (mashup platforms) is integrated in the persistence manager and therefore in the FAST ecosystem.

Building Block Repository. Once a component, for instance a screen or a screen-flow, is designed it must be stored in order to allow reuse at a later stage or even to create gadgets. The building block repository component is responsible for managing the existing building blocks' implementation. The acutal metadata is stored in the catalogue. By doing so, we separate between the actual code and metadata of the mashable components in the FAST platform.

Gadget Builder. When consultants finish their work and decide to create a gadget to be used in a mashup platform for execution, it is necessary to package the final gadget's code. It is the actual implementation of the designed functionality by using the modelled building blocks. The gadget builder is triggerd by the workspace manager of the FAST client and deals with this task. It processes each of the building blocks to create its associate code, and setting the defined relationships between them. The result is a self-contained, platform-independent gadget.

Gadget Storage and Deployment. The gadget code is stored and automatically adapted to the different mashup environments and their specifics. By attaching to the gadget's code the platform-compliant implementation of the target gadget API, the FAST gadget can be executed. The next section explains the FAST deployment concept in more detail.

3.4 Deployment of Multi-channel Gadgets

The final output of the FAST gadget development process is a gadget, which needs to be first stored and subsequently deployed to a chosen target destination, such as a start page (e.g., Netvibes, iGoogle, etc), mobile device, social networking site (e.g, Facebook, Bebo, etc), desktops of operating systems (e.g.: Windows Vista, Safari, etc) and finally, enterprise mashups (EzWeb).

In order to allow gadget deployment in one or multiple target platforms we have designed a flexible runtime gadget architecture. To achieve this platform independence, an important architectural design decision taken was to have the three layered approach as depicted in Fig. 5: The first layer corresponds to the *screen-flow implementation* of a specific enterprise-class gadget created by a user. The FAST platform empowers the user with the capability of emulating the runtime execution of the screen-flows, thus allowing for the experimentation of the final gadget. However, it is necessary the existence of a runtime execution environment, which corresponds to the other depicted two layers:

- *FAST Gadget Player.* This player enables building block interactions and guides the execution flow from one screen to another and keeps track of the facts.
- *FAST Gadget API.* This layer is responsible for the actual abstraction of the target destination mashup platforms.

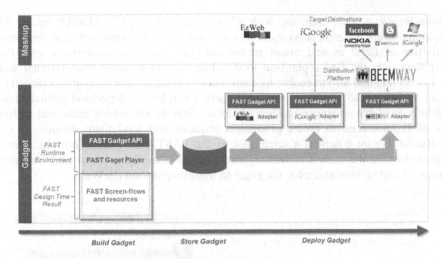

Fig. 5. Multi-Channel Gadgets

The three step deployment process begins after the FAST gadget has been created:

- **Build.** The first phase consists of packaging the complex gadget, namely the screen-flows and the corresponding resources, into a runtime environment that will execute independent of the FAST platform.
- **Storage.** With regards to deployment, it is important to take into consideration that most target destinations do not support the actual storage of gadgets. Therefore, the target destination usually keeps track of the URL where the gadget is stored. Consequently, once the gadget is built, it is placed within a repository.
- **Deployment.** This phase focuses on the placement of the gadget within the target designation platform, using the URL of where the gadget is stored. The actual deployment can take two alternative paths. First, the gadget is installed directly into the target destination platform by using an adapter. Second, the gadget is deployed via a distribution platform (e.g, Beemway[6]), which transparently installs the FAST gadget onto multiple destinations thus supporting the paradigm of build once, run everywhere.

4   Case Study: Cross-Organizational Promotion Scenario

After elaborating on the technical issues of the innovative FAST platform, this section is devoted to demonstrate the business value by means of a case study. Our demo scenario covers the usage of the FAST platform during the design, storage and deployment phase of the gadgets and the EzWeb[7] mashup platform for the building and execution of enterprise mashups in a cross-organizational context. The business scenario is involving two companies: The first company is a promotion agency

---

[6] http://www.beemway.com, last checked 2009-08-13.
[7] http://ezweb.morfeo-project.eu, last checked 2009-08-13.

PromoBueno, a SME company with 47 employees located in Madrid, Spain. The company offers different services to its customers, i.e. the organization of promotion activities at fairs/ events, brand promotion and marketing campaigns, etc. *PromoBueno* uses the FAST platform to develop gadgets to make their internal work more efficient and also to enable its customers to place promotion requests directly at them by using FAST gadgets. The latter gadget will be developed and published to a publicly available enterprise mashup platform, EzWeb, and allows interested customers of PromoBueno to create promotion requests and send them directly to PromoBueno. Figure 6 depicts a screenshot of the FAST prototype on how to define a screen-flow (in this case it consists of two screens - "available crew" and "incoming request") and on how to deploy the gaget to mashup platform (EzWeb).

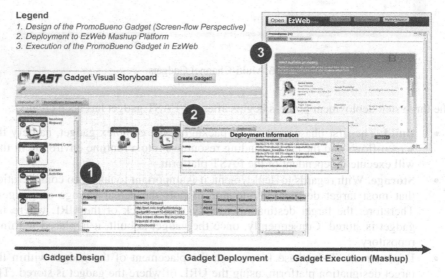

Fig. 6. Design, Deployment, and Execution of an enterprise-class Gadget

Now, the second company in our scenario (*AllSports*) is a sports equipment and nutrition producer, a large enterprise with 3227 employees located in Hamburg, Germany. Recently, *AllSports* created a new protein bar for high endurance athletes. The sales and marketing departments arrange and organize so-called point-of-sale (POS) promotion activities supported by different gadgets via the company internal enterprise mashup environment. When *AllSports* decides to introduce and sell their new product in Spain, they are interested in collaborating with different promotion agencies to request support for promotion activities at trade fair events. It is important for them that they can quickly establish the promotion request process with new agencies, as there are many available.

The created gadget can be used as follows to support the interconnection and collaboration between the two firms. A sales employee of *AllSports* has the need to request a promotion crew for a sport event. As it is her first time of organizing a booth at a fair in Spain, she needs the help of a local promotion agency. The sales employee of *AllSports* searches the gadget catalogue of the EzWeb platform and finds the published "Promotion Request Gadget" of PromoBueno. The integration of the new "Promotion Request Gadget" is done by a key user of *PromoBueno*. The sales employee now carries out the POS process including the booking of the event and also the staffing of the promotion crew directly via the gadget of the promotion agancy. The promotion manager at *PromoBueno* gets the incoming request displayed at her monitoring gadget and can send a confirmation back to *AllSports*.

5 Conclusion and Future Work

The aim of this paper is the design of an open and semantically-enriched platform which allows creating enterprise-class and multi-channel gadgets. In order to achieve this, first, we introduced the main terms related to enterprise mashups and identified the challenges in order to transfer consumer-driven mashup paradigm to corporate environments. In a second step, we present the FAST platform. By means of a life cylce model, the relationship of the mashable components of an enterprise-class gadget is described. The FAST gadget ontology and the resulting software architecture are presented. Finally, a first implemented mashup scenario in the marketing/ promotion event area demonstrated the potential of the FAST platform.

Apart from other existing mashup and gadget platforms [4], the presented FAST platform aims at providing intelligent or smart gadgets by leveraging semantics. The followed multi-channel deployment approach allows the usage of designed FAST gadgets in various environments. For example, users from the business unit are empowered to develop and publish gadgets on their daily portal environment (EzWeb) and also on mobile devices without involving the IT department.

What is still missing is a general concept on how to integrate existing legacy enterprise systems in enterprise mashup environments. Currently, the consumed resources from backend systems (SAP Enterprise Service) are integrated manually. Future reseach will also deal with the implementation of a complete version of the marketing/ promotion event scenario that covers the ad-hoc interaction between several parties across company borders.

Acknowledgments. This work is supported in part by the European Commission under the first call of its Seventh Framework Program (FAST STREP Project, grant INFSO-ICT-216048) and in part by Science Foundation Ireland under Grant No. SFI/08/CE/I1380 (Líon-2).

References

1. Chui, M., Miller, A., Roberts, R.P.: Six Ways to make Web 2.0 work. The McKinsey Quarterly (February 2009)
2. McAfee, A.P.: Enterprise 2.0: The Dawn of Emergent Collaboration. MIT Sloan Management Review 47(3), 21–28 (2006)
3. Tapscott, D., Williams, A.D.: Wikinomics: How Mass Collaboration Changes Everythink, Portfolio, New York (2006)
4. Carrier, N., Deutsch, T., Gruber, C., Heid, M., Jarrett, L.L.: The Business Case for Enterprise Mashups, Web 2.0 Technology Solutions, IBM White Paper (2008)

5. Hoyer, V., Stanoevska-Slabeva, K.: Towards a Reference Model for Grassroots Enterprise Mashup Environments. In: Proceedings of the 17th European Conference on Information Systems, Verona, Italy (2009)
6. Cherbakov, L., Bravery, A., Goodman, B.D., Pandya, A., Baggett, J.: Changing the Corporate IT Development Model: Tapping the Power of Grassroots Computing. IBM Systems Journal 46(4), 743–751 (2007)
7. Gootzit, D., Phifer, G., Valdes, R., Drakos, N., Bradley, A., Harris, K.: Hype Cycle for Web and User Interaction Technologies, Gartner Research G00159447 (2008)
8. Young, O.G.: The Mashup Opportunity: How to make Web 2.0 work, Forrester Resesarch, May 6 (2008)
9. The Economist Intelligence Unit: Serious Business – Web 2.0 goes Corporate, Report of the Economist Intelligence Unit (2008)
10. McKinsey Global Survey Results: Building the Web 2.0 Enterprise, The McKinsey Quarterly (2008)
11. Hoyer, V., Fischer, M.: Market Overview of Enterprise Mashup Tools. In: Bouguettaya, A., Krueger, I., Margaria, T. (eds.) ICSOC 2008. LNCS, vol. 5364, pp. 708–721. Springer, Heidelberg (2008)
12. Hoyer, V., Stanoevska-Slabeva, K., Janner, T., Schroth, C.: Enterprise Mashups: Design Principles towards the Long Tail of User Needs. In: Proceedings of the IEEE International Conference on Services Computing, Honolulu, Hawaii (2008)
13. Daniel, F., Matera, M., Yu, J., Benatalla, B., Saint-Paul, R., Casati, F.: Understadning UI Integration. A Survey of Problems, Technologies, and Opportunities. IEEE Internet Computing 11(3), 59–66 (2007)
14. Janner, T., Siebeck, R., Schroth, C., Hoyer, V.: Patterns for Enterprise Mashups B2B Collaborations to foster Lightweight Composition and End User Development. In: Proceedings of the IEEE 7th International Conference on Web Services, L.A, CA (2009)
15. Abbott, R.: Open at the Top, Open at the Buttom; and continually (but slowly) evolving. In: Proceedings of the IEEE Conference on Systems of System Engineering (2006)
16. Pautasso, C., Zimmermann, O., Leymann, F.: RESTful Web Services vs Big Web Services: Making the Right Architectural Decision. In: Proceedings of the 17th International World Wide Web Conference, Beijing, China (2008)
17. Maximilien, E.M., Hernan, W., Nirmit, D., Stefan, T.: A Domain-Specific Lanaguage for Web APIs and Service Mashups. In: Proceedings of the 5th International Conference on Service Oriented Computing (2007)
18. Rosenberg, F., Curbera, F., Duftler, M.J., Khalaf, R.: Composing RESTful Services and Collaboration Workflows. IEEE Internet Computing 12(5), 24–31 (2008)
19. Yu, S.: Innovation in the Programmable Web: Characterizing the Mashup Ecosystem. In: Proceedings of the 2nd International Workshop on Web APIs and Services Mashups (2008)
20. Bradley, A.: Addressing the Seven Primary Challenges to Enterprise Adoption of Mashups, Gartner Research G00164390 (2009)
21. Hoyer, V., Gilles, J.T., Stanoevska-Slabeva, K.: SAP Research RoofTop Marketplace: Putting a Face on Service-Oriented Architectures. In: Proceedings of the 7th IEEE International Conference on Web Services (ICWS), L.A., CA (2009)
22. Lizcano, D., Soriano, J., Reyes, M., Hierro, J.J.: EzWeb/FAST: Reporting on a Successful Mashup-based Solution for Developing and Deploying Composite Applications in the Upcoming Web of Services. In: Proceedings of the 10th International Conference on Information Integration and Web-based Applications & Services, iiWAS (2008)
23. Patel-Schneider, P.F., Hayes, P., Horrocks, I.: OWL Web Ontology Language Semantic and Abstract Syntax, Recommendation W3C (2004), http://www.w3.org/TR/owl-semantics
24. Möller, K.: Ontology and conceptual model for the semantic characterisation of complex gadgets, FAST Project Deliverable 2.2.1 (2009)

Message-Oriented Middleware with QoS Awareness

Hao Yang, Minkyong Kim, Kyriakos Karenos, Fan Ye, and Hui Lei

IBM T. J. Watson Research Center
{haoyang,minkyong,kkarenos,fanye,hlei}@us.ibm.com

Abstract. Publish/subscribe messaging is a fundamental mechanism for interconnecting disparate services and systems in the service-oriented computing architecture. The quality of services (QoS) of the messaging substrate plays a critical role in the overall system performance as perceived by the end users. In this paper, we present the design and implementation of Harmony, an overlay-based messaging system that can manage the end-to-end QoS in wide-area publish/subscribe communications based on the application requirements. This is achieved through a holistic set of overlay route establishment and maintenance mechanisms, which actively exploit the diversity in the network paths and redirect the traffic over links with good quality, e.g., low latency and high availability. In order to cope with network dynamics and failures, Harmony continuously monitors the link quality and adapts the routes whenever their quality deteriorates below the application requirements. Harmony can operate on top of different data transport layers. When the transport layer has built-in message scheduling capability, Harmony takes advantage of it and utilizes a novel budget allocation scheme to control the scheduling behavior. We have fully implemented the Harmony messaging system, and our empirical experience has confirmed its effectiveness in providing end-to-end QoS in dynamic wide-area network environments.

1 Introduction

We are witnessing major transformations to the enterprise computing landscape. One of such transformations is the ever increasing awareness of the real-world events and conditions through massive sensing, analytics and control capabilities, leading to a proliferation of cyber–physical systems (CPS)[1]. Another major transformation is the growing interconnection and interoperation of enterprise systems over a geographically distributed wide area, as triggered by business practices like mergers and acquisitions, off-shoring, outsourcing, and the formation of virtual enterprises. The second transformation has been driving an emerging engineering discipline around the system of systems (SoS) [2]. Message-oriented middleware (MOM) is widely recognized as a promising approach to the integration of both CPS and SoS, because messaging is a simple and natural communication paradigm for connecting the loosely-coupled and distributed components in those systems. However, CPS and SoS have also introduced new non-functional requirements on MOM. Specifically, MOM must

L. Baresi, C.-H. Chi, and J. Suzuki (Eds.): ICSOC-ServiceWave 2009, LNCS 5900, pp. 331–345, 2009.

be aware of and satisfy the unique quality-of-service (QoS) needs of these new systems in order for it to be practically useful.

Consider cyber physical systems being developed for a wide variety of application domains ranging from the smart grid of electricity to environmental monitoring and to intelligent transportation. Voluminous sensor event data needs to be transported from field sensors to backend enterprise servers for complex event processing and integration with the business processes. Sensor data is often time-sensitive in that the correct data that comes too late may become the wrong data. Therefore sensor data must be transported in a very responsive and reliable manner. Similarly, control directives carried in the reverse direction of traffic may drive various mission-critical systems. The control directives may have stringent requirements on delivery performance and security in order to avoid catastrophic consequences. On the other hand, the communication infrastructure for sensor data and control directives presents a number of challenges. Sensors are often deployed in potentially hostile environments, which make the sensors more prone to malicious attacks and natural hazards. Further, sensors are connected through wireless links that are inherently weak. There may be a high degree of variability in wireless bandwidth due to moving obstructions, RF interference, and weather. There may also be periods of intermittent disconnections. Such characteristics make it very difficult for MOM to effectively address the QoS requirements of CPS.

In the realm of system of systems, the constituent systems may be distributed over a large geographic area, e.g., across a nation or even spanning multiple continents. Messages between the systems often have to travel a long communication path, incurring much larger delay than local-area messaging. It is also harder for a long-haul communication path to maintain high availability due to the increased number of nodes and links on the path. Further, the systems are likely to be deployed and operated by separate organizations, which result in different security properties and degrees of trustworthiness to be associated with these systems. Despite technical challenges arising out of the communication infrastructure, many SoS applications require messaging capabilities with certain assurance on a range of QoS metrics including latency, throughput, availability and security. One example of such an SoS assimilated multiple systems used by US federal agencies (FAA, DoD, DHS, etc.) to facilitate the distribution of real-time national air surveillance data among these agencies [3].

Existing MOMs fall into one of two categories: enterprise messaging systems and real-time messaging systems. Intended to address traditional business needs, enterprise messaging systems provide message delivery assurance and transactional guarantees. They usually implement the JMS standard [4] and can transport messages over a wide area across multiple domains. However, they do not proactively manage messaging performance. As such, applications cannot predict or depend on when messages will arrive at the destination. Real-time messaging systems, on the other hand, offer QoS assurance by allocating resources and scheduling messages based on application-specific QoS objectives. They often conform to the DDS standard [5]. Unfortunately these systems are limited to

QoS management within a local area or a single domain. They are not designed for wide-area messaging involving multiple separate domains. Neither enterprise messaging nor real-time messaging is adequate for the emerging CPS and SoS, which require QoS awareness and enablement for messaging in a large geographic area and through federated domains.

The Harmony messaging system developed at IBM T. J. Watson Research Center is designed to combine the best of enterprise messaging and real-time messaging to suit the needs of the emerging CPS and SoS paradigms. Specifically, Harmony facilitates the interconnection of disparate messaging domains over large geographic areas and heterogeneous network infrastructure, and provides compatibility and interoperability with de-facto messaging standards including both JMS and DDS. One salient feature of Harmony is the holistic provisioning of dependable and predictable QoS by effectively addressing system and network dynamics, heterogeneity and failure conditions. It allows the specification of required performance properties (i.e., latency, throughput), availability and reliability models, and security constraints separately for each message topic or connection session; it further transports messages across autonomously administered domains respecting the above requirements end-to-end.

In this paper, we focus on the provisioning of end-to-end latency QoS in Harmony in the context of MOM for wide-area federated domains. This is achieved through a holistic set of overlay route establishment and maintenance mechanisms for managing the end-to-end latency, including both network latency and processing latency. In particular, the overlay routing mechanisms actively exploit diversity in the network paths and redirect messages over those links with good quality, e.g., low latency and high availability. In order to cope with network dynamics and failures, Harmony continuously monitors the link quality and adapts the routes whenever their quality deteriorates below the application requirements. Harmony can operate on top of different data transport layers. When the transport layer has built-in message scheduling capability, Harmony also adopts a novel budget allocation scheme to control its scheduling behavior and adapt to short-term network dynamics. Our experience from a testbed deployment demonstrates that Harmony can effectively manage the end-to-end latency with respect to the application requirements, despite the dynamics commonly seen in the wide-area networks.

The rest of this paper is organized as follows. Section 2 reviews our network and system models, and Section 3 presents our design of Harmony, a QoS-aware messaging middleware over wide-area networks. Section 4 describes our implementation efforts, and Section 5 reports our empirical experience from a testbed deployment. Section 6 compares the Harmony system to the literature. Finally, Section 7 concludes the paper.

2 Network and System Models

Our work targets the emerging CPS and SoS paradigms which require message-oriented middlewares to interconnect massively distributed components, services

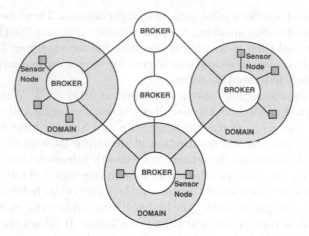

Fig. 1. Network Model

and systems over large geographic areas. Examples of such systems include Smart Grid for electricity distribution, smart city management and intelligent transportation. In all these applications, a large number of sensors and actuators are deployed in the field, and they must be interconnected with the event processing and analytics capabilities at the back end. A wide variety of event data and control directives are transported across different nodes in real time. This requires a messaging service that supports different communication paradigms, such as point-to-point, multicast and publish/subscribe. While the system we developed supports all these communication paradigms, we focus on the publish/subscribe aspect in this paper, because it provides the fundamental mechanism for asynchronous communication in distributed systems.

We assume that the endpoint nodes in the system are clustered into many local domains, and there is one broker node inside each domain. As shown in Figure 1, these brokers are inter-connected through an overlay network and collectively provide the publish/subscribe messaging service. Each endpoint node, such as a sensor, an actuator or a processing element, is attached to the local broker. There can be an arbitrary number of topics in the system, which can be defined either through administrative tools or dynamically using programming APIs. Each endpoint can publish and subscribe to one or multiple topics, while each broker can perform publish/subscribe matching, transport messages to local endpoints or neighboring brokers, and optionally perform message mediation (e.g., format transformation). Compared to the traditional approach using a single broker or a cluster of brokers, our overlay-based approach provides several architectural benefits as follow:

- *Scalability*: Each node only needs to know the local broker, while each broker only communicates with a small number of neighboring brokers. As such, we can avoid maintaining pair-wise connections, which is prohibitively expensive as the system scales up.

- *Federation*: The system is likely deployed and operated jointly by multiple organizations. In such a federated scenario, it is critical that each administrative domain can independently manage the access from/to its own nodes, which can be easily facilitated by the local brokers.
- *Heterogeneity*: The sensors are inevitably heterogeneous in a large-scale system. It is difficult, if possible, for any broker to understand all the protocols used by different nodes. With an overlay, the brokers can agree on a canonical protocol among themselves, and use a few adapters to communicate with the local sensor nodes.

Within each local domain, the sensor and actuator nodes can be connected to the broker through a variety of forms, e.g., wireless sensor networks. There have been numerous research in the sensor networking area, which is beyond our scope in this paper. Instead, we focus on providing Quality-of-Service (QoS) assurance within the broker overlay network. In the next subsection, we elaborate on the QoS model that we employ in this work.

2.1   Quality-of-Service Goals

Providing predictable QoS is an essential requirement for mission-critical applications. In particular, the messaging middleware should ensure timely and reliable delivery of critical messages, such as emergency alerts or real-time control commands. Formally stated, our goal is to provide QoS-aware publish/subscribe service in terms of *message latency and delivery rate between all matching pairs of publishers and subscribers*. Specifically, each topic is associated with a maximum delay that its messages can tolerate[1], and our system seeks to maximize the in-time message delivery rate, i.e., the percentage of messages that arrive before their respective deadline.

Note that the end-to-end delay for a given message consists of both processing delay at each intermediate broker and the communication delay between adjacent brokers. The former is affected by the load (i.e., message arrival process) of a broker, while the latter is affected by the characteristics of the network links. The broker processing delay also varies over time as each broker dispatches messages on multiple topics, and the messages may arrive in burst. Furthermore, since the sensors and actuators are deployed over a large geographic area, they will inevitably operate over wide-area networks, where the link quality fluctuates due to the dynamic traffic load. While some applications may employ dedicated networks, in general we do not assume the underlying network provides any QoS assurance. Such a relaxed network model allows our system to be applicable in different deployment scenarios, but it also poses challenges to our design as the messaging service must cope with such network and system dynamics, and ensure the end-to-end latency requirement is continuously satisfied.

---

[1] We consider per-topic latency requirement for ease of presentation. Our system can be easily extended to provide different QoS for individual publishers and subscribers.

3   Design

In this section, we present the design of *Harmony*, a message-oriented middleware with QoS awareness for wide-area publish/subscribe communication.

3.1   Overview

In order to meet the end-to-end latency requirements, our basic idea is to use overlay forwarding to bypass any congested network links or overloaded brokers, and to properly manage the network resources based on the message priorities. These techniques have been used in the literature for improving the QoS of point-to-point communication in the Internet [6][7][8]. However, there are a few non-trivial challenges in the context of publish/subscribe communication, where a topic may have many distributed publishers and subscribers. First, how can we establish QoS-aware overlay routes that interconnect all publishers and subscribers of a given topic, and adapt these routes in response to network dynamics such as link congestion and broker failures? Second, how can we coordinate the brokers along a route to collectively ensure the end-to-end latency performance?

Harmony addresses these challenges by a holistic set of overlay route establishment and maintenance mechanisms. Specifically, the brokers exchange control messages among themselves to discover remote subscriptions, and employ a distributed protocol to establish end-to-end overlay routes that satisfy the latency requirements. To handle network dynamics, each broker has a monitoring agent that keeps track of the latest processing latency and network latency to its neighboring brokers. These measurements are propagated among the brokers and used in the path computation to continuously find QoS-satisfied overlay routes. These overlay routing mechanisms can work with any data transport layer that supports publish/subscribe communication. Nevertheless, when the transport layer has additional message scheduling capability, Harmony allocates latency budgets for different topics at each hop, which are used to decide the scheduling priority of different messages at transmission time. This way, the system can handle short-term latency increase at one broker by increasing the latency budget at this broker, while reducing the budgets at other brokers. When the latency changes go beyond what can be handled by shifting budgets, however, new routing paths are computed to avoid congested links or overloaded brokers.

3.2   Overlay Routing

For simplicity, we assume that the set of brokers is known in advance, and the topology of the broker overlay is also decided a priori. Nevertheless, these brokers and links may fail and recover at any time. This assumption is reasonable in many application scenarios because the broker deployment only changes at very coarse timescales (e.g., once in a few weeks). In cases where brokers do frequently join and leave, a dynamic topology maintenance scheme is needed to adjust the overlay topology in runtime. We leave this issue for future study.

In general, there are two approaches for routing, namely link state (e.g., OSPF [9]) and distance vector (e.g., RIP [10]). While each approach has its own merits, our design follows the link state one which, as explained later, is more suitable for our specific context. We also employ several novel techniques to support QoS in distributed publish/subscribe communication.

Finding Subscribers.   As discussed in Section 2, each endpoint can subscribe to any topic at any time. Such subscriptions are sent to the local broker which this endpoint is attached to. Each broker maintains a *local subscription table* to record which topics each local endpoint subscribes to. The brokers then propagate these topics to other brokers. As a result, each broker knows which topics any other broker needs; it maintains such information in a *remote subscription table*.

When an endpoint publishes a message on a topic, say T, the message is sent to the local broker. This broker first checks the local subscription table and transmits to all local subscribers of T. It also checks the remote subscription table to finds all remote brokers that subscribe to T, and sends the message to these brokers using the overlay routes. Upon receiving this message, these brokers further forward it to their respective local subscribers. As such, the message will eventually arrive at all subscribers of topic T in the system.

Monitoring and Link State Advertisement.   Similar to OSPF [9], every broker periodically advertises its link states, including the measured processing latency for each topic and the network latency to each of its neighbors. Such link states are propagated to all other brokers through a simple neighbor forwarding mechanism [9]. Asa result, each broker has a local copy of the entire *network map*, i.e., the broker overlay topology with the latest latency measurements for all nodes and links.

Each broker employs a monitoring agent to measure processing and network latencies. It periodically pings neighboring brokers to obtain network latency. We use Exponentially Weighted Moving Averaging (EWMA) to avoid sudden spikes and drops in the measurements. On the other hand, if a neighbor fails to reply to three consecutive pings, it is considered to have failed and the link latency is marked as ∞. The monitoring agent also keeps track of the broker processing latency, including the time spent on publish/subscribe matching and the queueing delay. Both latency measurements are included in the link state advertisement so that each broker can build a complete network map.

QoS-aware Multipath Route Computation.   For both resilient and in-time message delivery, Harmony employs *multipath* routing in which a message may be delivered to the subscribers via multiple parallel paths. Since every broker maintains the complete overlay topology from the link-state advertisements, it can compute the QoS-satisfied paths individually and use a source routing protocol, which will be described shortly, to establish these paths. In what follows, we consider *resiliency level* (or simply *resiliency*) as the probability of delivering a message end-to-end over one or more paths, which can be measured over long periods of time. We provide a path computation algorithm that takes into account such failure probabilities towards choosing the most resilient combination of parallel paths. The failure probabilities of brokers and links are assumed to be known in advance, while our algorithm can accommodate various definitions of resiliency such as [11] or using historic information. For example, the percentage of time that a broker is *available* in a specific operational period of time can be extracted from traces such as the all-pairs-pings service.

Our algorithm takes as input the overlay network topology, the failure probability of each broker and each overlay link, the number of multipaths needed n, a delay constraint D and a maximum search depth k. The goal is to compute the n-multipath that provides the highest resiliency while satisfying the delay constraint. It first uses the k-shortest paths algorithm in [12] to find the k paths with the shortest delays between a source and a destination, in the order of increasing delays. It then excludes paths that exceed delay D. For the remaining k' paths we apply the provided failure probability of each broker to compute the resiliency of the remaining paths as follows: A path is considered available only when all brokers and all links along that path are also available. Thus, the resiliency of a path can be computed as $Pr(E) = \Pi_{i,j}(1 - p_i^n)(1 - p_j^l)$, where $Pr(E)$ is the resiliency of the path, and p_i^n and p_j^l are failure probabilities for brokers and links respectively. The algorithm then computes the resiliency of all the n-path combinations within the remaining k' paths, using *inclusion-exclusion* to compute $Pr(Q)$, i.e., the resiliency of the multi-path of n paths.

$$Pr(Q) = \sum_{j=1}^{n}(-1)^{j+1}\sum_{I\subseteq\{1...n\},|I|=j}Pr(E_I)$$

where, I is a subset containing j of the n paths, $Pr(E_I)$ is the probability that all the j paths are operational, meaning their brokers and links are all on. The sum is done over all subsets of size j, and over all sizes of j (from 1 to n).

Observe that the selection step is of exponential complexity due to its combinatorial nature. Another observation is that when adding an additional path say, p_i to a multipath Q the resiliency of the new multipath $Q\cup p_i$ is *at least* equal to Q. This observation motivates the utilization of a *branch-and-cut-based* heuristic search. We construct a tree, the root of which is the complete set of paths. Each broker of the tree represents a multipath. For each broker of the tree, its children are associated to all its sub-paths. Clearly, when a broker does not satisfy a resiliency value, none of its children will; thus it can be safely eliminated along with its children.

QoS Route Establishment.   In OSPF, each node independently runs Dijkstra's algorithm to determine the shortest path to every other node, and then populate its routing table accordingly. We do not directly apply this method in our broker overlay due to the need for controlling per-hop latency budget, as we shall describe in Section 3.3. Because each node on a route makes independent and possibly different decisions on how to reach the destination, the end-to-end routes change frequently; no single node can control the route. This makes it difficult to apply the budget allocation technique on a hop-by-hop basis.

Instead, we employ a novel source routing scheme, where a publisher broker locally computes the routes to all destinations (i.e., matching subscribers), and

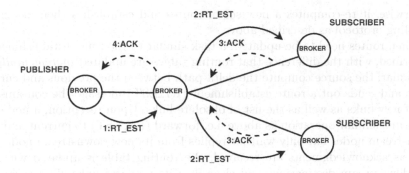

Fig. 2. Route establishment example. Numbers indicate the sequence of an operation.

uses a signaling protocol to set up these routes. As illustrated in Figure 2, the source node sends a route establishment (RT_EST) message to its next-hop neighbor on a route. The RT_EST message contains the topic name and all intermediate brokers on the route.

Upon receiving this message, a broker first checks whether it is the destination on the route. If so, it sends an acknowledgment to the upstream node from which it receives this message. Otherwise, it extracts its own next hops from the routes and forwards this RT_EST message to its next hop broker. When a node receives an acknowledgment from its downstream broker, it inserts the <topic,next_hop> pairs into its routing table, and then acknowledges to its own upstream node. Eventually, the source node receives the acknowledgment and the path is established. The process is repeated periodically to ensure the persistence of all QoS paths.

To briefly summarize, our scheme differs from OSPF in two fundamental aspects: 1) In OSPF, each node independently decides its next-hop nodes. In our scheme, the source node decides the entire routes. 2) In OSPF, a new link state advertisement may trigger an intermediate node to update its routing table, thus changing the end-to-end routes. In our scheme, once the routes are established, they remain fixed until the source node tears them down. To adapt to network dynamics, we employ a QoS-driven route maintenance mechanism.

Route Maintenance.   Harmony updates the overlay routes only when they cannot meet the latency requirement. This could happen when the route is disrupted by broker failure or network outage, or when the route quality deteriorates as the brokers are overloaded or the network is congested. All these cases can be easily detected by a source node, because it receives link state advertisement from all other brokers[2]. Specifically, when a source node receives a link state update, it checks whether the reported latency affects any of its routes. If so, it updates the end-to-end latency of the current routes and compares it to the latency requirement. If the requirement is still satisfied, no action is taken.

---

[2] Assuming the overlay is not partitioned by the failures.

Otherwise, it re-computes a new set of routes and establishes them using the signaling protocol as described above.

When routes need to be updated, a task similar to the route establishment is performed, with the difference that routing tables are updated *incrementally*. In particular, the source compute the delta-path between the previous and current paths and sends out a route establishment (RT_EST) message the contains the list of new links as well as the list of obsolete links. Upon reception, a node will perform a similar operation as above, i.e. forward (RT_EST) to current and new downstream nodes but only wait for replies from its new downstream nodes. As soon as acknowledgments are received, the routing table is updated with the new downstream destinations and cleared of its removed links. This technique ensures that no flow will be interrupted while the update process is executed.

3.3   Latency Budget Allocation

The Harmony overlay routing mechanisms can work on top of many different data transport layers. We have integrated the system with TCP/IP transport, a JMS-based publish/subscribe transport, and a real-time transport [13] with built-in message schedulers. In this subsection, we discuss how we take advantage of the scheduling capability in [13], which implements a laxity-based scheduling algorithm [14]. While message scheduling provides an important QoS mechanism of proactive network resource management, it does not always lead to globally desirable performance. In particular, the multiple brokers that a message traverses make independently scheduling decisions, and the resulting end-to-end latency may not satisfy the QoS requirement. While one could use a centralized algorithm to find globally optimal decisions based on the queue behavior (e.g., arrival process, steady states) of all brokers, such information changes fast and is difficult to maintain in practice.

Instead, we apply a heuristics algorithm where the latency margin, the different between the delay requirement and the current end-to-end delay, is divided among all brokers. This way, each broker will have some "buffer" to absorb sudden latency increases, provided they are small enough compared to the margin.

Consider a broker B which is currently on the forwarding routes for a set of topics $T_1, T_2, \ldots, T_I$. Let D_i be the end-to-end latency requirement for topic T_i. The routes for topic T_i has K_i hops, and the measured latency at each hop is d_i^j, where $1 \leq j \leq K_i$.

Our intuition is to give higher priority to those topics whose end-to-end latency is approaching the bound. To do so, we calculate the *end-to-end latency margin* for each topic (say T_i) as:

$$L_i = D_i - \sum_{j=1}^{K_i} d_i^j \tag{1}$$

We equally split this end-to-end latency margin among the K_i hops in the route. Thus the *per-hop latency margin* for topic T_i is:

$$L_i^j = (D_i - \sum_{j=1}^{K_i} d_i^j)/K_i \qquad (2)$$

Now the broker B can sort the topics in an increasing order of their per-hop latency margin. That is, the first topic has the smallest margin, thus should have the highest priority. Since laxity-based scheduling is used by the transmission queue, a high priority can be enforced by assigning a small latency budget for this topic. In general, for the n-th topic in the sorted list, we can assign a latency budget as (where δ is a step parameter):

$$LB_n = \min_{1 \le i \le I} T_i + n \times \delta \qquad (3)$$

Note that equal splitting is one simplest method for allocating latency margin among the brokers. It allows coordinated scheduling across brokers such that messages close to their delay bound get preferential treatment. We leave other forms of budget allocation, such as differentiated splitting, as future work.

4   Implementation

We have implemented the Harmony system within *IBM Websphere Message Broker (WMB)*, an industry-leading messaging platform. WMB introduces the concept of *message flows*; a message flow comprises of one or more incoming connections, a message processing component and one or more outgoing connections. Incoming connections are used by local domain applications to access the Harmony messaging service. Our implementation allows the applications to access the messaging service via standard *Java Messaging Service (JMS)* APIs [4]. Thus, those legacy applications that are already JMS-compatible can readily switch to a Harmony-enabled system, while JMS adapters can be easily built in order for non-JMS-compatible applications to leverage Harmony. Finally, Incoming and outgoing connections are also established to interconnect brokers across the wide area network.

Harmony control sits between the incoming and the outgoing connections, handling the process of routing various messages to the appropriate outgoing connections. In this way, WMB acts as the integrating agent between the Harmony routing control layer and the data transport layer. Therefore, Harmony routing control layer remains decoupled from any specific transport.

4.1   Topic Structure and Data Forwarding

To facilitate message forwarding, Harmony defines a different topic name space and naming convention to make a clear distinction between (i) topics coming from and destined for the local domain applications, and (ii) topics coming from and destined for the wide-area broker overlay. Harmony will then handle the topic name transformation from local domains to wide-area overlay. More precisely, in

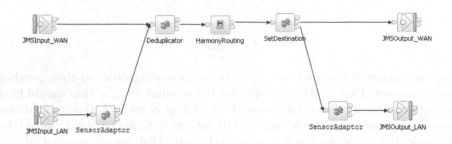

Fig. 3. WMB flow implementation of a Harmony overlay broker

the local domain, a global topic name T is transformed into the form /src/T when forwarded to Harmony and /dst/T when sent out from Harmony. At the overlay, topic T will be transformed according to the destination as /destID/T. This novel forwarding approach significantly simplifies the routing process by directly leveraging the underlying publish/subscribe infrastructure, without requiring for a separate forwarding protocol. Moreover, it can be readily used among different publish/subscribe engines beyond the current JMS implementation.

The overall implementation is illustrated in Figure 3 where the actual Harmony WMB flow components are shown. Two JMS input components are seen, one subscribing to local domain topics application publications (JMSInput_LAN) and one for incoming messages from remote brokers (JMSInput_WAN). Messages topics from the LAN are transformed via the Sensor Adapter component to internal Harmony names. Then, these messages along with incoming wide area messages are forwarded to the routing component which maintains the per-topic routing destinations. A de-duplication component removes possible duplicate messages received at the local node which could occur in the case of multipath routing. Finally, similar to the incoming messages, JMS output components are used for publishing out local domain (JMSOutput_LAN) and wide area messages (JMSOutput_WAN) according to destinations provided by the Harmony routing component.

5   System in Action

We have deployed Harmony in several distributed testbeds across the nation. For illustration purpose, we present a simplified operational example in which five brokers are each deployed at a major communication hub, namely Los Angeles, Seattle, Denver, Washington D.C. and Orlando. The presentation of the scenarios is facilitated by *Harmonitor*, an administrative tool for real-time visualization of the Harmony system, such as node/link status and per-topic paths.

In the scenario illustrated, two topics are published by the Seattle broker (more precisely, application endpoints attached to the Seattle broker). The first topic is subscribed by the Washington D.C. broker, while the second by Orlando. The topic to D.C. is considered of higher priority as its required end-to-end

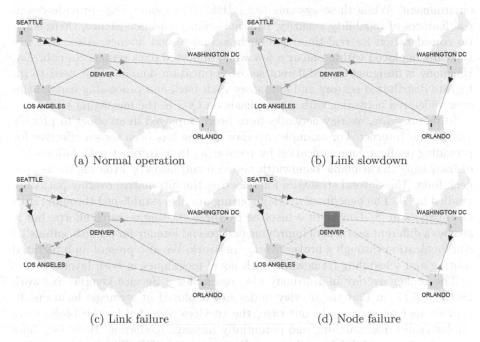

(a) Normal operation   (b) Link slowdown

(c) Link failure   (d) Node failure

Fig. 4. View of the deployed network from Harmonitor

latency is lower than that of the other topic. Figure 4(a) indicates the multipaths for each topic. Additional load is then introduced on the link between Seattle and Denver so as to slowdown that particular link, enough for the QoS of the first topic to be violated. As shown in Figure 4(b), Harmony provides differentiated service based on topic deadlines, and thus re-routes the higher priority topic away from the problematic link and through the Los Angeles broker. Note that while the second path is being reconfigured, data continue to flow within the QoS budget along the first path. In Figure 4(c), the previously slowed-down link is completely failed. The route for the topic that was flowing along the failed link, is immediately reconfigured to restore the multipath via the Los Angeles broker. Again observe that data delivery persists via the second path while the broken link is identified and the routes re-established. In the final Figure 4(d)), the Denver broker fails. The path that was routed via Denver is reset to forward traffic around the failed node from Los Angeles to Orlando and finally to Washington D.C.

6   Related Work

Message-oriented middleware has been widely used in today's enterprise IT infrastructure for integrating different applications and services in an SOA environment. While these systems (e.g., IBM WebSphere MQ) provide essential features of reliability, security, transactionality and persistence, there is little consideration for real-time QoS such as end-to-end latency. Also, they are typically deployed within one or a few well-connected data centers. In contrast, Harmony is designed for a different set of application domains that need to integrate distributed sensors and actuators with back-end processing capabilities over wide-area networks, with an emphasis on QoS in the messaging service.

In recent years, overlay networks have been employed in an effort to provide QoS in the Internet. For example, overlay routing has been shown effective for providing resilient communication by recovering from Internet path failures [6], or increasing the available bandwidth between end-hosts by avoiding the bottleneck links [15]. Several strategies for selecting the alternative overlay paths are studied in [7]. The benefits of overlay routing are also established through rigorous analysis in [8]. Our work is inspired by these existing research efforts, but it studies a different problem of improving end-to-end latency for publish/subscribe communication through a broker overlay network. We also present an integrated routing and scheduling framework, with novel techniques in both layers.

The broker overlay in Harmony also resembles a Service Overlay Network (SON) [16,17] in that the overlay nodes are deployed at strategic locations to provide specific services. In our case, the services provided by the brokers are publish/subscribe matching and potentially message mediation. However, there is one fundamental difference between Harmony and SON: The brokers in Harmony collectively provide the publish/subscribe service, while each broker in SON independently provides a service. There are several proposals for assuring QoS in a SON [17,18]. In particular, QRON [18] is a QoS-aware routing protocol that seeks to find paths satisfying QoS requirements yet balance the traffic on different overlay link and nodes. However, it only considers overlay routes between a pair of nodes, while Harmony provide QoS-aware group communication between multiple publishers and subscribers on the same topic.

7   Conclusion

In this paper, we presented the design and implementation of Harmony, a QoS-aware messaging middleware for supporting wide-area publish/subscribe communication. Harmony constructs an overlay network on top of the physical topology and provides a novel fusion of routing, scheduling and delay budget allocation to maintain the end-to-end QoS requirements. It allows for path adaptation and reconfigurations when either network outages or excessive delays occur along a delivery path. We have implemented Harmony in an industry-leading messaging platform and verified its feasibility and advantages through real deployment.

We are currently extending the Harmony system in several aspects. We plan to support dynamic topology construction and adaptation as nodes join and leave the overlay. We are also developing new path computation algorithms to accommodate multiple end-to-end QoS requirements in parallel. Finally, we plan to integrate mediation functionality in Harmony to allow applications to perform various types of actions, such as transformation and filtering, on the messages.

Acknowledgments

We would like to thank Parijat Dube, William Jerome, Zhen Liu, Dimitrios Pendarakis and Cathy Xia for their past contribution to the Harmony project. We are grateful to Maria Ebling, Francis Parr and Paul Giangarra for their support and valuable feedback. We also thank the anonymous reviewers for their insightful comments.

References

1. Lee, E.A.: Cyber-physical systems - Are computing foundations adequate? In: NSF Workshop on Cyber-Physical Systems: Research Motivation, Techniques and Roadmap (2006)
2. SOS: System of systems, http://www.sosece.org/
3. Comitz, P., Pinto, A., Sweet, D.E., Mazurkiewicz, J.: The joint NEO Spiral 1 program: Lessons learned, operational concepts and technical framework. In: Proc. Integrated Communications, Navigation and Surveillance Conference, ICNS (2008)
4. JMS: Java messaging service, http://java.sun.com/products/jms/
5. DDS: Data distribution service for real-time systems, http://www.omg.org/technology/documents/formal/data_distribution.htm
6. Anderson, D., Balakrishnan, H., Kaashoek, M., Morris, R.: Resilient overlay networks. In: Proc. ACM Symposium on Operating Systems Principles, SOSP (2001)
7. Fei, T., Tao, S., Gao, L., Guerin, R.: How to select a good alternate path in large peer-to-peer systems? In: Proc. IEEE Conference on Computer Communications, INFOCOM (2006)
8. Opos, J.M., Ramabhadran, S., Terry, A., Pasquale, J., Snoeren, A.C., Vahdat, A.: A performance analysis of indirect routing. In: Proc. IEEE International Parallel and Distributed Processing Symposium, IPDPS (2007)
9. Moy, J.: OSPF version 2. RFC 2328 (1998)
10. Malkin, G.: RIP version 2. RFC 2453 (1998)
11. Gu, X., Wang, H.: Online anomaly prediction for robust cluster systems. In: Proc. IEEE International Conference on Data Engineering, ICDE (2009)
12. Martins, E., Pascoal, M.: A new implementation of Yen's ranking loopless paths algorithm. 4OR: A Quarterly Journal of Operations Research 1(2), 121–133 (2003)
13. Astley, M., Bhola, S., Ward, M., Shagin, K., Paz, H., Gershinsky, G.: Pulsar: A resource-control architecture for time-critical service-oriented applications. IBM Systems Journal 47(2), 265–280 (2008)
14. Ramamritham, K., Stankovic, J.: Dynamic task scheduling in hard real-time distributed systems. IEEE Software 1(3), 65–75 (1984)
15. Lee, S.J., Banerjee, S., Sharma, P., Yalagandula, P., Basu, S.: Bandwidth-aware routing in overlay networks. In: Proc. IEEE Conference on Computer Communications, INFOCOM (2008)
16. Duan, Z., Zhang, Z., Hou, Y.: Service overlay networks: SLAs, QoS, and bandwidth provisioning. IEEE/ACM Transactions on Networking 11(6), 870–883 (2003)
17. Gu, X., Nahrstedt, K., Chang, R., Ward, C.: QoS-assured service composition in managed service overlay networks. In: Proc. IEEE International Conference on Distributed Computing Systems, ICDCS (2003)
18. Li, Z., Mohapatra, P.: QRON: QoS-aware routing in overlay networks. IEEE Journal of Selected Areas in Communications 22(1), 29–40 (2004)

Learning the Control-Flow of a Business Process Using ICN-Based Process Models

Aubrey J. Rembert[1] and Clarence (Skip) Ellis[2]

[1] IBM T.J. Watson Research Center, Hawthorne NY 10532, USA
[2] Department of Computer Science
University of Colorado at Boulder, Boulder CO 80306, US

Abstract. In this paper, we present a process mining algorithm that discovers Activity Precedence Graphs (APG), which are control-flow models in the Generalized Information Control Net (ICN) family of models. Unlike many other control-flow models discovered by process mining algorithms, APGs can be integrated with other business process perspectives.

1 Introduction

Process mining is the automatic discovery of process models and patterns from *process execution logs*. In this paper, we describe a process mining algorithm that discovers an Activity Precedence Graph (APG), which is a control-flow model in Generalized Information Control Nets (ICN) [1]. The area of process mining is over a decade old. It was first investigated by Cook and Wolf [2] in the context of software processes. Next, process mining was investigated by Agrawal et. al [3]. The concepts of process mining where extended with Petri-nets by Aalst et. al. in [4,5]. We extend the process mining literature by developing algorithms that discover APGs.

An ICN Activity Precedence Graph is an edge-colored, directed graph $\mathcal{G} = (A, E, \kappa)$, where A is a set of activities, $E \subseteq A \times A$ is a set of control-flow links, and κ maps an edge in E to a particular edge color. Let $\mathbf{a}, \mathbf{b} \in A$ be activities. The *predecessors* of $\mathbf{a}$ are denoted by $pred(\mathbf{a}) = \{\mathbf{b}|(\mathbf{b}, \mathbf{a}) \in E(\mathcal{G})\}$. The *successors* of $\mathbf{a}$ are denoted by $succ(\mathbf{a}) = \{\mathbf{b}|(\mathbf{a}, \mathbf{b}) \in E(\mathcal{G})\}$. Activities can be classified structurally as *simple*, *split* or *join*. A simple activity has at most one predecessor, and at most one successor. A split activity has multiple successors, and a join activity has multiple predecessors. It is important to note that a single activity can be both a split activity and a join activity. A control-flow link $(\mathbf{a}, \mathbf{b})$ is said to be *activated* once $\mathbf{a}$ has finished executing and selected it. In some instances, where $\mathbf{a}$ is a split activity, $\mathbf{a}$ must choose a subset of its control-flow links to activate. We now sketch our edge-coloring scheme. Given an activity $\mathbf{a}$, let $E_{succ(\mathbf{a})} = \{(\mathbf{a}, \mathbf{b})|\mathbf{b} \in succ(\mathbf{a})\}$. Each edge in $E_{succ(\mathbf{a})}$ is colored based on the execution semantics of the activities in $succ(\mathbf{a})$. For instance, if $\mathbf{b}, \mathbf{c} \in succ(\mathbf{a})$, and edges $(\mathbf{a}, \mathbf{b})$ and $(\mathbf{a}, \mathbf{c})$ are the same color, after $\mathbf{a}$ executes, $\mathbf{b}$ and $\mathbf{c}$ can be executed concurrently. If the edges are colored differently, a choice has be made to either execute $\mathbf{b}$, or $\mathbf{c}$. The set $E_{pred(\mathbf{a})}$ is defined analogously, and the color of edges in $E_{pred(\mathbf{a})}$ determine when $\mathbf{a}$ can be executed.

L. Baresi, C.-H. Chi, and J. Suzuki (Eds.): ICSOC-ServiceWave 2009, LNCS 5900, pp. 346–351, 2009.

2   Process Execution Logs

Our description of process execution logs and precedence dependencies is based on the descriptions given by Agrawal in the paper [3] and van der Aalst in the work [4]. Process execution logs consist of sets of process traces. Process traces consist of a sequence of events that were generated by activities that were executed in the same process instance. For the following definitions, let $\mathcal{L} = \{T_1, \ldots, T_{|\mathcal{L}|}\}$ be a process execution log. Also, let T be a process trace in $\mathcal{L}$. Additionally, let **a** and **b** be activities, and a and b be events generated by **a** and **b**, respectively.

Definition 1. *Event a precedes event b in T, denoted by $a \prec_T b$, if a occurs before b in T. (The T from $\prec_T$ can be dropped when the context is clear)*

Definition 2. *Activity **b** is precedence dependent on an **a**, denoted by $\mathbf{a} \rightarrow \mathbf{b}$, if in each process trace $T_i \in \mathcal{L}$, where $a, b \in T_i$, it is the case that $a \prec_{T_i} b$.*

Definition 3. *Activity **a** is precedence independent of activity **b** (and vice versa), denoted by $\mathbf{a} \perp \mathbf{b}$, if there exists traces T_i and T_j such that $b \prec_{T_i} a$ and $a \prec_{T_j} b$, where $j \neq i$.*

We can define a precedence dependency graph, and a precedence independency graph that represent the log-based precedence dependencies between activities. These two structures implicitly represent the structure and semantics of the underlying control-flow model.

Definition 4. *A directed graph $D_{\mathcal{L}} = (A, F)$ is a precedence dependency graph over $\mathcal{L}$, iff for each path $\mathbf{a} \rightsquigarrow \mathbf{b}$ in $D_{\mathcal{L}}$, there exists a log-based precedence dependence, $\mathbf{a} \rightarrow \mathbf{b}$.*

Definition 5. *An undirected graph $U_{\mathcal{L}} = (A, P)$ is a precedence independency graph, iff there exists an undirected edge between each pair of activities **a** and **b** in $U_{\mathcal{L}}$ where $\mathbf{a} \perp \mathbf{b}$.*

3   Learning APGs

The first phase of our algorithm is a straight-forward implementation of the Agrawal et. al. algorithm in the paper [3], with the exception that edges that appear in both directions are not discarded, but are used to construct a precedence independency graph. We will not present the full details of the modified Agrawal algorithm, and we will only consider the acyclic case due to space limitations. The reader, however, is referred to the work [6] for full details.

Example 1. Consider the process execution log $\mathcal{L} = \{abcef, acbef, adbef, acbef, abdef, abedf, abecf\}$. Figure 1(a) shows $D_{\mathcal{L}}$, after the Agrawal algorithm is executed on $\mathcal{L}$. Figure 1(b) shows $U_{\mathcal{L}}$ after the modified version of the Agrawal algorithm is executed on $\mathcal{L}$.

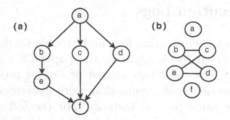

Fig. 1. (a) $D_{\mathcal{L}}$ (b) $U_{\mathcal{L}}$ based on the process execution log in Example 1

In the next phase, the semantics of splits and joins are made explicit. In particular, our algorithm, *LearnAPG*, constructs an APG by systematically exploring $D_{\mathcal{L}}$. The *LearnAPG* algorithm calls the *GrowAPG* sub-algorithm, which determines the semantics of splits and joins and extends a partially constructed APG. There are certain situations in which κ should map an edge to two different colors. In this situation, the *GrowAPG* algorithm calls the *HiddenActivitiySubstitution* sub-algorithm, which creates hidden activities in order to make the edge coloring scheme consistent. The input to the *LearnAPG* algorithm is a precedence dependency graph, $D_{\mathcal{L}}$, and a precedence independency graph, $U_{\mathcal{L}}$. The output of this algorithm is an APG, $\mathcal{G} = (A, E, \kappa)$, that explicitly represents the log-based dependencies captured in the precedence dependency and precedence independency graphs.

In the main iteration of *LearnAPG*, three sets of activities, $BLACK$, $GREY$, and $WHITE$ are maintained. The activities in the $BLACK$ set are activities that have been removed from $D_{\mathcal{L}}$ because they have no parents nor children in $D_{\mathcal{L}}$. The $GREY$ set contains activities from $D_{\mathcal{L}}$ that have no parents in $D_{\mathcal{L}}$. The $WHITE$ set contains activities such that all of the parents of each activity in $WHITE$ are in $GREY$, and there is no log-based precedence dependency between any of the activities in $WHITE$. Based on these sets, the *LearnAPG* algorithm constructs a *Family Graph*, a *Child Graph*, and a *Parent Graph*. Below we give definitions for these graphs. *LearnAPG* is presented in Algorithm 3.1.

Definition 6 (Family Graph). *Let children(a) be the children of activity* **a** *in graph* $D_{\mathcal{L}}$ *and parent(children(a)) be the parents of all the children in children(a). A family graph of activity* **a** $\in GREY$, *denoted by* $FG_{\mathbf{a}} = (A', F')$, *is an induced subgraph over* $D_{\mathcal{L}}$ *where* A' *is a set of activities such that* $A' = \{\mathbf{b}|(\mathbf{b} = \mathbf{a}) \vee (\mathbf{b} \in WHITE \wedge \mathbf{b} \in children(\mathbf{a})) \vee (\mathbf{b} \in GREY \wedge \mathbf{b} \in parent(children(\mathbf{a})))\}$

Definition 7 (Child Graph). *A child graph of a family graph* $FG_{\mathbf{a}} = (A', F')$, *denoted by* $CG_{\mathbf{a}} = (A'', P')$, *is an induced subgraph over* $U_{\mathcal{L}}$, *where* $A'' = \{\mathbf{b}|\mathbf{b} \in \{children(\mathbf{a}) \cap A'\}\}$.

Definition 8 (Parent Graph). *A parent graph of a family graph* $FG_{\mathbf{a}} = (A', E')$, *denoted by* $PG_{\mathbf{a}} = (A''', P'')$, *is an induced subgraph over* $U_{\mathcal{L}}$ *where* $A''' = \{\mathbf{b}|\mathbf{b} \in \{parents(children(\mathbf{a})) \cap A'\}\}$.

Algorithm 3.1. *LearnAPG($D_\mathcal{L}$, $U_\mathcal{L}$)*

1: $\mathcal{G} \leftarrow (\emptyset, \emptyset, \kappa)$
2: $color \leftarrow 0$ {We assume integers map to colors}
3: Set $GREY$ equal to the set of activities that don't have parents in $D_\mathcal{L}$.
4: **while** $GREY \neq \emptyset$ **do**
5:     Set $WHITE$ equal to the set of activities that are children only of activities in $GREY$ such
        that for any pair of activities $(\mathbf{a}, \mathbf{b}) \in WHITE$, it is the case that edge $(\mathbf{a}, \mathbf{b}) \notin D_\mathcal{L}^{-B}$
6:     Choose an activity $\mathbf{a}$ from $GREY$
7:     Compute $FG_\mathbf{a}$, $PG_\mathbf{a}$, and $CG_\mathbf{a}$
8:     **if** $|PG_\mathbf{a}| = 1$ **then**
9:         $GrowAPG(\mathbf{a}, CG_\mathbf{a}, \mathcal{G}, split, color)$
10:     **else if** $|PG_\mathbf{a}| > 1$ and $|CG_\mathbf{a}| = 1$ **then**
11:         Let $\mathbf{c}$ be the lone activity in $CG_\mathbf{a}$
12:         $GrowAPG(\mathbf{c}, PG_\mathbf{a}, \mathcal{G}, join, color)$
13:     **else if** $|PG_\mathbf{a}| > 1$ and $|CG_\mathbf{a}| > 1$ **then**
14:         Create hidden activity $\mathbf{h}$
15:         $GrowAPG(\mathbf{h}, PG_\mathbf{a}, \mathcal{G}, split, color)$
16:         $GrowAPG(\mathbf{h}, CG_\mathbf{a}, \mathcal{G}, join, color)$
17:     **end if**
18:     Remove all edges from $D_\mathcal{L}$ that correspond to edges in $FG_\mathbf{a}$
19:     **for** activities $\mathbf{g} \in GREY$ that have no more children in $D_\mathcal{L}$ **do**
20:         Remove $\mathbf{g}$ from $GREY$ and add it to $BLACK$
21:     **end for**
22:     Add all activities in $WHITE$ that have no parents in $D_\mathcal{L}$ to $GREY$.
23: **end while**

Algorithm 3.2. *GrowAPG($\mathbf{a}$, J, $\mathcal{G}$, ind, $color$)*

1: Add $\mathbf{a}$ to $A(\mathcal{G})$.
2: $C_J \leftarrow ConnectedComponents(J)$
3: **for** $C_i \in C_J$ **do**
4:     **if** C_i is a clique **then**
5:         **if** $ind = split$ **then**
6:             **for** each activity $\mathbf{c} \in C_i$ **do**
7:                 Add $\mathbf{c}$ to $A(\mathcal{G})$
8:                 Color edge $(\mathbf{a}, \mathbf{c})$ with $color$
9:                 Add edge $(\mathbf{a}, \mathbf{c})$ to $E(\mathcal{G})$
10:             **end for**
11:         **else**
12:             **for** each activity $\mathbf{c} \in C_i$ **do**
13:                 Add $\mathbf{c}$ to $\mathcal{G}.A$
14:                 Color edge $(\mathbf{c}, \mathbf{a})$ with $color$
15:                 Add edge $(\mathbf{c}, \mathbf{a})$ to $E(\mathcal{G})$
16:             **end for**
17:         **end if**
18:     **else**
19:         $HiddenActivitySubstitution(\mathbf{a}, C_i, \mathcal{G}, ind, color)$
20:     **end if**
21:     $color \leftarrow color + 1$
22: **end for**

The *GrowAPG* sub-algorithm computes the edge colors of, and extends a partially constructed APG. It takes as input a partially constructed APG, $\mathcal{G}$, an activity, $\mathbf{a}$, which is the place where the APG will be extended from/to, an undirected graph, J, that is either a child graph or a parent graph, and an indicator variable, *ind*, which determines if $\mathbf{a}$ is a split or join activity. To compute edge colors, the algorithm finds the connected components in J. Each connected component represents an edge color. All activities in the same connected component are connected to $\mathbf{a}$ with same colored edges. Activities in different connected

---

Algorithm 3.3. *HiddenActivitySubstitution*($\mathbf{a}$, K,$\mathcal{G}$, *ind*, *color*)

1: $Z \leftarrow (\emptyset, \emptyset)$
2: **if** K is a connected graph **then**
3:     $Z \leftarrow Compliment(K)$
4:     $Semantics(\mathbf{a}) \leftarrow OR$
5: **else**
6:     $Z \leftarrow K$
7:     $Semantics(\mathbf{a}) \leftarrow AND$
8: **end if**
9: $C_Z \leftarrow ConnectedComponents(Z)$
10: **for** each component $C_i \in C_Z$ **do**
11:     $k \leftarrow NULL$
12:     **if** $|C_i| = 1$ **then**
13:         Let $\mathbf{c} \in C_i$.
14:         **if** $ind = join$, $\kappa((\mathbf{c}, \mathbf{a})) = color$, and add edge $(\mathbf{c}, \mathbf{a})$ $E(\mathcal{G})$, otherwise $\kappa((\mathbf{a}, \mathbf{c})) = color$, and add $(\mathbf{a}, \mathbf{c})$ to $E(\mathcal{G})$
15:     **else**
16:         Create hidden activity $\mathbf{h_i}$
17:         $K' \leftarrow K[C_i]$ {K' is an induced subgraph of K over the activities in C_i}
18:         $HiddenActivitySubstitution(\mathbf{h_i}, K', \mathcal{G}, ind, color)$
19:         Add $\mathbf{h_i}$ to $A(\mathcal{G})$
20:         **if** $ind = join$, $\kappa((\mathbf{h_i}, \mathbf{a})) = color$ and add $(\mathbf{h_i}, \mathbf{a})$ to $E(\mathcal{G})$, otherwise $\kappa((\mathbf{a}, \mathbf{h_i})) = color$, and add $(\mathbf{a}, \mathbf{h_i})$ to $E(\mathcal{G})$
21:     **end if**
22:     **if** $Semantics(\mathbf{a}) = OR$ **then**
23:         $color \leftarrow color + 1$
24:     **end if**
25: **end for**

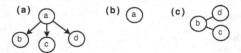

Fig. 2. (a) The family graph, $FG_\mathbf{a}$, of activity $\mathbf{a}$ from $D_\mathcal{L}$ based on Figure 1 (b) the parent graph $PG_\mathbf{a}$ (c) the child graph $CG_\mathbf{a}$

components are connected to $\mathbf{a}$ with different-colored edges. It must be noted that this only applies when the connected component is a clique. When a connected component found in J is not a clique, the algorithm makes a call to the sub algorithm *HiddenActivitySubstituion*. The *GrowAPG* algorithm uses the internal data structure $\mathcal{C}_J = \{C_1, \ldots C_w\}$, which is a set of connected components.

The *HiddenActivitySubstitution* sub-algorithm takes as input an activity $\mathbf{a}$, which is either a split or a join activity, an undirected graph, K, which is an induced subgraph over the connected component C_i from *GrowAPG*, $\mathcal{G}$, *ind*, and *color*. The *color* parameter represents the current color that edges should be colored. The output of this sub-algorithm is a partially constructed APG that contains a hidden activity to represent the semantics between activities in C_i and $\mathbf{a}$ that could not be represented directly. The algorithm maintains internal data structures K', which is a subgraph of K; Z, which is either equal to K or its compliment; $Semantics(\mathbf{a})$, which stores the control-flow semantics of $\mathbf{a}$. This algorithm also makes use of a the function *Compliment*, which takes a graph and returns the compliment of that graph. This algorithm is similar in principle to the work of Silva et. al. [7] and Herbst [8]. It is depicted in Algorithm 3.3.

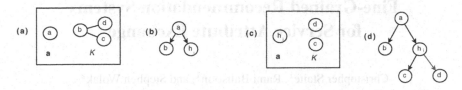

Fig. 3. (a)The first call to *HiddenActivitySubstitution* with the activity **a** and the child graph $CG_{\mathbf{a}}$ from Figure 2 and the resulting APG in (b). (c)A recursive call to *HiddenActivitySubstituion* and the resulting APG in (d).

4 Summary and Future Work

In this work, we have presented a control-flow discovery algorithm that discovers APGs. Additionally, since APGs can be integrated with other process models from the ICN family of models, future work will explore techniques for discovering other perspectives of a business process, especially the informational perspective. We are also exploring the development of correctness proofs of our control-flow discovery algorithm.

References

1. Ellis, C.A.: Formal and informal models of office activity. In: IFIP Congress, pp. 11–22 (1983)
2. Cook, J.E., Wolf, A.L.: Discovering models of software processes from event-based data. ACM Trans. Software Engineering Methodology 7(3), 215–249 (1998)
3. Agrawal, R., Gunopulos, D., Leymann, F.: Mining process models from workflow logs. In: Schek, H.-J., Saltor, F., Ramos, I., Alonso, G. (eds.) EDBT 1998. LNCS, vol. 1377, pp. 469–483. Springer, Heidelberg (1998)
4. van der Aalst, W., Weijters, T., Maruster, L.: Workflow mining: Discovering process models from event logs. IEEE Transactions on Knowledge and Data Engineering 16(9), 1128–1142 (2004)
5. Medeiros, A., Weijters, A., Aalst, W.: Genetic process mining: an experimental evaluation. Data Mining and Knowledge Discovery 14(2), 245–304 (2007)
6. Rembert, A.J.: Automatic Discovery of Workflow Models. PhD thesis, University of Colorado at Boulder (2008)
7. Silva, R., Zhang, J., Shanahan, J.G.: Probabilistic workflow mining. In: KDD 2005: Proceeding of the eleventh ACM SIGKDD international conference on Knowledge discovery in data mining, pp. 275–284. ACM Press, New York (2005)
8. Herbst, J., Karagiannis, D.: Workflow mining with involve. Comput. Ind. 53(3), 245–264 (2004)

Fine-Grained Recommendation Systems
for Service Attribute Exchange

Christopher Staite[1], Rami Bahsoon[1], and Stephen Wolak[2]

[1] School of Computer Science
University of Birmingham, United Kingdom
{C.Staite,R.Bahsoon}@cs.bham.ac.uk
[2] Vodafone Group Plc, Newbury, United Kingdom
Stephen.Wolak@vodafone.com

Abstract. The effectiveness of service oriented computing relies on the trust-worthiness of sharing of data between services. We advocate a semi-automated approach for information distribution and sharing, assisted by a reputation system. Unlike current recommendation systems which provide a user with a general trust value for a service, we propose a reputation model which calculates trust neighbourhoods through fine-grained multi-attribute analysis. Such a model allows a recommendation relevance to improve whilst maintaining a large user group, propagating and evolving trust perceptions between users. The approach is demonstrated on a small example.

1   Introduction

We address the problem of maintaining privacy where services interact with users. We suggest a recommendation system in order to assist sharing decisions and suggest semi-automation of sharing.

Current services maintain user profiles locally, which causes data to become outdated. The onus is on the user to provide a cross-service link between their profiles and manage authentication credentials. As a response, centralised Single Sign-On (SSO) services emerged permitting a single login. Popular implementations include Shibboleth [1] and OpenID [2]. This mechanism provides an easy framework for identifying users, but does not facilitate centralised profile storage.

Several systems attempt to centralise the storage of profile information. The most common is browser automatic form filling, which stores previous values. Although this assists profile creation, it does not allow services to access recent data. Other implementations such as SAML [3], OAuth [4] and OpenID Attribute Exchange [5] provide an interface to a central data repository. These permit centralised profile maintenance, assisting users on devices with restricted input abilities.

Sharing profile data between services raises many privacy questions, including: What trust should a user impart on a service? Which services should be allowed access to which parts of a users profile? How should data be transmitted between services? Where should the profile be stored? How can a user be assured that their data will not be used against the users' will? How can a service be sure that the user is not giving inaccurate information?

L. Baresi, C.-H. Chi, and J. Suzuki (Eds.): ICSOC-ServiceWave 2009, LNCS 5900, pp. 352–357, 2009.

As described in Section 2, research has attempted to solve the first question posed by using a recommendation system. Existing recommendation systems take coarse-grained approaches to analysis of trust by means of a single metric. Humans do not perceive trust on a per-service level, instead trust is dependant on factors such as the requested attributes. A user is constantly sharing their information as they utilise services, causing many requests from the central data. It is essential many of these operations are automated in order to produce a usable system. Services which have previously been given access could be given permanent access to certain fields. Initial access requests are hard to assess for trustworthiness from a mobile device. A recommendation from other users may provide a simple measure to assist.

We argue that there is a pragmatic need for semi-automated information distribution, assisted by reputation systems. By semi-automated we refer to the requirement of security to allow a user to make the decision in the case of sensitive data, but automatically distribute low-sensitivity data based on calculated trust. Reputation systems must analyse the requested attributes in order to accurately represent user opinion. In this paper we propose a mechanism, extending previous systems, in order to take attributes into account. Hence, we alter the analysis from the coarse-grained toward the fine-grained.

This paper is structured in the following manner: Section 2 discusses related work. Section 3 discusses the requirements for multi-factor trust analysis and proposes a formula which meets these requirements. A simple example is shown to detail the approach. Section 4 concludes.

2   Related Work

Current implementations of sharing mechanisms for the automation of attribute exchange (e.g. [6,7]) require a considerable setup effort from the user, such as defining the context and purpose of use.

Existing service recommendations are based upon whole service reputation [8,9,10]. [11] argues reputation systems are inadequate, due to the subtle differences between trust and reputation [12]. Trust defines a mental bias toward or against a service, whereas reputation is the conveyance of trust between people. The context sensitivity of trust causes it to be degraded by the use of coarse-grained reputation. We propose that reputation is more reliable when measured at a lower level (i.e. per-attribute).

[13] discusses methodologies for attribute exchange: although security in transmission is available, no mechanism utilises automation or recommendation.

[14] extends [13] in an attempts to enhance identity management online. Specifically, they provide users with the ability to see the purpose for request/retention details for each attribute, and the ability to revoke previously shared attributes [15]. This requires a large amount of screen space and bandwidth making its portability to mobile devices limited.

[16,17] extend authentication systems to achieve privacy oriented attribute exchange by utilising security conditions (similar to SAML [3]) and oblivious transfer [18]. The computational complexity is significant and unsuitable for deployment on mobile devices. Further, these methods do not allow for a persistent profile among user devices.

Collaborative filtering produces recommendations between items based on previous user input in order to make recommendations (e.g. user-based [19] and item-based

[20]). Both methods fail to apply multi-attribute to determine cross-attribute links (i.e. grouping users based on more than one attribute).

3 Approach

When a service requests personal information from a user it is assessed for trustworthiness. Abdul-Rahman & Hailes [10] discuss the three types of trust imparted by the user. *Interpersonal* trust is the trust between two individuals in a specific context. This is the context in which the service is accessed and which attributes are requested. *System* trust defines the general trust level in an institution. This relates to the provider of the service. *Dispositional* trust defines the natural trust a user has in a third party before they take any other aspect into consideration. Many people are willing to share their personal information freely on the internet, others prefer to preserve their anonymity due to their *disposition*.

A recommendation system attempts to group users based on their *dispositional* trust. It may then inform a user of *interpersonal* and *system* trust through analysis of similar users' previous decisions. Previous implementations fail to properly assess *interpersonal* trust due to their coarse-grained analysis.

Dispositional trust may evolve over time, the proposed system does not consider this factor. Hence, the database of previous interactions should degrade over time. For performance reasons the groupings may be calculated offline. By iteratively calculating the groupings offline there is a constant and recent grouping matrix available for fast trust calculations.

The trust measurement is taken from the decision to share information with a service. We define a binary variable $P_{u,s,a}$, where s identifies the service, a identifies the attribute requested and u identifies the user. The value is 0 if the information is withheld, or if a false value is given. If the attribute is supplied the value is defined as 1. $P_{u,s}$ refers to the set of attribute sharing values and may be in the state *undefined* if u has no experience with s. The correlation between two users $(u1, u2)$ produces a recommendation. This is performed for all values of P which are defined for both users $u1$ and $u2$. Where P is the set of all P_u for which $P_{u,s}$ are defined.

$$R_{u1,s} = \frac{\sum_{i=2}^{|u|}(P_{ui,s}Cor(P_{u1}, P_{ui}))}{\sum_{l=2}^{|u|}Cor(P_{u1}, P_{ul})}$$

$$Cor(P_{u1}, P_{ui}) = |P_{ui}|\sum_{j=1}^{|P_{ui}|}1 - \sqrt{\frac{\sum_{k=1}^{|P_{u1,sj}|}(P_{u1,sj,ak} - P_{ui,sj,ak})^2}{|P_{u1,sj}|}}$$

The correlation between two users is in a non-normalised form and used to provide the ratio of trust transference. This provides a non-negative value where 0 is defined as no similarities in past decisions, and increase in size the more similar previous decisions have been. A weighting value may be required in order to ignore lower correlation values. The multiplication by $|P_{ui}|$ ensures that users which have used more services similar to the user get preference over those who have similar, but limited, experience compared to the current user. The value of $R_{u1,s}$ is a vector with sharing recommendations for each of the attributes which may be sent to s. Each of the values in the

$$\begin{bmatrix} & & Service1 & Service2 & Service3 \\ Requested\ data & & \begin{Bmatrix} 0 \\ 1 \\ 1 \end{Bmatrix} & \begin{Bmatrix} 1 \\ 0 \\ 1 \end{Bmatrix} & \begin{Bmatrix} 1 \\ 1 \\ 0 \end{Bmatrix} \\ Alice & & \begin{Bmatrix} 0 \\ 1 \\ 1 \end{Bmatrix} & \begin{Bmatrix} 1 \\ 0 \\ 1 \end{Bmatrix} & \begin{Bmatrix} 1 \\ 1 \\ 0 \end{Bmatrix} \\ Bob & & \begin{Bmatrix} 0 \\ 0 \\ 1 \end{Bmatrix} & \begin{Bmatrix} 1 \\ 0 \\ 1 \end{Bmatrix} & \begin{Bmatrix} 1 \\ 0 \\ 0 \end{Bmatrix} \\ Charlotte & & \begin{Bmatrix} 0 \\ 1 \\ 1 \end{Bmatrix} & \begin{Bmatrix} 1 \\ 0 \\ 1 \end{Bmatrix} & undefined \end{bmatrix}$$

Fig. 1. A scenario showing three users transactions with three services

vector are between 0, meaning a strong recommendation not to share that attribute, and 1 which gives a strong recommendation to share the requested attribute. When the user has made their decision to share or withold attributes, the value of $P_{u,s,a}$ is set/altered.

We illustrate the use of the algorithm using a small example with the values given in Figure 1. In this table the requested attributes are shown for three services, followed by the previous sharing performed by three users, *Alice*, *Bob* and *Charlotte*. Both *Bob* and *Alice* have past transaction experience with all three services, *Service 1*, *Service 2* and *Service 3*. *Charlotte* only has past experience with *Service 1* and *Service 2*.

Charlotte visits *Service 3* and an attribute request is placed from the service to gain data items 1 and 2. A decision about which attributes to provide must be made, the recommendation system will aid the service judgement based on previous experiences. In order to provide the recommendation we calculate $R_{Charlotte,Service2}$.

$$Cor(P_{C,s1}, P_{A,s1}) = \sqrt{\frac{\sum_{k=1}^{|P_{C,s1}|} (P_{C,s1,ak} - P_{A,s1,ak})^2}{|P_{C,s1}|}}$$
$$= \sqrt{\frac{(0-0)^2 + (1-1)^2 + (1-1)^2}{3}} = \sqrt{0} = 0.$$

$$Cor(P_{C,s2}, P_{A,s2}) = \sqrt{\frac{\sum_{k=1}^{|P_{C,s2}|} (P_{C,s2,ak} - P_{A,s2,ak})^2}{|P_{C,s2}|}} = 0.$$

$$Cor(P_C, P_A) = 2((1-0) + (1-0)) = 4.$$

$$Cor(P_C, P_B) = 2((1 - \frac{1}{\sqrt{3}}) + (1-0)) = \frac{2}{\sqrt{3}}.$$

The value of $R_{C,s3}$ may be calculated using these correlations as groupings for users which *Charlotte* has similar sharing habits. The calculation that *Alice* has very similar habits to *Charlotte* as their correlation is much higher than that with *Bob*.

$$R_{C,s3} = \frac{\sum_{i=2}^{|u|} (P_{ui,s3} Cor(P_C, P_{ui}))}{\sum_{l=2}^{|u|} Cor(P_C, P_{ul})}$$

$$= \frac{\sqrt{3}((P_{A,s3} Cor(P_C, P_A)) + (P_{B,s3} Cor(P_C, P_B)))}{4\sqrt{3} + 2}$$

$$= \frac{\left(\left(\begin{Bmatrix} 1 \\ 1 \\ 0 \end{Bmatrix} \cdot 4\sqrt{3}\right) + \left(\begin{Bmatrix} 1 \\ 0 \\ 0 \end{Bmatrix} \cdot 2\right)\right)}{4\sqrt{3} + 2}$$

$$= \begin{Bmatrix} 1 \\ \frac{4\sqrt{3}}{4\sqrt{3}+2} \\ 0 \end{Bmatrix}.$$

We can present this recommendation to *Charlotte* in a percentage or bar form. She is given a 100% recommendation to share attribute 1, a 78% recommendation to share attribute 2 and a 0% recommendation to share attribute 3. The recommendation for attribute 3 is omitted as it was never requested by the service. Once *Charlotte* has made her decision of which information to share with the service the value of $P_{C,s3}$ is set for future reference by *Charlotte* and for producing recommendations for other users of the system.

Evolution of *dispositional* trust can occur as user opinion of a service becomes more or less trusting. The method given in this paper simply provides a method of calculating correlation based on past decisions. In order to allow for evolution of trust a time-based degradation may be performed before correlation calculation.

4 Conclusions

The need for automation and the role of recommendation systems have been outlined. Following, a mechanism to provide a recommendation has been proposed based on fine-grained past staring. The example provided an execution of the algorithm on a very small data set. A centrally accessible profile store is still required, following which an analysis of the effect of the proposed algorithm may be performed. The key to successful adoption of a serviced based web is the ability to exchange attributes without a large user effort.

References

1. Erdos, M., Cantor, S.: Shibboleth architecture draft v05 (2002), https://www.switch.ch/aai/docs/shibboleth/internet2/draft-internet2-shibboleth-arch-v05.pdf
2. Recordon, D., Reed, D.: Openid 2.0: a platform for user-centric identity management. In: DIM 2006: Proceedings of the second ACM workshop on Digital identity management, pp. 11–16. ACM, New York (2006)
3. Cantor, S., Kemp, J., Philpott, R., Maler, E.: Assertions and protocols for the oasis security assertion markup language (saml) v2.0 (2005), http://docs.oasis-open.org/security/saml/v2.0/saml-core-2.0-os.pdf

4. Atwood, M., Conlan, R.M., Cook, B., Culver, L., Elliott-McCrea, K., Halff, L., Hammer-Lahav, E., Laurie, B., Messina, C., Panzer, J., Quigley, S., Recordon, D., Sandler, E., Sergent, J., Sieling, T., Slesinsky, B., Smith, A.: OAuth Core 1.0. Technical report (2007)
5. Hardt, D., Bufu, J., Hoyt, J.: Openid atrribute exchange 1.0 - final (2007), http://openid.net/specs/openid-attribute-exchange-1_0.html
6. Cheng, W., Li, J., Moore, K., Karp, A.H.: A customer-centric privacy protection framework for mobile service-oriented architectures. In: IEEE International Conference on Services Computing, SCC 2008, Honolulu, HI, vol. 2, pp. 13–20 (2008)
7. Hong, J.I., Landay, J.A.: An architecture for privacy-sensitive ubiquitous computing. In: MobiSys 2004: Proceedings of the 2nd international conference on Mobile systems, applications, and services, pp. 177–189. ACM, New York (2004)
8. Herlocker, J.L., Konstan, J.A., Borchers, A., Riedl, J.: An algorithmic framework for performing collaborative filtering. In: SIGIR 1999: Proceedings of the 22nd annual international ACM SIGIR conference on Research and development in information retrieval, pp. 230–237. ACM, New York (1999)
9. Kinateder, M., Rothermel, K.: Architecture and algorithms for a distributed reputation system. In: Nixon, P., Terzis, S. (eds.) iTrust 2003. LNCS, vol. 2692, pp. 1–16. Springer, Heidelberg (2003)
10. Abdul-Rahman, A., Hailes, S.: Supporting trust in virtual communities, vol. 1, p. 9 (2000)
11. Resnick, P., Kuwabara, K., Zeckhauser, R., Friedman, E.: Reputation systems. Commun. ACM 43, 45–48 (2000)
12. Jøsang, A., Ismail, R., Boyd, C.: A survey of trust and reputation systems for online service provision. Decision Support Systems 43, 618–644 (2007) Emerging Issues in Collaborative Commerce
13. Pfitzmann, B., Waidner, M.: Privacy in browser-based attribute exchange. In: WPES 2002: Proceedings of the 2002 ACM workshop on Privacy in the Electronic Society, pp. 52–62. ACM, New York (2002)
14. Camenisch, J., Shelat, A., Sommer, D., Fischer-Hübner, S., Hansen, M., Krasemann, H., Lacoste, G., Leenes, R., Tseng, J.: Privacy and identity management for everyone. In: DIM 2005: Proceedings of the 2005 workshop on Digital identity management, pp. 20–27. ACM, New York (2005)
15. Pettersson, J.S., Fischer-Hübner, S., Danielsson, N., Nilsson, J., Bergmann, M., Clauss, S., Kriegelstein, T., Krasemann, H.: Making PRIME usable. In: Proceedings of the 2005 symposium on Usable privacy and security, pp. 53–64. ACM, New York (2005)
16. Fujiwara, S., Komura, T., Okabe, Y.: A privacy oriented extension of attribute exchange in shibboleth. In: IEEE/IPSJ International Symposium on Applications and the Internet Workshops, p. 28 (2007)
17. Takagi, T., Komura, T., Miyazaki, S., Okabe, Y.: Privacy oriented attribute exchange in shibboleth using magic protocols, pp. 293–296 (2008)
18. Rabin, M.: How to exchange secrets by oblivious transfer. Technical report, Technical Report TR-81, Harvard Aiken Computation Laboratory (1981)
19. Resnick, P., Iacovou, N., Suchak, M., Bergstrom, P., Riedl, J.: Grouplens: an open architecture for collaborative filtering of netnews. In: CSCW 1994: Proceedings of the 1994 ACM conference on Computer supported cooperative work, pp. 175–186. ACM, New York (1994)
20. Sarwar, B., Karypis, G., Konstan, J., Reidl, J.: Item-based collaborative filtering recommendation algorithms. In: WWW 2001: Proceedings of the 10th international conference on World Wide Web, pp. 285–295. ACM, New York (2001)

A Generative Framework for Service Process Composition*

Rajesh Thiagarajan, Wolfgang Mayer, and Markus Stumptner

Advanced Computing Research Centre, University of South Australia
{cisrkt,mayer,mst}@cs.unisa.edu.au

Abstract. In our prior work we showed the benefits of formulating service composition as a Generative Constraint Satisfaction Problem (GCSP), where available services and composition problems are modeled in a generic manner and are instantiated on-the-fly during the solving process, in dynamic composition scenarios. In this paper, we (1) outline the salient features of our framework, (2) present extensions to our framework in the form of process-level invariants, and (3) evaluate the effectiveness of our framework in difficult scenarios, where a number of similar and potentially unsuitable services have to be explored during composition.

1 Introduction

A vast number of proposals that exploit formal specifications of individual services to automatically select and compose individual services into executable service processes have been brought forward [1,2,3]. While most frameworks can successfully address basic composition tasks, many are based on ad-hoc algorithms or lack a precise representation of a service's capabilities. Therefore, the problem of configuring and tailoring the software that implements a given service is often left aside.

Constraint satisfaction based configuration techniques have been proposed as an alternative to address these challenges, where both type and instance information of services and relevant data must be considered [4,5]. Existing models compose services by treating services as components and assembling them. However, standard Constraint Satisfaction Problems (CSPs) are insufficient to model configuration problems where the number of components to be configured is unknown. Existing CSP-based composition techniques handle this by pre-specifying the number or type of services to be composed. In general, such estimation is difficult to make since such problem specific knowledge is not available a priori.

We present a generative consistency-based service composition approach that addresses these challenges [6]. We extend models that have been successfully applied to model and configure complex systems [7] to the software domain. The service composition problem is posed as a configuration task, where a set of service components and their interconnections are sought in order to satisfy a given

* This work was partially supported by the Australian Research Council (ARC) under grant DP0988961.

L. Baresi, C.-H. Chi, and J. Suzuki (Eds.): ICSOC-ServiceWave 2009, LNCS 5900, pp. 358–363, 2009.

goal. Our framework is based on a declarative constraint language to express user requirements, process constraints, and service profiles on a conceptual and also on the instance level. One of the major benefits of our approach is the provision to define problems independent of the number and type of services required, thereby overcoming the disadvantage of other models.

In this paper, we briefly outline our formalism that offers uniform (generic) constructs to represent service capabilities and semantics, represent data- and control flow between services (Section 2). We also present our extensions to the original model to unambiguously correlate conversations involving service instances or different parts of a workflow in a composition (Section 3). We also present the results from our evaluation on non-trivial pessimistic scenarios, where service compositions often fail (Section 4). Experimental results indicate that even in such pessimistic settings our framework's performance is quite competitive to other composition systems.

2   GCSP-Based Service Composition

CSPs[1] have successfully been applied in various domains including general planning [8] and service composition [4,5]. Generative CSPs (GCSPs) [7] extend standard CSPs by lifting constraints and variables to a meta-level, where *generic constraints* are the primary modeling element. Generic constraints abstract the actual CSP variables into so-called *meta variables* that are instantiated into ordinary constraints over variables in a classical CSP. Generative configuration can be seen as the problem of incrementally extending a CSP network until all the generic constraints are satisfied. In our formalism, when a component (C) of a particular type is added to the configuration, related variables and constraints (instances of the generic constraints of C) are activated in the configuration process. This dynamic activation of CSP variables makes GCSPs suitable for dynamic situations where a priori prediction of the problem structure is difficult.

A GCSP is characterized by the set of available component types, their attributes and ports (to connect to other components), and a set of generic constraints. In generic constraints, meta-variables act as placeholders for component variables. Generic constraints can be seen as prototypical constraints on a meta-level that are instantiated into *ordinary* constraints over variables in the CSP. For example, assume a generic constraint $X \sqsubseteq BudgetShipper \Rightarrow X.price < 1000$ is given, stating the invariant that the value of attribute *price* for any data object of type *BudgetShipper* must be less than 1000. A generic constraint over a meta-variable is said to be consistent if and only if the constraint is satisfied for all instances over active CSP variables. We extended the generative formalism in as follows [6]:

– We introduced connection components that act as connectors between services. The explicit representation of connectors provides a uniform interface

---

[1] A CSP consists of a finite set of variables, set of values that each variable can be assigned to (the variable's *domain*), and a set of constraints restricting the valid assignments of values to variables.

contract between services and also serves as a means to model the provider-consumer relationship between services.

- A connection component also holds a representation of the data values that may be passed along the connection.
- To capture their semantics, we treat complex data objects as components. This facilitates the uniform handling of service and data components in the configuration, and has the additional benefit that generic constraints can be used to impose invariants on data structures throughout a configuration.
- We introduced non-local process level constraints to model data flow, control flow, and structural invariants of service processes.

In our approach, a service composition problem is posed a as a configuration task expressed by an initial set of components and constraints that must be satisfied. During the configuration process, the CSP is dynamically extended by adding new variables and constraints. After each extension, the configuration is represented by a standard CSP constraint network (without generic constraints); therefore, standard algorithms can be applied to solve the CSP. An iterative deepening strategy that limits the number of components that may be introduced in the configuration prohibits the configuration from expanding indefinitely. Once that limit has been reached, the algorithm backtracks and attempts to find an alternative solution. If that fails, the limit is increased and the search is restarted. Detailed elaboration on the incremental configuration algorithm is given in [6].

3 Workflow Scope

The scope of a workflow or a sub-workflow defines the tasks it encapsulates in its behavioral process specification. For example, the Shipping process from the *Producer-Shipper* composition problem [9] encapsulates tasks *RequestGenerator* and *SendResponse* to process a request and acknowledge it, respectively. Existing specifications are insufficient if multiple instances of a sub-workflow exist within a composition. For example consider the process model in Figure 1a, where two users interact with two instances of the Shipping workflow.[2] The users would like to place a shipping order using the available shipping process, but are oblivious of each other. From a composition point-of-view, components in each sub-process are interchangeable. For example, the offer requested by *User 1* to *Shipper 1* may actually be sent to *User 2* (as in Figure 1a). Hence, means to ensure messages are directed to correct recipient must be provided.

To address this problem, we introduce explicit workflow *scope components* in our generic framework. Scope components, in addition to encapsulating a process specification, also differentiate between multiple instances of the same workflow by maintaining a *session ID* that is unique for each occurrence of the workflow. Figure 1b shows the scope component that encapsulates the Shipping process in our example. Formally, scope components and their connections to their process elements are also defined using generic constraints like other components

---

[2] We consider user interaction as an explicit part of the composition.

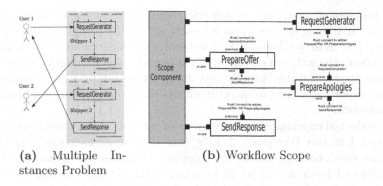

(a)   Multiple   In-   (b) Workflow Scope
stances Problem

Fig. 1. Process Specifications

in our framework. Connections between scope component and the process elements are also defined as generic constraints. While each workflow instance is identified by a unique ID attribute. Additionally, each constituent component in a composition is further distinguished by its unique component ID. Generic constraints make use of the scope components and IDs to ensure that the resulting service composition is well-formed by restricting the control and data flow between components.

4   Experimental Evaluation

We conducted an evaluation on a generalized version of the well-known *Producer-Shipper* problem [9], where a product ordering and shipping process must be composed from individual producers and shipper services, considering the capabilities and restrictions of individual services. Our largest problem with 28 parallel producer-shipper processes (1400 services) can be solved in roughly 3 minutes; a result quite competitive with other approaches [6]. The Producer-Shipper process is quite atypical in that is does not include complex chains of services or non-trivial transformations of data exchanged between services. We conducted further experiments to assess the performance of our framework in a scenario where items must be processed by a sequence of services in order to meet the goal requirements.

Assume the supply chain of a pie factory (at a fixed location) is to be configured using services. The factory requires supplies of flour and sugar to produce pies. Our model includes wheat and sugarcane farming *services* located in various Indian cities. In addition to the factory and farmers, the problem domain includes flour and sugar mills located in a number of South-East Asian destinations. The model also includes shipping services that ship products between locations. The aim is to compute a composition utilizing available services (farmers, mills, and shippers) in order to facilitate production operations in the pie factory while minimizing handling of the products (minimal number of shippers).

The problem structure in our scenario requires the solver to explore different alternative matching services, and for each alternative, longer chains of prerequisite services must be devised. This extensive exploration at each choice point better reflects the web service composition context, where a large number of services may appear suitable initially, but many fail to satisfy a given request. The following experiment aims to quantify effects of the changed search behavior on our framework.

We conducted experiments on a number of variants of our model. All our models contain 1 factory (the goal), 2 mills, and 12 farming locations. The smallest model involves choosing among 25 shipping locations. We gradually increase the number of locations up to 45 locations. Our smallest variant results in a composition with 13 services, and our largest requires 21 services.

We introduce another parameter *success factor* to vary the complexity of the problem. The higher the success factor is the more likely exploring an arbitrary branch will result in a successful match. A model with success factor 1 implies that exploring any out-going branch of the factory will definitely lead us to a matching service. The Producer-Shipper scenario model has a success factor close to 1 and hence exhibits near linear performance [6]. In this experiment we only consider models with success factors below 0.5 to simulate difficult composition problems. This setting reflects the assumption that many candidates that provide similar services exist, but only a few of those will be suitable. We vary the success factors of our models by replacing suitable services with ones that share similar profiles, but do not offer the required capabilities.

The first set of experiments employed the iterative deepening strategy discussed in [6]. The limit on the number of services in each experiment was initialized to 1 and was incremented by 1 in each iterative deepening step. The results are shown in Figure 2a. Our smallest problem with 13 services can be solved in roughly 45 seconds, and our largest problem with 21 services requires roughly 3

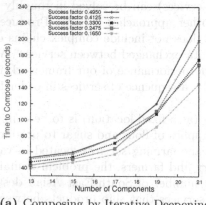

(a) Composing by Iterative Deepening

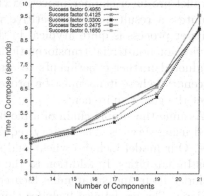

(b) Composing by Estimation

Fig. 2. Supply Chain Problem Results

minutes. This result is comparable in terms of problem size and complexity, and is quite competitive to other composition systems [5,9].

5   Discussion

We have shown that our approach exhibits competitive performance on complex process-level composition scenarios. However, the results in Figure 2a seem counter-intuitive as the problem instances with smallest success factor are solved fastest. Intuitively one would expect the opposite, since the chance of making a wrong choice and backtracking is more frequent in models with low success factor. To analyze this observation, we conducted another set of experiments where the number of service required in a composition is approximated beforehand (no iterative deepening). The results are presented in Figure 2b. It can be observed that the time taken to solve models with high success factor is lesser than that of model with low success factor. Therefore, backtracking caused by the iterative deepening strategy is the cause for the counter-intuitive observation in Figure 2a. We are currently exploring strategies to preserve solutions to sub-problems in the configuration while backtracking. In particular, we are investigating back jumping techniques that identify candidate variables to change based on previous successful and failing attempts to solve sub-problems.

References

1. Liu, Z., Ranganathan, A., Riabov, A.: A planning-based approach for the automated configuration of the enterprise service bus. In: Proc. ICSOC (2008)
2. Lécué, F., Delteil, A., Léger, A.: Optimizing Causal Link Based Web Service Composition. In: Proc. ECAI (2008)
3. Born, M., et al.: Semantic Annotation and Composition of Business Processes with Maestro. In: Bechhofer, S., Hauswirth, M., Hoffmann, J., Koubarakis, M. (eds.) ESWC 2008. LNCS, vol. 5021, pp. 772–776. Springer, Heidelberg (2008)
4. Karakoc, E., Senkul, P.: Composing semantic web services under constraints. Expert Syst. Appl. 36(8), 11021–11029 (2009)
5. Albert, P., et al.: Configuration Based Workflow Composition. In: Proc. ICWS (2005)
6. Mayer, W., Thiagarajan, R., Stumptner, M.: Service Composition As Generative Constraint Satisfaction. In: Proc. ICWS (2009)
7. Fleischanderl, G., et al.: Configuring large-scale systems with generative constraint satisfaction. IEEE Intelligent Systems 13(4) (1998)
8. Pralet, C., Verfaillie, G.: Using constraint networks on timelines to model and solve planning and scheduling problems. In: Proc. ICAPS (2008)
9. Pistore, M., et al.: Automated composition of web services by planning at the knowledge level. In: Proc. IJCAI (2005)

Achieving Predictability and Service Differentiation in Web Services

Vidura Gamini Abhaya, Zahir Tari, and Peter Bertok

School of Computer Science and Information Technology
RMIT University, Melbourne, Australia
vabhaya@cs.rmit.edu.au, {zahir.tari,peter.bertok}@rmit.edu.au

Abstract. This paper proposes a model and an admission control algorithm for achieving predictability in web services by means of service differentiation. We use real-time scheduling principles typically used offline, adapt them to web services to work online. The proposed model and algorithm is empirically evaluated by implementing it Apache Axis2. The implementation is benchmarked against the unmodified version of Axis2 for various types of workloads and arrival rates, given different deadlines. We meet 100% of the deadlines keeping a healthy request acceptance rate of 42-100% depending on the task size variation. Our solution outperforms Axis2, specially at instances with high task size variance, by a factor of 10 - 1000.

1 Introduction

Web service architectures and supporting infrastructure (such as SOAP engines and application servers) by design, lacks support for predictability in execution. For instance, they service requests in a *best effort* manner. As a result, specialised middleware (such as Real-Time CORBA [1]) has been the default choice for applications with real-time requirements.

Applications with real-time requirements are characterized by the equal importance placed on time taken for a result to be obtained as on the correctness of the computation performed. Herein, the notion of time taken for the result to be obtained is expected to be predictable and consistent invariably. Moreover, if the time taken to obtain the result is beyond a certain deadline, the result may be considered useless and might lead to severe consequences. As a result, real-time systems with stringent QoS levels require the service execution and middleware used to have very high predictability [2].

Although some research in web services has attempted to address Quality of Service (QoS) aspects [3,4,5,6,7], none of them guarantees predictability in all aspects of functionality, such as message processing and service execution. Moreover, there is no support for predictability from the operating system (OS) and the development platform. The work that comes close to achieving it [8], does it in a confined embedded environment where tasks and their resource requests are known in advance of the task occurrence. The challenge would be to achieve predictability in the totally dynamic environment that web services are used in.

Contribution. Our solution is unique due to several reasons. The solution achieves predictability in a highly dynamic environment with no prior knowledge of requests.

L. Baresi, C.-H. Chi, and J. Suzuki (Eds.): ICSOC-ServiceWave 2009, LNCS 5900, pp. 364–372, 2009.

Request acceptance is not pre-determined and happens *on-the-fly*. Moreover, it allows any web service request to be tagged with a target completion time, which on acceptance is guaranteed to be met. This is the first approach of scheduling web service requests based on a user requested deadline. Our solution is unique in adapting real-time scheduling principles designed for offline use, to a dynamic online environment.

2   Background

Two concepts considered in schedulability analysis, namely *processor demand* and *loading factor* [9] are defined here. Henceforth, we use a given task T_i, with release time of r_i, a deadline of d_i and an execution time requirement of C_i. Our proposed model is based on the following definitions.

Definition 1. *For a given set of real-time tasks and an interval of time* $[t_1,t_2)$, *the processor demand (h) for the set of tasks in the interval* $[t_1,t_2)$ *is*

$$h_{[t_1,t_2)} = \sum_{t_1 \leq r_k, d_k \leq t_2} C_k. \tag{1}$$

Definition 2. *For a given set of real-time tasks the fraction of the interval* $[t_1,t_2)$ *needed to execute its tasks is considered as its* loading factor (u) *that is,*

$$u_{[t_1,t_2)} = \frac{h_{[t_1,t_2)}}{t_2 - t_1}. \tag{2}$$

Definition 3. *The loading factor of the maximum of all such intervals, is considered as* absolute loading factor, *that is,*

$$u = \sup_{0 \leq t_1 \leq t_2} u_{[t_1,t_2)}. \tag{3}$$

Theorem 1 (Spuri [10]). *Any set of real-time tasks is feasibly scheduled by EDF algorithm if and only if*

$$u \leq 1. \tag{4}$$

3   Proposed Solution

3.1   Proposed Model

The proposed model is based on the notion of a *deadline*, specified by the client at the time of service invocation. The Deadline is considered to be the absolute time period the request has to be serviced within. The proposed solution has two parts. An *on-the-fly* schedulability check is conducted on the arrival of a task at the system, to evaluate the possibility of servicing it within the requested deadline, without compromising already accepted tasks. Then the accepted tasks are scheduled using a deadline based real-time scheduling algorithm.

In a pre-emptive scheduling system, execution of a given request could happen with several pre-emption cycles.

Definition 4. *For a given request T_i having n number of pre-emptions, where the start time of each execution is s_n and the end time of each execution is e_n, the Total time of the task execution E_i can be considered as,*

$$E_i = \sum_{j=1}^{n} (e_j - s_j). \tag{5}$$

Definition 5. *For a given request submitted to the system, with the execution time requirement of C_i, at any given point of time the remaining execution time R_i can be considered as,*

$$R_i = C_i - E_i. \tag{6}$$

Let T_{new} be a newly submitted task, with a release time of r_{new} and a deadline of d_{new} and an execution time requirement of C_{new}. Let P be the set of tasks already accepted and active in the system, with their deadlines denoted as d_p

With reference to definition 1, the processor demand within the duration of the newly submitted task can be defined as,

$$h_{[r_{new}, d_{new})} = \sum_{r_{new} \leq d_p \leq d_{new}} R_p + C_{new}. \tag{7}$$

With reference to definition 2, the loading factor within the duration of the newly submitted task can be defined as,

$$u_{[r_{new}, d_{new})} = \frac{h_{[r_{new}, d_{new})}}{d_{new} - r_{new}} \tag{8}$$

With condition 8, if the following condition is satisfied, the new task is considered schedulable together with tasks finishing on or before its deadline, with no impact on their deadlines.

$$u_{[r_{new}, d_{new})} \leq 1 \tag{9}$$

Let Q be the set of tasks already accepted and active in the system, required to finish after d_{new} (such that, with deadlines after d_{new}). Let q be the member of Q, with a deadline of d_q up to which the processor demand is calculated for,

$$h_{[r_{new}, d_q)} = h_{[r_{new}, d_{new})} + \sum_{d_{new} \leq d_i \leq d_q} R_i. \tag{10}$$

The result of 7 is used as part of the equation. This represents the processor demand of all tasks finishing on or prior to d_{new} and can be treated as one big task with a release time r_{new} and a deadline of d_{new} respectively. Next, the loading factor for the same duration is calculated.

$$u_{[r_{new}, d_q)} = \frac{h_{[r_{new}, d_q)}}{d_q - r_{new}} \tag{11}$$

The loading factor is also calculated on a per task basis for each member of Q. Subsequently, the calculated loading factor is compared to be less than or equal to 1, in order for all tasks leading up to q, to be satisfied as schedulable.

$$u_{[r_{new}, d_q]} \leq 1 \tag{12}$$

In summary, for a newly submitted task to be accepted to the system, condition 9 needs to be satisfied for tasks with deadlines on or before d_{new}, subsequently condition 12 needs to be satisfied, separately for each task with deadlines after d_{new}.

3.2 Proposed Algorithm

Based on the above model, Algorithm 1, will form the core of our solution in the implementation that follows. In devising the algorithm, we make the assumption that the execution time requirement or an estimation of it per parameter, for each service hosted would be available to the server.

Current time, deadline of the new request and the list of requests already accepted by the system as inputs. Current time is considered as the start time of the new request. As per the model described in 3.1, The check consists of two steps. First part determines the schedulability of a new request together with tasks finishing within its lifespan, while meeting all deadlines (Lines 2 to 14). For each request $P' \in P$, it is checked whether execution information is currently available (Line 4). If the request has been partially processed, the remaining execution time calculated as per equation 5, is obtained (Line 5). If the request is yet to be processed, the execution time requirement of the task (Line 7), is used alternatively.

Following equation 7, the processor demand within the duration of the newly submitted request is calculated by summing up the remaining execution times or execution time requirements of each task. Adding the execution time requirement for the new request (Line 10) completes the processor demand calculation for its lifespan. Following equation 8, we calculate the loading factor for the time period (Line 11). If the loading factor is greater than 1, the request is straightaway rejected. If the loading factor remains less than 100%, the check continues on to the second stage.

The second stage validates the effect of the newly submitted request on requests finishing thereafter. For this we select requests with deadlines later than that of the new task (Line 15). The check is done separately for each and every request selected. We make the process more efficient by, first sorting the list of selected requests in the ascending order of the deadlines (Line 16). For each request $Q' \in Q$, a further subset of requests from the list is selected. All requests required to finish between newly submitted and Q' are selected into set R (Line 19). For each request $R' \in R$, the processor demand is calculated by using either the remaining time of the request or its execution time requirement (Lines 21 to 26). To this, the remaining time or the execution time request of request Q' is also added (Line 27 to 29). Following equation 10, the processor demand calculated for the duration of the new request is added to it (Line 28 and 30). Finally, following equation 11, we calculate the loading factor for the same duration (Line 32). If the result exceeds 100%, the request is rejected (Line 33 to 35). If it is less than or equal to 100%, the check is repeated for members in Q, until a check fails or all of them are satisfied, at which point the request is considered schedulable.

Algorithm 1. Online Schedulability Check

Require: (S_{new}) Current time, (D_{new}) deadline of new
request N, (T) List of requests currently in the system
Ensure: true: if the task can be scheduled, false: if the
schedulability check fails
1: WPD ← 0; APD ← 0
2: P ← GetTasksFinWitnNewTask(T, S_{new} , D_{new})
3: **for all** P′ ∈ P **do**
4:     **if** execution information for P′ exists **then**
5:         WPD ← WPD + GetRemExTm(P′)
6:     **else**
7:         WPD ← WPD + GetExecTime(P′)
8:     **end if**
9: **end for**
10: WPD ← WPD + GetExecTime(N)
11: LoadingFactor ← $\frac{WPD}{(D_{new}-S_{new})}$
12: **if** LoadingFactor > 1 **then**
13:     **return** false
14: **end if**
15: Q ← GetTasksFinAftNewTask(T,D_{new})
16: Q ← SortByDL(Q)
17: **for all** Q′ ∈ Q **do**
18:     DL ← GetDL(Q′)
19:     R ← GetTasksFinBtwn(T, D_{new}, DL)
20:     **for all** R′ ∈ R **do**
21:         **if** execution information for R′ exists **then**
22:             APD ← APD + GetRemExTm(R′)
23:         **else**
24:             APD ← APD + GetExecTime(R′)
25:         **end if**
26:     **end for**
27:     **if** execution information for Q′ exists **then**
28:         APD ← APD + WPD + GetRemExTm(Q′)
29:     **else**
30:         APD ← APD + WPD + GetExecTime(Q′)
31:     **end if**
32:     LoadingFactor ← $\frac{APD}{(DL-S_{new})}$
33:     **if** LoadingFactor > 1 **then**
34:         **return** false
35:     **end if**
36: **end for**
37: **return** true

Sorting the requests by ascending deadlines ensures a failure happens as early as possible. Moreover, it avoids the check being repeated after a failure. The complexity of the algorithm results in $O(n^2)$.

3.3 Deadline Based scheduling

The requests accepted through the schedulability check are scheduled using a deadline based scheduling algorithm. It schedules tasks sequentially in the increasing order of their deadlines. The algorithm makes use of priority levels to control the execution of the worker threads in the system. This ensures predictability at execution level of the system.

4 Empirical Evaluation

The implementation is benchmarked against unmodified version of Apache Axis2. Since Axis2 by design works in a best effort manner, there would be no resultant task rejections. However, the number of tasks meeting their deadlines is used as the main metric to measure performance. A web service that allowed us to fine tune the task sizes with a single parameter was used for the experiments. We generated task sizes according to Uniform, Exponential and Pareto distributions. Moreover, we generated task arrival rates using a Uniform distribution.

4.1 Experimental Results

The success of our solution, depends on two primary factors. The number of requests accepted for execution and the number of requests meeting the requested deadlines. The aim was to achieve a high rate of task acceptance and to ensure that majority of them met their deadlines. The task size distribution, the execution time to deadline ratio and the arrival rates had an effect on this. Table 1 contains a summary of all experiments runs. The first two columns contain the various experiment runs conducted and the parameters used. The deadline for each run was calculated by multiplying the respective profiled execution time requirement by a value between 1.5 and 10 drawn out uniformly from the distribution.

Table 1. Comparison of Real-time Axis2 and Unmodified Axis2 performance

Distribution	Inter-arrival time(sec)	Real-time Axis2			Unmodified Axis2	
		% Acc.	% D. Mis.	% D. Met	% D. Mis.	% D. Met
Uniform	0.25 - 5	41.8	0	100	96.6	3.4
	0.25 - 10	81.2	0	100	83.6	16.4
Bounded Exponential $\lambda = 10^{-6}$	0.25 - 2	62.5	0.1	99.9	42.6	57.4
	0.25 - 5	99.3	0	100	0	100
	0.25 - 10	100	0	100	0	100
Bounded Exponential $\lambda = 10^{-5}$	0.25 - 2	100	0	100	0	100
	0.25 - 5	100	0	100	0	100
	0.25 - 10	100	0	100	0	100
Bounded Pareto $\alpha = 0.5$	0.25 - 2	100	0.3	99.7	0	100
	0.25 - 5	100	0.1	99.9	0	100
	0.25 - 10	100	0	100	0	100
Bounded Pareto $\alpha = 0.05$	0.25 - 2	99.4	0	100	0	100
	0.25 - 5	99.9	0	100	0	100
	0.25 - 10	100	0	100	0	100

4.2 Discussion

Task Acceptance. In a given period of time, real-time Axis2 accepts between 42% - 100% tasks it receives, depending on the mixture of tasks. If the request sizes take an Exponential or a Pareto type distribution, the task acceptance rate results a 100% in almost all the experiment runs. This happens due to the high concentration of small sized requests in the mix. A small task may have an execution time requirement of a few CPU cycles or even a fraction of a CPU cycle. As a result, it is possible to finish more small requests in a given period of time. Medium and large tasks having a higher execution time requirement tend to get accumulated to the backlog of tasks waiting to finish execution. This results in task rejections.

Impact of Arrival Rate. Varying the arrival rates of requests, it was observed that the number of tasks accepted is proportional to the arrival rate of tasks. A higher arrival rate results in the system receiving requests at a higher rate than it is completing requests. This leads to a build-up of unfinished requests in the system that leads to the eventual rejection of tasks. Moreover, a lower arrival rate results in the system finishing up execution of requests before the next task arrives at the system. This yields a higher task acceptance rate.

Deadline Achievement. With the real-time implementation, 100% of the requests achieve their deadlines, in most cases. It is clearly visible that the real-time implementation performs better than unmodified Axis2 in meeting request deadlines. When the requests received are predominantly small, both versions of Axis2 performs well with meeting deadlines of all tasks. Due to the small execution time requirements of the tasks the deadlines are easily achieved as it leads to no task build-up. Unmodified Axis2 performs marginally better than the real-time implementation in a couple of cases were the task mix consist of only very small sized requests.

Timeliness of execution. According to Fig. 1, with runs having a higher variety of task sizes, real-time Axis2 results in better execution times than unmodified Axis2 by very large factors. When the requests are predominantly small, both implementations achieve

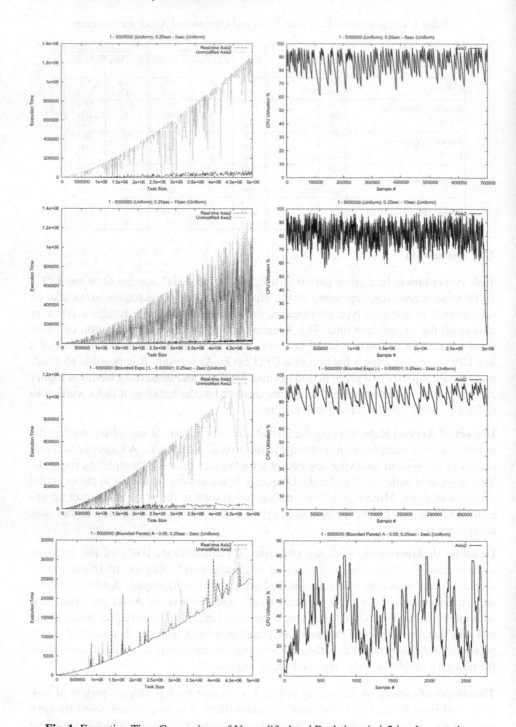

Fig. 1. Execution Time Comparison of Unmodified and Real-time Axis2 implementations

deadlines of almost all the requests. This is largely due to the best effort nature that unmodified Axis2 functions in. Accepting all requests and trying to execute as many as possible in parallel, results in all requests taking a longer time to finish execution. With the real-time implementation, a task is only accepted if its deadline could be met while not compromising that of the others already accepted. This results in lower execution times compared to unmodified Axis2. In some of the bounded exponential and pareto runs, Real-time Axis2 execution times have resulted in higher than normal execution times for certain task sizes. These are deviations intended behaviour by the real-time scheduler, in order to achieve the deadlines of other tasks.

CPU utilisation. In the runs where there was rejection of tasks, it is clearly visible from Fig. 1 that Real-time Axis2 has a very high utilization of the process during the experimental runs. Although it is reasonable to assume that the processor should be utilized 100% of the time by a process in such scenarios, practically this may not achieved due to thread level scheduling. However, with a real-time OS being used and a development platform that supports real-time systems, it is clearly visible that very high rates of processor utilisation can be achieved. Moreover, whenever tasks are rejected by the schedulability check, it is backed up by the high processor utilisation.

5   Conclusion

With the experiment results discussed in the previous section, it could be concluded that the devised model, schedulability check introduced and the real-time algorithm achieved their purpose. Moreover, it would be fair to conclude that real-time Axis2 achieves the goal of maximizing request deadline achievement. The result show a significant difference in the execution times achieved especially where there is a high variety of task sizes. The solution performs decently with a task acceptance rate of 42 - 100% varying with the arrival rates of tasks. Most importantly it performs well to achieve the deadline of all accepted tasks consistently.

References

1. Schmidt, D., Kuhns, F.: An overview of the Real-Time CORBA specification. Computer 33(6), 56–63 (2000)
2. Schmidt, D., Levine, D., Mungee, S.: The design and performance of real-time object request brokers. Computer Communications 21(4), 294–324 (1998)
3. Ran, S.: A model for web services discovery with QoS. ACM SIGecom Exchanges 4(1), 1–10 (2003)
4. Tian, M., Gramm, A., Naumowicz, T., Ritter, H., Freie, J.: A concept for QoS integration in Web services. In: Web Information Systems Engineering Workshops, Proceedings, pp. 149–155 (2003)
5. Yu, T., Lin, K.: The design of QoS broker algorithms for QoS-capable web services. In: IEEE International Conference on e-technology, e-commerce and e-service, EEE 2004, pp. 17–24 (2004)
6. Sharma, A., Adarkar, H., Sengupta, S.: Managing QoS through prioritization in web services. In: Web Information Systems Engineering Workshops, Proceedings, December 2003, pp. 140–148 (2003)

7. Tien, C.-M., Cho-Jun Lee, P.: SOAP Request Scheduling for Differentiated Quality of Service. In: Dean, M., Guo, Y., Jun, W., Kaschek, R., Krishnaswamy, S., Pan, Z., Sheng, Q.Z. (eds.) WISE 2005 Workshops. LNCS, vol. 3807, pp. 63–72. Springer, Heidelberg (2005)
8. Helander, J., Sigurdsson, S.: Self-tuning planned actions time to make real-time SOAP real. In: Eighth IEEE International Symposium on Object-Oriented Real-Time Distributed Computing, ISORC, pp. 80–89 (2005)
9. Stankovic, J.A., Spuri, M., Ramamritham, K., Buttazzo, G.C.: Deadline scheduling for real-time systems: EDF and related algorithms. Kluwer Academic Publishers, Dordrecht (1998)
10. Spuri, M.: Earliest Deadline scheduling in real-time systems. Doctorate Dissertation, Scuola Superiore S. Anna, Pisa (1995)

Incorporating Security Requirements into Service Composition: From Modelling to Execution

Andre R.R. Souza[1], Bruno L.B. Silva[1], Fernando A.A. Lins[1], Julio C. Damasceno[1],
Nelson S. Rosa[1], Paulo R.M. Maciel[1], Robson W.A. Medeiros[1],
Bryan Stephenson[2], Hamid R. Motahari-Nezhad[2], Jun Li[2], and Caio Northfleet[3]

[1] Federal University of Pernambuco, Centre of Informatics
{arss,blbs,faal2,jcd,nsr,prmm,rwam}@cin.ufpe.br
[2] HP Labs Palo Alto
{bryan.stephenson,hamid.motahari,jun.li}@hp.com
[3] HP Brazil
caio.northfleet@hp.com

Abstract. Despite an increasing need for considering security requirements in service composition, the incorporation of security requirements into service composition is still a challenge for many reasons: no clear identification of security requirements for composition, absence of notations to express them, difficulty in integrating them into the business processes, complexity of mapping them into security mechanisms, and the complexity inherent to specify and enforce complex security requirements. We identify security requirements for service composition and define notations to express them at different levels of abstraction. We present a novel approach consisting of a methodology, called Sec-MoSC, to incorporate security requirements into service composition, map security requirements into enforceable mechanisms, and support execution. We have implemented this approach in a prototype tool by extending BPMN notation and building on an existing BPMN editor, BPEL engine and Apache Rampart. We showcase an illustrative application of the Sec-MoSC toolset.

1 Introduction

There is an increasing need for considering security requirements in service composition. Service providers and service consumers need security guarantees to offer and use services. The users of composite services have requirements such as the confidentiality of their information being preserved by all service providers participating in the composition. Service providers may also sign SLAs (Service Level Agreements) with the service customers, which impose security requirements that must be satisfied when the service is being delivered.

Despite the importance, the incorporation of security requirements in service composition development is still a challenge for many reasons: no clear identification of security requirements for service composition, absence of notations to express them, difficulty in integrating them into the business process (behind the service composition), complexity of mapping them into actual security mechanisms, lack of monitoring

L. Baresi, C.-H. Chi, and J. Suzuki (Eds.): ICSOC-ServiceWave 2009, LNCS 5900, pp. 373–388, 2009.

mechanisms to check whether they are being satisfied at execution time and the complexity inherent to specify and enforce security requirements.

Current solutions on service composition and security usually concentrate on a particular aspect: incorporation of security requirements into the business process definition [10][14][11][12], executable composition [3][18][8][5][6] or enforcement of security at execution time [10][16]. However, there is little work that supports identification, expression and enforcement of security requirements for service composition at all levels of abstraction.

In this paper, we present an approach to deal with security requirements of service composition at various levels of abstraction. Our approach streamlines the modelling and enforcement of security requirements across multiple stages of business service development: from business process specification, to composite service design and development, and to business process execution.

We identify a collection of security requirements for service composition and propose a set of abstractions to express these security requirements. At the business level, we propose abstractions to express identified security requirements, which are represented by extending BPMN notations [19]. We present a methodology called Sec-MoSC (Security for Model-oriented Service Composition) through which composition logic, which is represented in standard BPMN, is annotated with security abstractions. The annotated model is translated into a BPEL process specification and configurations for security enforcement modules and mechanisms. The security requirements are enforced at runtime by an auxiliary engine, which complements the BPEL execution engine. We have implemented the approach in a prototype tool to demonstrate its viability and showcase it using an example.

This paper is structured as follows. Section 2 introduces an example scenario used throughout the paper. Section 3 presents security requirements and abstractions used to express them. Section 4 presents the Sec-MoSC methodology. Section 5 presents the architecture and implementation of the prototype tool and an example. Section 6 presents related works. Section 7 draws our conclusions and identifies future work.

2   Illustrative Scenario

We consider a virtual travel agency called VTA (Virtual Travel Agency), which provides services through an Internet portal for trip arrangements. The VTA portal is an interface between many different travel business companies/government services and end-users interested in travel.

Customers interact with VTA for service usage, payment and non-computational assets (e.g., receive the travel insurance policy). The operations are accessed through a Web interface available in the VTA portal. The VTA portal runs though the composition of services available in the Internet. We identified important security requirements including (i) encrypting credit card information in all communications, (ii) VTA and its partners need valid digital signatures, (iii) authentication mechanisms must be used in all interactions among web services accessed by VTA, (iv) logging all operations in the service composition for auditing purposes, and (v) VTA and its partners require that their Web services may only accept requests coming from specific IP addresses or domains.

3   Security Abstractions for Business Modelling to Execution

Our approach starts with the identification of security requirements that may be present in service composition. In the following, we identify these requirements and introduce a set of abstractions (modelling elements) that help understand, express and structure them in such a way that they can be incorporated into a service composition.

3.1   Security Requirements

By examining the VTA and other service applications that require composition of multiple Internet services across different service providers, we have identified the following common security requirements:

[NFR 01] Confidentiality. Critical information stored or exchanged in service interactions, such as credit card and personal identification information in the VTA example, needs to be disclosed only as needed to deliver the service.

[NFR 02] Data Retention. The information exchanged between services may have a time-to-live (TTL), i.e. it should be deleted after a certain time. For example, VTA must delete credit card information after sending the e-ticket to the customer.

[NFR 03] Access Control. Service providers must guarantee that only employees of the commercial department have access to customer data (e.g., the system designer cannot access this data).

[NFR 04] Authentication. Authentication ensures that only appropriate users have access to the sensitive or critical information held by the services, and also ensures that an action X was performed by a user Y and by nobody else (non-repudiation).

[NFR 05] Restricted Access. The composite service may filter communication with other services based on IP address or domain names. The VTA service relies on the IP addresses belonging to registered service providers to restrict access.

[NFR 06] Data Integrity. Stored and communicated sensitive customer data (such as credit card information) has to be checked against data corruption.

[NFR 07] Data Sharing. Service providers may be required to keep customer data within their company, or share it with sub-contractors in a limited way.

[NFR 08] Service Certification. Services used in the composition may need a certified abstraction of their behaviour. Any service whose behaviour is altered must be certified again. A Secure Capability Authority may be in charge of evaluating the compliance of Web services with respect to security capabilities and functionality.

[NFR 09] Auditing. Any operation performed by the service composition may need to be logged for auditing purposes.

[NFR 10] Monitoring. Anomalous behaviour in the composition that leads to violation of security constraints (e.g. leakage of information) should be monitored.

This set of security requirements has served as a basis for the proposed solutions presented in this paper.

3.2 Abstractions

In order to express the security requirements, we propose a set of abstractions by extending our previous work [15] to express non-functional requirements at modelling, development and run time: *NF-Attributes*, *NF-Statements*, and *NF-Actions*.

Table 1. Security requirements, NF-Actions and properties

Security requirement (Section 3.1)	NF-Action	Properties
NFR01	*UseCryptography*	Encryption Type (Symmetric / Asymmetric), Algorithm, Encrypted Message Parts , Key Length
NFR02	*DeleteInformation*	Type (Time/Event based), Time-to-live (TTL), Event (Before, After)
NFR03	*UseAccessControl*	Role, list of trusted entities, access level for each service
NFR04	*UseAuthentication* *UseDigitalSignatures*	Token Type (Username / X509 / Kerberos / SAML), Session Timeout
NFR05	*RestrictAccess*	Restriction Type (allow, deny), Source IP, Source IP Range, Destination Endpoint
NFR06	*CheckDataIntegrity*	Signature Type (HMAC_SHA1 / RSA_SHA1), Checked Parts (Header / Body)
NFR07	*ClassifyInformation*	Classification (Top Secret, Secret, Confidential)
NFR08	*CertifiedServiceBehavior*	Level of certification, The trusted entity
NFR09	*Log*	Level (DEBUG, INFO, WARN, ERROR)

NF-Attribute. It models non-functional characteristics such as *security* that may be defined in service composition. An NF-Attribute can be primitive or composite. A composite NF-Attribute is decomposed into primitive NF-Attributes that are closer to implementation elements. The composite NF-Attribute *Security* may be decomposed into primitive NF-Attributes *Integrity* and *Confidentiality*.

NF-Action. It models a software aspect or hardware feature that implements an NF-Attribute. Software aspects mean design decisions, algorithms, data structures, configurations and so on. Hardware features concern computer resources available for running the software system. NF-Actions are the abstractions to express the security enforcement mechanisms that must be implemented to achieve the NF-Attribute. For example, the realisation of the NF-Attribute *Authentication* may be carried out by implementing the NF-Action *UseAuthentication*. Finally, NF-Actions may be grouped to facilitate their reuse. They may have a set of properties like a tuple <name, value> that help to better characterise and implement them, e.g., the NF-Action *UseCryptography* has the property *<encryption type,* symmetric>.

NF-Statement. It models constraints defined on an NF-Attribute to guide decisions taken to implement the NF-Attribute. In the context of security, NF-Statements are defined in multiple levels such as *high, medium, low.* For example, *"High Confidentiality"* may require choosing public key-based encryption algorithm, whereas *"Medium Confidentiality"* may require 128-bit AES encryption.

In this paper, our focus is on "security" (a composite NF-Attribute). We define a set of primitive security NF-Attributes (*Integrity, Confidentiality, Authentication, Authorization, Audit, etc.*) and a set of NF-Actions (together with their properties) that may be used to realise the NF-Attributes (see Table 1), and four constraint levels to the NF-Statements (*High, Medium, Low* and *Other*). The identified NF-Attributes are realised by implementing these NF-Actions through configuring orchestration engines using existing standards, defining and implementing security modules, and so on.

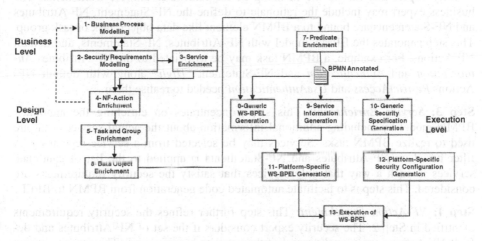

Fig. 1. Sec-MoSC Methodology

4 Sec-MoSC Methodology

We present a methodology, called Sec-MoSC, for incorporation of security requirements in service composition based on the following principles and assumptions: (i) different stakeholders (business users, security experts, service developers) are involved in defining and enforcing security requirements at various development stages. Following the principle of separation of concerns, we define three abstraction levels: *business, design* and *execution.* Security requirements are represented in different views corresponding to these layers; (ii) targeting business users, we adopt BPMN to express business processes; (iii) business users incorporate security requirements into the composition process during the business process definition using an extended BPMN notation; (iv) we use WS-BPEL to express the executable service composition specification. We provide a semi-automated approach to translate the annotated BPMN into executable BPEL along with enforceable security mechanisms. The runtime support is offered by complementing the orchestration engine with an auxiliary engine. Sec-MoSC methodology, shown in Figure 1, consists of the following steps:

Step 1: Business Process Modelling: This step refers to modelling the business process using BPMN abstractions such as tasks, task groups, data objects (business process information), predicates and so on. This step is performed by a business expert that has knowledge of the business process.

Step 2: *Security Requirements Modelling:* This step consists of defining security requirements and binding them to elements of the BPMN model. We extend BPMN elements by three new notations corresponding to NF-Attribute, NF-Statement and NF-Action. Considering the non-functional abstractions introduced in Section 3.2, this step initially defines NF-Attributes (composite *security* or primitive *confidentiality*, etc.) and NF-Statements (*High, Medium, Low* and *Other*) and binds them to BPMN elements. This step is performed by a business expert, possibly aided by a security expert that knows the meaning of NF-Attributes and NF-Statements. The business expert may include the rationale to define the NF-Statement. NF-Attributes and NF-Statements are bound to a BPMN element like data object, task or task group. This step annotates the BPMN model with NF-Attributes, NF-Statements, and default NF-Actions. For example, a BPMN task may be associated to the NF-Attributes *Authorization* and *Authentication* and NF-Statement *"High"* along with default NF-Actions *RestrictAccess* and *UseAuthentication* needed to realise them.

Step 3: *Service Enrichment:* This step concentrates on enriching the annotated BPMN model by including additional information about the actual services that are used to realize BPMN tasks. Services may be selected from a service repository. A filter based on NF-Attributes and NF-Statements is applied to the list of candidate services in such a way that only services that satisfy the security requirements are considered. This step is to facilitate automated code generation from BPMN to BPEL.

Step 4: *NF-Action Enrichment:* This step further refines the security requirements identified in Step 2. The security expert considers if the set of NF-Attributes and default NF-Actions are enough to realise the security requirements. The security expert may change (remove/add/alter) the default set of NF-Actions and their properties to satisfy the requested NF-Statement. Each NF-Action has a particular set of properties that serves as parameters in its use (see Table 1). These properties may be altered by the security expert to select the best parameters to meet NF-Statements.

Steps 5, 6 and 7: *Task and Group Enrichment, Data Object Enrichment* and *Predicate Enrichment:* Automatic mapping from BPMN to BPEL is intractable without additional information. Steps 3, 5, 6 and 7 are defined to enrich the BPMN model in order to facilitate automatic generation of executable service composition from the BPMN model to BPEL. Step 5 (*Task and Group Enrichment*) includes more information about the service defined in Step 3 such as URI, business type, and so on. Step 6 (*Data Object Enrichment*) consists of refining the definition of the BPMN data objects by associating data types and assigning variables to them. Finally, Step 7

(*Predicate Enrichment*) consists of explicitly solving predicates of the BPMN model (e.g., loop, decision commands).

Steps 8, 9 and 10: *Generic WS-BPEL Generation, Service Information Generation and Generic Security Specification Generation:* In these steps, we map the annotated BPMN model into an executable composition (WS-BPEL) along with the security configurations and enforcement mechanisms. This mapping is carried out in two steps as we choose to decouple the executable composition from any particular orchestration engine. Steps 8, 9 and 10 refer to the mapping of the annotated BPMN into platform-independent (which we call *generic*) WS-BPEL, service information and security configurations, and Steps 11 and 12 yield *platform-specific* BPEL and security configurations.

Step 8 (*Generic WS-BPEL Generation*) maps the annotated BPMN into a WS-BPEL composition that is independent from any particular WS-BPEL engine. The WS-BPEL composition only contains standard WS-BPEL elements. Step 9 (*Service Information Generation*) generates a file that contains generic information (XML file) about the services to be used in the executable service composition (see Steps 3 and 5). Finally, Step 10 (*Generic Security Configuration Generation*) is responsible for yielding a generic configuration file that includes needed security configurations to realise the security requirements defined in Steps 2 and 3. Internally, NF-Actions will be actually bound to WS-BPEL commands such as `invoke`, `receive`, `reply`, `sequence`, `assign`, `variable`, `eventHandler` and `throw`. NF-Actions have (in most cases) different meanings when they are bound to different WS-BPEL elements. For example, the NF-Action *UseCryptography()* bound to the WS-BPEL command `receive` means that once the receive is the entry point of the composition, the interactions between the client and the orchestration engine must be encrypted. On the other hand, when *UseCryptography()* is bound to the WS-BPEL command `invoke`, the interactions between the orchestration engine and the service provider must be encrypted.

Steps 11 and 12: *Platform-Specific WS-BPEL and Security Configuration Generation:* In these steps, the generic files generated in Steps 8, 9 and 10 are transformed into platform-specific WS-BPEL (Step 11) and security configuration files (Step 12). Step 11 (*Platform-Specific WS-BPEL Generation*) produces a WS-BPEL composition that is customised to run on a particular orchestration engine (e.g., Apache ODE in our work). Step 12 (*Platform-Specific Security Configuration Generation*) generates a set of configuration files to enforce the security requirements in a particular orchestration engine or security module (e.g., Apache ODE Rampart in our work).

Step 13: *Execution of WS-BPEL:* This step runs the WS-BPEL executable composition and enforces the security requirements at specified enforcement points using an auxiliary engine, which is described in more detail in Section 5.2.

5 Architecture, Implementation and Example

This section presents the Sec-MoSC solution architecture that supports security abstractions (Section 3) and the Sec-MoSC methodology (Section 4). Following this architecture, we have implemented a toolset to demonstrate the viability of the approach. We also detail how the prototype toolset can be used to support the modelling and development of the VTA use case introduced in Section 2.

5.1 Architecture

Figure 2 shows the architectural overview of the proposed solution, which includes a security extension of a BPMN editor (*Sec-MoSC Tool Editor*), a set of repositories (for *Security NF-Actions*, *Services* and *Log*), execution environment tools (*Auxiliary Engine* and *Orchestration engine*) and XML files.

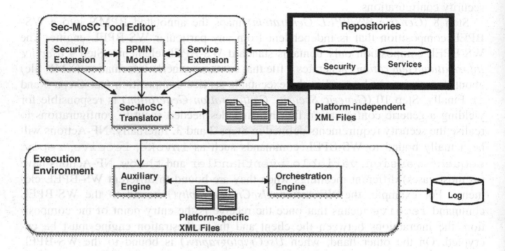

Fig. 2. Sec-MoSC Architecture

Sec-MoSC Tool Editor provides support at development time and is composed of four main components: *BPMN module*, *Security extension* module, *Service extension* module and the *Sec-MoSC Translator*. The *BPMN module* allows the developer to define a business process using the standard BPMN notation. The *Security extension* provides support to model the security requirements and bind them to BPMN elements. The *Service extension* is responsible for the annotation of service information (e.g., candidate services to execute a task) into the BPMN. Finally, the *Sec-MoSC Translator* is in charge of carrying out the mapping of the annotated BPMN model into WS-BPEL and other specification files. The repositories *Services* and *Security* store information about pre-registered services and supported security NF-Actions. These repositories support annotation of the business process model. The *Log* repository stores security log information generated at runtime.

The *Execution Environment* is responsible for executing the service composition and realising non-functional requirements. This realisation is performed by the enforcement mechanisms through generation of configuration files to the *Orchestration Engine*. This generation is performed by the *Auxiliary Engine*, which applies and manages configurations in order to execute the secure service composition. The

Orchestration Engine has the traditional role of executing the composition. The auxiliary engine has an internal component, the *MoSC Security Module* , that executes the security enforcement mechanisms by implementing needed NF-Actions either directly or by configuring existing engines such as Apache Rampart [1]. We provide three complementary views in the Sec-MoSC Tool Editor corresponding to the three levels of abstraction: business, design and execution. In the business view, the business user can use the editor to annotate a BPMN model with provided security annotations. The design view shows the corresponding BPEL code and security configuration files to the annotated BPMN model. The developer can inspect the generated code and further refine the configuration of NF-Actions. The execution view allows the user to deploy the composition logic into the Execution Environment and monitor and inspect the log of secured composition execution.

It is important to note that the functional BPEL code is not altered in order to insert enforcement points. In the presented approach, the enforcement points are specified in the configuration files generated by the Auxiliary Engine. For example, if the user specifies that a specific communication should be encrypted via the NF-Action of *UseCryptography*, the Auxiliary Engine will receive this requirement and will generate specific configurations in order to guarantee that the enforcement points will be performed. In this example (*UseCryptography*), the execution of the NF-Action will alter the SOAP request and SOAP response messages by encrypting/decrypting the message. This process is transparent to the functional execution of the application. An example of a configuration file will be presented in Section 5.3.

5.2 Implementation

Components of the Sec-MoSC architecture presented in Figure 2 are implemented as an Eclipse plugin. The *BPMN Module* was implemented by extending the BPMN editor [7] to support the BPMN concept of *TaskType* (this concept is present in the BPMN 1.2 specification). We used Eclipse GEF framework to implement the definition and binding of security and service information to the BPMN model. These extensions access the *Service* and *NF-Action* repositories at development time to assist the model annotation. The *Sec-MoSC Translator* has been implemented considering the BPMN elements and user annotations in the Sec-MoSC Tool Editor in order to generate platform-independent files containing all information required for the execution of the service composition and configuration of security mechanisms.

Figure 3 shows a screenshot of the *Sec-MoSC Tool Editor*. This figure is divided into three main areas. The palette on the right includes BPMN shapes (Task, Predicate and Data Object) and security shapes (NF-Attributes represented as cloud, NF-Statements as locker, Group of NF-Actions as dashed rectangle and NF-Actions as solid rectangle) used in the graphical modelling. The modelling area in the centre contains the business process and security definitions. The property area shows the properties of a particular BPMN shape (e.g., size) or security shape (e.g., *Encryption Type* for this particular example shown in the figure). The property area also includes service information bound to a BPMN task.

The *Auxiliary Engine* has been implemented in Java and it is able to generate both a *Platform-Specific WS-BPEL* (from the *Generic WS-BPEL* and service annotations) and a *Platform-Specific Security Configuration* (from *Generic Security Specification*);

and intermediate invocations/responses to/from the *Orchestration Engine*. The *Orchestration Engine* used is the Apache ODE [2] (based on Axis 2) due to its wide adoption and its support for security enforcement points provided by the Rampart security module [1]. Finally, the *Auxiliary Engine MoSC Security Module* was implemented based on Axis 2 that implements the NF-Actions not supported by Rampart, e.g., *RestrictAccess* and *Log* (see Table 1).

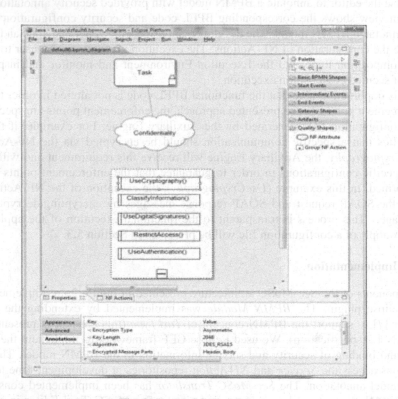

Fig. 3. Sec-MoSC Tool Editor

Figure 4 shows the architecture of *Execution Environment*. This architecture uses the orchestration engine Apache ODE [2], built under the framework Axis2 [17]. The service composition principle is based on the Axis2 message flow. The functional part of the application is translated to WS-BPEL 2.0 and is executed by the Apache ODE engine. The non-functional part of the application is handled by interceptors associated to the NF-Actions. When the Apache ODE sends/receives an invocation, the SOAP message crosses the Axis2 message flow; if the service to be invoked has an associated NF-Action, a handler will be invoked in order to perform this NF-Action. The Apache Rampart is able to handle a specific set of NF-Actions, e.g. *UseCryptography*, *UseAuthentication* and *CheckDataIntegrity*. However, there are some NF-Actions that Rampart is unable to manage; in this case, the Auxiliary Engine takes over the responsibility. The NF-Actions *RestrictAccess* and *Log*, for example, are managed by the Auxiliary Engine interceptors.

Note that the flow of messages inside the *Execution Environment* depends on the security requirements defined. For example, the implementation of the NF-Action *RestrictAccess* receives an invocation and then forwards it to the Auxiliary Engine that checks if the IP address in the output message has some kind of constraint. If the constraint is not satisfied, the message is not forwarded through other elements in the FlowOut. Otherwise (the IP address is allowed), the message is forwarded to Rampart that may enforce other NF-Actions (e.g., *UseCryptography*). Next, Rampart forwards the message to the web service that actually handles the request.

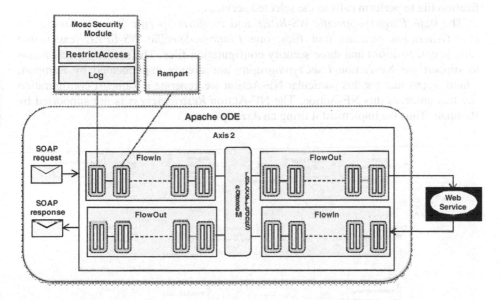

Fig. 4. Implementation of the Execution Environment in the Apache ODE

5.3   Illustrative Example

This section presents how the Sec-MoSC methodology and the tools have been used to model the example scenario presented in Section 2. We describe a use case in which the user buys a national air ticket. The security requirements defined in this business process are *Confidentiality* (NFR 01) and *RestrictAccess* (NFR 05), which are implemented by the NF-Actions *UseCryptography* and *RestrictAccess*.

Figure 5 presents the resulting business process model after steps *Business Process Modelling* and *Security Requirements Modelling*. This business process includes four Service Tasks (*Receive customer data, Check flight availability, Request authorisation payment* and *Send confirmation e-mail*), the NF-Statements bound to *Receive customer data* (locker) and *Request authorisation payment* (locker), the NF-Attribute *Confidentiality* and the NF-Actions *RestrictAccess* and *UseCryptography* that implement this NF-Attribute.

In step *NF-Action Enrichment* (shown in Figure 1), the properties of *UseCryptography* and *RestrictAccess* are configured. The next enrichment steps (*Data Object Enrichment, Task and Group Enrichment* and *Predicate Enrichment*) collect additional information from the users such that the remainder of the process can be automated. To perform the generic generation steps 8, 9, and 10, the *Sec-MoSC translator* takes the annotated BPMN model as input and generates three platform-independent files, which we term generic files. The security information file includes information for specific security enforcement actions expressed in the model. The service orchestration specification file is a platform-independent version of the functional executable code (WS-BPEL code). The service information file includes information (e.g. URI, partner links, operation names) needed to enrich the service orchestration specification file to perform calls to the selected services.

The steps *Platform-Specific WS-BPEL* and *Platform-Specific Security Configuration Generation* generate four files: one *Platform-Specific WS-BPEL* (executable service composition) and three security configuration files. The security mechanisms to support the NF-Action *UseCryptography* are already implemented by Rampart, which means that for this particular NF-Action we generate a Rampart configuration file that enforces this NF-Action. The NF-Action *RestrictAccess* is not supported by Rampart. Thus we implement it using an *Axis2 phase*.

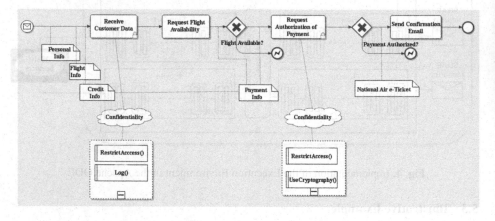

Fig. 5. Business Process and its security requirements

The following XML code refers to the specification of the security mechanism related to the NF-Actions *UseCryptography* and *RestrictAccess*. This code is generated by the Auxiliary Engine and provides configurations to the Apache Rampart (Line 9 to Line 11, and Line 17 to Line 19), in the case that the NF-Action can be implemented using this security module, and to the MoSC Security Module, in the case that Rampart do not provide support to the NF-Action (Line 21 to Line 27).

With respect to the NF-Action *UseCryptography*, this file specifies that the encryption algorithm TripleDESRSA15 (line 10) must be used. In addition, at line 18, it is stated that the body of the message must be encrypted. All of this information is used by Apache Rampart to guarantee that the user requirements will be respected.

In the case of the NF-Action *RestrictAccess*, the Apache Rampart does not support the enforcement. Therefore, the MoSC Security Module, part of the Auxiliary Engine, is responsible for the enforcement of this NF-Action. The associated configuration specification to this NF-Action can be found from Line 21 to Line 27 of the following code.

```
(1)   <wsp:Policy wsu:Id="SigEncr"
(2)   ...
(3)   <wsp:ExactlyOne>
(4)     <wsp:All>
(5)               <sp:AsymmetricBinding>
(6)                   <wsp:Policy>
(7)                   ...
(8)                   <sp:AlgorithmSuite>
(9)                         <wsp:Policy>
(10)                            <sp:TripleDesRsa15 />
(11)                         </wsp:Policy>
(12)                   </sp:AlgorithmSuite>
(13)                   ...
(14)                   </wsp:Policy>
(15)             </sp:AsymmetricBinding>
(16)             ...
(17)             <sp:EncryptedParts>
(18)                 <sp:Body />
(19)             </sp:EncryptedParts>
(20)             ...
(21)             <secmosc:SecMoscConfig>
(22)                 <secmosc:restrictAccess>
(23)                     <secmosc:restrictPartner policyType="allow">
(24)                         <secmosc:destinationEndpoint
     address="172.17.0.0/16"/>
(25)                     </secmosc:restrictPartner>
(26)                 </secmosc:restrictAccess>
(27)             </secmosc:SecMoscConfig>
(28)     </wsp:All>
(29) </wsp:ExactlyOne>
(30) </wsp:Policy>
```

The MoSC Security Module is also responsible for the enforcement of the NF-Action Restrict Access. When a service invocation is realized by the orchestration engine, the request message is intercepted by the MoSC Security Module that will call the handler to perform the NF-Action. The handler verifies whether the IP address of the web service to be invoked is valid based on the defined configuration (Line 24).

We learned that this model-driven approach facilitates the communication between the business analyst, security expert, and service developer to specify and refine security requirements. Having an intermediate platform-independent specification helps in both code generation and enforcement. In particular this enables the Auxiliary Engine to manage different orchestration engines and security modules.

6 Related Work

Existing research related to service composition and security usually concentrates on supporting security at one of the abstraction levels: the business process definition [10][14][11][12], the executable composition [3][18][8][5][6], or enforcement of specific security requirements at execution time [10][16].

At the business process modelling level, Menzel [10] and Rodriguez [14] have extended BPMN modelling notations with specific security elements to incorporate security requirements into business process specification. In contrast our modelling notation is minimal and generic (NF-Attribute, NF-Action and NF-Statement) and can be used to express any security requirement. Therefore, it is easily extendable. Basin [3] has complementary work focused on software modelling which offers specific notations for modelling access control requirements. Our approach handles all types of security requirements for business processes. In Neubauer's approach [11][12] the treatment of security requirements starts before defining the business process by supporting decision makers with elicitation of security requirements. Carminati [3] proposes an ontology-based method for modelling security requirements and provides a security vocabulary. In another approach, Phan et al [20] provide a framework for specification of high level security requirements as policy objectives and then translating them into WS-Policy fragments. However, they do not consider business processes and composite services, but focus on policies for atomic services.

Although conceptually a business process is mapped into an executable process, in most existing work that supports incorporating security requirements at execution time, the business process is directly defined using an executable language like WS-BPEL. For example, [18][8][5][6] extend WS-BPEL with security capabilities. Song [16] adopts an aspect-oriented approach that interprets the WS-BPEL process and plugs in calls to the security web service component. Menzel [10] reports generating only WS-SecurityPolicy fragments. In contrast, we automatically generate platform-independent configurations which are then automatically translated into platform-specific configurations which are enforced at execution time by security modules.

Another key advantage of our approach is that the extension to BPMN notation is managed separately from the BPMN model. This allows standard tools to be used with the BPMN model. Similarly, we do not modify the BPEL code corresponding to the BPMN model but rather identify the enforcement points and mechanisms in separate configuration files.

7 Conclusions and Future Work

In this paper, we presented a novel holistic model-driven approach and a toolset that supports security requirement modelling, automatic code generation and enforcement of security requirements. It facilitates the jobs of business users, security experts and developers of service composition solutions. The main contributions of the proposed approach include the definition of a set of non-functional abstractions to express security requirements at different abstraction levels, a methodology to incorporate security requirements and service information into BPMN, mappings of security and service information into executable elements, and providing execution support for security requirements. We have prototyped the Sec-MoSC solution architecture, which includes a security-extended BPMN editor to support service composition at modelling time, and an auxiliary engine that coordinates with security enhancement modules on top of Axis 2 to realise the security requirements at execution time.

In terms of future work, we concentrate on three areas: (1) to extend the binding of security requirements to other BPMN element types beyond tasks, task groups, and data objects; (2) to define and realise additional security requirements; and (3) to monitor security requirements at runtime in such a way that when a particular requirement is violated, the execution environment can provide evidence of and possibly correct violations.

Acknowledgement. This research is supported by Hewlett-Packard Brasil Ltda. using incentives of Brazilian Informatics Law (Law n° 8.2.48 of 1991).

References

[1] Apache Software Foundation (2008), Apache Rampart – Axis2 Security Model, http://ws.apache.org/rampart/ (last visit at May 3, 2009)

[2] Apache Software Foundation. Apache Orchestration Director Engine (ODE), http://ode.apache.org/ (last visit at May 3, 2009)

[3] Basin, D., et al.: Model driven security: From UML models to access control infrastructures, ACM Trans. Software Eng. Methodology 15(1), 39–91 (2006)

[4] Carminati, B., Ferrari, E., Hung, P.C.K.: Security Conscious Web Service Composition. In: Proc. International Conference on Web Services ICWS 2006, pp. 489–496 (2006)

[5] Charfi, A., Mezini, M.: Using aspects for security engineering of Web service compositions. In: Proc. IEEE International Conference on Web Services ICWS 2005, pp. 59–66 (2005)

[6] Chollet, S., Lalanda, P.: Security Specification at Process Level. In: Proc. IEEE International Conference on Services Computing (SCC 2008), pp. 165–172 (2008)

[7] Eclipse Foundation (2008), The BPMN Modeler, http://www.eclipse.org/bpmn

[8] Garcia, D.Z.G., Felgar de Toledo, M.B.: Ontology-Based Security Policies for Supporting the Management of Web Service Business Processes. In: Proc. IEEE International Conference on Semantic Computing, pp. 331–338 (2008)

[9] Han, J., Kowalczyk, R., Khan, K.M.: Security-Oriented Service Composition and Evolution. In: Proc. 13th Asia Pacific Software Engineering Conference APSEC 2006 (2006)

[10] Menzel, M., Homas, I., Meinel, C.: Security Requirements Specification in Service-Oriented Business Process Management. In: Proc. ARES 2009 (2009)

[11] Neubauer, T., Heurix, J.: Defining Secure Business Processes with Respect to Multiple Objectives. In: Proc. ARES 2008, pp. 187–194 (2008)

[12] Neubauer, T., Heurix, J.: Objective Types for the Valuation of Secure Business Processes. In: Proc. Seventh IEEE/ACIS International Conference on Computer and Information Science ICIS 2008, pp. 231–236 (2008)

[13] Ouyang, C., et al.: Translating BPMN to BPEL (2006), http://code.google.com/p/bpmn2bpel/ (last visit: May 10, 2009)

[14] Rodriguez, A., Fernández-Medina, E., Piattini, M.: A BPMN Extension for the Modeling of Security Requirements in Business Processes. IEICE - Trans. Inf. Syst. E90-D(4), 745–752 (2007)

[15] Rosa, N.S.: NFi: An Architecture-based Approach for Treating Non-Functional Properties of Dynamic Distributed Systems, PhD thesis, Centre of Informatics, Federal University of Pernambuco (2001)

[16] Song, H., Sun, Y., Sun, Y., Yin, Y.: Dynamic Weaving of Security Aspects in Service Composition. In: Proc. Second IEEE International Workshop Service-Oriented System Engineering SOSE 2006, pp. 189–196 (2006)

[17] Tong, K.K.L.: Developing Web Services with Apache Axis2, TipTec Development (2008)

[18] Wang, X., Zhang, Y., Shi, H.: Access Control for Human Tasks in Service Oriented Architecture. In: Proc. of ICEBE 2008, pp. 455–460 (2008)

[19] White, S.A.: Introduction to BPMN, Technical report, IBM Corporation (2004)

[20] Phan, T., Han, J., Schneider, J.G., Wilson, K.: Quality-Driven Business Policy Specification and Refinement for Service-Oriented Systems. In: Bouguettaya, A., Krueger, I., Margaria, T. (eds.) ICSOC 2008. LNCS, vol. 5364, pp. 5–21. Springer, Heidelberg (2008)

End-to-End Security for Enterprise Mashups

Florian Rosenberg[1], Rania Khalaf[2], Matthew Duftler[2], Francisco Curbera[2],
and Paula Austel[2]

[1] Distributed Systems Group, Technical University Vienna
Argentinierstrasse 8/184-1, Vienna, Austria
florian@infosys.tuwien.ac.at
[2] IBM T.J. Watson Research Center
19 Skyline Drive, Hawthorne, NY, 10532
{rkhalaf,duftler,curbera,pka}@us.ibm.com

Abstract. Mashups are gaining momentum as a means to develop situational Web applications by combining different resources (services, data feeds) and user interfaces. In enterprise environments, mashups are recently used for implementing Web-based business processes, however, security is a major concern. Current approaches do not allow the mashup to securely consume services with diverse security requirements without sharing the credentials or hard-coding them in the mashup definition. In this paper, we present a solution to integrate security concerns into an existing enterprise mashup platform. We provide an extension to the language and runtime and propose a Secure Authentication Service (SAS) to seamlessly facilitate secure authentication and authorization of end-users with the services consumed in the mashup.

1 Introduction

Mashups are an increasingly popular approach to develop new kinds of situational Web applications by combining content, presentation, and application functionality from disparate Web sources [1]. A vast number of mashup technologies and tools exist that provide a means of seamlessly "mashing" together several Web-based services and sources such as REST or SOAP services, feeds (RSS or ATOM) or plain XML or HTML sources. These mashup tools either provide a mashup language targeted for developers or provide an editor allowing a graphical mashup development such as Yahoo Pipes [2] or IBM Mashup Center [3].

In general, two different mashup types are dominant [4]: *Consumer mashups* are mostly for private use, combining data from several resources by unifying them using a common interface. *Enterprise mashups* combine different sources (content, data or application functionality) from at least one resource in an enterprise environment. An important distinction is the fact that enterprise mashups have some additional requirements such as security, availability or other quality of service items. Such enterprise mashups have an enormous potential by promoting assembly over development to reduce development costs and provision a new software solution within shorter time periods.

L. Baresi, C.-H. Chi, and J. Suzuki (Eds.): ICSOC-ServiceWave 2009, LNCS 5900, pp. 389–403, 2009.

However, current enterprise mashup tools lack the ability to consume and integrate different services in a secure way when having completely diverse security requirements in terms of authentication and authorization [5, 6]. As a consequence, many mashup tools can only integrate security-free services and data sources or hard-code authentication data in the mashup code. Clearly, this is a problem in enterprise environments because users are more reluctant to give their authentication information to third parties (in fact, company policy may even prohibit that), resources typically have custom security requirements, and resources may support any of several authentication protocols such as HTTP basic authentication, custom application keys or more Web 2.0 like protocols such as OpenID [7] and OAuth [8].

We argue that seamless security support for enterprise mashups, in particular related to secure credentials management is required and needs to be integrated in the mashup language and/or tooling because users are not willing and should not disclose their credentials for different resources in the mashup definition. The mashup environment has to provide support for authentication and authorization, and delegation control allowing the execution of a service on behalf of a given user.

1.1 Illustrative Example

An enterprise mashup scenario depicted in Figure 1 is used to illustrate the problem and concepts. In this scenario, the hiring manager at Acme Inc (left) is hiring for a new position. He uses the enterprise mashup to schedule the interview with and get the resume of the candidate (bottom right).

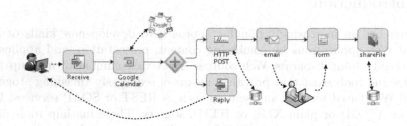

Fig. 1. Hiring Mashup Scenario

In order to do so, the mashup first makes a call to the hiring manager's calendar available via Google. Then, it forks: the bottom branch replies to the initial call and the top branch posts the available times to Acme's interview scheduling service, e-mails the candidate the final slot returned by that service and a link that should be followed to complete the process. Once the candidate clicks on the link, he finds a form where he fills in his personal information and attaches his resume. Finally, the mashup places the resume in the 'Files' file sharing service in LotusLive Engage, an online collaboration solution.

Interacting with multiple secured third-party services requires different sets of credentials and authentication protocols. For example, Google Calendar uses the OAuth protocol, Acme's scheduling service uses HTTP basic authentication, and the Files service requires an application key and the user in whose store the file is to be added. The Google Calendar call and the Files service call both require that the mashup interacts with them on the user's behalf - possibly after the user is no longer logged into the system.

1.2 Contributions

Seamlessly specifying and enforcing mashup security by supporting different authentication mechanisms requires both, a language extension and a runtime mechanism. In particular, this paper makes the following contributions to enable an end-to-end security solution for enterprise mashups:

- We provide a model and semantics for integrating security concerns directly into an existing business mashup platform (BMP), in particular the underlying lightweight workflow language Bite [9,10] to address authentication and authorization from a language perspective.
- We describe a framework and implementation for homogenizing the authentication and authorization process within a mashup application for authorization mechanisms (e.g., basic authentication, custom application IDs, OAuth, etc) by leveraging a trusted Secure Authentication Service (SAS).
- We elaborate on the seamless integration and user experience of the authentication process by describing several mechanisms to allow mashup users to securely enter their credentials directly at the service provider (if possible) or by using the SAS.

The remainder of this paper is organized as follows: In Section 2, we describe the BMP project and the underlying Bite engine as the target enterprise mashup platform. Section 3 outlines the proposed security solution. Section 4 describes the Bite language extensions to enable security support followed by a detailed description of the SAS in Section 5. Section 6 evaluates and discusses the proposed approach followed by a discussion of related work in Section 7. Finally, Section 8 concludes this paper and outlines future work.

2   BMP and the Bite Language

The Business Mashup Platform (BMP) provides a hosted development environment for rapid development of situational business processes or enterprise mashups. It overlaps with the system in [11]. The graphical mashup development is browser-based, leveraging a BPMN-style editor, a forms designer and a catalog of extension activities that are offered to the designer in a palette. Once a mashup has been completely specified, BMP allows one click deployment of mashups that are immediately invokable. In the backend Bite code is generated and executed on the server.

Bite Language and Runtime. Bite is an XML-based REST-centric composition language designed to facilitate the implementation of lightweight and extensible flows[1]. The process model implements a subset of the WS-BPEL [12] execution semantics that consists of a flat graph (except for loops) containing atomic actions (activities) and links between them. Loops may be created using a dedicated `while` activity, the only construct allowed to contain other activities. Graph execution logic is encoded in conditional transition links between activities. Error handling is provided by special error links to error handling activities. Bite provides a small set of built-in activities: (1) basic HTTP communication primitives for receiving and replying to HTTP requests (`receiveGET|POST`[2], `replyGET|POST`, `receive-replyGET|POST`) and making HTTP requests to external services (`GET`, `POST`, `PUT`, `DELETE`), (2) utility activities for waiting or calling local code, (3) control helpers such as external choice and loops.

```
 1 <process name="hiring">
 2   <receivePOST name="hrInput" url="/hiring" />
 3
 4   <!-- get Google calendar data -->
 5   <GET name="gcal" url="http://www.google.com/calendar/feeds/default/
         owncalendars/full">
 6     <control source="hrInput" />
 7     <input name=""></input>
 8     <input name=""></input>
 9     <security authtype="oauth" />
10   </GET>
11
12   <replyPOST name="hrReply" url="/hiring">
13     <control source="gcal" />
14     <input value=""/>
15   </replyPOST>
16
17   <!-- invoke interview scheduling service -->
18   <POST name="scheduleInterview" url="http://internal.acme.com/interview/
         schedule">
19     <control source="gcal" />
20     <input name=""></input>
21     <input name=""></input>
22     <security authtype="http_basic" notificationType="sametime"
           notificationReceiver="$:hrInput_User" />
23   </POST>
24
25   <!-- send an email to the candidate and collect candidate data using a
         special form activity -->
26
27   <!-- put all the collected candidate data on the Lotus file share -->
28   <shareFile name="storeApplication" ...>
29     <control source="collectCandidateData"/>
30     <!-- other parameter cut for brevity -->
31     <security user="$:hrInput_User" authtype="app_id">
32       <mapping>
33         <element name="par" label="Partner ID" applyTo="param" />
34         <element name="key" label="License Key" applyTo="param" />
35       </mapping>
36     </security>
37   </shareFile>
38 </process>
```

Listing 1.1. Hiring Mashup (simplified – without input parameters)

A Bite flow both calls external services and provides itself as a service. Sending an HTTP POST request to a flow's base URL results in the creation of a new flow instance that is assigned a new instance URL. This instance URL is returned

---

[1] We use 'mashup' and 'flow' interchangeably in this paper.
[2] The pattern [x]`GET|POST` denotes two different activities: [x]`GET`, [x]`POST`.

in the HTTP Location header field of the response. The instance URL contains a flow ID that is used for correlation of subsequent requests to that flow.

Each flow instance can define multiple receive activities corresponding to multiple entry points. These activities expose additional URLs as logical addresses of the instance's nested resources. POST requests directed to these URLs are dispatched to the individual receive activities in the flow model using the relative URLs defined in the activities' url attribute. This mechanism allows building interactive flows having multiple entry points for interacting with them. This behavior is leveraged by various activities such as Web forms that are designed as part of the mashup creation with the BMP.

A core concept of Bite is the extensible design that enables the developer community to provide additional functionality in a first-class manner by creating Bite extension activities and registering them with the Bite engine. This design allows keeping the language and its runtime very small and allows to implement other required activities as extensions. Extension activities can be created using Java or any scripting language supported by the Java Scripting API (e.g., Groovy, Ruby, Python, etc).

We show, in Listing 1.1, the (abbreviated) Bite code for the hiring sample in Figure 1. Each mashup has a root element called process (line 1). A new flow instance is created by sending a HTTP POST request to the relative URL /hiring of the initial receivePOST (line 2). The data associated with the POST request is implicitly available in variable hrInput_Output to all dependent activities. In this case the variable contains a map of all POST parameters. After completing the hrInput activity, the gcal activity is activated (lines 5–10). Transitions between activities are expressed by the control element (line 6). From lines 12–15, the mashup replies to the initial HTTP POST from the hiring manager informing him that he will receive an email with the selected interview date. The interview scheduling is executed in lines 18–23 by issuing a HTTP POST call to the interview scheduling service. Then, the other remaining steps are executed, e.g., sending an email using the sendMail activity and preparing the candidate form using the form activity – both implemented as Bite extension activities (not shown in the listing for brevity). Finally, the shareFile extension activity (lines 28–37) uploads the collected candidate data to LotusLive.

As stated in Section 1.1, the outgoing HTTP GET and POST call (gcal and scheduleInterview) and the shareFile activity require different security credentials that are required for successfully executing the mashup. The security element (lines 9, 22 and 31–36) and its semantics are presented in Section 4. For more details on Bite, its runtime and possible applications, see [9, 10].

3   Overview of the Enterprise Mashup Security Solution

Building security into an enterprise mashup platform requires to address (i) authentication of users at third-party services (i.e., verifying a user's claimed identity) and (ii) authorization in the sense that the user has to authorize the Bite engine to perform the task on the user's behalf. We have to distinguish two aspects: First, security has to be addressed on a language level to integrate security concerns into the Bite language. A core requirement is to keep the language extensions minimal and provide extensibility support for various authentication protocols in a seamless user-centric way. Second, an extensible mechanism is needed to realize authentication and authorization of trusted services having different authentication protocols. This process is transparently handled by a *Secure Authentication Service* (SAS) that offers an OAuth interface, as described in detail in Section 5.

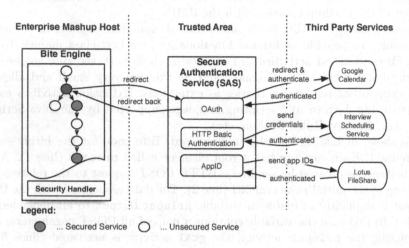

Fig. 2. End-to-End Security Solution Overview

In Figure 2, the basic overview of the security solution is depicted. The Bite engine including an executable flow is shown on the left (resembling the illustrative example from Figure 2). The white circles constitute services which do not require authentication, the gray ones require authentication. In the middle is the SAS which has to operate in a secure and trusted area within the company network as it manages credentials during the execution of a flow. On the right, the third-party services are depicted that will be invoked during the execution. Note that placement of the SAS is important: it must be in a trusted space. Some options include either at a third-party provider or a SAS at each service provider. As we are focused on enterprise mashups, it is viable that the SAS is a service provided by the enterprise itself making trust issues between users and the proxy infrastructure less of a problem. In this paper, we focus on an architecture and implementation whereby mashups can be secured using a security service; therefore, trust issues related to particular deployments are left to future work.

When the user triggers the execution of the flow by using the HTTP POST request in the Web form (or from another application), the mashup is executed and as soon as it reaches the first "secured" third-party service (cf. the `gcal` activity from Listing 1.1), the Bite engine will use a security handler to allow

the user to authenticate at the target service. The handler does this by interacting with the SAS. The SAS implements different security modules (OAuth,
HTTP Basic Authentication and AppID) to provide support for different security
mechanisms at the target service. The procedure for performing authorization
and authentication has two cases:

- *Synchronous Authentication*: In this case the user is already interacting with
  the flow via a Web application and can thus be simply redirected to the
  SAS to perform the authentication at the target service. In the flow, this
  means that `receiveGET|POST` has been processed without yet reaching a
  corresponding `replyGET|POST` activity. For example, this is the case for the
  `gcal` activity from Listing 1.1 (lines 5–10) which is in between a `receivePOST`
  and a `replyPOST`.
- *Asynchronous Authentication*: In this case the flow already returned to the
  user by executing a `replyGET|POST` activity. Alternatively, an activity called
  `receive-replyGET|POST` is used to receive and immediately reply to an in-
  coming request. Therefore, the user is no longer interacting with the flow
  and there is no connection that can be redirected to the SAS. For example,
  all activities from Listing 1.1 after line 18 (namely, `scheduleInterview`,
  `emailCandidate`, `collectCandidateData` and `storeApplication`). This requires contacting the user using asynchronous techniques to request him to
  authenticate at the third-party service. As shown later in the paper, we
  support email and instant messaging to do this.

The communication between the Bite engine and the SAS uses a slightly extended version of the OAuth protocol to seamlessly implement the handling of
authentication and authorization between Web applications (in our case the Bite
engine and the SAS). Therefore, the SAS design is generic and can be used by
any mashup tool by implementing the corresponding OAuth connector that is
capable of processing the proposed extensions.

4   Language Extensions for Security Specification

In order to enable security within Bite, the language needs to be extended to
capture the security requirements such as authentication and authorization. A
core requirement is to keep such language extensions minimal. On a language
level, we focus on the *outbound security* in this paper, i.e., security support
while calling an external service from Bite. *Inbound security*, i.e., authentication
and authorization of users that want to execute a mashup is also supported
but a detailed description is out of scope. For the sake of completeness, it is
mentioned that it is done on a runtime level whereby the user authenticates using
OpenID with an external authentication service and the authenticated user is
injected into the process context where it can be checked against user restrictions
on receiving activities (`receiveGET|POST`). If the user is allowed to access the
receive, the activity activates, stores the message and the user in the appropriate
variables, and completes. Otherwise, an error is sent back to the user and the

receive activity is not activated. If provided, user information from inbound security is stored at runtime in an implicit variable, [activity_name]_User. Hence, subsequent activities may use this variable to refer back to a particular user.

4.1   Security Extension and Semantics

A security extension element is provided and made optional for all outbound communication activities such as GET, POST, PUT, DELETE and all extension activities implementing custom behavior that may also require authentication.

Listing 1.1 has three security elements (lines 9, 22 and 31–36) in the flow. In Listing 1.2, we present the security element syntax.

```
1<security authtype="http_basic|oauth|app_id" user="string|expression"?
2          roles="string (comma-separated)"? scope="activity|flow"?
3          notification="http|email|sametime"?
4          notificationReceiver="string|expression"?/>
```

Listing 1.2. Security Extension Element

Attribute Description: The attributes available for the security element are:

- **authtype:** Specifies the authentication type for authenticating a user at the target service. Currently, we support OAuth [8], HTTP basic authentication and customized application IDs that are frequently used by various service providers in the form of single or multiple GET or POST parameters. Handling these authentication types is transparently supported by the Secure Authentication Service (SAS), described in Section 5.
- **user:** Defines the name of the user (as a string or an expression) on whose behalf a specific service is executed. This user attribute is relevant especially for extension activities that support the "on behalf of" semantics. For example, the hiring flow from Listing 1.1 uses LotusLive to upload and share files. This application supports the "on behalf of" semantics by explicitly defining who uploaded a document indicated by the **user** attribute in the Bite flow (this username is then used in LotusLive's file sharing service as the owner of the uploaded document).
- **roles:** Defines roles, that a user can have, in the form of comma-separated strings. If a role is used, role definitions must have been provided to the runtime.
- **scope:** It defines whether an activity's security credentials are propagated to the other activities for re-use. If the attribute value is **flow**, credentials are propagated thereby avoiding repeated logins by re-using credentials to a service that is called more than once in a flow for the same user. In case of an attribute value **activity**, the credentials are not propagated.
- **notification:** It defines how a user should be notified that a service requires authentication. In case of a *synchronous authentication*, **http** can be used by redirecting to the SAS to request authentication and authorization. In the *asynchronous case*, the flow has to get back to the user to request

authentication. This can be done by blocking the activity requiring security, sending an email to the user (attribute value `email`) or sending an instant message (attribute value `sametime`) pointing him to the SAS, and resuming the activity once authentication/authorization is complete. Our approach supports Lotus Sametime, a messaging software used at IBM; other protocols may easily be added.

- `notificationReceiver`: It is only needed when using the `notification` type `email` or `sametime` because then it is necessary to have the contact details (e.g., email address or sametime contact). In case of `http`, it is not necessary, because the user is still interacting with the flow in the browser and is thus redirected to the SAS to perform the authentication.

4.2   Execution Semantics

The effect of the security elements on the execution semantics of the Bite language is as follows: Once an activity that has a security element is reached in a flow, the values of the security element's attributes are evaluated and stored in a *security context*, itself stored in the *process context* which maintains the state of execution for the flow instance. This information is used to lookup a corresponding security handler in a handler registry. The security context and the message payload are provided to this handler, which interacts with the SAS to provide the required authentication and authorization. If no credentials are available, the handler contacts the user sending them to the SAS. The handler then makes the secure call and returns the result to the activity implementation, which in turn stores it in its output variable. If the `scope` attribute value is set to `activity`, the security handler contacts the SAS through its OAuth interface to proceed with the required security handling and the OAuth connection tokens are destroyed after the authentication. If it is set to `flow`, these OAuth tokens are stored in the process context and can be reused in case the same service is called again in the flow for the same user. Reusing the same OAuth tokens for connecting to the SAS allows it to determine whether the user has previously authenticated and authorized Bite to invoke a given third-party service on its behalf. For more details on the OAuth handling see Section 5.

While the asynchronous case has no further effects on flow semantics, the synchronous (http) case is more involved because if credentials are not available then it needs to reuse one of the flow instance's open connections to contact the user, redirecting him to the SAS, and then back to the flow. Bite allows several receiving activities to be open (i.e., not yet replied to) at the same time. Therefore, the right open connection must be identified. To do so, open receive activities in the flow instance are checked for a matching '_User' variable value to the one in the security element being handled. The 'reply status' of a matching receive activity is set to 'awaiting_redirect' and a key is created for it against which the redirection from the SAS back to the flow can be matched. A reply is sent to the receive's open connection that redirects the user to the SAS. Once the user completes working with the SAS, a client-side redirect sends him back to the flow. Also, the matched receive activity instance is found using the key and its reply status reset to 'open'.

If no match is found among open receives, then receives 'awaiting_reply' are checked as they will eventually become 'open' and may be used at that time. If no match is found among receives that are open or awaiting-redirect, the user is contacted as in the asynchronous case if contact information is provided in the security element definition. Otherwise, a fault is thrown.

A reply activity for a receive that is 'awaiting_redirect' must wait before it can send its response until the receive's reply status is again 'open' and no other security redirects are pending for that receive.

5 Secure Authentication Service

The Secure Authentication Service (SAS) is responsible for providing a proxy that can transparently handle various authentication types of different secure Web-based, e.g., RESTful services. Therefore, the SAS supports different security mechanisms and exposes itself using an OAuth interface, a popular protocol for managing authentication and authorization among Web-based APIs. The specification [8] defines it as follows: "OAuth protocol enables websites or applications (Consumers) to access Protected Resources from a web service (Service Provider) via an API, without requiring Users to disclose their Service Provider credentials to the Consumers."[3]. We provide a brief overview of the OAuth protocol and its extensions.

5.1 OAuth Principles

We leverage OAuth as the protocol for communicating with the SAS for two main reasons: OAuth is a well-understood and increasingly popular protocol for Web based applications and it implements a seamless way of handling authentication and authorization between a consumer and a provider. The consumer in our scenario is the Bite engine and the provider is the SAS itself. An OAuth provider has to provide three different request URLs: (1) a request token URL (relative URL /request_token); (2) a user authorization URL (/authorize); and (3) an access token URL (/access_token). A typical OAuth authentication and authorization is handled as follows: First, a consumer requests a request token using the request token URL (1) by sending a number of OAuth specific parameters, such a pre-negotiated consumer key to identify the consumer application, timestamp, nonce, signature etc. In case all parameters are correct and verifiable, the service provider issues an unauthorized *request token*. When the request token is received by the consumer, the user's browser can be redirected to the service provider to obtain authentication and authorization. This authorization ensures that the user sitting behind the browser explicitly ensures that the consumer Web application is allowed to access the service provider on its behalf.

---

[3] We are aware of the current security issue with OAuth [13], however, this will be fixed in a future version of the OAuth implementation that we currently use.

Once the authorization is performed, the service provider can redirect the user back to the consumer application (using a callback URL). Finally, the consumer has to exchange the request token for an *access token* at the service provider. This is typically granted if the user successfully performed the authentication and authorization in the previous step. This access token is one of the OAuth parameters that has to be sent with every further request to the protected service (among others such as consumer key, timestamp, signature, etc).

5.2   Third-Party Service Support

Transparently supporting a secure authentication and authorization of different third-party services through the SAS's OAuth interface requires extending the OAuth protocol. This allows the SAS to act as a "secure proxy" for various other authentication protocols. To do so, the SAS needs at least the URL and the authentication type of the target service. Since this information is available in the activity specification and the security extension in a Bite flow (e.g., Listing 1.1, lines 18–23), it just needs to be sent to the SAS to enable transparent third-party service authentication. Thus, a number of request parameters are added when the Bite engine requests a *request token* at the SAS as discussed below.

HTTP Basic Authentication. This type of authentication is widely used in practice although it is not very secure unless using SSL. It can be specified in Bite by setting the `authtype` to `http_basic` (cf., Listing 1.1, line 22). At runtime, the Bite engine contacts the SAS by requesting a *request token* by sending the following extended OAuth request:

```
http://sas.watson.ibm.com/request_token?oauth_consumer_key=bite_app
&oauth_timestamp=...&oauth_signature=...&oauth_...=...
&x-oauth_serviceurl=http://internal.acme.com/interview/schedule
&x-oauth_authtype=http_basic
```

The parameters `x-oauth_serviceurl` and `x-oauth_authtype` indicate the target URL of the secured third-party service and its authentication type from the `scheduleInterview` activity from Listing 1.1 (we prefix the extension with `x-` because this is a common pattern for HTTP header extensions too). In case of a synchronous authentication the user is redirected to the SAS Web interface, otherwise (in the asynchronous case) the user id specified in the `notification-Receiver` attribute receives a link that is used for authentication (basically the same that Bite redirects to in the synchronous case).

These two extension attributes are used by the SAS to make an outgoing call to the target URL in an iframe. It prompts the user for the credentials of the target service. If the authentication is successful, the HTTP `Authorization` header of the target service is intercepted by the SAS's proxying mechanism. A simple proxy servlet (`/proxy`) is used to achieve the proxying transparently at the SAS. The response of the target service is queued at the SAS, otherwise we would call the service twice: once for the authentication and once for the original service invocation. When the first "real" service invocation is executed, the SAS will return the queued response during the authentication process.

Custom Application IDs. Support for custom application IDs requires adding another OAuth extension parameter called x-oauth_appid_mapping, that encodes details on how application IDs are queried from the user in a dynamically rendered Web form at the SAS and how this data is sent to the target service (e.g., in the HTTP header or as GET or POST parameter). Therefore, the security extension element in the Bite flow defines a mapping element (cf. Listing 1.1, lines 31–36). More specifically, this mapping states that the target service requires two parameters for a successful authentication, par and key, that need to be added as HTTP POST parameters (because this extension activity internally uses POST). Additionally, each element defines a label attribute used as a label for the HTML input element in the dynamically rendered authentication form.

Upon execution of such an application ID based service, the Bite engine serializes the Bite XML mapping into a simple text based form that is transfered to the SAS using the aforementioned OAuth extensions. Then the dynamically rendered authentication form is shown to prompt for the application IDs.

OAuth. Support for OAuth is also transparently supported by the SAS. In this case, the SAS just adds another layer of redirection between Bite and the target service provider without storing any information. It would be possible to implement a customized security handler to consume OAuth-based services directly (because Bite is already an OAuth consumer for the SAS). However, going through the SAS when consuming OAuth-based services has the advantage of handling multiple security mechanism transparently for the Bite engine.

5.3   Implementation Aspects

Bite and the SAS have been implemented in Java 1.6. Bite can be run on either a servlet container or WebSphere sMash server. The SAS implementation is based on Google's Java OAuth implementation providing multiple servlets for the different endpoints (request token, access tokens, etc). These servlets have been extended to support the above mentioned security protocols transparently. The Bite engine implements the OAuth client by using a specific security handler upon calling services from an activity with a security element (SASSecurityHandler). All other calls use a NullSecurityHandler that does not involve the SAS.

6   Case Study and Discussion

We have implemented the approach and provided a simple case study based on the illustrative example from Figure 1. It uses three different authentication mechanisms that are transparently handled by the SAS.

Figure 3 illustrates the SAS's Web interface for the authentication and authorization for the shareFile activity from Listing 1.1 (lines 28–37) that uses custom application IDs as the "security" mechanism. Figure 3a shows the dynamically rendered authentication form based on the specification in Bite. When

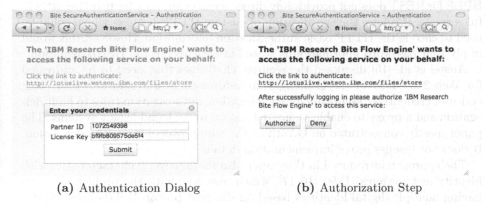

(a) Authentication Dialog   (b) Authorization Step

Fig. 3. Custom Application ID Authentication and Authorization Process

the user's browser is redirected to the SAS, the user sees the Web page as shown. By clicking on the link, the authentication box pops up and the user enters the credentials. After submitting the credentials, the user explicitly has to authorize Bite to call the service on its behalf (Figure 3b). When the user authorizes Bite, the flow proceeds its execution and the user is redirected back to the flow application (in the synchronous case), otherwise an error is thrown. The same user experience is available for HTTP basic authentication, however, the dialog box is not dynamically rendered but browser-specific.

The proposed approach based on the SAS effectively supports both, authentication and authorization of third-party services without the need to disclose the credentials to consumer applications (such as Bite in our case). A major focus was a seamless user-experience during the authentication and authorization process by automatically redirecting to the SAS to handle the authentication and authorization process. Therefore, it provides a mechanism for enterprise mashup solutions to transparently consume services in a secure way.

An important requirement for ensuring this end-to-end security is that the SAS has to run in a "trusted" environment because it stores intercepted credentials (for HTTP basic authentication) and stores the custom application IDs. Clearly, this is not an issue when using a third-party service supporting OAuth, because no credentials are disclosed to the SAS.

7   Related Work

Most existing mashup tools and products (e.g., Yahoo Pipes [2] or IBM Mashup Center [3]) do not address a secure end-to-end authentication and authorization of different services within a mashup. Most approaches use plain text to manage user credentials within a mashup definition.

Pautasso [14] proposed BPEL for REST, an extension to the WS-BPEL language to enable language support for RESTful services in business processes.

BPEL for REST does not provide any direct security support for invoking REST-ful services. It allows the specification of custom HTTP headers which could be used to encode the HTTP basic authentication information. However, this would imply that password information is stored in cleartext in the BPEL definition.

Austel et al. [15] discussed the security challenges that need to be addressed for Web 2.0. Many of the challenges are addressed in our solution: protecting end-user credentials, secure and open delegation, authorization rules to limit delegation and a proxy to enable secure delegation to back end legacy systems. The paper mostly concentrated on OAuth as the wire protocol for secure delegation. It does not discuss proxy implementation details.

The approach introduced in this paper also shares several characteristics with identity metasystems (IMs) [16,17], which also deal with the problem of users having multiple digital identities based on different protocols. IMs are typically used to allow clients to access Web applications on behalf of users. In the work presented here we consider the impact of multiple digital identities on the development and use of business mashups. The fundamental difference is our focus on a server side application (the mashup) acting on behalf of the end user.

A number of works have identified security issues for client-side mashups, i.e., running in a browser and communicating with other service through AJAX or related technologies. SafeMashups [18], for example, allows two web applications to communicate through a browser to securely authenticate each other and establish a trusted channel. Subspace [19] enables a secure cross-domain communication by providing a small JavaScript library to rule out a number of existing security flaws.

8   Conclusions and Outlook

In this paper we provided an end-to-end environment for securely consuming third-party services having diverse security requirements in a common service mashup application. The proposed approach was implemented as an extension to the Bite language and runtime by providing authentication and authorization transparently using a *Secure Authentication Service* (SAS) that can handle different security protocols common in the Web 2.0 area. The approach currently supports HTTP basic authentication, OAuth and customized application IDs that are frequently used in various RESTful services on the Web.

As future work, we plan to extend the support for further security mechanisms supported by the SAS, for example single sign-on approaches such as OpenID [7]. Additionally, we also want to reduce the need to explicitly specify the authentication type in the Bite flow, enabling automatic techniques to "guess" the security mechanism at the target service.

References

1. Yu, J., Benatallah, B., Casati, F., Daniel, F.: Understanding Mashup Development. IEEE Internet Computing 12(5), 44–52 (2008)
2. Yahoo! Inc.: Yahoo Pipes, http://pipes.yahoo.com (Last accessed: May 19, 2009)

3. IBM Corporation: IBM Mashup Center, http://www.ibm.com/software/info/mashup-center/ (Last accessed: May 19, 2009)

4. Hoyer, V., Fischer, M.: Market Overview of Enterprise Mashup Tools. In: Bouguettaya, A., Krueger, I., Margaria, T. (eds.) ICSOC 2008. LNCS, vol. 5364, pp. 708–721. Springer, Heidelberg (2008)

5. Lawton, G.: Web 2.0 creates security challenges. Computer 40(10), 13–16 (2007)

6. Koschmider, A., Torres, V., Pelechano, V.: Elucidating the Mashup Hype: Definitions, Challenges, Methodical Guide and Tools for Mashups. In: Proc. of the Workshop on Mashups, Enterprise Mashups and Lightweight Composition on the Web (MEM 2009), Madrid, Spain (2009), http://integror.net/mem2009/papers/paper14.pdf (Last accessed: May 21, 2009)

7. OpenID Foundation (OIDF): OpenID Authentication 2.0 - Final, http://openid.net/specs/openid-authentication-2_0.html (Last accessed: May 20, 2009)

8. OAuth Consortium: OAuth Core 1.0, http://oauth.net/core/1.0/ (Last accessed: May 20, 2009)

9. Rosenberg, F., Curbera, F., Duftler, M.J., Khalaf, R.: Composing RESTful Services and Collaborative Workflows: A Lightweight Approach. Internet Computing 12, 24–31 (2008)

10. Curbera, F., Duftler, M., Khalaf, R., Lovell, D.: Bite: Workflow Composition for the Web. In: Krämer, B.J., Lin, K.-J., Narasimhan, P. (eds.) ICSOC 2007. LNCS, vol. 4749, pp. 94–106. Springer, Heidelberg (2007)

11. Lau, C.: BPM 2.0 – a REST based architecture for next generation workflow management. In: Devoxx Conference, Antwerp, Belgium (2008), http://www.devoxx.com/download/attachments/1705921/D8_C_11_07_04.pdf

12. OASIS: Web Service Business Process Execution Language 2.0 (2006), http://www.oasis-open.org/committees/tc_home.php?wg_abbrev=wsbpel (Last accessed: May 28, 2009)

13. OAuth Consortium: OAuth Security Advisory 2009.1, http://oauth.net/advisories/2009-1 (Last accessed: May 20, 2009)

14. Pautasso, C.: BPEL for REST. In: Dumas, M., Reichert, M., Shan, M.-C. (eds.) BPM 2008. LNCS, vol. 5240, pp. 278–293. Springer, Heidelberg (2008)

15. Austel, P., Bhola, S., Chari, S., Koved, L., McIntosh, M., Steiner, M., Weber, S.: Secure Delegation for Web 2.0 and Mashups. In: Proc. of the Workshop on Web 2.0 Security and Privacy 2008, W2SP (2008), http://w2spconf.com/2008/papers/sp4.pdf (Last accessed: May 21, 2009)

16. OASIS: Identity Metasystem Interoperability Version 1.0, http://www.oasis-open.org/committees/download.php/32540/identity-1.0-spec-cs-01.pdf/ (May 14, 2009)

17. Microsoft: Microsoft's Vision for an Identity Metasystem, http://msdn.microsoft.com/en-us/library/ms996422.aspx (May 2005)

18. SafeMashups Inc.: MashSSL, https://www.safemashups.com (Last accessed: May 19, 2009)

19. Jackson, C., Wang, H.J.: Subspace: secure cross-domain communication for web mashups. In: Proc. of the International Conference on World Wide Web (WWW 2007), Banff, Alberta, Canada, pp. 611–620. ACM, New York (2007)

A Genetic Algorithms-Based Approach for Optimized Self-protection in a Pervasive Service Middleware

Weishan Zhang[1], Julian Schütte[3], Mads Ingstrup[1], and Klaus M. Hansen[1,2]

[1] Aarhus University
{zhangws,ingstrup}@cs.au.dk
[2] University of Iceland
kmh@hi.is
[3] Fraunhofer Institute for Secure Information Technology
julian.schuette@sit.fraunhofer.de

Abstract. With increasingly complex and heterogeneous systems in pervasive service computing, it becomes more and more important to provide self-protected services to end users. In order to achieve self-protection, the corresponding security should be provided in an optimized manner considering the constraints of heterogeneous devices and networks. In this paper, we present a Genetic Algorithms-based approach for obtaining optimized security configurations at run time, supported by a set of security OWL ontologies and an event-driven framework. This approach has been realized as a prototype for self-protection in the Hydra middleware, and is integrated with a framework for enforcing the computed solution at run time using security obligations. The experiments with the prototype on configuring security strategies for a pervasive service middleware show that this approach has acceptable performance, and could be used to automatically adapt security strategies in the middleware.

1 Introduction

Security is an important quality of service (QoS) requirement in pervasive computing systems. On the one hand, the higher security, the better. On the other hand, resource restrictions on pervasive computing devices may compromise the security requirements, as usually the higher security, the more resources are needed to implement and enforce them. Therefore, an interesting concern in relation to system quality is not how secure or efficient a system can be made, but rather how secure we can afford to make a system given the constraints set by available resources and other requirements, such as memory consumption and latency. Tradeoffs between security, performance, and resources are always involved, especially in pervasive computing systems.

Hence, an investigation on how to obtain an optimized solution following security, resource, and performance requirements is an interesting issue. Although

L. Baresi, C.-H. Chi, and J. Suzuki (Eds.): ICSOC-ServiceWave 2009, LNCS 5900, pp. 404–419, 2009.

several research contributions have been made towards making security mechanisms adaptable [1], we have found that most of this work focus on security in isolation rather than on managing an appropriate tradeoff between several quality attributes at runtime.

In this paper we present a way for systems to dynamically optimize the tradeoffs between security, resources and performance as users' preferences are changed to reflect, at run time, the relative importance of these three quality attributes. We have accomplished this by relying on a general architecture for self management developed in the EU-funded Hydra project[1], in which Genetic Algorithms (GAs) [2] are used to obtain optimized solutions at run time, from a number of conflicting objectives.

Approaching adaptive security from the perspective of making systems self-managing has particular merit because security is thereby managed alongside other quality attributes. Moreover, since even security mechanisms that are arguably simple to use are frequently misunderstood and applied incorrectly by end users [3], automating their configuration may make systems more secure by precluding their incorrect configuration by human operators, who express their goals declaratively as policies.

The remainder of the paper is organized as follows: First we explain the self-management architecture of Hydra and how its components interact to optimize self-protection (section 2). Our approach uses semantic models of resource consumption and security characteristics, which are described in Section 3. Section 4 describes a scenario of self-protection and the security strategies used within it. Next, section 5 describes how genetic algorithms are used to optimize protection in face of specific resource requirements. Section 6 presents our prototype implementation, and evaluations that show our approach can perform acceptably. Finally, we review related work (section 7) and conclude the paper (section 8).

2   Semantic Web-Based Self-management and Work Flow of Self-protection in Hydra

2.1   Self-management Architecture

The Hydra self-management features cover the full spectrum of self-management functionalities, including self-configuration, self-adaptation, self-protection, and self-optimization. The self-management of Hydra follows a three layer model proposed by Kramer and Magee [4] as detailed in Figure 1, where the interaction between different layers are through events via the Hydra Event Manager, following a publish-subscribe [5] communication style.

Besides the Event Manager, the Self-management component also needs to collaborate with other Hydra components, including the EventProcessingEngine component for Complex Event Processing (CEP), which is used to monitor dynamic resources and other context changes, and a QoS manager, which is used to retrieve the QoS properties for services/devices and monitor QoS changes.

---

[1] http://www.hydramiddleware.eu

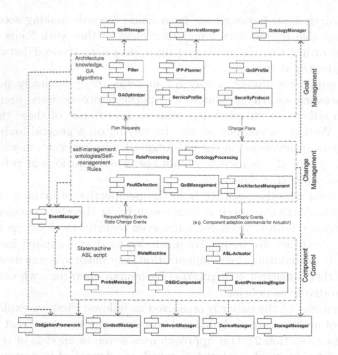

Fig. 1. Architecture of the Self-Management component in Hydra

Also, as we are adopting a Semantic Web-based self-management approach [6], the management of OWL[2](Web Ontology Language)/SWRL[3] (Semantic Web Rule Language) ontologies is handled by the Ontology Manager. The diagnosis results are stored via the Storage Manager for future analysis.

Component Control Layer. The component control layer has two responsibilities: to enable higher layers to monitor low-level events, and to actuate changes to the underlying system.

For detecting situations which require changes of the system's configuration, three components are available: device run time state monitoring via state machines, service invocations monitoring using message probes and detecting specific patterns of events through an event processing engine. Event patterns can be ordered in an increasingly abstract hierarchy, ranging from low-level events (e.g., raw sensor data) to high-level events (e.g., more complex situations like "fire in the hall"). In the Component Control layer, the EventProcessingEngine based on Complex Event Processing (CEP) is used to detect situations requiring changes of the system's security configuration, such as additional services or devices joining a network.

For the second purpose of the Component Control layer, the ability to actuate changes to a system's configuration by obligation policies triggering the execution

---

[2] http://www.w3.org/TR/swbp-n-aryRelations/
[3] http://www.w3.org/Submission/SWRL/

of ASL (architectural scripting language) [7] scripts is provided by its interpreter. This is shown as an *ASL-Actuator* component in Figure 1.

Change Management Layer. The Change Management layer is responsible for executing predefined schemes of self-management, i.e., this layer will respond to detected deficiencies in a system and execute strategies defined in advance or dynamically generated for a specific change event. A primary approach in Hydra is the usage of SWRL [6] to define these self-management capabilities. Further, QoS is considered if necessary for all self-management activities.

Goal Management Layer. Two complementary approaches are adopted in the Goal Management layer to achieve planning. First GAs are used for obtaining optimal solutions given some QoS goals and restrictions. Second, once a desired target solution has been chosen, it becomes input to the IPP planner [8] which generates an actuation plan.

A GA based approach [9] is used for optimization. Here, optimization (for example choosing the most suitable services for self-configuration) is one important task in self-management for pervasive service computing. These optimization tasks can be considered as problems of multi-objective services selection with constraints, where GAs are effective.

Non-trivial plans are generated with the IPP planner. Given a domain description, a start configuration and a condition describing the goal state, IPP planner can generate a sequence of actions available in the domain (architectural configurations in our case) that lead to a goal state.

2.2 Self-protection Work Flow

Figure 2 illustrates how the work flow of automatically re-configuring security settings in the middleware based on the components introduced above.

In the first step, situations are detected which might require a reconfiguration of security parameters and mechanism. For this purpose, events broadcasted on the event bus are being monitored and fed into the *EventProcessingEngine*, which then detects specific patterns of events. Once an event pattern has been detected (e.g. a new device with some additional managers joining the network), the EventProcessingEngine initiates the GAs to find the optimal configuration for the new situation.

In general, a number of steps is required to come from the current to the optimal solution identified by the GAs. Therefore, the optimal solution is at first sent to an *IPP planning engine* which calculates an enforceable plan leading to this solution. This execution plan is passed to an *obligation distribution point* (ODP) which is responsible for applying the individual steps of the plan to the system by sending appropriate obligations [10] to *enforcement points* (OEP). Obligations are signed by the Obligation Distribution Point (ODP) to prevent manipulation and to ensure authenticity of the obligation. When receiving an obligation, OEPs validate the attached signature and invoke appropriate enforcement plugins which are able to execute the actions stated within the obligation.

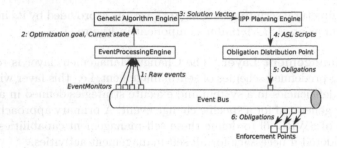

Fig. 2. Workflow of Self-Protection (components as boxes, communication as arrows)

After the enforcement process, OEPs can send back status report events indicating success or failure which can again be monitored by the component control layer.

From Figure 2, we can see that the proposed approach relies on two aspects: the underlying security contexts (implemented as ontologies) and an eventing mechanism for context provision. Therefore our approach is generic and is applicable to situations other than the Hydra middleware where the self-protection approach originated.

3   Security Ontologies

The Goal Management layer in Figure 1 requires information about security mechanisms that can be applied to the system to make proper decisions. This information is modeled in a set of security ontologies, which need to describe not only security mechanisms and their targeted protection goals, but also quality of those mechanisms which differentiate our security ontologies to the existing ones, such as the one from FIPA TC [11] and NRL ontology [12]. The ontology used in our approach is application-agnostic and provided as part of the middleware. Developers can add application-specific information by inserting additional instances into the predefined ontologies.

3.1   Modeling Protection Goals

For self-protection, the security ontology mainly serves two purposes: at first, it assigns each configuration to the protection goals it supports. Secondly, the ontology should provide information about the quality of a mechanism, i.e., describe how well it is suited to achieve the protection goals and how high the costs in terms of memory and CPU consumption will be. We will now describe the most important concepts of the ontology as depicted in Figure 3 and explain how they address those two purposes.

We model protecion goals as instances of the *SecurityObjective* class in order to describe which configuration of the system is suited to achieve a certain protection goal. This concept is modeled similarily to what is done in the NRL

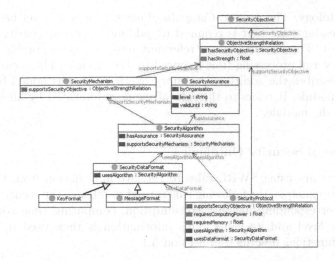

Fig. 3. Main concepts and properties of the Security Ontology

ontology, i.e. it comprises instances such as *Confidentiality, MessageIntegrity, ReplayPrevention*, etc.. Further, the concept *SecurityProtocol* represents the actual configuration that could be applied to the system. This concept is the only one whose instances refer to specific software modules or settings (e.g., OSGi[4] bundles or sets of preferences). As not all instances of *SecurityProtocol* are equally suited to fulfil a certain protection goal, we modeled an *n*-ary relation between *SecurityProtocol* and *SecurityObjective* using the *ObjectiveStrengthRelation* concept to overcome the lack of *n*-ary relations in OWL. In this way, we are able to express qualified relations using security levels like "RSA-512 serves *low* confidentiality". By querying the ontology given protection goals it is thus possible to retrieve a set of applicable implementations and configurations, ranked by the degree to which they address protection goals.

3.2 Modeling Resource Consumption

In most cases, security is not for free and so the second purpose of the security ontology is to provide information about the trade-off between the security level and the required performance costs for each instance of the *SecurityProtocols*. The resource consumption of each instance is represented by the properties *requiresComputingPower* and *requiresMemory*. Obviously, both properties vary depending on the platform and various other factors, so the values in the ontology may only be taken as a rough estimation. However, for our optimization approach the absolute values are not of interest but rather the relation of modules according to their resource consumption. Hence, we argue that in this case it is feasible to represent such platform-specific information in a system-wide

---

[4] http://www.osgi.org/

security ontology. The *requiresComputingPower* property describes the additional processing time that is required by adding a certain security module or configuration. That is, the values refer not only to cryptographic operations but to the overall processing time required by the module. The *requiresMemory* property describes the additional memory overhead that is added by applying a security module. It refers to the sum of memory allocated by all objects and methods of the module.

3.3   Usage of Security Ontologies

In Hydra, we are using SWRL rules to retrieve information from the security ontology. For example, the following rule is used to retrieve the security protocols and their corresponding memory consumption, computing time consumption, authenticity level and its value. This information is then used in the fitness evaluation functions described in Section 5.1.

> *Rule: SecurityResource*
> *SecurityProtocol*(?*protocol*) ∧
> *requiresComputingPower*(?*protocol*, ?*power*) ∧
> *requiresMemory*(?*protocol*, ?*memory*) ∧
> *authenticityObj*(?*protocol*, ?*auth*) ∧
> *hasStrength*(?*auth*, ?*value*)
> → *sqwrl* : *select*(?*protocol*, ?*memory*, ?*power*, ?*auth*, ?*value*)

Further, the security ontology is needed to automatically replace security mechanisms once they are considered to be insecure. From time to time, new attacks on cryptographic algorithms become feasible and their level of security decreases. Reflecting such changes in the security ontology by modifying the *ObjectiveStrengthRelation* (c.f. the following section) will trigger a re-configuration of the middleware, replacing outdated mechanisms by more secure equivalents. This work is still under investigation and will be reported in the near future.

4   Security Strategies and a Scenario for Self-protection in Hydra

In this section, we will describe how different security strategies described by the security ontology have been combined with the self-management architecture in order to realize self-protection in the Hydra middleware.

4.1   Security Strategies

A *Hydra device* is basically a set of *managers* (i.e. web services) which can either be hosted locally on a single platform or be distributed across devices. To protect communication between those managers (which we refer to as *Core Hydra*) a number of security modules with different properties are available. Besides the Core Hydra configuration, further security settings can be made in the middleware: the communication between Hydra devices can be protected in different ways, different trust models (e.g. OpenPGP, PKI-Common, etc.) can be used, and message formats such as XMLSecurity or S/Mime can be chosen. In this paper, however, we will focus on the Core Hydra configuration only, i.e. the selection of different security strategies for the communication between managers (the procedure for other configurations is analogous).

The protection of Core Hydra communication is realized by SOAP[5] security handlers implementing the following security strategies: *Null*, *XMLEnc*, *XMLEncSig* and *XMLEncSigSproadic* each representing a different protection level. These security handlers are hooked into the *web service handler chain*, a series of Java classes that is called immediately before a SOAP call is routed into the actual web service and immediately after the response leaves it. Thus, these Core Hydra handlers are supposed to be completely invisible for users of the middleware.

Null. This strategy switches off all message protection mechanisms and the Core Hydra security handler simply passes all messages on to the receiving manager. This strategy is obviously the most insecure but also the fastest way of sending messages in Core Hydra.

XMLEnc. This strategy applies XMLEncryption[6] to messages in Core Hydra. The message payload is encrypted using a 192 bit TripleDES key. This symmetric key is then attached to the message, encrypted by RSA 1.5 using the 1024 bit public key of the receiving manager. This strategy ensures confidentiality but does not fully prevent message modification or replay attacks.

XMLEncSigSporadic. For this strategy, nonces ("*number used once*") are added to messages in order to prevent replay attacks and XMLSignature[7] using RSA is applied in addition to XMLEncryption. Receivers will however only randomly verify a certain percentage of the arriving messages to save resources. While this strategy may allow attackers to send some individual forged messages, it is not possible to inject a whole sequence of faked messages. It depends on the messages content and the application whether this strategy adds any additional security – in the worst case it is equivalent to *XMLEnc*, in the best case it is equivalent to *XMLEncSig*.

XMLEncSig. For this strategy, messages are created in the same way as in the previous strategy. In addition, all signatures are verified by the receiver. So, the *XMLEncSig* strategy ensures confidentiality and authenticity as well as it prevents attackers from re-playing previously recorded messages.

Table 1 lists the security strategies with the degree of support for confidentiality and authenticity as well as their resource consumption, which are encoded in the security ontologies and will be used at run time as security contexts. For XMLEncSigSporadic, 50% of the arriving messages are verified in our case. The CPU processing time and memory consumption values have been obtained

---

[5] http://www.w3.org/TR/soap/
[6] http://www.w3.org/TR/xmlenc-core/
[7] http://www.w3.org/TR/xmldsig-core/

Table 1. Protection levels (0 to 10) and resource consumptions of security strategies

Strategy	Level of protection		Resource consumption	
	Confidentiality	Authenticity	CPU (ms)	Memory (KB)
Null	0	0	16.3	0.32
XMLEnc	4	4	21.4	28.96
XMLEncSigSporadic	4	7	102.4	54.97
XMLEncSig	4	9	114.3	57.52

by measuring the Hydra middleware with different security configurations on a VMWare Windows XP with 512 MB memory and an Intel Core2 Duo processor.

4.2   A Self-protection Scenario in Hydra

The Hydra middleware has been developed to interconnect heterogeneous embedded devices. In such scenarios developers have to deal with resource-constrained platforms and the performance versus security trade-off. Usually this requires design decisions to be made at development time and knowledgeable developers who know the benefits and deficits of different security mechanisms. The aim of self-protection is to relieve developers from this task as much as possible by automatically adapting security mechanisms to the current situation. As an example, we look at how the middleware automatically selects the security strategies that best fit the resource and security requirements of the application.

Suppose Hydra is the supporting middleware for an airport management system, a public area that needs high security. All of 10 different Hydra components are deployed on different devices: PDAs, PCs, and security checking machines, connected via the Internet. All data sent between the managers should be confidential, and – if possible – protected against modification and replay attacks. At the same time, resource constraints must be considered, i.e., the latency and memory consumption should not exceed limits. As there are 10 managers, there are $\binom{10}{2} = 45$ bi-directional connections/channels to consider. For each connection, three different security strategies are available (omitting the *Null* strategy as it does not provide any confidentiality). The problem space for finding the optimal solution is 3^{45}, a scale that works well for GAs. Therefore, the following goals for the overall system's security configuration (referring to all 45 channels) are passed as input to the Hydra Goal Management layer:

- *Authenticity* should be maximized (highest value is 10 for a channel)
- *Latency* must not exceed 2000 ms
- *Memory* should be minimized, not more than 2 Mbytes should be used

In the following section we will describe how the self-protection architecture finds an optimal solution to this problem, plans its execution and finally enforces all necessary steps.

5   Obtaining Optimized Protection Using GAs

First, we will formulate the abstract requirements as an optimization problem that can be solved using a GA engine.

5.1 Optimization Objectives and Constraints Formulation

The memory consumption of a Hydra device's security mechanisms (the M objective) is calculated by the sum of each channel's memory consumption as: $M = \sum_{i=1}^{n} \sum_{j=1}^{m} M_i \cdot E(i,j)$, where $E(i,j) = 1$ if for a channel i (with a scope of $[1,n]$) a security strategy that has memory consumption M_i is selected, otherwise $E(i,j) = 0$. j represents the sequence number of a concrete security strategy with a scope of $[1,m]$. In the scenario under consideration, $n = 45$ and $m = 3$. As we choose exactly one security strategy for each channel, there is exactly one $E(i,j) = 1$ and all other $E(i,j) = 0$ for all $j \in [1,m]$.

Similarly, we can formulate the CPU consumption (the P objective) to calculate the total processing time required by security mechanisms as: $P = \sum_{i=1}^{n} \sum_{j=1}^{m} P_i \cdot E(i,j)$, where $E(i,j) = 1$ if a component i (with a scope of $[1,n]$) that has power consumption P_i is selected, otherwise $E(i,j) = 0$. j represents the sequence number of a concrete component implementation with a scope of $[1,m]$.

Authenticity, as said, should be maximized. We instead minimize the un-authenticity to formulate all objectives in a similar way. The un-authenticity (the Ua objective) is calculated as: $Ua = n \cdot 10 - \sum_{i=1}^{n} \sum_{j=1}^{m} A_i \cdot E(i,j)$, where $E(i,j) = 1$ if a channel i (with a scope of $[1,n]$) that has authenticity A_i is selected, otherwise $E(i,j) = 0$. j represents the sequence number of a concrete security strategy with a scope of $[1,m]$.

5.2 Chromosome Encoding and Fitness Evaluations

A chromosome corresponds to a unique solution in the solution space. GAs can typically make use of booleans, real numbers and integers to encode a chromosome. The representation of chromosome in our case is using integers (starting from 0). That is to say, we are using an integer vector $V = [V_1, V_2, ...V_i, ..., V_n]$ (where n is the number of decision variables – in our case 45) to represent a solution. V_i is a natural number, acts as a pointer to the index of the security strategy of the ith strategy. For example, a chromosome $[0,1,2,1,2,0,1,1,2,1...]$ represents that a solution chooses the first security strategy for channel 1, the second security strategy for channel 2, the third security strategy for channel 3, and so on. In our case, this relates to *XMLEnc, XMLEncSigSporadic, XMLEncSig* (cf. Table 1). Based on the chosen security strategies, the GAs then decide fitness using the objective equations as introduced in Section 5.1, and will at the same time evaluate whether the constraints mentioned in Section 5.1 are met.

6   Prototype Implementation

In order to test the self-protection approach, we developed a prototype that has been integrated into the Hydra middleware. In this section we will discuss the architecture of the prototype implementation and the achieved performance.

6.1   Implementing GA-Based Optimization for Self-protection

As in our former evaluation of GAs for self-management [9], we used the JMetal GA framework[8] for the implementation of the self-protection optimization problem. As shown in Figure 4, we model a SelfProtectionProblem as a SelfManagementProblem. Evaluations of solution fitness using the formulas introduced in Section 5.1 are implemented in the SelfProtectionProblem class as usual when a developer is to implement self-management optimization problems. The GAEngine is the core class for the GA-based self-management planning, and defines the common methods for getting the solutions.

The package *evaluations* defines utility classes for obtaining the Pareto front/ set[9], and the evaluation of the solution quality uses the Hyper volume (HV) quality indicator [13], which is a quality indicator that calculates the volume (in the objective space) covered by members of a non-dominated set of solutions for problems where all objectives are to be minimized.

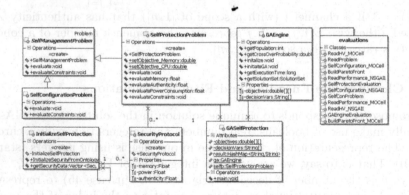

Fig. 4. GAs based Self-management optimization

6.2   Enforcement of Obligations

The enforcement architecture (c.f. Section 2.2) allows adding support for arbitrary obligations at runtime by loading appropriate enforcement plugins. We implemented one enforcement plugin that supports operations on the OSGi platform (such as starting and stopping bundles or setting preferences) and one that

---

[8] http://sourceforge.net/projects/jmetal/
[9] http://www-new.mcs.anl.gov/otc/Guide/OptWeb/multiobj/

supports the execution of ASL scripts. While for simple obligations such as used in our prototype example, the OSGi plugin provides a fast and direct access to OSGi management, platform-independent ASL scripts are better suited for heterogeneous platforms and more complex architectural restructurings [7]. The sequences of actions that constitute an obligation policy (and an ASL script) is generated by the IPP planner based on the target security configuration found by the GA optimization.

6.3   Performance Measurements and Quality Evaluation

Performance of Genetic Algorithms. For the measurement of performance of obtaining optimal solutions, the following software platform was used: JMetal 2.1, JVM 1.6.02-b06, Heap memory size is 256 Mbytes, Windows XP SP3. The hardware platform was: Thinkpad T61P T7500 2.2G CPU, 7200rpm 100G hard disk, 2G DDR2 RAM. The performance time measurements are in milliseconds.

We have done evaluations of two generic algorithms, NSGA-II and MOCell for their usage in pervasive computing [9]. In this paper, we want to validate whether our recommendations for these two algorithms are valid for different problem (where the problem space is much bigger and fitness evaluation algorithms are different). This time, the parameter settings for GAs are the same as in [9], and we are following the same steps as in [9] for evaluations.

The analysis for this evaluation (procedures as detailed in [9]) shows that our recommendations for parameter settings as in [9] are valid and NSGA-II is recommended for our self-management problems. Table 2 shows randomly chosen runs (from one of 100 runs for every parameter combination) for some of the parameter combinations (as detailed in the legend of Figure 5). We can see that for NSGA-II, which is recommended (and was recommended in [9]) in this case, the population size 64 to 100 with max evaluations of 5000 will have acceptable performance for getting optimized solutions within 342ms to 449ms, and has acceptable quality of solutions as shown in Table 2 and Figure 5. MOcell is not recommended as it has worse HV. We can see this in a direct way in Figure 5: MOCell solutions has many more points far from the Pareto front. We can also see that the *diversity* and *convergence* are satisfactory of NSGA-II, the solutions are spread uniformly along the true Pareto front, and the majority of the points in NSGA-II results are located at the Pareto front.

Table 2. Performance and quality of solutions

GA name	Population size	Max evaluations	cross over probability (CVP)	Avg. HV	Avg. Running Time
NSGA-II	64	5000	0.8	0.566524	342 ms
NSGA-II	81	5000	0.9	0.566524	419 ms
NSGA-II	100	5000	0.9	0.566524	449 ms
MOCell	1444	5000	0.8	0.459411	235 ms
MOCell	1600	10000	0.8	0.494775	576 ms

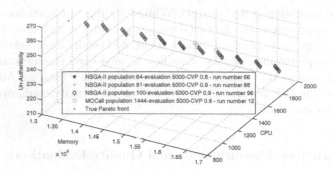

Fig. 5. Visualizing the solution quality

Performance of IPP Planner. We measured the performance of the IPP planner for the plans required in our implementation. With just one security strategy to be set, the planner generates the correct solution in just 10ms (average of 5 measurements, standard deviation 2 ms). In our case, at most four kinds of planning problems can occur, because the steps required to change a strategy depends only on the strategy being activated. Thus in practise the planner can be invoked once for each of these problems to produce a template plan/scheme which is stored in the Change Management layer and available for immediate execution once needed. Thus the test showing an execution time of just 10 ms is the worst case time for planning in our implementation. Other implementations of our approach may require more complex plans to activate a strategy. However, our previous experience with using the IPP planner for general architectural reconfiguration shows that it generates a plan within 100 ms [7].

Performance of Obligation Enforcement. Finally, we measured the performance of the enforcement process, i.e. the process of distributing a single obligation to the OEPs and executing the contained actions. The overall time (omitting network latency) amounts to 70.9 ms (standard deviation 14.21 ms) whereas the plain execution time is almost negligible (0.6%) due to the simple operation we use in our prototype example (changing the configuration of the Core Hydra module). The main computing costs come from signing and verifying the obligation, accounting to over 73% of the overall enforcement time. Another 21.7% is required by Axis 1.4 web service calls.

6.4   Discussion

The critical part of our self-management approach is obtaining the optimized solutions for all the communication channels. The search for the best solutions should be finished in a reasonable time. As we can see from Section 6.3, GAs can accomplish this within acceptable time and satisfactory quality. Combining the performance testing with IPP Planner for generating enforcement plans, and the performance of actual enforcement of security protocols from Section 6.3, in the best case we can get the self-protection ready within 520ms, which is acceptable for enabling the self-protection for the whole Hydra middleware. Even in the "worst" case, where the IPP planner needs to be invoked and the enactment of a strategy change is more complex than in Hydra, this would add less than 100ms or 20% to the execution time.

7 Related Work

In the Willow architecture [14] for comprehensive survivability, security threats are treated as one source of faults that the architecture provides mechanisms to avoid, eliminate, or tolerate. In contrast with our prototype, there is no dynamic adaptation or explicit modeling of the trade-offs involved in providing the protection. The ATNAC framework described by Ryutov et al. [15] detects malicious activity by analyzing failures and behavior patterns of the access control and trust negotiation process. Thus rather than trying to prevent an ongoing attack as such, a detected malicious activity is input to the access control and authorization process which thereby becomes more dynamic. The functionality is at the specific level orthogonal to our work, in that it is concerned with authentication. Further, the adaptation which is provided is focused on improving the accuracy of authentication, rather than on balancing multiple concerns against each other as in our approach. Another approach to multi-objective optimization is followed by the middleware CARISMA. In [16], the authors propose utility functions and auction-based negotiations to agree on an optimized trade-off between security and efficiency. Their decentralized approach however assumes each instance of the middleware acts honestly.

Event-condition-action policies as used in our obligation framework have been used for many policy-based management approaches before, where Ponder2 [17] is one of the most prominent examples. However, self-protection is scarcely considered in such approaches. Finally, a conceptually different approach to self-protection is used in artificial immune systems [18]. This approach is interesting but it is unclear yet how it can be combined with other self-* approaches in order to make acceptable tradeoffs between several different qualitative concerns. In our approach, multi-objective optimization can be used for other self-management features, as we have done for self-configuration [9].

8 Conclusion and Future Work

Self-protection is one of the important self-management capabilities of pervasive service computing. There is scarce reported work providing optimized self-protection, i.e. considering the characteristics of pervasive systems where resources are usually restricted. In this paper, we proposed a Genetic Algorithms-based approach for obtaining optimized security configurations. The optimized solutions can be used to enable corresponding security strategies, based on obligations generated from the IPP planner, and finally the obligation framework will execute these plans and make use of the chosen security protocols. The whole process is evaluated and it was show that our approach is feasible with acceptable performance and satisfactory quality. We will explore auction-based multi-attribute optimization [16], and investigate the replacement of outdated security mechanisms at run time using security ontologies.

Acknowledgments. The research reported in this paper has been supported by the Hydra EU project (IST-2005-034891).

References

1. Elkhodary, A., Whittle, J.: A survey of approaches to adaptive application security. In: Proc. of the 2007 International Workshop on Software Engineering for Adaptive and Self-Managing Systems, Washington, DC, USA. IEEE C.S, Los Alamitos (2007)
2. Mitchell, M.: An Introduction to Genetic Algorithms. Bradford Books (1996)
3. Whitten, A., Tygar, J.D.: Why johnny can't encrypt: A usability evaluation of pgp 5.0. In: Proceedings of the 8th USENIX Security Symposium (August 1999)
4. Kramer, J., Magee, J.: Self-Managed Systems: an Architectural Challenge. In: International Conference on Software Engineering, pp. 259–268 (2007)
5. Eugster, P., Felber, P., Guerraoui, R., Kermarrec, A.: The Many Faces of Publish/Subscribe. ACM Computing Surveys 35(2), 114–131 (2003)
6. Zhang, W., Hansen, K.M.: Semantic web based self-management for a pervasive service middleware. In: Second IEEE International Conference on Self-Adaptive and Self-Organizing Systems (SASO 2008), Venice, Italy, October 2008, pp. 245–254 (2008)
7. Ingstrup, M., Hansen, K.M.: Modeling architectural change - architectural scripting and its applications to reconfiguration. In: WICSA/ECSA 2009, Cambridge, England, September 2009. IEEE, Los Alamitos (2009)
8. Koehler, J., Nebel, B., Hoffmann, J., Dimopoulos, Y.: Extending planning graphs to an adl subset. In: Steel, S. (ed.) ECP 1997. LNCS, vol. 1348, pp. 273–285. Springer, Heidelberg (1997)
9. Zhang, W., Hansen, K.: An Evaluation of the NSGA-II and MOCell Genetic Algorithms for Self-management Planning in a Pervasive Service Middleware. In: 14th IEEE International Conference on Engineering Complex Computer Systems (ICECCS 2009), pp. 192–201. IEEE Computer Society, Washington (2009)
10. Pretschner, A., Hilty, M., Basin, D.: Distributed usage control. Communications of the ACM 49(9), 39–44 (2006)
11. FIPA Security: Harmonising heterogeneous security models using an ontological approach. Part of deliverable Agentcities. RTD, Deliverable D3.4 (2003)
12. Naval Research Lab: NRL Security Ontology (2007), http://chacs.nrl.navy.mil/projects/4SEA/ontology.html
13. Zitzler, E., Thiele, L.: Multiobjective evolutionary algorithms: a comparative case study and the strength Pareto approach. IEEE transactions on Evolutionary Computation 3(4), 257–271 (1999)
14. Knight, J., Heimbigner, D., Wolf, A.L., Carzaniga, A., et al.: The Willow Architecture: Comprehensive Survivability for Large-Scale Distributed Applications, Technical Report CU-CS-926-01, University of Colorado

15. Ryutov, T., Zhou, L., Neuman, C., Leithead, T., Seamons, K.E.: Adaptive trust negotiation and access control. In: SACMAT 2005: Proceedings of the tenth ACM symposium on Access control models and technologies, pp. 139–146. ACM, New York (2005)
16. Capra, L., Emmerich, W., Mascolo, C.: CARISMA: Context-Aware Reflective mIddleware System for Mobile Applications. IEEE Transactions on Software Engineering, 929–945 (2003)
17. Twidle, K., Dulay, N., Lupu, E., Sloman, M.: Ponder2: A policy system for autonomous pervasive environments. In: The Fifth International Conference on Autonomic and Autonomous Systems (ICAS) (April 2009)
18. Dasgupta, D.: Advances in artificial immune systems. IEEE Computational Intelligence Magazine 1(4), 40–49 (2006)

Role of Process Modeling in Software Service Design

Susanne Patig[1] and Harald Wesenberg[2]

[1] University of Bern, IWI, Engehaldenstrasse 12, CH-3012 Bern, Switzerland
susanne.patig@iwi.unibe.ch
[2] StatoilHydro ASA, Arkitekt Ebbels veg 10, Rotvoll, NO-7005 Trondheim, Norway
hwes@statoilhydro.com

Abstract. Service-oriented architecture technically facilitates business process management as it enables software to evolve along with changing business processes by simply recomposing software services. From a theoretical point of view it is, thus, natural to take business processes as a starting point for software service design. However, deriving software services strictly top-down from business processes is awkward from a practical point of view: The resulting services are too fine-grained in scope and too vast in number, and particular process control flows become cemented in service orchestrations. In this paper, another approach of software service design is described that, though starting from process models, avoids these drawbacks. The approach is illustrated by a practical example. The presented service design approach has been successfully applied in industry for more than 14 years and enables agile service implementation.

1 Motivation

Building large, mission-critical enterprise systems has always been challenging. During the last decades, these software systems have grown into tightly coupled mastodons that call for extensive efforts to keep in sync with the mutable business.

Service-oriented architecture (SOA) promises to ameliorate this situation: By structuring large software systems into smaller components (*software services*), adapting software to changed business processes amounts to recomposing software services. Consequently, SOA provides the technical foundation for business process management, where software evolves along with continuous process improvements.

Implementing SOA requires the definition of what constitutes a software service. SOA design approaches as sketched in Section 2 suggest that it works best to take business processes as a starting point for strict top-down derivation of software services, which realize process activities. However, practical experience indicates another way of software service design that can be justified by its favorable outcomes and, simultaneously, changes the view on the role of process models in SOA design.

In this paper we outline and generalize the service design approach used by StatoilHydro, which has proven since the mid-90s to facilitate service identification independently of technology and to create highly reusable and stable software services. Especially stability is a prerequisite for agile service development.

L. Baresi, C.-H. Chi, and J. Suzuki (Eds.): ICSOC-ServiceWave 2009, LNCS 5900, pp. 420–428, 2009.
© Springer-Verlag Berlin Heidelberg 2009

Section 3 explains the StatoilHydro approach of software service design abstractly and by means of a real-life example. Section 4 compares our approach with other practice-oriented ones, abstracts from the observations in the StatoilHydro case and draws some general conclusions on software service design for application systems.

2 Current Software Service Design Approaches

Basically, approaches to design software services for SOA fall into two groups: principles-driven approaches and hierarchical ones. *Principle-driven software service design approaches* (e.g., [3]) provide best practices that support SOA design princeples such as abstraction, standardized contract, autonomy, statelessness, discoverability etc. Often these recommendations are bundled into patterns (e.g., [4]) whose realization and combination is left to the user.

In contrast, *hierarchical software service design approaches* prescribe steps from some level of abstraction to a set of software services. They end either at the design stage (e.g., [7], [13], [16]) or include further stages of the service life cycle (e.g., [11], [1]). It can be distinguished between *top-down approaches,* which proceed from abstract information at the business level to the technical level of service implementation, and *bottom-up approaches* that increase the level of abstraction during design. *Hybrid approaches* combine bottom-up and top-down strategies (see Section 4).

Starting points for *top-down software service design approaches* are business goals [5], [9], functional business areas [13] or business processes [12], [7], [13], and [6]. *Goals* describe what should be achieved by a software service, *functional areas* are sets of related tasks referring to, e.g., departments or products, and *business processes* additionally consider the roles that perform these tasks as well as the order of tasks (*control flow*). Some of the top-down approaches rely on several types of business information [1]. The common idea of top-down approaches is a strict decomposition of business information into particular and usually fine-grained functions, which constitute service candidates. Process-oriented approaches are often favored as they enable the design of composite software services by orchestrating (atomic) software services according to the control flow between process activities [1], [11].

Current *bottom-up software service design approaches* (e.g., [16]) try to achieve service-orientation by wrapping existing application systems. They use reverse engineering techniques such as clustering to identify cohesive components. The functions these components provide form service candidates.

The direction top-down vs. bottom-up mainly refers to the *identification of service candidates.* Often the initial candidates are *refined* before they are specified: (1) Fine-grained services that have some logical affinity (in terms of, e.g., functions or communication [11]) are *grouped* into coarse-grained services; (2) *verification* and (3) *validation* check whether or not the candidate software services are conform to the SOA design principles [7], [2] and the stakeholders' needs [1], respectively.

Grouping and refinement can be found in top-down and bottom-up approaches. Only top-down approaches require *asset analysis* to map the identified and refined services either to existing application systems or to service implementation projects [2], [1], [7], [11]. Bottom-up approaches, on the other hand, need an analysis of business requirements and a corresponding *alignment* between IT and business [8].

The final step of *service specification* is always necessary. It defines the service interface (operations and their signatures, given by message types for inbound and outbound messages) and the conversations between services [1], [2], [13], [11].

3   A Practical Case of Software Service Design

3.1   SOA Development Context

StatoilHydro is an integrated oil and gas company with about 30,000 employees in 40 countries and more than 30 years domain experience. Part of the StatoilHydro value chain is the global sales and distribution of crude oil, an area that has been supported by a set of custom-made systems over the last 15 years. During the continued development of the application portfolio, the functional core of these systems was re-engineered as a set of services in the mid-90s, first as PL/SQL interfaces, then as web services. When developing these services (both PL/SQL and web), it was paramount to enable reuse and reduce duplication of code. Since the mid-90s, the services have been expanded, but the initially identified core has remained stable.

3.2   Service Design Process

There was no prescribed method for the design of the initial set of application services (*service inventory* [3]) at StatoilHydro when the project started. An academic ex-post analysis (by interviews, document and system analysis) of the service design process revealed recurring steps, which are depicted as BPMN activities [10] in Fig. 1 below. Section 3.3 illustrates the service design process by an example.

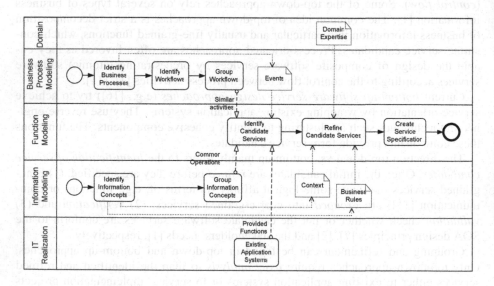

Fig. 1. Software service design process (in BPMN 1.1 [10])

Application services express the contribution of a software system to a business process on a logical level. They represent functions with high interdependencies in terms of data usage, user interaction or business rules. The (application) service design process followed a two-pronged approach focusing on business processes/ workflows and information concepts: Workflows were arranged in groups and analyzed to identify candidate services in a top-down way. Simultaneous bottom-up analysis of information concepts helped in generalizing these candidate software services to increase their stability and encourage reuse.

The identified candidate application services were *refined* (grouped or split) by using the following heuristics (for more examples see Section 3.3):

- An application service must refer to the same information concept in the same semantic *context*. For example, the information concept 'Cargo' has distinct interpretations depending on whether it is related to terminal operations, e.g., storing at the port, or to supply operations, e.g., lifting [15]. Hence, separate services are needed.
- An application service must stick to the same *business rules*.
- *Domain expertise* beyond the models must be used to check the candidate application services or to discover new ones.

As for *specification*, StatoilHydro decided to build small service interfaces containing only stable operations. In all, identification and refinement as described brought about three types of software services: (1) *entity services* (mainly CRUD – create, retrieve, update, delete - on information concepts), (2) *task services* (execution of operations more complex than CRUD and strongly guided by business rules) and (3) *technology services* that are not related to business, but needed for the systems to operate (e.g., services that provide a system with data from a data base). Currently, specification guidelines for these service types are prepared in the form of patterns.

3.2 Service Design Example

This section illustrates the service design process described in Section 3.2 by an excerpt from the current business process, workflow and service model of StatoilHydro. All pictures are real-life snapshots of the company's model repository. The models address human readers, contain both manual and IT supported activities and their execution is not automated, but relies on human interaction (*human-centric processes*). All models were already available due to governance requirements.

StatoilHydro has a supply business focusing on the delivery of crude oils and refinery products to customers all over the world. The high-level business process *Supply Operations* consists of the four sub-processes shown in Fig. 2 below.

Fig. 2. Business Process 'Supply Operations'

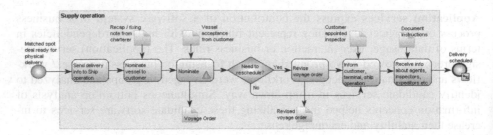

Fig. 3. Sub-process 'Schedule Delivery'

Each sub-process is detailed by workflows that are modeled with BPMN [10]. For example, Fig. 3 depicts the workflow of the sub-process 'Schedule Delivery'. The BPMN diagrams and candidate application services of the other sub-processes of Fig. 2 can be found in [14].

Top-down and bottom-up software service design were conducted simultaneously: The four sub-processes of the business process 'Supply Operations' form a natural group (*functional area*) to look for similar activities and information concepts. The candidate application services needed in a workflow were gathered by domain experience; Table 1 contains the results for the sub-process 'Schedule Delivery'. From workflow activities, both task and entity services (see Section 3.2) were derived, whereas information concepts initially brought about only entity services. The initial classification of the service types may change during refinement (see below).

Table 1. Identified candidate application services

Activity / Information Concept	Candidate Application Service	Service Type
Sub-process 'Schedule delivery'		
Send delivery info (information) to ship operations (A = activity)	Send Delivery info	Entity (Delivery)
Nominate vessel to customer (A)	Nominate Vessel, Update Vessel	Task (Nominate), Entity (Vessel)
Revise voyage order (A)	Reschedule Voyage	Task (Reschedule)
Inform customer, terminal... (A)	Send Voyage info	Entity (Voyage)
Receive info about agents, inspectors, expeditors etc. (A)	Receive Agent info, Receive Inspector info, Receive Expeditor info	Entity (Agent/Inspector/Expeditor information[1])
Vessel acceptance (IC = information concept)	Receive Vessel acceptance, Update Voyage	Entity (Vessel acceptance, Voyage)
(Revise) Voyage order (IC)	Send Voyage order	Entity (Voyage order)
Customer appointed inspector (IC)	Receive Inspector info, Update Inspector info	Entity (Inspector information)
Document instructions (IC)	Issue Document instructions	Entity (Document instructions)

---

[1] Information concepts whose names include the term 'information' represent relations between information concepts. Here, the relation exists between 'Cargo' and 'Agent', 'Inspector' etc.

After the initial identification of candidate application services for the workflow of each sub-process (see [14]), *refinement* was conducted in workshops with domain experts, software architects and software developers (see Table 2). There are three categories of refinement of candidate application services:

1. *Service type changes*: When more knowledge is gathered and a CRUD operation turns out to involve business rules, then the type of the candidate service is changed from 'entity' to 'task'. For example, 'Update Vessel' verifies that some selected vessel meets all legal requirements, which no longer is a CRUD operation.
2. *Grouping*: Candidate application services having the same names or working on similar information concepts in the same context are grouped. For example, initial services such as 'Update Vessel' and 'Update Voyage' form the service 'Maintain Cargo' as they work on the same, more general information concept 'Cargo'.
3. *Service Discovery*: The refined services 'Archive electronic documents' and 'Receive external documents' gathered from domain experts demonstrate that some services cannot be derived from workflow activities. Another example is the task service 'Calculation engine' that calculates transport costs, prices and volumes.

Table 2. Refined candidate application services

Refined Candidate Service	Identified Candidate Application Services[2]	Justification for Refinement	Service Type
Service Type Changes			
Update Vessel	Update Vessel	*Business Rule*: Before updating it must be checked, e.g., whether or not the vessel fulfils all legal requirements.	Task
Issue Document instructions	Issue Document instructions	*Business Rules:* A rules engine determines which document must be sent to which business partner.	Task
Grouping			
Maintain Cargo	Update {Cargo I Delivery I Volume I Transport costs I Gain/loss I Arrival info I ETA I Inspector info}	*Context*: All candidate services relate to attributes of a cargo. The refined service both creates and updates cargoes.	Entity (Cargo)
Receive external documents	Receive {Transport costs I Discharge documents I Cargo documents I ETA I Arrival info I Vessel nomination I Vessel acceptance}	*Domain expertise*: All candidate services relate to the reception of paper documents (by surface mail or fax). The scanned documents must be automatically processed and distributed electronically.	Task
Service Discovery			
Calculation engine	Calculate Transport costs	*Domain expertise:* Prices and volumes must be calculated in several activities.	Task
Archive electronic documents	Not applicable	*Domain expertise*: All legal documents related to a *cargo* must be stored in the corporate electronic archives. Archiving also adds necessary meta data.	Task

---

[2] To save space, terms common to the names of several service candidates are given outside the brackets '{}' and distinctive parts of the names inside, separated by 'I'.

Altogether, service refinement has reduced the number of application services handed over to software development teams from initially 33 candidates for the business process 'Supply Operations' to 21 [14]. Especially grouping increases reuse: The service 'Maintain Cargo' is used seven times in the workflows related to the business process 'Supply Operations'; further reuse occurs in other functional areas.

4 Generalization and Conclusions

The described approach to design application services has been successfully applied over 14 years in a complex industrial setting. In essence, candidate application services are functions related to (a) data handling (CRUD) of an information concept in the same context (*entity services*), (b) business rules (*task services*) or (c) IT (*technology services*). These service types are gathered both top-down (from activities common to a set of workflows) and bottom-up (from – potentially generalized – information concepts and domain experience). So, a service design process should be *hybrid*. If available, process models can be used as a source of domain knowledge; otherwise, a list of application (business) functions to be supported by IT is sufficient for service design. For human-centric processes, the control flow in the process models should be ignored to not artificially restrict process execution (see [14] for an example).

Table 3. Comparison of hybrid SOA design approaches

Approach		SOMA [1]	SOAF [2]	[6]	[7]	Statoil
Candidate Software Services						
Top-down	Goals	Decomposi-tion	—	—	—	—
	Functional Areas		Decomposi-tion	(SOA scope)	—	Similar activities in functional areas
	Business Processes	Activities, processes, CF	Activities of a use case	Activities, CF	Activities	
	Other	BR, variations	—	Stakeholder	Roles	Events
Bottom-up	Existing application	Available functions	Assessed functions	(Implemen-tation)	(Service list)	Available functions
	IC	(CRUD)	—	Only to group	(State changes)	CRUD
	Other	—	—	—	—	IT
Additional Design Rules				Low data trans-fer, not time-critical, reuse	SOA principles, service context/ layer, laws, reusability	SOA princi-ples
Refinement	Grouping	Logical affinity	Shared data/ code, scope, reuse	Entity / Task services		Same (gene-ralized) IC or BR
	Splitting	—	—	—	—	IC context
	Checks	VA	—	—	VE, VA, over-lap, feasibility	—
Specification		X	X	X	Specification schema	Small inter-face, stable operations

BR: Business rule, CF: Control flow, IC: Information concept, VA: validation, VF: Verification

Grouping of similar activities is essential in application service design to (1) keep the number of designed services small and (2) increase reuse. Grouping requires domain expertise and (preferably object-oriented) information models to guide *generalization*; thus, process modeling must be supplemented by information modeling. Finally, sometimes services must be *split* based on semantic *context* to enable reuse.

Table 3 compares the generalized StatoilHydro and other hybrid approaches of software service design. Shaded activities do not lead to software services.

The design of the StatoilHydro application services has proven to be stable for more than 14 years. As we look forward, agile software development is seeing widespread adoption across the software industry. Agile software development places less emphasis on upfront analysis and more emphasis on deferring decisions until more knowledge is available. In this setting, identifying stable application services at the right granularity before software service development starts is even more important, as identifying the wrong services can lead to extensive rework. We believe that the software service design process outlined in this paper has shown to facilitate service identification while, at the same time, significantly reducing the need for upfront analysis, making it immensely suitable for agile development projects.

References

1. Arsanjani, A., Ghosh, S., Allam, A., Abdollah, T., Ganapathy, S., Holley, K.: SOMA: A method for developing service-oriented solutions. IBM Systems Journal 47, 377–396 (2008)
2. Erradi, A., Anand, S., Kulkarni, N.: SOAF: An Architectural Framework for Service Definition and Realization. In: Proc. SCC 2006. IEEE, Los Alamitos (2006)
3. Erl, T.: SOA Principles of Service Design. Prentice Hall, Upper Saddle River (2008)
4. Erl, T.: SOA Design Patterns. Prentice Hall, Upper Saddle River (2008)
5. Kaabi, R.S., Souveyet, C., Rolland, C.: Eliciting service composition in a goal driven manner. In: Aiello, M., et al. (eds.) Proc. ICSOC 2004, pp. 305–308. ACM Press, New York (2004)
6. Klose, K., Knackstedt, R., Beverungen, D.: Identification of Services - A Stakeholder-based Approach to SOA development and its application in the area of production planning. In: Österle, H., et al. (eds.) Proc. ECIS 2007. St. Gallen, pp. 1802–1814 (2007)
7. Kohlmann, F.: Service identification and design - A Hybrid approach in decomposed financial value chains. In: Reichert, M., et al. (eds.) Proc. EMISA 2007, Koellen, Bonn, pp. 205–218 (2007)
8. Lämmer, A., Eggert, S., Gronau, N.: A Procedure Model for SOA-Based Integration of Enterprise Systems. Int. Journal of Enterprise Information Systems 4, 1–12 (2008)
9. Levi, K., Arsanjani, A.: A Goal-driven Approach to Enterprise Component Identification and Specification. Communications of the ACM 45, 45–52 (2002)
10. Object Management Group (OMG): Business Process Modeling Notation, V1.1. OMG Document Number: formal/20012-01-17,
    http://www.omg.org/docs/formal/012-01-17.pdf
11. Papazoglou, M.P., van den Heuvel, W.-J.: Service-oriented design and development methodology. Int. Journal of Web Engineering and Technology 2, 412–442 (2006)

12. Papazoglou, M.P., Yang, J.: Design Methodology for Web Services and Business Processes. In: Buchmann, A., Casati, F., Fiege, L., Hsu, M.-C., Shan, M.-C. (eds.) TES 2002. LNCS, vol. 2444, pp. 175–233. Springer, Heidelberg (2002)
13. Quartel, D., Dijkman, R., van Sinderen, M.: Methodological support for service-oriented design with ISDL. In: Aiello, M., et al. (eds.) Proc. ICSOC 2004, pp. 1–10. ACM Press, New York (2004)
14. Patig, S., Wesenberg, H.: Role of Process Modeling in Software Service Design. Preprint No. 219, University of Bern (May 2009)
15. Wesenberg, H., Landre, E., Rønneberg, H.: Using domain-driven design to evaluate commercial off-the-shelf software. In: Proc. Companion OOPSLA 2006, pp. 824–829. ACM Press, New York (2006)
16. Zhang, Z., Liu, R., Yang, H.: Service Identification and Packaging in Service Oriented Re-engineering. In: Chu, W.C., et al. (eds.) Proc. SEKE 2005, Skokie, pp. 620–625 (2005)

Assisting Trustworthiness Based Web Services Selection Using the Fidelity of Websites*

Lijie Wang, Fei Liu, Ge Li**, Liang Gu, Liangjie Zhang, and Bing Xie

Software Institute, School of Electronic Engineering and Computer Science,
Peking University, Beijing 100871, P.R. China
Key Laboratory of High Confidence Software Technologies, Ministry of Education,
Beijing 100871, P.R. China
{wanglj07,liufei08,lige,guliang05}@sei.pku.edu.cn,
{zhanglj06,xiebing}@sei.pku.edu.cn

Abstract. Web services selection aims to choose an appropriate web service among a number of service candidates. The trustworthiness of web services is an important metric for web services selection. Many trustworthiness based web services selecting methods have been proposed in the academic community. However, the fidelity of web service's supporting websites (e.g. the websites providing the service, or referencing the service.), as an important factor for the evaluation of web services' trustworthiness, is often ignored. This leads to that existing methods cannot provide service consumers with a comprehensive view of the web services. In this paper, we propose a method to estimate the fidelity of web services' supporting websites, and present a novel trustworthiness based web services selection approach using our estimation result. A case study conducted in this paper indicates that, by using our approach, we can provide active assistance for service consumers during web services selection.

Keywords: Web Services, Services Selection, Fidelity, Quality of Service.

1 Introduction and Related Work

With the increasing number of available web services on the internet, web services selection, which aims to select an appropriate web service among a bunch of functionally similar service candidates, is becoming a crucial task. Many researches on web services selection were proposed in the academic community in recent several years [3-6]. Recently, trustworthiness is introduced into services selection by many researches [5, 6]. In these researches, the trustworthiness of an individual web service is often acquired by collecting feedback from previous consumers, mainly in the form of rating on specific criteria of the service. However, all these existing researches mainly focus on using the quality or the trust of the individual service to conduct

---

* This work was supported by the National Basic Research Program of China (973) (SN: 2005CB321805), the Science Fund for Creative Research Groups of China (SN: 60821003), and the National Natural Science Foundation of China (SN: 60803010, 60803011).
** Corresponding author.

L. Baresi, C.-H. Chi, and J. Suzuki (Eds.): ICSOC-ServiceWave 2009, LNCS 5900, pp. 429–436, 2009.

selection of services. A comprehensive evaluation about the service is lacking in these researches.

For a specific web service on the internet, there are always some websites being related with the service. For instance, for a web service, there must be a website providing the executing environment for it, there must be some website(s) to publish the service, and there may be some website(s) providing reference links to the service. All these websites provide support for web services. In this paper, websites providing support for web services are called "*supporting websites*". Based on the different type of support they provide for services, we classify supporting websites into three types:

- **Service Provider** *(abbreviated as SP)*: The website providing the executing environment for the service. A service's *SP* is specified by an end point described in the service's WSDL document.
- **WSDL Hoster** *(abbreviated as WH)*: The website where the service is published on. Because a service is described by a WSDL document, publishing a service is actually hosting the service's WSDL document onto a website. Thus, we can get a service's *WH* from the URL of the service's WSDL document.
- **Service Reference** *(abbreviated as SR)*: The website containing reference links (i.e. hyperlinks) to the service. Because a web service is described by the service's WSDL document, a service's *SR* actually refers to the website containing hyperlinks to the service's WSDL document.

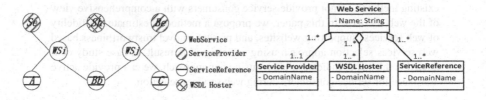

Fig. 1. Web services and supporting websites

The *fidelity* of a supporting website is the probability that it may provide valid web service information, it can be calculated using the proportion of valid web service information it provides.

Since there are three types of supporting websites for a web service, a website may play different roles for the same web service (or for different services). Actually, a website has different fidelity when it plays different roles. For example, all of the services provided by website *SiteX* are available, but many service hyperlinks on it are invalid. It means that website *SiteX* has high fidelity as a *SP*, but its fidelity is relatively low as a *SR*. Therefore, we treat a supporting website playing multi-roles as different ones, e.g. we treat '*SiteX*' as two websites, one plays the role as a *SP*; the other one plays the role as a *SR*. As shown in Fig 1, *Be* stands for the website *B* playing the role as a *SP*, *Bb* stands for the website *B* playing the role as a *SR*.

In real life, the fidelity of supporting websites provides valuable reference for a service consumer to judge the services at hand during web services selection. For instance, it is natural that a service consumer tends to choose a web service whose supporting websites have higher fidelity. The fidelity of supporting websites is an important factor for evaluation of the trustworthiness of services. It provides a comprehensive view of the services. However, existing evaluation mechanisms often ignore this factor and do not provide service consumers with a comprehensive view of web services. In this paper, we propose a method to assess the fidelity of supporting websites, and present a novel trustworthiness based web services selection approach using the fidelity of the service's supporting websites.

The rest of this paper is organized as follows. In section 2, we propose an approach to assessing the fidelity of supporting websites. The fidelity is used to assess the trustworthiness of web services in section 3. In section 4, we conduct a case study to evaluate our work. Section 5 draws the conclusion and some future work.

2 Assessing the Fidelity of Supporting Websites

2.1 Modeling the Relationship between Supporting Websites

When a service consumer uses a web service (represented as s), the typical sequence of supporting websites that he/she visits is from a *SR* of s to a *WH* of s, and then from the *WH* to the *SP* of s (the solid arrow shown in Fig 2). In other words, there exists linkage relation between the three types of supporting websites of a service. Z. Gyöngyi *et al.* argued that the trust of a website contributes to that of its linked websites [2]. The fidelity here also reflects a facet of trust for websites. We argue that there exists a fidelity transition relationship between the supporting websites of a service, along the sequence mentioned above, shown as the dotted arrow in Fig 2. The fidelity of a *SR* website contributes to that of its linked *WH* websites; the fidelity of a *WH* website contributes to that of its linked *SP* websites.

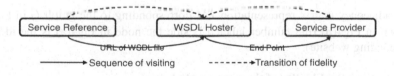

Fig. 2. Relationship between the supporting websites of a service

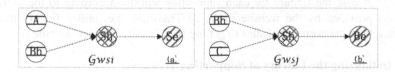

Fig. 3. Fidelity transition relationship between supporting websites of service *WSi* and *WSj* shown in Fig 1, respectively

We model the supporting websites of a web service (represented as s) and the fidelity transition relationship between them as a graph $G_s = (\mathcal{V}_s, \mathcal{E}_s)$ consisting of a set $\mathcal{V}_s$ of N_s sites (i.e. vertices, N_s is the number of the supporting websites of service s) and a set $\mathcal{E}_s$ of directed links (i.e. edges) that represent the fidelity transition relationship between the two linked websites. Thus, the fidelity transition relationships between the supporting websites of service WSi shown in Fig 1 are modeled as the graph shown in Fig 3(a).

The fidelity transition relationships between all of the supporting websites of all web services are modeled by combining the models of each individual service in the following way: $G = (V, E)$, where $V = \bigcup_{k=1}^{n} V_{ws_k}$, n is the number of web services,

$$E = \{< p,q,w_{pq} > \ | \exists E_{ws_i}, < p,q > \in E_{ws_i} \wedge w_{pq} = CountOf\ (< p,q >)\};$$

w_{pq} is the weight of edge $<p, q>$, and actually it is the number of the services co-supported by p and q. The weight of an edge reflects the closeness degree of the relationship between the two linked websites. According to the modeling method, the fidelity transition relationships between the supporting websites of the two web services shown in Fig 1 are modeled as a graph shown in Fig 4(a).

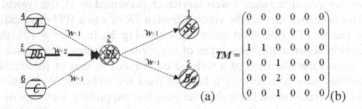

Fig. 4. Combined model of fidelity transition relationship between supporting websites for the web services shown in Fig 1

The adjacency matrix representation TM corresponding to the graph G in Fig 4(a) is shown in Fig4(b) (the number labeled beside the node in Fig4(a) is the id of the corresponding website).

2.2 Assessing the Fidelity of Supporting Websites

We divide the assessment of fidelity for supporting websites into two steps: 1) Initialization, i.e. initialize the fidelity for each supporting website according to the service information provided by the website itself; 2) Transition, i.e. utilize fidelity transition between related supporting websites to get the final fidelity for each website.

2.2.1 Initializing the Fidelity of Supporting Websites
For a supporting website e, we use $F_0(e)$ to represent the initial fidelity of e. We leverage the proportion of valid web service information a supporting website provides to initialize its fidelity.

Actually, the fidelity of supporting websites with different roles, i.e. SP, WH, and SR, has different meanings. The fidelity of a SP stands for the probability that it may provide available web services. The fidelity of a WH stands for the probability that it may host valid WSDL documents. The fidelity of a SR stands for the probability that it may provide valid hyperlinks to web services. Therefore, the initialization of the fidelity for supporting websites with different roles is different:

(1) For a supporting website with the role as a *SR*, we use the proportion of valid service hyperlinks it provides to initialize its fidelity. We set a service hyperlink to be valid only if service consumers could obtain the linked WSDL document which should confirm to the WSDL schema and could reach the referenced service successfully, otherwise invalid.

(2) For a supporting website with the role as a *WH*, we use the proportion of valid WSDL documents it hosts to initialize its fidelity. We set a WSDL document to be valid only if it confirms to the WSDL schema and service consumers could reach the declared service successfully, otherwise invalid.

(3) For a supporting website with the role as a *SP*, we use the proportion of available services it provides to initialize its fidelity. We send an empty testing SOAP message to the service's endpoint listed in the WSDL file and analyze the returned HTTP status codes to verify whether the service is active.

2.2.2 Utilizing Fidelity Transition between Supporting Websites

Based on the initial fidelity, we use the model described in section 2.1 to implement fidelity transition according the following three principles:

1) The fidelity propagated from a supporting website to its linked websites should be attenuated in some degree with respect to the source website's fidelity. We leverage a dampening coefficient β ($0<\beta<1$) to achieve such attenuation;

2) The more targets a website links to, the less fidelity propagated from this website to each target, i.e. the fidelity propagated from a website would be in inverse proportion with the out-degree of the source website;

3) Given a supporting website s, the closer the relationship between a linked website and s is, the more fidelity propagated from s to the target website. We leverage the weight of edges in the model described in section 2.1 to follow this principle.

Input:	*TM*	adjacency matrix of fidelity transition graph G
	F_0	initial fidelity vector produced in section 2.2.1
	P, H, R	the set of supporting websites with roles as *SP, WH, SR*, respectively
	α, β	α is the reservation factor, β is the dampening coefficient, $\alpha+\beta=1$
Output: *F*		vector of fidelity for each supporting website after transition

Begin

(step1) For each h in H

    $F(h) = \alpha \cdot F_0(h)$ //each website reserves a part of its initial fidelity

    For each i in R //the fidelity of a *WH* is influenced by the fidelity of the linking *SR*

$$F(h)+ = \beta \cdot F_0(i) \cdot [TM(i,h) / \sum_{j=1}^{N} TM(i,j)]$$

(step2) For each p in P

    $F(p) = \alpha \cdot F_0(p)$ //each website reserves a part of its initial fidelity

    For each i in H //the fidelity of a *SP* is influenced by the fidelity of the linking *WH*

$$F(p)+ = \beta \cdot F(i) \cdot [TM(i,p) / \sum_{j=1}^{N} TM(i,j)]$$

    return *F* //return the result

End

Fig. 5. Fidelity transition algorithm

The algorithm in Fig 5 illustrates the process of fidelity transition between supporting websites. Actually, according to the model described in section 2.1, fidelity only propagates from *SR* websites to *WH* websites (labeled as step 1), then from *WH* websites to *SP* websites (labeled as step 2). The transition strategies for step 1 and step 2 are similar, due to the limited space, we only explain step 1 in detail here.

Given a *WH* website (represented as *h*), its fidelity contains two parts: 1) one part is the reserved part of its initial fidelity (i.e. $\alpha \cdot F_0(h)$). 2) The other part is the fidelity propagated from its linking *SR* websites (i.e. $\beta \cdot F_0(i) \cdot [TM(i,h) / \sum_{j=1}^{N} TM(i,j)]$). β is the dampening coefficient introduced to follow principle 1, $F_0(i) \cdot [TM(i,h) / \sum_{j=1}^{N} TM(i,j)]$ is used to follow principle 2 and 3, where $TM(i,h)$ is the weight of edge $<i, h>$, $\sum_{j=1}^{N} TM(i,j)$ is the out-degree of website *i*.

3 Services Selection Using Trustworthiness

3.1 Assessing Trustworthiness for Web Services

In the section above, we get the fidelity of supporting websites. In this section, we will make use of the fidelity of websites to assess the trustworthiness of web services.

Given a service *s*, we use $T(s)$ to represent *s*'s trustworthiness. $T(s)$ can be measured in three dimensions, i.e. the dimensions of service's *SP*, *WH*, and *SR*. Thus, $T(s)$ can be represented as a triple: $T(s)=<T^P(s), T^H(s), T^R(s)>$, where $T^P(s)$, $T^H(s)$, and $T^R(s)$ is the trustworthiness measured in the dimension of *s*'s *SP*, *WH*, and *SR*, respectively. The computation is as follows:

$$T^P(s) = \frac{\sum_{p \in P_s} F(p)}{|P_s|} \cdot \sqrt{|P_s|}, T^H(s) = \frac{\sum_{h \in H_s} F(h)}{|H_s|} \cdot \sqrt{|H_s|}, T^R(s) = \frac{\sum_{b \in R_s} F(b)}{|R_s|} \cdot \sqrt{|R_s|}$$

P_s, H_s, and R_s is the set of service *s*'s *SP* websites, *WH* websites, and *SR* websites, respectively. In addition, we give rewards to the services which are more popular by multiplying the number of their supporting websites.

Then we convert the multi-dimensional representation into a single-dimensional representation in the following way:

$$T(s) = \chi \cdot T^P(s) + \delta \cdot T^H(s) + \gamma \cdot T^R(s), \quad \text{where } \chi + \delta + \gamma = 1 \qquad (*)$$

3.2 Services Selection Using Trustworthiness of Web Services

The essential purpose of services selection is to provide service consumers with a novel approach to choose the appropriate service more easily. The common practice is to provide a mechanism for ranking the functionally similar service candidates. Thus, in this section, by using services' trustworthiness, we propose an approach for ranking services candidates.

Assume the criteria used for services ranking is *K*. Given a service *s*, we use $K(s)$ to represent such criteria of *s*. $K(s)$ could be represented as a two-tuples: $K(s) = <M(s), T(s)>$, where $T(s)$ is the trustworthiness of *s* assessed using supporting websites' fidelity, and $M(s)$ is the evaluation of s with respect to some other metrics, e.g. availability[1]. An approach for comparing services according to K is needed.

We argue that the assessed trustworthiness of services reflects the quality of services in some degree; it plays the role as an assistant for services selection instead of a 'decision maker'. Thus, if the gap between $M(s)$ is larger than a given threshold, the comparing is determined on the aspect of $M(s)$, otherwise determined by $T(s)$.

4 Case Study

The scenario of the case is: A service consumer needs a service providing weather forecast. But there are a bunch of services providing this function, and the performance of them are roughly the same. Which service should the consumer select?

There are 16 web services providing weather forecast in our collected dataset[2]. We monitored the availability of these 16 services for two weeks[3]. Then we rank these 16 services in decreasing order of availability (the availability is used as $M(s)$ here). The top 6 services[4] in the ranked list are shown in the left part of Table 1. The first column from left is the ranking order; the second column from left is the ranked list in decreasing order of availability; the third column from left is the corresponding availability. The availability of the top 6 services ranges from 100% to 98%; it would be hard for users to choose a service from them just according to their availability.

Due to the small gap between the criteria of $M(s)$, we rank the 6 web services again using their assessed trustworthiness[5] (i.e. $T(s)$). The ranked list is shown in the right part of Table 1. The third column from right is the ranked list; the first column from right is the corresponding trustworthiness.

It is easy to notice the difference between the two ranked lists. For instance, in the left ranked list, the ranking order of service '*globalweather*' is 4; its ranking order is 1 in the right ranked list. Through analyzing the dataset, we find that the SP of service '*globalweather*' is '*webservicex.net*'. This website is a professional service provider which provides many fine web services. Moreover, service '*globalweather*' is also referenced by many websites among which there are several outstanding websites whose fidelity is high. In contrast, the fidelity of the supporting websites for service '*WeatherForecastService*' is relatively low; that is why its ranking order changes so much in the two ranked lists.

This case study indicates that the fidelity of web services' supporting websites does provide service consumers with a more comprehensive view of the services. With the

---

[1] We would not restrict the possible options for $M(s)$; we just use availability as an example here. Actually, the assessed trustworthiness of services could be used together with many metrics.

[2] The dataset was collected from the Internet according to the approach presented in [1] basically. We find these services in the dataset by searching with 'weather' 'forecast' as keywords firstly. Then we check the results manually.

[3] We check whether the service is available using the approach in section 2.2.1 once an hour. We use the ratio of successful check for each service as their availability.

[4] The reason for only listing the top 6 services is that their availability is high and very close with each other; it is hard for users to choose a service from them only using availability easily.

[5] α and β is set to 0.8 and 0.2; χ, δ and γ is set to 0.7, 0.2, and 0.1 respectively.

Table 1. Comparing of the two ranked lists

Rank	Rank according to $M(s)$		Rank according to $K(s)$		
	Service Name	$M(s)$	**Service Name**	$M(s)$	$T(s)$
1	WeatherWebService	100%	globalweather	99.2%	0.634
2	WeatherForecast Service	100%	WeatherWebService	100%	0.585
3	FastWeather	99.5%	FastWeather	99.5%	0.549
4	globalweather	99.2%	usweather	98.3%	0.549
5	usweather	98.3%	WeatherForecast	98%	0.527
6	WeatherForecast	98%	WeatherForecast Service	100%	0.43

comprehensive knowledge about web service candidates, service consumers can make a wiser decision in web services selection more easily.

5 Conclusion and Future Work

In this paper, we proposed a new feature for the trustworthiness of web service, i.e. the fidelity of supporting websites, to assist trustworthiness based services selection. Actually, the assessed trustworthiness of web service reflects the overall condition of the service's surrounding. However, we argue that the fidelity of supporting websites plays the role as an assistant instead of a 'decision maker'. The case study indicates the active effect of our approach. Some future work includes applying our approach on dynamic services selection, and proposing some other mechanisms to initialize the fidelity of supporting websites, etc.

References

1. Li, Y., Liu, Y., Zhang, L., Li, G., Xie, B., Sun, J.: An Exploratory Study of Web Services on the Internet. In: Proceedings of the IEEE International Conference on Web Services, ICWS, pp. 380–387 (2007)
2. Gyöngyi, Z., Garcia-Molina, H., Pedersen, J.: Combating Web Spam with TrustRank. In: Proceedings of the 13th International Conference on Very Large Data Bases, VLDB, pp. 576–587 (2004)
3. Liu, Y., Ngu, A., Zeng, L.: QoS Computation and Policing in Dynamic Web Service Selection. In: Proceedings of the 13th International Conference on World Wide Web, pp. 66–73. ACM Press, WWW (2004)
4. Zeng, L., Benatallah, B., Ngu, A., Dumas, M., Kalagnanam, J., Chang, H.: QoS-Aware Middleware for Web Services Composition. IEEE Transactions on Software Engineering 30(5), 311–327 (2004)
5. Maximilien, E.M., Singh, M.P.: A Framework and Ontology for Dynamic Web Services Selection. IEEE Internet Computing 8(5), 84–93 (2004)
6. Haddad, J.E., Manouvrier, M., Ramirez, G., Rukoz, M.: QoS-Driven Selection of Web Services for Transactional Composition. In: Proceedings of the IEEE International Conference on Web Services, ICWS, pp. 653–660 (2008)

Web Service Search on Large Scale

Nathalie Steinmetz[1,2], Holger Lausen[2], and Manuel Brunner[2]

[1] Semantic Technology Institute (STI) Innsbruck, University of Innsbruck,
Technikerstrasse 21, A-6020 Innsbruck, Austria
nathalie.steinmetz@sti2.at
[2] Seekda GmbH, Grabenweg 68, A-6020 Innsbruck, Austria
firstname.lastname@seekda.com

Abstract. The Web is nowadays moving from a Web of data to a Web of services. In this paper we present our approach for Web Service discovery on Web scale, targeted to support flexible and on-demand Web Service usage on the Web. The approach starts with crawling the Web for Web Services, gathering on the one hand WSDL service descriptions and related documents, and, on the other hand, Web APIs. We describe our methodology for building unique service objects from multiple Web resources. Then we provide an overview of how we extract basic service information from all the data and use it to semantically annotate the resulting services.

1 Introduction

The Web is currently changing from a Web of pages to a Web of services, that is instead of mainly assembling static documents the Web is more and more collecting and offering access to Web Services. With Web Services technologies all possible functionalities can be exposed and used in multiple ways. They can be flexibly integrated both in traditional software systems and in Web pages like for example Web 2.0 style portals. This way they provide a new ground for interoperability of business logics. Most Web Services are published using either WSDL (Web Service Description Language) or following a RESTful (Representational State Transfer) approach. For users to be able to use a service they need first to be aware of the existence its particular features.

In the beginnings of the Web Service era, UDDI[2] was proposed as solution to publish and search services, but the standard has not prevailed in the domain of publicly available Web Services. Today Web Services are often registered on specific portals (e.g. XMethods[1] or ProgrammableWeb[2]) or are simply put on the Web together with some Web pages describing the features of the service. This leads to two main ways how services are searched today: over the specific portal's search functionalities or using standard search engines and keyword search. [1] and [5] discuss the efficiency of these approaches and outline some related

---

[1] http://www.xmethods.net
[2] http://www.programmableweb.com/

L. Baresi, C.-H. Chi, and J. Suzuki (Eds.): ICSOC-ServiceWave 2009, LNCS 5900, pp. 437–444, 2009.

problems like outdated or missing data. [6] provides a quantitative analysis of
Web Service search using these methods.

Our approach allows discovery of publicly available Web Services, both WSDL
and RESTful ones, by (1) performing a focused Web crawl, (2) identifying relevant documents and (3) aggregating available information to lightweight annotations of the services. Using this approach we collected the largest pool of
(WSDL) Web Services known of (June 2009: more than 28.000 services from
around 8.000 providers).

2   Crawling the Web for Services

The big success of search engines today is only possible due to efficient crawling
solutions. A crawler exploits the fact that Web pages are interlinked with hyper-
references: by following the links found in a set of initial pages (seed) a crawler
discovers more URLs. These (yet) unvisited URLs build the frontier of a crawl,
distributed on multiple queues (e.g., one queue per host or per IP). The frontier
is dynamic and grows according to the scope of a crawl. A scope defines which
of the newly found URLs will be disregarded and which will be queued. Scoping
and priority assignments to queues and URLs are the most important aspects
in building a focused crawler like our Web Service crawler. To focus our crawler
on that part of the Web that is relevant to Web Services is important, as due
to (a) the size of the Web, (b) restricted resources and (c) time constraints, it is
unrealistic to provide a complete coverage of the whole Web.

Our focused crawler is based on the Internet Archive open-source crawler
Heritrix[3]. It has been designed in a modular way that allows extensions for all
relevant aspects such as scoping of URLs, queue assignment strategies, URL
precedence, etc. [8]. We focus our crawl on WSDL files, on related documents,
as well as on Web pages that informally describe Web APIs (a.k.a. RESTful
services).

2.1   WSDL Crawling Strategies

There are several aspects we need to take into account when crawling for WSDL
Web Services and related information:

Seeds. The seed URLs that we use to start a crawl are relevant for the success.
We collect them in a semi-automatic process that involves, e.g., screening of well
known sites, like the specialized portals mentioned in Section 1 and a selection
of URLs from previous crawls.

WSDL Identification. We concentrate our search on service descriptions and
related documents, which are mostly stored in textual files. That said, we do
by default reject a lot of content in our crawls, like images, audio or video

---

[3] http://crawler.archive.org/

files. We specifically want to look at pages like HTML, XML, PDF, other text documents, i.e. all types of files that could either contain a service description or a related information. During the crawl process we check whether a fetched XML resource is a valid WSDL description and whether it refers to publicly accessible endpoints.

Related Information Identification. Related information may consist of provider documentation of the service functionality, provider Web pages, Wikis, Blogs, FAQs, user ratings and many more. The documents may be pointing to the service, the service provider its service definition or may also not directly be linked to the service. As a first step we consider the inlinks and outlinks of the WSDL documents, i.e., those resources that include links pointing to the service interface description and vice versa. We can gather this information from the crawl link graph that is being written during a crawl iteration; the crawler follows the outlinks in a given page and writes the from-link and its outlinks into a link graph. The task of collecting related information is split onto the crawl run-time and the post analysis of the data because those documents that point to the WSDL descriptions, i.e. the inlinks, cannot be identified during the running crawl and are collected in a post-processing step by iterating through the crawl link graph (see also Section 4).

But it is not yet sufficient to collect related information only by relating outlinks and inlinks to the service descriptions: this way a lot of information may stay hidden to us (e.g., a price page published by the provider but not linking directly to the service description). This leads to another way of detecting information related to services: looking at term vector similarities. We assume that by looking at the term vectors of pages we are able to assess the similarity between documents and services and can thus conclude that they are related. We though calculate at crawl run-time the term vectors of all fetched pages and store them. The analysis, i.e., the term vector similarity comparison, is done afterwards in the postprocessing step. Clearly we cannot apply this approach blindly on all fetched documents, as this would require far too much computing power and time. We restrict our approach to checking the similarity of the term vectors of services to the term vectors of documents fetched from their respective provider domains, which we screen more intensively than other domains.

Queue and URL Scheduling. As we mentioned already before, queue and URL scheduling are very important means to focus a crawl. The crawler creates new queues per top-level domain, i.e. per host. Influencing the URL and queue scheduling means (in the specific case of Heritrix) allocating costs or precedences to URLs and/or queues before they are being scheduled by the frontier (low cost or high precedence meaning the URL or queue is being scheduled more upfront). We have developed an approach for URL cost assignment that is targeted on the prioritizing of (assumable) Web Service related documents. We set the cost of each new URL by default to 20. Then we check the URL for negative features that we penalize by increasing the costs (e.g. a lot of subdomains, more than one query string, more than one path segment). Afterwards we start privileging positive aspects of the analyzed URLs by reducing the costs (e.g. URLs that contain "?wsdl", "ws", "service", "api").

As last step we take into account a score that we calculate for the provenance page, i.e. for the 'from-link' URL whose outlinks we are currently assigning costs to. A high score means that it is rather probable that this page is somehow talking about Web Services; we assume that a page that is talking about services might with a high probability link to other pages that talk about services. We calculate the score based on the number and position of the occurrence of Web Service related terms in the page's content, taking as well into account HTML mark-up (e.g. words appearing in the title text or being marked bold). Finally we reduce the costs of the outgoing links by the score of the provenance page.

The aforementioned strategies to set, increase or reduce the costs of URIs cannot be applied to queues. Here we follow another approach: we set the precedence of the queues to the lowest cost that the URLs within those queues provide. This makes that URLs with low costs, i.e. interesting URLs, automatically enhance the precedence of the queue they are being scheduled in. This way the most interesting URLs should always be processed first. [11] provides a more detailed overview of the Service Crawler's queue and URL scheduling approach.

2.2   Web API Crawling Strategies

Detecting Web APIs on the Web is unlike harder than detecting WSDL files or even related documents. Web APIs are HTML documents, same as other Web pages, differentiated only by the fact that they expose a functionality that can be invoked by (in most cases) adding a specific query string to the URL that then calls a specific method in the background (e.g. `https://api.linode.com/api/?api_key=cakeisgood&action=domainGet&DomainId=45F33`). RESTful services, as introduced in [4], are usually a lot easier to create than WSDL services, use basic HTTP request methods (like GET, POST, PUT, DELETE) and are quite understandable for humans. We mostly use the term *Web API*, instead of REST service, as an API may represent a REST service, but it can also represent a service that is not strictly RESTful (following the definition in [4]). We have developed two different initial approaches to tackle the challenge of crawling Web APIs, which both are still in a rather experimental phase and not yet as well matured and evaluated as the WSDL crawling approach. We will outline the evaluation approach for the Web API crawling in Section 5.

Automatic Classification Approach. Our first approach follows a traditional data mining approach: text classification. Automated classification (also called categorization) of texts has become quite important as in recent years huge amounts of digital documents are becoming available[9]. There are two major types of text classification: supervised and unsupervised[7] learning approaches. In short, supervised learning works with a positive example set, i.e., a set of already classified documents, which is taken as input and used to produce a class label prediction (the so-called classification). Unsupervised learning functions are used when there is no training set available for the machine learning tool.

In our approach we use a supervised learning algorithm, concretely the Support Vector Machine (SVM) model[7]. We used Web API documents that we collected from ProgrammableWeb[4] as positive example set. The automatic classification is done within the crawler, by adding a classification processor into the regular crawl environment. As classifier we use the open-source data-mining tool RapidMiner[5].

Term Frequency Approach. Our second approach is based on term frequencies and tries to tackle, amongst others, the weaker aspect of the automatic SVM approach: the fact that it is only based on words and does not take into account HTML structures and mark-ups. We might as well want to take into account the URL of a Web document, which often contains words describing the topic of the page. Another relevant aspect covers the syntactical properties of the language used in Web API homepages. Most times they contain a higher amount of camel-cased words than random pages (e.g. getDocument) and often they contain fewer external links than usual. Often Web API homepages also contain internal links that target to the same domain, e.g., example calls for the described API.

We have created three indicators that group all the relevant parameters: *API*, *Documentation* and *Web*-related. The *API* indicator takes into account the appearance of keywords like "api", "developer", "lib", "code", "service", etc. in the URL and/or content of a page and looks for a high amount of camel-cased words. The *Documentation* indicator looks for keywords like "dev", "doc", "help", "wiki", etc. in the URL of a page and checks the page's content for the number of outlinks and camel-cased words. The *Web*-related indicator takes into account keywords like "rest", "web service", "api", etc. in the URL and/or content of a page and looks for a high amount of inner domain links in the page's content. [11] describes the parameters and indicators in more detail. Each of these indicators is regarded individually and is assigned a score that indicates to what level a specific document complies with this indicator: the three indicator scores need to be over a specific threshold in order to mark the specific page as Web API.

3   Building Unique Service Descriptions

After having harvested the Web for Web Service descriptions - both WSDLs and Web APIs - we remain with a large amount of service descriptions and related documents. But not all of these service descriptions correspond to exactly one unique service. That is, we do not have a one-to-one mapping from service descriptions to actual services. E.g., one WSDL can contain more than one single service, each bound to different endpoints. But even more usual is the case that multiple WSDLs are out there that resume to one single service. Often service

---

[4] http://www.programmableweb.com/

[5] http://rapid-i.com/content/blogcategory/38/69/

descriptions are hosted on more than one server, even sometimes from more than one provider.

We have developed an approach to deduplicate WSDLs, i.e. to build unique service objects that each represent single unique services. Our first step is to extract the provider from the service description endpoint. This is a non-trivial step, as it is not clear what is an authority and what is a registered domain. Since there is no algorithmic method for finding the highest level at which a domain may be registered for a particular top-level domain, we use the Public Suffix List[6] instead. An example would be the URL http://www.library.uibk. ac.at/test.wsdl, where the provider resolves to uibk.ac.at, the domain of the University of Innsbruck. Next we build a new unique (seekda) URL for the service. This URL contains first the provider's name and is then completed with the service name (e.g. http://seekda.com/providers/cdyne.com/IP2Geo).

If one service assembles a set of WSDLs under one umbrella, we, as last step, need to choose one service description that we present as the main one to the user. We do so by choosing the URL that has the shortest path and the less subdomains and - if available - belongs to the service provider domain. While this might not always be the right choice, we think of it as a good starting indication. This deduplication approach is so far restricted to the crawled WSDL service descriptions; for Web APIs we create a similar unique identifier for each, which contains the provider name and the hash value of the Web API URL instead of the service name (as we do not know the name of a service in that case).

After a crawl iteration where we have more than 200.000 WSDL service descriptions (see Section 2), we apply our algorithm for service deduplication on it and remain with more than 28.000 unique Web Services.

4   Automatically Enriching Service Descriptions

We do not stop the analysis of the data we gathered during the crawl at the deduplication of WSDL services. To each one of the unique service objects we try to append some more information. We store this service meta-data in RDF triples, using as structure ontologies that have partly been developed in the scope of the Service-Finder project: *Service-Finder Ontology*[7] and *seekda Crawl Ontology*[8].

The first meta-data that we store is the relation between services, their providers and their related documents, whereas these documents refer to both WSDLs and other documents. As already described in the sections 2 and 3, we collect this information by (a) going through the link graphs stored by the crawler and (b) when building the unique service objects.

Other meta-data that we collect refers to basic information that we can extract around the fetched Web Services. One information bit that we gather around the service endpoint is the geographic location of the service, that is the country

[6] http://publicsuffix.org./
[7] http://www.service-finder.eu/ontologies/ServiceOntology
[8] http://seekda.com/ontologies/CrawlOntology

where the service is located (i.e. hosted). Another basic information that we extract for all services is their liveliness, i.e. their availability and response times. seekda is monitoring and storing these data on a daily basis, and provides a corresponding availability graph with the service details.

Concerning the Web APIs we store initial meta-data concerning the three indicators that we have described in Section 2.2, i.e. the indicator scores, the number of camel-cased words, the number of external or inner links, etc. This information can be used in later stages to refine the focused crawl approach for this service type.

All the meta-data extracted about the two kinds of services as described above can be concluded by the crawler or a direct postprocessing analysis of the fetched data (without the need of complex information extraction, e.g.). This data can be used in several ways: to improve semantic service discovery, to provide service ranking (based e.g. on the availability of services) or to provide the users of a service discovery engine with more information on a service than only its technical description (see e.g. Service-Finder Portal, SOA4All studio).

5   Evaluation

We have evaluated our service crawling approach according to several indicators, which are different for the WSDL and Web API approaches.

The WSDL and related information crawling approach was evaluated by, on the one hand, pure performance measure indicators (e.g., documents crawled per second, kB crawled per second) and, on the other hand, indicators that refer to the quality of the resulting data, i.e. how much relevant information could be found (e.g., number of WSDL documents, number of extracted service identifiers). [3] provides detailed evaluation results using these indicators, comparing three different crawl iterations.

For evaluating the Web API crawling approach we have created three data sets: one set with random Web pages, one set with Web API Homepages from ProgrammableWeb.com and one set with Web pages from the domain of "programming languages", taken from the dmoz.org directory. We have then run our classifier over these three sets and evaluated the results. Detailed results of the evaluation can be found in [10].

6   Conclusion and Future Work

In the scope of this paper we have described our approach for discovering Web Services and related information on large scale, taking into account both WSDL services and Web APIs. We have showed how we focus a Web Crawler to retrieve as many as possible services and service-related information. The fact that there is no one-to-one mapping between WSDL service descriptions and actual services has led us to introduce new unique service objects and identifiers that assemble all duplicate services under one umbrella. We have shown how we relate the crawled data, i.e. the related information and the WSDLs, to the services and how we store this meta-data. Also we have provided an overview of what other meta-data can currently be extracted from the raw crawl data. Finally we have provided an overview of our evaluation approach for the three crawling approaches: one WSDL and related information approach and two Web API crawling approaches.

Some of the major issues that can be tackled in the future to improve the Web Service crawling and analysis include the deduplication of related documents, the detection of new means to find service related information on the Web, the refinement of the Web API crawling and the unification of the current two Web API classification approaches.

Acknowledgements

The work is funded by the European Commission under the projects Service-Finder and SOA4All.

References

1. Bachlechner, D., Siorpaes, K., Lausen, H., Fensel, D.: Web service discovery - a reality check. In: 3rd European Semantic Web Conference (2006)
2. Bellwood, T., Clément, L., Ehnebuske, D., Hately, A., Hondo, M., Husband, Y.L., Januszewski, K., Lee, S., McKee, B., Munter, J., von Riegen, C.: Uddi version 3.0 (July 2002)
3. Brockmans, S., Celino, I., Cerizza, D., Valle, E.D., Erdmann, M., Funk, A., Lausen, H., Schoch, W., Steinmetz, N., Turati, A.: D7.3 - assessment of tests for alpha release and revised testing scenarios and evaluation criteria for beta release (2009)
4. Fielding, R.T.: Architectural Styles and the Design of Network-based Software Architectures. PhD thesis, University of California, Irvine (2000)
5. Lausen, H., Haselwanter, T.: Finding web services. In: 1st European Semantic Technology Conference (2007)
6. Lausen, H., Steinmetz, N.: Survey of current means to discover web services. Technical report, STI Innsbruck (August 2008)
7. Moens, M.-F.: Information Extraction: Algorithms and Prospects in a Retrieval Context. Springer, Heidelberg (2006)
8. Mohr, G., Stack, M.: An introduction to heritrix. In: 4th International Web Archiving Workshop (2004)
9. Sebastiani, F.: Machine learning in automated text categorisation. Technical report, Consiglio Nazionale delle Ricerche (1999)
10. Steinmetz, N., Lausen, H., Brunner, M., Martinez, I., Simov, A.: D5.1.3 - second crawling prototype (2009)
11. Steinmetz, N., Lausen, H., Kammerlander, M.: Crawling research report - version 1 (2008)

Enabling Adaptation of Pervasive Flows: Built-in Contextual Adaptation*

Annapaola Marconi[1], Marco Pistore[1], Adina Sirbu[1], Hanna Eberle[2],
Frank Leymann[2], and Tobias Unger[2]

[1] Fondazione Bruno Kessler - Irst, via Sommarive 18, 38050, Trento, Italy
{marconi,pistore,sirbu}@fbk.eu
[2] Institute of Architecture of Application Systems,
Universitatsstrasse 38, 70569 Stuttgart, Germany
{eberle,leymann,unger}@iaas.uni-stuttgart.de

Abstract. Adaptable pervasive flows are dynamic workflows situated in the real world that modify their execution in order to adapt to changes in the execution environment. This requires on the one hand that a flow must be context-aware and on the other hand that it must be flexible enough to allow an easy and continuous adaptation. In this paper we propose a set of constructs and principles for embedding the adaptation logic within the specification of a flow. Moreover, we show how a standard language for web process modeling (BPEL) can be extended to support the proposed built-in adaptation constructs.

1 Introduction

In recent years, domains involving highly dynamic environments, such as pervasive computing and ambient intelligence, have turned their attention towards service oriented architectures (SOA). Indeed, even if SOA was initially designed for business contexts, its concept of building applications by exploiting and combining existing services matches very well the high variability, heterogeneity and dinamicity of these domains; this opens the possibility of re-using in these domains principles, methodologies and tools designed in the SOA framework. Conversely, for SOA, the dynamicity of these fields represents an important challenge that will contribute to speed up research on adaptability of service-based applications.

An example of this trend is the European project ALLOW [1]. The project exploits the well-known "workflow" concept, which has proven successful in the SOA field for modeling service-based applications, and uses it as the core of a new programming paradigm for human-oriented pervasive applications. More precisely, ALLOW's *Adpaptable Pervasive Flows* are workflows situated in the real world, i.e., they are logically or physically attached to entities like artifacts and people, move with them through different contexts. While being carried along, they model the behavior intended for their entity and the conditions on the execution context that guarantee a correct behavior. ALLOW's flows are hence capable to check deviations on the behavior of the entity they are attached to, as well as problems in the execution context, and to trigger adaptation.

There already exist pervasive computing infrastructures that use adaptation mechanisms (e.g., [6], [12]) . However, these mechanisms are mostly short-term, reactive

---

* This work is partially funded by the FP7 EU FET project Allow IST-324449.

L. Baresi, C.-H. Chi, and J. Suzuki (Eds.): ICSOC-ServiceWave 2009, LNCS 5900, pp. 445–454, 2009.

re-composition of services, or dynamic re-binding of components. The vision behind adaptable pervasive flows is to exploit the advantages of workflows to achieve kinds of adaptation beyond those already mentioned. *Short-term adaptation* will allow reacting to changes in the context by re-planning the structure of the running flow; it will be able to react not only to a change in the context, but also to detect that, given the current execution status, a constraint will be violated before a conflict actually occurs (proactive). Moreover, by analyzing information relative to past executions and adaptations of the flows, it will be possible to devise forms of *long-term adaptation*: the modifications on the flow produce produce a new generation of the flow model on which all future running flow will be instantiated.

A key enabling factor for all the aforementioned automated adaptation mechanisms is a convenient way of embedding the adaptation logic within the specification of a flow. The aim of this work is to present a set of modeling constructs and of tools that support the encoding of context-aware run-time flow adaptation. In particular, we propose a set of *built-in adaptation* modeling constructs that can be useful to add dynamicity and flexibility to flow models. For each built-in adaptation construct we provide a BPMN-like graphical representation and define a BPEL extension, with a clear syntax and operational semantics, that can be used to specify and execute Adaptable Pervasive Flows.

The paper is structured as follows. In Section 2 we present the adaptable pervasive flow paradigm proposed within ALLOW and we describe the main concepts concerning context-aware flow adaptation that drive the work described in this paper. Section 3 describes the built-in adaptation constructs that we propose for the encoding of context-aware adaptation within flow models. Finally, Section 4 presents some related works and draws conclusions, as well as on-going and future work.

2 Adaptable Pervasive Flows

Similar to the well-known workflows, adaptable pervasive flows (APF) consist of a set of activities and a corresponding execution order, which is specified using control elements such as sequence, choice, parallel operators.

A particular feature of APFs is that they are situated in the real world. This realizes the *pervasiveness* of the flows and is achieved in two ways. First, the flows are logically attached to physical entities (which can be either objects or humans) and move with them through different contexts. Secondly, they run on physical devices (e.g., PDAs, desktops). For instance, we can have a flow that models the shipment of a box and that is thus logically attached to that box; each fragment of a box flow is then potentially executed on different devices (e.g. the delivery part of the box flow is executed on the flow engine installed on the truck, while the storage part is executed on the PDA of the worker that in charge of storing the box).

Another important aspect of APFs is their *adaptiveness*. A flow is a dynamic entity that modifies its execution in order to adapt to changes in the execution environment. We consider different forms of flow adaptation. *Vertical* adaptation refines the flow or re-maps services to the flow without affecting the flow structure, while *horizontal* adaptation modifies the flow structure by adding, changing, or removing fragments of the flow. Moreover we distinguish between *instance-based* adaptation, were only the flow instance that triggers the adaptation need is modified, from *evolutionary* adaptation that, on the basis of previous flow executions and adaptations, proactively modifies the flow model on which all future flow instances will be based.

In the following we briefly introduce the most important concepts related to APFs. For a detailed description of adaptable pervasive flows we refer the reader to [9].

After an analysis and comparison [3] of todays workflow standards the ALLOW project has chosen BPEL [11] as a nucleus for the Adaptable Pervasive Flow Language (APFL).

An important characteristic introduced by APFL is the distinction between abstract and concrete activities. An *abstract activity* is a non-executable activity that allows to partially specify the flow model at design-time. It expresses properties which will be used at run-time to properly associate a concrete flow (a flow where all the activities are concrete). A *concrete activity* is an executable flow activity. Concrete activities include all standard BPEL basic and structured activities (e.g. sending/receiving of a message, data manipulation, control constructs, parallel forks) and a set of APF-specific activities that have been defined as BPEL extensions. *Human interaction* activities are activities that require an interaction with a human, e.g. displaying or getting information through a device. *Context events* are a special type of activities for receiving events broadcasted by a particular entity called Context Manager. We call *flow scope* a connected set of flow activities with unique entry and exit points. Moreover, we distinguish between a flow and a flow instance. A *flow instance* is a particular execution of a flow. To better underline the difference, we sometimes refer to flows as *flow models*.

Another basic element of the flow is the *constraint*, which can be used to annotate a flow, a flow scope or an activity. There are multiple types of constraints: security, contextual, adaptation, distribution etc. In its basic form, a constraint is a condition on the execution of the flow. The most relevant kind of constraint for the problem adressed in this paper is the contextual one, since it allows to specify conditions on the flow execution environment. A first extension that has been defined, on which we base the work in this paper, aims at providing a modeling approach to annotate BPEL processes with contextual constraints and an execution model to monitor those constraints during flow execution (see [8] for details).

To better understand the concepts described above, we will consider adaptation examples on a concrete flow model: the flow logically attached to a box, which describes how the box should be handled when reaching a warehouse (see Figure 1). The flow refers to the Warehouse Management Case Study of the ALLOW Project described in [2]. The drawing of flows is based on the graphical representation of APFL basic and structured activities defined in [7].

The basic flow in Figure 1 consists of two abstract activities Unload Me and Store Me. During the execution of the flow, we assume that the box is not damaged: we model this as a context constraint b.damaged == false.

An example of vertical adaptation is the refinement of the abstract activity Unload Me to obtain a concrete flow that can be executed. This refinement is done at run-time and can be achieved through different techniques, e.g. binding the abstract activity to a concrete activity (e.g. web service, human task...), or, as in this example, substituting the abstract activity with a concrete flow that can either be pre-defined or computed by composing other concrete activities/flows. The flow waits to receive a context event that it has been Picked Up by a worker, and then sends to the worker, through a human interaction activity, the information on the location where the box should be brought to. It then waits for a context event that it has been dropped. A characteristic of vertical adaptation is that, although a new flow is introduced, the structure of the original abstract flow remains unchanged.

On the contrary, horizontal adaptation affects the structure of the flow model. Consider for instance the situation where the context constraint not(b.damaged) is violated right after the unloading of a box. The adaptation mechanism tries to handle this assumption violation by modifying the flow instance structure. In particular, the damage extent is evaluated and, if the box can be repaired, the damage is fixed and the box can proceed with normal storage, otherwise the procedure for handling damaged items is started.

The adaptation cases presented so far are both examples of instance-based adaptation: a running flow instance is modified, refined or recomposed respectively, to react to an adaptation need. Now, suppose that analysing all past executions of Box Unloading flows, we find out that 10% of executions required to handle damaged boxes, and that in 90% of the cases, the horizontal adaptation variant devised in Figure 1 allowed to properly handle the violation of the flow constraint. We can decide to proactively embed this adaptation variant within the box flow model in such a way that all future executions will be able to cope directly with this adaptation need (evolutionary adaptation). Specifying such a flow requires having modelling tools that allow on the one hand to specify flexible, context and adaptation-oriented flows and on the other hand allow to keep trace of adaptation variants within the flow model.

The aim of *Built-in adaptation* is to tackle this problem, providing a set of constructs for embedding the adaptation logic within the specification of a flow. Although this is just a first (design-time, manual) form of adaptation, we believe it is not a trivial problem. Moreover, solving this problem will provide the modelling language that can be used when tackling automated adaptation problems.

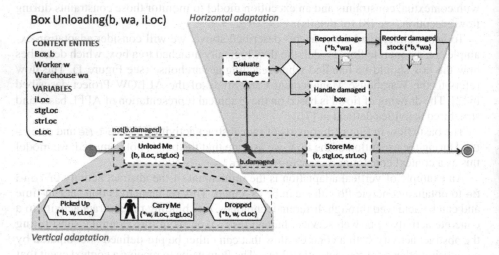

Fig. 1. Different Forms of Flow Adaptation

3 Built-in Adaptation Constructs

In the rest of this Section we present a set of built-in adaptation constructs that can support the encoding of context-aware adaptation within a flow model and for each construct we define the corresponding BPEL extension.

3.1 Basic Constructs: Context Conditions in Standard Control Constructs

The first and most simple kind of built-in adaptation constructs exploits the possibility to specify contextual conditions and applies it to standard BPEL control constructs (e.g. if, while).

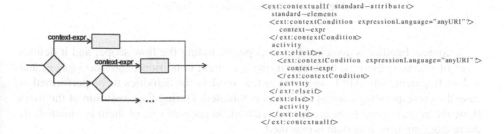

Fig. 2. <ContextualIf> Activity

For instance, the *Contextual If* construct, presented in Figure 2, allows to define several flow fragments as possible branches in the execution of the flow. Each flow fragment has an associated context condition. We can define also one flow fragment without a context condition, which will encode the default behavior. The syntax of the Contextual If is defined in Figure 2[1], where context-expr is a contextual condition and activity is any APFL simple or structured activity. The operational semantics of the construct is similar to a traditional if: the first fragment for which the context condition holds will be selected and executed.

Similarly, we can extend other BPEL traditional control constructs.

3.2 Context Handlers

Testing a context condition at a certain moment in time is not always sufficient. Rather, we might need to monitor the condition during the execution of several activities, and to react to changes of this condition. If we consider the example of Figure 1, it can be the case that while the box is unloaded/stored the staging/storage location is not free anymore (e.g. because some other worker dropped a box there), or the box gets damaged. It would be useful to have the possibility to specify that a certain context condition must be monitored during the execution of a flow/scope and, if it is violated, execute a set of predefined activities.

This possibility is offered by the *Context Handler* construct (see Figure 3).

---

[1] The syntax of all BPEL extensions is defined using W3C XML Schema language and, when not explicitly specified, refers to standard BPEL constructs.

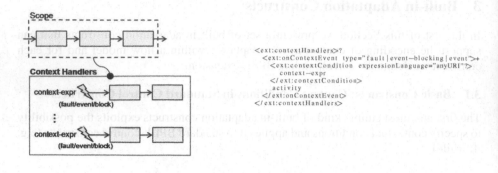

Fig. 3. <contextHandler> Activity

A context handler is associated to a scope, including the flow scope, and it defines a set of contextEvents, each specifying a context condition (context-expr) and a flow fragment (any APFL activity) that models the activities to be performed in case the corresponding context condition is violated. During the execution of the main flow, the context conditions are monitored and, as soon as one of them is violated, its corresponding flow fragment is executed.

We defined different kinds of context events within a context handler, namely fault, event-blocking, and event, which differ basically in the way their violation influence the execution of the scope to which the handler is attached.

When a fault-triggering condition is violated, the handling of the fault begins by stopping all active activities within the scope. Then, the flow fragment specified for that condition within the context handler is executed. The scope is considered to have not completed normally and as such is not eligible for compensation for that execution. Then normal process execution can resume from the point of the scope on. If this happens at the process level, then the process completes normally but would not be eligible for process instance compensation.

For what concerns event-triggering conditions, we propose two alternative kinds of context events: blocking and non-blocking. In the former case, whenever the condition is violated the execution of the scope is stopped, then the flow fragment specified within the context handler is executed and finally the scope execution is resumed. Whereas in the latter case the execution of the scope proceeds normally and the flow fragment specified within the context handler is executed concurrently.

Figure 5 presents an example of an event-blocking contextHandler used to check the availability of the assigned staging location during the unloading of a box.

3.3 Contextual One-of and Cross-Context Links

The aim of the *Contextual One-of* is to allow the design-time specification of a set of alternative flow fragments, each handling the execution of the flow within a specific context, and to allow at run-time to jump from one flow fragment to another, whenever the context changes or the assumptions on the context turn out to be wrong.

The Contextual One-of, as shown in Figure 4, consists of a set of alternative flow fragments, each of them associated to a contextual condition context-expr, modeling

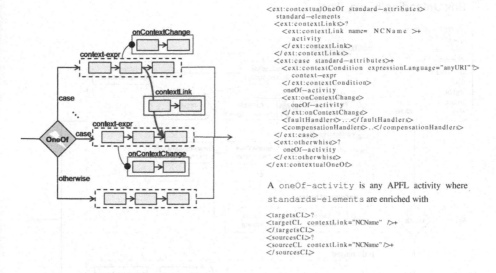

```
<ext:contextualOneOf standard-attributes>
    standard-elements
    <ext:contextLinks>?
        <ext:contextLink name= NCName >+
            activity
        </ext:contextLink>
    </ext:contextLinks>
    <ext:case standard-attributes>+
        <ext:contextCondition expressionLanguage="anyURI"?>
            context-expr
        </ext:contextCondition>
        oneOf-activity
        <ext:onContextChange>
            oneOf-activity
        </ext:onContextChange>
        <faultHandlers>...</faultHandlers>
        <compensationHandlers>..</compensationHandlers>
    </ext:case>
    <ext:otherwise>?
        oneOf-activity
    </ext:otherwise>
</ext:contextualOneOf>
```

A `oneOf-activity` is any APFL activity where
`standards-elements` are enriched with

```
<targetsCL>?
<targetCL contextLink="NCName" />+
</targetsCL>
<sourcesCL>?
<sourceCL contextLink="NCName" />+
</sourcesCL>
```

Fig. 4. `<contextualOneOf>` Activity

the context assumption for that fragment, and a roll-back flow, `onContextChange`, that can be executed to undo the partial and unsuccessful work of the fragment.

At run-time, the first flow fragment for which the property holds is chosen and executed. During the fragment execution, its context condition is monitored and, as soon as it is violated, the following actions are performed:

1. *stop execution*: all running activities within the fragment are stopped;
2. *undo partial work*: the roll-back flow associated to the current fragment is executed;
3. *context jump*: the first fragment for which the associated context condition holds is executed and its context condition is monitored.

Roll-back flows, like any other flow, can throw faults/exceptions (e.g. to handle the fact that the work done within the fragment cannot be undone), and in this case the flow is terminated following normal flow fault handling. If this is not the case, and the roll-back flow completes successfully, the main flow is considered successfully running, no matter how many times contextual one-of fragments are rolled back and re-executed.

It is possible (not mandatory) to specify a default flow fragment for which no context condition is specified. If this is the case, the defualt fragment is executed only if no other context condition holds and, during its execution, no context condition is monitored (that is, unless faults occur, it will complete its execution and the contextual one of will complete successfully). During the execution of a contextual one-of, if all the context conditions are evaluated to false and no default fragment is specified, a fault is thrown and the flow terminates abnormally.

For exemplification, consider again the box flow presented in Section 2. A first problem that can occur here is that the box can be damaged. The damage may have occurred either before, during transportation, but it may also occur at any point while the box is

Box Unloading(b, wa, iLoc)

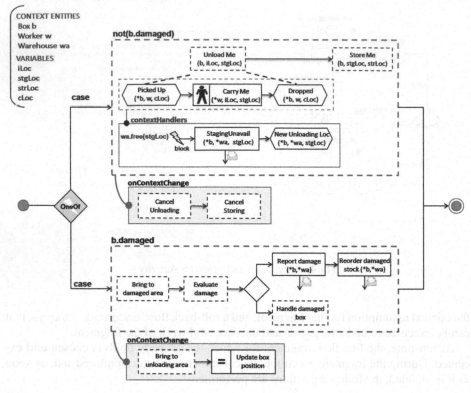

Fig. 5. Built-in Constructs at work: the Box Flow Example

being unloaded to the staging area, or moved to the storage area. In Figure 5 we use the Contextual OneOf construct to model the handling of damaged boxes.

When using the Contextual OneOf, it may be the case that, when jumping from one execution context to another, we do not want to undo the work done or the complete flow rollback is not possible. The *Cross-context link* (CL) is designed especially for this case. As can be seen from Figure 4, CLs connect two activities of different scopes within a Contextual OneOf. CLs allow adapting to a context change by jumping from a certain execution state of the current activity (source activity) to an execution activity (target activity) of another fragment suitable for the actual context. After the jump the flow instance must be in a consistent state. Therefore, a CL has an associate flow specifying the activities that are needed to prepare the flow to the jump.

At run time, if the contextual condition associated to the running scope turns out to be false, two possibilities are considered:

1. if there exists some context link leaving the active activity for which the context conditions holds
   (a) the roll-back flow associated to the cross-context link is executed

    (b) the monitoring for the new context condition is activated
    (c) the flow execution is re-started from the target activity of the cross-context link
2. otherwise the condition violation is handled as described for the standard Contextual one-of.

4 Conclusions and Future Works

We have provided an overview of the adaptable pervasive flows, a paradigm introduced in the ALLOW European project. We have presented the main concepts, as well as the associated adaptation methodology. After detailing the main adaptation strategies, we have focused on built-in adaptation, which is a design-time, evolutionary, horizontal, and fully manual strategy. For this particular strategy, we have presented several constructs which allow to encode the adaptation logic in the flow language and extended BPEL with suitable notations for the built-in adaptation constructs. These built-in adaptation constructs play an important role: they will serve as a basis for automated adaptation solutions.

Several adaptation approaches [13,4,14,5,10] have been proposed to address problems that are closely related to the built-in adaptation constructs presented in this paper. Most of them support the specification of context constraints within workflows [13,4,14,5] proposing different forms of context handling. In [10], the authors use an aspect-oriented programming (AOP) approach to adaptation.

Ongoing work aims at providing design tools and mechanisms for addressing automated flow adaptation. In particular, we are defining a formal language for APF that will enable the use of automated flow verification techniques [7]. Then, we plan to address run-time adaptation problems by providing a set of mechanism that can be used to compute adaptation variants during the execution of the flow instances. In the long term, we will devise mechanisms for analyzing historical data on flow executions and adaptations and that, on the basis of this analysis, proactively compute flow evolutions.

References

1. EU-FET Project 213339 ALLOW, http://www.allow-project.eu/
2. D2.1 Results of scenario analysis. ALLOW Project Deliverable (September 2008)
3. D3.1 Basic flow-model and language for Adaptable Pervasive Flows. ALLOW Project Deliverable (November 2008)
4. Adams, M., ter Hofstede, A.H.M., Edmond, D., van der Aalst, W.M.P.: Worklets: A Service-Oriented Implementation of Dynamic Flexibility in Workflows. In: Meersman, R., Tari, Z. (eds.) OTM 2006. LNCS, vol. 4275, pp. 291–308. Springer, Heidelberg (2006)
5. Baresi, L., Guinea, S., Pasquale, L.: Self-healing BPEL processes with Dynamo and the JBoss rule engine. In: Proc. of International workshop on Engineering of software services for pervasive environments (ESSPE 2007), pp. 11–20 (2007)
6. Becker, C., Handte, M., Schiele, G.: PCOM - A Component System for Pervasive Computing. In: Proc. of the International Conference on Pervasive Computing and Communications, PERCOM (2004)
7. Bucchiarone, A., Lafuente, A.L., Marconi, A., Pistore, M.: A formalisation of Adaptive Pervasive Flows. Submitted to WSFM 2009 (2009)
8. Eberle, H., Föll, S., Herrmann, K., Leymann, F., Marconi, A., Unger, T., Wolf, H.: Enforcement from the Inside: Improving Quality of Bussiness in Process Management. Accepted for ICWS 2009 (2009)

9. Herrmann, K., Rothermel, K., Kortuem, G., Dulay, N.: Adaptable Pervasive Flows – An Emerging Technology for Pervasive Adaptation. In: Proc. of the Self-Adaptive and Self-Organizing Systems Workshops (SASOW 2008). IEEE Computer Society, Los Alamitos (2008)

10. Kongdenfha, W., Saint-Paul, R., Benatallah, B., Casati, F.: An Aspect-Oriented Framework for Service Adaptation. In: Dan, A., Lamersdorf, W. (eds.) ICSOC 2006. LNCS, vol. 4294, pp. 15–26. Springer, Heidelberg (2006)

11. OASIS WSBPEL Technical Committee. Web Services Business Process Execution Language Version 2.0, 21, Committee Draft, work in progress (2005)

12. Roman, M., Hess, C.K., Cerqueira, R., Ranganathan, A., Campbell, R.H., Nahrstedt, K.: Gaia: A Middleware Infrastructure to Enable Active Spaces. IEEE Pervasive Computing, 74–83 (October–December 2002)

13. Wieland, M., Kopp, O., Nicklas, D., Leymann, F.: Towards Context-aware Workflows. In: CAiSE 2007 Proceedings of the Workshops and Doctoral Consortium (2007)

14. Wu, Y., Doshi, P.: Making BPEL Flexible: Adapting in the Context of Coordination Constraints Using WS-BPEL. In: WWW 2008 (2008)

A Service-Oriented UML Profile with Formal Support*

Roberto Bruni[1], Matthias Hölzl[3], Nora Koch[2,3], Alberto Lluch Lafuente[1],
Philip Mayer[3], Ugo Montanari[1], Andreas Schroeder[3], and Martin Wirsing[2]

[1] University of Pisa
[2] Cirquent GmbH
[3] Ludwig-Maximilians-Universität München

Abstract. We present a UML Profile for the description of service oriented applications. The profile focuses on style-based design and reconfiguration aspects at the architectural level. Moreover, it has formal support in terms of an approach called Architectural Design Rewriting, which enables formal analysis of the UML specifications. We show how our prototypical implementation can be used to analyse and verify properties of a service oriented application.

1 Introduction

Service-oriented computing is a paradigm centered around the notion of service: autonomous, platform-independent computational entities that can be described, published, discovered, and dynamically assembled for developing massively distributed, interoperable, evolvable systems and applications. However, services are still developed in a poorly systematic, ad-hoc way. Full fledged theoretical foundations are missing, but they are urgently needed for achieving trusted interoperability, predictable compositionality, and for guaranteeing security, correctness, and appropriate resource usage.

The IST-FET Integrated Project SENSORIA aims at developing a comprehensive approach to the engineering of service-oriented software systems where foundational theories, techniques and methods are fully integrated into pragmatic software engineering processes. The development of mathematical foundations and mathematically well-founded engineering techniques for service-oriented computing constitutes the main research activity of SENSORIA.

In this paper we present recent efforts within SENSORIA aimed to develop high-level modelling languages with strong formal support. More precisely, we present a novel extension of UML4SOA, our UML2 profile and define here its formal semantics. The presentation is illustrated on a simple example taken from the automotive domain (§ 2).

UML4SOA is an extension of UML2, the *lingua franca* of object-oriented software analysis and design. UML4SOA enhances UML2 with concepts for modelling structural and behavioural aspects of services. In § 3 we present for the first time an extension of the profile to support architectural styles [23] and dynamic reconfiguration.

The formal semantics of the extension is defined in § 4 in terms of *Architectural Design Rewriting* (ADR) [7], an approach for style-based design and reconfiguration of

---

* This work has been supported by the EU FET-GC2 IP project SENSORIA, IST-2005-016004.

L. Baresi, C.-H. Chi, and J. Suzuki (Eds.): ICSOC-ServiceWave 2009, LNCS 5900, pp. 455–469, 2009.

software architectures based on graphs and term rewriting, which supports both style-preserving and style-changing reconfiguration of service-oriented systems. In § 5 we show how the ADR formalisation and its prototypical implementation [4], can be used to analyse and specify properties of UML4SOA specifications.

2   Running Example

We illustrate our approach by exploiting the *On Road Connectivity* scenario from a SENSORIA case study where a road assistance group of services support car drivers activities. In the scenario, cars access wireless services via stations that are situated along a road. We use a UML component to represent a configuration of such a system. Figure 1 shows the white-box view of a system as a component (outer box) that contains other components (nested boxes) as parts of its internal assembly. A car is connected to the service access point of a station, which can be shared with other cars that are attached to the same station. A station and its accessing cars form a *cell*, which is dynamically reconfigurable, in the sense that cars can move away from the range of the station of their current cell and enter the range of another cell. A handover protocol permits cars to migrate to adjacent cells as in standard cellular networks.

Stations, in addition to the service access point, use two other communication ports that we call chaining ports. Such ports are used to link cells in larger *cell chains*. Stations can shut down, in which case their orphan cars are connected to other stations. This is tackled by appropriate system reconfigurations. We shall consider a shut down situation in which orphan cars switch from their normal mode of operation to a cell mode, in which case they become standalone ad-hoc stations (see the CarCells in Fig. 1).

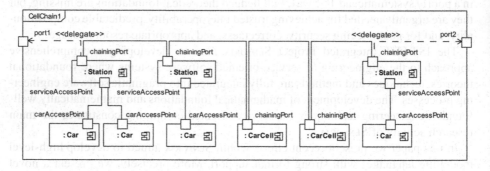

Fig. 1. Structure diagram of a configuration of the *On road connection* scenario

3   UML4SOA Extension

UML4SOA [17] is a UML profile for designing service-oriented software. UML4SOA is defined as a conservative extension of the UML2 metamodel. Such a UML Profile is the basis for the specification of a model-driven approach for the automated generation of service-oriented software through model transformations (c.f. [18]). UML4SOA uses extended internal structure and deployment diagrams. The extension for structure diagrams comprises service, service interface and service description [17]. A component may publish several services specified as ports, which are described by service descriptions. Each service may contain a required and a provided interface containing operations. The orchestration of these services defines a new service. The extension for deployment diagrams is restricted to different types of communication paths between the nodes of a distributed system: permanent, temporary and on-the-fly [25].

When modelling service oriented applications with our UML4SOA profile we observed the need for convenient mechanisms to model the inherent dynamic topologies of such applications: components join and leave the system, and connections are rearranged. Such dynamic reconfigurations exhibit a number of beneficial features, but require a suitable mechanism to constrain the possible evolutions of system configurations and to avoid ill-formed configurations. In order to express such constraints on topologies, it is common practice to use *architectural styles* [23], i.e. sets of rules specifying the legal constituents of a system configuration and the permitted interconnections between them. Unfortunately, UML offers a limited and unsatisfactory support for architectural styles. We propose a novel extension of UML4SOA to remedy this. In addition, we provide a methodology for modelling dynamic changes of configurations under architectural styles.

3.1 The UML4SOA Reconfigurations Profile

We present our UML4SOA extension to draw easily understandable diagrams for architectural styles and reconfigurations. UML4SOA models services with ports. For an enhanced readability we will omit in this paper the «service» stereotype on ports, as all ports in the following represent services. Service providers are represented by components, while (one-to-one) connectors are used to model service references.

Modelling System Configurations. We model system configurations with internal structure diagrams. Using such diagrams allows us to model services as ports of service providers. Internal structure diagrams are used to depict the interconnections of components contained within an architectural entity, together with their names, types, and multiplicities.

To model system configurations, we introduce the stereotype «fragment»(used in e.g. Chain), which may be applied to components and requires that all component fields (the elements pictured in the internal structure diagram) are typed with component or connector types, and interpret unspecified multiplicities as one. We constrain «fragment» components by forbidding the use of range or * multiplicities. Fig. 1 shows a sample system configuration of our scenario.

In internal structure diagrams, ports of the container classifier may be drawn on the border of the diagram; they may be connected to internal elements by «delegates» edges, stating that the port of the container component is a proxy an internal port. This allows the definition of named docking points to internal components, to which other components may be glued to. For «fragment» components, we require that all external ports must be a delegate of a port of its contained components. As the name implies, a «fragment» represents a fragment of a system configuration that

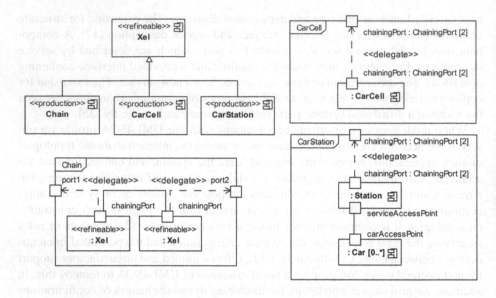

Fig. 2. Architectural style productions for the *On Road Connectivity* scenario

can be plugged together with other fragments. A complete system configuration is then modelled as a fragment without external ports.

Modelling Architectural Styles. UML internal structure diagrams provide a set of features to specify architectural styles. Indeed, such diagrams describe the static structure on the level of types, and allow to constrain multiplicities as well as interconnections between contained components. However, the service engineer is forced to model all alternatives allowed by a specific architectural style within one single diagram because of two reasons: first, there is no possibility to define abstract UML components, and second, using subtype polymorphism would introduce arbitrary many artificial composite components in the architecture. We believe that such mechanisms are not enough for a convenient specification of styles.

Our approach, instead, is based on a straightforward extension of the modelling of fragments with two modifications. First, the constraints on multiplicities are removed. Secondly, to define architectural styles in an inductive manner with composeable patterns, by using «refineable» components instead of concrete ones. Components used to define architectural style patterns are tagged with the stereotype «production». The non-terminal components marked with «refineable» may be replaced by any specializing «production» pattern (cf. Fig 2 for an example). In our scenario, for example, the «production» Chain contains two occurrences of «refineable» Xel components, which may be replaced by Chain, CarCell, and CarStation, as they all specialize the «refineable» Xel.

The «production» patterns define the legal wirings between components, and represent the basic building blocks of an architectural style. An architectural style is represented by a set of «production» patterns in the sense that every legal configuration must

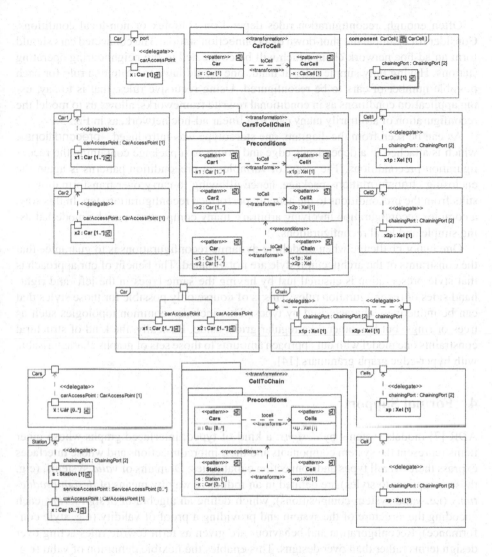

Fig. 3. Ad-hoc network reconfiguration rules for the *On Road Connectivity* scenario

be produceable by applying the production patterns of the architectural style, replacing «refineable» by specializing «production» patterns.

Modeling Reconfigurations under Architectural Styles. Reconfiguration rules are defined as «transformation» packages having two «pattern» stereotyped components with internal structure diagrams (a left hand side and right hand side pattern), linked with a «transforms» edge. The name of fields in «pattern» components is interpreted as variable names and the enclosing «transformation» package as their scope, hence allowing to share variables among left hand side and right hand side patterns.

Often enough, reconfiguration rules depend on complex or non-local conditions. Consider for example the shut-down of a connection station: The connected cars should form an ad-hoc network chain which will be connected to the neighbouring operating stations. Having only simple rules at hand, one would have to write one rule for each possible number of cars to be reconfigured. Using recursive rules, that is to say, using application conditions as in conditional rewrite frameworks, allows us to model the reconfiguration of arbitrarily many cars to a linear ad-hoc network, as in Fig. 3.

As can be seen from the diagram, one stereotype was introduced, «preconditions», which is attached to a dependency edge and points to a package containing the reconfiguration preconditions. The scope of variables in precondition patterns is again the enclosing «transformation» package, hence allowing to carry over transformation results from the preconditions to the actually performed reconfiguration step. In this way, a complex reconfiguration involving arbitrary many components may be modelled using simple and local reconfigurations.

One major challenge when modelling dynamic reconfigurations is to guarantee that the constraints of the architectural style are not violated. The benefit of our approach is that style preservation is ensured just by having the same types in the left- and right-hand sides of reconfiguration rules. This is of course only possible for those styles that can be inductively characterised by types. This includes common topologies such as trees or rings, but lets other, like regular grids, aside. Basically, the kind of structural constraints one model with our approach amounts to those sets of graphs characterisable with hyper-edge graph grammars [14].

4   Formal Support

ADR [7] models systems by *designs*: a kind of typed, interfaced graphs whose inner items represent the system components and their interconnections and whose interfaces express their overall types and connection capabilities. Domains of *valid* systems, (e.g. those compliant to styles) are defined in an inductive way by means of *design productions* (i.e. valid system compositions), which define an algebra of *design terms*, each encoding the structure of the system and providing a proof of validity (e.g. style conformance). Reconfiguration and behaviour are given as term rewrite rules acting over design terms rather than over designs. This enables the flexible definition of valid (e.g. style preserving) reconfigurations. A prototypical implementation is described in [4], where we also extended the approach to the treatment of hierarchical graphs and explained how to write system specifications and how to analyse them. ADR has been already validated over heterogeneous models such as network topologies, architectural styles and modelling languages. For instance, in [5] we presented a formalisation of reconfiguration aspects of Sensoria's business-level service modelling language.

4.1   ADR Semantics for the UML4SOA Reconfiguration Profile

This section describes, in an illustrative manner, the ADR formal semantics of the above presented UML4SOA profile. The main idea behind the formalisation is that «fragment»-stereotyped components, i.e. configurations, are represented by ADR designs,

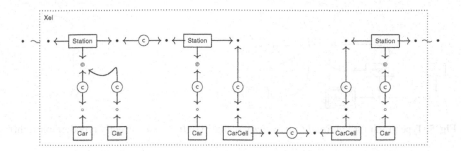

Fig. 4. The *On Road Connectivity* scenario of Fig. 1 as an ADR design

while the architectural constraints imposed by UML4SOA concepts such as multiplicity or productions are captured by appropriate ADR types and design productions. UML4SOA reconfiguration rules specified as «transformation» packages are represented by ADR rewrite rules. It is worth to recall that the main novel principles of the profile, i.e. style-consistent design-by-refinement and style-preserving, conditional reconfigurations are indeed the quintessence of ADR.

Modelling System Configurations in ADR. A design is a graph-based structure. Recall that a *graph* is a tuple $G = \langle V, E, \theta \rangle$ where V is the set of nodes, E is the set of edges and $\theta : E \rightarrow V^*$ is the tentacle function. Given a graph T (called the *type graph*), a T-*typed graph* is a pair $\langle G, t_G : G \rightarrow T \rangle$, where G is the *underlying* graph and $t_G : G \rightarrow T$ is a graph morphism. From now on we assume that graphs are T-typed.

Technically, a *design* is a triple $d = \langle L_d, R_d, i_d \rangle$, where L_d is the interface graph consisting of a single so-called *non-terminal edge* (the *interface*) whose tentacles are attached to distinct nodes; R_d is the body graph; and $i_d : V_{L_d} \rightarrow V_{R_d}$ is the total function that maps interface nodes to body nodes.

The visual representation of a design (see Fig. 4) depicts the interface as a dotted box with its type written in its top-left corner. The body is depicted inside the dotted box. Edges are represented as boxes (possibly rounded), tentacles as arrows (their order is given by their orientation) and nodes as small circles. The nodes being exposed on the interface are denoted by waved lines.

Fig. 4 exemplifies how UML4SOA «fragment» components of Fig. 1 can be mapped to ADR designs: «service» ports are mapped to ADR nodes, while the port type determines the node type (e.g. UML types ChainingPort, CarAcccessPort and StationAcccessPort are represented by node types •, ∘ and ⊚, respectively). Components are mapped to hyper-edges, where the component type determines the hyper-edge type. UML connectors are mapped to binary edges of a predefined type c.

The interface of the design is defined by the ports and the generalisation of the «fragment» component. The ports of the «fragment» define the set of interface nodes V_{L_d}, and each «delegates» edge defines a maplet of the mapping i_d from interface to body nodes V_{R_d}. The type of the so-produced graph, as defined by the UML4SOA model, is determined by the generalisation of each «fragment» (Xel in Fig. 1).

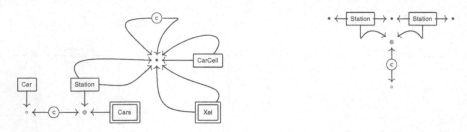

Fig. 5. Type graph for *On Road Connectivity* scenario (left) and a correctly typed graph(right)

Modelling Architectural Styles in ADR. The distinction between refinable components and non-refinable components amounts to the distinction between non-terminal and terminal edges in ADR. The underlying idea is the same: a non-terminal edge is an edge intended to be refined (i.e. replaced by an arbitrarily complex graph). Non-terminal edges can appear in designs, representing unspecified parts of a configuration (a refinable component) or in design productions (see later). Terminal edges instead represent parts of a graph that cannot be further refined (non-refinable components).

The style definition mechanisms of UML4SOA, i.e. internal structure diagrams and productions, are modelled by ADR type graphs and by design productions. Note however that some of the architectural constraints involved in class diagrams such as multiplicities cannot be directly mimicked by type graphs. Instead, they are dealt with at the level of design productions.

Consider the type graph on the left on Fig. 5. It is easy to see that each edge corresponds to a component (Car, Station, CarCell) or connector type (the overloaded symbol c). Non-terminal edges (Cars, Xel) are distinguished by their double border. In general, the type graph is obtained from the whole UML4SOA specification: adding terminal edges for each non-refinable component type, non-terminal edges for each refinable component type, nodes for port types, tentacles for component ports and edges for the connectors.

Type graphs do not impose any multiplicity constraint, i.e. they would amount to a UML [0..*] multiplicity constraint. A suitable way to impose a multiplicity constraint in ADR is by means of design productions. For instance, the treatment of sets of cars in the UML4SOA specification via multiplicities is dealt in ADR with the design productions NoCar, Car and Cars (see Fig. 6), which respectively allow to refine a generic set of cars as an empty set, a single car or the union of two other sets. In this way, UML4SOA productions are directly mapped into ADR design productions. For instance, in absence of production NoCar the multiplicity constraint would be [1..*]. We remark that productions allow to refine the architectural constraints imposed by a type graph alone. For instance, the graph on the right of Fig. 5 is well-typed but is not generated by our productions.

Technically, a design production is very much like a design but with an order on the non-terminal edges of the body graph (intuitively, the order of the arguments they represent). The *type* of a production p is $A_1 \times A_2 \times \ldots \times A_{n_p} \to A_p$, where A_k is the non-terminal symbol labelling the k-th non-terminal edge e_k of the body of the production. The functional type $A_1 \times A_2 \times \ldots \times A_{n_p} \to A_p$ associated to a production p means that

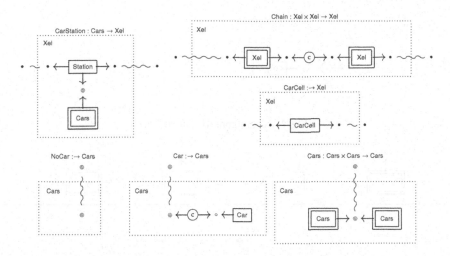

Fig. 6. Design productions for *On Road Connectivity* scenario

p can be considered a function that when applied to a tuple $\langle d_1, d_2, \ldots, d_{n_p} \rangle$ of designs of types $A_1, A_2, \ldots A_{n_p}$, respectively, returns a design $d = p(d_1, d_2, \ldots, d_{n_p})$ of type A_p. The definition is obvious: $d = (L_p, R_d, i_p)$, where R_d is obtained from R_p by replacing edge e_k in it with graph R_{d_k} respecting the tentacle function i_{d_k}, $k = 1, \ldots, n_p$.

This view corresponds to a bottom-up design development: a design is constructed by putting together some component designs. However, the dual view is also possible: a production can be seen as a refinement of an abstract component of type A as an assembly of concrete and abstract components, the latter being of type $A_1, A_2, \ldots A_{n_p}$.

Modelling Reconfigurations under Architectural Styles. UML4SOA transformations are represented by ADR rewrite rules, which are given in different flavours: e.g. in Meseguer's rewriting logic [19] or Plotkin's structural operational semantics (SOS) [22]. We just recall here that one of the advantages of ADR reconfigurations over other graph-based approaches is style-preservation, which is guaranteed by rewrites that do not change the overall type (they can actually change the type of certain sub-parts in the rule derivation of the overall reconfiguration).

Translating UML4SOA reconfiguration rules to ADR in the general case is done by translating the precondition rules, the «transforms» left- and right-hand sides of the rule conclusion, and translating transformation labels into their respective counterparts in ADR. In this process, «pattern» components are translated to ADR designs by first producing ADR design graphs (replacing components with [0..*] multiplicities by the corresponding non-terminal hyper-edge, as done in the example with Cars) and then parsing the result using the ADR productions generated from the UML4SOA productions.

The ad-hoc network reconfiguration is tackled by using inductive reconfiguration rules in SOS style. The base reconfiguration involves a single car (see Fig. 7):

$$\text{CarToCell} : \text{Car} \xrightarrow{\text{tocell}} \text{CarCell}$$

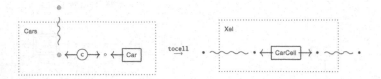

Fig. 7. Reconfiguration CarToCell

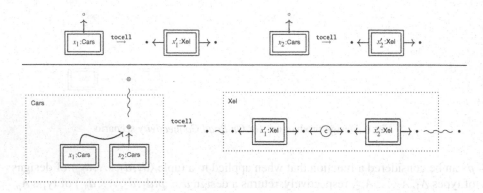

Fig. 8. Reconfiguration CarsToCellChain

The inductive case we consider is illustrated in Fig. 8, where the union of two collections of cars is reconfigured as the concatenation of the respective reconfigured cells, provided that these are possible:

$$\text{CarsToCellChain} : \frac{x_1 \xrightarrow{\text{tocell}} x_1' \qquad x_2 \xrightarrow{\text{tocell}} x_2'}{\text{Cars}(x_1, x_2) \xrightarrow{\text{tocell}} \text{Chain}(x_1', x_2')}$$

The cell with the station shutting down is reconfigured by the rule (see Fig. 9):

$$\text{CellToChain} : \frac{x \xrightarrow{\text{tocell}} x'}{\text{CarStation}(x) \longrightarrow x'}$$

Obviously, types are not preserved by CarToCell and CarsToCellChain and thus the right- and left-hand sides of the rewriting rule cannot be applied in the same contexts. Type changing allows for the modelling of reconfigurations that lead from one architectural style to another. However, this is not what we want in this example and thus labelled rules are given in SOS style. The last rule CellToChain, instead, is given as a conditional term rewrite rule, where the premise in its turn a rewrite rulle requiring a collection of cars to become a chain cell, while the conclusion actually transforms a chain of cells into a chain of cells. The type is preserved and the silent label makes it applicable in any larger context (unlike style-changing rewrites labelled tocell).

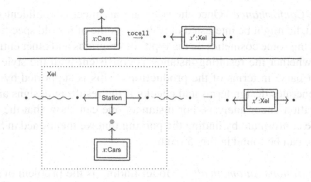

Fig. 9. Reconfiguration CellToChain

5 Analysis and Verification

This section emphasises the benefit of having a formal semantics for our UML profile by describing how the use of our implementation of ADR [4] can be used to analyse and verify properties of UML4SOA specifications. We remark that the translation of UML4SOA specifications to ADR specifications has not been implemented yet. On the other hand, a prototypical implementation of ADR is available for download [4]. Nevertheless, we offer sufficient evidence of the potential of our approach as a helpful support for software architects.

Analysing Styles. After a first development of a UML4SOA specification, a software architect might wonder whether the defined architectural styles enjoy some properties he desires. For instance, in our example scenario one could be interested in stating that no Xel production builds a configuration in which the left and right chaining ports are disconnected. It is easy to see that this property trivially holds in our example. However, as scenarios become complicated such properties become more subtle. Note that due to the inductive definition of styles it holds that if all Xel productions satisfy the property, then the property holds for any possible Xel configuration. This is indeed the case of the example property: all Xels are un-broken chains.

Our implementation includes a graph logic (Courcelle's MSO [11]) that allow us to reason about the structure of a graph. Such mechanism can be used to analyse the structure of UML4SOA productions by analysing the underlying graphs. The above example for instance is a well known property of graph connectivity which can be expressed in MSO by $\forall X.((\forall x, y(y \in X \land z \in R(y,z) \to z \in X \land \forall y.R(a,y) \to y \in X)) \to b \in X)$, where X is a set of nodes, x,y and z are nodes, R abbreviates the existence of an edge between two nodes, and a, b are shorthands for the left and right hand-side chaining ports. In words, we look for all sets of nodes X closed under the transitive closure of the relation R of direct adjacency and containing all nodes adjacent to a. If all such sets contain b too, then a and b are reachable from each other. The above formula holds for all body graphs of Xel productions. We can of course, write abbreviations for such formulae to construct a sort of library of structural properties.

Checking Style Conformance. Once the software architect is confident with the style he has designed, he might be interested in re-using some of his old specifications. After manually applying some cosmetics on the types of diagrams and other entities, he might want to know whether the resulting instance is consistent with the style. Roughly, he needs a correct parse in terms of the productions. This is supported by a mechanism that roughly generates design terms and checks if the resulting designs are isomorphic to the configuration under analysis. For instance, one can show that the configuration in Fig. 4 is style conformant by finding the parsing that we mentioned in Section 3.1. A counterexample can be found in Fig. 5 (right).

Finding Configurations Automatically. Model finding is the problem of analysing the state space of all possible instances of his architectural style. Such analysis serves as a computer-aided design process or as a debugging method to find out inconsistencies in models, styles or properties. Our model finding system is based on two mechanisms: one to generate a state space of models and one to explore it. In our approach we can define a rewrite theory that simulates a design-by-refinement process, roughly consisting of the context-free graph grammar obtained by a left-to-right reading of design productions. In order to explore such state spaces, we can use various mechanisms of Maude. Typically, the space of configurations is infinite and bounds are required. For instance, we can use search strategies to find configurations with at most 4 cars, 3 stations and 2 car cells and we obtain, among others, the design of Fig. 4.

Analysing Static Aspects of Configurations. Now that the software architect has adapted some of his old designs and possibly built new ones, he might want to reason about them. Returning to our example, we might wonder if a configuration has at least n cars or is free of cars in cell mode. Recall that our configurations have two levels: the more abstract level of design terms and the more detailed level of the diagrams. We can expect dual mechanisms for stating structural aspects. Indeed, we saw above that the properties of diagrams are supported by graph logics. Similarly, properties can be stated at the level of design terms. Our ADR implementation does this by means of spatial logics, the natural and structured way to reason about term-like specifications. Basically, for each design production f used to compose designs the logic incorporates a spatial operator f-so to decompose a design. For instance, formula Chain-so(ϕ_1, ϕ_2) is satisfied by all those designs of the form Chain(x1,x2), where design x1 satisfies formula ϕ_1 and design x2 satisfies formula ϕ_2.

Consider the property that states a collection of cars has at least n cars. We can inductively define it as follows: For n equal to zero the formula always holds. For $n + 1$ the formula holds whenever the term is decomposable as the composition via operation Cars of one car (Car-so) and a term with at least n cars. Using such formulas we can for instance check that the design of Fig. 4 satisfies the property stating that each station has at least one car and violates the property stating that each station has at least two cars.

Analysing Dynamic Instances of Configurations. At this point the software architect might be satisfied with the structural properties enjoyed by his configurations. The modelled application, however, has a dynamic architecture with various reconfiguration rules such as those we use in our running example. Can he express that some property is invariantly preserved or that some bad property will never happen? The standard way to reason about such properties is by means of temporal logics.

In our case temporal logics are supported by Maude's built-in LTL model checker. Properties regarding dynamic aspects of reconfigurations are expressed using the Linear-time Temporal Logic (LTL). Roughly, one is able to reason about infinite sequences of reconfigurations, by expressing properties on the ordering of state (i.e. configuration) observations. Such observations are predicates expressing structural properties as above mentioned.

As an example we can write the formula asserting that *it is always true that a collection of cars has at least 2 cars* as [] at-least-k-cars(2), where [] denotes the *always* temporal operator □. This property trivially holds for the design of figure 4. Indeed, no reconfiguration rule allows cars to leave the system so that their number remains constant.

6 Related Work

The Service Component Architecture (SCA) [9] focuses on policies and implementation aspects of services but is not based on UML. The work in [24] is based on UML models and transformations to executable descriptions of services. However, the approach lacks an appropriate UML profile preventing one from building models at the high level of abstraction; thus producing overloaded diagrams. The work of [13] proposes to use modes to address dynamic reconfiguration of service-oriented architectures and extends the UML to visualise such reconfiguration. The UML extension sticks to the mode terminology and does not include a visualisation of the transformation rules. The OMG is also working to standardise SoaML, a UML profile and metamodel for services [21]. The current version does not support styles or reconfigurations.

Structural aspects for services, modelled in UML, have also been addressed in several other works (e.g. [16]); however, as far as we know, none of them is based on a formal background like the one presented here. The only exception is the UML extension for service-oriented architectures that can be found in [2]. The approach includes refinement issues based on architectural styles and is formalised by graph transformation systems. It includes stereotypes for the structural specification of services. However, it does not introduce specific model elements for the orchestration of services, the notion of style there is less expressive (it basically amounts to our type graphs) and reconfigurations there are limited to unconditional ones.

A completely different approach to modelling architectural styles in UML would be to use constraints expressed in the OMG Object Constraint Language (OCL). To the best of our knowledge, however, there is no reconfiguration approach using solely OCL, which would have two drawbacks: OCL is a textual notation and it would introduce another language to the service engineer.

ADR has been mainly inspired by graph-based approaches to architectural styles [15,20] (see [7] for a comparison). The use of graphs and graph transformations to model architectural styles has been proposed by several authors (see [23], for instance) who based their approaches on the concept of *shapes* in programming languages. ADR shares also concepts with approaches based on process calculi with reconfigurable components (e.g. [1]). The main advantages of ADR are that the hierarchical and inductively based approach allows us to compactly represent complex reconfiguration rules, and that, style preservation is guaranteed by construction. ADR is also related to approaches that deal with reconfigurations in software architectures defined by an ADL (see [6]). The main advantages of ADR are the unified treatment of design, behaviours and reconfiguration, and the use of hierarchical, inductive reconfigurations. A comparison with a logic based architectural design methodology was given in [8].

7   Conclusion

We have presented a novel extension of UML4SOA, our approach for the modelling of service oriented architectures. The profile offers suitable ingredients to deal with architectural styles and reconfigurations. We have equipped the proposed profile extension with a formal semantics, offering support for analysis and verification from the very early stages of modeling. Thus, our approach is a comprehensive and pragmatic but theoretically well founded approach to software engineering for service-oriented systems. Our current efforts are aimed at completing our tool support. First, by automatising the translation of UML4SOA specifications, possibly by means of Maude-supported, MOF-based model transformations [3]. Second, by upgrading the prototypical implementation of ADR into a tool that can be used to formally analyse ADR models either specified directly or transformed from UML4SOA or other models. In future work we would like to integrate our approach in the SENSORIA suite of tools and techniques, which already includes some development [12] and re-engineering (legacy systems as services) [10] instruments.

References

1. Aguirre, N., Maibaum, T.S.E.: Hierarchical temporal specifications of dynamically reconfigurable component based systems. ENTCS 108, 69–81 (2004)
2. Baresi, L., Heckel, R., Thöne, S., Varró, D.: Style-based modeling and refinement of service-oriented architectures. SOSYM 5(2), 187–207 (2006)
3. Boronat, A., Meseguer, J.: An algebraic semantics for MOF. In: Fiadeiro, J.L., Inverardi, P. (eds.) FASE 2008. LNCS, vol. 4961, pp. 377–391. Springer, Heidelberg (2008)
4. Bruni, R., Lluch-Lafuente, A., Montanari, U.: Hierarchical design rewriting with maude. ENTCS 238(3), 45–62 (2009)
5. Bruni, R., Lluch Lafuente, A., Montanari, U., Tuosto, E.: Service Oriented Architectural Design. In: Barthe, G., Fournet, C. (eds.) TGC 2007. LNCS, vol. 4912, pp. 186–203. Springer, Heidelberg (2008)
6. Bruni, R., Lluch Lafuente, A., Montanari, U., Tuosto, E.: Architectural Design Rewriting as an Architecture Description Language. R2D2 Microsoft Research Meeting (2008)
7. Bruni, R., Lluch Lafuente, A., Montanari, U., Tuosto, E.: Style Based Architectural Reconfigurations. EATCS Bulletin 94, 161–180 (2008)
8. Bucchiarone, A., Bruni, R., Gnesi, S., Lluch Lafuente, A.: Graph-Based Design and Analysis of Dynamic Software Architectures. In: Degano, P., De Nicola, R., Meseguer, J. (eds.) Concurrency, Graphs and Models. LNCS, vol. 5065, pp. 37–56. Springer, Heidelberg (2008)
9. SCA Consortium, Service Component Architecture Policy Framework, Version 1.0 (2007)

10. Correia, R., Matos, C., Heckel, R., El-Ramly, M.: Architecture migration driven by code categorization. In: Oquendo, F. (ed.) ECSA 2007. LNCS, vol. 4758, pp. 115–122. Springer, Heidelberg (2007)
11. Courcelle, B.: The expression of graph properties and graph transformations in monadic second-order logic. In: Rozenberg, G. (ed.) Handbook of Graph Grammars and Computing by Graph Transformation, pp. 313–400. World Scientific, Singapore (1997)
12. Foster, H., Mayer, P.: Leveraging integrated tools for model-based analysis of service compositions. In: ICIW 2008. IEEE Computer Society Press, Los Alamitos (2008)
13. Foster, H., Uchitel, S., Kramer, J., Magee, J.: Leveraging Modes and UML2 for Service Brokering Specifications. In: MDWE 2008. LNCS, vol. 389, pp. 76–90. CEUR (2008)
14. Habel, A.: Hyperedge Replacement: Grammars and Languages. Springer, Heidelberg (1992)
15. Hirsch, D., Montanari, U.: Shaped hierarchical architectural design. ENTCS 109, 97–109 (2004)
16. Johnston, S.: UML 2.0 Profile for Software Services (2005)
17. Koch, N., Mayer, P., Heckel, R., Gönczy, L., Montangero, C.: D1.4a: UML for Service-Oriented Systems. Specification, SENSORIA Project 016004 (2007), http://www.pst.ifi.lmu.de/projekte/Sensoria/del_36/D1a.pdf
18. Mayer, P., Schroeder, A., Koch, N.: A Model-Driven Approach to Service Orchestration. In: SCC 2008, pp. 1–6. IEEE, Los Alamitos (2008)
19. Meseguer, J., Rosu, G.: The rewriting logic semantics project. TCS 373(3), 213–237 (2007)
20. Métayer, D.L.: Describing software architecture styles using graph grammars. IEEE Transactions on Software Engineering 24(7), 521–533 (1998)
21. Object Management Group (OMG). Service oriented architecture Modeling Language (SoaML), http://www.omg.org/cgi-bin/doc?ptc/09-04-01 (Last visited: July 2009)
22. Plotkin, G.D.: A structural approach to operational semantics. J. Log. Algebr. Program. 60-61, 17–139 (2004)
23. Shaw, M., Garlan, D.: Software Architecture: Perspectives on an Emerging Discipline. Prentice-Hall, New Jersey (1996)
24. Skogan, D., Grønmo, R., Solheim, I.: Web service composition in UML. In: EDOC 2004, pp. 47–57. IEEE Computer Society, Los Alamitos (2004)
25. Wirsing, M., Clark, A., Gilmore, S., Hölzl, M., Knapp, A., Koch, N., Schroeder, A.: Semantic-Based Development of Service-Oriented Systems. In: Najm, E., Pradat-Peyre, J.-F., Donzeau-Gouge, V.V. (eds.) FORTE 2006. LNCS, vol. 4229, pp. 24–45. Springer, Heidelberg (2006)

Designing Workflows on the Fly Using e-BioFlow

Ingo Wassink[1,2], Matthijs Ooms[1], and Paul van der Vet[1,2,*]

[1] Human Media Interaction Group
University of Twente
Enschede, The Netherlands
[2] The Netherlands Bioinformatics Centre (NBIC)

Abstract. Life scientists use workflow systems for service orchestration to design their computer based experiments. These workflow systems require life scientists to design complete workflows before they can be run. Traditional workflow systems not support the explorative research approach life scientists prefer. In life science, it often happens that few steps are known in advance. Even if these steps are known, connecting these tasks still remains difficult.

We have extended the e-BioFlow workflow system with an ad-hoc editor to support on-the-fly workflow design. This ad-hoc editor enables an ad-hoc design of the workflow with no predetermined plan of the final workflow. Users can execute partial workflows and extend these workflows using intermediate results. The ad-hoc editor enables its users to explore data and tasks representing tools and web services, in order to debug the workflow and to optimise parameter settings. Furthermore, it guides its users to find and connect compatible tasks. The result is a new workflow editor that simplifies workflow design and that better fits the explorative research style life scientists prefer.

1 Introduction

Life scientists are used to work in an explorative research style, without having a clear hypothesis [1–4]. Data is used as a source of inspiration, and few steps are known in advance. A workflow system will better fit the life scientist's needs if it supports this explorative research style [5]. Current workflow systems separate the design and execution of the workflow, which has led to a trial-and-error approach in using them.

We have extended our workflow system, e-BioFlow [6], to an ad-hoc workflow system. An ad-hoc workflow system enables an ad-hoc workflow design, with a small or no predetermined plan of the final workflow [7]. e-BioFlow presents new interactions with workflow systems and supports the explorative research style life scientists prefer. Scientists can execute partial workflows. The data produced are explicitly present in the workflow model, can be inspected and used as sources of inspiration to decide on the next steps in the experiment. These data are available as input for new tasks or tasks already in the workflow. New

---

* i.wassink@ewi.utwente.nl

L. Baresi, C.-H. Chi, and J. Suzuki (Eds.): ICSOC-ServiceWave 2009, LNCS 5900, pp. 470–484, 2009.

tasks can be inserted, connected to data produced by tasks in the workflow and executed in isolation. e-BioFlow simplifies workflow design, because it enables scientists to try things out and to insert tasks that may even be absent in the final workflow.

Even if the complete workflow model is known in advance, linking the parts is often difficult. Such problems are known as *plan composition problems* [8]. The real services to be used may be unknown and linking services often requires data conversion [9]. The ad-hoc editor will help the scientist to build the workflow. The scientist can run parts of the workflows and inspect intermediate results to test and debug the workflow, and to fine-tune parameter settings. The result of using the ad-hoc editor is a runnable workflow that can be stored as a generic file for future use. Due to e-BioFlow's support for late binding, it is independent of resources available at design time. Late binding means that tasks are abstracted from services until execution time. e-BioFlow can easily switch between alternative services without any change of the workflow model. Therefore, the workflow can be used as template for future experiments and shared with peers through web portals such as myExperiment [10, 11].

In this paper, we will first discuss the characteristics of an ad-hoc workflow editor. We will introduce our workflow system e-BioFlow. After that, e-BioFlow's ad-hoc workflow editor will be discussed. A use case will demonstrate the use of the ad-hoc workflow editor. Then, we will compare our approach to other systems that support ad-hoc workflow design. We will end with a discussion.

2   Ad-Hoc Editor: Characteristics

Although life scientists use data as sources of inspiration, workflow systems focus on tasks. The graph visualisation of the workflow consists of nodes representing the tasks and arrows representing the dependencies or data flows between the tasks. The data itself is absent and cannot be used to design the workflow. These workflow systems handle a *routine process-oriented mode*: the workflow needs to be designed in advance, before the workflow designer can run it [5]. Like in other visual programming environments, the workflow designer has to make many design choices without good data to direct his decisions [12]. This forces workflow designers to guess-ahead or to insert place-holders [8].

An ad-hoc workflow editor has characteristics of a traditional workflow editor, a workflow engine and a provenance system. It enables the workflow designer to execute partial workflows and extend them using the data produced by the tasks in the workflow that are already executed. It supports what Gibson et al. [5] call an *investigative data-oriented mode*.

Ad-hoc workflow systems have many advantages over traditional workflow interfaces:

- The tasks to be used are often unknown at design time. Tasks can be tried out in the ad-hoc editor.
- No need to know the complete workflow in advance, but extend and execute partial workflows.

- Speeds up of workflow design, because a small change in the workflow requires a rerun of just the tasks involved.
- Use intermediate results as sources of inspiration to decide on next steps of the workflow.
- No guess-ahead required about the data produced or consumed by the tasks.
- Fine-tune parameters and debug workflows by executing tasks in isolation.

Workflow systems have much in common with integrated development environments (IDE's) for visual programming languages and text-based programming languages. Most users of visual programming languages are not experts in programming and often do not want to be, but need to program for their daily working activities [4, 13], which is also true for most life scientists [14]. It is important that the visual language used matches the user's mental representation of the problem he wants to inspect [8, 12, 13]. The closer the programming world is to the problem world, the easier problem solving ought to be [8]. IDE's have implemented different techniques to help the programmer write correct program code through, among others, live editing, auto-completion and programming by demonstration. These three techniques are applicable to an ad-hoc workflow system as well. They will be explained in the context of workflow design.

The ad-hoc workflow editor explicitly presents the data to the workflow designer, which enables the designer to use these data to further design the workflow [2, 15]. The resulting environment supports what is called *live editing*, and is applied to textual programming languages [16]. A live editing environment supports explorative programming and gives programmers real-time feedback on the program's execution at edit time. The ad-hoc workflow system can be used as a live editing environment, but then to design workflows [15]. It enables the workflow designer to execute uncompleted workflows and gives feedback about the workflow's execution state by means of the data produced and consumed by tasks and about errors that may have occurred. In case of an error, the workflow designer can use the feedback to correct the workflow. In case of a successfully executed task, he can use the data produced to further design the workflow.

When data and input and output ports of tasks are syntactically and semantically typed, type information can be used by the ad-hoc workflow system to suggest new steps for the workflow design. The workflow editor has wizard-like functionality to help the workflow designer extend the workflow [15]. It supports what we call *guided workflow design*. The ad-hoc editor should support forward guiding, to propose tasks that can use the data produced as input [17], but also backward guiding, to find tasks that can produce the data required as input. Guided workflow design is close to the auto-completion functions found in many IDE's. Auto-completion helps the programmer, among others, to write correct programming code and to quickly discover methods [18].

Additionally the workflow system can guide data conversion. Data incompatibility forms a big problem in service composition [19–23]. Wassink et al. [9] have shown that at least 30% of the tasks in a typical bioinformatics workflow are devoted to data conversion. The workflow system can propose tasks that perform the data conversion required.

Some workflows are used only once, others repeatedly [11]. An ad-hoc workflow system should support both, workflows for one-time use and workflows intended for multiple-time use. The ad-hoc workflow system is a programming by demonstration environment. Programming by demonstration means the user shows what needs to be done, and the environment records these actions, generalises over them and translate them into a script [24]. A programming by demonstration environment acts like a macro recorder, but at the same time is able to recognise control structures such as iteration and conditional branching. In a workflow context, the workflow designer creates the workflow by demonstration; the ad-hoc workflow system abstracts from case specific properties, such as data and services, and translates the model into a template workflow.

Designing workflows by demonstration suits the dual mode of experiment design and experiment reuse. In the early phase of workflow design, scientists go through a fast cycle of hypothesis generation, experimentation, evaluation of the results and method selection [23]. After this phase, rationalisation is performed, in which scientists validate the results and formalise the process [5]. The ad-hoc workflow system enables the workflow designer to explore and to try things out in the early phase of workflow design. The result is a workflow that abstracts from concrete data and can be used as a template for future, similar experiments. The power of the template becomes even greater if the workflow system supports late binding, because then the workflow is independent of the resources used at design time.

3 e-BioFlow: Different Perspectives on Scientific Workflows

e-BioFlow [6] is an open source workflow system that provides its users a workflow editor and a workflow engine[1]. The workflow system uses a tabbed user interface to design and execute workflows and to analyse executed workflows. A tab is called a perspective. e-BioFlow contains six different perspectives at the moment:

Control flow perspective focuses on the order of tasks. It enables the workflow designer to model the order of task execution. The workflow designer can model sequential, parallel, iterative and conditional execution of tasks.

Data flow perspective is used to model data transfer between tasks, called pipes. Input ports and output ports contain type information (syntactical and semantical) about the data they respectively consume and produce.

Resource perspective is used to define the type of resources required to execute the task. The actual resource to execute the task is chosen at execution time of the workflow. The resources are called actors and are components that can execute tasks, such as invoking web services or executing scripts.

Workflow engine can execute workflows. It is responsible for scheduling tasks, performing the late binding and passing data between tasks. It is built on the YAWL engine [25], but supports late binding and passing data by reference.

---

[1] Available at: http://www.ewi.utwente.nl/~biorange/ebioflow

Provenance system automatically captures all process and data related information of workflow execution. It stores provenance data in Open Provenance Model [26, 27] compatible format. It contains a provenance browser, which is a graph visualisation to explore the provenance data.

Ad-hoc editor is able to perform ad-hoc design of the workflow. It will be discussed in more detail in the next section.

All perspectives except the provenance perspective directly communicate with the specification controller (Figure 1). This specification controller manages all workflows loaded into e-BioFlow. The perspectives send requests to the specification controller for a change in the workflow model when the user edits the workflow diagram. The specification controller applies the change and notifies all perspectives about the change.

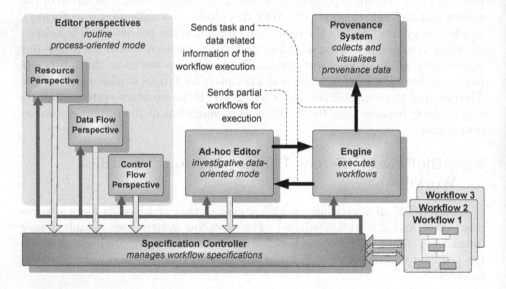

Fig. 1. All perspectives are registered to the specification controller to send and receive changes in the workflow model. The ad-hoc editor is a perspective that interacts with the engine.

The first three perspectives are introduced in previous work [6]. They are complementary: they edit the same workflow model, but each focuses on a specific aspect of the workflow. The ability to model control flow related information and data flow related information within a single workflow system makes e-BioFlow what is called a hybrid workflow system [28].

The engine can run the workflows managed by the specification controller in a routine process-oriented mode. It performs late binding using the task definitions. It tries to delegate the task to the default actor, if it is set and available, else it will try to find a compatible services. At the moment, e-BioFlow supports three types of actors: i) actors that can invoke SOAP/WSDL or BioMOBY services, ii) actors that can execute scripts written in, among others, Java[2], Perl[3] and R [29], and iii) actors that can interact with the user. The provenance system communicates with the engine. It receives all information related to the workflow execution, and stores this information. The provenance browser can be used to interactively explore these data.

4   Ad-Hoc Workflow Design in e-BioFlow

The ad-hoc editor combines features of an editor, an engine and a provenance system. The ad-hoc editor uses the workflow models shared by the other perspectives. Like other perspectives, the ad-hoc editor uses the specification controller to receive notifications about changes in the workflow models and to request changes in the workflow model when the workflow designer edits the workflow. The three characteristics live editing, guided workflow design and workflow by example will be used to explain the ad-hoc editor in more detail.

4.1   Live Editing

At first sight, the ad-hoc editor looks similar to the data flow perspective: the workflow designer can drag and drop tasks into the workflow diagram and define outputs of one task to be input for others. However, using the ad-hoc editor, the workflow designer can select one or more tasks and instruct the ad-hoc editor to execute these tasks. When the workflow designer instructs the ad-hoc editor to do this, the ad-hoc editor creates a partial workflow of the selected tasks based on the original workflow model. It adds two user interaction tasks to this new workflow. The first task, called the *input-task*, is added to the start of the workflow. This task shows a dialog containing the input data already available and fields for the missing data. The user can modify the already available data and enter the missing data using drop-down boxes in the case there are fixed sets of valid options or else using text fields. The second task is called the *output-task* and is added to the end of the workflow to show the results of the tasks.

The ad-hoc editor uses the workflow engine to execute this partial workflow. It automatically captures the data produced during workflow execution. These data are visualised as circles called data items (Figure 2). The ad-hoc editor uses arrows from the output ports to the corresponding data items to present the *created-by* relations. The workflow designer can inspect the data by selecting the circles. At the moment, e-BioFlow can visualise many data formats, such as plain-text, XML, PDF-files, bitmap graphics and vector graphics.

The workflow designer can create a connection between a data item and a task's input port to define this data item to be input for that task. This relation is called a *used-by* relation. The ad-hoc editor automatically adds a pipe between the output port of the task that has generated the data item and the input port

[2] http://www.java.sun.com
[3] http://www.perl.org

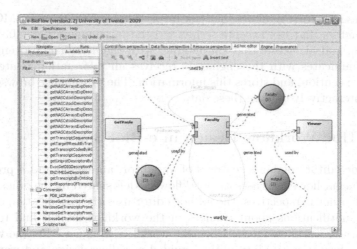

Fig. 2. A screenshot of the ad-hoc editor. Tasks are presented as boxes; data as circles connected to the output ports that have produced them and to the input ports that use them.

that uses the data item as input (Figure 3). When the user instructs the ad-hoc editor to execute this task, it uses this data item as input for that input port of the task. When multiple data items are defined to be input of the task, the input-task enables the user to choose which ones to use.

When an executed task has produced a data item related to an input port that is connected to an output port by means of a pipe, the ad-hoc editor automatically creates a used-by relation between the data item and the output port (Figure 4).

4.2   Guided Workflow Design

The ad-hoc editor helps the workflow designer to find new tasks to extend the workflow using the type information of data and the ports of tasks. When the workflow designer selects an input port of a task, the ad-hoc editor lists actors available and tasks already in the workflow that can produce compatible input. If the workflow designer chooses an actor from this list, the ad-hoc editor adds a task definition into the workflow for that actor. Additionally, it generates a pipe between the input port selected and the compatible output port of the new task. If the new task has multiple compatible output ports, the ad-hoc editor asks the workflow designer to which input port the pipe should be connected. If the workflow designer chooses a task already in the workflow, only the pipe is created.

In a similar way, the workflow designer can select output ports to find and add tasks or actors that accept the output data to as input. Data items can be selected to find and add tasks and actors that accept these data as input.

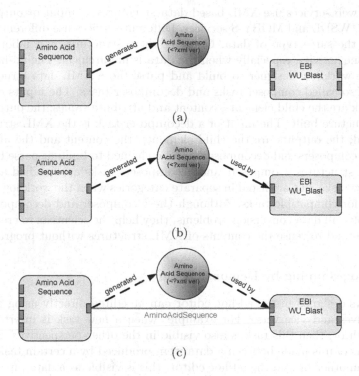

Fig. 3. (a) The "Amino Acid Sequence" task has generated a data item as output. (b) This data item is defined as input for the "EBI WU_Blast" task. (c) The ad-hoc editor automatically generates a pipe between the two tasks.

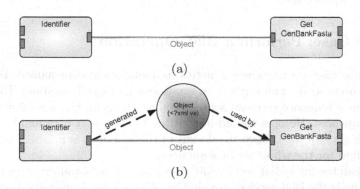

Fig. 4. (a) The output of the composer task "Object" is connected to the input of the task "Get GenBankFasta" task. (b) When the first task is executed, the ad-hoc editor automatically creates a data link between the data item produced and the next task.

Many web services use XML-based data structures as input or output, such as SOAP/WSDL and MOBY-S services. Different services use different formats, even for the same type of data. Creating these structures is a laborious and error-prone activity, especially when the data is hierarchical. The ad-hoc editor helps the workflow designer to build and parse these XML data structures by means of so-called composer tasks and decomposer tasks. The inputs of a composer task are the child elements, content and attribute values; the output is the XML structure built. The input of a decomposer task is the XML structure to be parsed; the outputs are the child elements, the content and the attributes. Multiple composers and decomposers can be chained to build or parse hierarchical XML structures. Composers and decomposers tasks are handled as normal e-BioFlow tasks, but are listed in separate categories when the workflow designer searches for compatible tasks. Although these composer and decomposer tasks do not solve all data conversion problems, they help the scientists to create XML structures and to reuse the contents of XML structures without programming.

4.3 Programming by Demonstration

Workflows designed in the ad-hoc editor can be edited directly using the other perspectives and vice versa. For example, when a new task is inserted in the ad-hoc editor, then this task is also visible in the other perspectives. Similarly, if a connection is made between a data item produced by a certain task and the input of another task in the ad-hoc editor, this is visible as a data pipe between the two tasks in the data flow perspective and vice versa. The relation is visible as a dependency relation in the control flow perspective, denoting the order of task execution. When the workflow is complete, it can of course also be run using the e-BioFlow workflow engine. The workflow can can be saved as a template for future experiments.

5   Use Case: Perform a Blat Operation

For the use case we introduce a fictitious bioinformatician named Tom, who wants to orchestrate web services to analyse a biological question. Tom wants to perform a sequence retrieval search against the zebrafish assembly for a set of 200 sequences. He uses the ad-hoc editor to construct a runnable workflow using a single sequence. Once the design of the workflow is finished, he will run the workflow for the whole set of sequences.

Tom searches for a Blat service [30], because it is a fast alternative for Blast. Soon, he finds the Blat service provided by Wageningen University, because this one provides fast access to the Ensembl [31] zebrafish assembly. He drags the Blat service to the workflow panel. The service requires two inputs, both MOBY-S objects. The first, named "User", is required for session information; the second, called "BlatJob", to provide the sequence and the database name. Tom does not know the XML structures required, and even does not want to. Luckily, the ad-hoc editor can help Tom to construct these complex data structures. Tom instructs the editor to add composer tasks for the "User" input by right clicking on this port. The ad-hoc editor shows compatible services and a composer task. Tom chooses the composer task and instructs the ad-hoc editor to execute it. The ad-hoc editor asks Tom to enter the e-mail address and password to construct the complex data structure. The service description tells Tom that any e-mail address and password will suffice. The ad-hoc editor shows the results of the composer task in the workflow panel. Additionally, two arrows are added to the workflow model, one connecting the composer's output port to the data item and one connecting the data item to the input port of the Blat task.

The "BlatJob" input is created in a similar way. This object is built of complex data input too (database and sequence information). The ad-hoc editor enables Tom to further compose these inputs. Tom instructs the ad-hoc editor to run these three composer tasks at once. The ad-hoc editor asks Tom to enter the database to be used and the sequence. The result is visualised as a red circle connected to the output port.

Now all the inputs required by the Blat task are available, Tom instructs the ad-hoc editor to execute the Blat task. The Blat service returns four outputs, namely a URL to the Blat report, a copy of the two inputs and the MOBY-S service notes. It seems that Tom has to download the Blat results using this URL, however, it is in MOBY-S XML format. By right-clicking on the URL data item, Tom selects the decomposer task for this MOBY-S object (Figure 5(a)). The data item is connected to the input of the decomposer automatically. Tom instructs the ad-hoc editor to execute this task. The output of the decomposer is the URL, this time in plain text.

The URL describes a location using a secure socket connection. Currently, e-BioFlow does not offer a task that can download content over a secure connection. Tom knows how to do this using Perl. He searches for a Perl task in the task panel and finds a "scripting task". Tom drags this task into the workflow panel. The scripting task has no inputs or outputs by default. When Tom selects the task, a configuration dialog pops to define the input (the URL) and the output (the Blat report) of the task, and the script to be executed. The scripting task requires Tom to select the language he wants to use. From the available languages, he chooses "Perl". Tom enters the code to be executed. The script panel supports syntax highlighting; the inputs and outputs are treated as normal variables, but are highlighted to distinguish them from the other variables.

When Tom has finished writing the code, he instructs the ad-hoc editor to run the scripting task. The ad-hoc editor shows an error message and complains about an unknown function. Tom reopens the configuration dialog of the scripting task and discovers he had forgotten to include a package. He inserts the import statement and re-executes the task. This time, the task runs successfully and returns the Blat report. The Blat report is in PSI format. Tom, however, wants the output in Blast format in order to inspect the alignment. He configures the Blat operation to generate the report in Blast format. He instructs e-BioFlow to rerun the Blat task, the decomposer and the download task. This time, the workflow generates the correct output (Figure 5(b)).

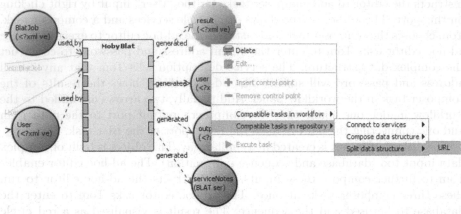

(a) Search for composer task.

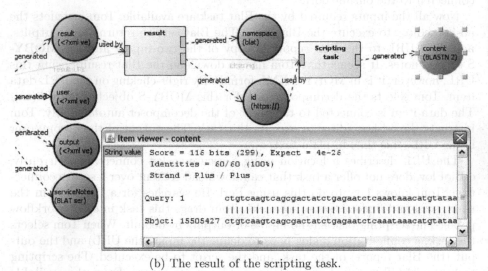

(b) The result of the scripting task.

Fig. 5. Screenshots of the design of the use case workflow in the ad-hoc editor

Now Tom has designed a correct workflow using a single sequence, he can use it to perform the sequence-based search for the complete set of sequences.

6   Related Work

Few systems support ad-hoc workflow design, but none of them fulfill all the features mentioned above. We will mention five different systems, all handling a different approach in supporting ad-hoc workflow design.

Workflow by Example (WbE) [32]. WbE records the operations the user performs on a database and translate them into a workflow for future applications in similar contexts. WbE, however, is task oriented and does not support direct data manipulation. Additionally, its focus is on automating querying databases instead of web service composition.

SeaHawk [17]. This tool provides an interface in which the user can explore data and request the tool for services that accept the data as input. Seahawk is not a workflow tool itself, but it can record the complete exploration history and export this to a Taverna workflow.

KNIME [33]. This is a data exploration system and mining. It provides access to many data analysis tools and they are presented as nodes of the workflows. KNIME enables its users to execute the tools in isolation and to explore the outputs. These outputs are, however, not explicitly presented in the graph. Additionally, KNIME does not support web services.

Data playground [5]. A Taverna [34, 35] extension that enable life scientists to "play" with MOBY-S services and to create small workflow snippets. This plugin system enables the scientist to transform these snippets to the standard process view of Taverna. Although the initial user experiences were promising, this extension is not further designed.

ADEPT2 [36]. ADEPT2 supports dynamic process adaptation Running processes can be modified at runtime. But ADEPT2 is directed to data-poor business administration workflows for which the workflow engine is idle most of the time during a run. Data, because it is scarce, cannot be used to decide about the continuation of the workflow.

e-BioFlow supports the workflow by example, the explorative reseach style of the Data playground and the guided experiment design of SeaHawk. It combines many features of these systems, and provides them through a single graphical user interface.

7 Discussion

The ad-hoc editor turns e-BioFlow into a workflow design and execution system that supports both the routine process-oriented mode and the investigative data-oriented mode to design workflows. The ad-hoc editor operates on the same workflow model and therefore workflows designed in this perspective can be edited using the other perspectives or run using the e-BioFlow engine. This editor enables the workflow designer to construct workflows in an explorative and intuitive way by giving real-time feedback of the state of the workflow and suggesting compatible actors, composers and decomposers. The workflow designer can run tasks in isolation, among others, to analyse intermediate results, to optimise parameters and to debug scripts.

The ad-hoc editor supports all actors provided by e-BioFlow. The ad-hoc editor fully supports the late binding capabilities of e-BioFlow. Workflows designed in this perspective are reusable templates for routine process-oriented mode to analyse other data sets and for sharing with other scientists through web portals such as myExperiment.

The use-case in this paper demonstrates a small but realistic scenario of using the ad-hoc editor to design a workflow. Many features the ad-hoc editor provides are shown, such as explorative design, composing and decomposing complex data structures, debugging the workflow and optimising parameter settings. The result of the use-case is a correct, runnable workflow that can be (re)used to perform a Blat analysis for a large number of sequences.

We [37] have tested the ad-hoc editor among life scientists and have found this editor to be a real improvement over traditional workflow editors.

Acknowledgement

This work was part of the BioRange programme of the Netherlands Bioinformatics Centre (NBIC), which is supported by a BSIK grant through the Netherlands Genomics Initiative (NGI).

References

1. Kell, D., Oliver, S.: Here is the evidence, now what is the hypothesis? BioEssays 26(1), 99–105 (2004)
2. Mahoui, M., Lu, L., Gao, N., Li, N., Chen, J., Bukhres, O., Miled, Z.: A dynamic workflow approach for the integration of bioinformatics services. Cluster Computing 8(4), 279–291 (2005)
3. Shao, Q., Sun, P., Chen, Y.: Efficiently discovering critical workflows in scientific explorations. Future Generation Computer Systems 25(5), 577–585 (2009)
4. Barga, R., Gannon, D.: Scientific versus business workflows. In: Taylor, I.J., Deelman, E., Gannon, D.B., Shields, M. (eds.) Workflows for e-Science, pp. 258–275. Springer, Berlin (2007)
5. Gibson, A., Gamble, M., Wolstencroft, K., Oinn, T., Goble, C.: The data playground: An intuitive workflow specification environment. In: Cox, S. (ed.) E-SCIENCE 2007: Proceedings of the Third IEEE International Conference on e-Science and Grid Computing, Washington, DC, USA, pp. 59–68. IEEE Computer Society Press, Los Alamitos (2007)
6. Wassink, I., Rauwerda, H., van der Vet, P., Breit, T., Nijholt, A.: e-BioFlow: Different perspectives on scientific workflows. In: Elloumi, M., Küng, J., Linial, M., Murphy, R.F., Schneider, K., Toma, C. (eds.) 2nd International Conference on Bioinformatics Research and Development (BIRD), Vienna, Austria, pp. 243–257 (2008)
7. Wainer, J., Weske, M., Gottfried, V., Bauzer Medeiros, C.: Scientific workflow systems. In: Proceedings of the NSF Workshop on Workflow and Process Automation in Information Systems, Athens, Georgia, pp. 1–5 (1997)
8. Green, T.R.G., Petre, M.: Usability analysis of visual programming environments: A cognitive dimensions framework. Journal of Visual Languages & Computing 7(2), 131–174 (1996)
9. Wassink, I., van der Vet, P., Wolstencroft, K., Neerincx, P., Roos, M., Rauwerda, H., Breit, T.: Analysing scientific workflows: why workflows not only connect web services. In: Zhang, L. (ed.) SERVICES 2009 (Part I), Los Angeles, USA, pp. 314–321 (2009)

10. Goble, C., De Roure, D.: MyExperiment: Social networking for workflow-using e-scientists. In: Deelman, E., Taylor, I. (eds.) WORKS 2007, Monterey, California, USA, pp. 1–2 (2007)
11. Goderis, A., De Roure, D., Goble, C., Bhagat, J., Cruickshank, D., Fisher, P., Michaelides, D., Tanoh, F.: Discovering scientific workflows: The myExperiment benchmarks. IEEE Transactions on Automation Science and Engineering (2008) (Submitted)
12. Whitley, K.: Visual programming languages and the empirical evidence for and against. Journal of Visual Languages & Computing 8(1), 109–142 (1997)
13. Costabile, M., Fogli, D., Mussio, P., Piccinno, A.: Visual interactive systems for end-user development: A model-based design methodology. IEEE Transactions on Systems, Man and Cybernetics, Part A: Systems and Humans 37(6), 1029–1046 (2007)
14. Kulyk, O., Wassink, I., van der Vet, P.E., van der Veer, G.C., van Dijk, E.M.A.G.: Sticks, balls or a ribbon? results of a formative user study with bioinformaticians. Technical Report TR-CTIT-08-72, CTIT, University of Twente, Enschede (2008)
15. Downey, L.: Group usability testing: Evolution in usability techniques. Journal of Usability Studies 2(3), 133–144 (2007)
16. Hundhausen, C., Lee Brown, J.: An experimental study of the impact of visual semantic feedback on novice programming. Journal of Visual Languages and Computing archive 18(6), 537–559 (2007)
17. Gordon, P., Sensen, S.: Seahawk: moving beyond html in web-based bioinformatics analysis. BMC bioinformatics 8(208), 1–13 (2007)
18. Robbes, R., Lanza, M.: How program history can improve code completion. In: Inverardi, P., Ireland, A., Visser, W. (eds.) 23rd IEEE/ACM International Conference on Automated Software Engineering (ASE 2008), Aquila, Italy, September 2008, pp. 317–326 (2008)
19. Wroe, C., Goble, C., Greenwood, M., Lord, P., Miles, S., Papay, J., Payne, T., Moreau, L.: Automating experiments using semantic data on a bioinformatics grid. IEEE Intelligent Systems 19(1), 48–55 (2004)
20. Neerincx, P., Leunissen, J.: Evolution of web services in bioinformatics. Briefings in Bioinformatics 6(2), 178–188 (2005)
21. Belhajjame, K., Embury, S., Paton, N.: On characterising and identifying mismatches in scientific workflows. In: Leser, U., Naumann, F., Eckman, B. (eds.) DILS 2006. LNCS (LNBI), vol. 4075, pp. 240–247. Springer, Heidelberg (2006)
22. Kappler, M.: Software for rapid prototyping in the pharmaceutical and biotechnology industries. Current Opinion in Drug Discovery & Development 11(3), 389–392 (2008)
23. Shon, J., Ohkawa, H., Hammer, J.: Scientific workflows as productivity tools for drug discovery. Current Opinion in Drug Discovery & Development 11(3), 381–388 (2008)
24. Lau, T.A., Weld, D.S.: Programming by demonstration: an inductive learning formulation. In: Maybury, M., Szekely, P., Thomas, C.G. (eds.) IUI 1999: Proceedings of the 4th international conference on Intelligent user interfaces, pp. 145–152. ACM Press, New York (1999)
25. van der Aalst, W., Aldred, L., Dumas, M., ter Hofstede, A.: Design and implementation of the YAWL system. In: Persson, A., Stirna, J. (eds.) CAiSE 2004. LNCS, vol. 3084, pp. 142–159. Springer, Heidelberg (2004)
26. Moreau, L., Plale, B., Miles, S., Goble, C., Missier, P., Barga, R., et al.: The Open Provenance Model (v1.01). Technical report, University of Southampton (2008)

27. Moreau, L., Freire, J., Futrelle, J., Mcgrath, R., Myers, J., Paulson, P.: The open provenance model: An overview. In: Freire, J., Koop, D., Moreau, L. (eds.) IPAW 2008. LNCS, vol. 5272, pp. 323–326. Springer, Heidelberg (2008)

28. Shields, M.: Control- versus data-driven workflows. In: Taylor, I.J., Deelman, E., Gannon, D.B., Shields, M. (eds.) Workflows for e-Science, pp. 258–275. Springer, Berlin (2007)

29. Ihaka, R., Gentleman, R.: R: A language for data analysis and graphics. Journal of Computational and Graphical Statistics 5(3), 299–314 (1996)

30. Kent, W.: Blat-the blast-like alignment tool. Genome Research 12(4), 656–664 (2002)

31. Flicek, P., Aken, B., Beal, K., Ballester, B., Caccamo, M., Chen, Y., Clarke, L., Coates, G., Cunningham, F., Cutts, T., Down, T., Dyer, S., Eyre, T., Fitzgerald, S., Fernandez-Banet, J., Gräf, S., Haider, S., Hammond, M., Holland, R., Howe, K., Howe, K., Johnson, N., Jenkinson, A., Kähäri, A., Keefe, D., Kokocinski, F., Kulesha, E., Lawson, D., Longden, L., Megy, K., Meidl, P., Overduin, B., Parker, A., Pritchard, B., Prlic, A., Rice, S., Rios, D., Schuster, M., Sealy, I., Slater, G., Smedley, D., Spudich, G., Trevanion, S., Vilella, A., Vogel, J., White, S., Wood, M., Birney, E., Cox, T., Curwen, V., Durbin, R., Fernandez-Suarez, X., Herrero, J., Hubbard, T., Kasprzyk, A., Proctor, G., Smith, J., Ureta-Vidal, A., Searle, S.: Ensembl 2008. Nucleic Acids Research 36(Database issue), D707–D714 (2008)

32. Tomasic, A., McGuire, R., Myers, B.: Workflow by example: Automating database interactions via induction. Technical Report CMU-ISRI-06-103, Carnegie Mellon University (2006)

33. Berthold, M.R., Cebron, N., Dill, F., Gabriel, T.R., Kötter, T., Meinl, T., Ohl, P., Sieb, C., Thiel, K., Wiswedel, B.: KNIME: The konstanz information miner. In: Preisach, C., Burkhardt, H., Schmidt-Thieme, L., Decker, R. (eds.) Data Analysis, Machine Learning and Applications, pp. 319–326. Springer, Berlin (2008)

34. Oinn, T., Addis, M., Ferris, J., Marvin, D., Senger, M., Greenwood, M., Carver, T., Glover, K., Pocock, M., Wipat, A., Li, P.: Taverna: a tool for the composition and enactment of bioinformatics workflows. Oxford Bioinformatics 20(17), 3045–3054 (2004)

35. Oinn, T., Li, P., Kell, D., Goble, C., Goderis, A., Greenwood, M., Hull, D., Stevens, R., Turi, D., Zhao, J.: Taverna/myGrid: Aligning a workflow system with the life sciences community. In: Taylor, I.J., Deelman, E., Gannon, D.B., Shields, M. (eds.) Workflows for e-Science, pp. 300–319. Springer, Berlin (2007)

36. Reichert, M., Dadam, P.: Enabling adaptive process-aware information systems with ADEPT2. In: Research on Business Process Modeling. Information Science Reference, pp. 173–203 (2009)

37. Wassink, I., van der Vet, P., van Dijk, E., Veer, G., Roos, M.: New interactions with workflow systems. In: European Conference on Cognitive Ergonomics 2009 (ECCE 2009), Otaniemi, Finland (in press, 2009)

Measuring the Quality of Service Oriented Design

Renuka Sindhgatta, Bikram Sengupta, and Karthikeyan Ponnalagu

IBM India Research Laboratory
Bangalore, India
{renuka.sr,bsengupt,pkarthik}@in.ibm.com

Abstract. Service Oriented Architecture (SOA) has gained popularity as a design paradigm for realizing enterprise software systems through abstract units of functionality called services. While the key design principles of SOA have been discussed at length in the literature, much of the work is prescriptive in nature and do not explain how adherence to these principles can be quantitatively measured in practice. In some cases, metrics for a limited subset of SOA quality attributes have been proposed, but many of these measures have not been empirically validated on real-life SOA designs. In this paper, we take a deeper look at how the key SOA quality attributes of service cohesion, coupling, reusability, composability and granularity may be evaluated, based only on service design level information. We survey related work, adapt some of the well-known software design metrics to the SOA context and propose new measures where needed. These measures adhere to mathematical properties that characterize the quality attributes. We study their applicability on two real-life SOA design models from the insurance industry using a metrics computation tool integrated with an Eclipse-based service design environment. We believe that availability of these measures during SOA design will aid early detection of design flaws, allow different design options and trade-offs to be considered and support planning for development, testing and governance of the services.

Keywords: Service Design, Business Process Model, Service Design Principles, Metrics.

1 Introduction

Service Oriented Architecture (SOA) represents the natural continuum of increasing levels of abstraction in software engineering that has previously seen the emergence of object-oriented programming and component based development. SOA is characterized by a greater focus on identifying business-relevant functionality that may be exposed as *services* to consumers (end-user applications or other services), a higher-level of decoupling of interfaces and implementation, and a thrust on open standards-based protocols (e.g. Web Services) for realizing this vision.

The design of a service is guided by a set of principles that help in achieving the goals of SOA. These principles have been well-documented in the literature [6, 7, 19] and include notions of cohesion, coupling, reusability, composability, granularity, statelessness, autonomy, abstraction and so on. However, the principles are largely

L. Baresi, C.-H. Chi, and J. Suzuki (Eds.): ICSOC-ServiceWave 2009, LNCS 5900, pp. 485–499, 2009.
© Springer-Verlag Berlin Heidelberg 2009

prescriptive in nature and there has been little work in defining how adherence to these principles may be quantitatively measured in practice. In some cases, metrics for a limited subset of SOA quality attributes have been proposed (e.g. [4, 5]), but most of these measures have not been empirically validated on real-life SOA designs. As a result, service design may proceed based on an informal or incomplete understanding of the principles, and without a sound measurement basis, could result in a flawed design. The generated services can provide all the functionality required by them and yet may not ultimately satisfy the design goals of SOA.

In this paper, we take a deeper look at how the key SOA quality attributes of service cohesion, coupling, reusability, composability and granularity may be evaluated, based only on service design level information. We review related work, adapt some of the well-known software design metrics to the SOA context and propose new measures where needed. We study their applicability on two real-life SOA design models from the insurance industry using a metrics computation tool integrated with an Eclipse-based service design environment. We also state the mathematical properties that the metrics adhere to (for lack of space, we do not include the proofs, which are straightforward). We believe that availability of these measures during SOA design will aid early detection of design flaws, allow different design options and trade-offs to be considered and support planning for development, testing and governance of services. The service consumer will also be capable of analyzing the quality of a service without having to analyze the details of the implementation (to which the consumer may not have access).

The rest of the paper is structured as follows. Section 2 sets the context by introducing the abstract service design model, case studies and tooling framework used in this paper. In Section 3, we define and evaluate a set of metrics for the SOA quality attributes of cohesion, coupling, reusability, composability, and granularity. Related work for each of the metrics is also discussed in detail and leveraged whenever possible. Section 4 presents directions for future research.

2   Setting the Context

We first describe the formal model and notation for service design that we use in this paper. Next, we introduce two large service designs in the Insurance Industry that we will use as running examples to compute and evaluate the metrics we propose. Finally, we briefly describe the service modeling environment on top of which our metrics computation tool has been built and our empirical studies conducted.

2.1   Model and Notations – Process, Service, Operations, Messages

To ensure common understanding of the metrics, we introduce the underlying service model and associated notations used in this paper. An enterprise adopting Service Oriented Architecture identifies a domain that needs to undergo SOA transformation.

- The business domain is supported by a set of business processes $P = \{p_1, p_2...p_P\}$.
- A set of services $S = \{s_1, s_2...s_S\}$ are identified and designed for automating the business process of the domain.

- A service $s \in S$ provides a set $O(s)$ of operations = $\{o_1, o_2,....o_O\}$ and $|O(s)| = O$
- An operation $o \in O(s)$ has a set of input and output messages that are used as data containers between the service consumers and the service. A message and its constituent data types are derived from an information model of the domain. $M(o)$ is set of messages and data types for the operation o, The set of messages and constituent data types of all operations of a service s is represented as $M(s)$ = $\bigcup_{o \in O(s)} M(o)$.
- $S_{consumer}(s) = \{Sc_1, Sc_2....Sc_n\}$, represents a set of consumers of the service s.

2.2 Case Studies

Insurance Application Architecture (IAA): IAA [20] is a comprehensive set of insurance specific models that represent best practices in insurance. IAA describes the business of the insurer and includes process and information models of the domain. In recent years, a set of services have been designed to accelerate SOA adoption. In the rest of the paper, we refer to this design as *ServiceDesignA*.

Insurance Property & Casualty Content Pack: IBM Websphere Industry content pack contains pre-built service-oriented architecture assets that are used to accelerate development of industry-specific business applications. The Insurance Property & Casualty Content Pack [21] for WebSphere Business Services Fabric focuses on property and casualty lines of business for insurance enterprises and provides a service design for the same. We refer to this design as *ServiceDesignB*.

Table 1 gives a high-level summary of the design of the two experimental systems.

Table 1. Case Studies for Measuring Quality of Service Design

Experimental System	# of services	# of operations	# of messages and types	# of Business Processes
ServiceDesignA	110	622	3000	292
ServiceDesignB	83	286	794	53

2.3 Service Design and Metrics Computation Tool

Rational Software Architect (RSA) [22] provides a mature environment for designing SOA solutions and is built over the Eclipse platform supporting plug-in development. Our tool for metrics computation on service design is an RSA plug-in. A UML model of the service design is taken as input. Eclipse EMF APIs are used to extract data on each service e.g. operations, messages, data types and business processes. This data is used to compute the metrics through a metrics calculator. The metrics is stored along with each service design element and can be analyzed.

We now move on to the main part of the paper – the definition and evaluation of a metric suite for different quality aspects of service-oriented design.

3 Service Design Metrics

SOA design principles emphasize the attributes of coupling, cohesion, reusability, composability and granularity. Below, we briefly introduce each attribute and survey related work on measuring them, for procedural and OO systems. We also review the (limited) research in quantifying these attributes for service-oriented systems. Finally, we propose a set of metrics for measuring each attribute and study their applicability and usefulness on our example service design models.

3.1 Cohesion

For any system, cohesion measures the degree to which the elements of the system belong together [1]. The notion is generic enough to be applied to different types or levels of encapsulation e.g. a module, class, component, service etc., although how it is measured would have to be adapted to the context. Highly cohesive designs are desirable since they are easier to analyze and test, and provide better stability and changeability, which make the eventual systems more maintainable [10].

For procedural systems, various categories of module cohesion were proposed in [1] such as Coincidental (weakest), Logical, Temporal, Procedural, Communicational, Sequential and Functional (strongest). For Object-Oriented (OO) systems, a different set of categories was defined in [11]: Separable (weakest), Multifaced, Non-delegated, Concealed and Model (strongest). However, some of this categorization is subjective in nature. Bieman et. al [8] measure the functional cohesion of procedures by identifying common tokens that lie in the data slices of the procedure. Perhaps the most well-known effort at quantifying cohesion for OO systems is the LCOM (Lack of Cohesion in Methods) metric introduced by Chidamber and Kemerer that has multiple definitions and has undergone several refinements [3, 9].

For service-oriented systems, Perepletchikov et. al [5] categorizes cohesion on the basis of data, usage, sequence and implementation, defines measures for these and aggregates based on their average. Of the proposed measures, Service Interface Data Cohesion (SIDC), that identifies cohesion based on commonality of messages of the operations in terms of contained data types, will be reviewed in more detail below. None of the metrics have been empirically validated.

In the following, we first adapt two variants of the LCOM metric in the services context ($LCOS_1$, $LCOS_2$). The metrics are applied on our case studies and their drawbacks are analyzed. We propose a new metric for measuring service cohesion (SFCI) and evaluate its performance. Finally, the properties of SFCI are discussed.

Lack of Cohesion of Service Operations (LCOS)

LCOM has been widely used as a measure of cohesiveness in OO systems. For each class, the methods that operate on the same attributes are considered cohesive. In the context of services, there are no service attributes but messages become relevant as operations use these to execute the business functionality. Service operations that use common messages or their constituent data types can be considered cohesive. Service messages typically represent business entities or artifacts and hence operations on the same business entity or artifact are functionally related. We evaluate LCOM definitions and redefine them for services. The definition is based on two widely used LCOM metrics [3, 9].

$LCOS_1$ is based on the [3] where pairs of operations on the same set of messages are identified and considered cohesive; similarly, pairs of operations that do not contain similar messages are considered non-cohesive.

For a service s with operations $O(s)$, let $M(o_i)$ be the set of messages (and data types) used by operation $o_i \in O(s)$. Let,

$P(s) = \{ (M(o_i), M(o_j)) \mid M(o_i) \cap M(o_j) = \emptyset, o_i, o_j \in O(s) \}$ and

$Q(s) = \{ (M(o_i), M(o_j)) \} \mid M(o_i) \cap M(o_j) \neq \emptyset, o_i, o_j \in O(s) \}$, then

$LCOS_1 (s) = |P(s)| - |Q(s)|$ if $|P(s)| > |Q(s)|$
$\qquad\qquad = 0$ if $|P(s)| < |Q(s)|$

As the above definition indicates, $LCOS_1$ is not normalized, similar to the original LCOM metric [6]. $LCOS_1$ is 0 (strong cohesion) when the number of operation pairs that share messages $(Q(s))$, is more than the number of pairs that do not $(P(s))$. Otherwise, the difference between the numbers is taken as the lack of cohesion measure. $LCOS_2$ is based on the [9]. The number of operations using a message m can be defined as $\mu(m)$ where $m \in M(s)$.

$$LCOS_2(s) = \frac{\left(\dfrac{1}{|M(s)|} \sum_{m \in M(s)} \mu(m) \right) - |O(s)|}{1 - |O(s)|}$$

$LCOS_2$ is bound between 0 and 1. If each operation uses all the messages ③(m) = |O(s)| and hence $LCOS_2 = 0$. If each operation uses a distinct message, then the numerator reduces to 1-|O(s)| and so $LCOS_2 = 1$.

In practice, we have found both $LCOS_1$ and $LCOS_2$ to suffer from some drawbacks when applied to service oriented systems. Apart from its lack of normalization, the discriminating power of $LCOS_1$ is low, and most services tend to be classified as highly cohesive. On the other hand, $LCOS_2$ tends to increase sharply with increase in the number of operations, and most services appear as lacking cohesion. This is because, with an increasing number of operations, it becomes very unlikely that each operation will require the same set of (all) messages, although they may still contain some core data types that are relevant to the service functionality and may thus be argued to be functionally cohesive. These observations motivated us to define the Service Functional Cohesion Index (SFCI) defined below.

Service Functional Cohesion Index (SFCI)
This metric defines the functional cohesion of the operations of the service based on the commonality of the *key* message(s) the operations use to perform the required functionality. As above, if the number of operations using a message m is $\mu(m)$ where $m \in M(s)$, and $|O(s)| > 0$, then

$$SFCI\ (s) = \frac{\max(\ \mu(m))}{|\ O(s)\ |}$$

We define SFCI(s) to be 0 when s contains no operations. In SFCI(s), we focus on the contained data types that defines the message that is most widely used across all the operations – the fraction of operations using this common message and types returns *SFCI*. The value of this metric is always between 0 (non-cohesive) and 1 (highly cohesive). The service is perfectly cohesive if all the operations use one common message – the intuition here is that *a cohesive service typically operates on a small set of key business objects (messages) relevant to that service,* so these objects should appear in most of its operations. But the operations may also need other messages as inputs to operate on the key objects, and these types can very well differ based on the nature of the operation. As our empirical studies will show, this metric is better indicative of the cohesion of service operations when compared to $LCOS_1$ and $LCOS_2$ and remains stable with increase in number of operations. To compute the above metric in practice, we recommend filtering out utility data types that are also part of the messages since otherwise, unrelated operations may appear cohesive. The classification of data types into utility and business-relevant types may be done by a domain expert. Utility data types (including those representing primitive types) usually appear in many/most operations, often across unrelated services, hence we may automatically identify potential utility data types based on their usage count, for validation and filtering by domain experts.

The Service Interface Data Coupling (SIDC) metric defined in [5] also considers common data types of messages across operations to measure service cohesion. However, like $LCOS_2$, cohesion is high in SIDC only when all operations have the messages with same data types. Also, the metric, which is defined as the ratio of two unrelated terms (the number of operations having the similar messages and the total number of messages) has not been normalized to range between 0 and 1. Finally, the metric has not been empirically evaluated.

Measuring and Evaluating Cohesion Metrics
We have evaluated $LCOS_1$, $LCOS_2$ and SFCI metrics on ServiceDesignA and ServiceDesignB, and the results are shown in Figure 1.Since $LCOS_1$ and $LCOS_2$ indicate lack of cohesion while SFCI measures cohesion; we plot $LCOS_1$, $LCOS_2$ and (1-SFCI). Along the X-axis, we have ordered the services in terms of their increasing number of operations.

In ServiceDesignA $LCOS_1$ indicates a value of 0 for all but 2 services, while in ServiceDesignB, it is 0 for all the services. Thus all services are deemed highly cohesive and are indistinguishable in this respect. Conversely, $LCOS_2$ displays a strong correlation with the number of operations, and cohesion is very low for all services with more than 5 operations. On the other hand, **the plot of SFCI shows better discriminating power compared to $LCOS_1$ and it remains stable as the number of operations increases, unlike $LCOS_2$.** To validate that SFCI is more meaningful as a cohesion metric than $LCOS_2$, we investigated a service PolicyAdministration having 9 operations, with $LCOS_2$ indicating *lack of cohesion of 0.85* and SFCI indicating *cohesion of 0.89*, which are very conflicting values. We found that all the 9 operations in PolicyAdministration are related to aspects of policy, and 8 of the 9 operations

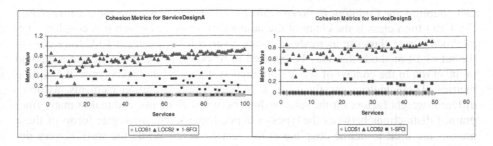

Fig. 1. Cohesion Metrics for ServiceDesignA and ServiceDesignB

process a business object called InsurancePolicy, hence from the design perspective, the service appears highly cohesive, as determined by SFCI, and the value of $LCOS_2$ appears misleading. We also reviewed a service with the lowest SFCI metric in ServiceDesignA. The service, LifePolicyManager has 19 operations dealing with different aspects such as terminating agreement, surrendering policy or requesting a loan, which could be refactored as multiple services. Note that there are several utility types that are defined to invoke an operation – e.g. RequestHeader, ResponseHeader and BusinessObject in ServicceDesignA. We filtered these types while computing the SFCI. It is seen that about 70% of the services in ServiceDesignA have an SFCI > 0.8. ServiceDesignB has 80% of the services with cohesion > 0.8. Thus both designs are very cohesive.

Validation of Cohesion Metrics
We verify the properties satisfied by the cohesion metric SFCI using the Properties based software engineering measurement framework [2]. SFCI is *not negative* and is *normalized* between 0 and 1 (*Non-negativity, Normalization*). SFCI is null when there are no messages or operations of a service (*Null Value*). SFCI is *monotonic* and does not reduce when more number of operations use some common messages. By adding more relationships between the messages and operations, $\mu(m)$ increases and hence the cohesion of the service cannot decrease (*Monotonicity*). SFCI of a service obtained by putting together two unrelated services (having disjoint message sets) cannot be more than the SFCI of either service (*Cohesive Service*).

3.2 Coupling

Coupling measures the strength of association or dependence between systems. Loosely coupled systems are easier to maintain [10], since a change in one system entity will have less impact on other entities. They are also easier to comprehend, reuse and test. Low coupling and high cohesion are thus fundamental to the design of any software system, including those that are service-oriented.

The concept of coupling was originally studied for procedural systems and classified into different types of coupling such as *Content(highest),Data, Control, Messages(lowest)* coupling [1]. For OO systems, additional complexities in coupling introduced by inheritance, polymorphism etc. have been studied and a number of coupling frameworks have been proposed [11, 12]. Two well-known metrics for

OO coupling are *Coupling Between Objects (CBO)* and *Response for a Class (RFC)* [3]. CBO for a class is the count of the number of classes to which it is coupled – i.e. methods of one class use methods or instance variables of another. RFC for a class is the set of all methods that may be invoked in response to the invocation of a method in the class. In the context of service-oriented systems, [4] defines 8 types of coupling metrics. These metrics mostly relate to service implementation elements, assumes different weight factors for the relationships between elements, and makes many fine-grained distinctions between the types of dependencies. The aggregate forms of these metrics are used to define coupling at the service level. While the work is very detailed, the measures have not been empirically evaluated. Unlike [4], we define coupling measures assuming the availability of only service design level information. The focus is on defining a small set of metrics that are easy for the service designer to act on and the service consumer to comprehend. Our approach has been motivated by the fact that coupling as a property, has a tendency to generate a multitude of measures often without offering newer insight, as a study by Briand et al have shown for OO systems [13].

In a service-oriented design, we believe that there is a need to distinguish between 2 categories of coupling: the dependence of a service on other services, and its dependence on *messages*. The dependence of one service on another has parallels with inter-class coupling, and the OO metrics of CBO and RFC may be suitably adapted, as we show below. However, the dependence of a service on messages is a characteristic of the services domain. Unlike in OO where a class encapsulates data (class attributes) and also operations on that data, messages are not bound to a service; rather, they are treated as first-class entities in a service-oriented design approach, and are defined by data architects based on the information model containing all the business entities of the domain. Services encapsulate operations that refer to and update the state of the business messages, and thus become coupled to them – business object models may get independently updated, thereby necessitating changes to the service operations that process them. Accordingly, we define metrics for both service coupling *(SOCI, ISCI)* and message coupling *(SMCI)*, below.

Service Operational Coupling Index (SOCI)
We analyze the dependence of a service on the operations of other services it uses for its functionality. Service Operational Coupling Index; SOCI can be represented as the number of operations of other services invoked by service s.

$$SOCI(s) = \left| \left\{ o' \in s' \mid \exists_{o \in s} calls(o, o') \land s \neq s' \right\} \right|$$

calls (o, o') denotes a call made by operation o of s to operation o' of s'. This measure considers direct coupling only. We can further use a transitive closure of the *calls* relation to get a measure of indirect service operational coupling, which is denoted as $SOCI_{indirect}(s)$. SOCI is an adaptation of the OO metric Response for a Class (RFC) [3], in the services domain.

Inter-Service Coupling Index (ISCI)
Inter-Service Coupling Index (ISCI) is defined as the number of services invoked by a given service s.

$$ISCI(s) = \left| \left\{ s' \mid \exists_{o \in s}, \exists_{o' \in s'} . calls(o, o') \wedge s \neq s' \right\} \right|$$

We can further use a transitive closure of the *calls* relation to get a measure of indirect inter-service coupling which is denoted as $ISCI_{indirect}(s)$. ISCI is similar in spirit to the OO metric of Coupling Between Objects (CBO) [3]. However CBO also includes dependencies on class attributes (in addition to methods), which is not relevant in the services context.

Service Message Coupling Index (SMCI)
SMCI measures the dependence of a service on the messages derived from the information model of the domain. These messages are those its operations receive as inputs, interpret and process, and those they need to produce as output, as declared in the interface. They also include messages the service needs to create in order to invoke operations in other services it is functionally dependent on. We represent SMCI as

$$SMCI(s) = \left| \bigcup M(o') \mid (o' \in s) \vee (\exists_{o' \in s'} \exists_{o \in s} calls(o, o') \wedge s \neq s') \right|$$

A low SMCI indicates less complexity for the service in interpreting and creating messages and less dependence on the domain information model. Note that $M(o)$ includes all the constituent data types.

Measuring and Evaluating Coupling Metrics
The ISCI and SOCI metrics, evaluated on ServiceDesingnA, are shown in Fig.2 (a) Overall, the system has moderate levels of coupling and of the 110 services, 36 services (~ 33%) are coupled to other services, while the rest are atomic services that do not depend on other services for their functionality. For most services, the SOCI and ISCI metric are the same. This indicates that a service is dependent on another service for only one of its operations. Moreover, we have determined that the *Indirect* versions of these metrics do not bring in any additional coupling. The maximum value of ISCI is 4. The service OperationalRiskAssessment is coupled to other services as it analyzes risk by requesting information from 4 distinct services related to Customer, Policy, Agreement and Payment. In the case of SystemDesignB, all 83 services were atomic services. The design consists of utility services on which other services can be defined. Figure 2 (b) shows the SMCI metric for the services in ServiceDesignA and ServiceDesignB In general, ServiceDesingA has higher message coupling than ServiceDesignB, as seen from the figure.

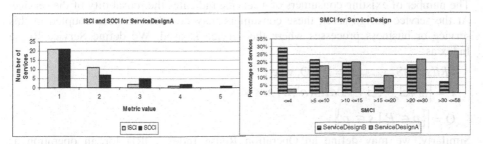

Fig. 2(a). ISCI, SOCI for ServiceDesignA   **2(b).** SMCI for ServiceDesignA and ServiceDesignB

Validation of Coupling Metrics

We now verify the properties of the coupling metrics [2]. The coupling metrics are *nonnegative* (*Nonnegativity*). ISCI, SOCI and SMCI are *null* if there are no coupled services or no messages for each of the service operations (*Null Value*). The metrics are *Monotonic* and *do not decrease* by adding more dependencies. SMCI may only increase if the number of messages of the service (or, in operations invoked by the service) increases (*Monotonicity*). The coupling of a service obtained by *merging two services* is less than or equal the sum of coupling of the two original services (*Merging of Services*). This is true for all the metrics. The coupling obtained by *merging two disjoint* services is equal to the sum of couplings of the two original services (*Disjoint Service Additivity*). Disjoint services are not consumers of each other, are coupled to different services and have disjoint message sets.

3.3 Reusability and Composability

We now discuss service reusability and composability, which are related concepts. Reusability is one of the key principles of service design. A service should ideally be designed for more that one service consumer. Service composability is a form of reusability. A service becomes a composition participant and can be reused along with other services to provide business functionality.

Reusability of an entity may be looked at from two perspectives: the characteristics of the entity that are predictors of reusability, and potential for future reuse of the entity based on usage that has already happened. The attributes of coupling and cohesion are generally good predictors of reusability. A service whose operations are cohesive and have less external dependencies will be more easily reusable. [14] computes *customizability*, *understandability* and *portability* metrics and uses them as predictors of reusability. Portability is measured in terms of the number of methods without parameters or return values. In [16], the average number of arguments per procedure is proposed as a measure of the understandability of the interface. For predicting reusability based on actual usage, contributions in terms of lines of code (LOC) [15] have been proposed for code assets. For OO systems, Depth of Inheritance (DIT) metric is used as a measure of reusability of a class [3]. However, neither of these metrics is relevant to services-oriented design, and we instead suggest measuring reusability based on use of the service by service consumers.

Service Reuse Index

The number of existing consumers of a service indicates the reusability of the service. At the service design level, these consumers may be other services coupled to this service or business processes where the service is used. We define Service Reuse Index as

$$SRI(s) = |S_{consumer}(s)| = P + Q, \text{ where}$$

$$P = \left| \left\{ s' | \exists_{o \in s}, \exists_{o' \in s'}.calls(o', o) \land s \neq s' \right\} \right|$$

$$Q = \left| \left\{ p \in P \mid s \in p \right\} \right|$$

Similarly, we may define an Operation Reuse Index (ORI) for an operation as the number of consumers of that operation across services and business processes.

Sometimes the reuse of a service is due to the reuse of one or few of its operations – ORI helps identify those important operations of the service.

While SRI predicts future reuse based on existing usage of a service, service reuse potential based on interface understandability (along the lines of component under-standability [16]) may be defined in terms of the complexity of the interface. The interface of a service is complex when it contains a high number of operations and messages, hence $|O(s)|$ and $|M(s)|$ may be used as indicators of understandability, with lower values implying better understandability (thereby higher reuse potential). How-ever, proving the value of such measures for reuse (i.e. being able to link actual usage to better understandability) is difficult and higher interface complexity often means more reuse opportunities, as our empirical studies reveal below.

Service Composability Index (SCOMP)

A composable service is designed to participate as an effective member of multiple compositions. We define service composability considering the compositions in which the service is a composition participant and the number of distinct composition participants which succeed or precede the service. *Neighbors(s, p)* returns the set of services which are neighbors (immediate predecessors and successors) of *s* in busi-ness process *p*. We define:

$$SCOMP(s) = |\bigcup_{p \in P} Neighbors(s, p)|$$

We may also extend this definition to include other services that may not be immedi-ate successors or predecessors of *s* but are participants of the same composition and would be present in the control flow of the composition. The composability of *s* with these services may be weighed by the inverse of its distance from *s* in these composi-tions (more distant is the neighbor, less is the composability).

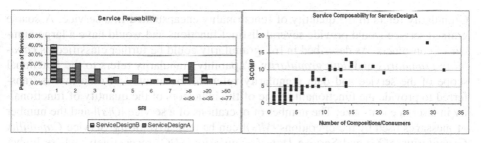

Fig. 3(a). SRI for ServiceDesignA and Ser-   3(b). SCOMP for ServiceDesignA
viceDesignB

Measuring and Evaluating Reusability and Composability

Figure 3(a) shows the percentage of services having a certain number of consumers. There are some instances of high reuse e.g. in ServiceDesignA, there is one service 'PartyNotification' having 77 consumers. Similarly, in ServiceDesignB, there are 4 services that have >30 service consumers, but there is also a significant percentage of services with very few consumers. We evaluate the operation reuse index of the Par-tyNotification service. There is one operation that is highly reused as compared to the others – notifyParty with 36 consumers. A change to this operation would have a high impact on the consumers of PartyNotification. SCOMP(s) for all the services of ServiceDesignA is measured as shown in Figure 3(b). As the number of compositions in which a service occurs increases, the number of distinct composition participants generally increases as well, and hence SCOMP increases. This correlation can be seen in the figure. This plot does not include the Party notification service that is used in 77 compositions and has SCOMP =32. We also found that for ServiceDesignA, service interface complexity ($|M(s)|$ and $|O(s)|$) has a positive correlation of > 0.5 with reusability: it seems that higher the complexity (arguably, lower the understandability), the larger is the scope of service functionality, and higher the number of consumers. While interface complexity/understandability is an issue that may concern consumers from outside the domain looking to use the service, it seems that within a domain it is the value and scope of the business functionality offered by a service that determines its reuse potential. We return to this issue when we discuss service granularity.

Properties of Reusability and Composability Metrics
Based on the inherent semantics of reusability and composability, we define a set of properties that their metrics should adhere to. The metrics cannot be negative (*Non-negativity*). They should be null where there are no consumers *(Null Value)*. Reusability of a service or an operation should not decrease by adding more service consumers; similarly, composability of a service should not decrease with more composition participants (*Monotonicity*). The reusability of a service obtained by merging two services is not greater than the sum of reusability of the two original services. This is also true for the composability metric. *(Merging of services)*. It may be shown that *SRI* and *SCOMP* satisfy these properties.

3.4 Service Granularity

Granularity refers to the quantity of functionality encapsulated in a service. A coarse grained service would provide several distinct functions and would have a large number of consumers. As described in [6], granularity could be further classified as *capability granularity* and *data granularity*. Capability granularity refers to the functional scope of the service and data granularity refers to the amount of data that is transferred to provide the functionality. One of the indicators of the quantity of functionality in a service is its size. The number of operations of a service $|O(s)|$ and the number of messages used by the operations $|M(s)|$ can be indicative of the Service *Capability Granularity (SCG)* and Service *Data Granularity (SDG)* respectively, where higher values may indicate coarser granularity e.g. larger functional scope. However, a high $|O(s)|$ can also result from decomposing coarser operations into multiple finer-grained operations that consumers need to call, hence there is a need to reason about service granularity also from the perspective of a business process where the service is used. If a service encodes many small units of capability, each exchanging small amounts of data, then complex business processes would need a large number of such services to be composed to yield the desired functionality – thus for a business process $p \in P$, the number of services involved (*Process Service Granularity or PSG(p)*) and number of operations invoked (*Process Operation Granularity or POG(p)*), may also indicate if the constituent services are of an acceptable granularity or not – too many (conversely, too few) services and operations constituting a business process may imply that the services in the design model are too fine grained (or, too coarse grained), and that there is a need to re-factor the services to get the granularity right. This is also related to the service identification process of *top-down decomposition* proposed by many methods (e.g. [18]), where a complex business process is successively decomposed into sub-processes, which ultimately map to services. The *Depth of Process Decomposition (DPD)* – the number of levels to which the process was decomposed before services were identified, can be an indicator of the granularity of the derived services and operations, with services/operations identified at a greater depth likely to be of finer granularity. Also, with each decomposition step, the potential number of services (and/or the number of operations in a service) may increase, thereby showing up as higher values of *PSG, POG, SCG* etc. Thus, service and process granularity metrics may need to be reviewed together, to obtain greater insight on design granularity.

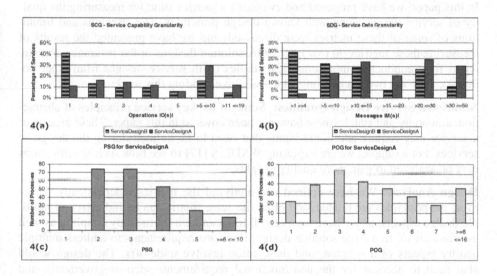

Fig. 4. Granularity Metrics for Service Design

Measuring Granularity Metrics

We measure the granularity metrics for both the designs. As shown in Fig. 4, a large number of services in ServiceDesignB are fine grained with one operation and < 4 messages and types. In ServiceDesignA, there are many services with > 5 operations and >20 messages and types, which is indicative of coarser granularity of the services. *PSG(p)* of the processes of ServiceDesignA is shown in Figure 4(c). There are about 20 processes that have one single service and invoke one operation as *POC(p)* =1. This indicates that the services used in the process are coarse grained. There are a few processes that involve around 10 services, and these may be explored to check if their granularity is too fine, but that is unlikely to be the case given that no process requires more than 16 operations. The DPD of the processes that we considered for the design is 1 or 2, which suggests that processes were not overly decomposed to obtain services, and the rest of the metrics seem to confirm this.

Properties of Granularity Metrics

We validate the granularity metrics against the mathematical properties of size, as the number of services, operations, and messages are size metrics. The granularity of a service and a process is *nonnegative (Nonnegativity)*. The granularity of a service/process is *null* if it does not have any operations (*Null Value*). The granularity of a service obtained by *merging two disjoint services* is equal to the sum of the granularity of the original services having different messages and operations (*Disjoint Service Additivity*).

4   Discussions and Future Work

In this paper, we have proposed and evaluated a metrics suite for measuring the quality of service design along well-known design principles. The strengths and limitations of some of these metrics were discussed, and we have presented the results of measuring these metrics on two large SOA solution designs in the Insurance domain. Apart from conducting more empirical studies (with service designs from other domains), there are two tracks along which we are extending this work:

Additional Service Design Qualities: Some of the key service principles of abstraction, autonomy and statelessness have not been covered in this paper. These aspects of a service may require additional inputs that need to be defined during the design of services. For example, we are exploring WSDL-S [17] to see how such specifications may be analyzed to gain more quality insights.

Design Analysis: We have defined and analyzed the metrics independently. However, the principles are related, and often the same metric can be indicative of multiple design aspects, as we have seen (e.g. |M(s)| can be used to study coupling as well as granularity). In a large solution design, there are requirements to address multiple quality aspects of a solution, and these often involve trade-offs. The design would also need to account for the non-functional requirements such as governance and performance. A more comprehensive analysis of the design, that would allow users to prioritize design attributes and would propose design alternatives that best meet the business needs, is an important direction that we intend to explore.

References

1. Stevens, W., Myers, G., Constantine, L.: Structured Design. IBM Systems J. 13, 115–139 (1974)
2. Briand, L.C., Morasca, S., Basili, V.R.: Property-Based Software Engineering Measurement. IEEE Trans. Software Eng. 22(1), 68–85 (1996)
3. Chidamber, S.R., Kemerer, C.F.: A Metrics Suite for Object Oriented Design. IEEE Trans. Software Eng. 20(6), 476–493 (1994)

4. Perepletchikov, M., Ryan, C., Frampton, K., Tari, Z.: Coupling Metrics for Predicting Maintainability in Service-Oriented Designs. In: Software Engineering Conference, ASWEC 2007, pp. 329–340 (2007)
5. Perepletchikov, M., Ryan, C., Frampton, K.: Cohesion Metrics for Predicting Maintainability of Service-Oriented Software. In: Seventh International Conference on Quality Software, pp. 328–335 (2007)
6. Erl, T.: SOA, Principles of Service Design. Prentice Hall, Englewood Cliffs (2007)
7. Artus, D.J.N.: SOA realization: Service design principles,
   http://www.ibm.com/developerworks/webservices/library/
   ws-soa-design/
8. Bieman, J., Ott, L.M.: Measuring Functional Cohesion. IEEE Transactions on Software Engineering 20(8), 644–657 (1994)
9. Henderson-Sellers, B.: Object-Oriented Metrics: Measures of Complexity. Prentice Hall, Englewood Cliffs (1996)
10. ISO/IEC, ISO/IEC 9126-1:2001 Software Engineering Product Quality – Quality Model, International Standards Organization, Geneva (2001)
11. Eder, J., Kappel, G., Schrefl, M.: Coupling and Cohesion in Object-Oriented Systems. In: ACM Conference on Information and Knowledge Management, CIKM (1992)
12. Briand, L.C., Daly, J., et al.: A Unified Framework for Coupling Measurement in Object-Oriented Systems. IEEE Transactions on Software Engineering 25(1), 91–121 (1999)
13. Briand, L.C., Daly, J., et al.: A Comprehensive Empirical Validation of Design Measures for Object-Oriented Systems. In: 5th International Software Metrics Symposium (1998)
14. Washizaki, H., Yamamoto, H., Fukazawa, Y.: A Metrics Suite for Measuring Reusability of Software Components. IEEE Metrics (2003)
15. Poulin, J., Caruso, J.: A Reuse Metric and Return on Investment Model. In: Advances in Software Reuse: Proceedings of Second International Workshop on Software Reusability, pp. 152–166 (1993)
16. Boxall, M., Arahan, S.: Interface Metrics for Reusability Analysis of Components. In: Australian Software Engineering Conference, ASWEC (2004)
17. Web Service Semantics – WSDL-S, http://www.w3.org/Submission/WSDL-S/
18. Arsanjani, A.: Service-Oriented Modeling and Architecture,
    http://www.ibm.com/developerworks/library/ws-soa-design1/
19. Reddy, V., Dubey, A., Lakshmanan, S., et al.: Evaluation of Legacy Assets in the Context of Migration to SOA. Software Quality Journal 17(1), 51–63 (2009)
20. Huschens, J., Rumpold-Preining, M.: IBM Insurance Application Architecture (IAA) – An Overview of the Insurance Business Architecture. In: Handbook on Architectures of Information Systems, pp. 669–692. Springer, Heidelberg (1998)
21. IBM Insurance Property and Casualty Content Pack:
    http://www-01.ibm.com/support/
    docview.wss?rs=36&context=SSAK4R&dc=D400&uid=
    swg24020937&loc=en_US&cs=UTF-8&lang=en&rss=ct36websphere
22. IBM RSA:
    http://www-01.ibm.com/software/awdtools/architect/
    swarchitect/

Specification, Verification and Explanation of Violation for Data Aware Compliance Rules

Ahmed Awad, Matthias Weidlich, and Mathias Weske

Hasso-Plattner-Institute, University of Potsdam, Germany
{ahmed.awad,matthias.weidlich,mathias.weske}@hpi.uni-potsdam.de

Abstract. Compliance checking is becoming an inevitable step in the business processes management life cycle. Languages for expressing compliance requirements should address the fundamental aspects of process modeling, i.e. control flow, data handling, and resources. Most of compliance checking approaches focus on verifying aspects related to control flow. Moreover, giving useful feedback in case of violation is almost neglected. In this paper, we demonstrate how data can be incorporated into the specification of compliance rules. We call these rules data aware. Building upon our previous work, we extend BPMN-Q, a query language we developed, to express these rules as queries and formalize these rules by mapping them into PLTL. In addition, whenever a compliance rule is violated, execution paths causing violations are visualized to the user. To achieve this, temporal logic querying is used.

Keywords: Compliance Checking, Business Process Querying, Violation Explanation, Temporal Logic Querying.

1 Introduction

Business process models are the means to formalize the way services are composed in order to provide an added value [1]. Evidently, the notion of a service in this context depends on the purpose of the process model. High-level models capture the way business goals laid by top management are achieved, whereas low-level models describe technical service orchestrations. When process models define how the day to day business is enacted in a certain organizational and technical environment, they are the best place to check for and enforce compliance to organization policies and external regulations.

Compliance rules originate from different sources and keep changing over time. Also, these rules address different aspects of business processes, for example a certain order of execution between activities is required. Other rules force the presence of activities under certain conditions, e.g. reporting banking transactions to the central bank, when large deposits are made. Violation to compliance requirements originating from regulations, e.g., the Sarbanes-Oxley Act of 2002 [2] could lead to penalties, scandals, and loss of business reputation. Therefore, compliance checking is crucial for business success.

As both compliance requirements and processes evolve over time, it becomes necessary to have automated approaches to reason about the adherence of process models to these requirements. In this context, there is a number of challenges. First, the question how to express the compliance requirements has to be addressed. Second, process models that are subject to checking within large repositories containing hundreds to

L. Baresi, C.-H. Chi, and J. Suzuki (Eds.): ICSOC-ServiceWave 2009, LNCS 5900, pp. 500–515, 2009.
© Springer-Verlag Berlin Heidelberg 2009

thousands of process models have to be identified. Third, there has to be an appropriate formalism for automatic checking of compliance rules against a process model. Fourth, users should be provided with useful feedback in case of violations.

While there are different notations available in order to express compliance rules, most of the approaches consider solely control flow aspects [3]. Moreover, the second challenge, that is automatic identification of processes that are subject to checking, was almost neglected in existing work. Further on, different formalism have been used to check for compliance. Here, model checking [4] is the most popular. The fourth challenge for compliance checking was neglected either. In case of violation, there is almost no feedback conveyed to the user in common approaches.

In a previous work [5], we demonstrated an approach that partially addresses these challenges. We employed BPMN-Q [6], a visual language we developed for querying business process models, to express compliance requirements (compliance rules) regarding execution ordering of activities (services) in process models. BPMN-Q was capable of expressing control flow aspects. Rules, expressed as BPMN-Q queries, were mapped into past linear time logic PLTL formulae [7]. Next, the resulting PLTL formulae were model checked [4] against the process models to decide about compliance.

Our contribution in this paper is twofold. First, we build upon work in [5] by incorporating data aspects. With data coming into play, the user can express so called data flow rules and conditional rules. Also, the mapping to PLTL is not straightforward. We achieve this by extending BPMN-Q with data aspects. Second, we introduce an approach to explain violations to compliance requirements. Whenever a rule is violated by the process model, we use temporal logic querying [8] techniques along with BPMN-Q queries to visually explain violations in the process model.

The use of BPMN-Q queries is manifold. First of all, BPMN-Q allows users to express compliance requirements in a visual way very similar to the way processes are modeled. That, in turn, simplifies application of our approach, as the business expert abstracts from the technical details. Second, a compliance rule that is defined as a query automatically determines the set of process models that are subject to checking in a repository. That is of particular importance, as such a repository might contain hundreds to thousands of process models. Finally, due to the nature of BPMN-Q query processing, the matching part(s) of the processes under investigation to the query are used to show execution scenarios causing violations directly on the process model level.

While we use BPMN for illustrating our contributions, results are applicable to other process modeling languages. The rest of the paper is organized as follows. Section 2 introduces an exemplary business process that needs to satisfy certain compliance rules. Section 3 is devoted to preliminaries on the applied techniques and Section 4 shows how BPMN-Q was extended to express data-aware compliance rules. Discussion of violation explanation is given in Section 5 and Section 6 gives details on our implementation. Related work is reviewed in Section 7, before we conclude in Section 8.

2   Motivating Example

A process model, expressed in BPMN notation, to open a correspondent bank account is shown in Fig. 1. The process starts with activity "Receive correspondent Account open request". Afterwards, the bank identity is looked up ("Identify Respondent Bank"). If

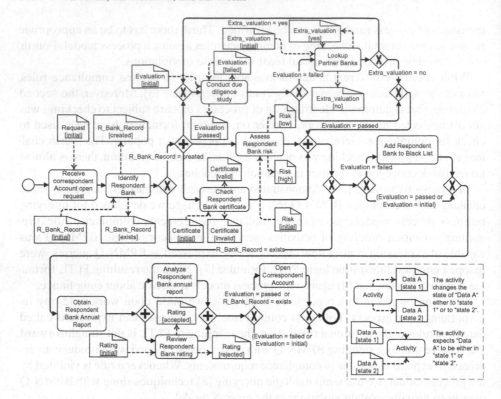

Fig. 1. A process model to open a bank account

this is the first time this bank requests to open an account, a new record is *created* and some checks must take place. The bank to open the account needs to conduct a study about the respondent bank due diligence, where the respondent bank may *pass* or *fail* this study. In case of failure, the bank inquires one of its partner banks about the respondent bank ("Lookup Partner Banks"). Then, it is decided, whether to make an extra study. It is also required to assess the risk of opening an account ("Assess Respondent Bank risk") resulting in either *high* or *low* risk. In the mean time, the respondent bank certificate is checked for *validity*. If the evaluation fails, the respondent bank is added to a black list. Subsequently, the bank obtains a report about the performance of the respondent bank ("Obtain Respondent Bank Annual Report"). This report is analyzed, and the respondent bank rate is reviewed. If the respondent bank passes the due diligence evaluation or it has already a record at the bank, an account is finally opened.

To prevent money laundering, various compliance rules are in place for the banking sector. We assume that the following rules must be checked for the process in Fig. 1.

R1: An account is opened only in case that risk is low.

R2: The respondent bank must always be added to the black list in case its due diligence evaluation fails.

R3: Before opening an account, the respondent bank rating must be accepted.

R4: In case the respondent bank rating review is rejected, an account must never be opened.

3 Preliminaries

3.1 Linear Temporal Logic with Past Operators (PLTL)

Linear Temporal Logic (LTL) allows expressing formulae about the future states of systems. In addition to logical connectors ($\neg, \wedge, \vee, \rightarrow, \Leftrightarrow$) and atomic propositions, LTL introduces temporal operators, such as *eventually* (F), *always* (G), *next* (X), and *until* (U). PLTL [7] extends LTL by operators that enable statements over the past states. That is, it introduces the *previous* (P), *once* (O), *always been* (H), and *since* (S) operators.

3.2 Data Access Semantics

Formalization of data access in process models is needed to be able to reason about. We formalized the semantics of accessing data objects by activities in a BPMN model in [9]. The semantics is inspired by the notion of business object lifecyles (cf. [10]), in which execution of activities might update the state of a data object. For instance, activity "Assess Respondent Bank risk" requires the data object "Risk" to be in state *initial* in order to execute. Since object lifecycles are merely state transition systems, at any point of execution a data object can assume only one state. Thus, an activity that has two or more associations with the same data object but with different states, e.g. activity "Lookup Partner Banks" with the data object "Extra_valuation" in Fig. 1, is interpreted as a disjunction of such states. This data processing semantics along with control flow execution semantics of BPMN given in [11] are used to generate the behavioral model of the process for model checking grounded on the following atomic propositions:

- The predicate **state**($dataObject, stateValue$) describes the fact that a data object assumes a certain state.
- The predicates **ready**($activity$) and **executed**($activity$) state that a certain activity is ready to be executed or has already been executed, respectively.

3.3 BPMN-Q

Based on BPMN, BPMN-Q [6] is a visual language that is designed to query business process models by matching a process to a query structurally. In addition to the sequence flow edges of BPMN, BPMN-Q introduces the concept of path edges as illustrated in Fig. 2(b). Such a path might match a sub-graph of a BPMN process — the highlighted part of the process in Fig. 2(a) is the matching part to the path edge of Fig. 2(b).

While such a path considers only the structure of a process, execution semantics have to be considered in the query if BPMN-Q is used for compliance checking. In this case,

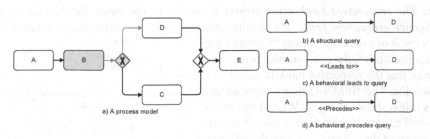

Fig. 2. BPMN-Q Path Edges

we type paths between two activities as being either *precedes* (cf. Fig. 2(d)) or *leads to* (cf. Fig. 2(c)) paths [5]. The former requires that before activity B is about to execute, activity A has already been executed. The latter, in turn, states that an execution of the first activity is *eventually* followed by an execution of the second activity. Considering Fig. 2(a), it is obvious that A *precedes* D is satisfied, while A *leads to* D is not.

Moreover, behavioral BPMN-Q queries are wrappers for PLTL expressions. That is, *leads to* paths are transformed into an implication with the *eventually* quantifier, whereas *precedes* paths map to an implication with the *once* operator. Thus, the mappings of the queries in Fig. 2(c) and Fig. 2(d) into PLTL are $G(\mathbf{executed}(A) \rightarrow F(\mathbf{ready}(D)))$ and $G(\mathbf{ready}(D) \rightarrow O(\mathbf{executed}(A)))$, respectively. The resulting expressions might then be checked against the process model's execution state space.

The path edge has one more property called the *exclude* property. Imagine a structural query with a path from activity A to activity E where *exclude* is set to D. Then matching this query to the process in Fig. 2(a) would yield the whole model except activity *D*. Setting the *exclude* property for behavioral paths affects the PLTL formula.

4   BPMN-Q for Data Aware Compliance Rules

In this section, we demonstrate how to express data aspects in compliance rules by extending the BPMN-Q language. Section 4.1 illustrates the extensions and introduces different kinds of data aware queries by using the aforementioned compliance rules as examples. We define the syntax for BPMN-Q in Section 4.2 and specify query semantics by mapping the queries into PLTL expressions in Section 4.3.

4.1   Examples for Data Aware Compliance Rules

R1: An account is opened only in case that risk is low. Data objects and data associations are used in BPMN-Q in the same way as in BPMN. BPMN-Q additionally introduces a new type of

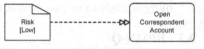

Fig. 3. Query for R1

association edges called behavioral associations. This association represents an implicit association between a data object and an activity. This captures R1, which requires that the data object "Risk" must be in state *low* when the activity "Open Correspondent Account" is about to execute. Fig. 3 depicts the query for R1. A behavioral association edge is visualized with a double arrow head. Rules specifying solely data dependencies for a single activity are called *data rules*.

R2: The respondent bank must always be added to the black list in case its due diligence evaluation fails. R2 requires that once the due diligence evaluation fails as a result of executing activity "Conduct due diligence study", the process must proceed in a way that the respective bank is added to a black list. The BPMN-Q query representing this rule is shown in Fig. 4. We call this rule a *conditional leads to* rule. It is a refinement of the *leads to* introduced above.

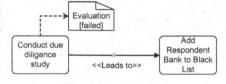

Fig. 4. Query for R2

R3: Before opening an account, the respondent bank rating must be accepted. This rule might be modeled similarly to R1. In this case, we want to be sure that the state of the "Rating" data object will always be *accepted* when the activity "Open Correspondent Account" is about to execute. Another way to model R3 is shown in Fig. 5(a). This query requires that when the activity "Open Correspondent Account" is ready to execute, the "Rating" was *accepted* as a result of the execution of activity "Review Respondent Bank rating". Unlike the first case, the state of the data object *may* change in between. We call the latter query a `conditional precedes` rule.

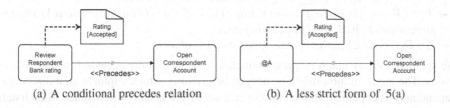

(a) A conditional precedes relation   (b) A less strict form of 5(a)

Fig. 5. Different BPMN-Q queries to capture R3

Fig. 5(b) shows an even less strict variant of the query in Fig. 5(a). Here, focus is only on the data condition that must have held once *before* the execution of activity "Open Correspondent Account". Using the BPMN-Q variable activity, denoted as an activity with the label "@A", relieves the modeler from explicitly mentioning the activity that sets the "Rating" to *accepted*. Rule R2 could have been modeled in the same way.

R4: In case the respondent bank rating review is rejected, an account must never be opened. This rule is another way of stating a requirement similar to this of R3. When a certain condition holds, i.e. the "Rating" is *rejected*, it has to be ensured that the activity "Open Correspondent Ac-

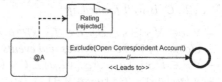

Fig. 6. Query for R4

count" will *never* be executed. The query in Fig. 6 captures this requirement. The variable activity "@A" with an association to the data object "Rating" with state *rejected* represents the data condition. Moreover, there is a `leads to` path from this activity to an end event with the *exclude* property set to the activity "Open Correspondent Account". That is interpreted as: activity "Open Correspondent Account" must never be executed from the point the data condition holds to the end of the process.

4.2   Syntax of Data Aware BPMN-Q Queries

After we have introduced data aware BPMN-Q queries by exemplary compliance rules, we define their syntax formally. Therefore, the notions of a *process graph* and a *query graph* as introduced in [5] have to be extended with data related concepts. We introduce these extensions formally solely for the query graph, as they subsume the extensions needed for the process graph. We begin by postulating infinite sets of activities $\mathfrak{A}$, data objects $\mathfrak{D}$, and labels of data object states $\mathfrak{L}$.

Definition 1 (Query Graph). *A BPMN-Q query graph is a tuple* $QG = (\mathcal{A}_Q, \mathcal{E}_Q, \mathcal{D}_Q,$ $\mathcal{P}, \mathcal{X}, \mathcal{C}, \mathcal{T}, \mathcal{L})$ *where:*

- $\mathcal{A}_Q \subset (\mathfrak{A} \cup \{@A\})$ *is the set of activities with @A as the distinguished variable activity,* $\mathcal{E}_Q \subseteq \{e_S, e_E\}$ *is the set of events that might contain a dedicated start and a dedicated end event, and* $\mathcal{D}_Q \subset \mathfrak{D}$ *is the set of data objects.* $\mathcal{A}_Q, \mathcal{E}_Q,$ *and* $\mathcal{D}_Q$ *are finite and disjoint sets.*
- $\mathcal{P} \subseteq (\{e_S\} \cup \mathcal{A}_Q) \times (\{e_E\} \cup \mathcal{A}_Q)$ *is the path relation.*
- $\mathcal{X} : \mathcal{P} \to \wp(\mathcal{A}_Q)$ *defines the exclude property for paths.*
- $\mathcal{C} \subseteq (\mathcal{D}_Q \times \mathcal{A}_Q) \cup (\mathcal{A}_Q \times \mathcal{D}_Q)$ *is the data access relation.*
- $\mathcal{T} : (\mathcal{P} \to \{leadsto, precedes, none\}) \cup (\mathcal{C} \to \{behavioral, none\})$ *assigns stereotypes to paths and data associations.*
- $\mathcal{L} : \mathcal{D}_Q \to \wp(\mathfrak{L})$ *assigns status labels to data objects.*

We see that a query graph might contain data objects that are accessed by data associations. The latter, in turn, might be of type *behavioral*, which captures an indirect data dependency as explained above. Moreover, a set of status labels is assigned to each data object. The labeling function $\mathcal{L}$, the set of data objects $\mathcal{D}_Q$, and the data access relation $\mathcal{C}$ are data related extensions that are applied for process graphs as well.

Definition 1 allows to define query graphs that are unconnected or show anomalies as, for instance, variable activities that are targets of a path. Therefore, we restrict the definition to *well-formed query graphs*. As a short-hand notation, we use $\mathcal{N}_Q = \mathcal{A}_Q \cup \mathcal{E}_Q$ for all nodes, $\mathcal{S}_Q = \{n_2 \in \mathcal{N}_Q | \not\exists n_1 \in \mathcal{N}_Q [(n_1, n_2) \in \mathcal{P}]\}$ for start nodes, and $\mathcal{T}_Q = \{n_1 \in \mathcal{N}_Q | \not\exists n_2 \in \mathcal{N}_Q [(n_1, n_2) \in \mathcal{P}]\}$ for end nodes.

Definition 2 (Well-Formed Query Graph). *A query graph* $QG = (\mathcal{A}_Q, \mathcal{E}_Q, \mathcal{D}_Q, \mathcal{P},$ $\mathcal{X}, \mathcal{C}, \mathcal{T}, \mathcal{L})$ *is well-formed, iff*

- $\forall n \in \mathcal{N}_Q [\exists s \in \mathcal{S}_Q, e \in \mathcal{T}_Q [s\mathcal{P}^*n \wedge n\mathcal{P}^*e]]$ *with* $\mathcal{P}^*$ *as the transitive reflexive closure of* $\mathcal{P}$, *i.e. activities and events are connected,*
- $\forall d \in \mathcal{D}_Q [\exists a \in \mathcal{A}_Q [(d, a) \in \mathcal{C} \vee (a, d) \in \mathcal{C}]]$, *i.e. data objects are accessed,*
- $\forall (n_1, n_2) \in \mathcal{P} [(n_2 \neq @A) \wedge (n_1 = @A \Rightarrow \exists d \in \mathcal{D}_Q [(n_1, d) \in \mathcal{C}])]$, *i.e. the variable activity is never target of a path and must have data access.*

We restrict our discussion to well-formed query graphs and use the term *query* as a short form for *query graph*. A query is called *compliance query*, if every path is of type `precedes` or `leads to`. Note that we do not consider paths of type `none` at this point. These paths are not applicable to specify compliance rules as BPMN-Q queries, as they specify structural requirements for the process model rather than behavioral requirements. Nevertheless, these queries are well-formed queries, which might be generated in order to explain violations of compliance rules. Depending on how data aspects are considered in the query, we distinguish *data queries*, *control flow queries*, and *conditional queries*. *Data queries* specify data constraints for solely one activity. In contrast, *control flow queries* are all BPMN-Q queries that do not consider any data dependencies. A *conditional query* combines data and control flow dependencies, such that a control flow dependency is required to hold under certain data conditions.

Definition 3 (Data Query). *A query* $Q = (\mathcal{A}_Q, \mathcal{E}_Q, \mathcal{D}_Q, \mathcal{P}, \mathcal{X}, \mathcal{C}, \mathcal{T}, \mathcal{L})$ *is called data query, iff* $|\mathcal{A}_Q| = 1$, $\mathcal{A}_Q \neq \{@A\}$, *and* $\mathcal{E}_Q = \emptyset$, *the query contains exactly one activity (not the variable activity), but no events.*

Definition 4 (Control Flow Query). *A query* $Q = (\mathcal{A_Q}, \mathcal{E_Q}, \mathcal{D_Q}, \mathcal{P}, \mathcal{X}, \mathcal{C}, \mathcal{T}, \mathcal{L})$ *is called* control flow query, *iff* $\mathcal{D_Q} = \emptyset$.

Definition 5 (Conditional Leads to / Precedes Query). *A query* $Q = (\mathcal{A_Q}, \mathcal{E_Q}, \mathcal{D_Q},$ $\mathcal{P}, \mathcal{X}, \mathcal{C}, \mathcal{T}, \mathcal{L})$ *is called* conditional query, *iff*

- $(|\mathcal{A_Q}| = 2) \vee ((|\mathcal{A_Q}| = 1) \wedge (\mathcal{E_Q} = \{e_E\}))$, *the query contains two activities or events, but no start event,*
- $(|\mathcal{P}| = 1) \wedge \forall (p_1, p_2) \in \mathcal{P} [p_1 \neq p_2]$, *that are connected by a path,*
- $\forall d \in \mathcal{D_Q} [\exists (a_1, n) \in \mathcal{P} [(a_1, d) \in \mathcal{C}]]$, *all data objects are written by the node that is the origin of the path.*

A conditional query is called conditional leads to query, *iff* $\forall p \in \mathcal{P} [\mathcal{T}(p) = leadsto]$, *or* conditional precedes query, *iff* $\forall p \in \mathcal{P} [\mathcal{T}(p) = precedes]$.

4.3 Mapping Queries into PLTL

After we specified the syntax for BPMN-Q queries, this section introduces the mapping of a query into a PLTL formula in order to model check them against process models. This mapping is based on the aforementioned classification of BPMN-Q queries. We focus on the mapping of *data queries* and *conditional queries*, and refer to [5] for a mapping of *control flow queries*.

Mapping Data Queries. The mapping into PLTL is straightforward. A certain data condition must always hold at the time an activity is about to execute.

Definition 6 (PLTL for Data Query). *For a data query* $Q = (\mathcal{A_Q}, \mathcal{E_Q}, \mathcal{D_Q}, \mathcal{P}, \mathcal{X},$ $\mathcal{C}, \mathcal{T}, \mathcal{L})$, *the corresponding PLTL formula* P_Q *is defined as:* $P_Q = G(\mathbf{ready}(a) \rightarrow$ $\bigwedge_{d \in \mathcal{D_Q}} P_d)$ *with* $a \in \mathcal{A_Q}$, $P_d = \bigvee_{s \in \mathcal{L}(d)} \mathbf{state}(d, s)$.

According to this definition, the mapping of the query in Fig. 3 into PLTL is $G(\mathbf{ready}(Open\ Correspondent\ Account) \rightarrow \mathbf{state}(Risk, low))$.

Mapping *Conditional Leads to* Queries. These queries can be distinguished into *presence* and *absence* queries, depending on whether the execution of an activity has to be ensured (presence) or prevented (absence). The query in Fig. 4 is an example for a *presence* query, whereas the query in Fig. 6 is an *absence* query.

   A mapping of these conditional queries to PLTL is not straightforward. Considering the query in Fig. 4, a first attempt to map this query might result in $G(\mathbf{executed}(Conduct\ due\ diligence\ study) \wedge \mathbf{state}(Evaluation, failed) \rightarrow$ $F(\mathbf{ready}(Add\ Respondent\ Bank\ to\ Black\ List)))$.

   At the first glance, the formula captures the requirement. Whenever the activity "Conduct due diligence study" is executed and the bank evaluation failed, the respondent bank must be added to a black list. Referring to the process in Fig. 1, we see that this requirement is satisfied. However, model checking this formula against the process model tells that the model does *not* satisfy the formula. The reason is that the formula has not been specified properly. Imagine the execution scenario where "Conduct due diligence study" is executed for the first time and as a result the evaluation fails, i.e., the condition of the above mentioned formula holds. Next, "Lookup Partner Bank" is executed with the result to make an extra diligence study. In the second execution of the diligence study, the "Evaluation" is *passed*. From that point the process continues without adding the respondent bank to the black list. Thus, the rule is violated.

As a result, the aforementioned mapping cannot be applied. Instead, for this specific example, we need the model checker to record that the evaluation failed only when there is no chance to pass the evaluation in the future. We say that the data object state, and consequently the predicates, $\mathbf{state}(Evaluation, failed)$ and $\mathbf{state}(Evaluation, passed)$ are contradicting. We assume that we have the knowledge about these contradicting states before we start the process of rule mapping. The corrected PLTL formula is $G(\mathbf{executed}(Conduct\ due\ diligence\ study)\ \wedge\ \mathbf{state}(Evaluation, failed)\ \wedge\ G(\neg\ \mathbf{state}(Evaluation, passed))\ \rightarrow\ F(\mathbf{ready}(Add\ Respondent\ Bank\ to\ Black\ List)))$.

Before we introduce the mapping of `conditional leads to` BPMN-Q queries into PLTL formulae, we introduce two auxiliary predicates that will be used in the mapping of all conditional queries.

Definition 7 (Full Data Condition Predicate). *For a set of data objects $\mathcal{D}_Q$ and a labelling function $\mathcal{L}$, the* full data condition *is a PLTL predicate defined as:* $PD_{(\mathcal{D}_Q,\mathcal{L})} = \bigwedge_{d \in \mathcal{D}_Q}(\bigvee_{s \in \mathcal{L}(d)} \mathbf{state}(d,s)) \wedge G(\bigwedge_{s_c \in \mathcal{L}_C(d,s)} \neg \mathbf{state}(d, s_c)).$

Definition 8 (Variable Activity Condition Predicate). *For a node n, the* variable activity condition *is a PLTL predicate defined as:*

$$PV_{(n)} = \begin{cases} \mathbf{true} & \textit{iff} \quad n = @A \\ \mathbf{executed}(n) & \textit{else} \end{cases}.$$

The full data condition requires all data objects to be in one state out of a set of states. In addition, it prohibits contradicting data object states. As mentioned above, we assume the knowledge about contradicting states to be part of the business context. This is formalized as a function $\mathcal{L}_C : \mathfrak{D} \times \mathfrak{L} \rightarrow \wp(\mathfrak{L})$ that returns all contradicting states for a pair of a data object and a state. The second auxiliary predicate, namely the variable activity condition, requires the execution of an activity. In case of the variable activity "@A" this predicate is simply true.

Definition 9 (PLTL for Conditional Leads To Query). *For a conditional leads to query $Q = (\mathcal{A}_Q, \mathcal{E}_Q, \mathcal{D}_Q, \mathcal{P}, \mathcal{X}, \mathcal{C}, \mathcal{T}, \mathcal{L})$, the corresponding PLTL formula P_Q is defined as:* $P_Q = G((PV_{(src)} \wedge PD_{(\mathcal{D}_Q,\mathcal{L})}) \rightarrow P_{tar})$ *with* $(src, tar) = p \in \mathcal{P}$,

$$P_{tar} = \begin{cases} \bigwedge_{a \in \mathcal{X}(p)}(\neg \mathbf{executed}(a))U(\mathbf{ready}(tar)) & \textit{iff} \quad p \in dom(\mathcal{X}) \\ F(\mathbf{ready}(tar)) & \textit{else} \end{cases}.$$

We distinguish *presence* and *absence* queries by the definition of the predicate P_{tar}, which is defined based on whether the exclude property is set for the path.

Mapping `Conditional Precedes` Queries. Similarly, we can derive the PLTL formula for a `conditional precedes` query. For instance, consider the rule in Fig. 5(a). Informally the rule states that at the point activity "Open Correspondent Account" is ready to execute, i.e. $\mathbf{ready}(Open\ Correspondent\ Account)$

holds, there was a previous state in which activity "Review Respondent Bank Rating" was executed and the "Rating" was *accepted*. In other words, the predicates **executed**(*Review Respondent Bank Rating*) and **state**(*Rating, accepted*) were true before. Following the argumentation on the change of data states given above, we need to be sure that the state of the data object "Rating" did not change to a contradicting state. Therefore, the PLTL formula to capture the query in Fig. 5(a) is defined as $G(\textbf{ready}(Open\ Correspondent\ Account) \rightarrow O(\textbf{state}(Rating, accepted) \wedge$ **executed**(*Review Respondent Bank Rating*) $\wedge\ G(\neg\,\textbf{state}(Rating, rejected))))$. For the rule in Fig. 5(b), the mapping is quite similar except the treatment of the variable activity (according to Definition 8).

While the former queries require the *presence* of an execution of a certain activity, *absence* queries can be mapped similarly. They require the absence of an execution of certain activities between two activities taking the data conditions into account. The `conditional precedes` query is mapped to a PLTL formula as follows.

Definition 10 (PLTL for Conditional Precedes Query). *For a conditional precedes query* $Q\ =\ (\mathcal{A}_Q, \mathcal{E}_Q, \mathcal{D}_Q, \mathcal{P}, \mathcal{X}, \mathcal{C}, \mathcal{T}, \mathcal{L})$, *the corresponding PLTL formula* P_Q *is defined as:* $P_Q = G(\textbf{ready}(tar) \rightarrow P_{src})$ *with* $(src, tar) = p \in \mathcal{P}$,

$$P_{src} = \begin{cases} \bigwedge_{a \in \mathcal{X}(p)}(\neg\,\textbf{executed}(a))S(PV_{(src)} \wedge PD_{(\mathcal{D}_Q, \mathcal{L})}) & \textit{iff}\quad p \in dom(\mathcal{X}) \\ O(PV_{(src)} \wedge PD_{(\mathcal{D}_Q, \mathcal{L})}) & \textit{else} \end{cases}.$$

Predicate P_{src} reflects the difference between presence/absence queries.

5   Explanation of Violation

When the rules R1 to R4 introduced in Section 4.1 are checked against the process model in Fig. 1, we get the following result. R2 is satisfied by the model, whereas R1, R3, and R4 are violated. That, in turn, leads to the question *why* a certain rule is violated.

We would like to answer this question by showing execution scenarios that violate the rule directly in the process model. One could think of using the counterexample returned by the model checker when the rule is not satisfied. However, there are two problems with that approach. Firstly, the counterexample is given as a trace of states that violate the rule. Therefore, we need to translate it back to the level of the model structure. Secondly, counterexamples given by a model checker are not exhaustive. That is, they do not show every possible violation to the rule, rather, they show the first met violation.

In order to tackle this problem we use a two-step approach. First, we extract the data conditions under which the violation occurred. Second, this violation is visualized on the process model level. For the first step we use Temporal Logic Querying (TLQ) [8]. For the purpose of visualizing the violations based on the results of the first step, we use BPMN-Q to formulate the so-called anti-pattern queries.

We briefly introduce TLQ in Section 5.1. Subsequently, Sections 5.2 to 5.4 demonstrate the application of this two-step approach for each category of queries.

5.1   Temporal Logic Querying

Temporal Logic Querying (TLQ) was first introduced by Chen in [8] in order to find software model invariants and gain understanding about the behavior of the model. So, model checking can be seen as a subproblem of temporal logic querying. In model checking, we issue Boolean queries only. In the general case of TLQ, we ask a TLQ solver (e.g. [12]) to find a propositional formula that would make our query hold true when seen as a temporal logic formula. The question mark '?' is used in a temporal logic query as a placeholder for such a propositional formula, which might also be limited to certain predicates. For instance, the query $G(?\{p, q\})$ looks for invariants that are based on the predicates p and q.

5.2 Explanation of Data Rules Violations

A data compliance query (cf. Definition 6) is violated if there is a state in which the respective activity (a) is ready to execute ($\textbf{ready}(a)$ holds), but the data condition is not fulfilled. This occurs in case the data objects that are relevant to the compliance rule, assume states other than specified in the rule. We issue the temporal logic (TL) query $G(\textbf{ready}(a) \rightarrow \textbf{state}(?_{dob}, ?_{st}))$ to discover the violation. Thus, we are asking about the data states that are set at the point $\textbf{ready}(a)$ holds. Here, the symbol $?_{dob}$ is a placeholder for the data objects that were mentioned in the compliance query; while $?_{st}$ is the placeholder for their respective states. In general, such a query delivers the different assignments of data object states that make the statement hold. The general form of the query result is $\bigwedge_{d \in \mathcal{D}_Q}(\bigvee_{s \in \mathcal{L}(d)} \textbf{state}(d, s))$.

For the case of rule R1, the result of the TL query $G(\textbf{ready}(Open\ Correspondent\ Account)$ $\rightarrow \textbf{state}(Risk, ?_{st}))$ is $\textbf{state}(Risk, low) \lor$ $\textbf{state}(Risk, high)$. Thus, there is a possible execution trace where the state of data object "Risk" is set to $high$ and remains in this state until activity "Open Correspondent Account"

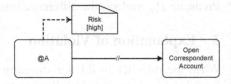

Fig. 7. Anti-pattern for R1

is ready to execute. In order to visualize this execution trace on the process model level, we need to find a path from some activity that sets the state of "Risk" to $high$ and another path from this activity to the activity "Open Correspondent Account". That is captured by the *anti-pattern*, which is illustrated in Fig. 7. Such anti-pattern matches the process part that causes the violation of the original compliance rule.

5.3 Explanation of *Conditional Leads to* Violations

Derivation of anti-patterns for *conditional leads to* compliance rules is straight-forward. Such a rule is violated when there is at least one execution trace in which the source activity is executed and the data condition holds, and the execution continues to the end of the process without executing the target activity. On the other hand, a *conditional absence*

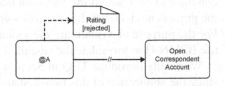

Fig. 8. Anti-pattern for R4

leads to rule is violated, if the activity required to be absent is executed in at least one possible execution trace. Rule R4 is an example for the latter kind of compliance rule. The corresponding anti-pattern query is shown in Fig. 8. Here, the path edge connects a variable activity at which the data condition holds to the activity "Open Correspondent Account". The type of path is *none*. Thus, we look for a structural match.

5.4 Explanation of *Conditional Precedes* Rules Violations

Explanation of violations of this type of rules is more complex than for the case of *conditional leads to* rules. According to Definition 10, a violation might be traced back to the following reasons.

1. $PV_{src} \wedge \bigwedge_{d \in \mathcal{D}_Q} (\bigvee_{s \in \mathcal{L}(d)} \text{state}(d, s))$ did not occur before activity *tar* is reached. That, in turn, might be traced back to one of the following reasons:
   (a) Either activity *src* was not executed at all, or
   (b) the data condition $\bigwedge_{d \in \mathcal{D}_Q} (\bigvee_{s \in \mathcal{L}(d)} \text{state}(d, s))$ was not fulfilled.
2. $G(\bigwedge_{s_c \in \mathcal{L}_C(d,s)} \neg \text{state}(d, s_c))$ was not fulfilled, i.e., the state of the data object had been altered to a contradicting data state before activity *tar* was ready to execute.

In order to identify the exact reason for the violation, we have to issue a sequence of TL queries. Depending on the results, anti-pattern queries are derived. First, we check whether the predicates for the execution of the source activity and the data condition hold when the target activity is ready to execute, i.e. $G(\text{ready}(tar) \rightarrow O(PV_{src} \wedge \bigwedge_{d \in \mathcal{D}_Q} (\bigvee_{s \in \mathcal{L}(d)} \text{state}(d, s))))$. Note that, again, we use the variable activity predicate PV_{src} (Definition 8) resolving to **executed**(src) for ordinary activities and to *true* for the variable activity "@A". If this query returns a positive result, we know that violation occurred owing to the second of the aforementioned reasons (2). That is, the states of the data objects are altered, such that $G(\bigwedge_{s_c \in \mathcal{L}_C(d,s)} \neg \text{state}(d, s_c))$ is not satisfied. The corresponding anti-pattern query is sketched in Fig. 9(a).

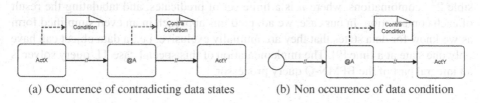

(a) Occurrence of contradicting data states   (b) Non occurrence of data condition

Fig. 9. Anti-pattern queries for conditional precedes

On the other hand, if the result is negative; either the source activity has not been executed at all before the target activity (reason 1a) or the data condition did not hold (reason 1b). In order to decide on a reason, we issue a TL query that checks, whether the source activity (src) is always executed before the target activity (tar), i.e. $G(\text{ready}(tar) \rightarrow O(PV_{(src)}))$. If this query is not satisfied, then we know that the target activity (tar) might be executed without executing the source activity (src) before. Thus, the violation can be identified by finding paths from the start of the process to the target activity without executing the source activity (which is captured by the exclude property). On the other hand, if this query is satisfied; we know that in *some* cases the data condition does not hold. To identify the data states that violate the data condition, we query the states of data objects that result from an execution of the source activity (src), as a TL query $G(\mathbf{ready}(tar) \rightarrow O(PV_{(src)} \wedge \mathbf{state}(?_{dob}, ?_{states})))$. For each resulting data state, a query as in Fig. 9(b) shows the violation in the process model.

Finally, the case of `conditional absence precedes` compliance rules adds one more potential reason for violation. That is, the excluded activities might have been executed. Again, the violation can be captured by issuing

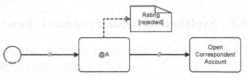

Fig. 10. Anti-pattern for R3

a query where there is a path from the start of the process to the activity that should be absent, and another path from this activity to the target activity. With respect to our examples, the anti-pattern query for rule R3 is illustrated in Fig. 10. This query matches the whole process model, such that activity "Review Respondent Bank Rating" is executed, the "Rating" is *rejected*, whereas activity "Open Correspondent Account" might be executed.

6   Implementation

Our approach has been implemented within the BPMN-Q query processor engine. The implementation covers mapping of the discussed rules into corresponding PLTL formulas as shown earlier. To prepare the investigated process models for model checking, the mapping proposed in [11,9] is used to generate the behavioral model.

For our work, we were not able to use existing temporal logic query solvers [12,13] as they support only CTL based queries. However, according to [14] it is possible to implement a temporal logic query solver by using a model checker and issuing all possible 2^{2^n} combinations, where n is a finite set of predicates, and tabulating the result of each combination. In our case, we adopted this approach in an even simplified form as we know for data states that they are mutually exclusive, i.e., a data object can have only one state at a time [9]. The implementation of this special case TL query solver is an integral part of the BPMN-Q query processor.

7   Related Work

There has been a large body of research interested in compliance checking on business process models. We focus on work done regarding execution ordering between activities on a business process. In this regard, we can divide work done on compliance into two areas, namely *compliance by design* and *post-design compliance checking*.

Compliance by design takes compliance rules as input for the design of new process models. Work in [15,16,17,18] shows how compliance requirements are enforced in the design process of new business processes. By definition, there is no chance for violations to occur. However, once a new compliance requirement is introduced or the process model is modified, the checking for compliance is needed.

Post-design compliance checking, in turn, targets checking for compliance for existing process models. Thus, it separates the modeling phase of a process model from the checking phase. Our approach belongs to this category. Similar approaches [19,20] also employ model checking to verify that process models satisfy the compliance rules. Although some of these approaches are able to express what we call conditional rules, it remains open how these approaches can be applied to express so-called data flow rules. Taking business contracts as a source for compliance rules, deontic logic was employed as a formalism to express these requirements in [21,22,23]. It is possible to express the notion of obligation and permission and prohibition. Thus, it is possible to express *alternative* actions to be taken when a primary one is not done. However, the data perspective is largely neglected. Further on, work in [24,10] addressed the consistency between business process models and lifecycles of business objects processed in these models. Yet, explanation of the points of deviation and their representation has not been addressed. A recent approach to measure the compliance distance between a process model and a rule was introduced in [25]. This approach enables measuring the *degree* of compliance on the scale from 0 to 1. Again, data aspects are not considered.

Another field of related work deals with resolution of compliance violations. In [26] an approach to check compliance of business processes and the resolution of violations was introduced. Although automated resolution is important, the paper discussed it from a high level point of view. We believe that this point needs further investigation and has to be tackled in future work.

Explanation of violations was also addressed in the area of workflow verification [27] as well as service orchestration [28]. In both approaches, the explanation was a translation of the output of the verification tools. Thus, it might be the case that some violation scenarios were not discovered.

The unique features of our approach are 1) the possibility of identifying process models subject to checking by means of queries and 2) giving explanations of possible violations on the process model level.

8   Conclusion

In this paper, we discussed an approach to model the so-called *data aware compliance rules*. These rules were realized by extending BPMN-Q. Including data aspects increased the expressiveness of the language. Nevertheless, formalizing these rules (queries), by mapping into PLTL, is not straightforward. Extra information, e.g. the notion of contradicting states, must be present. To explain violations, we applied temporal logic querying (TLQ). We demonstrated how feedback can be given — based on so-called anti-pattern queries that are derived automatically. To the best of our knowledge, we are the first to apply TLQ in the area of business process management.

The ability to provide explanations *why* a certain compliance rule is not satisfied has to be seen as a major step towards real-world applicability. Knowing just that a process violates a certain compliance rule is of limited use for common business scenarios. Owing to the intrinsic complexity of these scenarios, feedback on violations is crucial.

In future, we will investigate approaches for (semi) automated resolution of violations. In that case, other formalism has to be used as resolution of violation implies changes to the structure of the process models.

References

1. Weske, M.: Business Process Management. Springer, Heidelberg (2007)
2. United States Senate and House of Representatives in Congress: Sarbanes-Oxley Act of 2002. Public Law 107-204 (116 Statute 745) (2002)
3. Kharbili, M.E., de Medeiros, A.K.A., Stein, S., van der Aalst, W.: Business Process Compliance Checking: Current State and Future Challenges. In: MobIS, GI. LNI, vol. P-141, pp. 107–113 (2008)
4. Clarke, E.M., Grumberg, O., Peled, D.A.: Model Checking. MIT Press, Cambridge (1999)
5. Awad, A., Decker, G., Weske, M.: Efficient compliance checking using bpmn-q and temporal logic. In: Dumas, M., Reichert, M., Shan, M.-C. (eds.) BPM 2008. LNCS, vol. 5240, pp. 326–341. Springer, Heidelberg (2008)
6. Awad, A.: BPMN-Q: A Language to Query Business Processes. In: EMISA, GI. LNI, vol. P-119, pp. 115–128 (2007)
7. Zuck, L.: Past Temporal Logic. PhD thesis, Weizmann Intitute, Israel (1986)
8. Chan, W.: Temporal-logic queries. In: Emerson, E.A., Sistla, A.P. (eds.) CAV 2000. LNCS, vol. 1855, pp. 450–463. Springer, Heidelberg (2000)
9. Awad, A., Decker, G., Lohmann, N.: Diagnosing and Repairing Data Anomalies in Process Models. In: 5th International Workshop on Business Process Design. LNBIP. Springer, Heidelberg (to appear, 2009)
10. Küster, J.M., Ryndina, K., Gall, H.: Generation of Business Process Models for Object Life Cycle Compliance. In: Alonso, G., Dadam, P., Rosemann, M. (eds.) BPM 2007. LNCS, vol. 4714, pp. 165–181. Springer, Heidelberg (2007)
11. Dijkman, R.M., Dumas, M., Ouyang, C.: Semantics and analysis of business process models in BPMN. Inf. Softw. Technol. 50, 1281–1294 (2008)
12. Chechik, M., Gurfinkel, A.: TLQSolver: A temporal logic query checker. In: Hunt Jr., W.A., Somenzi, F. (eds.) CAV 2003. LNCS, vol. 2725, pp. 210–214. Springer, Heidelberg (2003)
13. Gurfinkel, A., Chechik, M., Devereux, B.: Temporal logic query checking: A tool for model exploration. IEEE Trans. Softw. Eng. 29, 898–914 (2003)
14. Bruns, G., Godefroid, P.: Temporal logic query checking. In: LICS, p. 409. IEEE Computer Society, Los Alamitos (2001)
15. Lu, R., Sadiq, S.W., Governatori, G.: Compliance aware business process design. In: ter Hofstede, A.H.M., Benatallah, B., Paik, H.-Y. (eds.) BPM Workshops 2007. LNCS, vol. 4928, pp. 120–131. Springer, Heidelberg (2008)
16. Goedertier, S., Vanthienen, J.: Designing Compliant Business Processes from Obligations and Permissions. In: Eder, J., Dustdar, S. (eds.) BPM Workshops 2006. LNCS, vol. 4103, pp. 5–14. Springer, Heidelberg (2006)
17. Goedertier, S., Vanthienen, J.: Compliant and flexible business processes with business rules. In: BPMDS. CEUR Workshop Proceedings, CEUR-WS.org, vol. 236 (2006)
18. Milosevic, Z., Sadiq, S.W., Orlowska, M.E.: Translating business contract into compliant business processes. In: EDOC, pp. 211–220. IEEE Computer Society, Los Alamitos (2006)
19. Yu, J., Manh, T.P., Han, J., Jin, Y., Han, Y., Wang, J.: Pattern based property specification and verification for service composition. In: Aberer, K., Peng, Z., Rundensteiner, E.A., Zhang, Y., Li, X. (eds.) WISE 2006. LNCS, vol. 4255, pp. 156–168. Springer, Heidelberg (2006)
20. Lui, Y., Müller, S., Xu, K.: A static compliance-checking framework for business process models. IBM Syst. J. 46, 335–362 (2007)

21. Governatori, G., Milosevic, Z.: Dealing with contract violations: formalism and domain specific language. In: EDOC, pp. 46–57. IEEE Computer Society, Los Alamitos (2005)
22. Governatori, G., Milosevic, Z., Sadiq, S.: Compliance checking between business processes and business contracts. In: EDOC, pp. 221–232. IEEE Computer Society, Los Alamitos (2006)
23. Sadiq, S.W., Governatori, G., Namiri, K.: Modeling control objectives for business process compliance. In: Alonso, G., Dadam, P., Rosemann, M. (eds.) BPM 2007. LNCS, vol. 4714, pp. 149–164. Springer, Heidelberg (2007)
24. Ryndina, K., Küster, J.M., Gall, H.C.: Consistency of Business Process Models and Object Life Cycles. In: Kühne, T. (ed.) MoDELS 2006. LNCS, vol. 4364, pp. 80–90. Springer, Heidelberg (2007)
25. Lu, R., Sadiq, S., Governatori, G.: Measurement of Compliance Distance in Business Processes. Inf. Sys. Manag. 25, 344–355 (2008)
26. Ghose, A., Koliadis, G.: Auditing business process compliance. In: Krämer, B.J., Lin, K.-J., Narasimhan, P. (eds.) ICSOC 2007. LNCS, vol. 4749, pp. 169–180. Springer, Heidelberg (2007)
27. Flender, C., Freytag, T.: Visualizing the soundness of workflow nets. In: Algorithms and Tools for Petri Nets (AWPN 2006), University of Hamburg, Germany, Department Informatics Report 267, pp. 47–52 (2006)
28. Schroeder, A., Mayer, P.: Verifying interaction protocol compliance of service orchestrations. In: Bouguettaya, A., Krueger, I., Margaria, T. (eds.) ICSOC 2008. LNCS, vol. 5364, pp. 545–550. Springer, Heidelberg (2008)

Generating Interface Grammars from WSDL for Automated Verification of Web Services*

Sylvain Hallé, Graham Hughes, Tevfik Bultan, and Muath Alkhalaf

University of California
Santa Barbara, CA 93106-5110 USA
shalle@acm.org, {graham,bultan,muath}@cs.ucsb.edu

Abstract. Interface grammars are a formalism for expressing constraints on sequences of messages exchanged between two components. In this paper, we extend interface grammars with an automated translation of XML Schema definitions present in WSDL documents into interface grammar rules. Given an interface grammar, we can then automatically generate either 1) a parser, to check that a sequence of messages generated by a web service client is correct with respect to the interface specification, or 2) a sentence generator producing compliant message sequences, to check that the web service responds to them according to the interface specification. By doing so, we can validate and generate both messages and sequences of messages in a uniform manner; moreover, we can express constraints where message structure and control flow cannot be handled separately.

1 Introduction

Service-oriented architecture (SOA) has become an important concept in software development with the advent of web services. Because of their flexible nature, web services can be dynamically discovered and orchestrated to form value-added e-Business applications. However, this appealing modularity is the source of one major issue: while dynamically combining cross-business services, how can one ensure the interaction between each of them proceeds as was intended by their respective providers? Achieving modularity and interoperability requires that the web services have well defined and enforceable interface contracts [20].

Part of this contract is summarized in the service's WSDL document, which specifies its acceptable message structures and request-response patterns. This document acts as a specification that can be used both to *validate* and to *generate* messages sent by the client or the service. This double nature of WSDL makes it possible to automatically produce test requests validating the functionality of a service, or to test a client by communicating with a local web service stub that generates WSDL-compliant stock responses.

As it is now well known, many web services, and in particular e-commerce APIs such as the Amazon E-Commerce Service, Google Shopping or PayPal,

---

* This work is supported by NSF grants CCF-0614002 and CCF-0716095.

L. Baresi, C.-H. Chi, and J. Suzuki (Eds.): ICSOC-ServiceWave 2009, LNCS 5900, pp. 516–530, 2009.

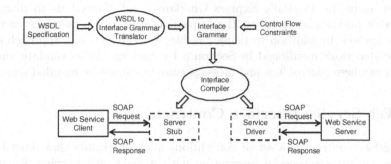

Fig. 1. Our web service verification framework

introduce the notion of *sessions* and constrain communications over several request-response blocks. The previous approach does not generalize to such scenarios. Apart from attempts at validation of service interactions through runtime monitoring of message sequences [5,6,18,13,14], for the most part the question of *generating* a control-flow compliant sequence of messages, for simulation, testing or verification purposes, remains open.

Interface grammars are a specification formalism that has been proposed to enable modular verification [16]. An interface grammar specifies the allowable interactions between two components by identifying the acceptable call/return sequences between them. In earlier work, we proposed their use for expressing the control-flow constraints on a client interacting with a web service [17]. However, message elements in these grammars were regarded as terminal symbols; to actually generate or validate a given message, hand-coded Java functions had to be written and hooked to their respective grammar counterpart. In this paper, we bridge the gap between control flow and message specifications by developing an automated translation of WSDL documents into interface grammar rules.

In Section 2, we present a real-world web service, the PayPal Express Checkout API. We exhibit constraints where the sequence of allowed operations and their data content are correlated, and express them with the use of interface grammars.

Our web service verification framework (Figure 1) consists of two tools: 1) a WSDL-to-interface grammar translator and 2) an interface compiler. First, the WSDL to interface grammar translator takes a WSDL specification as input and converts it into an interface grammar; this translation is described in Section 3. Constraints that are not expressed in WSDL (such as control-flow constraints) can then be added to this automatically generated interface grammar.

In Section 4, we use an interface compiler which, given an interface grammar for a component, automatically generates a *stub* for that component. This stub acts a parser for incoming call sequences; it checks that the calls conform to the grammar and generates return values according to that grammar. Moreover, the same grammar can be used to create a *driver* that generates call sequences and checks that the values returned by the component conform to it. The compiler was applied to perform both client and server side verification on two real-world services, including PayPal's Express Checkout, and allowed us to discover a number of mismatches between the implementation of the services and their documentation. In addition to being feasible and efficient, our approach differs from related work mentioned in Section 5 by enabling us to validate and test properties where control flow and message content cannot be handled separately.

2   Web Service Interface Contracts

An interface contract is a set of conventions and constraints that must be fulfilled to ensure a successful interaction with a given web service. Elicitation and enforcement of such contracts has long been advocated [20], and interface documents such as WSDL provide a basic form of specification for syntactical requirements on SOAP messages and request-response patterns. Although many web services are composed of such simple request-response patterns of independent operations, in practice a fair number of services also exhibit long-running behavior that spans multiple requests and responses. This is especially true of commerce-related web services, where concepts such as "purchase transactions" and "shopping carts" naturally entail some form of multi-step operations.

2.1   The PayPal Express Checkout API

A commercial web service suite provided by the PayPal company, called the PayPal Web Service API, is an example of a service that supports multi-step operations. Through its web site, PayPal allows to transfer money to and from credit card and bank accounts between its registered members or other financial institutions. In addition to direct usage by individuals, an organization wishing to use these functionalities from its own web site can do so through PayPal's web service API. All transactions can be processed in the background between the organization and PayPal by exchanging SOAP messages that replace the standard access to PayPal's portal.

PayPal's API is public and its documentation can be freely accessed [1]. The sum of all constraints, warnings, side notes and message schemas found in this documentation constitutes the actual interface contract to the web service API. We shall see that this contract is subject to data and control-flow constraints, and that these constraints can be formally specified using interface grammars.

To illustrate our point, we concentrate on a subset of PayPal's API called "Express Checkout", which allows for a simplified billing and payment between an organization and a customer. The organization simply sends PayPal a total amount to be charged to the customer; PayPal then performs the necessary background checks and confirmations with the customer, after which the organization retrieves a transaction number which can be used to execute the money transfer.

Express Checkout is performed in three steps, each corresponding to a request-response pattern of XML messages. The first step is to create an Express Checkout instance through the SetExpressCheckout message, whose structure, defined

```
<PaymentDetails>
   <Token>1234</Token>
   <OrderTotal>50</OrderTotal>
   <PaymentDetailsItems>
      <PaymentDetailsItem>
         <Name>...</Name>
         <Number>...</Number>
         <Quantity>...</Quantity>
         <Amount>...</Amount>
      </PaymentDetailsItem>
      ...
   </PaymentDetailsItems>
   <PaymentAction>Sale</PaymentAction>
</PaymentDetails>
```

(a) SetExpressCheckoutRequest

```
<Token>...</Token>
<PayerID>...</PayerID>
<PaymentDetailsItems>
...
</PaymentDetailsItems>
```

(b) GetExpressCheckoutDetails

```
<Token>...</Token>
<PayerID>...</PayerID>
<PaymentDetailsItems>
...
</PaymentDetailsItems>
<PaymentAction>Sale</PaymentAction>
```

(c) DoExpressCheckoutPaymentRequest

```
<Token>...</Token>
<PaymentInfo>
   <TransactionID>...<TransactionID>
   <GrossAmount>...<GrossAmount>
   <PendingReason>...<PendingReason>
</PaymentInfo>
```

(d) DoExpressCheckoutPaymentResponse

Fig. 2. Request and response messages from PayPal's Express Checkout API

in the WSDL specification, is shown in Figure 2(a). This message provides a total for the order, as well as (optionally) a list of items intended to detail the contents of the order the client is billed for. PayPal's response to this message consists of a single Token element, whose value will be used in subsequent messages to refer to this particular instance of Express Checkout. The PaymentAction element (Figure 2(c)) can take the value "Sale", indicating that this is a final sale, or "Authorization" and "Order" values indicating that this payment is either a basic or an order authorization, respectively.

The second step consists of obtaining additional details on the Express Checkout through the GetExpressCheckoutDetails operation. The request message simply requires a token identifying an Express Checkout instance; the response to this message is structured as in Figure 2(b). It repeats the payment details and token fields from the previous request, and adds a PayerID element. This element is then used in the last operation, DoExpressCheckoutPayment (Figure 2(c)); the response to this message (Figure 2(d)) completes the Express Checkout procedure.

2.2 Interface Grammars for Web Services

Interface grammars were proposed as a new language for the specification of component interfaces [15, 16]. The core of an interface grammar is a set of production rules that specifies all acceptable method call sequences for the given component. An interface grammar is expressed as a series of productions of the form $a(v_1, \ldots, v_n) \to A$. The $v_1, \ldots, v_n$ are lexically scoped variable names corresponding to the parameters of the non-terminal a. A is the right hand side of the production, which may contain the following:

$$start \rightarrow \text{!SECO}(\text{doc}_1, \text{items}, \text{token}, \text{action}); \text{¡SECO}(\text{doc}_2, \text{token});$$
$$start; details(\text{items}, \text{token}, \text{action}, \text{payerid}); start$$
$$| \quad \epsilon$$
$$details(\text{items}, \text{token}, \text{action}, \text{payerid}) \rightarrow \text{!GECOD}(\text{doc}_1, \text{token}); \text{¡GECOD}(\text{doc}_2, \text{token}, \text{payerid});$$
$$do(\text{items}, \text{token}, \text{action}, \text{payerid})$$
$$do(\text{items}, \text{token}, \text{``Sale''}, \text{payerid}) \rightarrow \text{!DECOP}(\text{doc}_1, \text{token}, \text{payerid}, \text{items}, \text{``Sale''});$$
$$\text{¡DECOP}(\text{doc}_2, \text{token}, \text{transactionid})$$
$$do(\text{items}, \text{token}, \text{action}_1, \text{payerid}) \rightarrow \text{!DECOP}(\text{doc}_1, \text{token}, \text{payerid}, \text{items}, \text{action}_2);$$
$$\text{¡DECOP}(\text{doc}_2, \text{token}, \text{transactionid})$$

Fig. 3. Interface grammar for a PayPal Express Checkout client

- nonterminals, written $nt(v_1, \ldots, v_n)$;
- semantic predicates that must evaluate to true when the production is used during derivation, written $[\![p]\!]$;
- semantic actions that are executed during the derivation, which we express as $\langle\!\langle a \rangle\!\rangle$;
- incoming method calls, written $?m(v_1, \ldots, v_n)$;
- returns from incoming method calls, written $\text{¿}m(v_1, \ldots, v_n)$;
- outgoing method calls, written $!m(v_1, \ldots, v_n)$;
- returns from outgoing method calls, written $\text{¡}m(v_1, \ldots, v_n)$.

For the purposes of web service verification, the method calls in the interface grammar correspond to the web service operations. For example, the interface grammar shown in Figure 3 represents the client interface for a simplified version of the PayPal service described previously. Terminal symbols SECO, GECOD and DECOP stand respectively for operations SetExpressCheckout, GetExpressCheckoutDetails and DoExpressCheckoutPayment; the ! and ¡ symbols denote the request and response message for each of these operations. The ? and ¿ symbols, which are not used in our example, would indicate that the server, instead of the client, initiates a request-response pattern.

Nonterminal symbols in interface grammars are allowed to have parameters [15]. The "doc$_i$" symbol in each message refers to the actual XML document corresponding to that particular request or response; it is assumed fresh in all of its occurrences. Remaining parameters enable us to propagate the data values from that document that might be used as arguments of the web service operations. Because we need to be able to pass data to the production rules as well as retrieve them, we use call-by-value-return semantics for parameters.

By perusing PayPal's API documentation, it is possible to manually define the simple interface grammar shown in Figure 3, which captures a number of important requirements on the use of the PayPal API:

1. Multiple Set, Get and Do operations for different tokens can be interleaved, but, for each token, the Set, Get and Do operations must be performed in order.

2. The PayerID field in the DoExpressCheckoutPaymentRequest must be the one returned by the GetExpressCheckoutDetails response with matching Token element.
3. If the action element of the SetExpressCheckout operation is set to "Sale", it cannot be changed in the DoExpressCheckoutPayment; otherwise, the Get and Do operations can have different action values.
4. To ensure that every Express Checkout instance is eventually complete, every SetExpressCheckout operation must be matched to subsequent GetExpressCheckoutDetails and DoExpressCheckoutPayment requests.

Although all these constraints are mentioned in the service's documentation in some form or another, none of them can be formally described through the WSDL interface document.

3   Translating WSDL to Interface Grammars

While interface grammars can express complex interfaces that involve both data-flow and control-flow constraints, writing such grammars manually requires a surprisingly large amount of boilerplate code. Crafting the appropriate data structures, verifying the result and extracting the data, even for one operation, requires as much code as the entire interface grammar. Moreover, parameters such as "items" and "token" refer to actual elements inside "doc", but the grammar in Figure 3 offers no way of actually specifying how the document and its parts are structured or related. To alleviate this difficulty, we developed a tool that uses type information to automatically translate the data structures associated with a WSDL specification into an interface grammar, without user input.

3.1   Translation from XML Schema to Interface Grammars

A WSDL specification is a list of exposed operations along with the type of the parameters and return values. It encodes all types using XML Schema. Since XML Schema itself is verbose, we use the *Model Schema Language (MSL)* formalism [10], which encodes XML Schema in a more compact form. More precisely, we define a simplified version of MSL that handles all the portions of XML Schema we found necessary in our case studies:

$$g \rightarrow b \mid t[g_0] \mid g_1\{m,n\} \mid g_1,\ldots,g_k \mid g_1|\ldots|g_k \qquad (1)$$

Here $g, g_0, g_1, \ldots, g_k$ are all MSL types; b is a basic data type such as Boolean, integer, or string; t is a tag; and m and n are natural numbers such that $m < n$ (n may also be ∞).

The MSL type expressions are interpreted as follows: $g \rightarrow b$ specifies a basic type b; $g \rightarrow t[g_0]$ specifies the sub-element t of g, whose contents are described by the type expression g_0; $g \rightarrow g_1\{m,n\}$, where $n \neq \infty$, specifies an array of g_1s with at least m elements and at most n elements; $g \rightarrow g_1\{m,\infty\}$ specifies an unbounded array of g_1s with at least m elements; $g \rightarrow g_1, \ldots, g_k$ specifies an ordered sequence, with each of the g_is listed one after the other; and $g \rightarrow g_1 | \ldots | g_k$ specifies choice, where g is one of the g_is. We denote the language of type expressions generated by Equation (1) to be $\mathcal{XML}$.

For example, the type for the DoExpressCheckoutPaymentResponse message (Figure 2(c)) is the following:

> **Token**[**string**], **PaymentInfo**[
> **TransactionID**[**string**], **GrossAmount**[**int**], **PendingReason**[**string**]]

As a more complex example, the SetExpressCheckoutRequest message (Figure 2(a)) is of the following type:

> **Token**[**string**]$\{0, 1\}$,
> **PaymentDetails**[
> **OrderTotal**[**int**],
> **PaymentDetailsItems**[
> **PaymentDetailsItem**[
> **Name**[**string**]$\{0, 1\}$, **Number**[**string**]$\{0, 1\}$, **Quantity**[**int**]$\{0, 1\}$,
> **Amount**[**int**]$\{0, 1\}$,
>]$\{1, \infty\}$
>]$\{0, \infty\}$,
> **PaymentAction**[**string**]$\{0, 1\}$]

These type expressions can be used to generate XML documents. However, to communicate with a SOAP server, we chose to use Apache Axis, a library that serializes Java objects into XML. Accordingly, we create Java objects from XML type expressions, and do so in the same way that Axis maps WSDL to Java objects.

XML Schema and the Java type system are very different and, hence, mapping from one to the other is not trivial. However, since such a mapping is already provided by Axis, all we have to do is the follow the same mapping that Axis uses:

1. $g \rightarrow b$ is mapped to a Java basic type when possible (for example, with Booleans or strings). Because XML Schema integers are unbounded and Java integers are not, we must use a specialized Java object rather than native integers.
2. $g \rightarrow t[g_0]$ is mapped to a new Java class whose name is the concatenation of the current name and t; this class contains the data in g_0, and will be set to the t field in the current object.
3. $g \rightarrow g_1\{0, 1\}$ is mapped to either **null** or the type mapped by g_1.
4. $g \rightarrow g_1\{m, n\}$ is mapped to a Java array of the type mapped by g_1.
5. $g \rightarrow g_1, \ldots, g_k$ is mapped to a new Java class that contains each of the g_is as fields.
6. $g \rightarrow g_1 | \ldots | g_k$ is mapped to a new Java interface that each of the g_is must implement.

The rules for the WSDL to interface grammar translation are shown in Figure 4. The translation is defined by the function $\mathbf{p}$, which uses the auxiliary functions $\mathbf{r}$ (which gives unique names for type expressions suitable for use in grammar nonterminals) and $\mathbf{t}$ (which gives the name of the new Java class created in the Axis mapping of $g \rightarrow t[g_0]$). By applying $\mathbf{p}[\![g]\!]$ to an XML Schema type expression g, we compute several grammar rules to create Java object graphs for all possible instances of the type expression g. The start symbol for the generated interface grammar is $\mathbf{r}[\![g]\!]$.

$$\mathbf{p} : \mathcal{XML} \rightarrow \mathbf{Prod}$$
$$\mathbf{r} : \mathcal{XML} \rightarrow \mathbf{NT}$$
$$\mathbf{t} : \mathcal{XML} \rightarrow \mathbf{Type}$$

$$\mathbf{p}[\![g = \text{boolean}]\!] = \left\{ \begin{array}{l} \mathbf{r}[\![g]\!](x) \rightarrow \langle\!\langle x = \textbf{true}\rangle\!\rangle, \\ \mathbf{r}[\![g]\!](x) \rightarrow \langle\!\langle x = \textbf{false}\rangle\!\rangle \end{array} \right\} \tag{2}$$

$$\mathbf{p}[\![g = \text{int}]\!] = \left\{ \begin{array}{l} \mathbf{r}[\![g]\!](x) \rightarrow \langle\!\langle x = 0\rangle\!\rangle, \\ \mathbf{r}[\![g]\!](x) \rightarrow \mathbf{r}[\![g]\!](x); \langle\!\langle x = x + 1\rangle\!\rangle \end{array} \right\} \tag{3}$$

$$\mathbf{p}[\![g = \text{string}]\!] = \left\{ \begin{array}{l} \mathbf{r}[\![g]\!](x) \rightarrow \langle\!\langle x = ""\rangle\!\rangle, \\ \mathbf{r}[\![g]\!](x) \rightarrow \mathbf{r}[\![g]\!](x); \langle\!\langle x = x\|c\rangle\!\rangle \quad \text{for every } c \end{array} \right\} \tag{4}$$

$$\mathbf{p}[\![g = \{c_1, \ldots, c_n\}]\!] = \{ \mathbf{r}[\![g]\!](x) \rightarrow \langle\!\langle x = "c_i"\rangle\!\rangle \quad \text{for every } c_i \} \tag{5}$$

$$\mathbf{p}[\![g = t[g']]\!] = \left\{ \begin{array}{l} \mathbf{r}[\![g]\!](x) \rightarrow \langle\!\langle \text{if } (x \equiv \textbf{null})\ x = \textbf{new } t[g']\rangle\!\rangle; \\ \mathbf{r}[\![g']\!](y); \langle\!\langle x.t = y\rangle\!\rangle \end{array} \right\} \cup \mathbf{p}[\![g']\!] \tag{6}$$

$$\mathbf{p}[\![g = g'\{0,1\}]\!] = \left\{ \begin{array}{l} \mathbf{r}[\![g]\!](x) \rightarrow \langle\!\langle x = \textbf{null}\rangle\!\rangle, \\ \mathbf{r}[\![g]\!](x) \rightarrow \mathbf{r}[\![g']\!](x), \end{array} \right\} \cup \mathbf{p}[\![g']\!] \tag{7}$$

$$\mathbf{p}[\![g = g'\{0,\infty\}]\!] = \left\{ \begin{array}{l} \mathbf{r}[\![g]\!](x) \rightarrow \langle\!\langle x = []\rangle\!\rangle, \\ \mathbf{r}[\![g]\!](x) \rightarrow \mathbf{r}[\![g']\!](y); \mathbf{r}[\![g]\!](x), \langle\!\langle x = x\|y\rangle\!\rangle \end{array} \right\} \cup \mathbf{p}[\![g']\!] \tag{8}$$

$$\mathbf{p}[\![g = g'\{0,n\}]\!] = \left\{ \begin{array}{l} \mathbf{r}[\![g]\!](x) \rightarrow \langle\!\langle x = []\rangle\!\rangle, \\ \mathbf{r}[\![g]\!](x) \rightarrow \mathbf{r}[\![g']\!](y); \langle\!\langle x = [y]\rangle\!\rangle, \\ \ldots \\ \mathbf{r}[\![g]\!](x) \rightarrow \mathbf{r}[\![g']\!](y_1); \ldots; \mathbf{r}[\![g']\!](y_n); \\ \langle\!\langle x = [y_1, \ldots, y_n]\rangle\!\rangle \end{array} \right\} \cup \mathbf{p}[\![g']\!] \tag{9}$$

$$\mathbf{p}[\![g = g'\{m,n\}]\!] = \left\{ \begin{array}{l} \mathbf{r}[\![g]\!](x) \rightarrow \mathbf{r}[\![g']\!](y_1); \ldots; \mathbf{r}[\![g']\!](y_m); \\ \mathbf{r}[\![g'']\!](x); \langle\!\langle x = [y_1, \ldots, y_m]\|x\rangle\!\rangle \end{array} \right\}$$
$$\cup \mathbf{p}[\![g'']\!] \cup \mathbf{p}[\![g']\!] \text{ where } g'' \rightarrow g'\{0, n-m\} \tag{10}$$

$$\mathbf{p}[\![g = g_1, \ldots, g_k]\!] = \{\mathbf{r}[\![g]\!](x) \rightarrow \mathbf{r}[\![g_1]\!](x); \ldots; \mathbf{r}[\![g_k]\!](x)\} \cup \bigcup_{i=1}^{k} \mathbf{p}[\![g_i]\!] \tag{11}$$

$$\mathbf{p}[\![g = g_1| \ldots |g_k]\!] = \bigcup_{i=1}^{k} \{\mathbf{r}[\![g]\!](x) \rightarrow \mathbf{r}[\![g_i]\!](x)\} \cup \mathbf{p}[\![g_i]\!] \tag{12}$$

For a nonterminal g, $\mathbf{p}[\![g]\!]$ is the set of associated grammar rules, $\mathbf{r}[\![g]\!]$ is a unique name suitable for a grammar nonterminal, $\mathbf{t}[\![g]\!]$ is the unique Java type for that position in the XML Schema grammar, and x and y designate an XML document or subdocument.

Fig. 4. MSL to interface grammar translation rules

Rule (2) translates Boolean types by simply enumerating both possible values. Calling $\mathbf{r}[\![g]\!](x)$ with an uninitialized variable x will set x to either **true** or

false. Rule (3) translates integer numbers to a Java instance by starting at 0 and executing an unbounded number of successor operations. If the number is bounded we can generate it more efficiently by creating one production for each value. However, Rule (3) allows us to generate an infinite number of values. We can also accommodate negative integers using Rule (3) and then choosing a sign.

Rule (4) translates strings to Java strings. It starts with an empty string and concatenates an unbounded number of characters onto it, to generate all possible string values. It should be noted that strings are frequently used as unspecified enumerations, have possible correlations with other parts of the object graph, or have some associated structure they should maintain (as in search queries), etc. Accordingly, the automatically generated grammar can be refined to something more restricted but also more useful by manually changing these rules.

Rule (5) takes care of enumerated types by providing one rule to generate each possible value of that type.

Rule (6) translates tags into Java objects. The rule is simple; we figure out which Java type Axis is using for this position using $\mathbf{t}[\![g]\!]$, if it is not already initialized (which can happen if we are applying Rule (11)) instantiate it, recursively process its contents, and then set the contents to the t field on the object we are currently working on. Rule (7) translates optional elements into Java objects by having two rules, one for **null** and the other to generate the object.

Rule (8) translates unbounded arrays into Java objects. We start with the base case of an empty array and concatenate objects onto it. Rule (9) translates bounded arrays into Java objects, by simply generating n rules, one for each potential object. Although we give this simple rule here for readability, in our implementation we handle this case more efficiently.

Rule (10) translates general arrays, that may have a minimum number of objects greater than 0, to a situation where one of Rule (8) or Rule (9) applies. Rule (11) translates sequences into Java objects; we simply apply each of the sub-rules to the object graph under examination in sequence. Rule (12) translates alternations into Java objects; we pick one of the sub-rules and apply it.

As an example of translation, consider the MSL type for the DoExpress-CheckoutPaymentResponse message in the PayPal WSDL specification mentioned above. First, the production rules for the basic types string and integer are:

$$string(\text{doc}) \rightarrow \langle\!\langle \text{doc} = \texttt{""} \rangle\!\rangle$$
$$string(\text{doc}) \rightarrow string(\text{doc}); \langle\!\langle \text{doc} = \text{doc}\|c \rangle\!\rangle \quad \text{for every character } c$$
$$int(\text{doc}) \rightarrow \langle\!\langle \text{doc} = \mathbf{0} \rangle\!\rangle$$
$$int(\text{doc}) \rightarrow int(\text{doc}); \langle\!\langle \text{doc} = \text{doc} + 1 \rangle\!\rangle$$

The message type consists of a sequence. For the first element of the sequence, we need to apply Rule (6) followed by Rule (4), resulting in the following grammar production:

$a(\text{doc}) \rightarrow \langle\!\langle \text{if } (\text{doc} \equiv \textbf{null}) \, \text{doc} = \textbf{new Token} \rangle\!\rangle; string(\text{doc}_1); \langle\!\langle \text{doc.\textbf{Token}} = \text{doc}_1 \rangle\!\rangle$

with start symbol a. Applying these productions can assign to *doc* a subdocument like <Token>abc</Token>. Nonterminal a is responsible for the creation of the Token element, and repeated application of the productions for the *string* nonterminal creates an arbitrary value for the string field.

For the second element of the sequence we apply Rule (6) which leads to another sequence. Then we apply Rule (11) followed by three applications of Rule (6), two applications of Rule (4) and one application of Rule (3). The resulting productions are:

$b(\text{doc}) \rightarrow \langle\!\langle \text{if } (\text{doc} \equiv \textbf{null}) \, \text{doc} = \textbf{new PaymentInfo} \rangle\!\rangle; c(\text{doc}_1); d(\text{doc}_1); e(\text{doc}_1);$
$\qquad\qquad \langle\!\langle \text{doc.\textbf{PaymentInfo}} = \text{doc}_1 \rangle\!\rangle$

$c(\text{doc}) \rightarrow \langle\!\langle \text{if } (\text{doc} \equiv \textbf{null}) \, \text{doc} = \textbf{new PaymentInfoTransactionID} \rangle\!\rangle; string(\text{doc}_1);$
$\qquad\qquad \langle\!\langle \text{doc.\textbf{PaymentInfoTransactionID}} = \text{doc}_1 \rangle\!\rangle$

$d(\text{doc}) \rightarrow \langle\!\langle \text{if } (\text{doc} \equiv \textbf{null}) \, \text{doc} = \textbf{new PaymentInfoGrossAmount} \rangle\!\rangle; int(\text{doc}_1);$
$\qquad\qquad \langle\!\langle \text{doc.\textbf{PaymentInfoGrossAmount}} = \text{doc}_1 \rangle\!\rangle$

$e(\text{doc}) \rightarrow \langle\!\langle \text{if } (\text{doc} \equiv \textbf{null}) \, \text{doc} = \textbf{new PaymentInfoPendingReason} \rangle\!\rangle; string(\text{doc}_1);$
$\qquad\qquad \langle\!\langle \text{doc.\textbf{PaymentInfoPendingReason}} = \text{doc}_1 \rangle\!\rangle$

with start symbol b. Finally, we apply Rule (11) one more time resulting in one additional nonterminal and production:

$$DoExpressCheckoutPaymentResponse(\text{doc}) \rightarrow a(\text{doc}); b(\text{doc})$$

3.2   Control-Flow and Messages

Using the translation scheme described above, terminal symbols standing for messages in the grammar of Figure 3 can be expanded into productions for validating or generating individual message instances. For example, the ¡DECOP terminal symbol refers to a message of type DoExpressCheckoutPaymentResponse. Generating such a message simply amounts to expanding the respective message productions according to the derivation rules we have just shown.

Recall that production symbols in an interface grammar can carry additional parameters that can be used to refer to specific elements of messages. These parameters can be passed on from message to message to express correlations between parameters across a whole transaction.

In the case of the ¡DECOP symbol, we attach two parameters: token and transactionid, standing for the values of message elements of the same name. We must therefore associate these two variables with the actual content of the production that relates to these values:

$$a'(\text{doc}, \text{token}) \rightarrow \langle\!\langle \text{if } (\text{doc} \equiv \textbf{null}) \text{ doc} = \textbf{new Token}\rangle\!\rangle; \, string(\text{token});$$
$$\langle\!\langle \text{doc}.\textbf{Token} = token\rangle\!\rangle$$

$$b'(\text{doc}, \text{transactionid}) \rightarrow \langle\!\langle \text{if } (\text{doc} \equiv \textbf{null}) \text{ doc} = \textbf{new PaymentInfo}\rangle\!\rangle;$$
$$c'(\text{doc}_1, \text{transactionid}); \, d(\text{doc}_1); \, e(\text{doc}_1);$$
$$\langle\!\langle \text{doc}.\textbf{PaymentInfo} = \text{doc}_1\rangle\!\rangle$$

$$c'(\text{doc}, \text{transactionid}) \rightarrow \langle\!\langle \text{if } (\text{doc} \equiv \textbf{null}) \text{ doc} = \textbf{new PaymentInfoTransactionID}\rangle\!\rangle;$$
$$string(\text{transactionid});$$
$$\langle\!\langle \text{doc}.\textbf{PaymentInfoTransactionID} = \text{transactionid}\rangle\!\rangle$$

Finally, the rule for ¡DECOP itself can be obtained by:

$$\text{¡DECOP}(\text{doc}, \text{token}, \text{transactionid}) \rightarrow a'(\text{doc}, \text{token}); b'(\text{doc}, \text{transactionid});$$

This mechanism is not restricted to primitive types; for example, the "items" argument of the !SECO message stands for the list of items; this element itself is formed of multiple item elements with values for name, amount, and so on.

This particular characteristic of our translation to interface grammars is fundamental. By expressing message structures, parameter values and control flow in a uniform notation, all such properties of a given service are taken into account in one specification framework. For example, by using the above rules to simulate an Express Checkout client, we have that: 1) if the client invokes Set-ExpressCheckout with some token i, then the client expects a response with the same token value; 2) the client is guaranteed to eventually invoke Get and Do with that same token i. Additionally, if the client invokes SetExpressCheckout with an action value of "Sale" for token i, then the DoExpressCheckoutPayment message that will be eventually sent for token i will also have the value "Sale". These constraints could not be handled if the messages were generated by a procedure independent of the control flow constraints.

4   Experiments

To demonstrate the value of our approach, we studied two web services: the Amazon E-Commerce Service provided by Amazon.com and the PayPal Web Service API that we used as a running example throughout the paper.

4.1   Amazon E-Commerce Service

The Amazon E-Commerce Service (AWS-ECS) [3] provides access to Amazon's product data through a SOAP interface specified with WSDL. It was analyzed in an earlier paper [17]; however, although it was not mentioned at the time, the interface grammar for the six key operations (ItemSearch, CartCreate, CartAdd, CartModify, CartGet, and CartClear) was generated automatically from the WSDL specification of the AWS-ECS. These six operations also have several control flow constraints that are not stated in the WSDL specification of the AWS-ECS. We extended the automatically generated interface grammar by adding these extra constraints. The data summarized below, and the interface grammar itself, are described in more detail in [17].

We used the interface grammar both for client and server side verification, as shown in Figure 1. The AWS-ECS client we used in our experiments is called the AWS Java Sample. This client performs no validation on its input data whatsoever. It is intended as a programming example showing how to use the SOAP and REST interfaces, not as something to use. Hence, it serves as a suitable vehicle to demonstrate the bug finding capabilities of our approach.

We fed the interface grammar for the AWS-ECS to our interface compiler and generated a service stub for the AWS-ECS. We combined this service stub with the AWS Java Sample for client verification. We used the Java PathFinder (JPF) [9] to systematically search the state space of the resulting system. Note that a model checker like JPF is not able to analyze the AWS Java Sample without the automatically generated service stub provided by our interface compiler.

We analyzed three types of errors that the client, were it doing proper input validation, would catch: type failures happen when the user enters a string when an integer is expected; data failures occur when the user attempts to add a nonexistent item to a nonexistent cart (the request is syntactically valid, but nonsensical); uncorrelated data failures involve two operations that are in the correct sequence, but the data associated with the two calls violates the extra constraints (for example, editing an item that was previously removed from the cart). We were able to discover the type failures in 12.5 seconds using 25 MB of memory, the data failures in 11.1 seconds using 25 MB of memory and the uncorrelated data failures in 20.8 seconds using 43 MB of memory.

For server verification, our interface compiler takes the interface specification as input and automatically generates a driver that sends SOAP requests to the web service. We ran ten tests using a sentence generator that chooses the next production randomly. In each of these tests, the sentence generator was run until it produced 100 SOAP message sequences, which were sent to the AWS-ECS server. The average execution time for the tests was 430.2 seconds (i.e., 4.3 seconds per sequence). On average, the driver took 17.5 steps per derivation, and each such derivation produced 3.2 SOAP requests.

These tests uncovered two errors, corresponding to mismatches between the interface grammar specification and the AWS-ECS implementation:

1. The AWS-ECS implementation does not allow multiple add requests for the same item, although this is not clear from the specification of the service.
2. We assumed that a shopping cart with no items in it would have an items array with zero length. However, in the implementation this scenario leads to a shopping cart with a null items array. This was not clarified in the AWS-ECS specification.

4.2   PayPal Express Checkout Service

As a second case study, we conducted server side verification for PayPal's Express Checkout API. The running example in earlier sections is a simplified version of this API. As we did for the server side verification of the AWS-ECS service, we used a random sentence generator algorithm that sends SOAP requests to PayPal's web service. Our tests uncovered two errors. Again, these errors correspond to discrepancies between the interface grammar specification and the API's actual implementation:

1. In a SetExpressCheckout request, elements CancelURL and ReturnURL cannot be arbitrary strings; they must be valid URLs. This is not written in the API documentation or in the WSDL, which only specify it must be a string. It took 5.7 seconds to find this error.
2. The implementation does not allow a client to set its own token in a SetExpressCheckout request. If the client does not use a token previously returned by another SetExpressCheckout request, it has to set the token to the empty string and reuse what SetExpressCheckout gives back. Again this constraint was not clear from the documentation. It took 2.5 seconds to catch this error.

Once we modified the interface grammar specification to reflect these constraints, the driver did not produce any more errors. The round-trip time to generate each new message from the grammar, send it, get and parse the response from PayPal took about 1 second.

5 Related Work

Earlier work has been done on grammar-based testing. For example, Sirer and Bershad [21] have developed a grammar-based test tool, *lava*, with a focus on validating Java Virtual Machine implementations. Test data has been generated using enhanced context-free grammars [19], regular grammars [8] and attributed grammars [12]. None of these tools focus on web service verification —they use grammars to characterize inputs rather than interfaces.

Some approaches attempt to automate the testing of web services by taking advantage of their WSDL definitions. Available tools like soapUI [2] allow a user to create so-called "mock web services" whose goal is to mimic the actual web service requests and responses; for each such operation, the tool generates a message skeleton that the user can then manually populate with data fields. Other works automate this process entirely by simulating a web service through the generation of arbitrary, WSDL-compliant messages when requested [4, 7].

On the other hand, other works attempt to validate incoming and outgoing messages to ensure they are WSDL-compliant. The Java API for XML Web Services (JAX-WS)[1] provides a validator for that purpose; the IBM Web Service Validation Tool[2] validates a trace of SOAP messages against WSDL specifications. Cacciagrano et al. [11] push the concept further and validate not only the structure of messages, but also additional constraints such as dependencies between values inside a message.

[1] https://jax-ws.dev.java.net/
[2] http://www.alphaworks.ibm.com/tech/wsvt

However, all these previous approaches treat request-response as patterns independently of each other; therefore, they do not allow properties where values generated in some messages constrain the control flow of the web service, as we have shown is the case in PayPal's Express Checkout.

6   Conclusion

We proposed and implemented a translator to automatically generate an interface grammar skeleton from a WSDL specification. This interface grammar skeleton can be combined with control flow constraints to generate an interface specification that characterizes both control and data-flow constraints in a uniform manner. Using the actual documentation and WSDL specification from the PayPal Express Checkout API, we have shown how such automatically generated grammar skeletons can be extended with control flow constraints to obtain interface grammars that specify the interaction behavior of web services. These interface grammars can then be automatically converted to web service stubs and drivers to enable verification and testing. We also applied these techniques to a client for the key interfaces of the Amazon E-Commerce Service and also to the Amazon E-Commerce Service server directly, and have demonstrated that our approach is feasible and efficient.

References

1. PayPal web service API documentation (2008), http://www.paypal.com
2. soapUI: the web services testing tool (2009), http://www.soapui.org/
3. Amazon web services, http://solutions.amazonwebservices.com/
4. Bai, X., Dong, W., Tsai, W.-T., Chen, Y.: WSDL-based automatic test case generation for web services testing. In: IEEE International Workshop on Service-Oriented System Engineering, SOSE 2005, pp. 207–212 (2005)
5. Barbon, F., Traverso, P., Pistore, M., Trainotti, M.: Run-time monitoring of instances and classes of web service compositions. In: Proceedings of the 2006 IEEE International Conference on Web Services (ICWS 2006), pp. 63–71 (2006)
6. Baresi, L., Guinea, S., Kazhamiakin, R., Pistore, M.: An integrated approach for the run-time monitoring of BPEL orchestrations. In: Proceedings of the First European Conference Towards a Service-Based Internet (ServiceWave 2008), pp. 1–12 (2008)
7. Bartolini, C., Bertolino, A., Marchetti, E., Polini, A.: Towards automated WSDL-based testing of web services. In: Bouguettaya, A., Krueger, I., Margaria, T. (eds.) ICSOC 2008. LNCS, vol. 5364, pp. 524–529. Springer, Heidelberg (2008)
8. Bauer, J.A., Finger, A.B.: Test plan generation using formal grammars. In: Proceedings of the 4th International Conference on Software Engineering, Munich, Germany, September 1979, pp. 425–432 (1979)
9. Brat, G., Havelund, K., Park, S., Visser, W.: Java pathfinder: Second generation of a Java model checker. In: Proceedings Workshop on Advances in Verification (2000)
10. Brown, A., Fuchs, M., Robie, J., Wadler, P.: MSL: a model for W3C XML Schema. In: Proceedings of the 10th International World Wide Web Conference, pp. 191–200 (2001)

11. Cacciagrano, D., Corradini, F., Culmone, R., Vito, L.: Dynamic constraint-based invocation of web services. In: Bravetti, M., Núñez, M., Zavattaro, G. (eds.) WS-FM 2006. LNCS, vol. 4184, pp. 138–147. Springer, Heidelberg (2006)
12. Duncan, A.G., Hutchison, J.S.: Using attributed grammars to test designs and implementations. In: Proceedings of the 5th International Conference on Software Engineering, New York, NY, USA, March 1981, pp. 170–178 (1981)
13. Hallé, S., Villemaire, R.: Runtime monitoring of message-based workflows with data. In: Proceedings of the 12th International Enterprise Distributed Object Computing Conference (EDOC 2008), pp. 63–72 (2008)
14. Hallé, S., Villemaire, R.: Browser-based enforcement of interface contracts in web applications with BeepBeep. In: Bouajjani, A., Maler, O. (eds.) CAV 2009. LNCS, vol. 5643, pp. 648–653. Springer, Heidelberg (2009)
15. Hughes, G., Bultan, T.: Extended interface grammars for automated stub generation. In: Proceedings of the Automated Formal Methods Workshop, AFM 2007 (2007)
16. Hughes, G., Bultan, T.: Interface grammars for modular software model checking. IEEE Trans. Software Eng. 34(5), 614–632 (2008)
17. Hughes, G., Bultan, T., Alkhalaf, M.: Client and server verification for web services using interface grammars. In: Bultan, T., Xie, T. (eds.) TAV-WEB, pp. 40–46. ACM, New York (2008)
18. Mahbub, K., Spanoudakis, G.: Run-time monitoring of requirements for systems composed of web-services: Initial implementation and evaluation experience. In: Proceedings of the 2005 IEEE International Conference on Web Services (ICWS 2005), pp. 257–265 (2005)
19. Maurer, P.M.: Generating test data with enhanced context-free grammars. IEEE Software 7(4), 50–55 (1990)
20. Meredith, G., Bjorg, S.: Contracts and types. Commun. ACM 46(10), 41–47 (2003)
21. Sirer, E., Bershad, B.N.: Using production grammars in software testing. In: Proceedings of DSL 1999: the 2nd Conference on Domain-Specific Languages, Austin, TX, US, pp. 1–13 (1999)

Satisfaction of Control Objectives by Control Processes*

Daniela Marino[1], Fabio Massacci[2], Andrea Micheletti[1], Nataliya Rassadko[2],
and Stephan Neuhaus[2]

[1] Fondazione Centro San Raffaele del Monte Tabor
e-Services for Life & Health Unit, Via Olgettina 60 - 20132 - Milano, Italy
surname.name@hsr.it
[2] Dipartimento di Ingegneria e Scienze dell'Informazione
Università degli Studi di Trento, via Sommarive 14 - 38100 Trento, Italy
name.surname@disi.unitn.it

Abstract. Showing that business processes comply with regulatory requirements
is not easy. We investigate this compliance problem in the case that the requirements are expressed as a directed, acyclic graph, with high-level requirements
(called *control objectives*) at the top and with low-level requirements (called
control activities) at the bottom. These control activities are then implemented
by *control processes*. We introduce two algorithms: the first identifies whether a
given set of control activities is sufficient to satisfy the top-level control objectives; the second identifies those steps of control processes that contribute to the
satisfaction of top-level control objectives. We illustrate these concepts and the
algorithms by examples taken from a large healthcare provider.

1 Introduction

Processes – no matter whether executed by people or by machines – are often governed
by desirable or prescribed features of their execution. For example, if an Italian hospital dispenses drugs to a patient, the identity of the person requesting the dispensation
must appear in an audit log, according to Legislative Decree no. 196 of 30 June 2003
"personal data protection code", "Computerized Authentication System", clauses 1, 2,
3 and 6 [25]. Processes that have these features are called *compliant*.

Designers of such processes are faced with a dilemma: the desirable features are
listed as high-level control objectives, e.g., "Processing operations may only be performed by persons in charge of the processing that act under the direct authority of
either the data controller or the data processor by complying with the instructions received", but the actions to which such control objectives pertain happen at a much lower
level, e.g., "look up the user's ID and check authorization". In order to know that the
action is influenced by the control objective, that objective must be successively decomposed until it is clear to which process steps it pertains. For example, a sub-objective of
"Personal data undergoing processing shall be kept [...] in such a way as to minimize
[...] the risk of their destruction or loss," [25, Section 31] could be "patient records may
only be deleted after authorization by at least two authorized persons".

---

* Research partly supported by the EU under the project EU-IST-IP-MASTER (FP7-216917).

L. Baresi, C.-H. Chi, and J. Suzuki (Eds.): ICSOC-ServiceWave 2009, LNCS 5900, pp. 531–545, 2009.

It may not be feasible to implement *all* the actions that are prescribed by control objectives. In this case, we want to know whether the subset that we *have* implemented is sufficient to guarantee the satisfaction of the high-level objective. For example, we could prescribe that patient records are anonymized even as they are assembled for sending to the local health administration. But failing to implement this anonymization would not be fatal if the records are anonymized during the sending process.

In this paper, we consider this problem on three levels:

- on the *design level*, we consider the decomposition of control objectives into sub-objectives. The objectives then become successively more specific on refinement until we consider them to be atomic. These atomic objectives can then be either implemented or not. We ask: "given a decomposition of objectives into sub-objectives and atomic objectives, and given that certain atomic objectives are implemented and others not, are the top-level objectives satisfied?" This allows us to claim compliance at the design level, when we plan to satisfy certain atomic control objectives, but don't have a concrete implementation yet.
- on the *implementation level*, we first consider the implementation of atomic objectives by processes. Steps in these processes will contribute to the satisfaction of different atomic control objectives. So we ask, "Does execution of a particular control process lead to the satisfaction of the top-level objectives?" This allows us to claim compliance by *adding independent controls*.
- on the *process level*, we recognize that control processes are usually woven into processes instead of being separate processes by themselves. For example, checking a user's authentication and authorization are usually parts of processes instead of being realized as separate processes. If we are given, for each process step, a list of atomic control objectives to whose satisfaction it contributes, we ask, "does every execution of this process lead to the satisfaction of the top-level control objective?" This allows us to claim compliance by *adding process-specific controls or by analysing controls that are already in place*.

Since control objectives are expressed in natural language, their decomposition and refinement, i.e., *design* is intrinsically a manual process requiring the presence of a human expert. We consider the automation of the rest, i.e. *implementation* and *process*, can be automated. So this paper is organized as follows: after introducing our case study (§ 2), we formalize the problem (§ 3). Then, we look at the problems of objective satisfaction through the implementation of atomic control objectives (§ 4) and compliance of control process. (§ 5). After that, we review related work (§ 6) and finish with conclusions and further work (§ 7).

2   Example: Outpatient Drug Reimbursement

The case study considered in this paper is based on a concrete process from Hospital San Raffaele (HSR) in Milano, Italy, and concerns drug reimbursement.

Private Hospitals with a officially recognized public functions (such as HSR) are charged with administering drugs or with providing diagnostic services to patients that use their structure (e.g,, because the corresponding public services are overbooked) and then are authorized to claim the cost of drug dispensation or diagnostic provisioning from the regional state health administration.

The Italian Direct Drug Reimbursement process is a mechanism that allows refunding hospitals for drugs administered or supplied in the outpatient departments to patients that are not hospitalized; this mechanism is called "File F" and guarantees continuity of care regardless of the different forms in which that care is provided.

As a consequence of their public function and because they treat sensitive data, the processes of HSR are highly regulated:

– First, the e-health services have to respect the Health Governmental Authority (e.g. Ministry, Regional Health authority, etc.) indications; these regulations or guidelines have to be followed by all the healthcare institutions and concern a wide spectrum of norms, e.g., from the Personal Electronic Health Record to the Accreditation procedures, from the clinical practice to the price of the hospital treatments. Moreover, the e-health services usually follow the healthcare standards related to a specific domain, such as HL7, DICOM, HIPAA, etc., depending on the service.

– Other regulations to consider are the Governmental indications about the privacy matters (personal data protection); the European framework is regulated by the "Directive 95/46/EC - privacy framework" that have to be implemented by each European state. There is also to consider the Directive 2002/58/EC concerning the processing of personal data and the protection of privacy in the electronic communications sector and other governmental regulations regarding digital signatures, health data storage, etc.

– The final regulatory framework consists of Information & Communication Technologies Security standards, such as ISO/IEC 27002 [16] "code of practice for In formation Security management", the ISO 15408 "Common Criteria for IT Security Evaluation" [17], the COBIT framework [15], ITIL [24], etc. Sometimes also business agreements between suppliers and customers impose security requirements.

In order to give an idea of the sheer volume of regulation, the simple process of authorization and accounting for the dispensation and recompensation of drugs (called "File F") is subject to the following (not exhaustive) set of regulations: Legislative Decree no. 196 of 30 June 2003 [25] "personal data protection code", "Additional Measures Applying to Processing of Sensitive or Judicial Data" clause 20; "Computerized Authentication System" clauses 1, 2, 3, 5; annex B, "processing by electronic means", "authorization system" clauses 12, and 13, as well as regional circular 17/SAN 3.4.1997, which is successively amended by various notes and circulars such as Circular No. 5/SAN 30_1_2004 [3], Circular No. 45/SAN 23_12_2004 [6], Note 30.11.2007 H1.2007.0050480 [5], Note 27.3.2008 H1.2008.0012810 [4], and Note 04.12.2008 H1.-2008.0044229 [7].

All the regulations and best practices above mentioned contribute to the definition of the control objectives of the HSR business process for performing regulatory compliance analysis. The set of control objectives for the File F process activities is augmented by various business objectives (also called business goals) that have to be satisfied to reach the correct process results.

3 Conceptual Model

Recall from Section 1 that we view processes as being governed by desirable or pre-scribed features of their execution, features which we called *control objectives*. In this section, we will formalize the concepts of objectives and objective decomposition, as well as the concept of implementing an atomic objective.

Control Objectives (COs) are requirements on the internal operations of a business that describe what needs to be done (e.g.,. follow certain industry best practices) or what needs to be achieved (e.g., certain states or outcomes). However, control objectives are not actionable because they are phrased as requirements, not as procedures.

Example 1 (Regulatory Requirement). For the File F process, one regulatory require-ment is "Legislative Decree no. 196 of 30 June 2003 'personal data protection code', 'Additional Measures Applying to Processing of Sensitive or Judicial Data', clause 20".

Example 2 (Control Objective). For the regulatory requirement described above, the following objectives (from ISO 27002) are particularly relevant: "access control" and "user access management".

Control objectives like "access control" are not actionable. Rather, they have to be re-fined to a level where it is clear to which part of the business these refined objectives pertain and such that further refinement is no longer needed. We call such atomic objec-tives *control activities* (CAs). They are the policies, procedures, mechanisms, and orga-nizational structures that are put in place to assure that control objectives are achieved. Control activities are embedded in business processes; that is they affect and change the inner workings of a business. Common synonyms include controls, countermeasures, and safeguards as well. Control activities, by definition, *are* actionable, because they are phrased as procedures.

Example 3 (Control Activity). One control activity that is pertinent to the control objec-tive would be (in ISO 27002 parlance) "User registration", or (in procedural parlance) "register users before granting them access".

The problem is now to translate somehow from control objectives to control activities so that if we implement and execute the control activities, we automatically satisfy the control objectives.

To this end, we introduce the concept of *control objective refinement*, i.e., the re-placement of a control objective by a number of more specific control sub-objectives that together contribute to the satisfaction of the control objective.

Example 4 (Objective Decomposition). The control objective "access control" in the File F example is achieved by having (from ISO 27002) "user access management" and "user responsibilities".

A decomposition can therefore be seen as a graph whose nodes are the *control objec-tives*, which have the property of being satisfiable. Control objectives have a number of sub-objectives that contribute to its satisfaction, which is expressed by drawing a di-rected edge from the objective to its sub-objective. We distinguish between two cases:

Fig. 1. Constructs of process decomposition. Composite processes are represented as boxes, tasks (atomic process that cannot be decomposed) are shown as rectangles with rounded corners. The flow of decomposition is denoted by an arrow. AND-decomposition (execution of all subprocesses required) is shown by a circle with plus inside, while (exclusive) OR (execution of at most one subprocess is required) is denoted as a circle with a O inside.

- When the satisfaction of a single sub-objective is sufficient to satisfy the objective, we call the objective *OR-decomposed*.
- When all sub-objectives need to be satisfied in order to satisfy the objective, we call the objective *AND-decomposed*.

Leaves (control objectives that have no sub-objectives) are so specific that they are actionable and are therefore *control activities*. For the purpose of checking compliance, they have the property of being *implemented* or not. It is also reasonable to assume that refinement is acyclic, i.e., that no objective ultimately depends on itself for fulfillment. More formally, we have therefore:

Definition 1 (Objective Model). *An objective model is a non-empty, directed, acyclic graph $G = (V,E)$, where V is a set of nodes that can be either control objectives or control activities, and where $(m,n) \in E$ if n is a sub-objective of m so that n contributes to the satisfaction of m. For $n \in V$, we write $n.\text{parents} := \{m \mid (m,n) \in E\}$ and $n.\text{children} := \{m \mid (n,m) \in E\}$.*

Since G is nonempty and acyclic, there exists a nonempty set of nodes n with $n.\text{parents} = \emptyset$. These are those objectives that do not function as sub-objectives to other objectives and are therefore called *global objectives*.

In our model, control activities they are implemented by *control processes* (CPs), including any configuration and maintenance work that is needed to keep the control operational. Control processes can be *structurally* composed of subprocesses, for which we use the notation shown in Fig. 1.

Example 5 (Process Decomposition). In Fig. 2 (left), we used a standard business process notation to show a process of File F dispensation. Its structural decomposition is shown in Fig. 2 (right). Namely, P_1 is the entire process depicted in Fig. 2 (left); P_2 is a sequence, consisting of all tasks before the first conditional diamond, P_3 is everything that is executed after the first conditional diamond. Note that P_2 and P_3 constitute an AND-decomposition of P_1. Next, P_2 is decomposed into and AND-structure consisting tasks $A2.1$, $A2.2$, $A2.3$. The decomposition of P_3 is more complex since it is the OR-decomposition consisting of the branches of the first conditional diamond. Therefore, it is either P_4, which is the YES-branch, or P_5, which is NO-branch.

Example 6 (Process-to-Objective Assignment). The overall conceptual model is shown on Fig. 3. The upper part of the figure is an objective model, where ovals and hexagons represent COs and CAs respectively. Namely, the global objective CO_3 can be satisfied

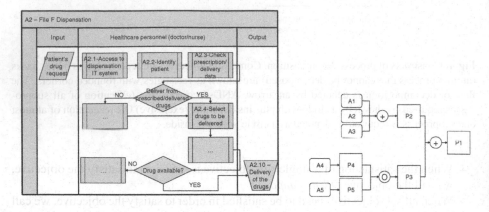

Fig. 2. File F Dispensation process (left) and its structural decomposition (right)

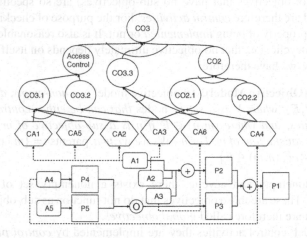

Fig. 3. Control objective satisfaction by executing control processes

if all CO_2 and $CO_{3.3}$ and AC (standing for *Access Control*) are satisfied. In their turn, satisfaction of CO_2 depends on satisfaction of both $CO_{2.1}$ and $CO_{2.2}$, where the first depends on implementation of activities CA_3 and CA_4 and the second depends on activity CA_3 only. On the other hand, the satisfaction of CO_3 requires an implementation of both CA_3 and CA_6. AC is satisfied if either $CO_{3.1}$ or $CO_{3.2}$ are satisfied. The satisfaction of the latter COs rely on implementation of $\{CA_1, CA_2, CA_5\}$ and CA_3 respectively. The explanation of all COs and CAs will be presented in Sec. 4.

The lower part of Fig. 3 is dedicated to an executable process P_1 which requires a necessary execution of both P_2 and P_3. The former is implemented by tasks A_1, A_2, A_3. The latter is decomposed into choice execution of P_4 and P_5 that are implemented by tasks A_4 and A_5 respectively.

During execution of a control process, we may contribute to the satisfaction of one of the sub-objectives of a global objective and hence ultimately to the satisfaction of that

Table 1. Control objectives, sub-objectives and control activities vs. regulatory requirements

Control objective (from ISO 27002)	Sub-objective (from ISO 27002)	Control activities (from ISO 27002)	Source of Regulatory Requirement
CO1: Access control	CO1.1: User access management	CA1 - User registration	Legislative Decree no. 196 of 30 June 2003 "personal data protection code", "Additional Measures Applying to Processing of Sensitive or Judicial Data" clause 20
		CA2 - User password management	Legislative Decree no. 196 of 30 June 2003 "personal data protection code", "Computerized Authentication System" clause 5. Legislative Decree no. 196 of 30 June 2003 "personal data protection code", "Additional Measures Applying to Processing of Sensitive or Judicial Data" clause 20
	CO1.2: User responsibilities	...	...
CO2: Information systems acquisition, development and maintenance	CO2.1: Correct processing in applications	CA3 - Control of internal processing	circular No.5/SAN 30.1.2004 and Note 30.11.2007 H1.2007.0050480 and Note 27.3.2008 H1.2008.0012810
		CA4 - Output data validation	circular No.5/SAN 30.1.2004 and Note 30.11.2007 H1.2007.0050480 and the Note 27.3.2008 H1.2008.0012810
	CO2.2: Technical vulnerability management	...	...

global objective itself. This is what we intuitively mean by *compliance* and what we show in Fig. 3 by a dotted line.

While process-to-objective assignment is an intrinsically human-related task [2], the compliance checking can be done automatically. For this purpose, we need to resolve the following problems:

1. Given a set of implemented CAs, we need to check whether the global COs are satisfied ("Problem of Satisfaction").
2. Given an implementation of CAs by tasks and (sub)processes, we need to check whether the entire process is compliant to the objective model ("Problem of Compliance").
3. Given the execution of a control process, we need to identify a set of (sub)processes, execution of which leads to a satisfaction of a concrete control objective ("Problem of Contribution").

Resolving the first problem will show us whether the mechanisms that we have (or want to have) in place are sufficient to satisfy our global objectives. The resolution of the last two problems will then make it possible for us to do check for compliance more effectively because, if we know exactly which sub-process contributes to which control objective, we can more easily establish what we need to monitor.

4   Specification: Control Objective Satisfaction

Considering the case study, starting from the Regulatory Requirements, we can obtain the control activities that have to be performed. In a practical way, it is possible to use standard control objectives, sub-objectives and control activities related to a specific

Table 2. Business objectives of the File F process

Process phase	Business/control objectives	Sub-objectives	Control activities (from ISO 27002)
A2. File F Dispensation	CO3: – Deliver the right drugs to the right patient; – Give input to logistic stock management	CO3.1: Doctors and nurses must have authorization and credentials for accessing the dispensation IT system	– CA1 - User Registration – CA2 - User Password management – CA5 - Review of User Access Right
		CO3.2: The original copy of prescription sheet with the signature of the doctor must be given to the nurse as dispensation request	– CA3 - Control of internal processing
		CO3.3: Prescription data must be univocally assigned to a patient	– CA3 - Control of internal processing – CA6 - Documented operating procedures

domain; for instance in our case we can consider the ISO 27002 "Information security management systems" standard. The specific control mechanisms to be implemented are then customized on the particular business process.

Table 1 reports an example of this methodology, where there is a mapping between the Regulatory requirements and the ISO control activities; the control mechanisms that will be implemented on our business process will have to satisfy the regulatory requirements[1].

On the other hand we can identify the control objectives, the sub-objectives and the control activities coming from the business objectives of our process, as shown in Table 2. Also in this case it is possible to refer to the ISO standard for having a common reference for the control activities.

Then control activities are implemented by processes compliant to regulations. However, for example, due to tight budget or other business/economical reasons, only a restricted set of activities can be implemented. However, the implemented activities should lead to the satisfaction of "global" control objectives.

In Fig. 4, we show our algorithm for satisfaction of global control objectives given the satisfaction of some control activities. The algorithm begins at the leaves (the CAs) of the objective model and proceeds upwards. To propagate satisfaction, we use an array UNTIL-SATISFIED that contains, for all nodes, a number of sub-nodes that need to be satisfied in order for the node to be satisfied as well. Lines 1–6 compute the initial value of UNTIL-SATISFIED: an implemented control activity is automatically satisfied; a non-implemented CA can never be satisfied. If a node is an AND-decomposed CO, all of its sub-objectives need to be satisfied; for an OR-decomposed CO, the satisfaction of a single sub-objective suffices.

We also use a queue that contains satisfied control objectives. Initially, the queue contains all satisfied leaves (implemented CAs). At each iteration of the **while** loop starting at line 7, one node is removed from the front of the queue and its parents are

---

[1] We do not include CO_1 (and its sub-objectives) into our objective model shown in Fig 3 because it is subsumed by $CO_{3.1}$.

Algorithm. PROBLEM OF SATISFACTION RESOLUTION

Input: A control objective model $G = (V, E)$
Output: Identifies if global COs are satisfied.
1: **for all** $n \in V$ **do**
2:     **if** n is a CA **then**
3:         UNTIL-SATISFIED $[n] := 0$ if n is implemented, 1 otherwise;
4:     **else**
5:         UNTIL-SATISFIED $[n] := |n.\text{children}|$ if n is AND-decomposed, 1 otherwise;
6: Insert into queue Q all nodes $n \in V$ with UNTIL-SATISFIED $[n] = 0$;
7: **while** Q is not empty **do**
8:     $n \leftarrow Q$;
9:     **for all** $n' \in n.\text{parents}()$ **do**
10:         **if** UNTIL-SATISFIED $[n] \neq 0$ **then**
11:             UNTIL-SATISFIED $[n'] :=$ UNTIL-SATISFIED $[n'] - 1$;
12:             **if** UNTIL-SATISFIED $[n'] = 0$ **then**
13:                 $Q \leftarrow n'$;

Fig. 4. Algorithm PROBLEM OF SATISFACTION RESOLUTION

examined. If the satisfaction of the current node is enough to also satisfy the parent, the parent is also marked as satisfied and appended to the end of the queue.

Theorem 1. *The algorithm is correct, terminates and has time complexity* $O(|V|^2)$.

In a nutshell, the correct outcome of algorithm run should result in UNTIL-SATISFIED $[CO] := 0$ if CO is satisfied, 1 otherwise; for any CO. This issue can be easily demonstrated by proof by contradiction. Termination of the algorithm is evident due to acyclicity of objective model and the fact that each node can be added to queue only once. Since in cycle **while** in line 7 lasts $O(|V|)$ iterations, $O(|V|)$ operations are performed in line 9 at each iteration, the complexity is $O(|V|^2)$.

5   Compliance of Control Processes

In this section, we want to tackle problems 2 and 3, namely which parts of a control process contribute to the satisfaction of control objectives.

Definition 2. *A Process-to-Activity Assignment is a mapping $\mathscr{A}$ from the set of processes to the set of control activities such that a process P is mapped to a control activity A if A is satisfied after P has completed. We write this assignment $P \rightarrow_{\mathscr{A}} A$ and say "P implements A".*

At the moment, we have no way of automating a process-to-activity assignment, so we assume that this is done manually.

Having identified process-to-activity assignment, we try to "dig" into each structural subprocess and to identify if this assignment may be alleviated. In other words, there might be many control processes assigned to one particular CA. This may happen not only because of the complexity of CA, but also because there is a need of "reserve" implementation that could be launched in the case of failure of the "main" implementation. Some of these assignments might be more costly to implement or difficult to audit, others might not. So, we want to identify the core subset of process-to-activity assignment which is necessary to implement in order to fulfill the root objectives. On the other hand, if we are able to distinguish some additional assignments leading to a "reserve" satisfaction of some COs, we will have a possibility to configure process-to-objective assignment in different ways w.r.t. our requirements to implementation cost or auditing difficulty.

Definition 3. *Let $G = (V, E)$ be a control objective model with a set G of global objectives, let $\{A_1, \ldots, A_n\} \subseteq V$ be a set of control activities, and let P be a process, composed of sub-processes $\{P_1, \ldots, P_m\}$ that implement control activities $A_1, \ldots, A_n$. Let $\mathcal{A}$ be a process-to-activity assignment. We call $\mathcal{A}$ correct if the global objectives in G are satisfied when P completes. In this case, we write $P \models G$.*

Given a process-to-activity assignment, we would like to test its correctness and also to identify which part of the process (1) is compliant with a particular control objective, and (2) contributes to a satisfaction of a particular control objective. We can answer these questions with the help of algorithm presented in Fig. 5. For this purpose, for each control objective $n \in V$, we maintain a set IMPLEMENTEDBY$[n]$ of those sub-processes of P that contribute to control objective satisfaction, and for each subprocess p of P, we maintain a set ACHIEVES$[p]$ that are implemented by that p.

The input of the algorithm is (1) a process-to-activity assignment, (2) the objective model, and (3) the control process and its sub-processes. From the process-to-activity assignment, we can easily instantiate IMPLEMENTEDBY and ACHIEVES for corresponding subprocesses and control objectives according to lines 7–10.

After this initialization, subprocesses start the propagation of their implementation to super-processes (parent processes). More precisely, each process p' implements those control objectives that are available for propagation of satisfaction from control objectives implemented by subprocesses of p'. To calculate such a reachability, we use the function Reach which is an algorithm PROBLEM OF SATISFACTION RESOLUTION having as input a set of satisfied control objectives or implemented CAs that are pushed into the queue. Respectively, values associated to the corresponding nodes in objective model are equal to "0", while the other nodes are associated the values according to the algorithm. The algorithm proceeds propagating satisfaction bottom-up. As soon as the algorithm terminates, satisfied control objectives represent the result of Reach function.

If super-process p' is AND-decomposed (flow or sequence of subprocesses), it satisfies all control objectives satisfied/implemented by each of its sub-processes. It means that we can propagate also satisfaction in the objective model. The satisfaction is propagated from the *union* of control objectives implemented by subprocesses of p'. On the other hand, if p' is OR-decomposed (choice), it can implement only those control objectives that are reachable from the *intersection* of control objectives implemented by subprocesses of p'. That is why OR-decomposition of process cannot implement AND-decomposition of objectives.

Theorem 2. *Algorithm PROBLEM OF COMPLIANCE AND CONTRIBUTION RESOLUTION is correct, terminates, and has time complexity $O((|V|^2 + |V|) \times |P|)$, where $|V|$ is the number of nodes in objective model, $|P|$ is the number of subprocesses of P.*

Proof. The correctness means that for each CO, IMPLEMENTEDBYCO contains only those elements that contribute to satisfaction of CO; for each p, ACHIEVESp contains only those elements that are satisfied by p.

Algorithm. PROBLEM OF COMPLIANCE AND CONTRIBUTION RESOLUTION

Input: A process-to-activity assignment $\mathscr{A}$, an objective model $G = (V, edges)$, an executable process P, composed of sub-processes $P_1, \ldots, P_n$.

Output: Structures that represent (1) compliance of each subprocess to a certain control objective, and (2) satisfaction of each control objective with a certain set of subprocesses of executable process.

```
1:  Put into Q_P all process that implement some CAs;
2:  for all nodes e of objective model do
3:      IMPLEMENTEDBY(e) = ∅;
4:  for all subprocesses and tasks P' of the executable process P do
5:      ACHIEVES(P') = ∅'
6:      VISITED[P'] := false;
7:  for all assignments P →_𝒜 {A_1, A_2, ..., A_n} do
8:      IMPLEMENTEDBY(A_i) := IMPLEMENTEDBY(A_i) ∪ {P};
9:      ACHIEVES(P) := ACHIEVES(P) ∪ {A_1, A_2, ..., A_n};
10:     VISITED[P] := true;
11: while Q_P is not empty do
12:     P' ← Q_P;
13:     for all p ∈ P'.superprocesses do
14:         if p is choice then
15:             ReachableObjectives := Reach(G, ∩_j{ACHIEVES(p.subprocesses())});
16:         else if p is flow or sequence then
17:             ReachableObjectives := Reach(G, ∪_j{ACHIEVES(p.subprocesses)});
18:         ACHIEVES(p) := ReachableObjectives;
19:         for all objectives CO ∈ ReachableObjectives do
20:             IMPLEMENTEDBY(CO) := IMPLEMENTEDBY(CO) ∪ {P'};
21:         if not VISITED[P'] then
22:             VISITED[P'] := true;
23:             Q_P ← P;
```

Fig. 5. Algorithm PROBLEM OF COMPLIANCE AND CONTRIBUTION RESOLUTION

We prove the correctness by the method of induction. The base of induction is a process-to-activity assignment $\mathscr{A}$, which is correct by default: for all assignments $P \to_{\mathscr{A}} \{A_1, A_2, \ldots, A_n\}$, the corresponding IMPLEMENTEDBY and ACHIEVES are calculated correctly.

Now let us consider any process p from process decomposition such that p $in\mathscr{A}$. Let's assume that for subprocesses of p, all ACHIEVES and corresponding IMPLEMENTEDBY are calculated correctly. Step of induction: ACHIEVES(p) is calculated correctly. Indeed, if ACHIEVES(p) is incorrect, then *ReachableObjectives* is calculated incorrectly. Since function Reach is correct by Theorem 1, then ACHIEVES of subprocesses of p are calculated incorrectly, which contradicts to the assumption of the induction step. Therefore, for all processes of process decomposition, ACHIEVES are calculated correctly.

Let us assume that there exists CO such that IMPLEMENTEDBYCO is calculated incorrectly. It means, that there exists a process p such that its *ReachableObjectives* is calculated incorrectly, which contradicts to the statement proved previously.

We will prove termination by showing that in cycle **while** in line 11, processes can be added to the queue at most once. Since process decomposition is finite and since one node is removed on every iteration, termination then follows. Initially (line 1), the elements of queue are all distinct. Line 13 guarantees that only super-processes are added to the queue. For an element to be added to the queue twice, it would therefore have to be its own super-processes which is impossible.

Finally, we prove the complexity result. The most complex calculation is hold in cycle **while** in line 11. Above, we have proved that the queue length is $O(|P|)$. At

Table 3. Result of algorithm run

CO	IMPLEMENTEDBY (CO)	P	ACHIEVES (P)
CA_1, CA_2, CA_5	A_1	A_1	$\{CA_1, CA_2, CA_5\}$
CA_3	A_2	A_2	CA_3
CA_4	$\{A_4, P_4\}$	A_3	CA_6
CA_6	A_3	A_4	CA_4
$CO_{3.1}, CO_{3.2}, CO_{3.3}, AC$	$\{P_2, P_1\}$	P_3, P_5, A_5	$\{\emptyset\}$
$CO_{2.1}, CO_{2.2}, CO_2, CO_3$	$\{\emptyset\}$	P_2, P_1	$\{CO_{3.1}, CO_{3.2}, CO_{3.3}, AC\}$
		P_4	CA_4

each iteration we pop exactly one process. For each popped process, in line 13 we check its parents. Due to the *structural* nature of our process decomposition model, each process has only *one* super process. Thus, for a single parent, we run algorithm Reach which has complexity $O(|V|^2)$ because of Theorem 1. In line 19, we have to update IMPLEMENTEDBY for some COs the total number which is less than $O(|V|)$. Thus the complexity is not more than $O((|V|^2 + |V|) \times |P|)$.

Example 7. In this example we will show the run of the algorithm PROBLEM OF COMPLIANCE AND CONTRIBUTION RESOLUTION. Since A_1, A_2, A_3 are composed into AND-execution (i.e., sequence in the original workflow), we have to calculate function Reach over the *union* of activities that they implement; and the union is CA_1, CA_2, CA_3, CA_5, CA_6. Thus, ACHIEVES(P_2) = Reach$(G, \{CA_1, CA_2, CA_3, CA_5, CA_6\})$= $\{CO_{3.1}, CO_{3.2}, AC, CO_{3.3}\}$, and P_2 is added to corresponding sets IMPLEMENTEDBY of control objectives respectively.

On the other hand, A_4 implements CA_4. And ACHIEVES(P_4) = Reach(G, AC_4) = $\{CA_4\}$. P_5 does not implement anything. Therefore at P_3 intersection of CA_4 with empty set is an empty set.

P_2 and P_3 are composed into sequence (AND-composition), therefore Reach will be calculated over ACHIEVES(P_2) ∩ ACHIEVES(P_3)=$\{CO_{3.1}, CO_{3.2}, AC, CO_{3.3}\}$. This will be a set of COs that are satisfied by P_1, the root objective is not in this set. Thus the root objective is not satisfied.

The complete output of the algorithm is shown in Table 3.

If we investigate column IMPLEMENTEDBY of Table 3, we will notice that there is a set of processes that do not satisfy any CO. These processes can be organized as a path of a tree-like structure of process decomposition model, e.g., $P_3 \rightarrow P_5 \rightarrow A_5$. Thus, we can detect the source of incompliance.

The situation that is described as in Example 7 could be fixed if A_5 were designed to implement some CA in objective model. It seems to be obsolete and even more non compliant to the hospital regulations and therefore it should be deleted. If we eliminate the process P_5, then P_3 obtains IMPLEMENTEDBY(P_4) = $\{CA_4\}$ and being united with IMPLEMENTEDBY(P_2) for calculation of IMPLEMENTEDBY(P_1) will result in the complete satisfaction of objective model.

6   Related Work

The problem of compliance to regulatory requirements was investigated from different angles and by means of different methodologies.

A recent survey on compliance checking [19] classifies various proposals either *design time* or *execution time* or *audit time* compliance checking. It's easy to see that our proposal can be attributed to the first class, i.e., design time compliance checking. Indeed, we reason on compliance by analysing business process structure, CO model, and process-to-objective assignment. There have been proposed other design time compliance checking methodologies.

A logical language PENELOPE proposed in [11] makes use of temporal deontic assignments from compliance requirements (obligations and permissions) to create state space. The latter is refined than in control flow. In contrast to [11], we do not consider workflow but rather its structural complexity, i.e., AND/OR decomposition.

A range of various model-driven proposals for compliance analysis were proposed, for example, in [18] (TROPOS [1]), [21] (pi-calculus and temporal logic), [22] (Deontic logic), [10] (REALM framework [9]). The idea of all these proposals is that requirements are modelled in the first turn either by means of logical prepositions or goal model, and then a workflow model is derived from requirements model. Thus, the derived business process should be compliant to requirement model by design.

Schmidt et al. [27] designed a compliance ontology w.r.t. regulations. The compliance checking is based on verification of instantiated classes of compliance ontology against process ontology. This automatic procedure could be used in ours at the stage of process-to-objective assignment which we assume to be a human-related task. Similar approach was proposed in [20], where semantic-based architecture for compliance checking was sketched. The difference is that compliance ontology is called *semantic policy* which is assumed to be enforced against business process semantic. The core policy ontology was designed as well.

The notion of *compliance pattern* (i.e., commonly occurring business process model which is proven to be compliant to some requirements) was introduced in [8]. Compliance patterns are used for compliance violation detection and also provide heuristic guidance to resolve non-compliance by modification of the business process.

An attempt to design a formal framework for business process compliance is presented in [23]. Basically, the framework relies on propositional logic to model risks, controls, business process activities.

A methodology that refines regulatory requirements to control activities according to risks (as in the current paper) was proposed in [26], [12]. After that, controls that is supposed to verify the compliance is encoded into prepositions of Formal Contract Language [13, 14].

7   Conclusion and Further Work

In this paper, we presented a methodology of design-time compliance checking between regulations and a control process. Our methodology is based on the notion of objective model which is derived from regulations and refined into simple instructions that can be easily implemented into small functions and procedures and later organized into a control process. The correctness of implementation can be checked by the algorithms presented in this paper. Namely, the proposed algorithms (1) verify the satisfaction of the root objective, (2) identify which subprocess contributes to satisfaction of which COs, (3) means to detect the source of incompliance.

Currently, we are working on the model of compliance of a *controlled* process that is process interwoven with a control process considered in the current paper. As the future work, we would like to develop an automated procedures for process-to-objective assignment which for now we assume to be performed manually by a human. Next, we are going investigate runtime compliance, i.e., compliance of business process execution traces to objective model. This will allow to include temporal COs into considerations and thus to extend the range of applicability of our methodology. Finally, we plan to introduce a notion of *compliance to some extend* in our methodology. Namely, we are working currently on the notion of key indicators which are metrics that are specific to business processes and so avoid one persistent metrics-related problem.

References

[1] Bresciani, P., Giorgini, P., Giunchiglia, F., Mylopoulos, J., Perini, A.: TROPOS: An agent-oriented software development methodology. Autonomous Agents and Multi-Agent Systems 8(3), 203–236 (2004)

[2] Curbera, F., Doganata, Y., Martens, A., Mukhi, N.K., Slominski, A.: Business provenance — a technology to increase traceability of end-to-end operations. In: Meersman, R., Tari, Z. (eds.) OTM 2008, Part II. LNCS, vol. 5332, pp. 100–119. Springer, Heidelberg (2008)

[3] DSRL. File f circular no. 5/san 30_1_2004 (2009),
http://www.sanita.regione.lombardia.it/circolari/04_05san.pdf

[4] DSRL. File f note 27.3.2008 h1.2008.0012810 (2009),
http://www.sanita.regione.lombardia.it/circolari/nota2008_12810.pdf

[5] DSRL. File f note 30.11.2007 h1.2007.0050480 (2009),
http://www.sanita.regione.lombardia.it/circolari/nota2007_50480.pdf

[6] Il Dirigente del Sanita Regione Lombardia. File f circular no. 45/san 23_12_2004 (2009),
http://www.sanita.regione.lombardia.it/circolari/04_45san.pdf

[7] Il Dirigente del Sanita Regione Lombardia (DSRL). File f note 04.12.2008 h1.2008.0044229 (2009), http://www.sanita.regione.lombardia.it/circolari/nota2008_44229.pdf

[8] Ghose, A., Koliadis, G.: Auditing business process compliance. In: Krämer, B.J., Lin, K.-J., Narasimhan, P. (eds.) ICSOC 2007. LNCS, vol. 4749, pp. 169–180. Springer, Heidelberg (2007)

[9] Giblin, C., Liu, A.Y., Müller, S., Pfitzmann, B., Zhou, X.: Regulations expressed as logical models (realm). In: JURIX 2005, pp. 37–48. IOS Press, Amsterdam (2005)

[10] Giblin, C., Müller, S., Pfitzmann, B.: From regulatory policies to event monitoring rules: Towards model-driven compliance automation. Technical Report RZ 3662, IBM Research (2006)

[11] Goedertier, S., Vanthienen, J.: Designing compliant business processes with obligations and permissions. In: Eder, J., Dustdar, S. (eds.) BPM Workshops 2006. LNCS, vol. 4103, pp. 5–14. Springer, Heidelberg (2006)

[12] Governatori, G., Hoffmann, J., Sadiq, S., Weber, I.: Detecting regulatory compliance for business process models through semantic annotations. In: 4th International Workshop on Business Process Design (2008)

[13] Governatori, G., Milosevic, Z.: A formal analysis of a business contract language. International Journal of Cooperative Information Systems 15(4), 659–685 (2006)

[14] Governatori, G., Rotolo, A.: An algorithm for business process compliance. In: Francesconi, E., Sartor, G., Tiscornia, D. (eds.) JURIX. Frontiers in Artificial Intelligence and Applications, vol. 189, pp. 186–191. IOS Press, Amsterdam (2008)

[15] ISACA. Cobit (2008), http://www.isaca.org/cobit/

[16] ISO/IEC. ISO/IEC 27001:2005: Information security management systems (2005)

[17] ISO/IEC. ISO/IEC 15408: Common criteria for information technology security evaluation (2009), http://www.commoncriteriaportal.org/thecc.html

[18] Kazhamiakin, R., Pistore, M., Roveri, M.: A framework for integrating business processes and business requirements. In: EDOC 2004, pp. 9–20. IEEE, Los Alamitos (2004)

[19] Kharbili, M.E., de Medeiros, A.K.A., Stein, S., van der Aalst, W.M.P.: Business process compliance checking: Current state and future challenges. In: MobIS 2008. LNI, vol. 141, pp. 107–113 (2008)

[20] Kharbili, M.E., Stein, S.: Policy-based semantic compliance checking for business process management. In: Loos, P., Nuttgens, M., Turowski, K., Werth, D. (eds.) MobIS Workshops. CEUR Workshop Proceedings, vol. 420, pp. 178–192. CEUR-WS.org (2008)

[21] Liu, Y., Müller, S., Xu, K.: A static compliance-checking framework for business process models. IBM Syst. J. 46(2), 335–361 (2007)

[22] Namiri, K., Stojanovic, N.: A model-driven approach for internal controls compliance in business processes. In: Hepp, M., Hinkelmann, K., Karagiannis, D., Klein, R., Stojanovic, N. (eds.) SBPM. CEUR Workshop Proceedings, vol. 251 (2007)

[23] Namiri, K., Stojanovic, N.: Towards a formal framework for business process compliance. In: Proceedings of Multikonferenz Wirtschaftsinformatik (MKWI 2008). GITO-Verlag, Berlin (2008)

[24] Office of Governance Commerce. IT infrastructure library (2009), http://www.itil.org/en/

[25] The President of the Italian Republic. Personal data protection code: Italian legislative decree no. 196 dated 30 june 2003 (2009), http://www.garanteprivacy.it/garante/document?ID=1219452

[26] Sadiq, S.W., Governatori, G., Namiri, K.: Modeling control objectives for business process compliance. In: Alonso, G., Dadam, P., Rosemann, M. (eds.) BPM 2007. LNCS, vol. 4714, pp. 149–164. Springer, Heidelberg (2007)

[27] Schmidt, R., Bartsch, C., Oberhauser, R.: Ontology-based representation of compliance requirements for service processes. In: ESWC 2007. CEUR Workshop Proceedings, vol. 251 (2007)

Effective and Flexible NFP-Based Ranking of Web Services

Matteo Palmonari, Marco Comerio, and Flavio De Paoli

University of Milano - Bicocca, viale Sarca 336, 20126 Milano, Italy
{palmonari,comerio,depaoli}@disco.unimib.it

Abstract. Service discovery is a key activity to actually identify the Web services (WSs) to be invoked and composed. Since it is likely that more than one service fulfill a set of user requirements, some ranking mechanisms based on non-functional properties (NFPs) are needed to support automatic or semi-automatic selection.

This paper introduces an approach to NFP-based ranking of WSs providing support for semantic mediation, consideration of expressive NFP descriptions both on provider and client side, and novel matching functions for handling either quantitative or qualitative NFPs. The approach has been implemented in a ranker that integrates reasoning techniques with algorithmic ones in order to overcome current and intrinsic limitations of semantic Web technologies and to provide algorithmic techniques with more flexibility. Moreover, to the best of our knowledge, this paper presents the first experimental results related to NFP-based ranking of WSs considering a significant number of expressive NFP descriptions, showing the effectiveness of the approach.

1 Introduction

Web Service (WS) discovery is a process that consists in the identification of the services that fulfill a set of requirements given by a user. Since more than one service is likely to fulfill the functional requirements, some ranking mechanisms are needed in order to provide support for the automatic or semi-automatic selection of a restricted number of services (usually one) among the discovered ones.

According to a gross-grain definition, the discovery process consists in first locating a number of WSs that meets certain functional criteria, and then identifying the services, among the discovered ones, that better fulfill a set of non-functional properties (NFPs) requested by actual users. The latter activity is called WS ranking and it is based on the computing of a degree of match between a set of requested NFPs and a set of NFPs offered by the discovered WSs. NFPs cover Quality of Service (QoS) aspects, but also other business-related properties, such as pricing and insurance, and properties not directly related to the service functionalities, such as security and trust.

The enrichment of WS descriptions based on WSDL by means of semantic annotation languages and ontologies (OWL-S, WSMO, SAWSDL) has been proposed to improve automation and precision of WS discovery and composition.

L. Baresi, C.-H. Chi, and J. Suzuki (Eds.): ICSOC-ServiceWave 2009, LNCS 5900, pp. 546–560, 2009.

Semantic annotations can be likewise exploited to support the description of NFPs and to improve ranking algorithms, as shown also by recent works such as [3,8,7,9,11,14]. Automated reasoning techniques based on semantic annotations are particularly suitable to mediate between different terminologies and data models considering the semantics of the terms used in the descriptions as defined by means of logical axioms and rules (e.g., at class-level, by making explicit that, in a given domain, the property *BasePrice* is equivalent to the property *ServicePrice*, or, at instance-level, by making explicit that a *fire insurance* is part of a *blanket insurance*). However, the crisp nature of matching-rules based on logical reasoning conflicts with the need to support ranking algorithms with more practical matching techniques; moreover, many reasoners show poor effectiveness when dealing with non trivial numeric functions (e.g., weighted sums) which are needed to manage more properties at the same time. As a consequence logic-based and algorithmic techniques need to be combined to provide for an effective and flexible approach to service ranking.

In this paper we present an effective and flexible approach to NFP-based ranking of Semantic WSs, which is based on PCM-compliant NFP descriptions. PCM (Policy Centered Meta-model) [6] is a meta-model that supports the description of the NFPs offered by a service, as well as requested by a user, by means of NFP expressions; NFP offers and requests are aggregated in sets called *Policies* to capture business scenarios by aggregating interdependent properties. A purpose of the PCM is to act as an intermediate and integrating meta-model that maps to significant subsets of popular languages (e.g., WSLA [10] and WS-Policy [17]).

The NFP-based WS ranking consists of a four-phase process: a **property matching phase** that identifies the NFPs in the offered policies that match with the NFP in the requested policy; a **local property evaluation phase** that computes a matching degree for each couple of matching NFPs; a **global policy evaluation phase** that computes a global matching degree between the requested policy and each offered policy; finally, services (and policies) are sorted according to their global matching degrees during a **policy ranking phase**. The ranking process has been tested by implementing the PoliMaR (Policy Matchmaker and Ranker) tool covering a significant set of NFP expressions for both requested and offered NFPs. Experimental results demonstrate the feasibility and the effectiveness of the approach.

The peculiar features of the proposed approach are the following:

- **expressivity**, by supporting rich descriptions of requested and offered NFPs addressing qualitative properties by mean of logical expressions on ontology values and quantitative properties by mean of expressions including ranges and inequalities;
- **generality**, by allowing semantic-based mediation in the matching phase with NFP descriptions based on multiple ontologies;
- **extensibility**, by supporting parametric property evaluation by customizing functions associated with operators;

- **flexibility**, by allowing incomplete specifications (i.e., unspecified properties and values in NFP requests and offers).

The paper is organized as follows: the problem of NFP-based WS ranking and the issues related to the NFP representations expressiveness are discussed in Section 2 through the introduction of a running example; Section 3 describes the PCM features and the ranking problem; Section 4 presents the approach to policy matchmaking and ranking; experimental results evaluating the scalability of the approach are discussed in Section 5; finally, the comparison with related works (Section 6) and concluding remarks (Section 7) end the paper.

2   Problem Context and Motivation

The problem of ranking a set of services can be defined as follows: given a set of service descriptions $S = \{s_1, ..., s_n\}$, and a specification R of non-functional requirements, define a sorting on S based on R. In this paper we assume that a set of services, namely *eligible services*, are identified by a discovery engine on the basis of their functional properties (FPs); the non-functional property descriptions of the eligible services form the set S to be ranked.

As discussed in [6], the distinction between FP and NFP is often ambiguous and no rules are available to qualify a property as FP or NFP. From our point of view this is a consequence of the fact that functional or non-functional is not an intrinsic qualification of a property, but it depends on the application domain and context. For example, the service location could be classified as a FP for a logistic service and as a NFP for a payment service. Moreover, from the requester perspective, the classification of requested properties as FP or NFP might be of little interest and counterintuitive. The requested properties represent the user preferences and could be mandatory or optional. In this paper, we adopt the proposal described in [1]. From the requester perspective, we considered hard and soft constraints to distinguish between the properties that are specified as mandatory or optional in a service request. From the provider perspective, we consider FPs those properties of a service that strictly characterize the offered functionality (e.g., service location for a shipment service) and NFPs those properties that do not affect or affect the offered functionality only marginally (e.g., service location for a payment service). Then, in order to support the matching between requested and offered properties, FPs and NFPs are mapped with hard and soft constraints respectively.

To illustrate the main aspects that need to be covered when dealing with NFP-based ranking, let us consider a running example based on the discovery scenario in the logistic domain presented in [1]. The scenario derives from an analysis of the logistic operator domain conducted within the Networked Peers for Business (NeP4B) project[1] and has inspired one of the current discovery scenarios in the Semantic Web Service Challange[2]. In this scenario, several logistic operators offer

---

[1] http://www.dbgroup.unimo.it/nep4b

[2] http://sws-challenge.org/wiki/index.php/Scenarios

one or more services (e.g., freight transport, warehousing) each one characterized by offered NFPs. A set of relevant NFPs in this domain are: (i) *payment method*: how the user can perform the payment; (ii) *payment deadline*: the maximum number of days that the user can wait to perform the payment after the service fulfilment; (iii) *insurance*: the type of compensation in case of failure applied to the service; (iv) *base price*: the amount of money to be paid to get the service; (v) *hours to delivery*: the number of hours required for the service fulfilment.

A freight transport service provider can specify the following NFP offered by its service: *"I offer a service that performs freight transportation in 24-48 hours with a base price equal to 100 Euros. I accept carriage paid payment within 45 days and I offer a blanket insurance on the transportation"*.

Users in this context might want to formulate quite rich requests to identify the best service according to their own stated criteria. An example of user request, written in natural language, is the following: *"I am interested in a service to perform a freight transportation in one or two days with a price less than or equal to 120 Euros. Moreover, I would like to use a service allowing, at least, a 15-days postponed payment with carriage paid or carriage forward payment method. Finally, I prefer a service offering a fire insurance or any insurance type that includes it"*.

A detailed discussion about the expressiveness of languages and models needed to represent NFPs in order to support WS discovery can be found in our previous work [6]. Here, we just observe that: NFPs may refer to either numerical values (e.g., 120) or world objects (e.g., *fire insurance*); some values can be undefined in the requests (e.g., in a lower bound expression such as *price less than or equal to 120 Euros*) or even in the offered NFPs (e.g., in a range expression such as *24-48 hours*); a user expresses constraints on different NFPs at a same time and may want to express preferences about what should be considered more important.

3   PCM-Compliant NFP Descriptions and Policy Ranking

The Policy Centered Meta-model (PCM) has been developed to address NFP representation and service ranking. In the PCM, requested or offered NFPs are grouped into policies; offered policies are associated with services and defined by an applicability condition for the properties composing them. As a result, the problem of ranking a set S of n WSs can be reformulated as the problem of ranking a set P of k policies on the basis of a requested policy RP, with $k \geq n$ since a service can be offered with more policies.

The PCM is defined by a language-independent conceptual syntax, whose semantics is defined by an ontology. Two concrete syntaxes of the PCM are provided in OWL and WSML. Since the implementation of the ranker presented in the paper uses the WSML language, in the following we will use a WSML-like notation with small variants to shorten the descriptions. In this paper we provide for a brief description of the PCM by means of examples, focusing on the elements that are more relevant in the ranking process. The reader can refer to [6] for details and formal definitions.

The following is an example of a section of a service description in the context of logistics operators.

```
< ONTOLOGY HEADING: namespace declaration, ontology import...>

instance premiumPolicy memberOf pcm#Policy
    pcm#ServiceReference hasValue
    "http://www.itis.disco.unimib.it/research/ontologies/WSSouthItalyOrdinaryTransport.wsml"
    pcm#hasCondition hasValue premiumCondition
    pcm#hasNfp hasValue [off.BasePrice1 memberOf nfpo#BasePrice]
    pcm#hasNfp hasValue [off.PaymentDeadline1 memberOf nfpo#PaymentDeadline]
    pcm#hasNfp hasValue [off.HoursToDelivery1 memberOf nfpo#HoursToDelivery]
    pcm#hasNfp hasValue [off.PaymentMethod1 memberOf nfpo#LogisticPaymentMethod]
    pcm#hasNfp hasValue [off.Insurance1 memberOf nfpo#LogisticInsurance]
    ...
```

The term *instance* introduces the name of the instance of the ontology, and *memberOf* specifies the class it belongs to. The namespace *pcm#* is for the PCM ontology and *nfpo#* for a domain-specific NFP ontology extending the PCM[3]. A policy is identified by a URI and associated with one or more WSs by *ServiceReference*. A *PolicyCondition* defines the requirements a client profile should fulfill to select that policy (e.g., the *premiumPolicy* is for frequent clients that subscribed for a significant number of shipments per years); NFPs are represented in the PCM by *PolicyNfps* and are expressed in terms of, possibly external, ontologies (e.g., *nfpo#BasePrice*). A NFP is specified by means of a *NfpExpression* that is characterized by a *ConstraintOperator* and by a set of attributes that depends on the constraint operator type. Different examples, referred to *premiumPolicy*, are synthetically represented on the right-hand side of Figure 1.

To explicitly take into account the requestor perspective, PCM introduces the concept of *RequestedPolicy* that is composed of *Requests* stating what values are acceptable for a certain property, and expressing the relevance of each required property. *Requests* are therefore defined extending *PolicyNfps* with the property *hasRelevance*, whose range is a rational within [0..1]. The requests formulated in the scenario in Section 2 are collected in the *LOReqPolicy1* in the left-hand side of Figure 1.

PCM makes distinction between qualitative and quantitative NFP expressions. Qualitative expressions refer to objects (their values are instances of given domain ontologies) and are further classified in *SetExpressions* and *CustomExpressions*. Quantitative expressions assume numeric values, whose measurement units is specified by a *unit* term; quantitative expressions are further classified into *SingleValueExpressions* and *RangeExpressions*.

Figure 2 shows the properties that characterize each class of NFP expressions, the respective ranges, and a set of *built-in* constraint operators, which are also exploited by the ranker proposed in this paper (the set of operators is extensible by mean of standard ontology import mechanisms). As for *SetOperators*, PCM

---

[3] All ontologies are available on-line at http://www.itis.disco.unimib.it/research/ontologies

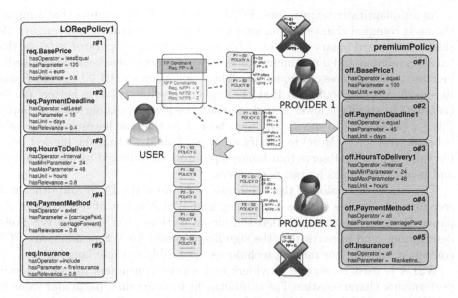

Fig. 1. The scenario revisited according to the PCM

introduces (i) the two standard logical operators *all* and *exist* with their logical meanings, and (ii) the operator *include*. Intuitively, a *include*-based request (e.g., *I need an insurance including fire insurance*) asks for values that *logically* include the selected values (e.g., *a blanket insurance*); logical inclusion is looked up by exploring hierarchical properties of different nature (e.g., *part-of, topological inclusion*). The set of *CustomOperators* allows domain experts to introduce other operators to deal with object values. As an example, a request based on *semanticDistance* operator may ask for values that are semantically close to the specified one.

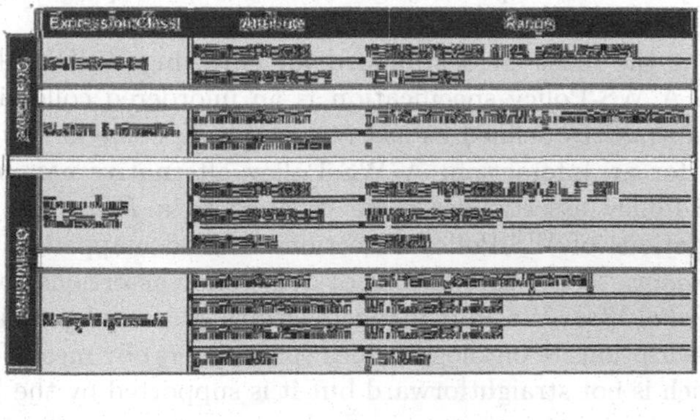

Fig. 2. Characterization of the four NFP Expression classes

As for quantitative expressions, PCM defines a set of operators that supports the most common clauses for numeric values (e.g., inequalities and ranges). Beside the standard binary operator $=$ (*equal*), and ternary operator *interval* that fixes a minimum and a maximum value, new operators have been introduced to increase expressiveness of inequalities. These operators are: (i) $\geq\uparrow$ (*greaterEqual*) to specify a lower bound, so that the highest possible value is better; (ii) $\geq\downarrow$ (*atLeast*) to specify a lower bound, so that the lowest possible value is better; (iii) $\leq\downarrow$ (*lessEqual*) to specify an upper bound, so that the lowest possible value is better; (iv) $\leq\uparrow$ (*atMost*) to specify an upper bound, so that the highest possible value is better. Observe that binary operators are followed by one parameter and ternary operators by two parameters.

The formal discussion of the relationships between the PCM and other well-recognized languages such as WS-Policy and WSLA is out of the scope of this paper. However, we can show that significant sections of WSLA and WS-Policy descriptions, and in particular, the significant subset for WS ranking, are PCM compliant, making our ranking techniques applicable to these languages.

WSLA is used by service providers and service consumers to define service performance characteristics. The commitment to maintain a particular value for a NFP (i.e., *SLAParameter*) is defined in the *Service Definition* section of a WSLA specification through the *Service Level Objectives*. A *Service Level Objective* is defined by an *Expression* based on quantification-free first order logic; the language includes ground predicates and logic operators, and easily maps to predicate logic. The simplest form of a logic expression is a plain predicate that can be mapped to a *PolicyNfp* characterized by an expression where the constraint operator and the parameter represent the *Type* (e.g., $=$, $\leq$) and the *Value* (e.g., numerical values) of the WSLA expression, respectively. Complex WSLA expressions are mapped as follows: implications are deleted and the resulting WSLA expression is put into a *disjunctive normal form* (a disjunction of conjunctions of ground predicates) exploiting standard techniques for predicate logic; each WSLA conjunction C is then represented by a *Policy* P composed of *PolicyNfps* representing the WSLA predicates in C; finally, for all the WSLA conjunctions C containing a predicate occurring in the head of an implication, an applicability condition representing the body of the implication is created for the *Policy* representing C.

WS-Policy is the most cited standard for enriching WSDL files with NFP specifications. A WS-Policy specification is an unordered collection of zero or more *policy alternatives* defined as *assertions* stating behaviors or requirements or conditions for an interaction. A WS-Policy alternative can be mapped to a *Policy*. WS-Policy assertions can be mapped to a *PolicyNfp* specification. "*And*" aggregations of WS-Policy assertions can be mapped to sets of *PolicyNfps* in a *Policy*. "*Or*" aggregations of WS-Policy assertions can be mapped to multiple *PolicyNfps*. WS-Policy specifications of nested policies need more articulated descriptions of ontology values (parameters) by means of *CustomExpressions*, which is not straightforward but it is supported by the WSML/OWL data-model.

4 Policy Matchmaking and WS Ranking: Combining Semantics and Algorithms for Policy Evaluation

The WS ranking process is composed of four phases: (i) **property matching phase**: for each *Request*, identify the set of *PolicyNFPs* to be evaluated; (ii) **local property evaluation phase**: for each identified *Request/PolicyNFP* couple, evaluate how the offered property satisfies the requested one - results are in range $[0, 1]$; (iii) **global policy evaluation phase**: for each policy, evaluate the results of the previous phase to compute a global satisfaction degree - results are values in range $[0, n]$; (iv) **policy ranking phase**: policies are ranked according to their global satisfaction degree.

The ranking process has been implemented in the PoliMaR tool. Figure 3 shows the components of the tool and their connection to external tools. As discussed above we assume that: (i) a number of PCM compliant policies are stored into an ontology repository; (ii) the eligible services are used by the *Ontology Loader* to make the reasoner load the knowledge needed to perform the ranking process; (iii) if NFPs are specified according to another model, the *PCM Wrapper* is used to transform the original descriptions into PCM-based descriptions.

The Matching Evaluator. The property matching phase is performed by the matching evaluator. According to the approach based on decoupling the matching phase from the evaluation phase, the matching evaluator has two goals: (i) discover the *PolicyNFPs* that match against the *Requests*; and (ii) retrieve all the data concerning these NFPs to support the other components in the evaluation tasks.

A mediator-centric approach is used to achieve these goals, according to the WSMO asset that exploits different kinds of mediators to solve semantic mismatches. In this case, the mediation is defined by logic programming rules. A first set of rules mediates among the possibly different ontologies on which offered and requested NFPs are based on. These rules retrieve a set of matching couples exploiting subclass relations. The following example of matching rule

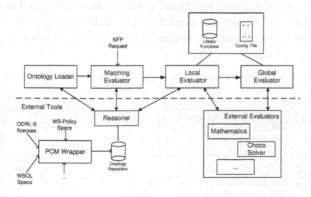

Fig. 3. The overall architecture of the PoliMaR tool

specifies that a request and an offer match if they belong to specific subclasses of *PolicyNfp*.

```
axiom BasePriceMatching
    definedBy
        matchCouple(?request,?nfp,baseprice) :−
            (?request memberOf nfpo#BasePriceRequest) and
            (?nfp memberOf nfpo#BasePrice) or
            (?nfp memberOf nfpo#ServicePrice)
```

A second set of rules is defined to retrieve the data related to the set of matched NFPs. The reasoner exploits standard mechanisms of variable binding to explore the PCM-compliant ontologies and retrieve the information for each NFP. Moreover, retrieval of such data is not straightforward because non monotonic rules are exploited to put results in a kind of normal form (e.g., some quantitative properties might be defined through binary operators in some policies and ternary operators in other policies). Formally, the results of the matching evaluator are provided by executing a query and consist in a table with all the relevant information necessary for the next phases. An example is sketched in Table 1.

The Local Evaluator. The local evaluator takes a result table, like the one shown in Table 1, as input. We call *matching couple* every couple <Request, PolicyNfp> in the table. The output of the local evaluator is a *local satisfaction degree* (*LD* for short) for each couple. A LD is expressed by a value in the range [0..1], where 0 means "no match" and 1 means "exact match". In our approach, the matching degree for each matching couple is calculated by a function that takes the form $e\,(cop_r, cop_o, norm\,(v_r), norm\,(v_o))$, where cop_r and cop_o are the requested and offered constraint operators; $norm\,(v_r)$ and $norm\,(v_o)$ are the requested and offered normalized values (i.e., values after a unit conversion when necessary). Observe that values of qualitative properties are objects in the ontology, which means that a default *object* unit can be considered; moreover, a qualitative property can refer to a set of objects (a property can assume multiple values).

The set of local evaluation functions is stored in a *Library Functions*. Links between functions and constraint operators are defined by a *configuration file* to supply a flexible and extensible solution. This is a crucial advantage to address

Table 1. A fragment of the table displaying the matching phase results

Policy/Req.Policy	NFP	Operator	MinParameter	MaxParameter	Unit	Relev.
LOReqPolicy1	req.BasePrice	lessEqual	120	null	euro	0.8
premiumPolicy	off.BasePrice1	equal	100	null	euro	-
goldPolicy	off.BasePrice2	interval	80	150	euro	-
...	...	...	...	...	...	...
...	...	...	...	...	...	...
LOReqPolicy1	req.Insurance	include	fireInsurance	null	null	0.6
premiumPolicy	off.Insurance1	all	blanketInsurance	null	null	-
silverPolicy	off.Insurance3	all	fireInsurance	null	null	-
	...	...	...	...	...	...

the development of effective tools. In the current implementation, a number of functions for matching qualitative and quantitative properties have been developed; the configuration file allows for links to new operators or to new tailored functions. Qualitative and quantitative NFPs need to be handled in a different way. The quantitative local evaluation functions currently in use have been introduced in [4]. As for qualitative local evaluation functions, the reasoner needs to be recalled to exploit inference mechanisms based on the NFP domain ontologies in use. In particular, we considered the *all* operator in the *PolicyNfps* and the operators *all*, *exist* and *include* in the *Requests*.

The operators *all* and *exist* have standard logical meaning; basic inferences based on identities need to be considered for both the operators (e.g., when a service ships to "Italy" and the request ask for a service shipping to "Italia"). Let V be the set of requested values and O the set of offered values. For the *Requests* based on the *all* operator, we evaluate a LD d within the range [0..1]. If $V \subseteq O$, then $d = 1$; If $V \cap O = \emptyset$, then $d = 0$. If $V \nsubseteq O$ and $V \cap O \neq \emptyset$, then $d = |V \cap O|/|V|$. For the *Requests* based on the *exist* operator, the LD d can assume the value 0 or 1. If $V \cap O = \emptyset$, then $d = 0$. If $V \cap O \neq \emptyset$, then $d = 1$.

Requests specified through an *include* operator need to consider specific dependencies among the values specified in the *PolicyNfps*. In the running example discussed in Section 2 the insurance ontology defines the *fireInsurance* as a *partOf* of the *blanketInsurance*. Therefore, policies offering a *blanketInsurance* satisfies requests asking for services that offer *fireInsurance*. A mediator centric approach is used. In the rule ontology, where mediation rules are stored, the axiom for the example states that the *partOf* relation among insurance is to be considered as an inclusion relation (see the listing below).

```
axiom insuranceInclusion
    definedBy
        include(?X,?Y) :-
            (?X memberOf ins#Insurance) and (?Y memberOf ins#Insurance) and ins#partOf(?X,?Y)
```

The local evaluation function for inclusion operators expands the set O of offered values according to the transitive closure for the inclusion relations involving offered and requested values. Then, LD is calculated as for the *all* operator.

The Global Evaluator. The global evaluator takes the set of LDs evaluated for each matching couple as input, and provides a *global satisfaction degree* (*GD* for short) as output. GD provides information about how much a *Policy* matches a *RequestedPolicy* and it is computed by taking into account the relevance associated with each *Request* in the *RequestedPolicy*. Different global evaluation functions can be defined and stored into the *Library Functions*. A possible function is the weighted sum of the LDs, where weights are the relevance values of the corresponding Requests. The global evaluator ranks the *Policies* according to their GD.

Observe that our approach is tolerant w.r.t. the incompleteness of the NFP specifications (i.e., *Requests* whose matching *PolicyNfps* are not specified in a *Policy*). In fact, the more *Requests* in the *RequestedPolicy* match with some

PolicyNfps for a given *Policy*, the greater the GD is; however, the evaluation does not crash when a *Request* in the *RequestedPolicy* does not match with any *PolicyNfps* of a given *Policy*.

5   Experimental Results

The current version of the PoliMaR tool has been implemented using Java JDK 1.6.0 update 11 for Linux 64 bit and provides all the components described in Figure 3 except for the PCM Wrapper. All the ontologies are represented in the WSML language. The ranker uses KAON2 (v2007-06-11) as ontology repository and reasoner and the Wsml2Reasoner API (v0.6.1) to communicate with the reasoner. PoliMaR is now part of the GLUE2 discovery engine [2] available at http://glue2.sourceforge.net.

The current implementation of PoliMaR has been tested to evaluate the scalability and the efficiency of the matching and evaluation components. The evaluation activity has been performed using an Intel Core2 Q6700 2.66 Ghz with 2GB RAM and Linux kernel 2.6.27 64 bits. Due to the lack of large and accessible sets of NFP descriptions to derive PCM-based descriptions, the experiment has been carried out starting from a set of randomly generated descriptions that consists of about 500 policies. The generated test set is a combination of the properties discussed in Section 2 to form policies that are described according to the *NFPO* ontology; constraint operators and parameters are selected randomly according to the ranges specified in the *NFPO*.

The *RequestedPolicy* (TRP) represented in Figure 1 was used as testbed. It is composed of three quantitative requests $r\#1$, $r\#2$, and $r\#3$; and two qualitative requests $r\#4$, and $r\#5$. Observe that $r\#4$ and $r\#5$ are based on two different constraint operators, namely *all* and *include*, that require different reasoning tasks for the evaluation. The performed tests were:

- TEST 1: Measurement of the overall execution time in the cases of single and multiple file storage;
- TEST 2: Analysis of the execution-time distribution between reasoning and algorithmic computation for single file storage;
- TEST 3: Analysis of the execution-time distribution among the ranking phases (matching, local and global evaluation) for single file storage;
- TEST 4: Measurement and comparison of the overall execution time with increasing complexity in the requested policy for single file storage.

TEST 1 (Figure 4a) highlights that: (i) the multiple file approach is efficient only for small numbers of policies. Moreover, the KAON2 reasoner was able to manage at most 136 WSML files containing a policy each; (ii) the required time increases exponentially for the multiple-file approach and polynomially for the single-file approach; (iii) there is an amount of time (approximately 5 seconds) that is independent of the input. It represents the time required to invoke the reasoner through the WSML2Reasoner API. The conclusion that can be driven from this first set of tests is that semantic tools available today make the single

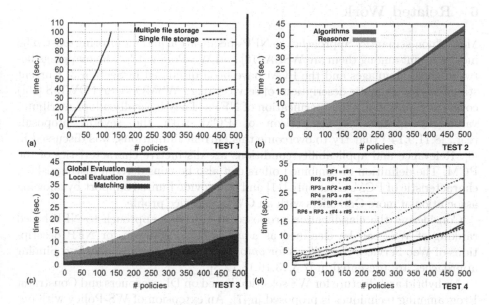

Fig. 4. Evaluation Tests

file approach compulsory. Ongoing research on large scale distributed reasoning might overcome this limit in the future.

TEST 2 (Figure 4b) highlights that the bottleneck for our evaluation is represented by the reasoner: the time required for the evaluation of quantitative NFPs and the global evaluation phase is very short.

TEST 3 (Figure 4c) highlights that: (i) the time required for the execution of the global evaluation phase does not influence significantly the evaluation time; (ii) the time used for the local evaluation phase is twice as long as the time for the matching phase.

TEST 4 has been executed considering six combinations of the single requests forming the TRP with increasing degrees of complexity. The first three requested policies were composed of quantitative requests only: $RP1$ was composed of $r\#1$ (written $RP1 = r\#1$); $RP2 = RP1 + r\#2$; $RP3 = RP2 + r\#3$. The next three requested policies considered also qualitative requests: $RP4 = RP3 + r\#4$ (the *all* constraint operator is used); $RP5 = RP3 + r\#5$ (the *include* constraint operator is used); $RP6 = RP3 + r\#4 + r\#5$ (both *all* and *include* are used).

The results of TEST 4 (Figure4d) highlight that: (i) the number of quantitative NFP constraints marginally affects the evaluation time (RP1, RP2 and RP3 show similar evaluation times); (ii) the evaluation of a qualitative NFP expressed with the *all* operator requires more time than one expressed with the *include* operator. Considering a Policy Repository with 500 policies, the introduction of an *all* constraint determines an increment of 12 seconds, instead the inclusion of an *include* constraint determines an increment of 4 seconds.

6   Related Work

Many "non-semantic" approaches to NFP specification and monitoring exist. The most relevant among them are WSLA [10] and WS-Policy [17]. The mappings between these languages and the PCM have been discussed in Section 3. Current standards for semantic descriptions of services (e.g., WSMO [5] and OWL-S [15]) cover only marginally the specification of NFPs. They basically adopt attribute-value descriptions. A comparison of PCM with the several proposals (e.g., [8,11,9,14]) that try to overcome this current limitations, was discussed in [6]. Relevance and applicability conditions are distinctive characteristics of the PCM. The definition of combined offers can also be considered a distinguishing characteristic of PCM, since only [11] and [9] provide limited support by allowing association of more QoS offers with an OWL-S service profile.

Considering the classification proposed in [19], our approach to NFP-based ranking of WSs can be classified as a *policy-based* solution for NFP descriptions of Web Services that allows for *ontology-based preference modeling*. Similar approaches are presented in [7,3,13,16,18,12,8]

An hybrid architecture for WS selection based on DL reasoners and Constraint Programming techniques is proposed in [7]. An extension of WS-Policy with ontological concepts to enable QoS-based semantic policy matching is presented in [3]. Approaches for the WS selection based on the normalization of QoS values are described in [13,16]. A NFP-based service selection approach that modifies the Logic Scoring Preference (LSP) method with Ordered Weighted Averaging (OWA) operators is proposed in [18]. A framework for WS selection that combines declarative logic-based matching rules with optimization methods is described in [12]. A WSMO-based hybrid solution to WS ranking based on the usage of axioms for requested and offered NFPs is defined in [8].

The comparison with these approaches is carried out focusing on the features described in Section 1: (i) *expressive NFP descriptions*; (ii) *semantic-based mediation*; (iii) *parametric NFP evaluation*; (iv) *tolerance to unspecified NFP*; (v) *experimental results*. Table 2 reports the results of the comparison (*yes/no* is used to show whether the approach achieves the requirement, and *low, average, high* to indicate at what level the approach reaches the requirement). The result of the comparison is that, among the considered approaches, only [12] presents an evaluation activity executed on a large number of policies. Test activities

Table 2. Comparison of NFP-based Web service ranking approaches

	Expr. Desc.	Mediation	Param. Eval.	Unspec. NFP	Experiment
Garcia et al. 2007 [7]	low	no	no	no	no
Chaari et al. 2008 [3]	low	no	no	no	no
Liu et al. 2004 [13]	low	no	no	yes	low
Wang et al. 2006 [16]	low	no	no	yes	low
Yu et al. 2008 [18]	low	no	no	yes	low
Lamparter et al. 2007 [12]	low	yes	no	yes	high
Garcia et al. 2008 [8]	high	yes	yes	no	low
Our Approach	**yes**	**yes**	**yes**	**high**	**high**

demonstrates that the semantic service selection described in [12] is more efficient. However, that approach is based on simpler NFP descriptions. Only the *equal* operator is allowed in the definition of qualitative NFP and quantitative NFPs defined as range of values are not considered. Moreover, the approach is less extensible and flexible since the algorithms are hard-coded.

The consideration of high-expressive NFP descriptions and the definition of parametric NFP evaluations are provided only by [8]. The proposed exploitation of axioms support complex and conditioned NFP definitions (e.g., if the client is older than 60 or younger than 10 years old the invocation price is lower than 10 euro). Our proposal differs for four different aspects. First, we support assertions about properties with undefined values by specifying them with a range of possible guaranteed values. This supports the evaluation of offers with some unspecified values. Second, we decouple the evaluation of policy/request matching and applicability conditions. This supports information retrieval without forcing the requester to know and specify all the information required to evaluate the applicability conditions. In case of incomplete requests, the user is involved to evaluate the actual applicability conditions. Third, our descriptions can be obtained by wrapping existing specifications defined in WSLA and WS-Policy. Fourth, our approach has been tested against a significant set of NFP descriptions.

7   Concluding Remarks

This paper represents an effort toward the development of feasible and practical ranking tools. The proposed solution overcomes some limits of the current approaches by combining high expressivity in NFP descriptions with a rich and extensible set of operators and evaluation functions. Experimental results show the effectiveness of the approach when dealing with a significant number of policy specifications, even if some desirable improvements emerged as necessary to reach high efficiency and increase performance.

Currently, our approach assumes the availability of PCM-based descriptions but we are working to fill these limitations by developing a wrapper to retrieve data from heterogeneous service descriptions defined using different languages and formats (e.g., WSLA and WS-Policy, but also RDF or generic XML files) and use them to define PCM-based Policies to be processed by PoliMaR. Moreover, our current research focuses on performance improvements by means of caching strategies for qualitative property evaluation. Future work will deal with the development of tools to support users in writing NFP descriptions and evaluation functions.

References

1. Carenini, A., Cerizza, D., Comerio, M., Della Valle, E., De Paoli, F., Maurino, A., Palmonari, M., Sassi, M., Turati, A.: Semantic web service discovery and selection: a test bed scenario. In: proc of the Int. Workshop on Evaluation of Ontology-based tools and the Semantic Web Service Challenge (EON&SWS-Challenge) (2008)

2. Carenini, A., Cerizza, D., Comerio, M., Della Valle, E., De Paoli, F., Maurino, A., Palmonari, M., Turati, A.: Glue2: a web service discovery engine with non-functional properties. In: Proc. of the Eur. Conf. on Web Services, ECOWS (2008)
3. Chaari, S., Badr, Y., Biennier, F.: Enhancing web service selection by qos-based ontology and ws-policy. In: Proc. of the Symp. on Applied computing, SAC (2008)
4. Comerio, M., De Paoli, F., Maurino, A., Palmonari, M.: Nfp-aware semantic web services selection. In: Proc. of the International Enterprise Distributed Object Computing Conference (EDOC), Annapolis, USA, pp. 484–492 (2007)
5. de Bruijn, J., Lausen, H., Pollcres, A., Fensel, D.: The web service modeling language: An overview. In: Sure, Y., Domingue, J. (eds.) ESWC 2006. LNCS, vol. 4011, pp. 590–604. Springer, Heidelberg (2006)
6. De Paoli, F., Palmonari, M., Comerio, M., Maurino, A.: A Meta-Model for Non-Functional Property Descriptions of Web Services. In: Proc. of the Int. Conference on Web Services (ICWS), Beijing, China (2008)
7. García, J.M., Ruiz, D., Ruiz-Cortés, A., Martín-Díaz, O., Resinas, M.: An hybrid, qos-aware discovery of semantic web services using constraint programming. In: Krämer, B.J., Lin, K.-J., Narasimhan, P. (eds.) ICSOC 2007. LNCS, vol. 4749, pp. 69–80. Springer, Heidelberg (2007)
8. Garcia, J.M., Toma, I., Ruiz, D., Ruiz-Cortes, A.: A service ranker based on logic rules evaluation and constraint programming. In: Proc. of the Non Functional Properties and Service Level Agreements in SOC Workshop, NFPSLASOC (2008)
9. Giallonardo, E., Zimeo, E.: More semantics in qos matching. In: Proc. of Int. Conf. on Service-Oriented Computing and Application, SOCA (2007)
10. Keller, L.H., The, A.: wsla framework: Specifying and monitoring service level agreements for web services. J. Netw. Syst. Manage. 11(1), 57–81 (2003)
11. Kritikos, K., Plexousakis, D.: Semantic qos metric matching. In: Proc. of the Eur. Conf. on Web Services (ECOWS), pp. 265–274 (2006)
12. Lamparter, S., Ankolekar, A., Studer, R., Grimm, S.: Preference-based selection of highly configurable web services. In: Proc. of the Int. Conf. on World Wide Web (WWW), pp. 1013–1022 (2007)
13. Liu, Y., Ngu, A.H., Zeng, L.Z.: Qos computation and policing in dynamic web service selection. In: Proc. of the Int. World Wide Web conference on Alternate track papers and posters (WWW-Alt), New York, NY, USA (2004)
14. Maximilien, E., Singh, M.P.: A framework and ontology for dynamic web services selection. IEEE Internet Computing 08(5), 84–93 (2004)
15. OWL-S. Semantic Markup for Web Services (2003), http://www.daml.org/services/owl-s/1.0/owl-s.html
16. Wang, X., Vitvar, T., Kerrigan, M., Toma, I.: A qos-aware selection model for semantic web services. In: Dan, A., Lamersdorf, W. (eds.) ICSOC 2006. LNCS, vol. 4294, pp. 390–401. Springer, Heidelberg (2006)
17. Ws-Policy. Web Service Policy 1.2 - Framework (2006), http://www.w3.org/Submission/2006/SUBM-WS-Policy-20060425/
18. Yu, H.Q., Reiff-Marganiec, S.: A method for automated web service selection. In: Proc. of the Congress on Services (SERVICES), pp. 513–520 (2008)
19. Yu, H.Q., Reiff-Marganiec, S.: Non-functional property based service selection: A survey and classification of approaches. In: Proc. of the Non Functional Properties and Service Level Agreements in SOC Workshop, NFPSLASOC (2008)

Combining Quality of Service and Social Information for Ranking Services

Qinyi Wu[1], Arun Iyengar[2], Revathi Subramanian[2], Isabelle Rouvellou[2], Ignacio Silva-Lepe[2], and Thomas Mikalsen[2]

[1] College of Computing, Georgia Institute of Technology
801 Atlantic Drive, Atlanta, GA 30332, USA
qxw@cc.gatech.edu
[2] IBM T.J. Watson Research Center
19 Skyline Drive, Hawthorne, NY 10532, USA
{aruni,revathi,rouvellou,isilval,tommi}@us.ibm.com

Abstract. In service-oriented computing, multiple services often exist to perform similar functions. In these situations, it is essential to have good ways for qualitatively ranking the services. In this paper, we present a new ranking method, ServiceRank, which considers quality of service aspects (such as response time and availability) as well as social perspectives of services (such as how they invoke each other via service composition). With this new ranking method, a service which provides good quality of service and is invoked more frequently by others is more trusted by the community and will be assigned a higher rank. ServiceRank has been implemented on SOAlive, a platform for creating and managing services and situational applications. We present experimental results which show noticeable differences between the quality of service of commonly used mapping services on the Web. We also demonstrate properties of ServiceRank by simulated experiments and analyze its performance on SOAlive.

Keywords: Cloud computing, Quality of service, Service ranking.

1 Introduction

Cloud computing is viewed as a major logical step in the evolution of the Internet as a source of services. With many big companies now offering hosted infrastructure tools and services, more and more businesses are using cloud computing. We envision an open, collaborative ecosystem where cloud services can be easily advertised, discovered, composed and deployed. In cloud computing, there are often software services that perform comparable functions. An example would be mapping services such as those available from Google, Yahoo!, and Mapquest. Users, service composers and service invokers alike are thus faced with the task of picking from a set of comparable services that meet their needs. A random selection may not be optimal for its targeted execution environment and may incur inefficiencies and costs. In this situation, it will be very valuable if users

L. Baresi, C.-H. Chi, and J. Suzuki (Eds.): ICSOC-ServiceWave 2009, LNCS 5900, pp. 561–575, 2009.

could be provided with some indication of the relative merits of comparable services. We propose a new ranking method to address this need.

Our methodology takes into account how services invoke each other via service composition. Service composition allows developers to quickly build new applications using existing services that provide a subset of the function they need. An address book service that takes as input an address and returns its geocoding is an example of a primitive service that provides a specialized function. A FindRoute service that takes as input the geocoding of two addresses and returns a route from the start address to the end address is a composite service. Composite services can also become the building blocks of other composite services. The ability to compose and deploy services quickly is a big draw for existing and prospective cloud customers. We therefore imagine that cloud environments shall abound in service networks, where services form client-server relationships. Having good methodologies for evaluating and ranking services will be critically important for selecting the right services in this environment.

Our service ranking methodology incorporates features from social computing. Social ranking features are available throughout the Web. The social rank of an item is the popularity of the item within a community of users. This community can be virtual or real. Recommender systems such as those by Amazon or Netflix collect reviews and ratings from users and record their preferences. They can then use this information to recommend products to like-minded users (a virtual social network of users). Social bookmarking sites such as del.icio.us allow an explicit community of users to be formed via user networks. del.icio.us provides listings of the most popular bookmarks at any point in time which can be tailored to specific communities. There has also been past work in ranking and matching web services [1][13]. Prior research deals with finding the services that best match a required interface, support certain functions, or satisfy certain rules or policies.

In our approach to rank services in the cloud, we start out with the assumption that some initial matchmaking has been performed to arrive at a set of comparable services which then need to be ranked. We therefore, do not dwell on the aspects of matching interfaces, service descriptions, semantics, etc. Instead, we focus our energies on drawing the parallel between social networks and service networks. In social networks, users rate services. In service networks, services can rate other services based on how successful the service invocations were. The high rank (or popularity) of a service is influenced not just by a large number of service clients, but also by the satisfaction expressed by these service clients. A hike in the rank of a service S propagates favorably down the line to other services that it (S) depends upon.

The contributions of this paper are as follows:

- We present a new algorithm, referred to as ServiceRank, for ranking services which combines quality of service (QoS) aspects such as response time and availability with social ranking aspects such as how frequently the service is invoked by others.
- We show through experimental results that our algorithm is efficient and consumes minimal overhead.

– We study the performance of different mapping services on the Web. Our results indicate that the different services exhibit different behavior which is a key reason that quantitative methods are needed to rank services.

In the rest of this paper, we first define the ServiceRank algorithm in Section 2. We then describe an implementation of ServiceRank in Section 3. Experiments are presented in Section 4. We describe related work in Section 5 and conclude in Section 6.

2   ServiceRank

ServiceRank incorporates features from social computing by taking into account how services invoke each other via service composition. Figure 1 shows an example. A circle represents a service. A directional arrow represents a service invoking another service to fulfill its functionality. We call the service sending a request the *client* and the service processing the request the *server*. In this example, services s_1 and s_2 are clients. s_4 is their server. s_3 dynamically invokes either s_4 or s_5 to balance its load between these two services. s_4 and s_5 are grouped into a category because they provide the same functionality. From ServiceRank's perspective, a request is regarded as a rating from the client to the server. The client evaluates all the requests to compute a local rating of the server. Local ratings are eventually aggregated to compute global ranks for all the services. ServiceRank considers three factors for the aggregation. The first factor is how many clients a service has. In this example, we expect that s_4 gains a higher rank than s_5 because it has more client services. The second factor is how frequently a service is invoked. If s_3 sends more requests to s_5 than s_4, s_3 will rank s_5 higher under the condition that the quality of both services is similar. The third factor considers QoS in terms of response time and availability. For example, if s_5 has better response time than s_4, its rank should be raised even though it has fewer clients. In the rest of this section, we explain how ServiceRank combines all three factors to compute global ranks for services.

2.1   Local Ratings

A service network consists of a set of services $S = s_1, s_2, ..., s_n$. If s_i sends a request to s_j, s_i is a *client* of s_j, and s_j a *server* of s_i. We use $R_{ij} = \{r_{ij}^1, r_{ij}^2, ..., r_{ij}^m\}$

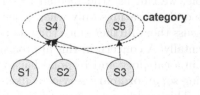

Fig. 1. A service network example

to denote all the requests between s_i and s_j and r_{ij}^u the u-th request. In ServiceRank, a request r_{ij}^u is regarded as a rating from s_i to s_j. If s_i processes it successfully, s_i gives s_j a positive rating: $rate(r_{ij}^u) = 1$, otherwise $rate(r_{ij}^u) = -1$. s_i's total rating to s_j, denoted by l_{ij}, is the sum of the ratings of all the requests.

$$l_{ij} = \sum_u rate(r_{ij}^u) \tag{1}$$

l_{ij} considers how frequently a service is invoked, and whether requests are successfully processed. However, QoS is a critical factor in service composition as well. It is important that ranks of services can be differentiated based on their performance. The ServiceRank algorithm achieves this goal by comparing the average response time of a service with that of other services with the same functionality and using the comparison ratio to adjust local ratings. Next we introduce a few more notations to explain how this is done.

For a service s_j, its average response time, rt_j, is computed by averaging the response time of all the requests it receives. Let B_j denote its client set.

$$rt_j = \frac{\sum_{s_i \in B_j} \sum_{r_{ij}^u \in R_{ij}} response\ time(r_{ij}^u)}{\sum_{s_i \in B_j} |R_{ij}|} \tag{2}$$

Services with the same functionality are grouped into a category, denoted by c_u. We use $min\ c_u^{rt}$ to denote the minimal average response time of services in c_u. Services with no requests are not considered. Suppose s_j belongs to c_u, the total rating from s_i to s_j is adjusted as follows:

$$\hat{l}_{ij} = (\sum_u rate(r_{ij}^u)) * \frac{min\ c_u^{rt}}{rt_j} \tag{3}$$

In the above equation, if s_j achieves the minimal average response time in category c_u, the total rating remains the same. Otherwise, the rating will be adjusted by a constant less than 1. $\frac{min\ c_u^{rt}}{rt_j}$ brings category knowledge into local ratings. This unique feature differentiates ServiceRank from earlier ranking algorithms in which local ratings are solely based on local knowledge [5][7]. With this new feature, if a client sends the same amount of requests to two services in a category, the client will give a higher rating to the one achieving better response time. Note that there are other ways to adjusting local ratings with category knowledge. For example, we can use the median of services' average response time and put penalties on local ratings only when a service performs below the average. We do not discuss them further since they do not change the definition of Equation 3 fundamentally. A concern in this approach is that a malicious service can register itself in a category and respond back to its malicious partners instantaneously. In doing so, an ordinary service is likely to be penalized due to its "bad" performance. This problem can be avoided if we use average response time from well-established services as an adjusting baseline.

2.2   Normalizing and Aggregating Local Ratings

In social ranking, we wish that the rank of a service is decided by both the ranks and ratings of its clients. ServiceRank computes the global rank of s_j by aggregating the local ratings from its client, defined as

$$w_j = \sum_{s_i \in B_j} \hat{l_{ij}} w_i \tag{4}$$

It is important to normalize local ratings to remove noisy data and protect the ranking system from a malicious party which creates bogus services and commands them to send requests to a service to artificially raise its rank. ServiceRank normalizes local ratings in two steps. First, it evaluates the eligibility of a local rating l_{ij} by two criteria: 1) the total number of requests exceeds a constant number T such that $|R_{ij}| > T$; 2) successful rate exceeds a threshold β such that $\frac{|R_{ij}^{succ}|}{|R_{ij}|} > \beta$, where R_{ij}^{succ} denotes those requests that satisfy $rate(r_{ij}^u) = 1$. T and β are two configurable parameters. The two criteria ensure that two services must establish a stable history before ServiceRank considers its local rating. This helps remove noisy data such as ratings from testing requests or ratings for unavailable services. In the second normalization step, only eligible ratings are considered. A local rating from s_i to s_j is divided by l_{ij} with the total number of requests sent by s_i:

$$r_{ij} = \frac{\hat{l_{ij}}}{\sum_j \hat{l_{ij}}} \tag{5}$$

With Equation 4, the global rank values of services $w = (w_1, w_2, ..., w_n)$ are the entries of the principal left eigenvector of the normalized local rating matrix $R = (r_{ij})_{ij}$, defined as follows:

$$w^T = w^T R \tag{6}$$

The above definition does not consider prior knowledge of popular services. In a service network, some services are known to be trustworthy and provide good quality. Similar to the early approach [5], ServiceRank uses this knowledge to address the problem of malicious collectives in which a group of services sends requests to each other to gain high global ranking values. Let Q denote a set of trusted services. We define the vector q to represent the pre-trusted rank values. q_i is assigned a positive value if $s_i \in Q$, otherwsie $q_i = 0$. q satisfies $\sum_i q_i = 1$. The global rank values of services are now defined as:

$$w^T = aw^T R + (1 - a)q^T \tag{7}$$

where R is the normalized local rating matrix and a a constant less than 1. Equation 7 is a flow model [4]. It assumes that the sum of global ranks is a constant, and the total rank value is distributed among services in a network. q serves as a rank source. This model states that starting from a trusted source, the global ranks are unlikely to be distributed to untrusted services if there are no links from trusted services to untrusted services. Therefore, malicious collectives can be prevented if we can effectively control the number of links between these two groups.

3   System Prototype and Runtime Traffic Monitoring

ServiceRank has been implemented on SOAlive [12] which is an approach to provide smart middleware as a service. The SOAlive platform allows users to create, deploy, and manage situational applications easily. Each application may include one or more services which may be invoked at runtime, and which in turn, may invoke other services. For our experiments, we used a SOAlive implementation on WebSphere sMash [http://www.projectzero.org/]. WebSphere sMash is an agile web development platform that provides a new programming model and a runtime that promotes REST-centric application architectures. Logically, the SOAlive platform can be broken down into i) system components; and ii) hosted applications and their runtimes.

Figure 2 shows the key SOAlive components. The service catalog, the repository, the application manager, the application installer, and the router work in concert to provide a simplified development and deployment experience.

- The **SOAlive repository** allows modules, the building blocks for applications, to be uploaded and shared.
- The **SOAlive Application Manager** lets users create deployed applications from deployable modules in the repository.
- The **SOAlive Application Installer** is responsible for downloading, resolving, and installing user applications on worker nodes.
- The **SOAlive catalog** stores metadata about hosted artifacts, in addition to storing metadata about external artifacts which are of interest to users of the SOALive platform. It also acts as the hub for collaborative development.
- The **SOAlive router** is the first stop for any request coming into SOAlive and provides a suitable extension point for monitoring functions.

SOAlive supports several different topologies ranging from the one in which all the system components and managed applications run on a single node to a truly distributed topology where individual system components are themselves distributed across several nodes, and applications execute in one or more worker nodes based on system policies. SOAlive defines several extension points as a way to build upon its core functionality. One of these extension points allows for different runtime monitors to be added as logical extensions to the routing component.

Monitoring is enabled on a per-application basis. Each application includes a "monitor" flag that must be set for monitoring to occur. When monitoring is enabled for a given application, the server will invoke all registered application monitors for each application request/response pair. The monitor will be invoked on the application request thread, after the response is available. The monitor's caller

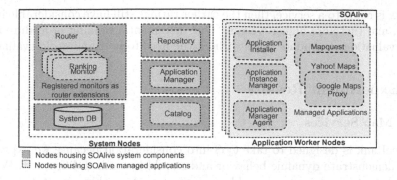

Fig. 2. SOAlive system architecture

assumes that the monitor will return as quickly as possible, and that it will defer any processing for a later time and on a separate thread. The following figure shows the sequence of events when SOAlive receives a request to a managed application that has monitoring enabled. For inter-application requests (i.e., where one hosted SOAlive application invokes another hosted SOAlive application), the runtime for the source application adds headers to the out-bound request that identifies the source application and the specific method in the source application from which the call originated. This allows the SOAlive monitoring and logging facilities to fully determine the source of a request. This header injection feature is also used to propagate the correlator for a chain of invocations. For instance, if application A_1 called A_2 that called A_3 and A_4, then the paths $A_1 \rightarrow A_2 \rightarrow A_3$ and $A_1 \rightarrow A_2 \rightarrow A_4$ have the same correlator. This correlator is a unique ID generated by SOAlive at the start of a chain of requests.

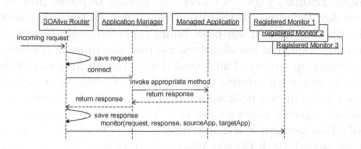

Fig. 3. SOAlive monitoring flow

Using the information gathered from the ranking monitors, ranks are computed periodically and incrementally in SOAlive. Weights are assigned to each evaluation, with the more recent evaluations having higher weights. The assigned weights also depend upon service lifecycle events - for example, if a service is entirely rewritten, then its previous evaluations are assigned low weights. If a minor bug fix is made to a service, then the earlier ratings still have considerable importance, and therefore higher weights. Our incremental ranking procedure allows new evaluations to update ranks without the need to re-examine old evaluations.

4   Experiment Results

4.1   Map Services

ServiceRank is designed to take QoS into consideration because we expect services demonstrate dynamic behavior and should be ranked differently. We conducted experiments on real-world services to confirm this expectation. In our experiments, we collected traffic data from three well-known map services: Google Maps, Yahoo! Maps, and Mapquest. They were chosen because all of them have standard APIs that take the geocoding of an address and return its local map. Moreover, the returned results all contain similar map data. Therefore, it is meaningful to characterize and compare their performance in terms of response time and failure rate.

Experiment setup. To obtain the traffic data of three map services through SOALive, we create three proxies. Each proxy is responsible for forwarding a request to the real map service and forwarding back the result to its client. We implement a workload generator that periodically sent requests to three proxies at a configurable interval. At each turn, the workload generator uniformly chooses the geocoding of an address in the US from a database that contains hundreds of entries. We collect the traffic data for each service for seven consecutive days. The time interval is set to be 30 seconds. The traffic data was collected from 7:00pm (EDT) August 4th, 2008 to 7:00pm (EDT) August 11th, 2008.

Experiment results. Figure 4 shows the average response time at different times in the day. We can see three phenomena. First, all three map services have degraded response time during peak hours (approximately between 8:00 and 18:00). Second, MapQuest has slightly worse response times in general compared to the other two map services. Third, even though Google Maps and Yahoo! Maps have similar response time during non-peak hours, Google Maps performs worse than Yahoo! Maps during peak hours. Figure 5 shows the percentage of failed invocations at different times in the day. The figure does not show anything for Yahoo! Maps because it did not return any failed invocations during our experimental period. Both Google Maps and MapQuest have very small failure rates with MapQuest being slightly higher.

From these experiment results, we can see that real-world services do demonstrate different behavior over time. Therefore, it is very important to rank them dynamically to characterize their latest performance. From Figure 4, we see that Google Maps has degraded response time during peak daytime hours. The most likely explanation is that Google Maps is more loaded during that period. Yahoo! Maps demonstrates better average response time during the same period. QoS-based ranking can provide valuable information to assist applications that have

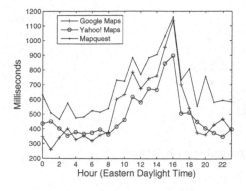

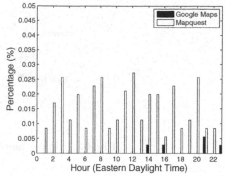

Fig. 4. Average response time

Fig. 5. Percentage of failed invocations. Yahoo! Maps does not have bars because it did not return any failed request. Google Maps has few bars because it returned failed requests only in some of the hours.

critical requirements on performance. For example, travel planning services that want to integrate a map service would do well to choose Yahoo! Maps during peak hours.

The relative performance of Google Maps, Yahoo! Maps, and Mapquest may have changed since the time these measurements were made. For a large number of customers, all three services offer performance and availability which are more than adequate. We do not have sufficient data to judge one of the services as currently being superior to another. The key point is that at any given point in time, different services offering the same functionality will often show noticeable differences in performance. In addition, there may also be considerable variations in performance based on the time of day.

4.2 ServiceRank Properties

We now demonstrate the properties of ServiceRank through a hierarchical service network model. In this model, a set of services form a hierarchical structure. The structure is divided into layers $l_1, l_2, ..., l_n$. Services at the same layer belong to the same category. The lowest layer is l_1. Services at l_i are clients of services at l_{i+1}. Requests are sent by a root service s_0 to services at l_1. To process a request, a service at l_1 invokes one of the services at l_2, which will in turn uses a service at l_3 and so on. The response time of a request at a service is the service's own processing time plus the round trip time spent at upper layers.

Experiment 1. We intend to show how the rank of a service changes with the number of times it is invoked. A simple topology suffices for this purpose. We use the one shown in Figure 6. An arrow represents a client-server relationship. We gradually adjust the percentage of requests between s_1 and s_2 and observe how

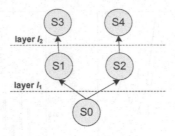

Fig. 6. A simple hierarchical service network

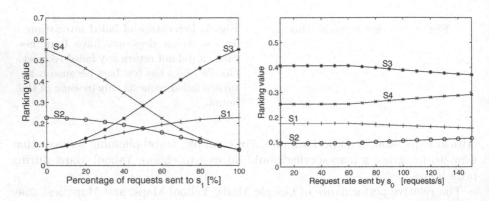

Fig. 7. Impact of request frequency on ranking values

Fig. 8. Impact of response time on ranking values

the ranks of s_3, s_4, s_5, and s_6 change. To see only the impact of request frequency, we do not consider the two other factors: failure rate and response time. In other words, each request is successfully satisfied, and services in the same category have similar response times. The results are shown in Figure 7. We can see that the ranking values of both s_1 and s_3 increase as they consume a higher percentage of requests compared to their counterparts. The ranking values of s_2 and s_4 decrease correspondingly. We can also see that the ranking value of a service is impacted not only by the percentage of requests it receives, but also by the ranking values of its client. In this case, s_3's ranking value increases faster than s_1 because both s_3's request percentage and s_1's ranking value get increased. This property is a desirable feature of social ranking because it takes into consideration both popularities of services and the amount of workload they share.

Experiment 2. We now evaluate how the rank of a service is impacted by the quality its requests receive. We continue to use the topology in Figure 6. We assume that the percentage of requests between s_1 and s_2 follows the 80-20 rule in which s_1 receives 80% of requests while s_2 receives 20%. The experiment runs in cycles. In each cycle, s_0 sends requests at a given rate to both s_1 and

s_2, which will invoke their corresponding services at the next upper layer. We simulate the average response time of a service by a function, which remains constant when the request rate below a threshold and increases linearly after that. In the experiment, we configure the threshold to be 50. Figure 8 shows the result. Without considering the factor of response time, the ranking values of all services would not change over the course of the experiment because the percentage of requests at all services does not change. After taking response time into consideration, the number of ratings a service receives from its clients will be adjusted by how well the requests are served. From Figure 8, we can see that the ranks of services do not change when the number of requests is below 50. After that, the ranks of s_1 and s_3 begin to drop because their response times start to increase. This is to simulate the situation in which a service shows degraded performance when overloaded. As a result, the ranks of s_1 and s_2 start to converge. s_3 and s_4 demonstrate similar trends. In real applications, this property motivates service writers to improve service response times in order to keep service ranks from declining when the services are overloaded due to high request rates. It also provides more accurate information to guide new traffic to services that are less overloaded.

4.3   Monitoring Overhead in SOALive

SOALive collects the traffic data of services when they are serving customers. It is very important that the monitoring procedure does not interfere with the ordinary operation of services. The experiment in this section measures the monitoring overhead.

Experiment setup. We set up two services s_i and s_j in SOALive. s_i uses s_j's functionality by sending a sequence of HTTP requests. The monitoring service in SOALive is responsible for recording the round trip time of each invocation and its status. s_j has an empty function body. It returns back to s_i as soon as

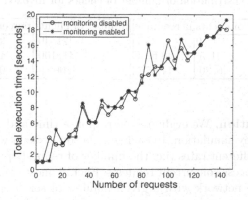

Fig. 9. Monitoring overhead in SOALive

it receives a request. Therefore, the total amount of time to process a batch of requests will be close to the overhead introduced by SOALive.

Experiment result. Figure 9 shows the results. We gradually increase the total number of requests between s_i and s_j. For each configuration, we collect total processing time with and without monitoring enabled. We run the experiment five times and compute the average. Figure 9 shows that the overall processing time with monitoring enabled is only slightly higher than the case with monitoring disabled. This demonstrates that an efficient monitoring service can be implemented in a cloud. The current experiment is only run in a small setting. For large settings with hundreds or even thousands of services deployed, we can use different optimization techniques such as sampling to collect traffic data.

4.4 ServiceRank Performance

In SOALive, ServiceRank periodically analyzes traffic data and computes the ranking values of services. It is important that ServiceRank can scale up to large numbers of services to provide ranking values in a timely fashion. We have implemented the ServiceRank algorithm by using the power method to compute the left principal eigenvector of Equation 7. Since we do not have enough services in SOALive to test the algorithm for a large number of services, we evaluate its performance for a high number of services by simulation.

Service network model. The topology of a service network is determined by both the number of services and the service invocations. We assume that within the cloud, services with different popularities exist. For an invoked service, the number of its clients conforms to a power law distribution as shown in Table 1. In this setting, 35% of services are only clients and do not provide services to others. A majority of services (60.36%) have clients ranging between 1 and 20. Less than 1% services have more than 100 clients.

Table 1. Distribution of number of clients for invoked services

number of clients	percentage	number of clients	percentage
0	35%	[21, 40]	2.26%
[1, 5]	48.69%	[41, 100]	1.39%
[6, 20]	11.67%	[100, +]	0.99%

Simulation execution. We evaluate the response time and throughput of our ranking algorithm by simulation. In each simulation cycle, a workload generator sends requests at different rates (i.e. the number of requests per second). We use a thread pool to process concurrent requests. Each request computes the ranking values for a service network with a given number of services. The services are connected according to our service network model. To measure average response time, we run our workload generator for three minutes and average the response

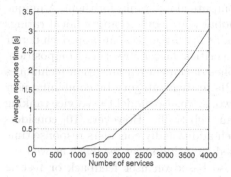

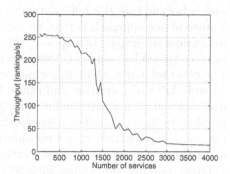

Fig. 10. Average response time for service networks with different number of services

Fig. 11. Throughput per second for service networks with different number of services

time of each request. To measure maximum throughput, we adjust request rates and observe the values of throughput at different rates for three minutes. The maximum throughput is the point when the throughput does not increase any more with the increase of request rate.

Hardware configuration. All experiments are conducted on a 64-bit GNU Linux machine with Intel(R) Core(TM)2 Quad CPU 2.83GHz, 4GB RAM.

Experiment results. Figure 10 shows the results for the measurement of response time. Figure 11 shows the results for the measurement of throughput. As the number of services increases in a service network, the response time is less than tens of milliseconds on average until the number reaches at around 1500 services. Correspondingly, the throughput of ServiceRank scales well for service networks with less than 1500 services. After that the throughput gradually drops from hundreds of rankings per second to less than ten rankings per second. We expect in a real cloud, rankings are not workload-intensive. There may be many seconds between successive rankings. Therefore, ServiceRank should be able to scale up to large settings with many thousands of services.

5   Related Work

Past work addresses the ranking problem by analyzing relationships between different parties. Mei et. al. [7] analyze binding information in service WSDL specifications and apply the PageRank algorithm [9] to compute global ranks of services. The binding relationships are static and cannot distinguish services different in runtime qualities. Gekas et.al. [3] analyze semantic compatibility of input/output parameters of services and select the best matching service for an output request. We focus on QoS metrics for service composition. Two pieces of work are close to ours. One is EigenTrust [5], which works on peer ranking on P2P networks. EigenTrust considers how frequently two parties interact with each other and uses this information to compute global ranks for them. A unique feature of our approach is that we use global knowledge to adjust local ratings to consider the impact of response time. This feature makes our approach better suitable for service ranking in that QoS is a critical factor for service composition. The other related work is [10], which applies document classification techniques for web API categorization and ranks APIs in each category by combining user feedback and utilization. Similar to their work, we also model the service ranking problem by using statistics collected from web traffic. However, [10] considers the factor of popularity only. Our approach additionally considers response time and failure rate and can be easily extended to include user feedback as well.

Other ranking approaches include those based on user feedback or testing techniques. In [2], the authors propose to rank services based on users' ratings to different QoS metrics. These ratings are then aggregated to compute global ranks of services. In [8], gaps between users' feedback and actually delivered QoS from service providers are measured to rank services. These approaches have limited application in service networks because human feedback may not be available for those backend services that do not have direct interactions with customers. Tsai et.al. [14] propose a ranking technique in which pre-developed testing cases are executed periodically to check the current status of services. Services are ranked according to their deviation from the expected output.

Several ranking frameworks are proposed to rank services by combining many aspects of QoS into the same picture. Liu et al. [6] proposed to rank services based on prices, advertised QoS information from service providers, feedback from users, and performance data from live monitoring. Sheth et. al [11] proposed a service-oriented middleware for QoS management by taking into consideration time, cost, reliability and fidelity. Bottaro et al. [1] proposed a context management infrastructure in which services are dynamically ranked based on application contextual states at runtime (e.g., physical location of mobile devices). These frameworks target a broader spectrum of QoS domains and mainly focus on the design of expressive QoS specification languages and algorithmic solutions to aggregating metrics from different subdomains. By comparison, our work provides a unique solution to incorporate QoS into service ranking and can be adopted as part of a broader ranking framework covering other aspects.

6   Conclusion

In cloud computing, services are discovered, selected, and composed to satisfy application requirements. It is often the case that multiple services exist to perform similar functions. To facilitate the selection process for comparable services, we propose a new ranking method, referred to as ServiceRank, that combines quantitative QoS metrics with social aspects of services to provide valuable ranking information. Services form a social network through client-server invocation relationships. The ServiceRank algorithm ranks a service by considering not only its response time and availability but also its popularity in terms of how many services are its clients and how frequently it is used. By combining all these factors, the rank of a service will be raised if it attracts a higher amount of traffic and demonstrates better performance compared to other comparable services. In the future, we plan to integrate service level agreements into our current work. With this feature, the rank of a service will be impacted by both its performance and its fulfillment of service-level contracts.

References

1. Bottaro, A., Hall, R.S.: Dynamic contextual service ranking. In: Lumpe, M., Van-derperren, W. (eds.) SC 2007. LNCS, vol. 4829, pp. 129–143. Springer, Heidelberg (2007)
2. Chan, H., Chieu, T., Kwok, T.: Autonomic ranking and selection of web services by using single value decomposition technique. In: ICWS, pp. 661–666 (2008)
3. Gekas, J., Fasli, M.: Automatic web service composition based on graph network analysis metrics. In: Meersman, R., Tari, Z. (eds.) OTM 2005. LNCS, vol. 3761, pp. 1571–1587. Springer, Heidelberg (2005)
4. Jósang, A., Ismail, R., Boyd, C.: A survey of trust and reputation systems for online service provision. Decis. Support Syst. 43(2), 618–644 (2007)
5. Kamvar, S.D., Schlosser, M.T., Garcia-Molina, H.: The eigentrust algorithm for reputation management in p2p networks. In: Proceedings of the 12th international conference on World Wide Web, pp. 640–651. ACM, New York (2003)
6. Liu, Y., Ngu, A.H., Zeng, L.Z.: Qos computation and policing in dynamic web service selection. In: Proceedings of the 13th international World Wide Web conference on Alternate track papers & posters, pp. 66–73. ACM, New York (2004)
7. Mei, L., Chan, W.K., Tse, T.H.: An adaptive service selection approach to service composition. In: Proceedings of the 2008 IEEE International Conference on Web Services, Washington, DC, USA, 2008, pp. 70–77. IEEE Computer Society, Los Alamitos (2008)
8. Ouzzani, M., Bouguettaya, A.: Efficient access to web services. IEEE Internet Computing 8(2), 34–44 (2004)
9. Page, L., Brin, S., Motwani, R., Winograd, T.: The pagerank citation ranking: Bringing order to the web. Technical Report 1999-66, Stanford InfoLab (November 1999)
10. Ranabahu, A., Nagarajan, M., Sheth, A.P., Verma, K.: A faceted classification based approach to search and rank web apis. In: Proceedings of ICWS 2008, pp. 177–184 (2008)
11. Sheth, A., Cardoso, J., Miller, J., Kochut, K.: Qos for service-oriented middleware. In: Proceedings of the Conference on Systemics, Cybernetics and Informatics (2002)
12. Silva-Lepe, I., Subramanian, R., Rouvellou, I., Mikalsen, T., Diament, J., Iyengar, A.: Soalive service catalog: A simplified approach to describing, discovering and composing situational enterprise services. In: Bouguettaya, A., Krueger, I., Margaria, T. (eds.) ICSOC 2008. LNCS, vol. 5364, pp. 422–437. Springer, Heidelberg (2008)
13. Sriharee, N., Senivongse, T.: Matchmaking and ranking of semantic web services using integrated service profile. Int. J. Metadata Semant. Ontologies 1(2), 100–118 (2006)
14. Tsai, W.-T., Chen, Y., Paul, R., Huang, H., Zhou, X., Wei, X.: Adaptive testing, oracle generation, and test case ranking for web services. In: Proceedings of the 29th Annual International Computer Software and Applications Conference, Washington, DC, USA, 2005, pp. 101–106. IEEE Computer Society, Los Alamitos (2005)

Web Services Reputation Assessment Using a Hidden Markov Model*

Zaki Malik[1], Ihsan Akbar[2], and Athman Bouguettaya[3]

[1] Department of Computer Science, Wayne State University
Detroit, MI, 48202 USA
zaki@wayne.edu
[2] Department of Electrical Engineering,
Virginia Tech Blacksburg, VA. 24061 USA
iakbar@vt.edu
[3] CSIRO, ICT Center. Canberra, Australia
athman.bouguettaya@csiro.au

Abstract. We present an approach for reputation assessment in service-oriented environments. We define key metrics to aggregate the feedbacks of different raters, for assessing a service provider's reputation. In situations where rater feedbacks are not readily available, we use a Hidden Markov Models (HMM) to predict the reputation of a service provider. HMMs have proven to be suitable in numerous research areas for modelling dynamic systems. We propose to emulate the success of such systems for evaluating service reputations to enable trust-based interactions with and amongst Web services. The experiment details included in this paper show the applicability of the proposed HMM-based reputation assessment model.

1 Introduction

The next installment of the World Wide Web will be a shift from the current data-centric Web to a service-centric Web [14]. In this regard, the Web, services, and semantic technologies (e.g. in the form of ontologies) will come together to create an environment where users (and applications) can query and compose services in an automatic and seamless manner. The *Service Web* will build upon and extend the Semantic Web to treat services as first class objects. Web services are slated to be the key enablers of the new service computing paradigm [14]. A Web service is defined as a self-describing software application that can be advertised, located, and used on the Web using a set of standards such as WSDL, UDDI, and SOAP. The Service Web is expected to be a place where a large number of Web services will compete to offer similar functionalities [9]. Thus, enriching the Web with semantics would facilitate the organization and location of these services, and most importantly enable quality-based querying. It is expected that Web services would fully leverage the Semantic Web to outsource

---

* This work is funded in part by the U.S. National Science Foundation grant number 0627469.

L. Baresi, C.-H. Chi, and J. Suzuki (Eds.): ICSOC-ServiceWave 2009, LNCS 5900, pp. 576–591, 2009.

part of their functionality to other Web services [20]. In this case, some services may not have interacted before, while others may act maliciously to be selected, thus negatively impacting the quality of collaboration. A key requirement then is to provide *trust* mechanisms for quality access and retrieval of services [8].

Over the years, a number of techniques have been proposed for establishing trust online. These techniques fall under two main categories: security-based solutions, and social control-based solutions. The former includes mechanisms as authentication, access control, etc, while the latter is based on recommendations and reputation. In this paper, we focus on reputation as a means to establish trust among different services.

Reputation is regarded as a predictor of future behavior. It is a subjective assessment of a characteristic ascribed to one entity by another based on past experiences. In the context of the Service Web, we refer to the aggregated perceptions that the community of service requesters have for a given Web service provider as service *reputation*. Experimental studies have shown that people rely on reputation systems (e.g. eBay's Feedback Forum) to make trust-enabled decisions regarding their daily Web-enabled activities [8]. Reputation systems rely on the feedbacks or ratings provided by the members of the community for a given subject. At times, due to various reasons, majority of the members may not be willing to engage in the rating process. In such situations of *ratings scarcity*, the accuracy of the reputation system may be compromised. We address the issue of ratings scarcity by approximating ratings aggregation and *predicting* the reputation of a given subject based on historical data.

In terms of prediction accuracy, machine learning algorithms have provided better results over other traditional techniques [16]. For instance, Artificial Neural Networks (ANNs) and Hidden Markov Models (HMMs) exhibit high predictive power, especially with large data sets [16]. Since ANN performances depend greatly on the chosen architecture, and a user may need to perform extensive model training by considering almost every feature, we prefer to use HMMs for reputation prediction. Moreover, an HMM allows a user more control than an ANN, with comparable accuracy. HMMs have been used successfully in pattern recognition (voice and face), hand writing recognition, natural language domains, DNA sequence analysis, finger print matching, prediction of stock market prices, etc [16]. We build on that success to predict the reputation of Web services through HMMs.

Several reputation systems have been proposed in the literature. The spectrum of these reputation management solutions ranges from "purely statistical" techniques to "heuristics-based" techniques. While statistical techniques focus on providing a sound theory for reputation management, heuristics-based techniques focus on defining a practical model for implementing a robust reputation system. Bayesian systems [5], [13] and belief models [6], [24] are the major examples of purely statistical techniques. Bayesian systems work on binary ratings (honest or dishonest) to assess the reputation, by statistical updating of beta probability density functions. In a belief model, a consumer's belief regarding the truth of a ratings statement is also factored in reputation computation. The techniques for combining beliefs vary from one solution to the other. For example, [24] uses the Dempster's Rule, while Subjective Logic is used in [6]. The complexity of purely statistical solutions has prompted researchers to present heuristics-based solutions. These solutions aim to define a practical, robust, and easy to understand/construct reputation management system. For example, [23] and [4]. In the following, we present a hybrid solution defining key heuristics, and a statistical model (HMM-based) for reputation assessment.

2   Web Services Reputation

A Web service exposes an interface through which it may be automatically invoked by Web clients. A Web service's interface describes a collection of operations that are network-accessible through standardized XML messaging [9]. Invoking a Web service involves three entities: the *service provider*, the *service registry* and the *service consumer*. The service provider is the entity that owns and/or manages the service. It advertises the capabilities of the service by publishing a description to the service registry. This description specifies how the service can be invoked (i.e., its address, operations, parameters, etc.) The service registry is a repository of service descriptions. Finally, the service consumer is the entity that invokes the service.

In traditional Web service models, service selection is not trust-based, and an invocation can be made directly after discovering the service through the registry. However, in our model this selection is based on the reputation of each individual service from the list retrieved through the service registry. The service consumer gathers the feedbacks of the providers from its peer service consumers, and then sorts the providers according to the assessed reputation. The higher the reputation of a service provider, the *better* the service. Service consumers then *invoke* the best available Web service through one of its listed operations. We assume that at the end of the interaction the service consumer *rates* the provider according to some pre-determined criteria (e.g., using an ontology[9], [23]). The service ratings are used to compute the provider reputations accordingly.

We view the reputation of a Web service as a reflection of its *quality*. The Quality of Service (*QoS*), is defined as a set of quantitative and qualitative characteristics of a system, necessary to achieve the required functionality of an application [17]. We adopt a similar definition of *QoS* and extend its application to the Service Web with related constraints (similar to [17], [10]). We term this as the quality of Web service (QoWS). QoWS is a mapping between a set of quality parameters defined through a common ontology, and a set of values or ranges of values. Examples of quality parameters include security, privacy preservation, a services' response time, availability, reliability, etc.

Let S and T be the set of provider Web services and the set of service consumers respectively. Let Φ be the universal set of quality parameters. Φ may be represented as a p-element vector $(\phi_1, ..., \phi_p)$ where ϕ_k is the kth quality parameter. Each Web service $s_j \in S$ advertises a promised quality $QoWS_p(s_j)$, which assigns values or ranges of values to each quality parameter ϕ_k. When a service requester $x \in T$ invokes the service s_j, each quality parameter ϕ_k in Φ gets assigned a delivered quality value ϕ_k^{xj} (post-transaction completion). For this invocation of service s_j, the vector $QoWS_d(s_j, x) = \{\phi_1^{xj}, .., \phi_p^{xj}\}$ is called the delivered quality of Web service.

It is outside the scope of the current discussion exactly how values are assigned to different $QoWS$ attributes. We assume a service publication model presented in [17], where service providers publish their $QoWS_p$ values in the service registry (say UDDI) with the service descriptions ([20] proposes a similar technique). Other similar models where the QoWS information can be added to the WSDL file using WS-Policy, can also be used [8]. Post-transaction completion, observing the variation between $QoWS_p$ and $QoWS_d$, *reputation* values can be created [17], [20], [8].

We suggest that since the Service Web cannot be easily monitored due to its expanse, each service consumer records its own perceptions of the reputation of only the services it actually invokes. This perception is called *personal evaluation (PerEval)*. For each service s_j that it has invoked, a service consumer x maintains a p-element vector $PerEval_j^x$ representing x's perception of s_j's reputation. Thus, personal evaluation only reflects the QoWS performance of a provider in the consumer's own view.

2.1 Reputation Assessment

A consumer intending to assess the reputation of a service provider may inquire several peer consumers in its community (the one its is registered with), and aggregate their respective personal evaluations for s_j. Identifying the entities responsible for collecting and disseminating reputations, and defining the procedures involved in such reputation exchanges are important aspects of a reputation management system, which require independent research. We assume a reputation collection model presented in [22], and extend it to the Web services domain using methods presented in [12]. Note that other collection models as [1], [17] can also be used. A single value is obtained as a result of the aggregation of personal evaluations collected. This derived value is defined as the service provider's *aggregated reputation* in that consumer's view. Different service consumers may employ different aggregation techniques. Therefore, the aggregated reputation value for the same provider may be different for each consumer, i.e., it may not be consistent across all consumers. Formally, the reputation of s_j, as viewed by a consumer is defined as:

$$Reputation(s_j) = \bigwedge_{x \in L} (PerEval_j^x) \tag{1}$$

where L denotes the set of service raters and $\bigwedge$ represents the aggregation function. It can be as simple as representing the union of personal evaluations where the output is a real number, or an elaborate process that considers a number of factors to assess a fairly accurate reputation value.

Equation 1 provides an approximation of how the service reputation may be calculated. In the following, we build upon this equation to define the "RATEWeb metrics" for accurate reputation assessment. We aim to counter attacks related to deception in reputation management, i.e., identifying, preventing, and detecting malicious behavior of peers or a set of colluding peers acting as either service providers or raters. Problems as free riding, fake identities, ratings incentives, etc. are outside the scope of this paper.

Credibility of Raters: The foremost drawback of feedback-only based systems is that all ratings are assumed to be honest and unbiased. However, in the real world we clearly distinguish between the testimonies of our sources and weigh the "trusted" ones more than others [19]. A Web service that provides satisfactory service (in accordance with its promised quality $(QoWS_p)$), may get incorrect or false ratings from different evaluators due to several malicious motives. In order to cater for such "bad-mouthing" or collusion possibilities, a reputation management system should weigh the ratings of highly credible raters more than consumers with low credibilities [4], [3], [18], [15], [23]. In RATEWeb, the reputation score of the provider is calculated according to the credibility scores of the raters (used as the weight). Thus, Equation 1 becomes:

$$Reputation(s_j) = \frac{\sum_{x=1}^{L}(PerEval_j^x * C_r(x))}{\sum_{x=1}^{L} C_r(x)} \qquad (2)$$

where $Reputation(s_j)$ is the assessed reputation of s_j as calculated by the service consumer and $C_r(x)$ is the credibility of the service rater x as viewed by the service consumer. The credibility of a service rater lies in the interval $[0,1]$ with 0 identifying a dishonest rater and 1 an honest one. The processes involved in calculating raters' credibilities are described in detail in [8].

Personalized Preferences: Service consumers may vary in their reputation evaluations due to their differences in QoWS attribute preferences over which a Web service is evaluated. For instance, some service consumers may label Web services with high reliability as more reputable while others may consider low-priced services as more reputable. We allow the service consumers to calculate the reputation scores of the Web services according to their own *personal preferences*. Each service consumer stores its QoWS attribute preferences in a *reputation significance vector* (RSV). This allows the consumers the ability to weigh the different attributes according to their own preferences. Let $\phi_h(s_j, u)^x$ denote the rating assigned to attribute h by the service rater x for service provider s_j in transaction u, m denote the total number of attributes and RSV_h denote the preference of the service consumer for attribute h. Then, the local reputation for s_j as reported by service rater x is defined as:

$$PerEval_j^x = \frac{\sum_{h=1}^{m}(\phi_h(s_j, u)^x * RSV_h)}{\sum_{h=1}^{m} RSV_h} \qquad (3)$$

Reputation Fading: Reputation information of a service provider decays with time [9][11]. Hence all the past reputation data may be of little or no importance.

For instance, a Web service performing inconsistently in the past may ameliorate its behavior. Alternatively, a service's performance may degrade over time.
It may be the case that considering all historical data may provide incorrect reputation scores. In order to counter such discrepancies, we incorporate temporal
sensitivity in our proposed model. The rating submissions are time-stamped to
assign more weight to recent observations and less to older ones. This is termed
as "reputation fading" where older perceptions gradually *fade* and fresh ones
take their place. We adjust the value of the ratings as:

$$PerEval_j^x(t) = PerEval_j^x(t-1:t-v) * f_d \qquad (4)$$

where $PerEval^{xj}$ is as defined above and f_d is the reputation fader. t is the
current time instance and $t-1:t-v$ specifies the time interval from previous 1
to v transactions. In our model, the recent most rating has the fader value 1 while
older observations are decremented for each time interval passed. When $f_d = 0$,
the consumer's rating is not considered as it is outdated. The "time interval" is
an assigned factor, which could be anywhere from a single reputation inquiry,
ten inquiries or even more than that. All inquiries that are grouped in one time
interval are assigned the same fader value. In this way, the service consumer can
define its own temporal sensitivity degree. For example, a service can omit the
fader value's effect altogether by assigning it a null value. We propose to use
a fader value that can then be calculated as: $f_d = \frac{1}{\sqrt{P_u}}$, where P_u is the time
interval difference between the present time and the time in which the rating
was collected from the rater. This allows the convergence of reputation to a very
small value as time passes. Note that the consumer can assign a group of ratings
collected at different times to have the same time-stamp, and hence lie in the
same time interval.

Incorporating the defined metrics together (denoted RATEWeb metrics), the
equation for overall reputation calculation becomes:

$$Reputation(s_j) = \frac{\sum_{x=1}^{L} [\frac{\sum_{h=1}^{m}(\phi_h(s_j,u)^x * RSV_h)}{\sum_{h=1}^{m} RSV_h} * f_d * C_r(x)]}{\sum_{x=1}^{L} C_r(x)} \qquad (5)$$

Through experimental evidence we have found that the above equation provides
a comprehensive assessment of the reputation of a given service provider. Some
evaluation results are presented in Section 3. For a thorough review, the interested reviewer is referred to [9]. Other aspects of our RATEWeb framework
relating to reputation bootstrapping are defined in [10], and are outside the scope
of this paper. As mentioned earlier, the providers' reputations calculated above
may not always be available. This may either be due to the reluctance of the
raters or other unforseen circumstances as power outages, network congestion,
etc. We propose to use HMM-based "prediction" methods to evaluate service
reputations based on past behavior in situations where the current feedbacks
are not available.

The proposed methodology is shown in Figure 1. Each service consumer's
HMM first trains itself using the feedbacks provided by its peers. Once a reliable

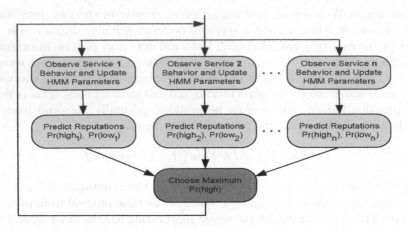

Fig. 1. Predicting Reputations using HMMs

model is developed, the high and low reputations of the services are predicted. In the next step, the service consumer compares all the predicted provider reputations. The provider that has the highest predicted reputation for the next time instance is chosen for interaction. After each interaction, the observed behavior values and present feedbacks are input to the HMM, and the model is refined.

2.2 HMM-Based Reputation Assessment

A Hidden Markov Model (HMM) is a finite state machine in which the observation sequence is a probabilistic function of a fixed number of states. In our case, it provides a probabilistic framework for modelling service reputations. Since their introduction in the 1970s, HMMs have proven to be very powerful prediction tools [16]. Some of the advantages of HMMs include: (1) strong mathematical and statistical basis, (2) more control through easy manipulation of training and verification processes, (3) mathematical/theoretical analysis of the results, (4) efficient prediction of similar patterns, and (5) ability to incorporate new knowledge robustly.

An excellent tutorial describing the basics and use of HMMs is available in [16]. In brief, an HMM (denoted ζ) is characterized by:

- the number of states in the model (N).
- the number of observation symbols per state (M), where each symbol corresponds to the actual output (here, reputation) being modelled.
- state transition probability matrix ($P = \{p_{ij}\}$), where p_{ij} represents the probability of transition from state i to state j.
- output probability matrix ($B = \{b_j(y_k)\}$), where $b_j(y_k)$ represents the probability of generating symbol y_k at state j.
- initial state distribution ($\pi = \{\pi_i\}$), where π_i gives the probability of being in a particular state at the start of the process.

With N and M (which depend on the observation data and the application objective) specified, an HMM is denoted as $\zeta = \{P, B, \pi\}$, with $\sum_j p_{ij} = 1$, $\sum_k b_j(y_k) = 1$, and $\sum_i \pi_i = 1$, where p_{ij}, $b_j(y_k)$, $\pi_i \geq 0$, $\forall i, j, k$.

There are established algorithms and techniques for the estimation of the parameters of an HMM. We have used the Bayesian Information Criterion (BIC) (one of the most accurate and frequently used order estimation techniques [16]) to estimate N for our reputation model: a 2-State HMM was selected. The estimation of the total number of states of HMM is an open question that still needs to be solved satisfactorily. "In the case of HMM, the problem of model selection (and in particular the choice of the number of states in the Markov chain component model) has yet to be satisfactorily solved" [7]. Similarly, in [2], it is stated that "the order estimation problem in an HMM is difficult because of our poor understanding of the maximum likelihood in HMMs." The likelihood of a process in case of HMMs, increases as the number of states increases. However, even though a higher state HMM is expected to perform well, it does not guarantee to provide optimal results [7], [2]. BIC is defined as:

$$\hat{x} = min[-2(\sup_{M^x} logPr(y_1^n)) + klog(n)] \tag{6}$$

where k is the dimension of a HMM, n is length of the observed reputations sequence, M^x represents the HMMs with different number of states, and $\hat{x}$ represents the selected HMM with optimal number of states. Using BIC over past reputations, we train HMMs with different number of states and obtain their corresponding log-likelihood (denoted l) values. The model with the minimum BIC value is then chosen. For instance, Table 1 shows the BIC order estimation process for a number of HMMs evaluated using experimental reputation data for different service providers. Experiment details are presented in the next section. Since 4.6861×10^3 is the lowest value obtained, BIC selects a 2-state HMM as the model of choice. Note that the number of HMM states that the BIC estimator selects, are specific to the training data. Thus, the number of states that different service consumers obtain for their respective HMMs, may also differ (since each consumer aggregates reputations according to his own preferences, knowledge, etc).

Note that all the models (2-state, 3-state, and 15-state HMMs shown) produce similar l-values, upon reaching the local maxima. Moreover, the number of iterations required to get to the local maxima are also similar. In terms of accuracy,

Table 1. Estimating BIC values of different HMMs

Model	k	$-l$	BIC
2-State HMM	4	2321.8056	4.6861×10^3
3-State HMM	9	2321.7719	4.7391×10^3
4-State HMM	16	2321.6676	4.8131×10^3
5-State HMM	25	2320.8490	4.9070×10^3
6-State HMM	36	2320.4865	5.0230×10^3

the different state models show similar results. But since greater the number of states in an HMM, greater is the complexity of the prediction process [21]. Therefore, we use the minimal state HMM (2-state HMM).

In defining M, we use a simple strategy that outputs one of two reputation symbols for the results obtained through Equation 5. One symbol represents a *trustworthy* service (i.e., high reputation), while the second symbol represents an *untrustworthy* (with low reputation) service. The choice of only two symbols is made only for simplifying the model explanation, and the number can be extended easily. Although the reputation values obtained from Equation 5 may be continuous, we distinguish the results to two discrete symbols by setting a threshold. For example, on a scale from 0 to 10 (0 being the lowest) with the threshold set at 5, reputation values graters than 5 are treated as trustworthy and untrustworthy otherwise. Other techniques (e.g., vector quantization) may also be used. Defining the system with just two reputation symbols suffices the need of our application. The service consumer either interacts with a trustworthy service, or it does not interact with an untrustworthy service. The need for "middle-ground" or "fuzzy" decision making arises only in cases where no trustworthy service is available. However, this can also be handled by adding a clause that lets the consumer choose the *best* provider from the remaining (untrustworthy) services.

In using the HMM, one major task is to find the probability (Pr) of generating the reputation sequence given the model ζ. This can be written as:

$$Pr(y_1^T|\zeta) = \pi B(y_1)PB(y_2)...PB(y_T) \qquad (7)$$

where $y_1^T = [y_1, y_2, ..., y_T]$ with each y_k having either high or low reputation (i.e., one of the 2 symbols), and $B(y_k)$ denotes the probability of generating symbol y_k from different states. We use the "Forward-Only algorithm" to compute $Pr(y_1^T|\zeta)$. Moreover, we use the Baum-Welch Algorithm (BWA) [16] (a form of the Expectation-Maximization (EM) algorithm) to estimate the parameters, and find the model that best explains the observed data. Due to space restrictions, details of the algorithms are not presented here. The interested reader is referred to [16].

Figure 2 shows the steps (simplified to elucidate) involved in using an HMM to assess a provider's reputation. To decide on interacting with a particular service provider, feedbacks from different raters are collected and aggregated (to derive the provider's reputation). In situations of ratings scarcity, aggregate reputations from previous instances are used to predict future provider behavior. The reputations, initial conditions (if any), etc. are used as inputs to the BWA to extract HMMs (with different number of states). BIC is then used to estimate the optimal number of states for the HMM. The selected model is then used to predict future service reputations, to aid in the interaction decision process. Any subsequent re-estimations are performed on the selected model.

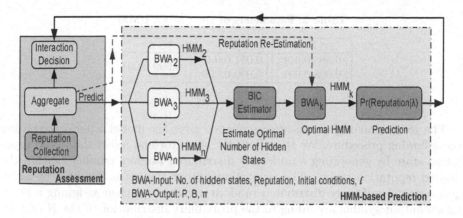

Fig. 2. HMM-based Prediction Processes

3 Evaluation

We performed preliminary experiments to evaluate the RATEWeb approach and show the accuracy of HMM-based reputation assessment. The experiments are divided into two phases. In the first phase, the effectiveness of RATEWeb metrics is evaluated. In the second phase, the assessed reputations from the first phase are used to train an HMM. The HMM is then used to predict future provider behavior. In the following, we provide the experiments related to HMM prediction (phase 2). Extensive evaluation of RATEWeb related to phase 1 is presented in [8], [9].

Setup: We created a Web services environment where the *actual* behavior of service providers is accurately captured, i.e, we can monitor each service's behavior. The providers' behaviors are simulated using data similar to the behavior of sellers at *eBay*. The service community consists of 100 Web services, and the interactions are conducted over 6000 time iterations. Although each QoWS parameter is rated individually, we use only the aggregated scalar aggregated reputation value to facilitate comparison. We assume that QoWS values are assigned accurately according to a pre-defined rating scheme. The minimum performance value is 0 while the maximum is 10.

The accuracy of the hidden Markov model is evaluated by observing the variance between the actual behavior and predicted reputation. We check the validity of our HMM-based reputation prediction by comparing the results with another formal prediction model (ANN) and with an ad hoc model in which no prediction is used. The type of ANN that we have used (through MATLAB) incorporates adaptive filtering which allows the network to adapt at each time step to minimize the error and predict in a relatively short time. The parameters of the HMM (from the processes in Figure 2) we use in the experiments are shown in Table 2.

Table 2. Parameters of the Chosen HMM

P	B	π
$\begin{bmatrix} 0.988 \ 0.011 \\ 0.008 \ 0.991 \end{bmatrix}$	$\begin{bmatrix} 0.051 \ 0.948 \\ 0.990 \ 0.009 \end{bmatrix}$	$\begin{bmatrix} 0.999 \ 0.001 \end{bmatrix}$

The generation of the reputation sequence given the model is performed using the following procedure. We start from the π vector and select the initial reputation state by generating a uniformly distributed random number (within the desired reputation range). The reputation output symbol is obtained by again generating a uniformly distributed random number and then assigning a reputation output symbol according to the probability distribution of the B matrix. The next reputation state is then obtained by again generating a uniformly distributed random number and selecting the next reputation state according to the probability distribution of the previous reputation state from the P matrix. We then go back and find the reputation output symbol according to the probability distributions of different reputation symbols using the B matrix. We continue till the required number of reputation output symbols are obtained. An HMM is most useful for random data that shows some pattern. We have generated a data set in which service reputations oscillate between high (above 5) and low (less than 5). The reputation data is random such that the service provider can shift from a high to low state and vice versa at any time. The time spent in each state is random and not uniform. However, the data exhibits memory since the service follows the pattern of staying in one state and moving to the other after 'sometime.' Note that the service provider does not change states at almost every time instance (as in memoryless systems).

Figure 3 shows the original reputation data generated for one service provider, and the comparison of the original data against HMM-based and ANN-based predicted reputation. The original data is represented by a continuous line (in color: blue) while the predicted reputations are shown as dotted lines (in color: red). In Figure 3-A, the original values for 5000 iterations are shown. However, Figures 3-B and -C show the zoomed-in values for iterations 1200 to 1600 for explanatory purposes. We have trained the HMM and ANN over 1000 iterations and then predicted reputations for 5500 future iterations. The predicted reputations shown in Figure 3 are not *completely* identical to the original ones. There is some "error" associated with each reputation prediction. However, the error is not disruptive to the prediction process due to its small size. The predicted reputation values obtained using the HMM (Figure 3-B) and the ANN (Figure 3-C) are very close to the original reputation. Therefore, we can safely conclude that the generated values are representative of the original service behavior allowing fairly accurate trust decision making.

Both the prediction models predict the reputation in a fairly accurate manner. This proves that both ANN and HMM-based methods are viable. Note that the duration of the provider's "stay" in either state (high or low reputation) is random and no two intervals are equal. Still, the HMM and ANN are able

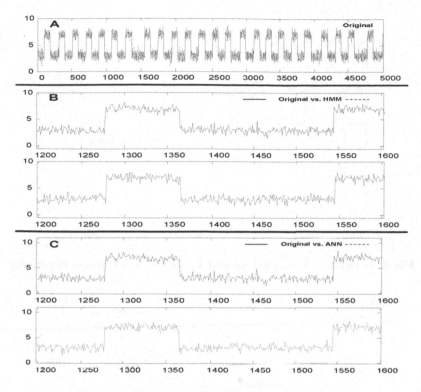

Fig. 3. Predicted Reputation Comparisons

to predict the reputation fairly accurately. However, the predicted values for HMM are closer to the original values in comparison with the ANN. Therefore, HMMs get our preference over ANNs. Moreover, the strong mathematical basis of HMMs is also a plus, which the ANNs lack. Since there is some cost associated with each of the above mentioned prediction models, either of these is of help to the service consumer only if the accuracy obtained through reputation prediction is more than the reputation values calculated in an ad hoc manner.

To capture the effects of reputation assessment when no prediction is involved, we have performed the experiments on the same data set of original reputations. Figure 4, shows the result of 1000 interactions out of a total 6000 interactions. The first 1449 interactions are those in which rater feedbacks are present. The 1450th. interaction onwards, no peer feedback is available about the service provider. Since no prediction is involved here, the future reputation evaluations hover around the reputation value that was observed at the last time instance. Since service consumer's *own* experience is also not factored in the reputation computation, we see an almost stationary reputation graph.

Figure 5 shows the effects of incorporating the service consumer's personal experience in calculating the provider reputation, when no peer feedbacks are available and no prediction is used. Around 600 iterations are shown for this case

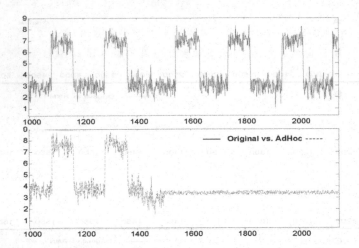

Fig. 4. Reputation Evaluation without Prediction and Personal Experience

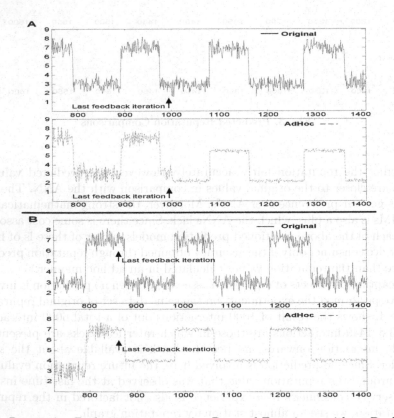

Fig. 5. Reputation Evaluation incorporating Personal Experience without Prediction

out of a total of 6000 iterations. In Figure 5-A, the last set of peer feedbacks
is received at the 980th. iteration, which gives an overall *low* value (around 3)
for the provider's reputation. Starting from the 981st. interaction, the service
consumer incorporates his own personal experience into the last calculated aggregate reputation to reassess the provider's reputation. Since, the consumer's
own testimony is weighed in highly, therefore the "general trend" of the evaluated reputation moves towards the original. However, since majority feedbacks
are still centered around 3, an accurate assessment is not possible and the values
are off by some degrees. Figure 5-B, provides a similar picture, but in this case
the last feedbacks receiving iteration (960), leaves the service consumer with an
aggregate reputation of 7. Subsequent reputation evaluations using the personal
experience provide accurate results when the *actual* provider performance is high
but inaccurate results when the actual provider performance is low. The reason
is similar to the previous case, that since majority of the ratings are around 7,
if the service consumer evaluates the provider as a low performer, the general
trend of reputation evaluation moves in that direction but the high majority
rating keeps the assessment inaccurate.

In light of the above experiments, we conclude that using a prediction model,
we can assess the reputation of a service provider fairly accurately even if no
rater feedbacks are present. We have also seen that HMMs have a slight edge
over ANNs in computing service reputations. In contrast, if no prediction model
is used then the reputation values that are assessed are inaccurate.

4   Conclusion and Future Work

We have presented an HMM-based reputation management framework to establish trust among Web services in situations where rater feedbacks may not be
readily available. We have provided evaluation results for reputation prediction
based on past service provider behavior using both an ANN and an HMM. In the
future, we intend to build upon our proposed reputation management framework.
We would refine the service interaction model to define a reputation model for
composed Web services. Similarly, information dissemination techniques, change
detection and interpretation for both individual and composed services will also
be studied.

References

1. Buchegger, S., Le Boudec, J.-Y.: Performance Analysis of the CONFIDANT Protocol. In: Proc. of the 3rd ACM Intl. Symposium on Mobile Ad Hoc Networking
   and Computing, June 9-11, pp. 226–236 (2002)
2. Cappe, O., Moulines, E., Ryden, T.: Inference in Hidden Markov Models. Springer,
   Heidelberg (2005)

3. Delgado, J., Ishii, N.: Memory-Based Weighted-Majority Prediction for Recommender Systems. In: ACM SIGIR 1999 Workshop on Recommender Systems: Algorithms and Evaluation (1999)
4. Huynh, T.D., Jennings, N.R., Shadbolt, N.R.: Certified reputation: how an agent can trust a stranger. In: AAMAS 2006: Proceedings of the fifth international joint conference on Autonomous agents and multiagent systems, pp. 1217–1224. ACM Press, New York (2006)
5. Josang, A., Ismail, R.: The beta reputation system. In: 15th Bled Conference on Electronic Commerce (June 2002)
6. Josang, A.: A logic for uncertain probabilities. Int. J. Uncertain. Fuzziness Knowl.-Based Syst. 9(3), 279–311 (2001)
7. MacDonald, I.L., Zucchini, W.: Hidden Markov and Other Models for Discrete-valued Time Series. Chapman and Hall, Boca Raton (1997)
8. Malik, Z., Bouguettaya, A.: Rater Credibility Assessment in Web Services Interactions. World Wide Web Journal 12(1) (March 2009)
9. Malik, Z., Bouguettaya, A.: Reputation-based Trust Management for Service-Oriented Environments. VLDB Journal 18(4) (August 2009)
10. Malik, Z., Bouguettaya, A.: Reputation Bootstrapping for Trust Establishment among Web Services. IEEE Internet Computing 13(1) (January-February 2009)
11. Marti, S., Garcia-Molina, H.: Limited Reputation Sharing in P2P Systems. In: Proc. of the 5th ACM Conference on Electronic Commerce, New York, NY, USA, May 2004, pp. 91–101 (2004)
12. Medjahed, B., Bouguettaya, A.: Customized delivery of e-government web services. IEEE Intelligent Systems 20(6) (November/December 2005)
13. Mui, L., Mohtashemi, M., Halberstadt, A.: A computational model of trust and reputation. In: Proceedings of the 35th Annual Hawaii International Conference on System Sciences, January 2002, pp. 2431–2439 (2002)
14. Papazoglou, M.P., Georgakopoulos, D.: Serive-Oriented Computing. Communcications of the ACM 46(10), 25–65 (2003)
15. Park, S., Liu, L., Pu, C., Srivatsa, M., Zhang, J.: Resilient trust management for web service integration. In: ICWS 2005: Proceedings of the IEEE International Conference on Web Services (ICWS 2005), Washington, DC, USA, pp. 499–506. IEEE Computer Society, Los Alamitos (2005)
16. Rabiner, L.R., Juang, B.H.: An introduction to hidden markov models. IEEE ASSP Magazine 3(1), 4–16 (1986)
17. Ran, S.: A model for web services discovery with qos. SIGecom Exch. 4(1), 1–10 (2003)
18. Sonnek, J.D., Weissman, J.B.: A quantitative comparison of reputation systems in the grid. In: The 6th IEEE/ACM International Workshop on Grid Computing, November 2005, pp. 242–249 (2005)
19. Tennenholtz, M.: Reputation systems: An axiomatic approach. In: AUAI 2004: Proceedings of the 20th conference on Uncertainty in artificial intelligence, Arlington, Virginia, United States, pp. 544–551. AUAI Press (2004)
20. Tian, M., Gramm, A., Ritter, H., Schiller, J.: Efficient selection and monitoring of qos-aware web services with the ws-qos framework. In: International Conference on Web Intelligence, Washington, DC, USA, pp. 152–158. IEEE Computer Society, Los Alamitos (2004)

21. Turin, W.: Digital Transmission Systems: Performance Analysis and Modeling. McGraw-Hill, New York (1998)
22. Udupi, Y.B., Singh, M.P.: Information sharing among autonomous agents in referral networks systems. In: 6th International Workshop on Agents and Peer-to-Peer Computing (May 2007)
23. Xiong, L., Liu, L.: PeerTrust: Supporting Reputation-based Trust for Peer-to-Peer Electronic Communities. IEEE Trans. on Knowledge and Data Engineering (TKDE) 16(7), 843–857 (2004)
24. Yu, B., Singh, M.P.: An evidential model of distributed reputation management. In: AAMAS 2002: Proceedings of the first international joint conference on Autonomous agents and multiagent systems, pp. 294–301. ACM Press, New York (2002)

MC-Cube: Mastering Customizable Compliance in the Cloud

Tobias Anstett, Dimka Karastoyanova, Frank Leymann, Ralph Mietzner,
Ganna Monakova, Daniel Schleicher, and Steve Strauch

Institute of Architecture of Application Systems, University of Stuttgart, Germany
lastname@iaas.uni-stuttgart.de

Abstract. Outsourcing parts of a company's processes becomes more
and more important in a globalized, distributed economy. While architectural styles and technologies such as service-oriented architecture and
Web services facilitate the distribution of business process over several departments, enterprises and countries, these business processes still need
to comply with various regulations. These regulations can be company
regulations, national, or international regulations. When outsourcing IT-
functions, enterprises must ensure that the overall regulations are met.
Therefore they need evidence from their outsourcing partners that supports the proof of compliance to regulations. Furthermore it must be
possible to enforce the adherence to compliance rules at partners. In this
paper we introduce so-called compliance interfaces that can be used by
customers to subscribe to evidence at a provider and to enforce regulations at a provider. We introduce a general compliance architecture that
allows compliance to be monitored and enforced at services deployed in
any emerging cloud delivery model.

1   Introduction and Motivation

Service-oriented architecture has emerged as the architectural style that allows
to recursively compose services that are run in a distributed fashion on heterogeneous infrastructures. Service-oriented systems are often used in conjunction
with business process execution engines to build cross-organizational IT-support
for the business processes in and across enterprises.

   With upcoming service delivery models such as infrastructure as a service
(IaaS), platform as a service (PaaS) and software as a service (SaaS) enterprises
can outsource computing and middleware resources to the cloud and use them
"on demand". This allows enterprises to focus on their core competencies that
may not lie in the acquisition and management of an IT infrastructure. As a consequence from financial and other scandals in the last years, companies are faced
with more and more regulations that they need to obey to. These regulations
range from internal regulations, such as business ethics or sustainability rules to
external regulations, such as privacy laws that need to be obeyed or frameworks
such as BASEL II [3] or SOX [20] that regulate financial transactions.

   Many of these regulations mandate enterprises to provide enough evidence to
auditors so that those auditors can judge whether regulations have been obeyed

L. Baresi, C.-H. Chi, and J. Suzuki (Eds.): ICSOC-ServiceWave 2009, LNCS 5900, pp. 592–606, 2009.

or violated. In the case of outsourced IT services, the gathering of evidence can be partially delegated to the outsourcing provider. However, some regulations still hold an enterprise (or even the CEO of an enterprise) liable even if an outsourcing provider violated a regulation. Furthermore as complex business processes can be partially supported by IT systems running at different providers and in the own data-center, the evidence must later be aggregated to provide a comprehensive view on the whole business process.

In this paper we deal with cross-organizational business processes that use services provided at multiple outsourcing providers in multiple delivery models. In such a setting, compliance to regulations is of utmost importance and has implications on the IT-infrastructure of both providers and consumers of services. Thus there is a need to monitor and correct the execution of business processes after reaching a service-level agreement. Therefore we introduce the notion of a *compliance interface* that allows enterprises to gather evidence from providers as well as enforce rules on these providers. We show that providers must allow their clients to customize the evidence they provide depending on the regulations the client has to be compliant with. The approach presented in this paper is very flexible and does not focus on a certain legal framework. However, specific focus is paid on outsourcing parts of applications, which must maintain the overall compliance rules imposed on the whole application.

We introduce a running example in Section 2 that will be used while presenting the main contributions of the paper. We then describe the requirements and architecture for a general compliance framework that we gathered from the case studies in various projects (Section 3). We apply this framework to different delivery models in Section 4. In Section 5 we then discuss how the compliance interfaces could be realized. We show a prototypical implementation in Section 6, compare our approach to other approaches in Section 7 and finish with a conclusion and an outlook to future work that we plan in the field.

2 Running Example

In [2] we investigated how security and trust issues affect the execution of WS-BPEL [16] processes in the cloud and discussed requirements on the middleware supporting the execution of WS-BPEL processes in the different cloud delivery models. In contrast, in this paper we investigate how compliance of business processes can be ensured during outsourcing.

Therefore we introduce the example of a fictional EU-based company manufacturing and shipping drugs named Pharmazon. Figure 1 illustrates a simplified view on the business process that Pharmazon follows when selling drugs.

Of course the company Pharmazon and its business processes have to comply to several European laws and national laws for example concerning production, distribution, advertising and labeling of medical products for human and veterinary use [6]. For example, Pharmazon must be compliant to directive 2001/83/EC [21] of the European Parliament and Council, which deals among other things with the advertising of medicinal products for humans. Their

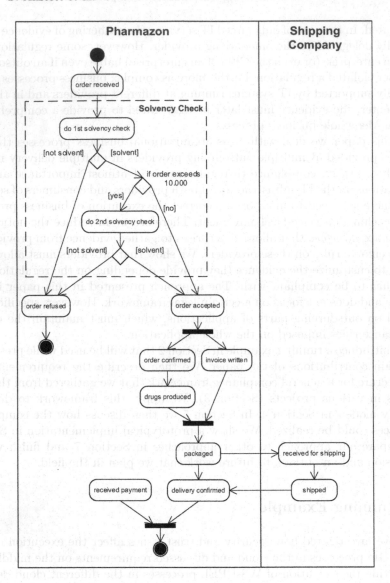

Fig. 1. Simplified view on Pharmazon's business process

business processes also have to be compliant to their own internal regulations. Examples for such internal rules are: *'Every time an order is received, a solvency check has to be done. If the amount exceeds € 10.000 a second solvency check has to be done by a person different from the first one'* or *'Every order has to be delivered within 24 hours'.*

Pharmazon is forced to maintain lower costs to stay competitive. The first step in reducing cost is to reduce the enormous shipping costs to non European countries by subcontracting pharmaceutical companies in the US and Asia

Pacific countries. Furthermore parts of the business process such as the above mentioned solvency check have to be outsourced.

While outsourcing parts of the business (process) it must be ensured that the outsourcee still complies with the European, national or internal regulations that formerly were ensured by the company itself. Thus Pharmazon has to have the possibility to check, whether the outsourcee complies to the given regulations imposed on Pharmazon's processes.

In this paper we will use the example with focus on the internal regulations mentioned above, ensuring that the outsourced solvency check is made as defined and the cross-cutting business concern of orders delivered within 24 hours is achieved.

3   Requirements and Resulting Architecture

As mentioned in Section 1 it is required that a specified set of compliance constraints is ensured during a business process execution.

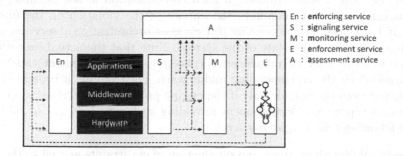

Fig. 2. Abstract Compliance Supporting Architecture / Infrastructure

Figure 2 presents an abstract architecture using compliance services to enable the control and assessment of compliance. Here the term En is a shortcut for **enforcing service**, S for **signaling service**, M for **monitoring service**, E for **enforcement service** and A for **assessment service**. The architecture as well as terms used in this paper are based on the research work [13] in the European Community's FP7 project MASTER [1].

In the following each compliance service is described in detail:

Signaling Service: Provides evidence in form of events emitted on action state changes. An example of an action state can be state *ready*, denoting that an action is ready to be executed, state *running*, denoting that an action is currently executing or a state *completed*, denoting that an action was executed. Signaling services can be implemented at any level of abstraction where events must be

---

[1] http://www.master-fp7.eu

emitted, e.g. at application, platform middleware or hardware level. Logically they are however related to a certain business process behavior as evidence to prove the satisfaction of constraints.

Runtime Monitoring Service: Aggregates events based on its situation information, payload or any other data, which can be resolved using an external service (such as a database entry lookup or a Web service call). Thus, runtime monitoring services can also be viewed as complex event processing, for short CEP [14], services. Depending on the aggregation rules, events may either provide evidence for a compliant execution of the process or the detection of a constraint violation.

Enforcement Service: In order to prevent a violation the enforcement service reacts to an event denoting a possible threat of violation and guides (controls) the system in such a way that the invalid state (the state, which violates the constraint) cannot be reached. In case of a detected violation the goal of the reactive process is to transfer the system from the current invalid state into a valid one. This can be done through the compensation of the actions, which caused the invalid state transfer. If such compensation is not possible, other actions can be taken to minimize the impact of the violation on the business value. In both cases, an enforcement process is an orchestration of services, which are able to influence the state of the system. Note that the actual execution of the services can only be influenced if corresponding enforcement capabilities are provided by the corresponding middleware. For example a process can be terminated from the outside only if the engine provides an interface supporting a *terminate* operation. A component providing such enforcement capabilities is in the following called *enforcing service*.

Assessment Service: Assess the satisfaction of constraints as well as the effectiveness of the implemented enforcement process.

Because compliance concerns may vary between different business processes an infrastructure realizing the presented architecture has to allow dynamic configuration of its services. Compliance policies allow to describe the configuration of the compliance services required to monitor and enforce a certain compliance constraint. The configuration can be divided into the following blocks: i) description of the signals (events) required to monitor the behavior of the system, ii) description of the monitoring rule (predicate), which allows detection of the violation or a violation threat, iii) description of the reactive and preventive actions and iv) description of the assessment function.

When translating compliance regulations to compliance policies, for short doing compliance regulations refinement, the responsible person has to take decisions about the granularity of events, where they occur and where and how they can be aggregated to express the required semantics. Depending on the capabilities of the underlying execution environment these events can be emitted and aggregated at different levels. For example an event denoting the read access to a specific database resource could be emitted by the database using its trigger mechanism, by a service that provides an interface to the database functionality or by the business process that initiated the access. Furthermore the required *signaling* and *runtime monitoring* capabilities can be part of the business process itself, implemented as internal controls, or provided as *compliance services*. Reactions to certain events, e.g. to enforce the satisfaction of constraints, may be realized by single operation calls or require more complex *reactive* processes. In Section 5 we present a concrete example using the running example of Section 2.

4 Refining the General Architecture to Cloud Delivery Models

One of the biggest challenges of mastering compliance in the cloud is that the customer is not able to transfer its obligations regarding compliance regulations to the outsourcing provider. This section discusses the requirements as well as responsibilities of customer and provider in outsourcing scenarios. We describe the requirements for the following three categories of delivery models, namely infrastructure as a service (IaaS), platform as a service (PaaS) and software as a service (SaaS).

4.1 IaaS

In this delivery model a customer basically rents the required hardware from an IaaS provider. Like in the traditional on-premise model, he has to take care for configuring the platform and application on his own. Amazon Elastic Compute Cloud (Amazon EC2)[2] is a prominent example of an infrastructure as a service. The configuration of the platform includes the installation of *operating system*, *platform middleware* such as database management system (DBMS), enterprise service bus (ESB) or a BPEL engine, and *application*. In the following compliance services are considered as a specialized platform middleware. Although only responsible for providing the hardware the provider may also provide signaling, monitoring and enforcement capabilities for its hardware. A provider may offer these compliance services as agreed in the service agreements with the customer. He may also require compliance services for ensuring his own compliance. E.g. he has to check that his hardware works as expected and furthermore is not abused to run illegal software like file sharing servers.

Using IaaS a customer will always trust his own installation and therefore does not have to worry about the validity of the events generated by this software.

4.2 PaaS

The PaaS model offers both, the *infrastructure* (hardware) as well as the *platform middleware* to deploy *applications*. The customer neither has to take care for

---

[2] http://aws.amazon.com/ec2/

reserving hardware resources nor for configuring the platform. Google's App Engine[3] is an example of platform as a service.

In PaaS the customer has to specify his functional and non-functional requirements to the provider and the provided infrastructure. While the functional requirements might for example only specify the need for a certain type of middleware, the non-functional part includes the specification of the compliance requirements on the provided middleware or even hardware. For example the customer might specify that the BPEL engine, which is part of the platform, must be able to send events about the actual state of process instances. Furthermore the engine must allow to enforce certain actions on process instances and must therefore provide a specific enforcement interface. If the customer is for example interested in using monitoring or enforcement services, he has to provide its configuration using the compliance policies. The provider is in charge of installing and executing these policies on his middleware in a similar way he would have to do it when deploying a BPEL process on a BPEL engine. Thus policies can be considered at the level as BPEL processes, which realize applications. This allows PaaS providers to offer monitoring, enforcement and assessment services in a SaaS delivery model. Because signaling and enforcing services are bound to specific platform middleware they can not be outsourced independently of that platform middleware.

In contrast to the IaaS model, the provider may not be able to offer all the required information or services to the customer or even may decide to offer only a limited subset of information he could generate for use by its customers. Thus the customer is constrained to the offered granularity and semantics of the provided events as well as monitoring and enforcement capabilities of the provider.

One of the main deficiencies of using PaaS in this context is the perceived lack of trust, that events provided to the customer are authentic. Because everything except the business process model and its explicitly generated events are hosted, the customer must trust his provider. There are several ways to increase the trust level. On the one hand the trust level could be increased by applying more complex monitoring rules, which execute additional checks on the middleware or even hardware event level. On the other hand there is need for a compliance certification agency to increase trust and allow chains of trust similar to Verisign's[4] role and functionality in the Internet. Certification agencies might base their certificates on audits of the assured compliance, refined compliance policies and the implementation of compliance services. This also leads to the need for trusted middleware.

4.3   SaaS

Software as a service provides different customers the functionality of an application that is completely hosted in the cloud. The user does not have to worry about the required infrastructure or setting up and configuring the platform.

---

[3] http://appengine.google.com
[4] http://www.verisign.com

When recalling the presented compliance architecture, which is mainly based on the presence of signaling services to provide evidence, the concept of variability becomes very important not only for SaaS but also for the other delivery models. The set of supported events must be made available to the user at each level of abstraction. These abstraction levels should support but not be limited to the categorization used throughout this paper, namely *hardware, platform middleware* and *application*, but also introduce more convenient perspectives such as *resources, actions* and *states*. Based on a the provided compliance capabilities the customer should be able to define the compliance policies.

5   Technical Architecture

In this section we discuss how the signaling and enforcement capabilities can be described. For this purpose we extend the model described in [5], which is based on relations between *actions, resources, services* and *events*. As motivated in Section 1 and discussed in Section 3 the customer requires evidence of the behavior of the actual executed business process. This behavior is defined by the set of actions being executed and their ordering relations. Thus the behavior can be represented by and reconstructed from event traces [1] [23] [22]. An event basically represents a specific execution state of the process or an action within the process and contains additional payload information such as resources.

The description of the signaling capabilities contains the following information:

- actions the service performs
- states an action supports, e.g. [7] describes the states BPEL activities support
- resources the service uses
- events emitted on action state change
- resource/information an event may contain
- event properties such as event timestamps

The description of the enforcement capabilities contains the following information:

- enforcement actions the service performs. The enforcement actions are specific actions, which can be used to influence the service execution.
- resources on which the enforcement action is performed
- end point reference (EPR) of the enforcement action to enable action invocation

Figure 3 illustrates the model for describing signaling and enforcement capabilities. The relation *onState* is an abstract relation, which can be subtyped with the relations *onStarted, onRunning, onFaulted, onTerminated, onCompleted*, depending on the states the corresponding action supports. Note that because an enforcement action is a subtype of the general action concept, events also can be emitted on the state changes of the enforcement action. Note also that because

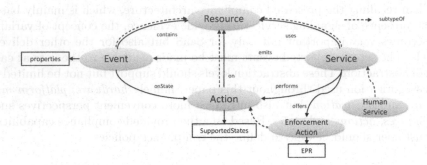

Fig. 3. Signaling and Enforcement Model

action is a subtype of a resource, an enforcement action can be executed on another action, e.g. an enforcement action *block* can be executed *on* action *check*. A signaling policy is a serialization of the events of a concrete instance of this model. An enforcement policy is a serialization of all actions of type *EnforcementAction*. If both customer and provider specify their requirements/capabilities using the same model with domain specific actions and resources, two signaling as well as enforcement policies can be matched using policy matching algorithms (for example that of WS-Policy [25]) to determine if the service provider provides sufficient evidence and actions for external control.

As described in Section 2 Pharmazon decided to outsource the solvency check part of its business process. To be compliant with internal regulations, Pharmazon wants to ensure that the *check* action is performed twice in case the order exceeds € 10.000 and that these check operations are performed by different persons. Thus, Pharmazon requires events every time a *check* action was executed, denoting the completion of this action, on action state *completed*, containing information about the person who executed this action. Figure 4 shows an example of a solvency check process signaling and enforcement description offered by an SaaS provider.

Note, that this model does not describe the structure of the solvency check process. The provider can in addition describe the structure of the process using existing standards, such as abstract BPEL [16].

In general there are two options to bind to a service: i) dynamic binding and ii) static binding. Dynamic binding as defined in [25] is based on the operations publish, find and bind. A service requestor finds a service by providing its requirements to the discovery facility, which is responsible for matching service descriptions as well as policies. If a service matching the required capabilities is found, the service requestor binds itself to the service to use it. Because the customer also has to subscribe to the events he described within his signaling policy the bind step has to include the subscription to the events using the compliance interface offered by the provider. A compliance interface has to provide the following operations, which could be implicitly contained in the service description (WSDL [25]) or offered as a standalone service:

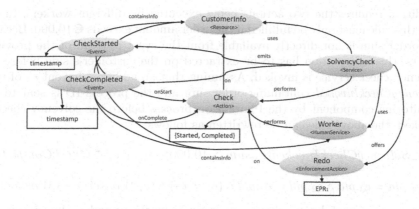

Fig. 4. Signaling capabilities of the service provider

- getSignalingCapabilities(service) returns the signaling policy for the specified service
- getEnforcementCapabilities(service) returns the enforcement policy for the specified service
- subscribeTo(service, event) subscribes to a specific event of the service

Static binding assumes that a suitable service was already found and only the subscription to signaling events has to be done manually. For example a SaaS provider could offer a graphical user interface to describe an abstract view on the business process including signaling and enforcement capabilities available for this process. The customer can use the offered tooling to select the events he wants to subscribe to and the provider automatically performs the subscription in the background. Especially in SaaS delivery models this approach might be interesting because providers already allow customers to customize the provided business processes using variability descriptors [15].

However, which of the discussed approaches is used, the events, a customer has subscribed to, have to be monitored to provide evidence for a compliant execution of the process or the detection of a constraint violation. In Pharmazon's case it has to be ensured that every time an order exceeds € 10.000 two check operations are performed by different persons.

Using the provided description of the signaling capabilities, the monitoring rule for the seperation of duties (SoD) objective can be specified as follows:

$$\forall r \in SolvencyCheck \; \exists e_1, e_2 \in CheckCompleted :$$

$$(e_1.pid = r.pid) \wedge (e_2.pid = r.pid) \wedge (e_1 \neq e_2) \wedge (e_1.Worker \neq e_2.Worker)$$

where *pid* denotes the id of the current process instance run. This rule states that at least two different events of type *CheckCompleted* should be available for every run of the *SolvencyCheck* service. This implies that the action *Check* must be performed at least twice for every process run. In addition, the above condition requires the two actions being executed by different workers. In our case this rule must only be fulfilled if the order amount exceeds € 10.000. Because the order sum is not directly available from the event payload of the provided events, this information has to be extracted on the customer's side before the solvency check service is invoked. Assuming that an additional event e_3 of type *SolvencyCheckInvoked* containing order sum and the process ID is sent to the monitoring component by the Pharmazon process before the solvency check is invoked, the above rule can be rewritten as follows:

$$\forall e_3 \in SolvencyCheckInvoked(e_3.sum > 10.000) \rightarrow \exists e_1, e_2 \in CheckCompleted :$$

$$e_1.pid = e_3.pid \wedge e_2.pid = e_3.pid \wedge (e_1 \neq e_2) \wedge (e_1.Worker \neq e_2.Worker)$$

If the separation of duties criteria was not met by the provider, Pharmazon can for example enforce the compliance of its process by invoking a reactive process, which enforces a *redo* on one of the *check* activities.

If the outsourcing provider always executes the check operation twice and the check operations are performed by different persons, then the monitoring rule is not violated. Because checking things twice may take significant longer than not doing so, Pharmazon's business process has to wait longer for the reply of solvency checks made for orders less than € 10.000. Because Pharmazon has to be also compliant to its internal regulation *Every order has to be delivered within 24 hours* this might not be applicable. Thus another monitoring policy is needed to express the relation between the order volume, time available and checks to be performed. This policy could trigger an enforcement process, which either skips the activity waiting for the result of the solvency check if the order is less than € 10.000, and the first check evaluated to true, or changes the shipping partner or method to a faster one depending on the time left.

6   Implementation Aspects

In this section we show a prototype, which fulfills the requirements of Section 3 and can be used to implement the described architecture.

We extended the Apache ODE BPEL engine[5] with the capability of sending events to the outside. Apache ODE supports BPEL 2.0 process models.

Figure 5 shows where the BPEL engine is placed in a compliance supporting architecture. It also shows the signaling service (S) and the enforcing service (En), which are part of the engine. The enforcing service provides operations to for example influence the running processes on the engine.

During the execution of a process the BPEL engine produces many events and stores them in an internal database called the *audit trail*. These events can be used to check compliance concerns. In order to fulfill the requirement of emitting events to the outside, the engine has been extended with two Web services. The first one is a publish-subscribe Web service, which provides operations to

---

[5] http://ode.apache.org

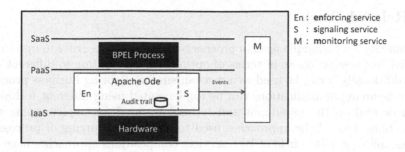

Fig. 5. Placement of BPEL engine in a compliance supporting architecture

subscribe to certain events occurring during process execution. For technical details of the subscription mechanism we refer to [24]. The second Web service is a signaling Web service. It sends the events as SOAP messages to the subscribers. These events are based on the common base event model proposed by IBM[6]. This model for example comprises information of the service, which sent a certain event and in what situation it was sent.

In [7] a static event model for BPEL is proposed. In this context static means, that every activity has a static set of events and one could subscribe to all events at any time. There is no way of constraining the events, which are visible outside of the BPEL engine. This document also contains definitions of all events, which can be emitted during execution of a BPEL activity. This is useful for subscriptions to certain events of a particular activity.

To process the events emitted by a BPEL engine a monitoring service (M) could for example subscribe to certain events to check the validity of the running processes in the BPEL engine. If a violation has occurred a new event can be issued to a so called *enforcement service.* The enforcement service then could carry out reactive actions in order to respond to compliance violations. Actions, which react to a compliance violation, can for example stop the business process running in the domain of the business partner. Such actions could also be modeled in a business process. This process is then called a *reactive process.*

The life cycle management operations, ODE provides, can be used as enforcement capabilities. ODE is capable of pausing, resuming, terminating, and deleting of process instances. So this prototype can be used as an enforcement component specified in Section 3. The engine is also capable of blocking a process instance when a certain event has occurred. This is in some cases useful when a decision has to be made before the process could continue.

For example, if someone has placed an order to buy drugs from Pharmazon exceeding the price of € 100.000 the process will be blocked and an event will be emitted notifying the enforcement service. The engine then can be unblocked by the enforcement by invoking a reactive process, which then takes the necessary actions to unblock the process.

---

[6] http://www.ibm.com/developerworks/library/specification/ws-cbe/

7   Related Work

Outsourcing is a technique used in process re-engineering in order to optimize or improve business processes in terms of optimization according to different criteria. Additionally it can be used as a mechanism for adapting business processes. The outsourcing of applications can be implemented using different techniques, which depend on the paradigms and technology used for implementing these applications. One of the approaches used to enable outsourcing of processes is process splitting. In the field of Web services compositions approaches have been created for outsourcing service compositions in order to optimize the processes they implement with respect to organizational resources or infrastructure performance. E.g. the approach in [11] enables splitting of BPEL processes into so-called partitions, which can be run as stand-alone processes on different BPEL engines at different locations/organizations in such a manner that the overall semantics of the original business process is maintained. The work in [4] reports on another approach for splitting service compositions in an optimal manner according to criteria like execution time, response time, cost etc. The approach allows for splitting a composition in the so-called strata and is based on the concept of stratified transactions, while the communication among strata is enabled via a queuing infrastructure (MOM in general). This approach views a service composition as a transaction and all the tasks of a composition - as nested transactions. The resulting stratified compositions maintain the original logic but improve its performance. The work introduces several algorithms for optimal stratification of service compositions. Multiple coordination protocols for partitioned/split processes exist and they are dependent on the approach used for the splitting. Worth mentioning are the WS-BA [17], which is a part of the WS protocol stack; for the above mentioned approaches there are corresponding coordination protocols based on either WS-Coordination Infrastructure [12] or on other coordination mechanisms. To enable the communication among the parts of a global process that run at different locations and hence be able to coordinate these partitions/fragments each service composition engine needs to provide information about events related to the life-cycle of process instances. Usually, an engine implements an event model, which is used to publish information for the purposes of monitoring; this has been used for enabling monitoring [9], adaptation [15] [8] [9] and a framework for coordination of service compositions [10]. These are all examples of the use of the events published by the engine, based on an event model. The existence of such an model is crucial also for enabling the outsourcing of parts of service-based applications and enabling their compliance. Compliance to a global process logic in the area of process splitting has been enabled by design in the approaches presented in [11] and [4]. Compliance of processes to a process model has been enabled by the work of [18] for the case of adaptation by means of model evolution. The difference with respect to the subject of compliance between this approach and the one we present here is that our approach focuses on ensuring compliance of process instances, whereas the approach of [19] enables the compliance or correctness of adaptation/modifications on the process model level only.

8   Conclusion and Future Work

In this paper we presented MC-Cube, an approach to deal with compliance requirements in cross-organizational applications build upon a service-oriented architecture. We introduced compliance interfaces as a means to allow subscribers of services to customize the evidence they need from a provider. On the other hand when enforcing compliance at an oursourcing provider the enforcement part of the compliance interface can be used. We introduced a general architecture for outsourcing and compliance and mapped this infrastructure to different delivery models such as IaaS, PaaS and SaaS. We described a prototype that shows how the presented concepts can be applied to a BPEL engine that can then be used at providers to offer customizable compliance to their customers. In future work we will extend this work to describe how suitable services that offer the required compliance can be automatically discovered. We will also investigate in detail how changes to compliance requirements will affect running applications and how this affects the underlying middleware (such as BPEL engines).

Acknowledgments

The work published in this article has partially received funding from the European Community's 7th Framework Programme Information Society Technologies Objective under the COMPAS project[7] contract no. FP7-215175, the MASTER project[8] contract no. FP7-216917 and under the Network of Excellence S-Cube[9] contract no. FP7-215483.

References

1. Agrawal, R., Gunopulos, D., Leymann, F.: Mining Process Models from Workflow Logs. In: Schek, H.-J., Saltor, F., Ramos, I., Alonso, G. (eds.) EDBT 1998. LNCS, vol. 1377, p. 469. Springer, Heidelberg (1998)
2. Anstett, T., Leymann, F., Mietzner, R., Strauch, S.: Towards BPEL in the Cloud: Exploiting Different Delivery Models for the Execution of Business Processes. In: IWCS 2009 (2009)
3. Basel Committee on Banking Supervision. International Convergence of Capital Measurement and Capital Standards (2006)
4. Danylevych, O., Karastoyanova, D., Leymann, F.: Optimal Stratification of Transactions. In: ICWS 2009 (2009)
5. Flegel, U., Kerschbaum, F., Miseldine, P., Monakova, G., Wacker, R., Leymann, F.: Insider Threats in Cybersecurity - And Beyond. Springer, Heidelberg (to appear, 2009)
6. Gordon, J.W., Appelbe, E.: Dale and Appelbe's pharmacy law and ethics. Pharmaceutical Press (2005)

---

[7] http://www.compas-ict.eu
[8] http://www.master-fp7.eu
[9] http://www.s-cube-network.eu

7. Karastoyanova, D., Khalaf, R., Schroth, R., Paluszek, M., Leymann, F.: BPEL Event Model. Technical Report Computer Science 2006/10
8. Karastoyanova, D., Leymann, F.: BPEL'n'Aspects: Adapting Service Orchestration Logic. In: ICWS 2009 (2009)
9. Karastoyanova, D., Leymann, F., Nitzsche, J., Wetzstein, B., Wutke, D.: Parameterized BPEL Processes: Concepts and Implementation. In: IWCS 2009 (2009)
10. Khalaf, R., Karastoyanova, D., Leymann, F.: Pluggable Framework for Enabling the Execution of Extended BPEL Behavior. In: WESOA 2007 (2007)
11. Khalaf, R., Leymann, F.: A Role-based Decomposition of Business Processes using BPEL. In: ICWS 2006 (2006)
12. Khalaf, R., Leymann, F.: Coordination Protocols for Split BPEL Loops and Scopes. Technical Report Computer Science 2007/01
13. Lotz, V., Pigout, E., Fischer, P.M., Kossmann, D., Massacci, F., Pretschner, A.: Towards Systematic Achievement of Compliance in Service-Oriented Architectures: The MASTER Approach. Wirtschaftsinformatik (2008)
14. Luckham, D.: The Power of Events: An Introduction to Complex Event Processing in Distributed Enterprise Systems. Addison-Wesley Longman, Amsterdam (2002)
15. Mietzner, R., Leymann, F.: Generation of BPEL Customization Processes for SaaS Applications from Variability Descriptors. In: IEEE SCC (2008)
16. OASIS. Web Services Business Process Execution Language Version 2.0 – OASIS Standard (2007)
17. OASIS. Web Services Business Activity (WS-BusinessActivity) Version 1.2 – OASIS Standard (2009)
18. Reichert, M., Dadam, P.: ADEPT flex - Supporting Dynamic Changes of Workflows Without Loosing Control. Journal of Intelligent Information Systems (1998)
19. Reichert, M.U., Rinderle, S.B.: On Design Principles for Realizing Adaptive Service Flows with BPEL. In: EMISA 2006 (2006)
20. Sarbanes, P., Oxley, M.: Sarbanes-Oxley Act of 2002. The Public Company Accounting Reform and Investor Protection Act. Washington DC: US Congress (2002)
21. The European Parliament and the Council of the European Union. Directive 2001/83/EC of the European Parliament and the Council. Official Journal of the European Communities 311 (2001)
22. van der Aalst, W.M.P., van Dongen, B.F., Herbst, J., Maruster, L., Schimm, G., Weijters, A.J.M.M.: Workflow mining: A survey of issues and approaches. Data Knowl. Eng. (2003)
23. van der Aalst, W.M.P., Weijters, A.J.M.M., Maruster, L.: Workflow Mining: Discovering Process Models from Event Logs. IEEE Transactions on Knowledge and Data Engineering (2004)
24. van Lessen, T., Leymann, F., Mietzner, R., Nitzsche, J., Schleicher, D.: A Management Framework for WS-BPEL. In: ECOWS 2008 (2008)
25. Weerawarana, S., Curbera, F., Leymann, F., Storey, T., Ferguson, D.F.: Web Services Platform Architecture: SOAP, WSDL, WS-Policy, WS-Addressing, WS-BPEL, WS-Reliable Messaging, and More. Prentice Hall PTR, Englewood Cliffs (2005)

Another Approach to Service Instance Migration

Nannette Liske[1], Niels Lohmann[2], Christian Stahl[3], and Karsten Wolf[2]

[1] Humboldt-Universtität zu Berlin, Institut für Informatik,
Unter den Linden 6, 10099 Berlin, Germany
[2] Universität Rostock, Institut für Informatik, 18051 Rostock, Germany
{niels.lohmann,karsten.wolf}@uni-rostock.de
[3] Department of Mathematics and Computer Science, Technische Universiteit
Eindhoven, P.O. Box 513, 5600 MB Eindhoven, The Netherlands
c.stahl@tue.nl

Abstract. Services change over time, be it for internal improvements, be it for external requirements such as new legal regulations. For long running services, it may even be necessary to change a service while instances are actually running and interacting with other services. This problem is referred to as *instance migration*. We present a novel approach to the behavioral (service protocol) aspects of instance migration. We apply techniques for finitely characterizing the set of all correctly interacting partners to a given service. The approach assures that migration does not introduce behavioral problems with *any* running partner of the original service. Our technique scales up to services with thousands of states, including models of real WS-BPEL processes.

1 Introduction

Service-oriented computing aims at creating complex systems by composing less complex systems called *services*. A service interacts with an environment consisting of other services. Such a complex system is subject to changes. To this end, individual services are substituted by other services. This becomes particularly challenging as services rely on each other and often nobody oversees the overall system—for example, if the individual services belong to different enterprises.

As a service is stateful rather than stateless, its exposed operations have to be invoked in a particular order, described by its business protocol. Throughout this paper we restrict ourselves to *business protocol changes* [1]; that is, we assume that nonfunctional properties (e.g., policies, quality of services) and semantical properties are not violated when changing a service S_{old} to a service S_{new}.

In our previous work we presented a procedure to decide for given services S_{old} and S_{new} whether S_{new} can substitute S_{old} [2]. The approach ensures that every service S that interacts properly with S_{old} also interacts properly with S_{new}. A properly interacting service is called a *partner*. In [3], we have applied these techniques to WS-BPEL processes.

However, this approach only covers the static and not the *dynamic* business protocol evolution. A service has *running instances*. In case a service is long

L. Baresi, C.-H. Chi, and J. Suzuki (Eds.): ICSOC-ServiceWave 2009, LNCS 5900, pp. 607–621, 2009.

running (e.g., an insurance), it is not feasible to wait until a running instance has terminated. Instead, instances have to be *migrated* to the new service definition. In this paper, we extend our previous work towards instance migration.

Given a running instance in a state q_{old} of S_{old}, instance migration is the task of finding some state q_{new} of S_{new} such that resuming the execution in state q_{new} does not affect any partner of S_{old}. We call the transition from q_{old} to q_{new} a *jumper transition*. Clearly, not for every state q_{old} may exist a jumper transition to a state q_{new}. Sometimes it might be necessary to continue the instance on S_{old} until a state is reached, where a migration is then possible. As a service may have arbitrary many running instances, we do not calculate suitable jumper transitions for each individual instance, but calculate them independently of actually running instances.

A jumper transition models that an engine is stopped, an instance is frozen and migrated to the new service definition. As our approach only guarantees behavioral correctness, a jumper transition may later disqualify for other reasons; for example, it may violate a data dependency or domain-specific restrictions. Hence, the set of jumper transitions can be seen as a safe overapproximation of possibilities to migrate an instance. That means, any *additional* jumper transition can introduce behavioral problems such as deadlocks in the interaction with some partner of S_{old}.

The contribution of this paper can be summarized as follows. We present an algorithm to compute the *maximal* set of jumper transitions. An implementation of this algorithm justifies the applicability of our approach to real-world WS-BPEL processes. In contrast to most existing approaches we assume an *asynchronous* communication model for services, because services are intended to communicate asynchronously rather than synchronously [4]; furthermore, we do not put restrictions on the structure of S_{old} and S_{new} and the way they are changed. We only require that every partner of S_{old} is a partner of S_{new}.

The necessary background from our previous work is introduced in Sect. 2. In Sect. 3, we formalize the problem of instance migration in terms of the introduced concepts. Our actual approach to migration is explained in Sect. 4. In Sect. 5, we report on an implementation and a case study. We compare our contribution to related work in Sect. 6 and, finally, we conclude the paper in Sect. 7.

2   Behavior of Services

We model a service as a *service automaton*. This model reflects the control flow and the business protocol while abstracting from semantics and nonfunctional properties. To a limited degree, data aspects may be coded within the states of a service automaton.

Definition 1 (Service automaton). *A service automaton $S = [C_{in}, C_{out}, Q, q_0, \delta, \Omega]$ consists of two disjoint sets C_{in} of inbound message channels and C_{out} of outbound message channels, a set of states Q including an initial state q_0 and a set of final states Ω, and a nondeterministic labeled transition relation $\delta \subseteq Q \times (C_{in} \cup C_{out} \cup \{\tau\}) \times Q$.*

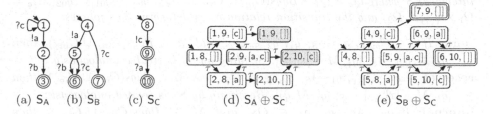

Fig. 1. Running example: service automata and their composition

We shall use indices for distinguishing the ingredients of different service automata. C_{in} and C_{out} establish the interface of S. Messages can be received from inbound channels and sent to outbound channels. In figures, we represent the interface implicitly by appending the symbol "?" to inbound channels and the symbol "!" to outbound channels. A transition with a label $a \in C_{in}$ receives a message from channel a. It is blocked if no message is available in the channel. A transition with a label $b \in C_{out}$ sends a message to channel b. We assume *asynchronous communication*, so sending transitions are never blocked. A transition with label τ ($\tau \notin (C_{in} \cup C_{out})$) represents any internal (i.e., non-communicating) activity. We shall write $q \xrightarrow{x}_S q'$ for $[q, x, q'] \in \delta$. Final states symbolize a successful completion of a service execution.

Example. As a running example, consider the service automata in Figs. 1(a)–(c). We use the standard graphical notations for automata and denote initial states by an inbound arrow and final states by double circles.

The interaction between services is defined through the concept of composition. For formalizing composition, we need to introduce *multisets*. A multiset is similar to a set, but permits multiple occurrences of elements. Formally, the number of occurrences of an element is represented as a mapping into the set $\mathbb{N}$ of natural numbers (including 0).

Definition 2 (Multiset). *A multiset A ranging over a set M is a mapping $A : M \to \mathbb{N}$. Multiset $A + B$ is defined by $(A + B)(x) = A(x) + B(x)$, for all x. A singleton multiset, written $[x]$ means $[x](x) = 1$ and $[x](y) = 0$, for $y \neq x$. The empty multiset $[]$ assigns 0 to all arguments. Let $Bags(M)$ be the set of all multisets ranging over set M.*

In the definition of composition, we use multisets in particular for representing the messages that are pending in channels. If, for some channel a, $M(a) = k$, then k messages are pending in channel a. Using multisets instead of queues, we assume asynchronous communication in which messages may overtake each other.

Definition 3 (Composition). *Services S_1 and S_2 are composable if $C_{in_1} = C_{out_2}$ and $C_{out_1} = C_{in_2}$. For composable services S_1 and S_2, the composition $S_c = S_1 \oplus S_2$ is the transition system (i.e., a service automaton with empty*

interface) S where $Q_c = Q_1 \times Bags(C_{in_1} \cup C_{in_2}) \times Q_2$, $q_{0c} = [q_{01}, [\,], q_{02}]$, $\Omega_c = \Omega_1 \times \{[\,]\} \times \Omega_2$, and the transition relation δ_c is determined as follows:

send: *If* $x \in C_{out_1}$, $q_1 \xrightarrow{x}_{S_1} q_1'$, $q_2 \in Q_2$, *and* $M \in Bags(C_{in_1} \cup C_{in_2})$, *then*
$[q_1, M, q_2] \xrightarrow{\tau}_{S_c} [q_1', M + [x], q_2]$. *Sending by* S_2 *is treated analogously.*

receive: *If* $x \in C_{in_1}$, $q_1 \xrightarrow{x}_{S_1} q_1'$, $q_2 \in Q_2$, *and* $M \in Bags(C_{in_1} \cup C_{in_2})$, *then*
$[q_1, M + [x], q_2] \xrightarrow{\tau}_{S_c} [q_1', M, q_2]$. *Receiving by* S_2 *is treated analogously.*

internal: *If* $q_1 \xrightarrow{\tau}_{S_1} q_1'$, $q_2 \in Q_2$, *and* $M \in Bags(C_{in_1} \cup C_{in_2})$, *then*
$[q_1, M, q_2] \xrightarrow{\tau}_{S_c} [q_1', M, q_2]$. *Internal transitions in* S_2 *are treated analogously.*

Example (cont.). The service automata S_A and S_C as well as S_B and S_C are composable (we assume all three services have three channels a, b, and c). Figures 1(d)–(e) depict the respective compositions.

Of course, only states reachable from the initial state are relevant. Using the notion of composition, we may define our correctness notion. We call an interaction correct if no *bad states* are reached in the composed system. We distinguish two kinds of bad states: deadlocks and overfull message channels. A deadlock is a non-final state where no transition is enabled. An overfull message channel is a state where some message channel contains more than k messages, for some given value k. As we treat the particular value of k as a parameter, we actually talk about k-*correctness*.

Definition 4 (k-correctness, k-partners). *Let* $k > 0$ *be a natural number. The interaction between composable services* S_1 *and* S_2 *is called* k-correct *if the composed system* $S_1 \oplus S_2$ *enables at least one transition in every non-final state* $q \in Q_{S_1 \oplus S_2} \setminus \Omega_{S_1 \oplus S_2}$, *and, for all states* $[q_1, M, q_2]$ *reachable from* $q_{0_{S_1 \oplus S_2}}$ *and all message channels* x, $M(x) \leq k$. *If the interaction between* S_1 *and* S_2 *is* k-correct, *we call* S_1 *a* k-partner *of* S_2, *and we call* S_2 *a* k-partner *of* S_1. *We write* k-Partners(S) *for the set of all* k-partners *of* S.

Example (cont.). The composition $S_A \oplus S_C$ contains two bad states (shaded gray). In contrast, the composition $S_B \oplus S_C$ does not contain any bad state, and in every reachable state at most one message is pending on each channel. Hence, S_B and S_C are 1-partners.

Treating overfull message channels as bad states has the advantage that a composed system has only finitely many reachable good states. This is essential for our approach. Besides, a crowded channel may indeed indicate a problem in the mutual interaction. In the real WS-BPEL processes we have analyzed so far, there is hardly any process in which more than a single message pending on a channel made sense. In practice, the value of k may stem from capacity considerations on the channels, from static analysis of the message transfer, or be chosen just sufficiently large. In the sequel, we shall assume that one particular value of k is fixed and we shall use the terms *correct* and *partner* without the preceding k.

In previous work, we were able to show that the (usually infinite) set *Partners(S)* can actually be finitely characterized. We provided an algorithm [5] and a tool for computing that characterization. The characterization exploits the fact that the set $Partners(S)$ actually contains a top element in the simulation preorder (i.e., it can exhibit all behavior that any service in $Partners(S)$ may exhibit).

Definition 5 (Simulation, most-permissive partner). *Let S_1 and S_2 be services with the same interface. A relation $\varrho \subseteq Q_1 \times Q_2$ is a simulation relation iff the following conditions are satisfied:*

Base: $[q_{01}, q_{02}] \in \varrho$;
Step: *If $[q_1, q_2] \in \varrho$ and, for some x, $[q_1, x, q'_1] \in \delta_1$ then there exists a state q'_2 such that $[q_2, x, q'_2] \in \delta_2$ and $[q'_1, q'_2] \in \varrho$.*

If there exists such a simulation relation, we say that S_2 simulates S_1. An element $S^* \in Partners(S)$ is called most-permissive partner *of S iff S^* simulates all elements of $Partners(S)$.*

In [6], we showed that a (not necessarily unique) most-permissive partner exists for every service S unless $Partners(S) = \emptyset$.

A simulation relation shows that the behavior of every partner of S is embedded in the behavior of a most-permissive partner. Hence, our finite characterization of *all* partners of S extends a most-permissive partner with Boolean annotations. They determine *which* embedded behaviors of the used most-permissive partner are actually in the set $Partners(S)$. The formulas constrain the outgoing edges from states as well as the set of final states.

Definition 6 (Annotated automaton, matching). *An annotated automaton $A = [S_A, \phi]$ consists of a service automaton S_A and a mapping ϕ that assigns to each state of S_A a Boolean formula. The formulas use propositions from the set $C_{in_A} \cup C_{out_A} \cup \{\tau, final\}$.*
A service automaton S matches with A if it uses the same interface as S_A and there is a simulation relation $\varrho \subseteq Q_S \times Q_{S_A}$ such that, for all $[q, q'] \in \varrho$, formula $\phi(q')$ is satisfied under the following assignment. Proposition x is true if there exists a state q_1 with $q \xrightarrow{x}_S q_1$. Proposition final is true if $q \in \Omega_S$.
With $Match(A)$, we denote the set of all services that match with A.

The main result of [5] is:

Proposition 1 (Operating guidelines). *For every service S with $Partners(S) \neq \emptyset$, there exists an annotated automaton $A = [S_A, \phi]$ (called operating guidelines of S or $OG(S)$) such that S_A is a particular most-permissive partner of S, subsequently referred to as $MPP(S)$, and $Partners(S) = Match(A)$.*

The most-permissive partner $MPP(S)$ used as the underlying structure of operating guidelines has two important structural properties. First, it is deterministic (i.e., transitions leaving a state have different labels) no matter whether the service S is deterministic or nondeterministic. This fact makes the search for simulation relations rather efficient. Second, there exist transitions $[q, \tau, q]$ in every state. We are going to use this fact as an argument in subsequent proofs.

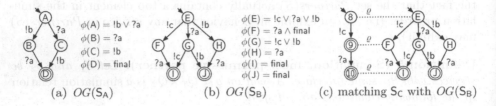

$\phi(A) = !b \vee ?a$
$\phi(B) = ?a$
$\phi(C) = !b$
$\phi(D) = final$

$\phi(E) = !c \vee ?a \vee !b$
$\phi(F) = ?a \wedge final$
$\phi(G) = !c \vee !b$
$\phi(H) = ?a$
$\phi(I) = final$
$\phi(J) = final$

(a) $OG(S_A)$ (b) $OG(S_B)$ (c) matching S_C with $OG(S_B)$

Fig. 2. Running example: operating guidelines and matching

Example (cont.). The operating guidelines of S_A and S_B (cf. Fig. 1) are depicted in Figs. 2(a)–(b). To increase legibility, we refrained from showing the τ-loops. The formula $\phi(A) = !b \vee ?a$ can be interpreted as a partner must send a message to channel b or receive a message from channel a; $\phi(F) = ?a \wedge final$ means that a partner must be in a final state, but still be able to receive a message from channel a. For the ease of presentation we also do not show the τ-disjunct in each annotation. For example, $\phi(F)$ is $\phi(F) = (?a \wedge final) \vee \tau$; that is, a partner may also execute an internal step. As S_C is a partner of S_B, it matches with $OG(S_B)$. The simulation relation ϱ is depicted in Fig. 2(c). It can be easily verified that the formulas are also satisfied. As S_C is not a partner of S_A, there is no matching between S_C and $OG(S_A)$.

We have already described a number of applications of operating guidelines to problems related to service behavior, including test case generation [7], service correction [8], and service transformation [3]. One that we actually shall apply subsequently is related to *substitutability* (i.e., static business protocol evolution). Informally, substitutability states that every service that interacts correctly with S_1 will also interact correctly with S_2. This means that S_1 can be safely substituted by S_2 (this time assuming that there are no running instances).

Definition 7 (Substitutability). *Service S_1 is substitutable with service S_2 if $Partners(S_1) \subseteq Partners(S_2)$.*

Substitutability (which is an inclusion between infinite sets) can be checked using operating guidelines [2]. We need to check a simulation relation and implications between annotations:

Proposition 2 (Checking substitutability). *Let S_1 and S_2 be services with the same interface, $Partners(S_1) \neq \emptyset$, and $Partners(S_2) \neq \emptyset$. Let $OG(S_1) = [MPP(S_1), \phi_1]$ and $OG(S_2) = [MPP(S_2), \phi_2]$ be the corresponding operating guidelines. Then S_1 is substitutable with S_2 if and only if there is a simulation relation $\varrho \subseteq Q_{MPP(S_1)} \times Q_{MPP(S_2)}$ such that, for all $[q_1, q_2] \in \varrho$, the formula $(\phi(q_1) \implies \phi(q_2))$ is a tautology (i.e., true in all assignments).*

Implementations of all techniques referred to in this section are available at http://www.service-technology.org/tools.

Example (cont.). By checking Proposition 2, we can verify that $Partners(S_A) \subseteq Partners(S_B)$; that is, S_A is substitutable with S_B. As we saw earlier, the converse does not hold, because $S_C \notin Partners(S_A)$ (cf. Fig. 1(d)).

3   Formalization of Instance Migration

Assume throughout this section that we want to migrate an instance of a service S_{old} to an instance of S_{new}. We generally assume that S_{old} and S_{new} have the same interface. Furthermore we require that S_{old} is substitutable with S_{new}. The assumption of substitutability is reasonable as it allows us immediately to migrate an instance of S_{old} being in its initial state to an instance of S_{new} being in its initial state. Furthermore, substitutability in connection with the assumption $S \in Partners(S_{old})$ gives us $S \in Partners(S_{new})$ which is also a desirable property.

An actual migration can be modeled as an internal transition from a state q_{old} of service S_{old} into a state q_{new} of service S_{new}. We call such a transition *jumper transition*. This kind of modeling abstracts from technical details like the process of freezing S_{old} (with all its parallel threads) in some intermediate state, transferring data to the new service and finally to start S_{new} in some non-initial state. In this sense, our approach considers behavior in isolation and abstracts from other aspects which are indeed relevant for instance migration.

Formally, we are not just interested in one particular jumper transition. Instead, we would like to find *all* feasible jumper transitions. That is, we aim at the calculation of a largest possible set $J \subseteq Q_{old} \times Q_{new}$ of jumper transitions. This way, a single calculation of J may help in migrating *all* running instances of S_{old} regardless of how far the execution of instances has progressed.

It is worth mentioning that there may be states of S_{old} for which there is no corresponding state in S_{new}. In such a state, migration is not possible. Instead it is necessary to let S_{old} proceed to another state where a migration can take place.

Using relation J, the process of instance migration can be expressed in terms of a single model. In fact, we can place S_{old} next to S_{new} and insert all jumper transitions as internal transitions. This model captures all possible migration scenarios reflected in J. In the literature, the term *hybrid model* has been coined for this approach [9]. The following notation formalizes the idea and introduces a notation.

Definition 8 (Hybrid model). *Let S_1 and S_2 be services with disjoint sets of states ($Q_1 \cap Q_2 = \emptyset$) and equal interfaces. Let $J \subseteq Q_1 \times Q_2$. Then the* hybrid model $S = \langle S_1 \overset{J}{\rightleftharpoons} S_2 \rangle$ *is a service automaton defined as follows.* $Q_S = Q_1 \cup Q_2$, $C_{in_S} = C_{in_1} = C_{in_2}$, $C_{out_S} = C_{out_1} = C_{out_2}$, $q_{0S} = q_{01}$, $\Omega_S = \Omega_1 \cup \Omega_2$, $\delta_S = \delta_1 \cup \delta_2 \cup \{[q_1, \tau, q_2] \mid [q_1, q_2] \in J\}$.

As the jumper transitions are internal to S_{old} and S_{new}, their occurrence is under full control of the provider of these service. For this reason, the hybrid model indeed reflects the process of migration of arbitrary instances of S_{old}.

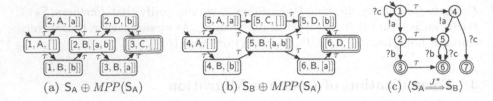

(a) $S_A \oplus MPP(S_A)$ (b) $S_B \oplus MPP(S_A)$ (c) $\langle S_A \overset{J^*}{\Longrightarrow} S_B \rangle$

Fig. 3. Running example: constructing the hybrid model

Using the notion of a hybrid model, we may state the correctness requirement on J. Essentially, we would like that every partner S of S_{old} interacts correctly with the hybrid model. In other words, interaction does not lead to bad states before, during, or after the migration.

Definition 9 (Feasible migration). *Let S_{old} and S_{new} be services. The migration relation $J \subseteq Q_{old} \times Q_{new}$ is feasible if $Partners(S_{old}) \subseteq Partners(\langle S_{old} \overset{J}{\Longrightarrow} S_{new} \rangle)$.*

4 Migration Approach

In this section, we first exhibit a particular migration relation J^*. Then we show that J^* is feasible. We continue with a discussion on the maximality of J^*.

The next definition shall determine J^*. To this end, remember that a migration must be correct independently of the interacting partner S of S_{old} and the state of S. A jumper transition $[q_{old}, q_{new}]$ means that we switch from a reachable state $[q_{old}, M, q]$ of $S_{old} \oplus S$ into state $[q_{new}, M, q]$. Of course, we are on the safe side if $[q_{new}, M, q]$ is a reachable state of $S_{new} \oplus S$. This is due to the fact that S is a partner of S_{old} and, by substitutability, a partner of S_{new}, too. Being a partner, no bad states can be reached from $[q_{new}, M, q]$ which is all we desire.

This observation leads straight to the definition of J^*, with just one modification. Instead of considering an arbitrary service S, we consider the particular service $MPP(S_{old})$ (which we can compute from S_{old}). This is a reasonable choice as $MPP(S_{old})$ embeds the behavior of all partners of S_{old}.

Definition 10 (Migration relation J^*). *Let S_{old} and S_{new} be substitutable services. Then $J^* = \{[q_{old}, q_{new}] \mid$ for all $[q_{old}, M, q] \in Q_{S_{old} \oplus MPP(S_{old})}$ holds: $[q_{new}, M, q] \in Q_{S_{new} \oplus MPP(S_{old})}\}$.*

Example (cont.). As S_A is substitutable with S_B, we can calculate the migration relation to migrate states from instances from S_A to S_B. The compositions with the most-permissive partner of S_A are depicted in Figs. 3(a)–(b). Among the states, we have $\{[2, A, [a]], [2, B, [a, b]], [2, D, [b]]\} \subseteq Q_{S_A \oplus MPP(S_A)}$ and $\{[5, A, [a]], [5, B, [a, b]], [5, C, []], [5, D, [b]]\} \subseteq Q_{S_B \oplus MPP(S_A)}$. From Definition 10, we can conclude that $[2, 5] \in J^*$: We can safely migrate state 2 to state 5 without jeopardizing correctness. The resulting hybrid model is depicted in Fig. 3(c).

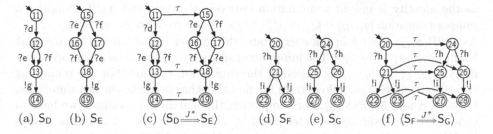

Fig. 4. Further migration examples

Figures 4(a)–(c) show an example in which migration is not possible in every state of the old service: state 12 of service S_D cannot be migrated to a state of S_E. Only after S_D proceeds to state 13, migration to S_E is again possible.

In the remainder of this section, we will focus on feasibility and maximality of the migration relation.

Feasability of the Migration Relation

We will first show that the migration relation J^* is indeed feasible; that is, the jumper transitions induced by J^* do not introduce bad states in the interaction with running partners of S_{old}.

Theorem 1. J^* is feasible.

Proof. Assume the contrary. Then there exists a service $S \in Partners(S_{old}) \setminus Partners(\langle S_{old} \xrightarrow{J^*} S_{new} \rangle)$. For not being a partner of $\langle S_{old} \xrightarrow{J^*} S_{new} \rangle$, there must be an execution in $\langle S_{old} \xrightarrow{J^*} S_{new} \rangle \oplus S$ that leads to a bad state. Consider first the case that the sequence does not contain any jumper transition. Then the sequence is actually a sequence in $S_1 \oplus S$ which contradicts the assumption $S \in Partners(S_{old})$.

Consider now the case that a jumper transition $[q_{old}, q_{new}]$ occurs in the considered execution. By our construction, only one such transition can occur. We now produce a contradiction by exhibiting a partner S_{bad} of S_{old} which is not a partner of S_{new}. This contradicts the assumed substitutability of the involved services.

As $S \in Partners(S_{old})$ there is a simulation relation $\varrho \subseteq Q_S \times Q_{MPP(S_{old})}$ such that the conditions of Definition 6 are met. Let $S_{bad} = \langle MPP(S_{old}) \xrightarrow{\varrho^{-1}} S \rangle$. We first show $S_{bad} \in Partners(S_{old})$. By Proposition 1, it is sufficient to show that S_{bad} matches with the operating guidelines $OG(S_{old}) = [MPP(S_{old}), \phi]$. To this end, consider the relation $\varrho_{bad} = \varrho \cup id_{Q_{MPP(S_{old})}}$ between S_{bad} and $MPP(S_{old})$.[1] ϱ_{bad} is actually a simulation. For states in $MPP(S_{old})$ this is easily verified

---

[1] By construction of S_{bad}, we have $Q_{MPP(S_{old})} \subset Q_{S_{bad}}$, so $id_{Q_{MPP(S_{old})}}$ can be seen as a relation between $Q_{S_{bad}}$ and $Q_{MPP(S_{old})}$.

as the identity is indeed a simulation between a service and itself. Consider a jumper transition $[q_1, q_2] \in Q_{MPP(S_{old})} \times Q_S$. We arrive with $[q_1, q_1] \in id_{Q_{MPP(S_{old})}}$. As $MPP(S_{old})$ has τ-loops in every state, the jumper transition can be matched, leading to the pair $[q_2, q_1]$. The jumper transition $[q_1, q_2]$ has been introduced only if $[q_2, q_1] \in \varrho$. So, $[q_2, q_1]$ is indeed in the simulation relation. For the remaining transitions, simulation follows from the fact the ϱ has been chosen as a simulation between S and $MPP(S_{old})$. For completing the matching procedure, we have to show that the assignments determined by S_{bad} satisfy the related annotations in $MPP(S_{old})$. For those states of S_{bad} which are in $MPP(S_{old})$, this is obvious as $MPP(S_{old})$ is indeed a partner of S_{old} and the identity is a valid simulation relation. For those states of S_{bad} which are in S, satisfaction of the annotations follows from the choice of ϱ.

We conclude our proof by showing that S_{bad} is not a partner of S_{new} which contradicts the assumed substitutability. For this purpose, return to the assumed execution sequence that brings $\langle S_{old} \xrightarrow{J^*} S_{new} \rangle \oplus S$ into a bad state. We replay this sequence in $S_{bad} \oplus S_{new}$. Assume that the jumper transition $[q_{old}, q_{new}]$ occurred in the context of state q of S and a bag M of pending messages. In other words, the composed system $\langle S_{old} \xrightarrow{J^*} S_{new} \rangle \oplus S$ contained the transition $[q_{old}, M, q] \xrightarrow{\tau} [q_{new}, M, q]$. As $MPP(S_{old})$ embeds the behavior of S, we can find a corresponding sequence in $S_{old} \oplus MPP(S_{old})$ that reaches a state $[q_{old}, M, q^*]$ such that $[q, q^*]$ are in the simulation relation between S and $MPP(S_{old})$. The latter sequence is also executable in S_{bad}. Now, let the jumper transition $[q_{old}, q_{new}]$ occur, followed by the jumper transition $[q^*, q]$ in S_{bad}. The resulting state is $[q_{new}, M, q]$. This is exactly the state reached by the jumper transition in the originally considered sequence. Hence, the remainder of the original sequence may be appended and shows that $S_{bad} \oplus S_{new}$ may reach a bad state. □

Maximality of the Migration Relation

Now we turn to the question of maximality of J^*. For this purpose, consider a transition $[q_{old}, q_{new}] \in Q_{old} \times Q_{new}$ which is not contained in J^*. By Definition 10, this means that there exists at least one service (e.g., $MPP(S_{old})$) and a reachable state $[q_{old}, M, q]$, from where the migration leads to a state $[q_{new}, M, q]$, is not reachable in the composition $S_{new} \oplus MPP(S_{old})$. As $MPP(S_{old})$ is most-permissive, this means that actually *no* service in $Partners(S_{old})$ is able to reach $[q_{new}, M, q]$. That is, migration would bring us into a part of S_{new} which is not intended to be reached by *any* partner of S_{old}. Though continuation from such a state may or may not lead to bad states, we believe that it is very unplausible to continue interaction there. In this light, we may claim that our migration relation is the largest possible set of jumper transitions.

5   Case Study and Implementation

For evaluating our proposed approach, we have implemented the computation of the migration relation J^* of Definition 10. The algorithm takes the two service automata S_{old} and S_{new} as its input. First, it computes the most-permissive partner $MPP(S_{old})$. According to the technique used in [6], this calculation returns not only $MPP(S_{old})$, but also the set of states $Q_{S_{old} \oplus MPP(S_{old})}$. Consequently, a second calculation is only required for producing $Q_{S_{new} \oplus MPP(S_{old})}$. The two sets of states are then sorted according to a criterion that enables an efficient verification of the implications in Definition 10.

The services used in the case study were anonymized real WS-BPEL processes provided by a small German consulting company. They implement several business processes from different domains such as government administration, industrial production, and customer services. To apply our formal framework, we first translated these WS-BPEL processes into service automata [10].

Table 1 lists the size of the interface (i.e., the number of inbound and outbound channels) and the number of states of the service automata. Due to complex internal behavior such as fault and compensation handling, the services have up to 14,569 states. The forth column contains the number of states of the most-permissive partner. For the considered services, the most-permissive partner usually has less states, because it only describes the interaction behavior and does not contain internal behavior other than the τ-loops mentioned in the remarks below Proposition 1.

In the case study, we migrated each service to its *public view*. The public view of a service S is a service $PV(S)$ that can be canonically derived from the operating guidelines $OG(S)$ such that holds: $OG(PV(S)) = OG(S)$. Hence, the public view $PV(S)$ is (1) by design substitutable with the original service S. Being constructed from the operating guidelines, however, it (2) abstracts from internal behavior and usually has no structural relationship to S. For these reasons, we chose the public view to benchmark the migration approach. The last column of Table 1 lists the number of states of the public views.

Table 2 lists information about the migration. To calculate the migration relation J^*, the composition of the most-permissive partner of the original service S (called "S_{old}" before) and the public view of S ("S_{new}") has to be considered. At maximum, this composition contained more than 100,000 states. The third column ("search space") lists the number of states to check in Definition 10. As

Table 1. Numbers on the services used in the case study

service S	$|C_{in_S} \cup C_{out_S}|$	$|Q_S|$	$|Q_{MPP(S)}|$	$|Q_{PV(S)}|$
Travel Service	10	34	192	202
Purchase Order	10	402	168	176
Ticket Reservation	9	304	110	118
Internal Order	7	1,516	96	104
Contract Negotiation	11	784	576	588
Deliver Finished Goods	14	182	1,632	1,394
Passport Application	11	14,569	1,536	1,540

Table 2. Numbers on the calculation of the maximal migration relation

migration $S \Rightarrow PV(S)$	$|Q_{MPP(S) \oplus PV(S)}|$	search space	$|J^*|$	time (sec)
Travel Service	2,976	3,333,120	49	2.1
Ticket Reservation	1,031	4,886,940	359	0.6
Purchase Order	2,545	19,851,000	429	1.3
Internal Order	1,455	34,460,220	1,613	0.9
Contract Negotiation	17,331	856,844,640	866	12.9
Deliver Finished Goods	60,753	1,050,783,888	197	123.1
Passport Application	100,975	990,199,624,400	22,382	518.1

this number depends on several state spaces, it heavily suffers from state explosion and nearly reaches 10^{12} states for the Identity Card service. Nevertheless, this number is only a theoretical bound, because (1) only two generator sets are kept in memory (the state spaces of the compositions with the most-permissive partner), and (2) these generators are sorted and represented to quickly detect violation of the criterion of Definition 10.

The forth column of Table 2 lists the size of the maximal migration relation J^* (i.e., the number of jumper transitions). Compared to the states of the involved services and the search spaces, this relation is rather small. The last column shows that most results were available in a few seconds. The maximal calculation took a bit more than eight minutes.[2] Though the implementation is only a prototype to prove the concept, we claim that these numbers are acceptable: The whole setting of instance migration is motivated by long-running services in which a few minutes of calculation is negligible. Furthermore, once the jumper transitions have been calculated, they can be applied to any number of running instances.

The case study of this paper can be replayed using the Web-based implementation of the tools available at `http://service-technology.org/live/migration`. At the same URL, the tools and the examples of the case study can be downloaded.

6   Related Work

Instance migration (or dynamic business protocol evolution) is a hot topic which has been studied by many researchers. Our proposed approach is inspired by the notion of state replaceability in [11], where all pairs of states (q_{old}, q_{new}) of S_{old} and S_{new} are determined such that S_{old} and S_{new} are forward and backward compatible. Backward compatible means that every path from the initial state of S_{old} to q_{old} is a valid path from the initial state of S_{new} to q_{new}. In contrast, forward compatible means that every path from q_{old} to a final state in S_{old} is

---

[2] The reported experiments were conducted on an Apple MacBook with a 2.16 GHz Intel Core 2 Duo processor. No calculation required more than 1 GB of memory.

also a valid path from q_{new} to a final state in S_{new}. Besides state replaceability, several weaker notions are presented in [11].

We identify the following differences to our approach: In [11] it is guaranteed that a service can always reach a final state, whereas our approach only guarantees deadlock freedom. As a restriction, synchronous communication is assumed in [11]. In contrast, service automata model asynchronous communication, as services are intended to communicate asynchronously rather than synchronously [4]. Although not explicitly mentioned, the approach in [11] is restricted to deterministic services, as forward and backward compatibility only relies on trace inclusion. For example, if we assume *synchronous communication*, then services S_F and S_G in Figs. 4(d) and 4(e) cannot be migrated. A service that first executes h and then expects i is a partner for S_F but not for S_G (S_G may enter the right branch causing a deadlock). However, by looking at traces, this counterexample cannot be detected. Moreover, the states 20 and 24 are forward and backward compatible. In contrast, our proposed method works for deterministic and non-deterministic services. As the crucial difference, we do not compare the structures of S_{old} and S_{new} but use information about all partners of S_{old} to compute the jumper transitions.

Dynamic evolution has been in particular studied in the field of workflows; see [12,13] for an overview. Some approaches [14,15] calculate the part of the workflow definition that is affected by the change (i.e., the change region). If an instance of S_{old} is not in the change region, it can be safely replaced by S_{new}. Other approaches like [16] and [17] are restricted to acyclic workflow models. In addition, [17] and also [18] take only the history into account to decide migration. Hence, the migrated instance may deadlock.

In [19] inheritance (i.e., branching bisimulation) is proposed for relating two workflows S_{old} and S_{new}. Transfer rules are presented to map a state of S_{old} to a state of S_{new}. The transfer rules ensure proper termination of an instance in S_{new}. The approach can also be combined with dynamic change regions in [15] to widen the applicability. However, branching bisimulation is too strict; for example, services S_F and S_G in Figs. 4(d) and 4(e) are not branching bisimular, and hence could not be migrated. In contrast, using our approach a migration can be computed (see Fig. 4(f)).

The ADEPT2 framework [13] offers support to dynamically change a workflow definition and to migrate running instances of the old workflow definition to the new one. The approach guarantees that no deadlocks or livelocks are introduced. Furthermore, the history of the migrated instance can be replayed on the new workflow definition. Thereby ADEPT2 also takes the data flow into consideration and ensures data consistency. However, the approach is restricted to workflows, whereas we consider services.

7   Conclusion

We provided an approach to the automated calculation of the maximal set of jumper transitions which model the possible migration of service instances. We addressed the behavioral aspect and took care that migration does not introduce reachable bad states. Other than this, the set of jumper transitions is reasonably large. The calculation of the set is possible within seconds to few minutes, considering real WS-BPEL processes. As instance migration is typically relevant for long-running services, this amount of time negligible. Though the results base on service automata, they can be easily applied to other service description languages once a translation to automata is specified. As such a translation is usually straightforward, the choice of service automata as formal model poses no intrinsic restrictions.

We are of course aware that our approach only considers behavior while it is necessary to obey several restrictions in several other aspects. Therefore, it is very well possible that some of our jumper transitions disqualify for reasons of data integrity or domain specific reasons. However, these issues can hardly avoid problems if the service runs into a bad state. Hence, our approach can be understood as a first overapproximation which reasonably reduces the combinatorics for subsequent consideration of other aspects for correct migration. Furthermore, data dependencies can be detected by techniques used in the area of static program analysis [20]. For WS-BPEL there exist such techniques already [21,22,23].

Due to the lack of tools and the fact that usually thousands of running instances have to be migrated, we think that our approach is a significant step towards supporting instance migration.

An interesting line of further research is to investigate the data aspect in more detail. As a result, we may get a smaller overapproximation. Furthermore, as a service composition may run on different servers another interesting line of further work is to migrate the state of each service separately rather than migrating the whole composition at once.

Acknowledgements. Niels Lohmann and Karsten Wolf are funded by the DFG project "Operating Guidelines for Services" (WO 1466/8-1).

References

1. Papazoglou, M.P.: The challenges of service evolution. In: Bellahsène, Z., Léonard, M. (eds.) CAiSE 2008. LNCS, vol. 5074, pp. 1–15. Springer, Heidelberg (2008)
2. Stahl, C., Massuthe, P., Bretschneider, J.: Deciding substitutability of services with operating guidelines. In: Jensen, K., van der Aalst, W. (eds.) ToPNoC II. LNCS, vol. 5460, pp. 172–191. Springer, Heidelberg (2009)
3. König, D., Lohmann, N., Moser, S., Stahl, C., Wolf, K.: Extending the compatibility notion for abstract WS-BPEL processes. In: WWW 2008, pp. 785–794. ACM, New York (2008)
4. Papazoglou, M.P.: Web Services: Principles and Technology. Pearson - Prentice Hall, Essex (2007)
5. Lohmann, N., Massuthe, P., Wolf, K.: Operating guidelines for finite-state services. In: Kleijn, J., Yakovlev, A. (eds.) ICATPN 2007. LNCS, vol. 4546, pp. 321–341. Springer, Heidelberg (2007)

6. Wolf, K.: Does my service have partners? In: Jensen, K., van der Aalst, W. (eds.) ToPNoC II. LNCS, vol. 5460, pp. 152–171. Springer, Heidelberg (2009)
7. Kaschner, K., Lohmann, N.: Automatic test case generation for interacting services. In: Feuerlicht, G., Lamersdorf, W. (eds.) ICSOC 2008. LNCS, vol. 5472, pp. 66–78. Springer, Heidelberg (2009)
8. Lohmann, N.: Correcting deadlocking service choreographies using a simulation-based graph edit distance. In: Dumas, M., Reichert, M., Shan, M.-C. (eds.) BPM 2008. LNCS, vol. 5240, pp. 132–147. Springer, Heidelberg (2008)
9. Casati, F., Ceri, S., Pernici, B., Pozzi, G.: Workflow evolution. In: Thalheim, B. (ed.) ER 1996. LNCS, vol. 1157, pp. 438–455. Springer, Heidelberg (1996)
10. Lohmann, N., Massuthe, P., Stahl, C., Weinberg, D.: Analyzing interacting WS-BPEL processes using flexible model generation. Data Knowledge Engineering 64(1), 38–54 (2008)
11. Ryu, S.H., Casati, F., Skogsrud, H., Benatallah, B., Saint-Paul, R.: Supporting the dynamic evolution of web service protocols in service-oriented architectures. TWEB 2(2) (2008)
12. Rinderle, S., Reichert, M., Dadam, P.: Correctness criteria for dynamic changes in workflow systems - a survey. Data Knowl. Eng. 50(1), 9–34 (2004)
13. Reichert, M., Rinderle-Ma, S., Dadam, P.: Flexibility in process-aware information systems. In: Jensen, K., van der Aalst, W. (eds.) ToPNoC II. LNCS, vol. 5460, pp. 115–135. Springer, Heidelber (2009)
14. Ellis, C.A., Keddara, K., Rozenberg, G.: Dynamic change within workflow systems. In: COOCS 1995, pp. 10–21. ACM, New York (1995)
15. van der Aalst, W.M.P.: Exterminating the dynamic change bug: A concrete approach to support workflow change. Information Systems Frontiers 3(3), 297–317 (2001)
16. Agostini, A., Michelis, G.D.: Improving flexibility of workflow management systems. In: van der Aalst, W.M.P., Desel, J., Oberweis, A. (eds.) Business Process Management. LNCS, vol. 1806, pp. 218–234. Springer, Heidelberg (2000)
17. Sadiq, S.W.: Handling dynamic schema change in process models. In: Australasian Database Conference, pp. 120–126 (2000)
18. Casati, F., Ceri, S., Pernici, B., Pozzi, G.: Workflow evolution. Data Knowl. Eng. 24(3), 211–238 (1998)
19. van der Aalst, W.M.P., Basten, T.: Inheritance of Workflows: An Approach to Tackling Problems Related to Change. Theoretical Computer Science 270(1-2), 125–203 (2002)
20. Nielson, F., Nielson, H.R., Hankin, C.: Principles of Program Analysis, 2nd edn. Springer, Berlin (2005)
21. Lohmann, N.: A feature-complete Petri net semantics for WS-BPEL 2.0. In: Dumas, M., Heckel, R. (eds.) WS-FM 2007. LNCS, vol. 4937, pp. 77–91. Springer, Heidelberg (2008)
22. Moser, S., Martens, A., Gorlach, K., Amme, W., Godlinski, A.: Advanced verification of distributed WS-BPEL business processes incorporating CSSA-based data flow analysis. In: SCC 2007, pp. 98–105. IEEE Computer Society, Los Alamitos (2007)
23. Heinze, T.S., Amme, W., Moser, S.: Generic CSSA-based pattern over Boolean data for an improved WS-BPEL to Petri net mappping. In: ICIW 2008, pp. 590–595. IEEE Computer Society, Los Alamitos (2008)

Distributed Cross-Domain Configuration Management

Liliana Pasquale[1], Jim Laredo[2], Heiko Ludwig[2], Kamal Bhattacharya[2],
and Bruno Wassermann[3]

[1] Politecnico di Milano, Italy
pasquale@elet.polimi.it
[2] IBM TJ Watson Research Center, USA
{laredoj,hludwig,kamalb}@us.ibm.com
[3] University College London, UK
b.wassermann@cs.ucl.ac.uk

Abstract. Applications make extensive use of services offered by distributed platforms ranging from software services to application platforms or mere computational resources. In these cross-domain environments applications may have dependencies on services or resources provided by different domains. A service management solution based on a centrally managed configuration management database (CMDB) is not viable in these environments since CMDB federation does not scale well to many domains. In this paper we propose a distributed configuration management approach by applying standard technologies (e.g., REST services, ATOM feeds) to provide access to and distribution of configuration information. A domain exposes individual configuration items as RESTful web service resources that can be referred to and read by other domains in the context of service management processes. Using this distributed approach, organizations can engage in effective service management practices avoiding the tight integration of CMDBs with their service providers and customers.

1 Introduction

Applications make extensive use of services offered by distributed platforms hosted in different domains. These platforms range from software services (Software-as-a-Service, SaaS), to application platforms (e.g., facebook.com) to mere computational resources (e.g., Amazon Elastic Compute Cloud). Often, applications make use of different services from different providers, e.g., for storage and application platforms, and may be also integrated with in-house, dedicated software. Hence applications may depend on services or resources provided by different organizational domains. In such a loosely-coupled environment, providers are not even aware of the set of other organizations currently using their services. Furthermore, the wide adoption of web standards to consume and provide services facilitates the easy establishment and the change of these cross-domain configuration relationships. If providers conduct changes independently of their

L. Baresi, C.-H. Chi, and J. Suzuki (Eds.): ICSOC-ServiceWave 2009, LNCS 5900, pp. 622–636, 2009.

clients, the clients services may be disrupted. For this reason clients need to understand on which external configurations they depend on.

Configuration management plays a crucial role for other service management processes, e.g. incident management, change management, or process management, whose activities depend on configuration information of the environment. Hence, management activities have to take into account the distribution of configuration information across organizational boundaries due to the presence of inter-domain dependencies. Moreover, when a configuration changes it is necessary to provide some mechanisms to manage these changes, notifying interested clients. This becomes of high importance especially in those environments in which an outage caused by an unmanaged configuration change may be propagated along a chain of dependencies.

Current service configuration management approaches rely on a centrally managed configuration management database (CMDB) [1], which collects the state of hardware and software entities, represented by Configuration Items (CIs) [2]. When changes happen in a CI, specific operations need to be performed on other CIs that depend on it. A service management solution based on a central CMDB is not viable in cross-domain environments since CMDB federation does not scale well to many domains and different organizations are often reluctant to provide direct access to their CMDBs.

In general there are different issues configuration management must address for distributed, loosely coupled environments:

- **Discovery:** The lack of scope and access to resources of other domains makes hard to discover CIs outside ones' own management domain,
- **Dependency management:** Detect the management domains an CI depends on is not an easy task.
- **Cross-Domain configuration analysis:** It is not always feasible to aggregate and combine configuration information of different domains in a straightforward way, to ease management activities.

In this paper we propose a distributed configuration management approach by applying standard Web technologies (e.g., REST services, ATOM feeds) to help to solve the issues described above and provide access and distribution of configuration information. A domain exposes individual CIs as RESTful web service resources that can be referred to and read by other domains in the context of service management processes. Domains can manage dependencies on outside resources in the form of URLs. Using this distributed approach, organizations can engage in effective service management practices while not requiring tight integration with their service providers and customers. This approach and the specific application to change management has been shown in [3] and [4].

The paper is organized as follows. Section 2 analyzes the problems of cross-domain configuration management using an example. Section 3 gives an overview of the architecture of our solution. Section 4 explains the approach of Smart Configuration Items, including their publication, consumption, and format. Subsequently, section 5 illustrates how configuration information can be aggregated across domains. Finally, section 6 discusses implementation, section 7 summarizes related approaches, and section 8 concludes the paper.

2   Problem Analysis

In this section we discuss the main challenges of cross-domain configuration management using an example scenario, shown in Figure 1. A startup company, E-Shop, integrates different retailers, to advertise and sell their products. E-Shop relies on a distributed application infrastructure whose elements are owned and managed by different organizations. In our example, *Domain A* provides an application server (*AS-A1*), hosting the service which advertises the products to sell (*Advertise*). *Domain A* also hosts a database management system (*DBMS-A1*) which controls several databases (e.g., *DB-A1*, etc.). Both the application server and the DBMS are hosted on a virtual machine, represented through its address (*131.34.5.20*). Each machine can provide one or more file systems. The same situation holds for *Domain B*, which provides the service that performs payments (*Payment*), and some storage facilities.

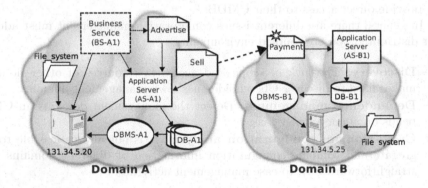

Fig. 1. Running Example

In the scenario we have intra-domain dependencies between CIs, represented through straight arrows, and inter-domain dependencies, represented through dashed arrows. For example, services provided by *Domain A* depend on the application server on which they are deployed. While file systems, application servers and DBMSs depend on the machine in which they are installed. Moreover, databases depend on the DBMS by which they are managed and application servers depend on local/remote DBs used by applications deployed on them (e.g., through a Web services connection). Furthermore each application may depend on services of another domain. In our example, application *Sell* depends on service *Payment*, provided outside its domain.

Finally, E-Shops marketing campaign is carried by several business services that can be considered as "abstract" CIs relying on "concrete" elements of the infrastructure. Figure 1 shows a business service (*BS-A1*) that depends on those CIs that implement it (service *Advertise*, application server *AS-A1* and the machine *131.34.5.20*). This case highlights the need to trace properties and dependencies of CIs that do not correspond to an element provided by the underlying infrastructure (e.g., business services), since changes on the infrastructure may also impact on these abstract elements.

This example illustrates the main functional issues that need to be addressed by a cross-domain configuration management approach:

- **Publication of configuration information:** Management domain must select internal CIs relevant for other domains and provide them in a convenient way.
- **Identification of cross-domain dependencies:** When performing discovery in a domain, a configuration management system must identify those CIs that depend on external CIs and manage the dependency (e.g., receiving notifications when external CIs change).
- **Multi-domain configuration analysis:** In the course of service management processes, analysis is conducted through entire configurations, e.g., for root cause analysis. Organizations must be able to aggregate configuration information from multiple domains.

These functions enable a management domain to conduct configuration management in a multi-domain environment involving multiple service providers.

3   Overview of the Approach

Our approach deals with configuration information for each single domain of the infrastructure. This information is published on one or more web servers authoritative for a domain and can be consumed in a standard way through REST and ATOM [5] protocols. Local configuration management also provides distributed and cross-domain benefits, since information about the overall infrastructure can be easily published and obtained aggregating that available for each local domain. Figure 2 shows the application of our solution for our running example. It provides two main functionality: Smart Configuration Management and Cross Domain Aggregation.

Smart Configuration Management. All CIs are detected for each resource of a domain, through a discovery process *(1)*. We call these configuration items Smart Configuration Items (SCIs): they represent the properties and the inter- and intra-domain dependencies of an element of the infrastructure. Our discovery process is also able to resolve cross-domain dependencies, that in general are hard to identify, through the DSM Registry *(2.b)*. SCIs and their dependencies may also be established manually, when elements they represent cannot be detected through the discovery mechanisms (e.g., the business service we adopted in our example). Each SCI is associated with a feed document carrying on its changes. SCIs and feed documents generated after the domain configuration discovery

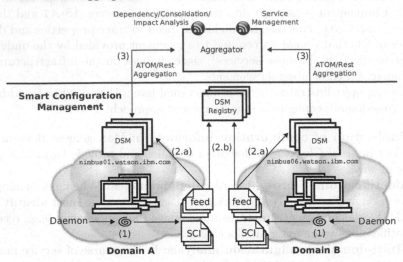

Fig. 2. Solution Architecture

are periodically published *(2.a)* on a authoritative web server known as Domain Service Manager (DSM), which serves local information via REST or as ATOM feeds to interested parties.

Cross-Domain Aggregation. Information about the overall infrastructure is obtained querying to an Aggregator that is in charge to communicate to all DSMs of the infrastructure *(3)*. This information is provided through a REST or an ATOM aggregation. The first one is synchronous and offers information about all SCIs of the infrastructure or all SCIs of a particular type. While, the latter is asynchronous and generates notifications if some changes happened in one or more SCIs that comply to specific features. Aggregation provides configuration information in a flexible way and eases the adoption of this information to perform several kinds of analysis (e.g. dependency, consolidation, impact analysis, compliance analysis) or to perform service management operation (e.g., change management, incident management, etc.).

The basic tenet of our approach is to use Web-based techniques for dealing with cross-domain management issues. The flexibility of the REST-based approach and the wide availability of tooling to create/consume SCIs and their associated feeds makes possible to easily manage configuration information also for cross-domain environments. For example, we can hypothesize to have listeners from *Domain A* for a change in service *Payment* of *Domain B*. In this case, after a feed listener in *Domain A* is notified about the change of parameter `AcceptedPayments` of service *Payment* it can trigger a new internal change process (supposed that this change is relevant), resulting in the participation of *Domain A* in *Domain B*'s change process.

4   Smart Configuration Items

DSM is the enabling element for domain configuration management. It tracks in its internal registry all available SCIs in a domain. Each SCI is associated with a unique id, a set of properties/dependencies (address, port, type, etc.) able to unambiguously identify it and two paths in the domain file system pointing respectively to the location of the SCI document and the feed document containing configuration changes. We also provide a DSM Registry, which associate each DSM with the hosts it is authoritative for. A DSM Registry may be available in a single domain and is in charge to communicate with other DSM Registries provided by other domains. The DSM offers RESTful services to retrieve, create, modify or delete discovered SCIs. Users can access to SCI information through a simple GET operation on the SCI URL constructed as follows:

```
http://<DSM_HostName>:8080/sci?id=<id>
```

where `<DSM_HostName>` is the address of the DSM and `<id>` is the identifier of the requested SCI. While the feed document associated with an SCI can be retrieved at the following URL:

```
http://<DSM_HostName>:8080/feed?id=<id>
```

Feeds can also be consumed through a standard feed reader. DSM also provides a graphical interface system administrators can use to perform several operations on local SCIs. It allows to visualize information about all SCIs available in a domain (URL, type, properties and dependencies). It also permits to recursively traverse the dependency chain of an SCI, with the possibility to reach SCIs involved in a inter-domain dependency, which are not local. For example, from the SCI associated with application *Payment* of *Domain A*, it is possible visualize information about its application server (*AS-A1*). This is still valid if the requested SCI is managed by another DSM, e.g., belonging to *Domain B*.

We also allow domain administrators to add a new SCI to represent configuration information that is not discovered automatically. This functionality is adopted when we need to add SCIs representing business services (e.g., *BS-B1*, in our example) that rely on infrastructural resources, but cannot be detected through the standard configuration discovery algorithms. The interface also permits to manually modify an existing SCI e.g., adding inter-domain dependencies when they cannot be discovered automatically.

4.1   Configuration Data Model

An SCI status is represented through an extensible XML document, able to address the descriptive requirements of different configuration domains.

In Figure 3 on the left we show the SCI logic schema, while on the right we propose an example of SCI document associated with application *Sell* of the proposed scenario. Each SCI is described through a set of mandatory attributes: `uri`, which represents the URL that uniquely identifies the SCI (on the DSM which is actually keeping it); `type`, which is the type of the represented item (DBMS, application server, database, etc.). In Figure 3 attribute `type` is set to `application`

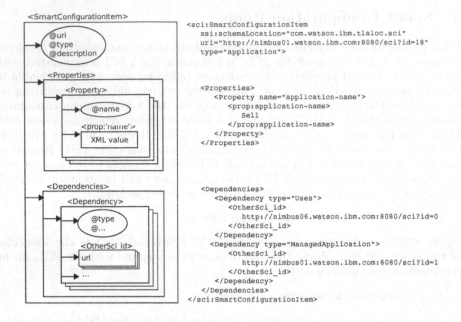

```
<SmartConfigurationItem>
    @uri
    @type
    @description

    <Properties>
        <Property>
            @name
            <prop:'name'>
            XML value

    <Dependencies>
        <Dependency>
            @type
            @...
            <OtherSci id>
            url
            ...
```

```
<sci:SmartConfigurationItem
    xsi:schemaLocation="com.watson.ibm.tlaloc.sci"
    uri="http://nimbus01.watson.ibm.com:8080/sci?id=18"
    type="application">

    <Properties>
        <Property name="application-name">
            <prop:application-name>
                Sell
            </prop:application-name>
        </Property>
    </Properties>

    <Dependencies>
        <Dependency type="Uses">
            <OtherSci_id>
                http://nimbus06.watson.ibm.com:8080/sci?id=0
            </OtherSci_id>
        </Dependency>
        <Dependency type="ManagedApplication">
            <OtherSci_id>
                http://nimbus01.watson.ibm.com:8080/sci?id=1
            </OtherSci_id>
        </Dependency>
    </Dependencies>
</sci:SmartConfigurationItem>
```

Fig. 3. SCI document schema and example

and attribute uri indicates that the SCI is kept in the DSM authoritative for *Domain A*, since it starts with hostname nimbus01. watson.ibm.com. SCIs can also have optional attributes (e.g., description, which gives a human readable description of the SCI).

An SCI can have any number of properties, defined by a name and an XML value. The property name is equal to the local name of the XML tag enclosing the property value. This mechanism allows users to define their own properties that can have values compliant to an arbitrary schema. In the proposed example the application is described through property: application-name.

An SCI has zero or more dependencies, specified by a type and a list of URLs identifying SCIs on which the item depends. Extension points are provided to insert new attributes and elements describing the nature of the dependency. In our example we have two kinds of dependencies: ManagedApplication and Uses. The first is on the SCI representing the application server in which application *Sell* is deployed. While the latter indicates a dependency on the adopted service (*Payment*). This last dependency is not local since the corresponding SCI is available on the DSM authoritative for *Domain B* (nimbus06.watson.ibm.com).

Besides the representation of the current SCI in the DSM, the discovery process produces a feed outlining SCI changes compared to the previous discovery. Possible changes are: add/delete/modify property, add/delete dependency, or add/delete a SCI pointer into a dependency. An example of the feed document associated to web service *Payment* is shown in Figure 4. It is updated after the input message of operation *PayOrder* change type from tns:RPType to `tns:RPAllowedType`. Change descriptions are enclosed into element `<entry>` in the feed document. In the example we have two entries. The first is created when an SCI associated with web server *Payment* is added for the first time to the authoritative DSM, while the second one advertises the change of operation *PayOrder*. Change information is carried on by element `<property-change>` and is described through the following attributes: `type` that represents the kind of change happened (`ChangePropertyValue`); `xpath`, which points to the modified property/dependency (in this case, property `alias-name`); `uri`, that is the url of the corresponding SCI; and `feed-uri` that is the feed url. Each change is described through two sub-elements: `<old>`, which contains the previous value of the property/dependency and `<new>`, which contains the new value of the considered property/dependency. If the change is an addition or a deletion of a property/dependency, element `<old>` or `<new>`, respectively, are not inserted in the change description.

```
<entry>
    <title>SCI Added</title>
    <id>random id</id>
    <updated>2008-12-14T18:30:02Z</updated>
    <content type="TEXT">
        A new service was added to DSM nimbus06.watson.ibm.com;
    </content>
</entry>
<entry>
    <title>Modify Property Entry</title>
    <id>random id</id>
    <updated>2008-12-14T19:30:02Z</updated>
    <content type="XHTML">
        <!-- the element Property is modified -->
        <pc:property-change xmlns:pc="com.ibm.tlaloc.propEntryContent"
            type="ChangePropertyValue"
            xpath="//Property[@name='operationq']"
            uri="nimbus06.watson.ibm.com:8080/sci?id=0"
            feed-uri="nimbus06.watson.ibm.com:8080/feed?id=0"
            propertyName="operations">
            <pc:old>
                ...
                <wsd:operation name="PayOrder">
                    <wsdl:input message="RequstPayment" type="tns:RPType"/>
                ...
            </pc:old>
            <pc:new>
                <wsd:operation name="PayOrder">
                    <wsdl:input message="RequstPayment" type="tns:RPAllowedType"/>
                ...
            </pc:new>
        </pc:property-change>
    </content>
</entry>
```

Fig. 4. An example of configuration change

4.2   Domain Configuration Discovery

SCIs rely on a local discovery mechanism to report the dependencies and properties of each CI. The local discovery gives us another level of granularity removing the need of any centralized repository, ideally for a more distributed approach, yet given the complexity of comprehensive discovery mechanisms it is necessary to make trade-offs as to how close to the CIs we can place the discovery engine given their resource requirements.

A discovery process must detect the main SCIs available on those virtual machines that it covers and, for each of them, it must find their main properties and dependencies on other SCIs (that can belong to that domain or to other domains). For example, it must discover the basic properties of virtual machines, e.g., their operating system and the hostnames associated with them. Moreover, a discovery process must find the servers installed on each host (e.g., DBMSs, application servers, http servers), their main properties (e.g., for a DBMS, the ports it listens to, its type and version), and dependencies (e.g. a DBMS is associated with the host in which it is installed). A discovery process must also detect SCIs managed by the servers installed on a host (e.g., applications managed by an application server). From the discovered properties and dependencies we also want to identify each SCI uniquely, among other SCIs of the same type. For example, a DBMS can be uniquely identified through the host in which it is installed and the ports it listens to. Finally we also require discovery to be performed periodically and automatically upon configuration change (e.g., with a specific periodicity or when something happens, for example a new component is installed or an existing one is upgraded).

Taking into account these requirements we demonstrated our approach using Galapagos [6], a lightweight discovery mechanism acting on a per virtual node basis. In particular we embedded in our discovery agent the Galapagos capability. The agent converts information discovered by Galapagos into several SCI state representations. The adoption of Galapagos satisfies our requirements since it is able to detect all basic elements provided by common virtual machines (file systems, http servers and their virtual hosts, databases, DBMSs, application servers, etc.). Furthermore, Galapagos is primarily tailored for IBM software (e.g., DB2, IBM HTTP Server, WebSphere Application Server, etc.), for which it can discover a wider set of properties. Finally we allow to perform discovery periodically depending on specific needs in terms of times and frequency of scans, or it can be triggered by particular events, like failures, software/hardware upgrades, etc.

4.3   SCI Dependency Resolution and Management

The discovery agent inspects all CIs starting from those that have no dependencies (e.g. a virtual machine) up to those that may have numerous dependencies (e.g. application servers, applications).

If we consider host *131.34.5.20* of *Domain A*, discovery will follow the following steps:

1. **host (mandatory):** It leverages data describing the host *131.34.5.20* in which discovery is performed to create an SCI of type host which has no dependencies and has at least two properties: os, which represents its operative system, with a name (Linux) a version (2.6.18 - EL5.02), etc., and lan,

which carries on hostnames associated with that host (`nimbus03.watson-.ibm.com`).

2. **File Systems (mandatory):** It transforms information regarding mounted file systems into an SCI of type `file_system`, which is described by the following properties: `fs-device` (file system device), `fs-mount-point` (mount point), `name` (file system name), `fs-mode` (read only/write mode). It also depends on the host providing its mount point, represented by dependency `HostedBy`. This dependency is within the domain and the corresponding SCI is detected at step 1.

3. **DBMSs:** An SCI of type `dbms` is created for `DBMS-A1`, found during discovery. It is characterized by a hostname (property `host-name`) and a set of ports it listens to (property `ports`). Each dbms depends on the SCI created at step 1 and associated with the host in which it is actually installed (dependency `HostedBy`).

4. **Databases:** Database `DB-A1` found during discovery is transformed into an SCIs of type `db`, described through a database name (property `databasename`) and an alias name (property `alias-name`). It also depends on the SCI associated with its DBMS (`DBMS-A1`). For this reason, dependency `ManagedDB` is created: it is within the domain and the corresponding SCI is created at step 3. Discovered DBs may also depend on other databases they refer to (dependency `Uses`) which can be managed on other hosts (this last case is not illustrated in our scenario).

5. **Application Servers:** Application server *AS-A1* found during discovery is associated with an SCI of type `application_server`, we already shown in Section 4. This SCI also has an inter-domain dependency on databases hosted on other domains of the cloud.

6. **Applications:** Applications *Advertise* and *Sell* found during discovery are associated with an SCI of type `application`. They are described through their name (property `application_name`). Furthermore they may be composed of several ejb/java/web modules (dependency `ComposedOf`). They depend on the application server on which they are deployed (dependency `ManagedApplication`). Both these dependencies are within the domain and the corresponding SCIs are created in the previous steps.

During discovery it is necessary to identify URLs of SCIs that are referenced in the dependencies. These SCIs can be local to the domain or they can belong to other domains. An SCI URL can be automatically constructed knowing the hostname of its authoritative DSM and the id through which the DSM reference it in its internal table. Hence, when a dependency refers to a local SCI (which has the same authoritative DSM of the depending item) it is only needed to know its id. This id can be retrieved from the local DSM giving in input some properties/dependencies inferred during discovery. The DSM searches in its table the rows that have properties/dependencies matching those given as input and returns the associated ids. When an SCI is not local, it is also necessary to know what DSM maintains it.

For example, in our scenario we need to identify URL of the SCI associated with service *Payment* on which application *Sell* depends. Information retrieved

during discovery about service *Payment* is its endpoint http://131.34.5.25/-
FlexPayService.wsdl. From this property we know the host on which service
Payment is deployed (131.34.5.25). At this point the discovery needs to know
what is the DSM authoritative for the SCIs of host 131.34.5.25. Discovery
process gets this information from DSM Registry, issuing the query below:

http://nimbus06.watson.ibm.com:8081/machine?address=131.34.5.25

It is worth to note that each host of the domain knows the address of the authoritative DSM Registry, since it is given to the discovery process as a configuration
parameter.

The DSM Registry returns the hostname of the required DSM (nimbus06-
.watson.ibm.com) that keeps the SCI of service *Payment*. Finally, what the
discovery needs to do is to request to the DSM the SCI id of service *Payment*
through a query of this type (single URI):

```
http://nimbus06.watson.ibm.com:8080/
  sciRegistry?type=web_service&
  properties=<property name=ws-endpoint>
    <prop:ws-endpoint>
      http://131.34.5.25/FlexPayService.wsdl
    </prop:ws-endpoint>
  </property>
```

The DSM Manager returns the id of the SCI associated to service Payment
(i.e., 0). This way the discovery process is able to construct the URL of the SCI
associated with service Payment as follows:

http://nimbus06.watson.ibm.com:8080/sci?id=0

Before terminating discovery the set of detected SCIs is given as input to the DSM
authoritative for that domain. DSM keeps the set of SCIs already detected in the
previous discovery phase. Hence it compares discovered SCIs with the previous
ones grouping them into three sets: ADDED (new SCIs that were not discovered
previously), DELETED (old SCIs that are not detected in the last discovery phase)
and MODIFIED (pairs of SCIs detected in two subsequent discovery phases). Association between SCIs that refer to the same component in two subsequent discovery phases are detected as follows: the DSM checks if the properties/dependencies
that allow to uniquely identify an SCI are still the same. For example, to uniquely
identify an SCI associated with a db among all SCI of type db, we need property
database-name and dependency ManagedDB (the corresponding dbms). If a previous SCI is detected with properties/ dependencies matching those given as input, both the previous SCI and the new one are inserted in the set MODIFIED.
Otherwise the new SCI is put in the set ADDED. Old SCIs that do not have a
corresponding new SCI, are put in set DELETED.

For each SCI in set ADDED the DSM adds a new entry in its internal table
with a unique id, the discovered attributes that allow to uniquely identify it
and the paths to the locations of the configuration information. A new feed
document is also created and associated to that SCI, with an entry that advertise

its creation. For all SCIs in set DELETED, DSM adds a new entry in their feed documents to advertise their deletion. DSM also marks as "deleted" the row state in its internal table pointing to that SCI. Configuration files will be deleted after a certain time for space reasons. All couples of SCIs put in the set MODIFIED are compared to find differences in the SCI documents that reveal possible modifications. If a modification is detected a suitable entry is added to the feed document associated with that SCI to advertise the change.

5 Cross Domain Aggregation

SCIs availability in each domain via the authoritative DSM allows all interested stakeholders to get higher level views on the configuration of the overall infrastructure according to specific needs. These views transcend the perspective of a particular domain and are created through the combination and the reinterpretation of existing SCIs or feed documents. Cross-domain aggregation is enabled by the adoption of mashups relying on one or more Aggregators, which collects and aggregates the information exposed by each DSM. To aggregate SCIs and feeds coming from the whole distributed platform, Aggregators ask the DSM Registry what are the hostnames of all DSMs available in the infrastructure.

Aggregators provide overall information about items configuration and their changes through respectively a REST or an ATOM aggregation. REST aggregation allows to combine several SCIs according to some criteria. In our current prototype we provide the following aggregations we considered significant for service management processes:

All SCIs available in the infrastructure. It provides a global view of all items available in all domains of the distributed platform. For example, it can be useful when a cloud provider receives a request from a user who wants to deploy his/her applications. In this case, the provider needs a global overview of all SCIs of the infrastructure to know which machines of its cloud are more suitable to host those applications.

All SCIs a business application relies on. It is useful for business analysts who may want to retrieve SCIs a specific business application relies on.

All SCIs associated with items of the same type. It is useful for administrators who need to perform maintenance on items of the same type. For example, an administrator may ask for all SCIs of type dbms when he/she has to perform an upgrade to a next version of DB2, to all DBMS of the infrastructure. In fact he/she needs to view the version of all DBMS available in the infrastructure to know which of them has to be upgraded.

A specific SCI together with those SCIs referenced in its dependencies. During incident management processes, detecting the cause of a failure in an CI may require to inspect the configuration of other items it depends on.

ATOM cross-domain aggregation allows stakeholders to subscribe on changes that can affect any item of the overall infrastructure, without knowing the URLs of the feeds associated with each SCI. We provide some predefined criteria to aggregate feeds:

– *All feeds available in the infrastructure.* It eases change management processes. For example, interested users may be notified when an item in the infrastructure changes (e.g. service *Payment*) and, if this change is relevant for their business, they can perform maintenance actions on the affected items (e.g., change the parameters adopted to invoke service *Payment*).

– *All feeds associated with items of the same type.* It is useful, for example, when an administrator is interested in knowing all changes affecting all DBMS of the infrastructure, to perform suitable corrective actions.

– *A specific feed together with those feeds associated with SCIs an items depends on.* It shows configuration and changes relative to a specific SCI and its dependencies. If we consider a business service, it may be necessary to know changes in all items it depends on to perform impact analysis or activate change management processes.

Other SCI/feed aggregations may be offered easily since the infrastructure already provides all necessary configuration information. For example we may support aggregation that collects SCI/feeds of a component having particular properties, e.g., all DBMSs of type DB2, or we may want to collect feeds carrying specific kinds of changes to apply a suitable patch. We also provide a graphical interface to view aggregated SCI and feed documents.

Even if each DSM only keeps the current SCI version it is possible to go back to previous versions inspecting the corresponding feed document. This is important for incident management processes where stakeholders want to inspect configurations before a failure happened and analyze the cause of a problem. It is possible to retrieve the last SCI configuration, inspect the changes that happened after a particular time instant (that in which the failure happened), starting from the last one up to the first one and apply these changes in a backward way. For example, if an entry advertises a change in a property/dependency, it is sufficient to substitute the XML value of the property/dependency with that carried on by element `<old>` in the entry content. We may need to get the SCI version associated with service *Payment*, before its signature for operation `PayOrder` is changed. In this case we have to change the input parameter is changed from `tns:RPType` to `tns:RPAllowedType` (see second feed entry in Figure 4).

6   Implementation

The viability of the SCI approach was validated by implementing a prototype comprising the following components: the configuration discovery agent, the feed generator, the DSM, the DSM Registry and the Aggregator. The domain discovery process is a script that triggers the execution of Galapagos discovery and translates its results into a set of SCIs, and generates the ATOM feed entries associated to the detected changes. The DSM, the Aggregator and the DSM Registry are implemented through WebSphere sMash [7], a development and runtime environment for RESTful services and mash-ups.

The platform was tested in a laboratory environment using scenarios like that outlined in section 2. The tests showed that the platform permits to maintain

configuration information automatically. Configuration exchange among different domains takes place easily, by simply retrieving or aggregating XML documents using Web browsers and feed readers. Service management processes
or interested stakeholders can access configuration information using common
tools. Finally, the application of filters to customize the SCIs/feeds aggregation
offers to service management processes the information they exactly need.

7 Related Work

Distributed system management is the central focus of two standards: Web Services Distributed Management (WSDM) [8] and Web Services for Management
(WS-M) [9]. Both propose the idea to expose management information as Web
services and represent resource information through extensible models. To trace
associations among resources WSDM provides the concept of relationship, which
includes our notion of dependency. While, even if WS-M proposes a rich configuration model, i.e., CIM [10], it does not support dependencies. Furthermore,
WSDM and WS-M provide limited discovery capabilities. Our solution represent a significant improvement over these standards because it offers a global
approach that continuously maintains resources after they are discovered, updates their configuration when changes are detected, and notifies interested users
about these changes. WSDM and WS-M support allow users to subscribe on
events generated after resources' changes and being notified according to respectively WS-Notification [11] or WS-Eventing [12] standards. These standards
do not provide a clear way to represent resources changes and their low dif-
fusion, discourages their adoption. Instead, our approach adopts ATOM/RSS
feeds, offering a standard way to represent changes (encoded into a feed entry),
and consume them through any feed reader, with the possibility to rely on its
subscription and filtering capabilities.

CMDB federations [1] are an approach to use CMDBs across domain boundaries, enabling access to information held in different CMDBs. This approach
has high setup costs since all parties must establish explicit relationships, which
it is not feasible in loosely coupled environments. Treiber et al. [13] proposed a
concrete information model to represent both static and dynamic changes in web
services and encapsulate them in atom feed entries. The authors also relate each
change to its cause and to the stakeholders who may be interested in. Despite
our approach focuses on static configuration properties, it has the main advantage of dealing with cross-domain environments, representing intra- and inter-
domain dependencies among CIs. Moreover our solution keeps the information
model light, enabling different business analysis through several cross-domain
aggregations.

8 Conclusions

Loosely coupled applications spreading an SOA over multiple management domains requires a configuration management approach that takes into account

the the absence of central service management and a central CMDB. The SCM approach proposes to decentralize configuration management in a way in which service providers can expose configuration information to their users in a standard format based on domain discovery information while service users are able to discover and trace CIs outside their own management domain boundaries. The use of RESTful interfaces to CIs and ATOM feeds to distribute updates on configuration changes enables the use of very commonly available tools to expose and process configuration information. The feasibility of the approach was demonstrated in a proof-of-concept implementation. As next steps we will further validate the approach and work on improvements related to interaction with existing discovery technology, selective publication of SCIs, and programming models for aggregation. We also plan to remove the architectural bottleneck generated by the DSM Registries organizing them in P2P networks.

References

1. Clark, D., et al.: The Federated CMDB Vision: A joint White Paper from BMC, CA, Fujitsu, HP, IBM, and Microsoft, Version 1.0. Technical report
2. IBM: Tivoli: Change and Configuration Management Database, http://www-01.ibm.com/software/tivoli/products/ccmdb/
3. Ludwig, H., Laredo, J., Bhattacharya, K., Pasquale, L., Wassermann, B.: REST-based management of loosely coupled services. In: Proceedings of the 18th International Conference on World Wide Web (2009)
4. Wassermann, B., Ludwig, H., Laredo, J., Bhattacharya, K., Pasquale, L.: Distributed cross-domain change management. In: Proceedings of the International Conference on Web Services (2009)
5. Network Working Group: The Atom Syndication Format (2005), http://www.ietf.org/rfc/rfc4287.txt
6. Magoutis, K., Devarakonda, M., Joukov, N., Vogl, N.: Galapagos: Model-driven discovery of end-to-end application-storage relationship in distributed systems. IBM Journal of Research and Development (2008)
7. IBM: Projectzero, http://www.projectzero.org/
8. OASIS: Web services distributed management: Management using web services
9. DMTF: Web Services for Management (WS-Management)
10. DMTF: Common Information Model (CIM) Specification, Version 2.2
11. OASIS: Web Services Base Notification 1.3 (WS-BaseNotification) (2006)
12. Box, D., et al.: Web Services Eventing (WS-Eventing) W3C Member Submission
13. Treiber, M., Truong, H.L., Dustdar, S.: On analyzing evolutionary changes of web services. In: Feuerlicht, G., Lamersdorf, W. (eds.) ICSOC 2008. LNCS, vol. 5472, pp. 284–297. Springer, Heidelberg (2009)

A Pluggable Framework for Tracking and Managing Faults in Service-Oriented Systems

Daniel Robinson and Gerald Kotonya

Computing Department, InfoLab21, South Drive,
Lancaster University, Lancaster, United Kingdom
{robinsdb,gerald}@comp.lancs.ac.uk

Abstract. Practical fault management in service-oriented systems requires dynamic monitoring of services for SLA violations, failures and undesirable changes in the system runtime environment. It should also include effective fault recovery strategies, and be transparent and lightweight to enhance trust and to minimise the load on the consumer and providers. This paper describes a technology-independent fault management approach that uses a pluggable brokerage model to track and resolve service changes and faults. A case study is used to illustrate the efficacy of the approach.

Keywords: Service-oriented systems, Fault tracking, Change management.

1 Introduction

Failures in service provision, Service Level Agreement (SLA) violations and changes in the system runtime environment can impact adversely on the quality of a service-oriented system. There are several initiatives based on monitoring that are designed to track changes and detect SLA violations. However, these generally support static rather than dynamic analysis and provide poor support for resolving undesirable changes and violations [1]. In addition, most are designed to support service providers avoid SLA violations, rather than help the service consumer to detect and respond to problematic QoS [3]. Effective fault management in service-oriented systems requires a consumer-centred approach that actively monitors services for SLA violations, failures and undesirable changes; and provides strategies for minimising their adverse effects.

Our solution has been to develop a failure management approach that uses a consumer-centred, pluggable brokerage model to track and renegotiate service faults and changes. The brokerage model is reported in [2]. Our approach is service-technology independent and incorporates pluggable support for different monitoring and negotiation models in addition to assessing provider reputation. To help with the automation of negotiation and monitoring processes, and to ensure a shared set of terms for describing services, our approach also incorporates pluggable support for a service ontology. We will show using a service-oriented case study and different fault and change scenarios how our framework tracks and manages faults and changes.

L. Baresi, C.-H. Chi, and J. Suzuki (Eds.): ICSOC-ServiceWave 2009, LNCS 5900, pp. 637–638, 2009.

2 An Overview of the Approach

Figure 1 shows the framework on which the approach is based. Service consumers and providers supply the brokerage system with templates that specify strategies for the services they require or provide. For consumers, the strategy describes the ideal QoS requirements of the functional services they wish to use. The brokerage incorporates an engine builder component, which uses the templates to assemble a custom service broker engine for processing negotiation messages and service proposals. The proposal engine creates and evaluates service proposals. The broker engine contains a separate negotiation engine for each negotiation protocol it supports. The negotiation engine concurrently negotiates with multiple parties. The engine maintains a separate negotiation session for each negotiation.

The framework provides a service monitoring system, which actively monitors the quality of negotiated services for emergent changes, SLA violations and failure. The primary monitoring approach adopted by the framework is a passive model, which transparently intercepts service requests and responses between service consumers and providers.

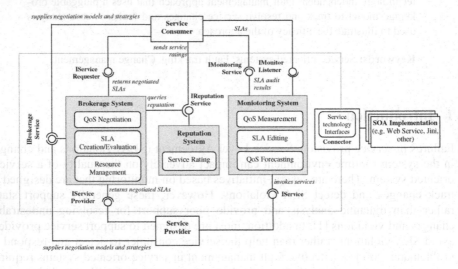

Fig. 1. Pluggable Service brokerage framework

References

1. Saunders, S., Ross, M., Staples, G., Wellington, S.: The Software Quality Challenges of Service-Oriented Architectures in E-Commerce. Software Quality Control 14(1), 65–75 (2006)
2. Robinson, D., Kotonya, G.: A Runtime Quality Architecture for Service-Oriented Systems. In: Bouguettaya, A., Krueger, I., Margaria, T. (eds.) ICSOC 2008. LNCS, vol. 5364, pp. 468–482. Springer, Heidelberg (2008)
3. Hoffman, R.: Monitoring, at your service. ACM Queue 3(10), 34–43 (2005)

Distributed Access Control Management – A XACML-Based Approach

Erik Rissanen[1], David Brossard[2], and Adriaan Slabbert[1]

[1] Axiomatics AB, Electrum 223, 164 40 Kista, Sweden
{erik,adriaan}@axiomatics.com
[2] BT Innovate, Adastral Park, IP5 3RE Martlesham Heath, England
{david.brossard}@bt.com

Abstract. Enterprises are increasingly pervasive with users and services belonging to different domains. Cross-enterprise business collaborations are soaring and so are business relationships with complex access control rules. Business rules no longer come from a single source. There is a need for multiple administrators to define rules that apply to their part of the collaboration. Traditional access control models are not sufficient. This demonstrator illustrates an authorization service developed by Swedish SME Axiomatics. It implements the eXtended Access Control Markup Language (XACML), a policy- and rule-based access control language which allows the expression of fine-grained access control rules in distributed environments.

Keywords: SOA, security, authorization, access control, XACML.

1 Introduction

Distributed access control and authorization services allow access policies to be enforced in a multi-administrative environment. Traditional models tend to rely on a single-administrator model where policies are authored by the same authority within a single domain.

The dynamic nature and level of distribution of the business models typical of service-oriented infrastructures (SOI) [4] mean that one can no longer rely on a set of known users or fixed organizational structures with access to only a set of known systems. Furthermore, access control policies need to be aware of the context within which an access control request is being issued as it can impact the final decision.

The dynamic multi-administrative nature of an SOI necessitates a new model for access control and the development of new models that cater for these characteristics of the infrastructure while combining the best features from role-based, attribute-based, and policy-based access control (RBAC, ABAC and PBAC respectively).

This demonstrator presents the Axiomatics Authorization Service (AuthZ-PDP) and illustrates how it can be used in distributed environments. Axiomatics is also working with OASIS, to drive the evolution of the XACML [2,3] standard.

A demo video can be seen at http://www.gridipedia.eu/gt-axiomatics.html.

L. Baresi, C.-H. Chi, and J. Suzuki (Eds.): ICSOC-ServiceWave 2009, LNCS 5900, pp. 639–640, 2009.

2 System Description

The AuthZ-PDP allows the necessary decision making for distributed enforcement of access policies by multiple administrators, ensuring compliance, accountability and audits. Current access control models are extended with (1) validity conditions for each policy, (2) policy issuance whereby administrators digitally sign the policies they write, and (3) administrative delegation policies that lets an administrator define who can issue policies about what actions on which resources. Key functions include:

- *Policy-based access control*: applicable policies are stored on the system and are analyzed by the PDP. The PDP makes its decision and returns the decision.
- *Constrained Administrative Delegation:* the delegation mechanism is used to support decentralized administration of access policies. It allows an authority (delegator) to delegate all or part of its authority to another user (delegate). The specific authorization can then be delegated further.
- *Obligation*: an obligation is a directive from the PDP to the Policy Enforcement Point (PEP) on what must be carried out before or after access is granted. If the PEP cannot comply with the directive, the granted access will not be realized.
- *Segregation of policy stores*: by means of PDP instantiation, it is possible to have instances of the PDP service that each act as a single standalone PDP.
- *Flexible*: the PDP is standards-based and can be deployed in a variety of ways.

3 Benefits

The innovations that differentiate the solution from other access management capabilities include the delegation of administrative authority: policy authoring and management is controlled by constraint-delegation policies that put constraints on the access management policies that administrators can author and allow the run-time creation of dynamic chains of delegation of administrative authority without assuming prior knowledge of an organization's structure. Authenticity, integrity and accountability are guaranteed: policy authoring rights are granted to issuers whose accountability is enforced by use of digital signatures. This is only possible through the introduction of the Policy Issuer element in XACML and through the rigorous implementation of the standard by the PDP put forward. Lastly, the AuthZ-PDP is context-aware and can be contextualized enabling its use in multi-tenancy scenarios. It can be provisioned in the SaaS pattern.

Acknowledgments. This demonstrator was partly produced within BEinGRID [1].

References

1. The BEinGRID project, http://www.beingrid.eu
2. OASIS, XACML 3.0 (core specification and schemas) (May 18, 2008)
3. OASIS, XACML 3.0 administration and delegation profile, (October 10, 2007)
4. Gresty, C., et al.: Meeting customer needs. BT Technology Journal 26(1)

Engage: Engineering Service Modes with WS-Engineer and Dino

Howard Foster[1], Arun Mukhija[2],
David S. Rosenblum[2], and Sebastian Uchitel[1]

[1] London Software Systems, Dept. of Computing, Imperial College London,
180 Queen's Gate, London SW7 2BZ, UK
{hf1,su2}@doc.ic.ac.uk

[2] London Software Systems, Dept. of Computer Science, University College London,
Gower Street, London WC1E 6BT, UK
{a.mukhija,d.rosenblum}@cs.ucl.ac.uk
http://icsoc09.ws-engineer.net

Abstract. In this demonstration[1] we present an approach to engineering service brokering requirements and capabilities using the concepts of Service Modes. The demonstration illustrates building service modes in UML2 with Rational Software Modeller, transforming modes in WS-Engineer and generating artefacts for runtime service brokering.

1 The Service Modes Approach

A mode, in the context of service engineering, aims to provide an easily accessible mechanism for developing adaptive service brokering requirements. Service modes are an abstraction of a set of services that collaborate to achieve a task or sub-tasks. A *Service Modes Architecture* consists of specifying the service components, their configuration and behaviour required or provided, and their interface specifications. We developed and apply a UML Service Modes Profile [1] to identify various elements of the service configuration elements for service brokering, and reuse this in the approach to identify required and provided services in modes. A service modes model consists of a number of mode packages, which themselves contain collaborations with configurations of service components and their requirements or capabilities. If a service component is specified as required, it identifies the service component for service discovery. Alternatively, if a service component is specified as provided, it identifies the service component as *offered* in service discovery. Additionally, service component bindings may reference binding constraints, offering non-functional requirements or capabilities (such as expected response times for the service specified).

We also provide transformations from service mode models to service brokering requirements and capability specifications (initially for a specific service broker *Dino* from University College London). The transformations generate documents which are deployed on to a runtime broker. Thus, at runtime the requirements documents are used by service clients to create a new brokering session and trigger discovery of required services. Capabilities may also be registered with the service broker, which offers provided services and adds service capability to discoverable services.

---

[1] Sponsored by the EU funded project SENSORIA (IST-2005-016004).

L. Baresi, C.-H. Chi, and J. Suzuki (Eds.): ICSOC-ServiceWave 2009, LNCS 5900, pp. 641–642, 2009.

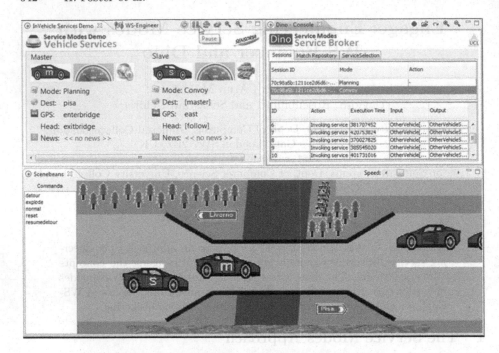

Fig. 1. Demonstration of In-Vehicle Service Modes

2   The Demonstration

The demonstration illustrates service modes for an In-Vehicle Services Architecture. The scenarios used as requirements for this example consider two vehicles in different roles, namely a Master role (planning mode) and a Slave role (convoy and detour modes). The demonstration takes place in three core stages. Firstly, a service mode model for several modes of an In-Vehicle Services Architecture is described. The audience is taken through a series of mode packages illustrating both the approach of constructing service configuration specifications using the UML Modes profile and those elements which are referenced to the core UML model. More specifically, service brokering requirements and capabilities are highlighted. The second stage takes this model and mechanically transforms the model modes to service brokering runtime documents. The audience is taken through these documents, their structure and how this links to elements of both the model and runtime requirements. Finally, the generated documents are used directly for a runtime example of brokering in a simulation (as a vehicle animation illustrated in Figure 1) of the In-Vehicle Services scenario.

References

1. Foster, H., Mukhija, A., Uchitel, S., Rosenblum, D.S.: A Model-Driven Approach to Dynamic and Adaptive Service Brokering using Modes. In: Bouguettaya, A., Krueger, I., Margaria, T. (eds.) ICSOC 2008. LNCS, vol. 5364, pp. 558–564. Springer, Heidelberg (2008)

FAST-SE: An ESB Based Framework for SLA Trading

Jose Antonio Parejo, Antonio Manuel Gutiérrez,
Pablo Fernandez, and Antonio Ruiz-Cortes

University of Sevilla

Abstract. SLA driven service transaction has been identified as a key challenge to take advantage of a SOA. FAST System provides a software framework for the automated creation of SLAs. In particular it have been developed as an extension to the ESB (Enterprise Service Bus) paradigm to create a transparent SLA management layer that drives any service invocation. Our framework has been successfully applied in two different scenarios and provides an extensible architecture to address new domains.

1 Introduction

As SOC has evolved into a mature paradigm, new challenges appear in the horizon. In particular, the automatic provision of services is a promising field that could lead to a new generation of organizations that adapt "on demand" to rapid changes in its business environment.

FAST system addresses a core element of the automatic provision of services: the creation of SLAs (Service Level Agreements) that will describe the rights and obligations of the service consumer and the service provider during the transaction. The terms of the agreement could refer to either functional (such as the type of service – i.e. the interface-) or non-functional (such as the availability of the service) features. In doing so, our approach provides an architecture based on components to extend a JBI Enterprise Service Bus with a new element: the FAST-SE (FAST Service Engine). This element provides an extensible software framework to deal with different service domains: On the one hand, the system defines standard data models (information, proposals, counterparties, agreements, etc.) that can be refined with a specific vocabulary of the domain. On the other hand a flexible orchestration system is provided to allow different SLA creation transactions.

A short video demonstration of the system can be found in[1]

2 FAST Extension Capabilities

The FAST (Framework for Automatic Service Trading) system provides an architecture based on components that are interconnected with a set of linking choreographies and generic data models. The implementation of linking choreographies is independent of the vocabulary of the information so they can be adapted to different domains.

---

[1] http://www.isa.us.es/fast

L. Baresi, C.-H. Chi, and J. Suzuki (Eds.): ICSOC-ServiceWave 2009, LNCS 5900, pp. 643–644, 2009.

Also, the components develop a set of generic roles executed as autonomous process so their behavior can be orchestrated.

Adapting to a specific domain only requires defining the domain vocabulary: i.e. the specific (functional and non-functional) properties. Once the framework is instantiated the parties (consumers and providers) specify their SLA creation preferences in the trading process using the domain vocabulary. Finally, a domain can also specify the component orchestration to model the trading process that will create the SLA. Following, a short description of two domains already implemented is described.

Computing Marketplace Domain. In this case, a set of providers trade with a computation service according to different properties as cost, computation time or delay. The interaction choreographies are implemented in a distributed deployment scenario and the agreement conditions are obtained optimizing domain constraints between consumer requirements and providers features. Additionally, it is important to remark that the application of the framework in this scenario provides the feasibility of adapting the trading process stages in each provider.

Federated bus government. The framework is applied to govern services in a federated bus inside a corporation. The system creates agreements to plan service invocations inside a federated bus with different service providers   according to certain conditions as reliability, performance or priority. The linking choreographies are implemented to adapt a high performance environment. Moreover, the framework provides an extensible environment to adapt new corporate services or constraints with minimal effort. Currently, the system is in a pre-production test stage and it is deployed to federate corporative services implemented by several departments in a wide-size organization for a regional government.

3 Conclusions

The system has been deployed successfully in two different scenarios proving their adaptability to their vocabulary and interaction needs. Currently, the system is being extended to enrich the expression language in properties and preference. A set of generic components is developed to deal with complex negotiations and CSP-based selection.

Gelee: Cooperative Lifecycle Management for (Composite) Artifacts

Marcos Báez, Cristhian Parra, Fabio Casati, Maurizio Marchese,
Florian Daniel, Kasia di Meo, Silvia Zobele, Carlo Menapace, and Beatrice Valeri

University of Trento, Italy
{baez,parra,casati,marchese,daniel}@disi.unitn.it,
{katarzyna.dimeo,silvia.zobele}@studenti.unitn.it,
{carlo.menapace,beatrice.valeri}@studenti.unitn.it

Abstract. In this demonstration we introduce *Gelee*, our online platform for the hosted specification and cooperative execution of lifecycles of artifacts of any kind. With Gelee we aim at filling two lacks we identify in current cooperative software systems when it comes to unstructured, artifact-based works (e.g., the writing of a project deliverable): the lack of state and the complete lack of automated actions. Lifecycles allow us to model the state of any object, and if we focus on online resources (e.g., a Google Doc) then we can also automate some lifecycle actions. If we apply Gelee to composite artifacts, e.g., a set of web services, lifecycles provide for the human-driven orchestration of services.

Keywords: Lifecycle Management, Artifacts, Online Resources, Gelee.

1 Introduction

Historically, the spectrum of cooperative software has been divided into two macro-areas: *process-centric* systems (e.g., workflow management or service orchestration systems) and *document-centric* systems (e.g., groupware or sub-versioning systems). The former typically suffer from a too rigid imposition of the process logic, not allowing users to easily adapt or change a running instance; as a consequence, such systems do not suit unstructured, creative works without predefined process. Ad-hoc or adaptive workflow management systems or case handling systems only partially introduced flexibility into process-centric systems. Document-centric systems, on the other hand, typically come without any explicit notion of state for the work being assisted by the system (the state is represented by the data in the system) and, hence, there is no automated coordination of the work or support for automated actions.

We argue that everything has a *lifecycle*, a real-world object (e.g., a car) the same way as a creative work (e.g., the writing of a deliverable). If modeled in terms of phases and transitions, the lifecycle of an artifact allows us to capture some notion of state of the artifact. While in general we cannot automate the progression of a lifecycle for a given object, the people working on the artifact know how it changes during its life. So we rely on humans to progress lifecycles. In projects where multiple artifacts are manipulated, this already grants the project coordinator visibility into the

L. Baresi, C.-H. Chi, and J. Suzuki (Eds.): ICSOC-ServiceWave 2009, LNCS 5900, pp. 645–646, 2009.

state of each artifact (e.g., to fill a progression report), a feature that is only scarcely supported by any project management tool on the market (if at all). We then specifically focus on online resources, which typically come with an API (a web service) that allows the enactment of actions on the resource. By binding a lifecycle to specific resource (e.g., a Google Doc), Gelee allows for the automation of the API's actions by extending the lifecycle model with resource-specific actions (e.g., the translation into PDF), thus alleviating the work of human actors. Composite artifacts (e.g., the writing of a paper and its submission to a conference) can be obtained by combining atomic artifacts, and lifecycles can be used to coordinate the interaction with their APIs, practically yielding a human-orchestrated service composition.

In this demo we show Gelee at work, and we show that it indeed is an answer to many situations that cannot be adequately managed with existing cooperative software. The demo introduces the Gelee online platform, the lifecycle editor, the execution environment, and the monitoring tool. Gelee itself implements a SOA and allows one to plug in new services through a dedicated registry. The platform includes a SOA middleware for resource management, with on top the lifecycle management applications.

2 Demonstration Flow

In this demonstration we will show the Gelee prototype at work. This prototype implements the concepts in [1] providing artifact lifecycle modeling, progression, and monitoring. The goal of this demonstration is to introduce the user to the Gelee features and underlying concepts in the following flow:

1. First, we put Gelee into context to explain what the key contributions and the novel features of the tool are.
2. Then we show the Gelee system at work, starting from the Gelee *workspace*.
3. From the workspace we move to the *modeling environment* to describe the modeling features with an example of a deliverable lifecycle.
4. We follow then this example to describe the *execution environment*, in which we bind the actual deliverable (e.g., in Google Docs) to the lifecycle defined in the modeling environment. In particular, we show how we operate on the resource by executing and configuring lifecycle actions.
5. After introducing both environments, we briefly show the *monitoring widgets* and how they can be included into web dashboards (e.g. iGoogle).
6. Finally, we summarize the demonstration and we mention our ongoing and future work.

A short video describing the above demonstration flow is available at the following address: http://project.liquidpub.org/gelee/docs/gelee-demo.wmv.

References

[1] Báez, M., Casati, F., Marchese, M.: Universal Resource Lifecycle Management. In: ICDE 2009, pp. 1741–1748 (2009)

Hosted Universal Integration on the Web: The mashArt Platform

Florian Daniel[1], Fabio Casati[1], Stefano Soi[1], Jonny Fox[1],
David Zancarli[1], and Ming-Chien Shan[2]

[1] University of Trento, Italy
{daniel,casati,soi,fox,zancarli}@disi.unitn.it
[2] SAP Labs- 3410 Hillview Avenue, Palo Alto, CA 94304, USA
ming-chien.shan@sap.com

Abstract. Traditional integration practices like Enterprise Application Integration and Enterprise Information Integration approaches typically focus on the application layer and the data layer in software systems, i.e., on limited and specific development aspects. Current web mashup practices, instead, show that there is also a concrete need for (i) integration at the presentation layer and (ii) integration approaches that conciliate all the three layers together. In this demonstration, we show how our *mashArt* approach addresses these challenges and provides skilled web users with *universal integration* in a hosted fashion.

Keywords: Hosted Universal Integration, Mashups, Services Composition.

1 Introduction and Contributions

Mashups are online applications that are developed by composing contents and functions accessible over the Web [1]. The innovative aspect of mashups is that they also tackle integration at the user interface (UI) level, i.e., besides application logic and data, they also reuse existing UIs (e.g., many of today's applications include a Google Map). We call this practice of integrating data, application logic, and UIs for the development of a composite application *universal integration*.

Universal integration can be done (and is being done) today by joining the capabilities of multiple programming languages and techniques, but it requires significant efforts and professional programmers. There is, however, also a growing number of *mashup tools*, which aim at aiding mashup development and at simplicity more than robustness or completeness of features. For instance, Yahoo Pipes focuses on RSS/Atom feeds, Microsoft Popfly on feeds and JavaScript components, Intel Mash Maker on UIs and annotated data in web pages, while JackBe Presto also allows putting a UI on top of data pipes. None of these, however, covers the three application layers discussed above together in a convenient and homogeneous fashion.

Building on research in SOA and capturing the trends of Web 2.0 and mashups, in this demo we propose an integrated and comprehensive approach for universal integration, equipped with a proper hosted development and execution platform called *mashArt* (a significant evolution of the work described in [2]). Our aim is to do what service composition has done for integrating services, but to do so at all layers, not

L. Baresi, C.-H. Chi, and J. Suzuki (Eds.): ICSOC-ServiceWave 2009, LNCS 5900, pp. 647–648, 2009.

just at the application layer, and to do so by learning lessons and capturing the trends of Web 2.0 and mashups, removing some of the limitations that constrained a wider adoption of workflow/service composition technologies.

The mashArt approach aims at empowering non-professional programmers with easy-to-use and flexible abstractions and techniques to create and manage composite web applications. Specifically, mashArt provides the following, unique contributions:

- A *unified component model* that is able to accommodate and abstract UI components (HTML), application logic components (SOAP or RESTful services), and data components (feeds or XML/relational data) using a unified model.
- A *universal composition model* that allows mashArt users to develop composite applications on top of the unified component model and conciliates the needs of both UI synchronization and service orchestration under one hood.
- A *development and execution platform* for composite applications that facilitates rapid development, testing, and maintenance. mashArt is entirely hosted and web-based, with zero client-side code.

2 Demonstration Storyboard

The live demonstration introduces the three contributions of mashArt by means of a joint use of slides (for the conceptual aspects) and hands-on platform demos (for the practical aspects). In particular, the demonstration is organized as follows:

1. *Intro:* introduction of the conceptual and theoretical background of the project, its goals and ambitions, and its contributions.
2. *UI integration:* explanation of the idea of UI integration and how UI components and the composition logic look like.
3. *UI integration demo:* demonstration of how to do UI integration with mashArt starting from a set of existing mashArt UI components. Two minutes suffice to show how to develop and run a simple application that synchronizes a search component and a map component for geo-visualization of results.
4. *Universal integration:* description of mashArt's component model and its composition model, which characterize the universal integration approach.
5. *Universal integration demo:* demonstration of how to combine service, data, and UI integration in mashArt. Again, two minutes suffice to show how to add an RSS reader component to the previous scenario and to feed it with data sourced from a RESTful service and transformed via a Yahoo! pipe.
6. *Architecture:* functional architecture of mashArt to show that mashArt is (or will be) more than what is shown in the demo.
7. *Conclusion and future works:* summary and outline of future works.

A short version of the demo can be previewed here: *http://mashart.org/mashArt.wmv*.

References

[1] Yu, J., et al.: Understanding Mashup Development and its Differences with Traditional Integration. Internet Computing 12(5), 44–52
[2] Yu, J., et al.: A Framework for Rapid Integration of Presentation Components. In: WWW 2007, pp. 923–932 (2007)

Sec-MoSC Tooling - Incorporating Security Requirements into Service Composition

Andre R.R. Souza[1], Bruno L.B. Silva[1], Fernando A.A. Lins[1], Julio C. Damasceno[1], Nelson S. Rosa[1], Paulo R.M. Maciel[1], Robson W.A. Medeiros[1], Bryan Stephenson[2], Hamid R. Motahari-Nezhad[2], Jun Li[2], and Caio Northfleet[3]

[1] Federal University of Pernambuco, Centre of Informatics
`{arss,blbs,faal2,jcd,nsr,prmm,rwam}@cin.ufpe.br`
[2] HP Labs Palo Alto
`{bryan.stephenson,hamid.motahari,jun.li}@hp.com`
[3] HP Brazil
`caio.northfleet@hp.com`

Abstract. The Sec-MoSC Tooling supports modelling and enforcement of security abstractions in business processes and service composition. It offers a novel approach consisting of abstractions and methods for capturing and enforcing security requirements in service composition.

1 Introduction

There is an increasing need for considering security requirements during service composition. However, no holistic and consistent approach exists for the identification, modelling and enforcement of security requirements in service composition that covers all levels of abstraction from modelling to execution.

The Sec-MoSC Tooling is a novel set of tools and programming components that enables the high-level specification, modelling, mapping and enforcement of security requirements in business processes and service composition. Sec-MoSC enables traceability of security requirements at different levels of abstraction, automatic generation of configuration files containing enforceable security actions for the composed services and the involved security tools. Security requirements are defined once and enforced across many services.

The architecture of this solution is presented in Figure 1. The *Sec-MoSC Tool Editor* allows the user to define a business process based on BPMN standard and annotate it with security requirements. The repositories store information related to the participant services and security properties. The *MoSC Security Module* implements security enforcement mechanisms. The *Auxiliary Engine* coordinates the operation of Security Module and the orchestration engine. While the Tool Editor provides support at development time, the *Execution Environment* components shown in Figure 1 are responsible for executing the service composition and realising the security mechanisms.

We introduce three non-functional abstractions to express security requirements: NF-Attribute, NF-Statement and NF-Action. NF-Attribute models non-functional requirements (e.g. confidentiality). The NF-Statement represents constraints related to

L. Baresi, C.-H. Chi, and J. Suzuki (Eds.): ICSOC-ServiceWave 2009, LNCS 5900, pp. 649–650, 2009.

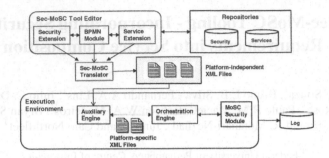

Fig. 1. Architecture of the Sec-MoSC Tooling

NF-Attributes (e.g. "high" confidentiality) and NF-Action refers to detailed technical mechanisms that realize NF-Attributes, (e.g. use cryptography to encrypt data).

2 Demonstration Scenario

To illustrate the application of Sec-MoSC Tooling, we use a service composition example called Virtual Travel Agency (VTA). Our demonstration starts with a BPMN model of the VTA. We show how a business person can annotate a BPMN model using the provided security annotations. Several security requirements across composed services and their enforcement mechanisms are demonstrated including confidentiality, data integrity, and restricting access. In order to enforce the security requirements we follow a model-driven approach for code generation. Specifically, from the annotated BPMN we generate three platform-independent files: WS-BPEL code, XML-based security configuration (in particular WS-SecurityPolicy), and service configuration. The Auxiliary Engine transforms the platform-independent files to platform-specific configuration files for the chosen security enforcement modules and orchestration engines. The platform-specific files are deployed to the execution environment to enforce security requirements. We finally demonstrate how the user can monitor service interactions to verify enforcement of security requirements.

All the components in the Sec-MoSC Tooling are implemented as an Eclipse plugin. We choose Apache ODE as our WS-BPEL orchestration engine and Apache Rampart for enforcing message-level security requirements. The editor is built on top of the Eclipse BPMN Modelling Editor. Additional information can be found in [1].

Acknowledgement. This research is supported by Hewlett-Packard Brasil Ltda. using incentives of Brazilian Informatics Law (Law n° 8.2.48 of 1991).

References

[1] Souza, A.R.R., et al.: Incorporating Security Requirements into Service Composition: From Modelling to Execution. In: 7th International Joint Conference on Service Oriented Computing (ICSOC&ServiceWave 2009), Stockholm, Sweden (2009)

Services Inside the Smart Home:
A Simulation and Visualization Tool*

Elena Lazovik**, Piet den Dulk**, Martijn de Groote**, Alexander Lazovik***,
and Marco Aiello***

University of Groningen, Nijenborgh 9, 9747AG Groningen, The Netherlands
{A.C.T.den.Dulk,M.de.Groote}@student.rug.nl,
{e.lazovik,a.lazovik,m.aiello}@rug.nl

Abstract. Pervasive systems, and domotics in particular, is an application area where heterogeneity is the norm, with thousands of autonomous heterogeneous devices live together and need to interoperate. One of the greatest difficulties in developing middleware for smart homes is that this kind of systems are extremely difficult to test and verify. We propose to reduce the testing costs by replacing actual home services with virtual stubs behaving as if they were actual hardware installed somewhere in the house and, most importantly, to visualize the behaviour of the home to give the user the impression and feedback of being in a real home.

1 Introduction

Service-Oriented Computing (SOC) is a leading paradigm to create state of the art information systems. It is widely used in the development of complex software artifacts that require high interoperability, scalability, security, and reliability. Software of this kind can be seamlessly integrated with other systems that are possibly written in different programming languages and are deployed under different operating system. High interoperability is achieved through usage of standard platform-independent protocols, such as the web services stack. Pervasive systems and domotics applications are concerned with technology that pervades the home in order to make it more pro-active and aware with the final goal of increasing security and comfort of its inhabitants. SOC is a natural candidate to address the major requirements of domotics needs. Examples of are the Java based Jini technology (http://www.jini.org) or web services [2].

In this paper, we concentrate on smart homes, that is, homes that contain interactive and pro-active devices, that adapt their behavior to the needs of the home inhabitant through extensive interoperation and user interaction. For example, a movie may be automatically paused when the user leaves the room, and then launched again when s/he is back; windows are automatically opened

---

* This research is supported by the EU through the STREP project FP7-224332
  Smart Homes for All, http://www.sm4all-project.eu
** Master in Computer Science.
*** Distributed Systems Group.

L. Baresi, C.-H. Chi, and J. Suzuki (Eds.): ICSOC-ServiceWave 2009, LNCS 5900, pp. 651–652, 2009.

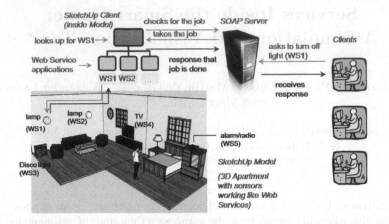

SketchUp Client
(inside Model)   checks for the job   SOAP Server

looks up for WS1→   takes the job   Clients

Web Service   response that   asks to turn off
applications   job is done   light (WS1)

WS1 WS2 ...   receives
response

lamp ○   lamp ○   TV
(WS1)   (WS2)   (WS4)

alarm/radio
(WS5)

Disco light   SketchUp Model
(WS3)   (3D Apartment
with sensors
working like Web
Services)

Fig. 1. Architecture of the domotics simulation environment ViSi

to regulate the air condition or as a reaction to gas leak, and so on. One of the greatest challenges in domotics is verification of the proposed solutions.

We propose to reduce the testing costs by replacing actual home services with virtual stubs behaving as if they were actual hardware installed somewhere in the house. To this end, we extend Google SketchUp (http://sketchup.google.com) with a set of tools that extend its visual representation of the house with virtual interactive home web services supporting SOAP messages. This allows not only to visualize the potential smart home but also to provide a full featured simulation of any possible domotics scenario. In addition, it is possible to model the user and its interaction with the home. The realized simulation and visualization environment is named ViSi (Smart Home Visualization and Simulation) [1].

The framework may be used in conjunction with hardware supporting the web service stack. For instance, we have included in our test a controller of a fridge implementing WSDL and SOAP over HTTP on an ethernet connection. Figure 1 provides an overview of the implementation: the visualization component is written as a set of plug-ins for Google SketchUp, the communication mechanism is based on the Ruby SOAP implementation. As typical of web services, the clients are language-independent and can be written in any language that supports the web services stack. In our experimentation we have used Java and various BPEL engines. The implemented framework ViSi is not limited to domotics applications. Google SketchUp is a domain-independent drawing tool, and our framework may be used to simulate and visualize network applications, distributed systems, telecommunications, to name some application areas.

References

1. ViSi demo (2009),
   http://www.sm4all-project.eu/index.php/activities/videos.html
2. Aiello, M., Dustdar, S.: A domotic infrastructure based on the web service stack. Pervasive and Mobile Computing 4(4), 506–525 (2008)

SLA Management and Contract-Based Service Execution

Matthias Winkler[1], Josef Spillner[2], and Alexander Schill[2]

[1] SAP Research CEC Dresden, SAP AG, Chemnitzer Str. 48,
01187 Dresden, Germany
matthias.winkler@sap.com
[2] TU Dresden, Nöthnitzer Str. 46, 01187 Dresden, Germany
{josef.spillner,alexander.schill}@tu-dresden.de

Abstract. In the Internet of Services vision, services are traded via internet service marketplaces. Service provisioning is regulated by service level agreements (SLAs). In this demonstration[1] we present an infrastructure which supports SLA creation and negotiation as well as service provisioning and monitoring based on SLAs in the context of service marketplaces. It is an implementation of the work presented in [1] and [2] and an intermediate result of the TEXO project[2].

1 The SLA Management Infrastructure

We present a novel system for end-to-end SLA handling during design time, negotiation, and runtime which improves existing work by increasing automation of SLA management. The system is also different from existing ones because of its centralized SLA negotiation and monitoring support via the marketplace instead of requiring consumer-provider negotiation. Our system supports contract-bound tradable service execution through a distributed service infrastructure with ubiquitous support for WS-Agreement[3]. SLAs are created, negotiated, and monitored by specialised components on the infrastructure for engineering, trading, and executing services.

The ISE development environment consists of tools for modelling and describing services. The Service Management Platform (SMP) provides service marketplace functionality for offering and searching services, SLA negotiation and monitoring, and billing. The Tradable Services Runtime (TSR) supports service execution and monitoring at the provider side. Multiple distributed service runtimes are interacting with the central service marketplace. The communication between the SMP and the TSRs is realized via a message-oriented middleware which supports the exchange of information regarding deployed services, negotiated SLAs, and monitoring data. Figure 1 provides an overview of the infrastructure of ISE, SMP and TSR.

---

[1] Associated video:
http://texo.inf.tu-dresden.de/servicewave-texo-video

[2] The project was funded by means of the German Federal Ministry of Economy and Technology under the promotional reference "01MQ07012". The authors take the responsibility for the contents.

[3] WS-Agreement: http://www.ogf.org/documents/GFD.107.pdf

L. Baresi, C.-H. Chi, and J. Suzuki (Eds.): ICSOC-ServiceWave 2009, LNCS 5900, pp. 653–655, 2009.

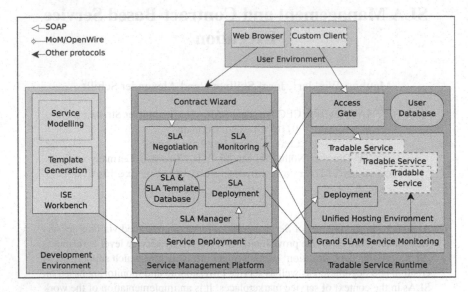

Fig. 1. Infrastructure for SLA management of tradable services

SLA template generation and deployment: SLA templates, which form the base for SLA negotiation, are created at design time by the *SLA Template Generation* component [2] of ISE. It takes a USDL (Universal Service Description Language) service description as input and generates a WS-Agreement SLA template via a model-to-text transformation. This automates part of the work of a service provider.

Negotiation of SLAs: The negotiation of SLAs is supported by the *SLA Manager* component, which provides the agreement provider interfaces defined by WS-Agreement. The *Contract Wizard* and the *ISE SLA Negotiation Wizard* provide front ends for the negotiation of SLAs for service consumers and composite service creators, respectively. While the Contract Wizard was implemented as a web application, the ISE SLA Negotiation Wizard was implemented as a plug-in for the ISE workbench. Upon the successful negotiation of an SLA, different runtime components are activated in order to prepare service provisioning and monitoring.

Service Execution and Monitoring: Once an SLA was negotiated, the respective service can be consumed. Service requests are checked by the *Access Gate* SOAP proxy for user authentication and SLA-based authorisation. Invocation-related statistics are injected into the SLA-driven monitor *Grand SLAM*. Further system and service metrics are measured by its monitoring sensors. They are aggregated and evaluated according to the negotiated SLA conditions. In the case of detected problems a violation event is sent to the SLA Manager. Adaptive execution environments can react on this event.

References

[1] Spillner, J., Winkler, M., Reichert, S., Cardoso, J., Schill, A.: Distributed Contracting and Monitoring in the Internet of Services. In: Senivongse, T., Oliveira, R. (eds.) DAIS 2009. LNCS, vol. 5523, pp. 129–142. Springer, Heidelberg (2009)
[2] Winkler, M., Springer, T.: SLA Management for the Internet of Services. In: Proceedings of the Third International Workshop on Architectures, Concepts and Technologies for Service Oriented Computing (ACT4SOC), Sofia, Bulgaria (2009)

Author Index